THE HORSE IN HUMAN HISTORY

The horse is surely the "aristocrat" of animals domesticated by man. This book documents the origins of horse domestication on the Pontic-Caspian steppes some 6,000 years ago and the consequent migration of equestrian tribes across Eurasia to the borders of sedentary states. Horse chariotry and cavalry in effect changed the nature of warfare in the civilizations of the Middle East, India, and China. But, beyond the battlefield, horse-power also afforded great advances in transport, agriculture, industry, and science. Rapidity of horse communications forged far-flung equestrian empires, where language, law, weights, measures, and writing systems were standardized and revolutionary technologies and ideas were disseminated across continents. Always recognizing this dual character of horsepower – both destructive and constructive – this work discusses the politico-military and economic importance of the horse in the rise of Hittite, Achaemenid, Chinese, Greco-Roman, Arab, Mongol, and Turkic states. Following Columbian contact, Old and New World cultures are con-trastively evaluated in terms of presence or absence of the horse. And Spanish conquest of the horseless Americas is seen as the model for subsequent European equestrian colonization of horseless territories around the planet.

Pita Kelekna holds a Ph.D. in anthropology from the University of New Mexico. Early fieldwork in indigenous societies of the Americas and later research conducted across the Middle East, Central Asia, and East Asia have well equipped her for this worldwide analysis of the importance of the horse in human society. She is a member of the New York Academy of Sciences and the American Anthropological Association.

THE HORSE IN
HUMAN HISTORY

PITA KELEKNA

CAMBRIDGE
UNIVERSITY PRESS

CAMBRIDGE UNIVERSITY PRESS
Cambridge, New York, Melbourne, Madrid, Cape Town, Singapore, São Paulo, Delhi

Cambridge University Press
32 Avenue of the Americas, New York, NY 10013-2473, USA

www.cambridge.org
Information on this title: www.cambridge.org/9780521736299

First published 2009

Printed in the United States of America

A catalog record for this publication is available from the British Library.

Library of Congress Cataloging in Publication data

Kelekna, Pita, 1938–
The horse in human history / Pita Kelekna.
    p.   cm.
Includes bibliographical references and index.
ISBN 978-0-521-51659-4 (hardback) – ISBN 978-0-521-73629-9 (pbk.)
1. Horses – History.   2. Animals and civilization.   I. Title.
SF283.K437   2009
636.1009 – dc22   2008043690

ISBN 978-0-521-51659-4 hardback
ISBN 978-0-521-73629-9 paperback

To
my sons,
John and Tiran

CONTENTS

Acknowledgments   *page* xiii

1 **Introduction to Equestrian Man and to *Equus***   1

   Six Thousand Years of Human–Equine Relations   2
   Wild Equids – c 60 Million Years Ago to the Present   6
   Equid Paleontology   7
   Extant *Equus* in the Wild   12
   Equus ferus in the Old World   16

2 ***Equus caballus*: Horse Domestication and
   Agro-Pastoralism across the Eurasian Steppes**   21

   The Transition from Food Procurement to Plant and
      Animal Domestication   22
   The Concomitant Development of Metallurgy   25
   Emergence of the Centralized Alluvial State   27
   Peripheral Farming and Eneolithic Exploitation of the
      Horse on the Eurasian Steppes   28
   Why the Domestication of the Horse?   39
   Criticisms – and Near Eastern Comparisons   41
   Yamnaya Horizon – Steppe Expansion West and East
      (3500–2400 BC)   44
   Andronovo Horizon – Steppe Expansion East and
      South (2000–900 BC)   49
   Equestrian Penetration of the Eastern Deserts   55
   Indo-European Diaspora   57
   Summary   64

Contents

3 Nomadic Horse Culture of the Steppes   67

Mobile Dwellings of the Steppes   68
Steppe Technology and Weaponry   73
The Horse – Sacred Symbol of Rebirth   78
Steppe Kurgans and Ritual Burial   79
Regalia of the Pazyryk Kurgans   82
Scythian Rituals of Sacrifice, Dismemberment,
   and Regeneration   86
The Nomad Ritual of *Buzkashi*   89

4 Expansion from the Steppes to Southwestern and Southern Asia   92

Early Indo-European Invasion across the Near East   93
   The Hittite State in Anatolia   93
   The Chariot in Warfare   95
   Training of the Chariot Horse   98
   War Chariots of Kadesh and Troy   99
   The Appearance of the Military Steed in Battle   104
Aryan Expansion from the Steppes through
   Central Asia   107
   Aryan Migrations South   108
   The *Rgveda*   110
   The Vedic *Asvamedha* Horse Sacrifice   113
   Aryan Equestrian Migrations West   116
   Ancient Iranians   119
   The Achaemenid Equestrian Empire   120
   Europe's Defiance of Achaemenid
   Equestrian Might   126

5 China and the Steppes beyond Its Borders   135

Equestrian China   135
   Arrival of the Horse in China   136
   The Qin Equestrian Conquest of China   141
   Xiongnu Nomads   143
   Chinese Equestrian Expansion   145
Equestrian Cultures of Cosmopolitan Central Asia   150
   From Vedic Roots, Buddhism Travels North
   to China   151

On Horseback West Meets East – the Silk Road 155
Via Nomadic Central Asia, China's Early Impact on
the West 160

6 **Equestrian Europe – Solar Edifices, Hippodromes, and
Arthurian Chivalry** 165

Early Indo-Europeans in Europe 165
Prehistoric Solar Edifices 166
Celtic Migrations across Europe 171
The Horse in Greek War and Myth 175
Cavalry Wars between Rome and Carthage 181
Resistance to Rome and the Boudican Revolt 184
Roman Equestrian Might 187
Solar Edifices of Rome 191
Equestrian Invasions from the Steppes 195
The Arthurian Epic – Chivalry in the West 199
Byzantium – Equestrian Bastion of Christianity in
the East 204

7 **Arabian Conquest from the South** 209

Turn of the Era to Mid-First Millennium AD 209
Crossroads of Continents 209
Byzantine and Sasanian Imperial Policies
toward Arabia 212
The Prophet Muhammad 214
Military Expansion of the Islamic State out
of Arabia 216
Horses of the Deserts 217
Equestrian Expansion of Islam Eastward 221
The Umayyad Caliphate and the Shia Schism 223
The Twelve and Seven Imams 224
The Epic Drama of *Taziyeh* – Opera on Horseback 226
Abbasid Caliphate and Turkic Incursion 231
Equestrian Expansion of Islam Westward 235
Islamic Advance across the Iberian Peninsula and
Defeat at Poitiers 237
The Song of Roland 239
The Heavy-Armored European Knight 241
Al-Andalus 242

Arabic Efflorescence 244
Berber Cavalry Rebellion from Africa 247

8 **Turkic-Invader Converts to Islam and Crusader Opponents** 253

The *Shahnameh* 253
Equestrian Invaders from the East 259
Equestrian Invaders from the West 259
The Enduring Legacy of the Equestrian Warrior Orders 272

9 **From the Steppes, the Altaic Nomad Conquest of Eurasia** 281

The Mongol Equestrian Expansion across Eurasia 281
The Epic of the Horsehair Spirit Banner 282
Emergence of Mongol Power 285
Equestrian Conquests in the West 293
Death of Genghis Khan 297
Successors of Genghis Khan 298
Mongol Trade across Asia and Multicultural Efflorescence 304
Khubilai Khan and Yuan China 304
The Cosmopolitan Ilkhanate – Arts and Sciences across Equestrian Asia 309
The Mongol Impact across Asia to Europe 313
Successor States to Nomadic Equestrian Militarism 317
Warrior Horsemen East of the Asian Mainland 318
Equestrian Conquests in West Asia and West of Asia 324
Steppe Nomad Legacy across Eurasia 330

10 **From Europe, *Equus* Returns to Its Continent of Origin** 333

Europe toward the End of the Middle Ages 334
The Palio of Siena 338
Late Medieval Warfare 341
The Spanish Reconquista 344
Equus Extinct in the Western Hemisphere and *Equus* Returns 348
Mesoamerica and the Spanish Conquest of Tenochtitlan 354
The Andes and the Spanish Conquest of Tawantinsuyu 359
Post-Conquista Europe 365
Horses of Rebellion in the Americas 371

Contents

11 Horses Are Us   380

  Hemispheres with and without Horses   380
  The Impact of Equestrianism around the World   387
  Homo equestriens   398

References   407

Index   449

ACKNOWLEDGMENTS

First, I must recognize my debt to three scholars from very different branches of anthropology: Patricia Draper, mentor and longtime friend, who in my research urged me "to leave no stone unturned"; Robert Carneiro of the American Museum of Natural History, whose great knowledge and generosity have inspired and encouraged many a fledgling anthropologist returning from the Amazon; and finally, the late Alfonso Ortiz, whose tutelage in Tewa mythology and extraordinary erudition in the sphere of ritual symbolism prepared me well for the interpretation of the many epics accompanying the horse across the ages.

Comparably, this book is built on the pioneering efforts of numerous scholars of diverse nationalities. From opposite ends of Eurasia, J. P. Mallory's linguistic analyses of Indo-European complement Victor Mair's literary and archaeological studies of ancient China and Persia, with emphasis on the centuries-long role of *Kulturvermittlers* played by Iranians. The many archaeologists and other specialists to whose work I am indebted include Juliet Clutton-Brock, Elena Kuzmina, Mary Aiken Littauer, Joost Crouwel, Renate Rolle, Sandor Bokonyi, Asko Parpola, E. N. Chernykh, Hans-Georg Huettel, Dmitry Telegin, Janos Harmatta, Ann Hyland, Stuart Piggott, Robert Drews, Peter Andrews, David Owen, Kazuya Maekawa, Anatoly Khazanov, Brian Fagan, John Saunders, Thomas Allsen, Jack Weatherford, and Trevor Dupuy. I am deeply appreciative of the research of Sandra Olsen, David Anthony, and Dorcas Brown, whose dogged fieldwork of decades has furnished Western readers with critical information on the archaeology of the Eurasian steppes.

I most gratefully acknowledge the generous financial assistance provided by the Leonard Hastings Schoff Fund of Columbia University

Seminars in meeting publication costs and the sympathetic support of Robert Belknap and his administrative staff. It was in the Ecological Systems and Cultural Evolution seminar where I first learned from Ross Hassig of the logistical problems encountered by pedestrian Aztec armies in confrontation with Spanish equestrian forces. Realization of this extraordinary difference between New and Old World capability in war, transport, trade, and communications ultimately led to my undertaking cross-cultural evaluation of horse presence/absence worldwide. Progress in the book was additionally stimulated through presentation and discussion of my data in this and other Columbia seminars, namely, Latin America and Brazil, all of whose chairs and members I sincerely thank: Carol Henderson, Martin Poblete, Laura Randall, Roberta Delson, Diana Brown, Miguel Pinedo-Vasquez, Barbara Price, Malva Filer, Harriet Klein, and Anne Whitehouse. I wish also to express my gratitude to my anonymous reviewers, whose recommendations greatly strengthened my work; to my gifted and gracious editor, Beatrice Rehl; and to James Dunn, Karin Horler, Peggy Rote, and other members of Cambridge's crack production team.

Special thanks go to dear friends whose curiosity and criticisms have spurred me across the rough stretches of my manuscript: Jane Townsend, Kathleen Killorin, Carol Joiner, Margaret Lanzetta, David Packer, Jim Fulop, Barbara Bode, Laila Williamson, Lilian Scott, Nina Swidler, Helen Lukievics, Stuart Guthrie, John Ryan, Bill Peace, and Bruce and Shirley Hyland. Finally, I thank my family, Gail, Jake, Kelly, and Brian, for their tolerance of my foibles and eccentricities while in "writing" harness.

THE HORSE IN HUMAN HISTORY

INTRODUCTION TO EQUESTRIAN MAN
AND TO *EQUUS*

THIS BOOK EXAMINES THE EMERGENCE OF HORSEPOWER IN HUMAN society and its cultural ramifications around the globe over the last 6,000 years. Within anthropology, cultural advance has traditionally been viewed in the context of the sedentary agricultural state. But the horse, in its original evolution in North America and repeated radiations and extinctions worldwide, developed the anatomical features to become the fastest distance-running quadruped on earth in arid regions of poorest forage. To assess the impact of the horse on human culture then, we must turn first, not to the well-watered heartlands of pristine civilization, but to the steppes and deserts of our world. Consideration of these peripheral zones will both challenge and complement existing theory by exposing important data entirely overlooked in previous interpretations. Analysis of man's symbiosis with the domesticated horse necessarily takes the reader to regions remote from urban centers and pays special attention to mobile elements of nomadic society, too often deemed marginal or transitory. Horse domestication probably first occurred in the fourth millennium BC on the Eurasian steppes, a great expanse of grasslands stretching eastward from Hungary for more than 6,400 km to the borders of China. Tribes of that vast peripheral area were notoriously responsible for the depredations and invasions that over the millennia threatened the heartlands of civilization to the west, south, and east. While it is true that mobile horsemen from the steppes relentlessly harassed the imperial armies of sedentary states, it is also true that their far-ranging routes across forbidding mountains and deserts afforded rapid transport of distant trade goods, both essential and exotic. With trade went cultural exchange: adoption of different cultigens, implementation of new technologies, introduction of foreign inventions, dissemination of ideas, diffusion of religions, the spread of science and art. The history of the horse and its extraordinary impact on human culture explores this dual reality. On the one hand, the increasing effectiveness of the war horse – its sophisticated armature, weaponry, and superior military force – wrought utter destruction in war; yet in the wake of conquest, rapid horsepower greatly extended the scale and complexity of civilization. The current work traces the rise of Old World equestrianism across Asia, Europe, and North Africa and in the final chapters describes the devastation of the equestrian conquest of horseless Amerindian societies, citing it as model for subsequent Atlanto-European planetary expansion and colonization. Throughout the book ideology is considered: the great epics that inspire and inflame equestrian militarism.

SIX THOUSAND YEARS OF HUMAN–EQUINE RELATIONS

From the perspective of movement from the periphery and always noting the dual character of horsepower, its destructive and constructive qualities, this work undertakes to identify the technology, tactics, and ideology that allowed equestrians of different epochs and geographical areas to dominate with the horse wide expanses of arid and semiarid lands and, by successfully traversing these barren regions, to disperse important new ideas and inventions across continents. To document early nomadic movement across the Eurasian steppes and later military invasions with the horse of sedentary centers of civilization in the Old World and later the New World, six major migrations of progressively broader scale are recognized.

1. FOURTH TO THIRD MILLENNIUM BC: PASTORALIST PIONEERS ACROSS THE EURASIAN STEPPES. In the fourth millennium BC, Indo-European agriculturalists of the Pontic-Caspian region, already practicing herding and metallurgy, initially domesticated the horse. The resultant horse culture facilitated early extension west into Europe and rapid advance eastward across the Eurasian steppe interior with successful adaptation to that inhospitable environment. Techniques of adaptation are discussed in terms of steppe exploration: wheeled vehicles, portable dwellings, weaponry, primitive irrigation, and bronze, gold, and iron metallurgy. Nomad ethos is also examined in the art and ceremony of the great funerary tumuli scattered the entire length of the steppes. The extreme mobility of agro-pastoralism ranging over thousands of

kilometers is contrasted with the sedentariness of circumscribed alluvial states emerging in Asia and North Africa during this epoch.

2. SECOND TO FIRST MILLENNIUM BC: STEPPE INVASIONS OF
OLD WORLD CIVILIZATIONS. After 2,000 years of successful agro-
pastoralism, the high mobility achieved allowed expansion out of the
marginal steppe habitat, military invasion of urban centers of sedentary
civilization, and the establishment by horse charioteers of states in those
ancient nuclear areas. In the Near East, North Africa, Iran, India, and
China, iron weaponry and war chariots dominated the battlefield, the
ancient scriptures of the *Rgveda* and *Avesta* reflecting this expansionary
might. In the second millennium BC, the Hittites employed rigorous
techniques in training the chariot horse and were the first to deploy
horsepower in the coercive relocation of vanquished populations to
frontier zones of their Anatolian state. At the end of the second millennium BC, the recurved composite bow facilitated the transition from
battle chariot to war horse. At the beginning of the first millennium BC,
while steppe mass chariotry attacked China in the east, military cavalry first appeared on the western steppe. Through selective breeding,
the Iranian-speaking Medes produced a larger horse fully capable of
carrying an armed warrior with combat weapons. Cavalry and chariot conquests culminated in the first far-flung equestrian empires that
effectively absorbed earlier nuclear states, the Achaemenid in the west
stretching from India to the Mediterranean, the Qin in the east encompassing the whole of China. Astonishingly, introduction of advanced
horse technologies to these two regions, separated by vast distances,
triggered identical parallel developments at opposite ends of Asia. In
both empires thousands of kilometers of roads were constructed for
equid transport; a unitary language and writing system were imposed;
and coinage, weights, and measures were standardized across the realm.
Burgeoning overland trade consequently spurred maritime commerce.
In China canals were built to transport foreign commodities from southern ports deep into the interior. In the west a canal, wide enough for
two ships to pass, was dug between the Red Sea and the Nile to link
trade from the Indus to the Mediterranean.

3. TURN OF THE ERA: MEDITERRANEAN EQUESTRIAN MILITARISM.
By the end of the first millennium BC, the war chariot and then cavalry had been introduced to all centers of civilization across Eurasia

and North Africa, whether by outright conquest or deliberate acquisition. The ancient megalithic structures of prehistoric Europe are first described in their important ceremonial function as solar centers of equestrian ritual. Europe's equestrian militarism is then discussed in terms of early intercontinental confrontation during the Trojan war, later Greco-Macedonian defiance of Asia's Persian might, Hannibal's Punic invasion of Spain and Italy, and Rome's near defeat and subsequent adoption of Carthaginian cavalry tactics to colonize most of Europe and the Mediterranean littoral. Rome's military power was celebrated with great pomp in the solar racetracks and amphitheaters of the empire. By the turn of the era, trade was bustling along the nomads' Silk Road as exotic products were exchanged between Occident and Orient. Great religions – Buddhism, Judaism, and Christianity – also diffused on horseback along the routes linking Europe, India, and China. But as warring equestrian tribes continued to invade Europe from the steppes, Rome's strength ebbed. In the sixth century AD, the Mongol Avars brought an important Chinese invention west, the metal stirrup, which allowed the rider to grip the lance in a couched position and to attack an adversary with the full force of his charging horse, a factor of critical significance in the later development of medieval knightly warfare. As Rome retreated, Arthurian legends of great equestrian heroes arose in the north to inspire medieval traditions of chivalry.

4. LATE FIRST MILLENNIUM AD: ARAB EQUESTRIAN ASSAULT FROM THE SOUTHERN DESERTS. In the south, Byzantine dominance in the Mediterranean was challenged in AD 636 by equestrian nomads from a new periphery, not the northern steppes as before, but the southern deserts. Supported by the dromedary, Arab horses sped across the deserts of the Middle East and North Africa, conquering as far as Sasanian Persia in the east, Visigothic Spain in the west, and south across the Sahara to tap the gold wealth of Ghana. Building on earlier Egyptian, Babylonian, Jewish, Hindu, and Greek scholarship, Arabic learning soared to new heights of human endeavor as scientists and philosophers of different ethnic backgrounds pursued knowledge in diverse disciplines, with rapid communications permitting an exchange of ideas unprecedented in earlier civilizations. But religious strife struck stark divisions in Islamic society; bitter feuding occurred between Umayyads and Abbasids, Sunni and Shia, schisms that to this day rend the region apart and are ever immortalized in the great epic of *Taziyeh*. This political strife was further exacerbated around the turn of the millennium

by nomadic Seljuk incursions into the region and the later Crusader challenge to Islam from the west. During the Crusader-Saracen conflict in the Levant, from western Europe to the eastern Mediterranean, there developed the world's first systematic long-distance maritime transport of horses. We also note during this period the emergence of the equestrian military orders – Christian warrior monks and Muslim slave Mamluks – and their enduring influence over political developments of later centuries respectively in Europe and the Middle East, until the time of Napoleon.

5. EARLY SECOND MILLENNIUM AD: ALTAIC NOMAD CONQUEST OF EURASIA. From 2000 BC to AD 1000 armies invading from the peripheral steppes and deserts had succeeded only in partial conquests of Eurasia; this invasion pattern, however, was shortly to escalate. Early in the second millennium AD there erupted in furthermost Mongolia an equestrian military force that was to convulse both continents. Employing Chinese siege technology as no nomads had before and following audacious military strategy, the Mongol conquest extended from the Pacific to the Baltic to persist for several centuries in the form of distinct khanates. In the aftermath of brutal massacres and tumultuous destruction of the environment, technicians were exchanged across the length and breadth of Asia, luxury industries resulted that reflected the talents of many lands, intercontinental trade flourished, and scientific exchange followed; great Chinese inventions – printing, gunpowder, and forged steel – flowed west to Europe to bridge the gap between the medieval and modern eras. With the sack of Constantinople in 1453, the Ottomans emerged as successors to the Mongols, with Turkish horses invading Europe as far west as Vienna. In the face of this latest invader from the steppes, countries of western Europe turned desperately to the oceans in order to circumvent the Muslim stranglehold of Middle Eastern trade routes.

6. LATE SECOND MILLENNIUM AD: ATLANTO-EUROPEAN EQUESTRIAN WORLD CONQUEST. Having successfully traversed the Atlantic, on his second voyage to the Americas in 1493 Columbus astutely introduced 50 warhorses to the hemisphere where the horse had been extinct for 9,000 years. Profiting from Crusader experience in long-distance horse transport across the Mediterranean, from Europe's westernmost fringe Spain promptly dispatched hundreds of horses, enabling mounted Christian knights to topple two advanced civilizations and in a brief few years to

conquer more than 25 million people. Contrast is drawn between the technological achievements of Old and New World cultures at the time of contact, with notable differences attributed to horse presence and absence in the two hemispheres. Absence of the horse clearly placed Amerindians at a disadvantage in terms of military organization and inter-polity communication. The devastation of Europe's equestrian conquest of horseless Amerindian societies is then described as model for subsequent European maritime exploration in which, financed by the vast wealth of the New World, nations of the Atlantic seaboard took to the oceans with their ships and horses to colonize other horseless lands around the globe. In uncharted regions, horses provided vital transportation for the development of agriculture and industry. But as gunboat diplomacy reigned at sea, equestrian warfare raged on land. By successfully introducing horse rearing to arid Australia in the early nineteenth century, then shipping half a million Australian warhorses to military campaigns across Asia and Africa, Britain quickly gained the competitive edge in empire building to outstrip all European colonial rivals. Thus, while accelerating the rate of progress, well into the twentieth century the horse's speed and strength also conferred a military might that inflicted untold suffering on millions. As heirs to six millennia of horse power, in today's hypermechanized era of "iron horses," "horseless carriages," and "winged Pegasuses" encircling the earth, we must recognize that rapid technological advance and economic expansion often have been accomplished at great human cost and have contributed significantly to environmental degradation. As our wars continue unabated, the final chapter examines critically our horse legacy from the past – the modern obsession with speed, our insatiable consumption of the world's resources, and, in our unrelenting drive for acceleration, the irreversible destruction of our planet.

WILD EQUIDS – c 60 MILLION YEARS AGO TO THE PRESENT

Before we embark on man's high-speed adventure on horseback, first let us try to recapture a more ancient epic, that of the wild horse itself – long, long before its domestication. *Homo* as a bipedal hominid first evolved some six or seven million years ago. The genus *Equus*, which includes the modern horse and its closest relatives, the asses and zebras, by contrast is the result of more than 55 million years of highly specialized evolution in the development of rapid forward locomotion, revealed to us in an abundant trail of robust fossil limbs across most continents.

Equid Paleontology

The family *Equidae,* the horse family in its broadest sense, subsumes modern *Equus* and all fossil relatives derivative from the ancestral line as far back as the Eocene. In that distant epoch, the earliest equid to become differentiated from ancestral *Perissodactyla* was *Hyracotherium,* or "dawn horse." A timid herbivore between 25 and 50 cm in height, it was adapted to browsing succulent leaves, soft seeds, and fruits of the forest. Over the next 60 million years many evolutionary changes would transform this diminutive creature into the robust horse we know today. In *Hyracotherium,* the heel of all four feet was raised above the ground, the weight of the body being carried on padded digits[1] or toes. This, combined with the slight lengthening of the toe and shin bones, gave added distance from knee to ground that greatly facilitated running (Simpson 1951:116–119). Another perissodactyl innovation was the astragalus bone in the ankle joint, which has two raised parallel ridges at the point of articulation with the tibia. This type of joint permits ease of flexure in a fore and aft direction but minimizes wasteful lateral movement and the possibility of dislocation, an early adaptation, it would seem, to high-speed travel over distance (Hulbert 1996:17). By 58 million years ago, hyracotheres had encircled the planet, only to become extinct in Eurasia during the Oligocene. This pattern of global radiation and Old World extinction would occur repeatedly before modern *Equus* finally evolved in North America (Fig. 1.1).

Equids survived in North America to follow a distinct evolutionary course. During the Oligocene, a series of changes occurred in *Mesohippus* and *Miohippus,* both of which stood about 6 hands or 60 cm.[2] One significant feature of the hind leg distinguished *Miohippus* from *Mesohippus.* The cannon bone, that is, the metatarsal of the middle toe, previously in contact with a single ankle bone, now articulated with the outer ankle bone, thereby forming a broader, stronger joint. All four feet of these two equids had only three toes (tridactyly), the middle toe being much larger than the side toes (Simpson 1951:124, 127); retention of side toes probably provided greater traction on muddy surfaces and lateral stabilization when turning at speed to avoid bushes and trees (MacFadden 1992:259). The late Oligocene was an important time of

---

[1] In all perissodactyls, the first digit (equivalent of the human thumb or big toe) is missing on fore- and hindfeet, as is the fifth digit on hindfeet.

[2] An equid's height is calculated in hands; 1 hand equals 4 in. or 10.16 cm. This measurement is taken from ground level to the highest points of the horse's withers.

branching and radiation as different lines developed from *Miohippus*. But, again during the Miocene, many of these equids became extinct as increasing global aridity led to the reduction of forests and the spread of grasslands, conditions under which many other browsing herbivores perished at that time (MacFadden 1992:160–161; Hulbert 1996:23–24).

In these open terrains of the Miocene a new rich food supply became available – grass. As a mixed feeder *Parahippus* was transitional between browsing and grazing. But grasses were hard to digest because the cell walls contained highly resistant lignin and silica. In the new equid adaptation of grazing, extensive chewing was required to break down the tough phytoliths in order to release the nutritious cell contents. To exploit this new food source, radical transformations were needed in dentition (MacFadden 1992:229; Simpson 1951:131). To cope with the harsh diet of grass mixed with abrasive grit, hypsodonty (long-toothedness) evolved progressively in the successive genera of *Parahippus* and *Merychippus*. High-crowned cheek teeth with deep ridges were developed. With this increase in crown height, only the end of the crown protruded from the gum, leaving the remainder buried in the socket, reserved for future use. With wear the whole tooth kept moving outward to maintain an efficient grinding surface over a prolonged period, significantly extending the lifetime of the animal. The final result, completely developed in *Merychippus*, was cheek dentition admirably adapted for laterally grinding the lower jaw against the upper. Also important for long-distance travel across grasslands was the equid digestive track, which, in contrast to the bovid divided stomach with rumen, had alongside the large intestine a developed cecum, housing symbiotic microorganisms that digest the cellulose of grass. The cecum in modern Equus measures 1.25 m in length and has a capacity of 30 L. This meant that equids, unlike cattle, did not need to rest after feeding in order to ruminate (Clutton-Brock 1992:21–22; MacFadden 1992:237; Simpson 1951:132–135).

In both *Parahippus* and *Merychippus*, while the two vestigial side toes persisted, all body weight was supported by the convex hoof of the third central digit. Also, the ulna of the lower forefoot in *Merychippus* had fused solidly with the radius to form a more rigid structure in adaptation to fast running on hard surfaces. Strong ligaments ran from the central metapodial to the rear of the lengthened toe bones to provide support and springlike action to the foot, developments occasioned by the real need for a more rapid gait (Hulbert 1996:24). Geological evidence of this epoch points to increasing aridity and open

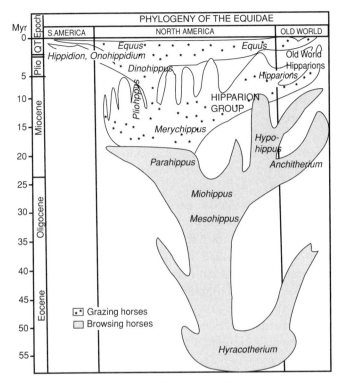

FIGURE 1.1. Evolution of equid genera leading to the emergence of Equus 4.5 million years ago (after MacFadden 1992:fig. 5.14). Reprinted with the permission of Cambridge University Press.

country. As body size increased to 10 hands so did equid longevity and home range. During different seasons of the year, equids would have ranged widely in the search of patchy food resources. Such increased cursoriality would have led to the development of greater stamina in the locomotory system of equids. At the same time, in an open habitat the equids were more visible and thus more vulnerable to predation. Speed was therefore at a premium, not only for finding food, but also for escaping swift mammalian predators (MacFadden 1992:260). These important adaptations occurred at a time when abundant grasslands afforded a new ecological niche for equid evolution.

The late Miocene was characterized by great generic diversity in which these new adaptations were further developed into the Pliocene by successive species of tridactyl grazers. *Merychippus* was superseded by tridactyl *Hipparion*, which in terms purely of dentition was the most advanced equid ever and effectively migrated across the Old World

(Hulbert 1996:27). But the next extremely important innovation took place in eastern North America. There in *Pliohippus* the two side toes were lost, becoming vestigial splints beneath the skin of the upper portion of the foot and resulting in one digit per foot – monodactyly (Fig. 1.2). The "chestnuts" and "ergots," horny outgrowths of skin visible on the limb surface, are vestiges of these ancestral toes. Toward the end of the Miocene, in the west later monodactyls evolved in the arid intermontane basins of Utah to become the earliest members of the *Equus* lineage. Around this time global climates underwent drastic change, transitioning into cyclic glacial/interglacial ages. The rich savannas were replaced by less diverse grasslands, and many savanna species became extinct. Better suited to earlier moist habitats, tridactyls perished in North America by the late Pliocene, only hipparionines persisting in parts of the Old World until the mid-Pleistocene.[3] As will be seen in the chapters ahead, such massive extinctions of tridactyls would have future repercussions for human culture. Monodactyls, superbly suited to drier climes, would spread widely across the arid and temperate zones of the planet but never adapt to the earlier tridactyl habitat in moist regions – particularly the tropics. After 7 million years ago, the monodactyl *Dinohippus* dominated the North American continent until c 4.5 million years ago when *Equus* finally emerged. By the mid-Pleistocene *Equus* had spread to South America, where it coexisted with earlier immigrants, the monodactyl *Hippidion* and *Onohippidium*. In an intricately branching and radiating process, *Equus* also populated the Old World. Early differentiated in the sub-Saharan Pleistocene were the progenitors of modern zebras. The other groups of *Equus*, the asses and the horse (ancestor of modern wild and domestic horses), probably originated in North America 1.5 million years ago, the asses dispersing to the Old World 900,000 years ago, the horse somewhat later becoming very successful across Eurasia (Hulbert 1996:28–32).

Ironically having populated most of the globe and successfully survived the last Ice Age, *Equus* became extinct 9,000 years ago in South and North America, the latter the locus of its 60 million years of evolution. It is unclear what precipitated this extinction. Vast herds roamed during the Pleistocene and the prairies were relatively unaffected by the glaciers, but camelids and mastodons too became extinct in North

---

[3] The Quaternary geologic period is divided into the Pleistocene epoch, which began 1.6 million years ago, and the most recent Holocene epoch, dating from 10,000 years ago.

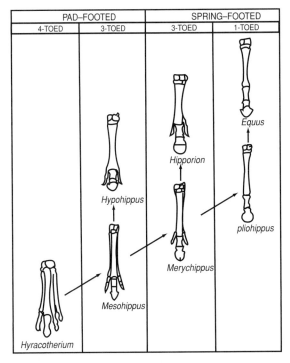

PAD–FOOTED		SPRING–FOOTED	
4-TOED	3-TOED	3-TOED	1-TOED

FIGURE 1.2. Selected stages in the evolution of the forefoot of equids, from four-toed to one-toed. Drawn about the same size and not to scale, for comparison (Simpson 1951:fig. 31). By permission of Oxford University Press.

America. Yet bison that subsist on similar forage as *Equus* persisted undiminished. Disease is unlikely for it probably would have impacted a large variety of animals, including the bison. The entrance of Amerindians into the New World, human harassment, and primitive overhunting may have been contributing factors (Simpson 1951:148–150).

At the close of the Ice Age, *Equus* finally stood between 12 and 13 hands.[4] Ever alert to predator approach and poised for instant flight, *Equus* had a long neck and especially long head that enabled it to feed on the low grass while its eyes remained high and watchful. In the elongated muzzle the first premolar (wolf tooth) had disappeared as had commonly the canines in mares, widening even further the diastema between front and cheek teeth that was to be invaluable for future placement of the bit (mouthpiece of the bridle) in domestication (Clutton-Brock 1992:21; Duncan, Ryder, Asa, and Feh 1992:3–4).

4 The exception is Grevy's zebra, which measured closer to 15 hands.

In terms of locomotion, *Equus* had increased the effective length of the leg where it counted the most, at the lower end. With the long metacarpals/metatarsals elevated high above the ground, the animal walked permanently on the tip of one hoof. Slender but extremely strong, in a hard run, one leg could sustain the full weight of the animal. The toe had highly complex digital ligaments that furnished a spring mechanism. In running, upon landing on one foot the middle toe was strongly flexed by impact, thereby stretching the elastic ligaments and creating potential energy. This spring facilitated remarkably fast and efficient action in equids of increasing weight (Simpson 1951:198–201). Morphological changes resulted as a consequence of this springing motion: greater density of the trabeculae improving the strength of the limb bones, reorientation of upper limb bones and musculature for a more powerful stride, and increased restriction of lateral limb motion. Its speed mechanisms could bear little more weight. *Equus* had become as fast as mechanically possible for an animal of its size, its powerful limbs supporting a body mass in modern times often in excess of 500 kg and massive compressive stress on the skeleton during running. Today's racehorse is capable of galloping at 65 km per hour and of completing more than two strides per second, the upper range for all mammals. For short distances the cheetah exceeds the speed of the horse, but over long distances the speed, strength, and stamina of *Equus* are unparalleled (MacFadden 1992:246–247, 259).

Extant Equus *in the Wild*

Wild *Equus* thus spread to every continent on earth except Australia and Antarctica. Wherever the preferred diet of grasses was too sparse, as in deserts or winter, the Equus was an effective consumer of coarse forage – digestible parts of bushes and trees. In the wild today, the modern genus *Equus* is represented by four subgenera: zebras, Asian asses, African asses, and horses. All species of wild *Equus* have short upright manes and a dark dorsal stripe along their coat. The gestation period of today's wild equids is approximately one year, 20 percent longer than that of ruminants of comparable size, ensuring that equid foals are born at an advanced stage of development and able to keep up with the moving band (Duncan et al. 1992:5).

Striped equids are limited to Africa and fall into three distinct species: Plains zebra (*Equus burchelli*); Mountain zebra (*Equus zebra*); and Grevy's zebra (*Equus grevyi*). Numbering over half a million, **Plains**

zebras are the most abundant and widespread of modern wild equids, formerly occupying the grasslands and savannahs of Africa south of the Ethiopian Massif and the Zaire rain forest (Duncan and Gakahu 1992:12–13). By contrast, **Mountain zebras** are encountered only from southern Angola to Cape Province along the edges of deserts through semiarid to savannah grasslands, preferring rocky or mountainous terrain; in winter they can range up to 20 km from a water source (Novellie, Lloyd, and Joubert 1992:7–8). **Grevy's zebras** are possibly the most primitive morphologically and certainly the largest of the wild equids, with adult males weighing up to 450 kg and adult females 10 percent less. They inhabit the semiarid scrub/grassland of northern Kenya and neighboring areas of Ethiopia and Somalia (Rowen and Ginsberg 1992:10).

The **Asian wild asses**, in historic times, covered the desert areas from the Black Sea eastward to the Gobi desert, and south as far as Arabia, Persia, and northwest India (Fig. 1.3). In the twentieth century, however, their populations shrank to a fraction of this range (Clark and Duncan 1992:17). The largest species, the **kiangs** (*Equus kiang*) are well adapted to the high elevations of the Tibetan and Ladakh plateaus, rising as high as 4,100–4,800 m. Equipped with hard lips and a horny palate, in level areas they feed on coarse grasses and swamp plants, which would wreck the mouths of other equids. In August and September, at the peak of forage availability, kiangs acquire a thick layer of insulating fat for the winter ahead. The other species of Asian ass is the **hemione** (*Equus hemionus*), shorter in stature and with a smaller head than the kiang but with longer, slender limbs and a lighter coat. Local names abound for the hemione, among which the kulan of Central Asia and the onager of the Middle East are perhaps the most familiar (Woodward 1996:198–199). Another species of wild ass, *Equus hydruntinus*, of uncertain ancestry, survived in southern Europe into the Holocene and was eaten in Spain and eastern Europe during the Neolithic, but shortly thereafter became extinct (Anthony 1994:186).

The **African wild ass** (*Equus africanus*), originally widespread from the Moroccan Atlas across North Africa to Nubia, Sudan, and Somalia (possibly extending into the Arabian peninsula), is the most endangered of extant equids. An elegant, fine-limbed animal, it trots freely over rocks and gallops at high speed across the desert. Today, perhaps as many as 3,000 of these animals inhabit remote arid grasslands and bushlands of Ethiopia and Somalia, where temperatures soar in summer to 50°C. To a larger extent than their Asian counterpart, occupying harsh, rocky terrain, they feed upon forbs as well as grass and also browse. It is known that in recent times in the Hoggar mountains of Algeria, herdsmen used to tether domestic donkey mares in heat out on the range near a water hole to be covered by a wild stallion of the Atlantic ass subspecies. This and the fact that domestic asses frequently wandered off to join the wild population resulted in genetic swamping. The genomes of wild and domestic asses became extensively mixed. This process of introgression was probably the primary factor accounting for the disappearance of the wild African ass from the northern territories of its range (Moehlman 1992:15–16).

Today *Equus* has two different social systems, which are linked to two types of mating patterns. In equids of extremely arid habitats, namely, the African wild ass, Grevy's zebra, and the Asian wild asses, a dominant male often defends a large territory for a long period and has mating rights over all estrous females, whenever they occur on his territory. Lasting bonds are not established between adults. Thus African and Asian asses and Grevy's zebras form loose groups, sometimes in aggregations of more than 100 individuals, where the only long-term relationship is between a mother and her offspring, often until the age of two. Young males roam as bachelor groups without access to females to the point that they are able to defend a territory of their own (Duncan et al. 1992:4).

A second type of behavior, apparently unique among ungulates, is found in the Plains zebra, the Mountain zebra, and the wild horse (*Equus ferus przewalskii*).[5] Nonterritorial by contrast, these species form smaller (occasionally numbering as many as 17 animals), long-term family groups of one stallion, a harem of one to six mares, and their young. To reduce direct inbreeding, offspring of both sexes move out from the natal group. Fillies leave at two years of age to join another reproductive unit, although often observing an experimental period of moving across different groups before settling into the permanent unit. Once integrated they rarely change and among mares observe a linear dominance hierarchy based on age. Males in the natal group mature later, after three, when they may harass mares in estrus and are expelled by the father. These lower-ranking stallions spend a couple of years in company of other bachelors practicing the fighting skills necessary to assemble a harem. These stallions may establish temporary alliances with other stallions of comparable rank to cooperate in defending a harem against rivals. But by the age of four or five, a dominant stallion

---

[5] Also encountered in *Equus caballus*, the domestic horse.

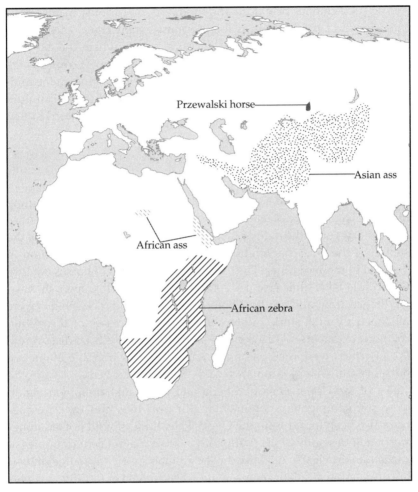

FIGURE 1.3. Extant *Equus* in the wild.

emerges to repulse other males and to secure the harem as his own; only highly aggressive individuals succeed in this. The celibate bachelors may be joined by sick or older males that have been ousted from their family band by a younger challenger. In the family band, during migration the highest-ranking mare leads the way; other mares follow in order of dominance, each one accompanied by their foals in ascending order of age. Protecting the family against predators, the dominant stallion keeps the band moving from the rear (Clutton-Brock 1992:22; Duncan et al. 1992:5).

The predicament of wild equids today is precarious. Increasingly, intensive land use by man is forcing most extant *Equus* species into peripheral habitats outside their ancestral range, where the environment scarcely offers a secure refuge. Not yet discussed of course is the wild horse, a species that in Eurasia actually became extinct in the mid-twentieth century AD, but miraculously by the end of the millennium has been restored to its natural habitat in the wild. Let us turn to that unique story.

Equus ferus *in the Old World*

Information on the wild horse in the Old World is rather ragged, coming to us from a diversity of sources. We will attempt to trace its prehistory and history not to the date of domestication by man, which will be the subject of the next chapter, but to the point of its tragic extinction in the wild in modern times. The earliest human record of horses dates to the Middle Paleolithic (100,000–35,000 BP). As is well known, in western France, Italy, and northern Spain great caves and rock shelters were inhabited by prehistoric hunters. Deep in the recesses of these low-ceilinged chambers, over 2,000 animal paintings have been discovered, 610 of which were rock paintings, engravings, or portable effigies of horses (Bouman and Bouman 1994:5). Similarly, far across Asia in the valley of the Upper Lena of Siberia and the Mankhan-Somon region of western Mongolia, monumental cliff drawings and cave frescoes have also been found from the Upper Paleolithic of wild horses alongside antelopes and woolly mammoths. These magnificent examples of rupestrian art clearly celebrated prey animals as a vital source of food but also employed their representation as symbols of fertility in rituals surrounding the hunt and propitiation of deities (MacFadden 1992:1–3; Okladnikov 1990:56–57).

From cut marks on bones recovered by archaeologists, it is known that in those remote times horses were butchered for their skin and meat on a massive scale. Our best knowledge of primitive hunting tactics comes from the site of Solutre in central France, where recurrent collective horse hunts were conducted during the Upper Paleolithic. In their seasonal migrations there, wild horses followed a natural corridor between two limestone ridges from their winter floodplain habitat on the Saône up into the summer pastures of the western foothills. In this valley, a cul-de-sac served as a natural corral into which panicked horses were driven, whether by placing piles of stone or brush in convergent lines or by controlled brush fires and torches. Whatever the ancient techniques, the kill site at Solutre covered approximately 1 ha, reached over 9 m in depth, and contained the remains of an estimated 32,000–100,000 horses (Olsen 1996a:43–45). As a consequence of overpredation, following the close of the Ice Age, horses in Europe became increasingly rare and by the Neolithic (8,000–4,500 BC) appear to have been extirpated in most of the continent, with small pockets remaining only in central Europe and Spain. However, to the east, skeletal remains of the same horse species once present in the west, although varying in size, have been found to extend into Central Asia. On the plains of the Ukraine and Russia, horses continued to be abundant and as a steppe animal thrived there. Thus, despite intensive hunting and extreme climatic fluctuation, the wild horse persisted in the Old World into the Holocene (Bouman and Bouman 1994:5–7).

In more recent classic times, continued wild horse presence on the steppes was noted by Greek and Roman historians. During the Middle Ages wild horses known as *tarpans* were hunted by nobility in the forests of eastern Europe. And in eighteenth-century Mongolia hundreds of wild horses were reported killed in an imperial hunt by the Manchus (Bouman and Bouman 1994:7–8). Under the Russian tsars various exploratory expeditions were organized deep into Asia, the most famous of which was undertaken by the Polish geographer Colonel Nikolai Michailovich Przewalski. From Kirghiz nomads he obtained the hide and skull of a wild horse, which in 1881 at the Zoological Museum of the Academy of Science of St. Petersburg was accorded the formal name *Equus ferus przewalskii*.

Today we know *Equus ferus* stands between 12 and 14 hands at the withers and is characterized by a compact body build, convex head, and a yellowish dun coat. To withstand the cold a shaggy ashen coat is developed in winter. As in Paleolithic parietal art, the mane of the Przewalski horse is upright, rarely in excess of 20 cm. A dark dorsal stripe runs from the mane along the back onto the lower half of the tail; sometimes a shoulder or half shoulder stripe is evident, as are sharp zebra markings on the lower leg. The food quest governs daily wanderings. With its hard hooves, the horse knows how to dig out plants from under the snow. Normally able to subsist two to four days without water, the wild horse avoids water-hole dependence in winter by utilizing pools of snowmelt. It also obtains water in summer by digging holes with its hoof in salt brine pans (Mohr 1971:41, 45, 59, 66). Grazing with head down, horses have greater than 300° vision, seeing almost in all directions (Houpt and Boyd 1994:230). When confronted by a challenger, a stallion rushes forward to administer lightening bites with the aim of bringing down the enemy. Once an opponent is downed, the dominant stallion keeps him there and may continue fighting until his adversary's legs are broken, skin and ears ripped to shreds, and entrails torn out. When frightened, a band of wild horses runs off in single file, a young stallion in the lead and foals in the middle with their dams. The dominant stallion positions himself on the side of the predator or if hunted from behind guards the rear. When a young foal lags behind, its mother first whinnies encouragingly to it. But it is the stallion that hurries the foal along, pushing it with his nose, grasping it at the withers with his teeth and pulling it, kicking the air threateningly, or throwing the foal in the air to animate it. The stallion will turn to attack a predator, rearing up and striking it with his hooves; similarly a mare will kick with her hind legs (Mohr 1971:67, 72–73).

Nineteenth-century explorer reports of extant wild horses in eastern Asia attracted the attention of many European zoologists. However, even with the aid of Asian nomads from the Altai, early endeavors to capture the wild horse alive were not fruitful. The steppe horses were so rare that weeks would elapse before any were sighted, and once spotted the animals would disappear like a windstorm. Finally, the only viable approach was to attempt in early spring to separate the young foals from the family band. After a long chase in which frequent remounts were required, this was accomplished with the *urak/arkan* (a long stick with a loop of rope at the end). Kept alive on domestic mares' milk supplemented by goats' and sheep's milk, these small animals were bagged to be borne one on either side of a camel to the Trans-Siberian railroad for transportation to European zoos and reserves. During one 1901 expedition 52 foals were captured. To realize such a catch, at least 25 harems had needed to be raided and adult animals shot. In this lamentably misguided all-out effort to preserve the wild species, of the original 52 foals captured only 28 reached Europe alive (Bouman and Bouman 1994:19–22). Subsequently, the numbers of captive wild horses in Russia were significantly diminished during the Bolshevik revolution, although not before Baron Friedrich von Falz-Fein, a rancher in the Ukraine, had successfully trained an imported wild stallion to be ridden (Mohr 1971:69). Later in the twentieth century, the cataclysm of World War II would obliterate many other Przewalski horses across Europe.

The initial breeding of Przewalski wild horses within small groups in isolated zoos was not marked by success. Consanguineous matings and overemployment of specific stud stallions had detrimental genetic effects, combining in the long run to increase juvenile mortality, decrease life span, and reduce the fitness of succeeding generations (Ballou 1994:102, 107). But in time, with Volf's International Studbook and Bouman's computerized pedigree card system, propagation in captivity became more systematically organized as guidelines were formulated for a comprehensive program of international exchange of animals, placing great emphasis on outcrossing to preserve the viability of the gene pool. Success was such that by 1990 in 33 countries across the world, the population of captive wild horses reached a total of 961 (Bouman and Bouman 1994:31–35; Knowles and Wakefield 1992:22).

But while progress had been made in the zoos, not all was well in the wild. During the 1950s zoologists had recorded the presence of several bands of wild horses in Mongolia totaling perhaps as many as 100. However as pastoralism and predation intensified, the rapid-fire modern rifle reached even the remotest regions, where it allowed hunters to annihilate an entire band of wild horses in short shrift. By the 1960s, observed wild-horse presence had dwindled to only sporadic sightings and occasional tracks (Mohr 1971:32). After 1968 no further sighting of wild horses could be confirmed, and it was then assumed that the Przewalski horse was finally extinct in the wild (Bouman and Bouman 1994:31). But with a burgeoning international zoo population, it now became feasible to reintroduce zoo animals back to their historic range on the Asian steppes. To ensure the transfer of a heterozygotic gene pool from captivity to steppe, a broad selection of relatively unrelated individuals was recruited. The objective was to establish the species in a secure wild habitat, where wild predator pressure should not be excessive and, to avoid hybridization, contact with domestic or feral horses had to be prevented (Knowles and Wakefield 1992:23). Semireserves were established first in Xinjiang, China, in 1988, then in Mongolia in 1990. The Przewalski horses were received with great pride and excitement by the Mongolians, for the wild horse is featured in many of their traditional songs and poetry. The horses were gradually acclimatized to location and natural vegetation. Most importantly, they adjusted successfully to one another to form a normal social structure, banding together in their cohesive units in order to withstand predation by wolves, lynxes, and polecats. Today local nomads trained as reserve scouts monitor their progress (Bouman, Bouman, and Boyd 1994:255–262). As the world population of captive wild horses soars past 1,000, similar reserves for preservation of the species *Equus ferus* have been established in other countries. At a time when so many wild species are being extinguished on our planet, one can only hope that this quest for the survival of *Equus ferus przewalskii* in the wild – or *takhi* as it is known in Mongolia – meets with success.

To conclude this rather fleeting introduction to wild equids from the Eocene to the present, it is clear that over the last 60 million years the horse, subject to rigorous selective pressures, has evolved multiple anatomical features that assure it great speed, strength, and stamina. Furthermore, in the course of its repeated world migrations it has adapted to extremes of climate across many continents, in terms of temperature, altitude, and aridity. In that the equid digestive tract allows the animal to survive on poorest quality vegetation, the horse subsists successfully over a vast range of habitats. All these awesome qualities of the wild horse in time would become appreciated and utilized by *Homo* – whose own six million odd years of bipedal evolution had fostered extraordinary brain development. Highly intelligent, yet as a biped agonizingly slow, man would learn to harness the horse's speed and strength through domestication of *Equus caballus*. The remainder of this book recounts that adventure – the story of man's 6,000 years of horse domestication – a partnership of the world's brainiest biped and the world's fastest quadruped.

2

EQUUS CABALLUS: HORSE DOMESTICATION AND AGRO-PASTORALISM ACROSS THE EURASIAN STEPPES

AS DISCUSSED IN CHAPTER 1, WILD EQUIDS PROLIFERATED THROUGH-out the Pleistocene but became extinct in the western hemisphere at the close of the Ice Age. *Equus*, however, had migrated widely over the Old World, failing to occupy only the equatorial rain forests, Australia, the Arctic, and Antarctica. In the Holocene, zebras and asses extended over wide areas of Africa and Asia, while wild horses roamed the Eurasian lowlands largely north of the great mountains, but due to extensive hunting continuing into the Mesolithic,[1] horses became limited in distribution. Following the retreat of the glaciers, only on the semiarid steppes of Eurasia did the horse continue to flourish in large numbers (Mallory and Adams 1997:274–275). This vast region will be the focus of our initial analysis, but to learn how the wild horse came to be controlled there by man, it is necessary first to become acquainted with the earliest building blocks of civilization – to understand the events that led to the subsistence change from hunting wild game and gathering wild plants to the cultivation of crops and the domestication of animals. The horse was not among the first animals to be domesticated. In fact, its domestication came several thousand years after husbandry of those animals that today form the basis of our food economy. Yet, the initial domestication of the horse was integrally related to the agricultural complex and subsequently contributed to the expansion of both farming and herding. Inevitably, it also led to economic and political developments well beyond the subsistence sphere. To begin to comprehend these phenomena, we turn to the immediate post-Pleistocene era.

---

[1] The transitional period between the Paleolithic (Old Stone Age) and the Neolithic (New Stone Age), when the agricultural revolution took place.

The Transition from Food Procurement to Plant and Animal Domestication

In Eurasia, as glaciers shrank there was population movement northward to occupy areas hitherto covered by ice or polar desert (Zvelebil
2000:69–70). Reindeer and seal hunting were undertaken in the boreal
zones. To the south, a mixed hunter-gatherer economy exploited wild
plants and animals such as deer, boar, auroch, bison, and horse alongside fishing and fowling technologies. Settlement was mostly limited to
river valleys, where forager mobility adhered to a well-defined territorial range (Kozlowski and Kozlowski 1986:102). Increased world temperatures with resultant moister climates fostered new plant growth. By
10,000 BC, the resource-rich locations of the Near East were occupied by
sedentary foragers who, while hunting wild sheep, goats, and gazelles,
also developed intensive techniques of plant exploitation. This Natufian
culture flourished over the coastal strip from southern Turkey to the Nile
valley. Much of the wild food was obtained from herbaceous legumes
and stands of large-seeded grasses. Settlements were fairly permanent
with storage chambers as an integral part of the stone house. Natufian
sedentary life preceded and made possible the subsequent development of agriculture and animal husbandry (Fagan 1986:230–231). The
earliest, unambiguous evidence for agriculture in Eurasia dates to the
eighth millennium BC and is from southwest Asia, along the woodland and steppe oases of the Levantine corridor and the mid-Euphrates
valley. The most numerous plant remains in these early farming villages were from three cereals: emmer wheat, einkorn wheat, and barley,
but also present were pulses, legumes, and flax. Seed-crop agriculture
then spread across the Levant-Euphrates region, northward and eastward where it was encountered, in the late seventh millennium BC, in
Anatolia at Cayonu, Can Hassan, and Hacilar and in the Zagros mountains at Jarmo and Ali Kosh.

By the seventh millennium BC, in the lower montane valleys of the
Taurus and Zagros ranges, we find the earliest firm indications of ovicaprid domestication (Harris 1996:554, 558). Sheep and goats, of course,
were not the first animals to be domesticated; they were long preceded
by the dog. Mutual association between man and dog possibly began
in the Paleolithic, when wolfhound participation in the chase increased
the efficiency of the hunt; in this context, young puppies may have
been captured as pets and tamed. A tame animal of course is not auto-
matically domesticated. Domestication requires selective breeding of
a tamed population, ideally genetically isolated from wild relatives.

But given the high value accorded canine olfactory prowess, by the Mesolithic the domestic dog had become visible as a distinct animal in the zoo-archaeological record (Uerpmann 1996:229–231). But whereas the dog was trained as a hunting companion, camp guard, and sled dog, sheep and goats were domesticated primarily for meat. Sheep, of course, were domesticated secondarily for wool. As a result of mutations reinforced by artificial selection, clearly shown in a clay figurine from Tepe Sarab in western Iran (Bokonyi 1994:18), c 5000 BC the wild bristly coat had changed to wooly fleece in the domesticated animal, allowing shearing to be practiced. The pig, one further participant in the farming complex and valued for its quick growth and high prolificacy, fulfilled the important role of scavenger in recycling scraps. Together these animals served as a valuable buffer against the risks of crop failure during the period of dry farming.

Cattle, browsing and grazing ruminants, came under human control in the Near East perhaps a thousand years later than caprines. Not an easy domesticate, cattle needed to be fenced at night, which interfered with grazing and rumination and resulted in marked animal size reduction. Besides meat, cattle furnished important pack and draft capability and, by 4000 BC, were providers of milk, although the goat, whose copious supply of milk exceeds that of sheep, may have preceded the cow in this service (Clutton-Brock 1981:62–68). Like cattle, wild equids, as large and fast animals, were not easily tamed. Probably the first wild equid to be domesticated for its meat and milk was the African ass, most likely the Nubian subspecies. The earliest evidence of equid transport dates to the fourth millennium BC at Maadi in Lower Egypt, when the cattle-rearing people of Nubia trained the domestic donkey (*Equus asinus*) to become a pack animal, outperforming bovids, which covered little more than 3 km per hour and necessarily depended on a rest period in which to ruminate. Capable of carrying loads of 100 kg, the domestic donkey was a hardier work animal that could be maintained at low cost on poor forage. It played a vital role in the development of trade routes across the desert, to the east reaching the Red Sea from the Nile valley in trade with Arabia. In antiquity, donkeys of Nubian origin were even established on the island of Socotra, 300 km off the Horn of Africa, where subsequently in a feral[2] state they were reduced in stature to

---

[2] *Feral* refers to an animal when it or its ancestor, once domesticated, escapes confinement to revert to a state of self-sufficiency in the wild.

1 m at the withers.[3] On the Nile floodplain, the donkey was alternatively deployed in agriculture to plow, tread seeds, and thresh the harvest. Pictorial evidence from the third millennium BC shows that probably the donkey was ridden, but because of its low withers, neck, and head carriage, to avoid falling forward the rider needed to sit well back on the high, broad rump. Unfortunately, the constant jolting of the donkey's hind legs prevented any travel at high speeds. By the end of the fourth millennium BC, the domestic donkey had spread to southwest Asia, where in later centuries it played a key role in the transport of important metals from mountainous regions, primarily Afghanistan, to the great centers of alluvial civilization in the Middle East (Clutton-Brock 1992:40, 66; Woodward 1996:202–203).

There is certain evidence to suggest that in the third millennium BC the Persian onager was herded east of the Tigris and perhaps in northern Mesopotamia (Maekawa 2006). It appears, though, that the onager was difficult to tame and did not breed well in captivity. Numerous cuneiform records on clay tablets instead indicate that c 2800 BC it was common practice to interbreed donkeys and onagers for purposes of traction. All existing species of *Equus* today are capable of interbreeding. While the resultant offspring are almost invariably sterile, they nevertheless exhibit heterosis in that the hybrid has larger body size, has greater endurance, and survives better on poor forage than either parent. The hybrid most frequently produced is the mule, the progeny of a male donkey and a female horse; the hinny or jennet is the progeny of a male horse and a female donkey (Clutton-Brock 1992:42–44). Hybridization has even extended to the Plains zebra, the domestication of which was attempted by the Boers in South Africa. The zebra was interbred with both horse and donkey in the hope it would confer immunity to disease (lethal distemper) in the offspring (Clutton-Brock 1992:47–49).

To return to the founder assemblage of southwest Asian cultigens and domestic livestock, it is clear that seed-crop agriculture of cereals and pulses yielded a well-balanced diet of vegetable proteins, lipids, and carbohydrates that in combination with animal husbandry provided all essential nutrients. As a result of sedentarization and the adoption of this self-sufficient dietary package, there was a marked tendency for the mixed farming communities not only to increase numerically but also to

---

[3] In marginal environments of limited resources, it is common for equids to assume miniature proportions, as in the case of the ponies of Iceland, the Shetland Isles, Exmoor, and the barrier islands of eastern North America.

expand geographically (Harris 1996:556–557). Following its establishment in the nuclear area, Near East agriculture underwent rapid expansion, west to Europe and east across southwestern Asia to the Indian subcontinent. In the seventh millennium BC it appeared in Greece, in the sixth in the Danube Basin, Caucasia, and Turkmenia, a little later south in the Nile Valley; in the fifth millennium farming culture extended across central Europe and the Mediterranean littoral (Zohary and Hopf 2000:246). As agriculture radiated outward to distant lands and different climes, experimentation was conducted with local wild species. Oats were domesticated in Europe, sorghum and millet in North Africa, and the water buffalo in India. This Neolithic transition was a regionally variable and piecemeal process. The conversion from a hunter-gatherer economy to agriculture was largely accomplished through technology transfer and assimilation rather than through warfare and population displacement (Zvelebil 2000:61–68). Nevertheless, some evidence for disruptive contact and eviction exists (Keeley 1996:38), where farming practices negatively impacted forager space and mobility.

The Concomitant Development of Metallurgy

As agriculture was undergoing widespread adoption, another extremely important technological innovation occurred along the pathway to civilization – metallurgy. Dating to the eighth millennium BC, in aceramic Anatolia, the first uncontested copper artifacts were found at Cayonu Tepesi on the upper reaches of the Tigris (Muhly 1988:5). By the beginning of the fifth millennium BC, across Anatolia, Mesopotamia, and as far afield as Iran, entire cultures had modest copper assemblages and lead ornaments (Chernykh 1992:3). The discovery that hard, intractable rock could be turned into malleable metal was momentous. Since copper deposits are found on or near the surface in many places around the world, it was the first metal to be used widely and on a large scale. Drawing on the experience of stone working, native copper was initially hammered to shape, then reworked by heating in the fire and repeated hammering – the process of annealing. In time, annealing led to the actual melting of native copper and casting metal into molds (Wertime 1973:880). As metalsmiths came to appreciate the efficacy of pyrotechnology applied to metalliferous rocks, they instigated techniques to separate from ores the metals linked by strong chemical bonds of oxygen, sulfur, and carbon. Smelting and pottery manufacture appeared at approximately the same time. Pots were first fired in the hearth where early experimentation was undertaken with metallic pigments as decoration. To achieve more predictable results, in the fourth millennium BC, the kiln was constructed with its thick cover, heat-retaining walls, and flue-assisted natural draft, thereby reaching temperatures well beyond 1000°C to refine the smelting process. Depending on the ore from which the copper was derived, the metal might contain traces of arsenic, lead, tin, or other minerals. Alloying, the deliberate removal of undesirable elements and the increase of useful properties, was the next step. The first metal to appear in smelted copper in proportions significant enough to indicate intention was arsenic. Encountered as high as 7 percent in many utensils, far in excess of natural occurrence, the addition of enriched arsenical ores improved the ease of smelting and casting and greatly strengthened the metal (Raymond 1984:10–17, 25). Across Europe, the Middle East, and the Indian subcontinent, the first alloys were predominantly arsenic. In the Carpatho-Balkan metallurgical complex, gold production was attested in 4300 BC, in the abundant gold and copper funerary objects concentrated in just a few of the many Varna graves in Bulgaria. These magnificent items, associated with elite burials, indicated a level of production above the household. They were also an explicit expression of the wealth generated by the metal trade. But trade was not the only means of acquiring metals. Plunder and tribute exacted in war were major contributions to the supply of metal and technology in most periods. In the third millennium BC, a Sumerian expedition to Iran seized not only precious metals, but also the skilled artisans with their tools and molds for casting (Chernykh 1992:49–50; Moorey 1988:29).

Arsenical copper persisted as the most common metal well into the second millennium BC. But as early as the fourth millennium, tin was recognized as the metal alloying best with copper to form bronze. By the third millennium BC, silver was a sumptuary product and served as the chief unit of exchange. These varied advances in polymetallism were critically important in promoting the mass reduction of ores and paving the way chemically for the much later industrial utilization of iron (Wertime 1973:883). In the mid-third millennium BC, an iron dagger and welded head of a bronze pin were manufactured on the Russian steppes by Yamnaya pastoralists (Anthony 1998:104). In 2100 BC a sword with gold hilt and iron blade of low nickel content was interred in the Royal tombs of Alaca Huyuk, Anatolia (Wertime 1973:885). In western Eurasia, iron was produced from mined iron ore in smelting furnaces by reacting the ore with a form of carbon, usually charcoal. In that this process never achieved temperatures much beyond 800°C, pure iron, which melts at about 1537°C, was never truly liquefied. It was only chemically changed to a pasty solid iron mass, bloom, that had to be wrought by repeated hammering to drive out the slag in order to achieve a useful engineering material (Raymond 1984:55–56). As will be seen in future chapters, a long series of intertwined events would need to transpire, in which the horse was destined to play a critical role, before efficient steel manufacture (steel is iron with carbon content between 0.1 and 0.8 percent) would be realized in the west.

Emergence of the Centralized Alluvial State

With the intensification of farming and metallurgy, in fact long, long before the invention of iron, another important evolutionary development had occurred – the emergence of the state. The first pristine state, Sumer, arose at Uruk in Mesopotamia toward the end of the fifth millennium BC; Egypt emerged in the fourth millennium; and the Harappa civilization of India in the third. The Tigris-Euphrates, Nile, and Indus valleys shared one feature in common: all three were areas of abundant fertile agricultural land but were circumscribed by inhospitable deserts, mountains, or seas. According to Carneiro (1970), the concentration of rich river alluvium attracted large numbers of people who came into conflict over the premium territory. In the ensuing warfare, however, because of environmental restriction, defeated groups could not flee to the forbidding, arid hinterland but instead were forced into subjugation by their victors and incorporated into increasingly complex political units. In this manner it is thought the centralized state first evolved, encompassing large populations, collecting taxes, enforcing laws, organizing systematic flood control and extensive irrigation, and drafting men to work and war. The environmentally circumscribed alluvial states of the Middle East thus set the course of early civilization in the Old World. By contrast, in the moister, noncircumscribed regions, as we have seen, agricultural populations were free to expand into different habitats, there to develop new strains of cultigens. In their early fluid dispersal from the sixth to the third millennium BC, tribal farmers developed different craft specializations and coalesced in autonomous fortified settlements, but nowhere did they attain the extraordinary political centralization of the circumscribed alluvial state. Yet population increase, naturally resulting from sedentary adaptation, exerted pressure on land and impelled splinter groups to migrate further and further afield into outlying areas only marginally suited to agriculture. It is to one of these fringe areas of mixed farming and herding on the eastern borders of Europe that we must now turn to view the inception of a mobile equestrian subsistence adaptation, which would take millennia to mature but which in time would collide with and challenge the sedentary circumscribed civilizations that had emerged in the south.

Peripheral Farming and Eneolithic[4] Exploitation of the Horse on the Eurasian Steppes

David Anthony, a leading American archaeologist in the study of horse domestication and riding, with colleagues saw fit to introduce a recent article (Anthony, Brown, and George 2006) with a quote from Grahame Clark's 1941 article "Horses and Battle-axes" (Clark 1941): "The importance of the horse in human history is matched only by the difficulties inherent in its study; there is hardly an incident in the story which is not the subject of controversy, often of a violent nature."

From the preceding very brief synopsis of the beginnings of farming and metallurgy in southwest Asia, it is clear that the horse was not an immediate domesticate of the early Neolithic; nor was it native to the Near East, site of so many items of primary domestication. Throughout much of western and central Europe, exploitation of the horse as a food source had drastically decreased its numbers; while small pockets of wild horse populations possibly still persisted, these were too rare to play any essential role in the domestication of *Equus caballus* (Bokonyi 1994:20). To find the first domesticators of the horse, it is necessary to look for protracted human interaction with wild horses. This occurred only in the transitional area between the forest and grasslands of the Eurasian steppes, an ideal habitat for wild horses where large numbers had managed to survive into postglacial times (Anthony 1994:186). It is to this new ecozone that we must follow the farmer-herder-metallurgist in his initial adaptation to the steppes to understand fully the significance of man's earliest symbiosis with the horse and the nature of agropastoralist expansion across Eurasia. From Grahame Clark's statement above, it should be clear that even in 1941 the inquiry into early human-equine relations had long been fraught by bitter controversy. Let the reader be warned that multiple decades later the furor of the debate has

---

4 The Eneolithic, also known as the Chalcolithic or Copper Age, is the transitional period between the Neolithic and the Bronze Age.

not diminished any! Most scholars today recognize the Pontic-Caspian steppe as the general location where domestication of the horse initially occurred, but exactly when and where this first happened and how the horse transitioned from being a food animal to its transport role in riding and driving continues to be the subject of vigorous international disputation. As we trace successive phases of demic expansion eastward from the edge of the steppes across Eurasia, also westward into Europe, our discussion will attempt to summarize the salient points of scholarly contention.

CRIS (5600 BC). The earliest food-producing economies, whereby cattle, ovicaprids, pigs, cereals, ceramics, and hammered copper technology were first introduced onto the western steppes, originated in the lower Danube valley. Later contributors to the steppes were early cultures of the Caucasus and Bactria-Margiana. But initially, c 5600 BC, avoiding the barren lowland steppe and entering the upland Moravian forest-steppe fringe mosaic of meadow and woodland, the Danubian Cris culture encountered thriving hunting-fishing peoples in the North Pontic region and settled in a fertile area west of the Prut River. The Mesolithic population east of the Prut soon implemented certain aspects of Cris subsistence, giving rise to the first indigenous Neolithic culture of the region, the Bug-Dniester, as ceramic technology diffused to foragers along river valleys to the north and the east (Fig. 2.1).

CUCUTENI-TRIPOLYE (4900–3400 BC). Shortly into the fifth millennium BC, processes of social integration resulted in the establishment of another agricultural and stockbreeding culture from the Danube region, the Cucuteni-Tripolye, which extended from the Carpathian piedmont across the forest-steppe to the Dnieper River (Anthony 1991a:256–257). This society was characterized by hierarchical organization, fortified settlements comprising hundreds of households, and craft specialization – notably elaborate polychrome ceramics and Old Europe female figurines with exaggerated hips and buttocks (Anthony 1990:905; Gimbutas 1997a:362). Mining and metallurgy were practiced, and hundreds of copper tools were cast in molds. Linked to the Ai Bunar mining center in the Carpatho-Balkan complex, Cucuteni-Tripolye traded large quantities of copper and gold artifacts east to the lower Volga (Chernykh 1992:35–42). At the Dnieper valley, Cucuteni-Tripolye contacted the Dnieper-Donets foraging groups of the Mesolithic, which of late had adopted many farming subsistence practices (Anthony 1990:906).

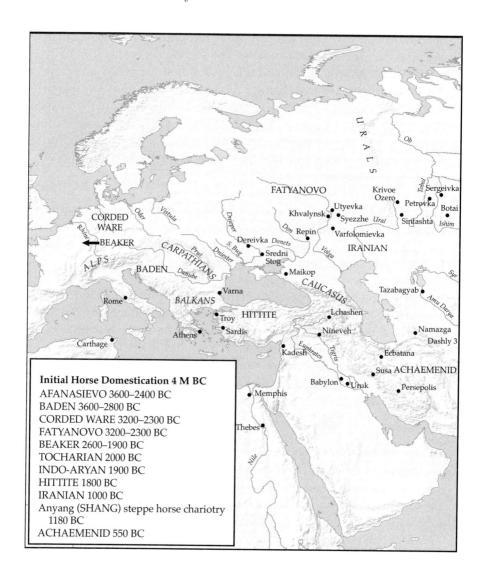

Initial Horse Domestication 4 M BC
AFANASIEVO 3600–2400 BC
BADEN 3600–2800 BC
CORDED WARE 3200–2300 BC
FATYANOVO 3200–2300 BC
BEAKER 2600–1900 BC
TOCHARIAN 2000 BC
INDO-ARYAN 1900 BC
HITTITE 1800 BC
IRANIAN 1000 BC
Anyang (SHANG) steppe horse chariotry
   1180 BC
ACHAEMENID 550 BC

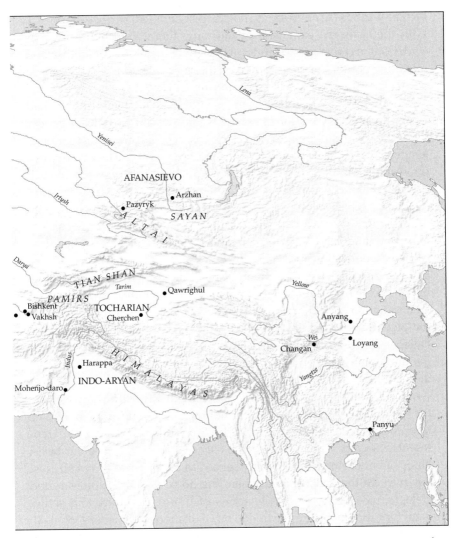

FIGURE 2.1. Eurasian steppes, fourth through first millennium BC, showing area of initial horse domestication and Indo-European expansions across and beyond the steppes.

DNIEPER-DONETS (PERIOD I, 5100–4600 BC; PERIOD II, 4600–4100 BC). With the eastward expansion of farming, there were indications, as evidenced in cemetery size and complexity, of increasing sedentism and mounting population densities along the river valleys north of the Black Sea. Before the transition to agriculture, Dnieper-Donets I, a cultural tradition markedly different from Old Europe Cucuteni-Tripolye, had focused on the exploitation of rich wild game within the riverine gallery forest. But these steppe-forest borderlands, ever subject to fluctuation in temperature and precipitation, risked periodic exposure to severe stress. Interestingly, Binford (1972:440) has argued that it is precisely in such marginal habitats subject to stress that innovative exploitative measures are most likely to be adopted. Specifically, by Dnieper-Donets II, with the adoption of agriculture and stockbreeding, the attendant clearance of gardens and pastures in the constricted steppe-zone river valleys had caused deforestation and reduction of wild resources. In the face of fish and game scarcity, to supplement the meat supplied from stockherding, hunters were forced to turn to the steppe. Between the Carpathian and Ural mountains, wild onager, horse, and *Equus hydruntinus* (extinct by the Neolithic) had been hunted during the Mesolithic. Now during Dnieper-Donets II, wild horses from the nearby steppe fringes became the dominant game animal, contributing over 25 percent of the meat diet (Anthony 1991a:257–260; Anthony and Brown 2003:58).

At a slightly later date, between the Ingul River on the west and the middle Volga on the east, even more intensive utilization of equine resources was encountered. The **Sredni Stog** culture (4200–3500 BC) represents a society where horses were early exploited on a regular basis. Finds of antler tines that possibly served as bridle cheekpieces suggest this may be the general area where the horse was first domesticated (Telegin 1986:15–17, 82–88). In terms of lithics, ceramics, and settlement type, Sredni Stog appeared to be an offshoot of Dnieper-Donets II; burials of certain individuals could be elaborate, suggesting increasing hierarchy in society. Agriculture and stock rearing were practiced with some dependence on wild game. Other aspects of material culture differed and might be attributed to the expansion of the resource base into the steppe environment. Households were three times larger, reflecting perhaps the greater flexibility needed in dealing with dispersed economic resources that require simultaneous labor. Also cemeteries were smaller, implying a more mobile adaptation. The largest faunal sample occurred at the (phase IIa) site of **Dereivka**. Among the roughly 4,000 animal bones identified, 2,555 or 61 percent were from horses, a remarkable increase over Dnieper-Donets II. The absence of old indi-viduals and the preponderance of young adult or juvenile males in the equine remains suggest these animals were less likely to have been obtained during predation and more probably were the ones culled for slaughter in a managed herd (Anthony 1991a:261–263, 269; Bibikova 1986). Unfortunately, it is extremely difficult to identify specific skele-tal traits that reliably differentiate the earliest domesticated horse from its wild cousin. However, the Dereivka horse bones were found to be highly variable in terms of robustness, a trait again perhaps indicative of domestication (Anthony 1996:73).[5] Interacting with Cucuteni-Tripolye, Sredni Stog spread 650 km westward as far as present-day Romania and Hungary. At the same time, copper ornaments of Cucuteni-Tripolye type and spectrographic composition were encountered 900 km to the east beyond the Volga, presumably carried by Sredni Stog traders. As a leading proponent for early horse domestication on the steppes, David W. Anthony contends this span of over 1,500 km denotes a culture of high mobility – such as might be conferred by horse riding (Anthony 1996:81).

Anthony and Bibikova's conclusions regarding the Dereivka data as evidence of horse domestication in the fourth millennium BC have met with certain criticism, notably by Levine (1990:738–739), who argues forcefully that the high incidence of males slaughtered at Dereivka attests to a wild horse population, in which stallions either protect-ing the mares and foals of their bands or in bachelor groups were killed by human hunters, not horse keepers. On the basis of horse remains at the nearby Mesolithic site of Mirnoe, specialists Benecke (1998) and Hausler (2000) concur with this position. In face of this skepticism, Anthony points to further signs of domestication, observing that during the Mesolithic, horses, like other equids, were just hunted animals; their bones received no special treatment. But, in the course of the Neolithic as food-producing economies diffused eastward across the steppes, c 5000 BC cattle and ovicaprid bones had come to feature prominently

---

5 Initial excavations at Dereivka in 1964 had uncovered the ritual burial of a stallion's skull (Telegin 1986), on which the lower second premolar displayed signs of bit wear characteristic of bridling (Anthony 1991a). While as many as 10 radiocarbon dates attest to the overall Eneolithic age of the Dereivka site, ranging centrally from 4300 to 3900 BC, separate tests conducted by Oxford and Kiev laboratories in 1997 later dated the cult stallion to the first millennium BC. In all probability, the horse skull had been placed in a 1 m deep pit dug into the Eneolithic layer during the Scythian Iron Age and therefore is irrelevant to discussion of Eneolithic horse keeping (Anthony and Brown 2003:55).

in the archaeological record, appearing frequently in ritual context with human burials. By the Eneolithic, horse bones were also found in ritual association with cattle and ovicaprid bones in graves across the Pontic-Caspian region. For Anthony, this new symbolic role of the horse in mortuary ritual signaled closer involvement of the horse in the world of humans. In an economy where cattle, sheep, goats, and horses supplied most of the meat in the diet, it now seemed the horse too had become a managed food resource.

Other evidence of horse ritual is encountered on the middle Volga at Khvalynsk (5000–4500 BC), a very early outpost of trade linked by long exchange chains to the copper-using cultures of southeastern Europe. Located above 12 human burials, ochre-stained shallow depressions with pottery fragments appeared to represent funerary ceremonies enacted alongside the grave. Four deposits contained the head and lower-limb bones of caprines or cattle; three deposits contained horse lower limbs or phalanges – in two grouped with sheep or cattle bones. Within the actual graves, many cattle skulls and bones, horse phalanges, sheep bones, and one sheep head-and-hoof offering were interred. With the exception of a single boar-tusk ornament, no obviously wild animal remains were included in these ritual deposits. Near Khvalynsk at Syezzhe in the Samara valley, similar graveside deposits, deeply stained with red ochre, featured the crania and lower extremity bones of two horses, seemingly a horse head-and-hoof offering, comparable to those of cattle and sheep at Khvalynsk (Anthony and Brown 2003:58–62). This ancient practice of sacrifice, in which, following the ceremonial consumption of meat, the skin still retaining skull and hoofs was suspended on a pole over the burial, extended across Asia to the northern European plain and until recent times persisted among nomadic herders of the Altai mountains. Retention of the bones in the head, feet, and tail helped maintain the form of the hanging horse, which from afar might be perceived as in flight (Piggott 1962:110–111; Fig. 2.2).[6] Thus, by the Eneolithic, Anthony claims, there was clearly an important association between man and horse; the horse in fact had come to play a prominent role not only in subsistence practices but also in the belief system and mortuary rites of the western steppes. This latter point is further substantiated by the presence of ritually carved

---

[6] Mair (2007:34) has commented on the ritual association between horse sacrifice and sacred groves. In Norse mythology, the greatest tree of all, Ygdrasil or Terrible Horse ("Terrible" was an epithet for Odin), was the *axis mundi*, whose branches and roots held together heaven, earth, and hell.

FIGURE 2.2. Steppe horse sacrifice (Lubinski 1928; cited in Mair 2007:fig. 4).

bone horse figurines in Eneolithic burials at Khvalynsk, Syezzhe, and Varfolomievka, in the Volga drainage (Anthony and Brown 2000:80–81), and of horsehead effigy maces or scepters of exotic porphyry or diorite, with incised lines possibly representing bridles or halters, scattered in prestige graves from the Balkans to the Caspian c 3500–3000 BC (Anthony 1996:76; Gimbutas 1997b:78).

Further support for Anthony's thesis comes from the east beyond the Urals. The Surtanda, Tersek, and **Botai** culture sites in the Tobol-Ishim drainage on the north Kazakh steppe date to c 3500–3000 BC. In this northern zone of thin saline soils and harsh winters, where snow covers the ground from December to April and temperatures plummet to −50°C, agriculture was nonviable (Olsen 1996b:50). Prior to the fourth millennium BC, the inhabitants of this area practiced a mobile foraging economy, living in small, temporary riverside camps, where deposits show varied animal bones numbering only in the low hundreds. However, c 3500 BC a major shift occurred, whereby the earlier Botai occupation of 4 households now ballooned to more than 150 (Anthony, Brown, and George 2006:144, 146). While Surtanda herded some cattle (Anthony 1998:104), these related people relied primarily on horses for their meat; the site of Botai alone yielded in excess of 300,000 animal bones of which 99 percent were from the horse.

In this stark environment, Sandra L. Olsen of the Carnegie Museum of Natural History finds mounting evidence to support the argument for incipient horse domestication at Botai, in which equestrian horse-hunters maintained at least some horse herds for riding. Different bone items unearthed at the site help substantiate Olsen's hypothesis that Botai horsemen were hunting indigenous wild horses (Olsen 1996b:50–51). The archaeological record shows that along with stone arrowheads and spearpoints, formidable harpoons, fashioned from horse metapodials, were deployed in the hunt to inflict large oval wounds on horse bones, distinct from the narrow, lenticular apertures left by arrowheads. Conversely, as shown by a deep fracture on a horse upper maxilla, poleaxing was probably also practiced at Botai. This slaughter technique, commonly conducted on domestic animals, requires that two ropes tied around the neck be held taut by persons on opposite sides of the horse, while a third person approaches from the front to strike a fatal blow between the eyes (Olsen 2003:85–86). Other bone artifacts, nonexistent in most prehistoric sites but numerous at Botai, were horse mandibles that functioned as thong smoothers. This tool, easily recognized by its broad notch with microscopic striae running perpendicular to the edge, served in the manufacture of rawhide thongs needed in an equestrian economy. Even today, thongs utilized as lassos, bridles, reins, whips, and hobbles are still vital elements of nomad equipment (Olsen 2003:93). One further element encountered at Botai indicative of horse herding were large concentrations of horse manure, suggesting penning and possible use of horse dung as insulating material in house construction, a steppe custom persisting to the present (Olsen 2006:105). Of recent interest, the meeting brief "Third International Symposium on Biomolecular Archaeology: Trail of Mare's Milk Leads to First Tamed Horses" (Travis 2008) recently reported on research undertaken by Natalie Stear of the University of Bristol. From residue left on 55,000-year-old Botai potsherds, Stear identified the hydrogen isotope deuterium, indicating mare's milk. Since it is impossible to milk a wild mare, these data together with new evidence of bit wear are strongly supportive of early horse domestication and riding at Botai.

Given Botai's broad economic dependence on the horse, Olsen, like Anthony, finds the horse conspicuously represented in ceremonial observances. Perhaps the most exotic bone artifacts encountered were 46 elaborately incised horse phalanges. Ritual sacrifice was evidenced in intramural horse-head burials beneath houses; in one instance human skeletons were encircled by the skulls, vertebrae, and pelves of 14 horses. Such simultaneous sacrifice of so many animals strongly implies the availability of a domesticated herd; to procure such a number from the wild would require transport over distance of 6,350 kg of horseflesh. The dog, the only other domestic animal at Botai, was

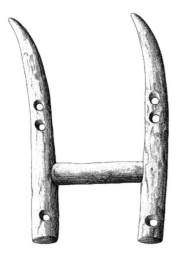

FIGURE 2.3. A later organic bit: cheekpieces of antler, mouthpieces of bone (c 1500 BC) from Corcelettes, Switzerland. Drawing by Brigitte Gies and Manfred Ritter (Huettel 1981; cited in Drews 2004:fig. 4.6). By kind permission of Taylor and Francis Books. Courtesy Hans-Georg Huettel.

also featured alongside the horse in burials, this spiritual association perhaps mirroring the animals' secular relationship in life – their partnership in hunt and in herding as practiced on the Kazakh steppe till this very day (Olsen 2003:94, 98–99; Weed 2002:59).

Anthony further buttresses Olsen's argument through reference to the Amerindians of the Plains who, by domesticating feral mustangs, with minimal apparatus successfully rode in the great buffalo hunts of North America (Anthony and Brown 2003:65). On the steppes, the earliest bridles similarly may have consisted of a leather thong looped around the jaw or later involved a simple halter with ropes or reins attached. However, to exert firmer control over the horse, a bit needed to be employed. Apparently, the first bits were organic, consisting of a mouthpiece of rope, leather, or wood fitted into two cheekpieces made from bone or antler (Fig. 2.3). The bit was thus placed between the diastemata of the lower jaw, the mouthpiece providing braking power, the cheekpieces permitting human direction of the horse to left or right. Since the bit was designed to inflict pressure on the corner of the lips, the tongue, and the toothless jaw between incisors and molars, to relieve discomfort the horse tended to cast off the bit from the soft tissues of the mouth to where it abraded the premolars, leaving a characteristic mark on the enamel (Dietz 2003:192; Mallory and Adams 1997:275–276). For the Botai horses, 26 percent of mature measurable second premolars (P_2) examined had significant bevel measurements.

Information on horse P_2 bevel has been derived from systematic, longitudinal experimentation conducted with organic bits on previously unbitted modern domestic and feral horses (Brown and Anthony 1998:331). These investigations demonstrated that bit wear causes a distinctive, quantifiable signature. After 150 hours of riding with bits made of leather, bone, hemp rope, or horsehair rope, not only did the bits display signs of being chewed on by the horse, but most significantly, the P_2s showed microscopic abrasion on the occlusal enamel and a pronounced increase in beveling on the mesial corner of the tooth, the highest attrition occurring with hemp and bone bits. These bevels measured at 2.0–2.5 mm, two standard deviations above the mean bevel measurements for never-bitted horses (0.78, SD 0.66). In the general archaeological context, horse P_2 mesial bevels have been recorded at Egyptian, Roman, Greek, Scythian, Avar, Russian, and Iranian Bronze Age archaeological sites. The P_2 bevels at Botai ranged from 3.0 mm to 6.0 mm. Since mesial bevels of 3.0 mm or more are common only among bitted horses, Anthony and Brown conclude (2000:82–83) that some Botai horses were bitted and likely ridden for hundreds of hours. Botai horses were certainly large enough to ride, with 70 percent standing at 13–14 hands, larger than the average horse ridden by the Roman cavalry.

Antler cheekpieces excavated in the graves of **Afanasievo**, 1500 km east of Botai, also appear to be evidence of horse riding. The Afanasievo (c 3600–2400 BC), a Europoid culture whose funerary practice of supine flexed burial under a low mound derives from the western traditions of the Pontic-Caspian steppe, introduced metallurgy, wheeled vehicles, pottery, agriculture, and stock raising including horses to the eastern steppes and highlands between the Altai mountains and the Minusinsk Basin of the Yenisei River (Anthony 1991a:267; 1998:104–105; Mallory and Adams 1997:4), subsequently spilling south toward Mongolia and northern China (Mallory and Mair 2000:294–296). Originating possibly from Repin in the Don-Volga drainage, in their easterly migration across the Kazakh steppes the Afanasievo folks likely transmitted horse riding to the indigenous foragers of the Botai region. Moreover, in the centuries that followed, it appears some contact was maintained between the Altai and the western steppes (Anthony 2007:264–265, 308). At a later date, bit wear was also evidenced at Sergeivka (2800–2600 BC), where domesticated cattle and sheep bones were associated with those of the horse and significant bevels were present in 30 percent of horse P_2s; Utyevka VI (2000 BC), where bevels of 6.0 and 5.0 mm were encountered in a stallion with accompanying ornate cheekpieces; and Alakul-Petrovka (1800 BC), where a bevel of 4.0 mm was uncovered (Anthony and Brown 2000:83–84). From the above, Anthony and Brown contend the data strongly suggest that as populations migrated eastward from Europe across the sparsely inhabited Eurasian steppes, the horse, first hunted as a prey animal, was later herded for meat, and by the fourth millennium BC was utilized as a mount in riding.

Why the Domestication of the Horse?

With successful stock rearing of bovids and ovicaprids, one might ask what was the impetus to domesticate the horse. The horse is an extremely fast, aggressive, and intelligent animal. If cornered, both males and females will attack an opponent; the male uses its forelegs, the females the hind legs, also spattering urine in the pursuer's eyes. In mate-defense polygyny, the stallion is regularly accustomed to fight other stallions both to capture and to defend his mares; the mare fights to protect her foals. Such spirited tactics pose significant problems for capture or control of this animal. It is possible, though, that cold-weather adaptability to steppe winters may have been the motivating factor in the exploitation of the horse as a low-maintenance food source. To graze in snowy conditions, both sheep and cows push their snouts through the snow, bloodying and incapacitating themselves as a result; without fodder they starve. By contrast, the high gait of the horse allows it to move through snows that paralyze sheep. With its tough hoofs, it scrapes away snow in order to feed and breaks through ice-covered waterholes in order to drink; this clearing away of snow subsequently allows other animals to forage. Far better equipped for severe winter weather than cattle, sheep, or goats, the horse survives extreme conditions (Anthony 1991a:272). To withstand long steppe winters, notably the brutal cold of Botai, human populations required high consumption of fat to insure sufficient caloric intake. It is therefore interesting to note that by comparison to ruminants, horse meat is low in saturated and high in polyunsaturated fats (Olsen 2003:89), and is also high in amino acids, minerals, and vitamins. It is significant that steppe folk beliefs commonly attribute unusual medicinal and nutritional properties to horse products (Levine 1999:8).

In hunting wild horses, human groups have typically utilized the cooperative drive, as was seen at Solutre during the Upper Paleolithic. Possibly with this method, animals driven into a trap or corral often were numerous, too numerous to be immediately killed and consumed. As a consequence, some horses may have been held in the stockade or alternatively hobbled and allowed to feed as meat on the hoof, to be dispatched later when needed. Another play might have been to catch small foals or to capture a heavily pregnant, consequently less mobile, mare; her captive offspring would be highly malleable. The experienced stockbreeder no doubt would soon be alert to the potential of his new quarry. In fact, cattle herders, well accustomed to large ruminant herbivores, were most qualified to transition to the role of horse herder (Anthony 1991a:271–272). Parallels exist between cattle and horse behavior. Earlier, discussing the Przewalski horse, it was shown that the wild horse reproductive unit was the family band composed of the dominant stallion, his mares, and their young. As was earlier noted, among mares of a band a hierarchy prevails, in which the lead mare chooses the daily route and is duly followed by the other mares and their foals. In the cattle herd too there is the corresponding lead cow. By controlling the lead cow or mare, the herder knew how to control the herd. Recently, mitochondrial DNA studies (Jansen et al. 2002) have shown that the female-derived part of the equine bloodline is far more diverse than the male. Such genetic disparity possibly can be attributed to the high irascibility of wild stallions. In their efforts to augment their herds, horse breeders likely preferred to capture the more docile females to add to the harem of an already domesticated and satisfactorily tractable male (Olsen 2006:81). To eliminate any subsequent undesirable traits, in selective breeding a certain proportion of young males was probably castrated; as geldings their presence would not be disruptive, therefore tolerated by stallions. In this manner several horse bands could graze together as a herd (Kuzmina 2008:28; Levine 1990:729). Given certain similarity in the behavior of bovid and equid grazers, it is not altogether surprising that the African donkey of Nubia and the Eurasian horse of the steppes both were domesticated by frontier cattle herders within roughly the same timeframe, that is, the fourth millennium BC.

Having eaten his way through most of the planet's megafauna, one wonders what finally curbed man's voracious gustatory appetite. But in those early times cattle, originally domesticated for meat and milk, were already being used as baggage animals. As we have seen, in Africa the donkey had proven to be a superior transport animal to cattle. Given the exigencies of expanding mixed agriculture on the steppes, while still appreciated for its meat the horse probably was soon utilized as a pack animal. A simple halter would have been sufficient to control the horse, and its strength would have been invaluable for lugging loads over uneven ground. As familiarity between humans and horse grew, the first experiments in bareback riding would have been undertaken. Handling a few horses on foot might have been possible at first, but as Levine (1999:10) discovered in ethno-archaeological research in Kazahkstan and Mongolia, even today's nomads recognize any large herd requires a mounted herder. Other archaeologists agree that riding was a prime requirement for horse breeders (Azzaroli 1998:41; Mallory and Adams 1997:276). Thus, according to Anthony's interpretation, the newly arrived-at equestrian skills would have immensely facilitated the pursuit, capture, and domestication of many more horses and furthermore would have mobilized herd management of cattle, sheep, and goats, effecting immediate broadening of the resource base and leading to progressive penetration of new zones for eventual exploitation.

Criticisms – and Near Eastern Comparisons

Despite their multifaceted research, opposition to Anthony, Brown, and Olsen's dating of horse domestication and riding to the fourth millennium BC has been raised on a variety of counts. Again, Levine maintains that the horses at Botai, as at Dereivka, were a wild population and dismisses Anthony and Brown's work on bit wear, charging that a large bevel can be produced naturally through pathological malocclusion (1999:11–12). In response to this objection, in collaboration with Christian George, Anthony and Brown (Anthony, Brown, and George 2006:140–141) undertook analysis of 74 mature[7] equid P_2s, retrieved from a 1.5 million-year-old Pleistocene deposit in Florida – the largest sample of never-bitted equid P_2s ever examined in this manner. These Leisey equids, although not assigned to *Equus caballus*, nevertheless were similar to horses in stature, diet, and dentition. The mean bevel measurement of the Leisey premolars was 1.1 mm with a standard deviation of 0.71 mm; only one never-bitted P_2 in the Leisey sample had a bevel greater than 2.5 mm. This indicates that a bevel of 3 mm, encountered at Eurasian steppe sites, is not characteristic of wild equids and therefore should be considered possible evidence for the use of bits.

Historian Robert Drews (2004) disagrees with Levine with regard to domestication and supports the position that horses were probably domesticated around the fourth millennium BC. He recognizes that

---

7 Horses under three years of age are excluded from the sample because their newly erupted premolars display many irregularities.

during the Paleolithic the horse was hunted extensively for its meat, but notes that the late Mesolithic saw a drop in horse population and, by the sixth millennium BC, the once-plentiful wild horses had disappeared from Europe west of the steppes (Bokonyi 1978:21–22). Notwithstanding, on the Pontic-Caspian steppe dependence on the horse continued, albeit with a slight decline and subsequent rebound in the Dnieper region. Drews interprets this local resurgence along with the dramatic increase in the number of horse bones in deposits across the Dnieper, Don, Volga, Ural, and Ishim valleys as clear evidence of horse domestication. He finds these data are further corroborated by the reappearance – after a total absence of three millennia – of high numbers of butchered horse bones in the osteological assemblages of eastern and central Europe, which he attributes to domestication of the horse as a food animal, diffusing westward from the steppes into adjacent regions toward the end of the fourth millennium BC (Bokonyi 1978; Drews 2004:11–12).

Drews also remarks the dramatic first appearance of the horse in funerary context in central Europe during the third millennium BC. In an Austrian grave near Gross-Hoflein, a nanny goat and kid, ewe and lamb, cow and calf, and mare and foal were interred alongside a man and child. Such ritual association with other livestock next to the human burial certainly implies the horse as domesticate (Drews 2004:24–25). While keenly supportive of fourth-millennium-BC horse domestication, Drews nevertheless is exceedingly critical of Telegin's early identification of the rough antler objects at Dereivka as bridle cheekpieces. He states that few materials in nature are sharper and more durable than stag antlers. For this reason, from ancient times across Eurasia, often in sites where the horse was totally absent, antlers were used for a wide variety of tools: awls, picks, and borers. Drews considers that the single perforation present in the Dereivka antler tines simply allowed for the insertion of the tool's rotator. Drews insists that antler tines were not effectively shaped as cheekpieces until the second millennium BC, when, as evidenced on the incised *Stangenknebel* of the Hungarian plain, one large perforation served for insertion of the bit mouthpiece and several smaller ones for the straps or reins (Drews 2004:16–18; Huettel 1994: 208–210).

Drews then delivers his sharpest criticism against Anthony's claim that horse riding originated in the fourth millennium BC, asserting that no clear pictorial depiction of a horse rider exists anywhere much before

FIGURE 2.5. Mesopotamian clay plaque of rider seated in a donkey position (Littauer and Crouwel 1979:fig. 37).

definitively by future excavations. What is certain, however, is that in the course of the fourth millennium BC the **Yamnaya** (Pit grave) horizon, a series of diverse societies adopting a common stockbreeding-agricultural economy, developed seminomadic pastoralism on the western steppes. Derived from the Sredni Stog and Khvalynsk cultures that first ventured onto the steppe, Yamnaya effectively accomplished the earliest systematic grassland occupation, extending west to the Danube delta and east to the Ural River. Yet another major innovation, the acquisition of ox-drawn wheeled technology, helped facilitate this expansion in all directions. Between 3400 and 3100 BC, carts and wagons appeared over a large area almost simultaneously: Mesopotamia, eastern Hungary, southeastern Poland, northern Germany, and the Russian-Ukrainian steppes, reaching to the Rhine and the Indus by 3000 BC. Weighing as much as 670–700 kg (Piggott 1992:17), these solid-wheeled vehicles were slow and cumbersome yet delivered the critical bulk transport capability so vital to Yamnaya mobile adaptation. By transporting cultivators and tools to the field and carrying farm produce to the settlement, they improved overall farm efficiency to render the single-family work unit viably operative. They also made systematic manuring possible, thereby opening areas of less productive soils to agricultural development (Anthony 1995:558, 563; Mallory and Adams 1997:627). Across the steppes, wheeled vehicles provided the additional function of transporting the supplies necessary for herders to live dispersed in remote

45

areas with their animals for protracted periods (Anthony 1998:102–103). Along with stocks of provisions, bedding, tents, and personal accoutrements, the very young, old, and infirm could travel safely, driving their herds to seasonal pastures. Alternatively, with its arched tilt of mats or felt, the covered wagon afforded habitation (Fig. 2.6); in Pit graves, covered carts that constituted houses on wheels have been unearthed (Shilov 1989:123). Such was the mobility of agro-pastoralism after this time that Yamnaya steppe settlements were scarcely apparent in the archaeological record. But Yamnaya cemeteries, markers of ancestral territories, occurred in pastures as much as 80 km away from major river valleys (Khazanov 1984:93). Under a kurgan (tumulus), the deceased, saturated with ochre, was interred on one side or in supine position with legs flexed (Mallory and Adams 1997:651). Wheeled vehicles were not merely an adjunct to subsistence; they were ceremonially valued for the mobility they conferred. From the Danube to the Ural, in hundreds of Yamnaya burials, clay models or actual carts and wagons have been found, accompanied by sacrificial offerings of cattle, sheep, and horses. Subsequently, the ceramic votive offerings were supplanted by copper representations (Piggott 1992:19–23).

Pole-and-yoke draft was originally designed for paired bovids drawing the plow, the yoke attached to the horns or resting on the oxen's necks. Such a system, however, when applied to hauling a wagon, was ill suited to equine anatomy, horses having slenderer necks and much higher head carriage. When a horse was harnessed in this primitive manner, there was a tendency for the yoke to slip back, bruising and chafing the horse's withers; if the yoke were secured forward, straps constricting the animal's throat reduced tractive power (Littauer and Crouwel 1979:11, 28–29). Unquestionably, the two-wheeled cart was the lighter, more resilient vehicle. From the archaeological record it is clear that concerted efforts were underway, such as wickerwork sides of the cart and fenestrated openings in heavy wheels, to lessen overall vehicular weight (Mallory and Adams 1997:627) – very probably in order to adapt the cart to horse traction. Because of its speed and considerable height above the ground, as Drews asserts, the horse presumably also functioned as a pack animal, invaluable in traversing stretches of rugged terrain and fording rivers and streams (Mair 2003:181). Across the steppes, there occurred localized areas of rich resource concentration, notably river valleys, but mostly separated by wide stretches of arid territory. Wheeled draft and pack horses enabled Yamnaya groups to traverse these inhospitable zones, then to fan out in search of new

FIGURE 2.6. Restored second-millennium-BC disc-wheeled wagon with arched tilt from Barrow 9, Lchashen, Armenia (Piggott 1968:pl. 22).

lands for cultivation and pasturage (Anthony 1991a:266). As we have seen, donkey riding was probably undertaken at Kish during the third millennium BC. We have no reason to believe steppe pastoralists were any less athletic than their Near Eastern counterparts! Very likely, in the context of Yamnaya migrations, incidental riding took place, as a pliant mare or gelding would be mounted to lead a pack train. Incipient riding capability would then be generalized to other situations (Khazanov 1984:93). Scouting on horseback would have facilitated maximal exploration of the steppe environment. The mobility of even inefficient horse riding would have allowed a mounted herder to control more livestock than a shepherd on foot,[8] to tap the seasonal availability of diverse pastures, and, in times of drought, to split his flocks and herds in multiple directions to survive crises through optimal exploitation of scarce resources (Shilov 1989:123–124).

Thus, unlike earlier steppe cultures centered along forested river valleys, by 3000 BC the Yamnaya had penetrated deep into the steppe

---

[8] Steppe ethnographic accounts indicate that on foot a single herder can manage 150–200 sheep; on horseback one person can control 500 (Khazanov 1984:32).

interior, as evidenced by the hunting of the saiga antelope and camel. Yamnaya mobility was also critical in the exploration of new mineral sources, the transport of metals, and the spread of metallurgy. With the Bronze Age, metal production shifted from the Balkans to the southern region of the Caucasus, where the first agricultural tools were manufactured, notably bronze sickles (Chernykh 1992:64). In exchange for cattle, horses, and hides, the abundant gold, silver, and copper of the Transcaucasian deposits were traded to steppe agro-pastoralists, who acting as intermediaries passed the metals north to the foraging inhabitants of the forest steppes and boreal forests. This long-distance trade in exotic prestige goods transformed the traditional bartering system. Even more importantly, Yamnaya metalworkers themselves were the first to intensively exploit steppe ores; they alloyed arsenic with copper to make tanged daggers, pins, and flat axes; they even experimented with iron (Anthony 1998:103–104).

In the latter half of the fourth millennium BC, as early Usatovo sites began to replace the declining Tripolye culture, Yamnaya groups with their metal tools also dispersed westward, migrating into the lower Danube valley and Carpathian Basin as far as Bosnia, Croatia, and Poland. The resultant Baden culture featured hilltop fortifications, dispersed settlements, and with the horse pronounced dependence on animal husbandry. Westward contacts further north extended from the upper Volga to the Rhine and were reflected in the Corded Ware Culture, again a mobile pastoral economy characterized by flexed inhumation under tumulus accompanied by battle axes. An eastern variant of the Corded Ware horizon, the Fatyanovo-Balanovo culture, also marked by burials with battle axes, introduced domestic livestock and metallurgy into the northerly forest region of Russia (Mallory and Adams 1997:43, 127, 196). Very probably, linguistic divisions occurred at this time as pre-Germanic/Italic/Celtic languages started to become differentiated c 3300–3000 BC; pre-Slavic/Baltic became detached slightly later, c 2800 BC; and pre-Greek, sharing traits with pre-Phrygian/Armenian, possibly separated c 2500 BC. As asserted earlier, Anthony attributes the success of Yamnaya expansion to raiding with the horse; but he also recognizes that as the intruding herders established control over lands suited to pasturage, their chieftains granted in alliance legal status to indigenous agriculturalists, as evidenced by a common term for patron-client contract shared across the differentiating language groups (Anthony 2007:100, 191, 369–370).

But Europe was already heavily populated with agriculturalists; moreover, its woodlands and mountains presented obstacles to rapid travel. Pastoralist expansion was therefore most effective to the east, where horse and wheeled transport opened up the Eurasian steppes, which previously had only been a barrier to population movement. Freed from logistical dependence on river valleys, agro-pastoralists moved steadily across the western steppes as far as the Ural valley. Of course, pastoralist cultures splintering away from the core had dispersed even further afield. As we have seen, Afanasievo in the east had reached the Minusinsk basin, just as Corded Ware in the west extended to the Rhine – thus spanning a total distance of 5,600 km.

Andronovo Horizon – Steppe Expansion East and South (2000–900 BC)

Apart from the Botai and Afanasievo early extensions eastward, it was not until c 2300 BC that systematic agro-pastoralism spread far to the east beyond the Ural River, probably initially in response to the need for metal ores from the Ural mountains in order to manufacture hard bronze weapons. While seminomadic pastoralism was pioneered during the Yamnaya phase, it would fall to Andronovo to fully develop sophisticated metallurgy across the steppes. In fact, it was the widespread demand for valuable metals that led to far-flung exploratory prospecting in distant zones. Migrations penetrated deep into the eastern steppes and forests, to areas previously uninhabited or only sparsely populated by hunter-gatherers. Hundreds of new sources of copper ores were located in Kazakhstan, the Altai, and the desert regions of Central Asia. From the Don-Volga to the upper Ural basin, the important bronze production culture of Abashevo was established predominantly in forest-steppe zones. Seams were reached by open quarry or drift mine. Eventually tin deposits, rare in the west, were located as far afield as the upper Irtysh, gold was mined in the Dzungarian Alatau mountains, and with the transition to the Iron Age, bimetallic (bronze and iron) tools began to appear (Anthony 1998:107; Chen and Hiebert 1995:249, 285).

By this time, population movement was no longer in a single direction; initial migration was followed by counterstream, returning to the place of origin with reports of outlying opportunities and inciting new efforts at exploration and further colonization; lessons learned from novel situations were thus shared across society. The **Andronovo** horizon, a blanket term for a series of regional cultures, stretched from the

Ural mountains to the Yenisei River, with later subgroups – Fedorovo and Semirechye – extending even further east to introduce gold and advanced wheeled technology to China (Kuzmina 2008:84, 112). In the Minusinsk Basin, rock drawings of equestrian figures (1700–1300 BC) attest to horse riding on these eastern steppes (Drews 2004:46). Andronovo men wore trousers, sleeved kaftans, caps – knitted, felted, or leather – with high conical tops and attached earflaps, and tall boots, the last item earlier evidenced in Pit-grave burials of the Ukraine. Subsequently, pointed caps, often with ceremonial insignia, were worn by many other Indo-Europeans: Hittites, Scythians, Phrygians, Thracians, Medes, and Persians (Kuzmina 2007:103–104).

A related culture, the **Srubnaya** (Timber-grave), 1800–1200 BC, extended west from the Urals to the Dnieper valley. From the Altai mountains in the east, c 1900 BC the Seima-Turbino tradition of the forest steppe, distinguished by its use of tin bronze and mastery of lost-wax casting, transmitted westward new techniques of casting thin-walled celts, chisels, and socketed spears – the strong all-metal cast socket a momentous innovation for its time (Chernykh 1992:200; Kuzmina 2007:252–253). Across these diverse regions, metallurgy served as one of the most significant stimuli for social interaction. Advances in technology were discovered and disseminated; casting was undertaken in closed molds; with universal use of tin bronzes new levels of bronze smithing were attained in the mass production of new tools; and metals were distributed in the form of ingots or finished products, promoting exchange and intertribal connections across Eurasia (Kuzmina 2007:96). Also, possibly derivative of earlier Catacomb culture (2500–1900 BC),[9] migration southward from the western steppe into the Aegean occurred during the first half of the second millennium BC, leading to the formation of the Mycenaean Shaft Grave dynasty (Kristiansen and Larsson 2005:182–185). In all, these related Srubnaya/Andronovo groups shared a similar agro-pastoral economy and traditions of horse training and bronze metallurgy, the former group laying the foundation for later Iron Age Cimmerian/Scythian/Sarmatian cultures of the west, the latter for the Aryan extension south.

---

[9] Catacomb was roughly intermediate between the rudimentary Yamnaya Pit-grave and later elaborate Srubnaya Timber-grave cultures. By late third millennium BC, a side chamber accommodating the corpse and a rich array of grave goods distinguished the Catacomb grave. This form was succeeded in the second millennium BC by the Srubnaya Timber grave, in which a subterranean wooden house was erected over the deceased (Drews 2004:26).

With regard to the Andronovo southern migration, Parpola (1999: 183) has noted similarity in design between fortresses protecting mineral deposits and areas of large-scale metalworking in the southern Urals and a temple-fort complex located far south in Bactria at Dashly 3. On the Ural-Tobol steppe (2200–1900 BC), in early steppe sites of **Sintashta** and **Petrovka**, immediate predecessors of Andronovo situated in regions rich in copper and gold ores, advances in furnace construction had involved chambered and dome-shaped hearths, permitting firing at higher temperatures and the production of first arsenical and eventually tin bronze (Kuzmina 2008:44–45). Forts characteristically were surrounded by a ditch and two rows of defensive walls composed of clay blocks and vertical pine logs with a timber palisade above. Traces of numerous fires and rebuilding attest to an unstable military situation and the necessity of fortifications for frequent defense of mines and metallurgy production centers (Kuzmina 2007:32, 223). Funerary architecture was also becoming increasingly sophisticated for the emergent chiefly class. Tumulus burial featured a tholos-like vaulted dome, constructed of mud bricks based on a cosmology of the quadrant open circle (Kristiansen and Larsson 2005:177). In these strongholds, excavations of the 1970s uncovered in cemeteries no fewer than 14 early spoke-wheeled chariots. These formative cultures (2300–1900 BC) of the eastern steppe, clearly derivative from the western steppe, featured elaborate burials in which deceased warriors equipped with weaponry were accompanied by the sacrificial head and forelegs of horses; other elements, such as exposure of dead before burial and the fire cult, help establish the proto-Aryan identity of these Bronze Age people (Mallory and Adams 1997:520–521). Alongside funereal remains, chariots were interred, as shown by stains outlined on the earth of vehicle superstructure, wheel rim, and spoke shape. These mortuary offerings followed a thousand-year-long western-steppe tradition for which more than 100 cart and wagon burials have been discovered; the chariot axle length was practically the same as the earlier steppe wagons, arguing for local evolution rather than foreign borrowing.

Such findings provide the earliest incontrovertible record of rapid horse transport. Weighing less than 34 kg, one-twentieth the weight of ancient wagons (Piggott 1992:17–18), horse-drawn chariots were a new breed of vehicle, infinitely lighter and swifter than the older solid-wheeled conveyances. Sintashta draft horses were purebred, had rather thin legs, and stood 13–14 hands at the withers (Kuzmina 2008:44). The Sintashta-Petrovka chariot wheels featured 8 to 12 spokes mortised into

FIGURE 2.7. Battle wagons from the "Standard of Ur" (Littauer and Crouwel 1979: fig. 3).

a separate navel. Clearly, extensive experimentation had been undertaken in order to engineer this sophisticated vehicle for the express purpose of harnessing the superior speed of the horse. Some 130 km north of Sintashta, at Krivoe Ozero, two horse skulls interred with a chariot yielded a date of 2026 BC. Next to the two horse skulls, amidst projectile points and a bronze axe and dagger, lay four disc-shaped bone cheekpieces; horse bones together with similar shaped cheekpieces have been found in sites across the Volga, Don, and Donets regions (Anthony and Vinogradov 1995:38–40; Kuzmina 2000:119). In fact, it appears that widespread experimentation with different types of bridling was well under way at this time. The early type of the bridle had one strap on the horse's nose fastened by simple cheekpieces; subsequent development entailed a cheek-strap fixed by more complex cheekpieces with multiple minor orifices. Concurrent usage of shieldlike (with or without tenons), grooved, and rodlike cheekpieces indicates an intensive quest for the most efficient form (Kuzmina 2007:115; 2008:52).

To the south in the Near East, solid-wheeled battle wagons (Fig. 2.7) drawn by teams of donkeys or donkey-onager hybrids had been deployed in Mesopotamian warfare since 2800 BC. As attested by seal impressions at Karum Kanesh II (Kultepe), a four-spoke-wheeled war chariot – driven by a single figure brandishing a battle-axe and drawn by two horses controlled by lines attached to nose rings (Fig. 2.8) – was operative in Anatolia c 1950–1850 BC. Not only did the light horse-drawn chariot render the clumsy battle wagons of the third millennium immediately obsolete (Anthony and Vinogradov 1995:38–40; Kuzmina 2000:119), the critical innovation of harnessing with bridles, bits and reins soon replaced the archaic methods of nose-ring and nose-band equid control throughout the Near East (Drews 2004:49–51). Utilized for hunting, military, and ceremonial purposes, by the mid-second millennium BC the light horse chariot also diffused rapidly westward to

FIGURE 2.8. Karum Kanesh II (Kultepe) seal impression of a four-spoke-wheeled war chariot (Littauer and Crouwel 1979:fig. 29).

the Aegean and central Europe and south across the steppes to India, extending east to China later in the millennium (Pare 1992:16; Parpola 1999:200). Advances in bridling may not have been limited to the chariot. Possibly, effective bits for riding had also evolved by this time. Rectangular bone plaques with serrated inner edges dating to c 1700–1300 BC were encountered next to a horse skull at Komarovka on the upper Volga (Piggott 1983:99). Because a single horse instead of a team was interred in this human burial, Drews (2004:55) considers these cheekpieces evidence of riding, rather than driving.

Anthony (1995:562) has proposed that compact fortified settlements, chariotry, sumptuous mortuary ritual, and horse sacrifice, important traits first displayed together on the steppes, also characterized the Aryans, who from the north across Central Asia invaded the Indian subcontinent. Like Parpola, Anthony identifies intriguing features that link Sintashta, Petrovka, and subsequent Andronovo to the south. His details of the Sintashta-Petrovka burials show remarkable affinity with rites specified in the *Rgveda* of ancient India. For example, in one instance of a chariot team of two horses, the hides with skulls and lower front legs attached were deposited in the grave, the detached hind legs

meticulously segmented, then laid out separately. This paralleled ceremonies described in the *Rgveda* in which the sacrificial horse was dissected and offered in a strictly prescribed sequence, the remaining flesh
ritually consumed in a feast. As extolled in the *Rgveda*, at Sintashta
the deceased was interred in a wooden chamber covered by a mound.
But even more strikingly, in the Rgvedic hymn of the fire priest, son
of Atharvana, the Asvin twins cut off his head and replaced it with a
horse head through which to learn the secret of the sacred mead libation. Amazingly, at a Sintashta-Petrovka variant site on the Volga, a
decapitated sacrificial human victim was discovered in a burial fitted
with such a horse head (Anthony and Vinogradov 1995:40–41).

Further evidence of steppe agro-pastoralist movement southward
comes from the BMAC, Bronze Age agriculturalists without the horse
who c 2200 BC had moved north from the Iranian highlands to practice
irrigation agriculture in desert oases south of the Aral Sea (Hiebert
1998:151–153).[10] Interaction between the encroaching horse herders
from the steppes and the settled agriculturalists of Margiana was initially hostile, as evidenced by Namazga VI settlements destroyed by
fire (Kuzmina 2008:73). But later Andronovo ceramics encountered in
BMAC fortified citadels indicate social interaction between the two
groups, particularly in temple rituals involving fire altars and the preparation of hallucinogenic beverages extracted from ephedra. These fire
altars and accompanying ash pits closely matched the fire cult later
elaborated in the *Rgveda* and *Avesta*. By 1500 BC, an Andronovo variant, Tazabagyab, had settled near the Aral sea to engage in small-scale
irrigation agriculture. Even further south in Tajikistan it appears other
Andronovo groups became established at Bishkent and Vakhsh. Here,
dichotomous mortuary practices associating rectangular hearths with
male inhumations and round hearths with female, rituals known to
characterize later Swat cultures of Pakistan and those of Vedic India,
mark the path of Indo-Aryan migration southward toward the subcontinent (Mallory and Mair 2000:260–266). In that India lies outside
the habitat of the wild ancestor of the horse, the indigenous Aryan
hypothesis claiming the horse was domesticated in Harappan culture
has been categorically rejected by paleozoologists. Following BMAC
trade contacts, it was the Andronovo horse from the Eurasian steppes

---

[10] Interestingly, the usual complement of herd animals was now joined by the Bactrian
camel, domesticated in the latter part of the fourth millennium BC in southern Turk-
menistan (Kuzmina 2008:66–67).

that entered India via Afghanistan during the second millennium BC, the agro-pastoralists traveling in covered carts with their chariots disassembled. The Bolan pass in Baluchistan led directly to the Indus, but more difficult paths through the Pamirs and Hindukush were also traveled. At night the carts formed a ring in which to guard the livestock. Light, transportable sectional dwellings were utilized. When circumstances were propitious, these Indo-Aryan invaders would stop to sow and harvest a crop of barley. Along this invasion route lay Andronovo ceramics and the Andronovo-Fedorovo marker, a trumpet-shaped earring; in Khurab an axe with a camel depicted; and at Kuruksetra, site of the epic battle, a celt of Andronovan type. Also evident were images of horses, chariots, and at Chibarnalla a sun-headed man with a bow shooting at the enemy – the ancient Aryan sun god Mithra. Over the ruins of the Harappan settlement at Hathala, Andronovo kurgans were built to entomb cremated corpses and ritual offerings of horse skulls and leg bones (Kuzmina 2007:324–328, 336–339). Such mobility across a wide range of habitats, the adjustment by seminomadic cultures to the extreme aridity of Central Asia, and their ability to incorporate new subsistence strategies bespeak adaptive flexibility on the part of these ancient steppe agro-pastoralists.

Equestrian Penetration of the Eastern Deserts

Nowhere was the adaptability to oasis environment more keenly evidenced than in the eastern deserts of the Tarim Basin,[11] where proof of equestrian penetration comes to us from a surprising source. In the late nineteenth century, different international scientific expeditions to this remote area of the Taklimakan Desert encountered the astonishing remains of mummified Europoids, also hundreds of Europoid skeletons. The mummies were by no means the product of deliberate embalming techniques as practiced in pharaonic Egypt but rather resulted from burial in soils of high salinity in climatic conditions of extreme aridity and winter cold (Mallory and Mair 2000:29). Subsequent modern archaeological research has indicated that these Europoid oasis settlements in the Tarim were likely first populated c 2000 BC from the northwest, with similarities in physical type, mortuary ritual, and ceramics linking them to the Afanasievo agro-pastoralists who, as previously noted, c 3600 BC had migrated from the Volga region to the Altai (Chen

[11] Today China's Uighur Autonomous Region of Xinjiang.

and Hiebert 1995:243; Mallory and Mair 2000:314–316); the wheat farming and stockbreeding practiced in the Tarim were unequivocally of western provenance. Encased in coffins sealed with hides or carpets, the Europoid corpses were wrapped in a woolen blankets, wore ornaments of jade, and carried bags of ephedra, used widely in steppe ritual (Mallory and Mair 2000:137–138). The best-preserved mummies were retrieved from Cherchen (Zaghunluq) and date to about 1000 BC. The most notable was a man, over 190 cm tall, with light-brown hair flecked with gray, heavy beard, high-bridged nose, and round eye sockets characteristic of Europoids (Mallory and Mair 2000:16). The Cherchen man wore colored woolen pants, a sleeved shirt, and white deerskin boots. Also excavated at Cherchen was a felt hat, molded into the shape of a cap curving up to a peak but flipped over at the bottom to form a cuff around the head, almost identical to the famous headgear of the Phyrgian archers who invaded Anatolia in the first millennium BC (Barber 1999:33–34, 64). Plaid textiles and iron objects were also encountered in the Tarim (Mallory and Mair 2000:147, 217–218). Suggestive of *suttee*, three corpses of women accompanied the Cherchen man. Alongside lay a separate burial of an infant, his eyes closed with two blue stones, a nursing bottle fashioned from a sheep's udder by his side. In the entrance to the main tomb, a leather horse saddle was placed atop a white felt blanket; above lay the head and front leg of a horse (Barber 1999:45, 50–52). Saddle, trousers, and boots! Without doubt these Europoids rode horseback!

A later related phenomenon, an equally astonishing find, was reported at Dunhuang in 1907 by the famed explorer Sir Aurel Stein. By gaining the confidence of a Taoist priest, he uncovered a cave crammed with hundreds of ancient manuscripts, all miraculously preserved, their diverse languages attesting to extensive contact over the centuries between east and west. The most marvelous discovery, however, were texts dating to the fifth through ninth centuries AD in a hitherto unknown Indo-European language, Tocharian, which differed markedly from nearby Iranian languages on the steppes, resembling instead ancient Celtic languages of the west; its influence on the Chinese language is evidenced in *mjit* "honey" taken from Tocharian B *mit* "honey" (cognate with English *mead* and Sanskrit *madhu*) (Boltz 1999:87; Wood 2002:64). The fair-haired and fair-skinned Europoid mummies whose abundant remains are so widely distributed across the Tarim Basin are therefore thought to have been Tocharian speakers and have been tentatively identified as the ancestors of the Yuezhi, a numerous and powerful tribe, documented historically by the Han Chinese to have inhabited this region during the late first millennium BC. From the first millennium AD, frescoes of red- or fair-haired monks and horsemen with blue eyes further corroborate long-term Europoid presence in the area (Mallory and Mair 2000:25).

Indo-European Diaspora

Thus far we have traced the spread of agriculture and stock rearing across the Eurasian steppes far into the inhospitable eastern deserts, where c 2000 BC Europoid equestrians penetrated the arid Tarim Basin on the northwestern borders of China. Furthermore, it is documented that these pioneers likely spoke a somewhat enigmatic Indo-European language, Tocharian. In order to understand more about Tocharian, we must now turn to an area of inquiry barely broached previously, comparative or historical linguistics, where we will tread *gingerly* on what has been termed the minefield of Indo-European origins. The concept of Indo-European languages originated in 1786, when a Welsh judge in India, Sir William Jones, not only demonstrated the interrelatedness of ancient Sanskrit, Latin, and Greek but also noted their connection to Persian, Germanic, and Celtic tongues; he therefore advanced the hypothesis of common descent from one ancestral language. Over the last few centuries, proposals as to where to set the Indo-European homeland have ranged – rather erratically – from the Baltic to the Hindu Kush to North Africa. One recent theory, combining archaeology and the linguistic research of Gamkrelizde and Ivanov (1983), attributes the spread of Indo-European languages to the expansion of agriculture from Anatolia west to Europe (Renfrew 1990:168–174) and east to India (Renfrew 1990:189–197). Opposition to this proposition, however, stems largely from knowledge that the territories, allegedly traversed in the latter proposed migration, are known to have anciently been occupied by speakers of numerous non-Indo-European languages (Mallory 1996:150, 178–179).[12] By contrast, the existence in the Tarim of Tocharian, an offshoot of Afanasievo – itself a derivative from the western steppe – has prompted other linguists and archaeologists to explore the possibility that the Eurasian steppe might be the original center from which Indo-European

---

[12] Europe itself is eliminated as the original homeland since multiple ancient remnant non-Indo-European languages persisted on its southern periphery, such as Basque, Etruscan, Iberian, Tartessian, and Linear A, among others, suggesting earlier distinct linguistic diversity prevailing across this continent (Mallory 1996:147).

languages radiated west, south, and eastward across Europe and Asia (Anthony 1991b; Mallory 1996; Mallory and Mair 2000; Parpola 1999).[13]

In the search for linguistic origins, it is necessary to recognize that the one constancy of language is that it is always changing in response to an endlessly shifting real world. Languages spread, diversify, and act upon one another. However, in that speakers – within a specific region and time frame – observe a course of relatively similar linguistic change, continuity in language can be discerned. Loan words or convergence from other language families may pose problems but can be handled by an arsenal of linguistic techniques (Mallory 1996:22–23, 112). Thus, historical comparison across languages undertakes to reconstruct a reasonable facsimile of phonological patterning and to compile a lexicon of the remote common ancestral language, that is, a language spoken long ago but no longer spoken today, the ancient predecessor from which more recent languages have evolved (Goodenough 1970:254). For example, by examining cognates for "sheep" in related but geographically dispersed languages, Sanskrit *avis*, Greek *o(w)is*, Latin *ovis*, Lithuanian *avis*, and English *ewe*, it is possible to determine the ancestral word *owis* in proto-Indo-European (PIE).[14] Besides vocabulary, similarities are apparent in grammatical systems and inflections of Indo-European languages. Not only can historical relatedness be demonstrated across languages, it is also possible through examination of the reconstructed cultural vocabulary to infer background information on the habitat of the original population. In PIE, botanical and zoological lexica both indicate a temperate zone, where subsistence appears to have been based on stock breeding with some farming. Terms for agriculture exist, for example, *agros* "field" and *semo* "seed," but far more prominent are words for domesticated animals: *owis* "sheep," *sus* "swine, sow," *porkos* "pig," *aig* "goat," *uksan* "castrated ox," *gwows* "cattle," and *ekwos* "horse," features obviously concordant with the western steppe environment (Mallory 1996:113–119).

Perhaps the most telling evidence in locating the Indo-European homeland is the important cleavage in the Indo-European language phylum, the distinction between *centum* and *satem* languages. Both terms signify a hundred, the former in Latin, the latter in Old Persian. The centum languages comprise Celtic, Italic, Germanic, Greek,

---

[13] Proposals along these lines were earlier sketched by Schrader (1890), Childe (1926), and Goodenough (1970) and in part submitted by Gimbutas (1997b).

[14] Conventionally, the reconstructed ancestral language is marked by the prefix "proto-" and its words or sounds are preceded by an asterisk.

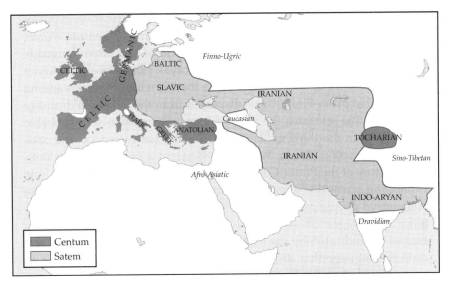

FIGURE 2.9. Division of Indo-European languages into centum (*darker*) and satem (*lighter*) subgroups, with subsequent formation of Indo-European language families (*uppercase*) by the end of the second millennium BC. Neighboring non-Indo-European language groups (*lowercase*) are also shown.

Anatolian, and Tocharian, all of which have preserved the hard PIE **k*, as in PIE **k'mtom* and Latin *centum*. By contrast, the satem languages, Baltic, Slavic, Albanian, Armenian, and Aryan (Iranian and Indo-Aryan), have relinquished the hard sound and adopted instead the palatalized s sound as in *satem* (Mallory and Mair 2000:121). As can be seen in Figure 2.9 (with the notable anomaly of Tocharian) this division splits the Indo-European languages virtually in half, centum in the west, satem in the east. Importantly, such partition implies that linguistic expansion was centrifugal in character, emanating from a central homeland, rather than simply a lineal extension from one extreme to the other.

The next question, of course, is when and where such centrifugal expansion took place. Again historical linguistics may provide the answer. A significant quantity of PIE loanwords occur in the proto-Finno-Ugric language spoken during the third millennium BC in the northern forests between the Volga and the Ob rivers, and also to the south in the proto-Caucasian language spoken in the mountains between the Black and Caspian seas (Anthony 1995:559). For this to have happened, PIE speakers had to have been situated on the steppes between the two populations. We know, of course, that in this time period agro-pastoralists of the steppes were actively trading metals from

spoken in the Bactria-Margiana settlements and in the Hindu Kush, early separated from proto-East-Aryan just as Indian Dasa diverged south toward the Sindh, Punjab, and the upper Ganges. By 1800–1700 BC West Aryan and East Aryan were established, the former to be associated with the Srubnaya culture west of the Ural River, the latter with the Andronovo to the east. Parpola prefers the West/East Aryan distinction to the customary Iranian/Indo-Aryan, in that while many Dasas[15] migrated south deep into India, other Bactrian Dasas remained in Central Asia, where their language likely later evolved into the little-known Nuristani dialects spoken today in the isolated northern valleys of Afghanistan and Pakistan. During the second millennium BC, the Dasa languages of Bactria, Margiana, Ferghana, and Gurgan were heavily influenced by an East Aryan offshoot, proto-Sauma-Aryan, which itself evolved into the Rgvedic languages of Gandhara, Swat, and the Punjab, later becoming Vedic as it overlaid late Indian Dasa on the plains of northern India. Pirak (1700 BC) on the Kachi plain furnishes the earliest direct evidence of horse riding on the subcontinent, in the form of terracotta figurines of horse riders with birdlike faces and legs bowed around the body of the horse (Parpola 1988:150). But, by the first millennium BC, East Aryan languages had become heavily influenced by West Aryan, with proto-Saka assimilating late East Aryan in Kazakhstan and Avestan assimilating Sauma-Aryan in Sistan. Mitanni-Aryan, an offshoot of Sauma Dasa that had diffused westward to the south Caspian-eastern Anatolian region, in Central Asia was overlaid by West Iranian later to evolve into Medean and Old Persian; West Iranian influences may even have extended to Vedic India. On the steppes c 800 BC, West Aryan came to be differentially represented as Cimmerian-Scythian around the Pontus/Ukrainian/Caucasus region, Sarmatian from the Don eastward across the Ural, Saka east on the Kazakh steppe, and Medean and Persian toward the Iranian plateau.

Changing ecology of the steppes may have in part triggered this vast movement of Aryan peoples. By the twelfth century BC climatic

---

[15] Because accounts in the *Rgveda* refer to the Dasas as dark-skinned enemies, it was earlier thought they were non-Aryan speakers. However, it now appears that as the first Andronovo migrated south, they intermarried with local indigenous populations, constructing the Dasa forts to protect their territories. Sanskrit *pur* is etymologically related to Greek *polis*. The myth of Tripura (fort with three concentric circular walls) recounts how the Vedic gods and Aryan kings destroyed the Dasa forts. The Dasas apparently understood the Sauma-Aryan language, but neither worshipped Indra nor practiced the cult of pressing sauma/haoma. In classical Sanskrit "Dasa" signifies war captive – slave (Parpola 1988:109–110, 121–122, 131).

deterioration and lowering of temperatures (Kuzmina 2000:121) had also forced West Aryan Iranian speakers to move their large herds through an annual circuit, hundreds of kilometers long, to exploit the steppes' feathered grasses across seasonal pastures (Khazanov 1984:94–95). This transfer to extensive pasturing had certain drawbacks, however. In remote regions of the steppes, herds were ever vulnerable to alien predation. This stimulated the intensification and diversification of offensive weapon production, with horse riding now at a premium. But the mounted warrior was only as effective as his control over his steed. Thus, earlier leather bits and horn cheekpieces soon were replaced by superior metal fittings. Along with these improvements went the progressive development of other horse equipment and better defensive armor for the equestrian combatant (Kuzmina 2007:412).

Thus, the dramatic shift to full-fledged pastoral nomadism was certainly aided by wheeled technology, but now equestrianism was in full operation. We have seen how over the centuries organic bits had become more complexly structured. By the latter part of the second millennium BC, rodlike cheekpieces were in widespread use from Carpathians to the Altai (Kuzmina 2007:358). Toward the end of the millennium sophisticated bits were being produced in both bronze and iron. Initially used in chariot bridling, by the turn of the millennium metallic bits were also deployed on the steppes to achieve truly *efficient* horseback riding (Bokovenko 2000:304–305). As noted in the Tarim, by 1000 BC the Cherchen man was using a leather saddle, woolen breeches, and riding boots; a felt peaked hat, similar to that worn by the Phrygians of Anatolia, was also found at Cherchen. A pad saddle or thick saddle blanket protected a man from injury, as with the bronze bridle he now exerted full mastery over the ridden horse. At speeds of 50 km per hour, pants and boots helped prevent chafing of the rider's legs. By the last quarter of the second millennium BC, the recurved composite bow had also appeared, contributing to the horseman's military success and to the diminishing importance of the chariot (Kuzmina 2007:138). Short and light, the bow in hunt and war permitted rapid discharge of arrows, as many as a dozen a minute. It further facilitated agile archery from the saddle, by allowing shooting while in retreat (Fig. 2.11) – essential when pursued by ferocious lions or wild bulls. These developments occurred on the western as well as the eastern steppe. In the west, a bronze figurine of a horse rider dating c 1000 BC was retrieved from a Koban burial on the northern slope of the Caucasus. In the Siyalk cemetery, just east of the Zagros mountains near the Nisaean plain, together with bronze cheekpieces and bit, a seal showing two archers wearing pants and mounted on horseback was unearthed and dated to the ninth or eighth century BC (Drews 2004:47–48, 78–79, 82, 101–102). Such extended migrations and diffusion of new technologies bespeak the extraordinary mobility gained through the adoption of first chariot transport, then efficient horseback riding. The constant intermingling of language and dialectical groups also shows the back-and-forth, wide-ranging interconnectedness of these nascent nomadic cultures.

Summary

In the Pontic-Caspian region, domestication of the horse, an animal indigenous to the Eurasian steppes, was the outcome of a complex interplay of social, economic, and ecological factors. As a result of farming and animal husbandry, deforestation and impoverishment of wild game in the river valleys of the western steppe caused stresses that required expansion of the resource base by way of increased utilization of the eastern steppe lands. At first hunted, the horse was initially domesticated on the steppe as a low-maintenance food source; it would later serve as a mount and a pack and draft animal. No doubt, ongoing research and debate will eventually clarify the precise development of these different equine functions. But in the agro-pastoralist migrations of the mid-fourth to mid-third millennium BC, as far east as the Minusinsk basin and as far west as Bosnia – a total distance of 5,600 km – if the horse were not yet ridden efficiently, we can reasonably surmise that at least it was utilized as a pack animal.[16] Following a lead mare, a small caravan of pack horses could be organized in efficient transportation, each loading 90 kg (Drews 2004:24). While riding may have been initiated earlier by some tribes in the core area of horse domestication, it is probably in the context of migrations that rudimentary riding first came to be regularly practiced. Once accustomed to bearing heavy burdens on its back, the pack horse may have become more amenable to being mounted by an agile youth, intent upon leading the pack train; riding would then be generalized to activities such as scouting, herding, and hunting, albeit at first on a limited scale due to the risks inherent in mounting bareback.

---

[16] The llama, capable of carrying only half the load half as fast as the horse, facilitated Bronze Age Inka expansion over 3,000 km along the length of the Andes.

FIGURE 2.11. Cylinder seal, first millennium BC, showing a steppe rider shooting to the rear (Littauer and Crouwel 1979:fig. 85).

With the advent of ox-drawn, wheeled transport toward the end of the fourth millennium BC, every effort was made to adapt the cart to harnessing the superior speed of the horse. The primitive organic bit, developed during incidental riding, was applied to paired-horse traction. Weighed down by the heavy disc-wheeled cart, unable to bolt (Dietz 2003:190), the horse was now malleable to meticulous experimentation with bit technology, so necessary at this point to control two horses traveling at far greater speeds than the lumbering ox. Correspondingly, modifications were made to cart structure and wheel assemblage to lessen their weight, culminating a millennium later in the appearance of the light horse-drawn chariot. Speed of travel was dramatically increased by a factor of 10, from 3 km per hour for ox draft to 33 km per hour for the spoke-wheeled chariot (Piggott 1983:89). The chariot provided a broad field of fire; it allowed hunters to carry more weapons, including large javelins; and it permitted more meat to be packed back to bases distant from the hunt site. The swift horse-drawn chariot also functioned as a lethal instrument of war, in the course of the second millennium BC invading east, west, and south across Eurasia.

And by 1000 BC, riding skills honed over centuries of herding, hunting, and raiding had progressed to full military competence. In conjunction with the short recurved composite bow, mass-produced socketed arrowheads helped deliver penetrating fire from the saddle (Anthony, Brown, and George 2006:152). High-speed riding constituted a radical innovation in human locomotion. It dramatically reduced geographic distance, forever changing the sociopolitical landscape. In the face of increasing aridity, it allowed the pastoralist to transition to full-fledged nomadism – the most mobile and extensive form of herd management. The Eurasian steppe was finally open; what once had been a hostile ecological barrier to human settlement was transformed into an intercontinental corridor of rapid communication. Successful traversal of the steppe on horseback resulted in expansion of tribal territories, with consequent flourishing of trade in all directions. Inhabitants of adjoining forests and deserts also adopted the new technology to more fully exploit the grassland habitat. But with large-scale movement of peoples came intensification of tribal conflict, resulting in equestrian conquest of the great nuclear alluvial civilizations in the Near East, India, and China. As will be seen in the chapters ahead, military cavalry would first complement and then supersede chariotry in warfare. Notwithstanding, the chariot would long be revered in myth and ceremony as the sacred vehicle of heroes and the gods.

NOMADIC HORSE CULTURE OF THE STEPPES

IN BRIEF DETAIL, THE PREVIOUS CHAPTER DOCUMENTED THE 4000–
1000 BC spread of horse culture from the Pontic-Caspian region west to
Europe and east and south across Central Asia. The current chapter will
continue in part to dwell on these early millennia, but its main focus will
be the high degree of prosperity achieved in the course of the Iron Age
by the Eurasian nomadic pastoralists. These intrepid horsemen were not
just hardy, competent herders, they were also enterprising traders, successful prospectors of minerals, skilled metallurgists, and consummate
artists, accomplished in diverse media. In this increasingly technical
environment, innovative tools and weapons were developed along with
the evolution of chariotry. In this increasingly hierarchical society, the
monumental tumuli of chiefly burials were sites of extravagant horse
and human sacrifice. And in mythology and ritual, we will note the
emergence during this epoch of complex religious concepts that greatly
influenced life across the steppes and eventually far beyond. To gain
an understanding of these phenomena we rely as always on the tools
of archaeology, but our enquiry is also informed from Chinese, Persian,
and Greek historical sources. First, though, let us consider an invention
integral to the nomad's adaptation to the Eurasian steppes, important
both functionally and ritually, his portable house – the trellis tent. This
collapsible bentwood structure fashioned with sophisticated metal tools
allowed nomadic horsemen to lead their herds to the remotest pastures,
to penetrate the most rugged terrains, and to survive the harshest climate of the continental interior. Unfortunately, this mobile habitation is
rarely discernible in the archaeological record. So for information on its
ingenious architecture, we are obliged to turn to modern ethnographic
studies of today's equestrian nomadic cultures.

Mobile Dwellings of the Steppes

From the Yamnaya horizon of the fourth millennium BC, we know of course that the first mobile habitation was the nomads' covered wagon with hooped canopy (Piggott 1992:23). But from models and pictographs encountered in later burial mounds, it seems that a primitive tent was early placed atop the wagon. This structure likely evolved from the Central Asian hunter's *tipi* lean-to of saplings covered with bark or animal skins. In fact, the later ceremonial tent of a Mongol chieftain traditionally was covered by numerous snow leopard pelts. The initial simple wooden frame, covered by matting or weatherproof felts, probably was easily lifted from the wheels to provide a stable dwelling in camp, while allowing for quick return to mobility as needed. At first conical and then domical, as the architecture became more sophisticated, the structure was made collapsible for transport by pack animals (Andrews 1999:17–18). Temporary round frame houses are known from Andronovo times, and ancient Indian texts attest that Vedic Aryans were fully acquainted with folding transportable dwellings constructed from poles and mats (Atharvaveda 9.3 cited in Kuzmina 2007:66, 154–155). Today thousands of sturdy tents, known to us as the Mongol *ger* or the Turkish *oy* or *yurt*, continue to dot the steppes. Dating from the first millennium BC, in its inception this trellis tent of the nomads was well constructed to withstand fierce winter winds. Style and detail vary from tribe to tribe, but the basic bipartite design of vertical walls and dome-shaped roof is the same (Fig. 3.1). The tent frame, largely of willow, consists of a cylindrical trellis wall more than 1.5 m high joined by a set of radially converging, curved roof struts to the rim of a roof wheel, which is placed horizontally to form the top of the dome approximately 3 m above the ground. The trellis is made with an outer and an inner layer of wooden laths fastened together at cross points by rawhide thongs. The laths are equally spaced in both layers so that when the trellis is erected, they form a network of diamond-shaped interstices. At the top, bottom, and ends, the laths extend slightly beyond the last crossing to form a series of V-shaped protrusions known as the heads, feet, and junctions. For ease of handling the trellis wall is divided into several sections that are fitted together at the vertical junctions, with overlapping lath ends to make a secure joint. The feet of the trellis provide friction to prevent the wall from being dislodged from its position on the ground. The doorposts of the entranceway ensure that the trellis ends fit closely to complete the continuity of the wall. Wall stability is

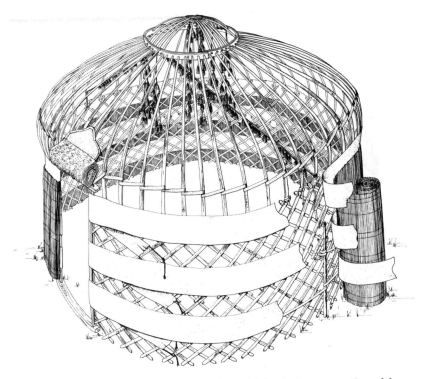

FIGURE 3.1. Modern nomads' trellis tent from Afghanistan, perspective of frame with cordage and screen (Andrews 1997: Vol. 2, b7).

established by one or more encircling girths secured around the entire structure from doorpost to doorpost, drawing post firmly toward trellis and placing both lintel and threshold under tension. Narrower bands, brightly patterned, are also bound spirally around the trellis junctions to prevent collapse. With four trellis sections of approximately equal length, the junctions naturally occur at the back and on either side of the tent.

Roof wheels are about 2 m in diameter and varied in design, made entirely of bentwood or a combination of bentwood rims with cut and shaped spokes. The rim is pierced radially with slots at regular intervals to receive strut tips and an arrangement of spokes. Instead of being arranged regularly all around the circumference, the spokes are grouped in two or more sets crossing the circle diametrically and bound together at the center with rawhide pins. Alternatively, they may form a cross or fan pattern, the double curvature providing additional strength. The spokes serve to brace the potentially fragile rim while providing support for the woolen felt spread over the top of the wheel. Since the spokes are cut longer than the internal diameter of the rim, they bow upward to form a dished wheel about 30 cm deep at the center. This dishing of the wheel forms a convex surface over which it is easy to pull the front edge of the roof felt back or forward with a rope operated from the ground, in order to afford a smoke hole or simply a window admitting light and air. As the curved roof struts have an inherent tendency to tip sideways, it is essential that they be held upright. This is accomplished by wrapping a long band of webbing around each strut at the point of maximum curvature. Two wrapping girths are utilized, one at the front of the dome and one at the rear. The ends of these beautiful, intricately woven tent bands are fastened to the trellis near a junction. The descending ends thus cross each other at each side of tent, securing dome to trellis and completely stabilizing the rigid structure. During construction, adjustments may be made in the internal architecture. In the winter season, the trellis is erected with a smaller diameter simply by opening it less fully. In this manner the roof struts slope at a steeper angle and are better able to shed snowfall on the roof. Another device for stormy weather is a system of cordage hung from either side of the roof wheel that can be weighted by a heavy sack or lashed to a stake driven into the ground (Andrews 1997:25–29, 33).

The ger is regarded by the nomads as the microcosm of the universe – the dome of its arched roof, the firmament; the smoke hole, the door to heaven. Three cosmic levels are reflected in the interior coloration of the Mongol shelter, where around the roof aperture the uppermost parts of the roof struts are painted a solar gold; the slightly lower parts, a celestial blue; and the ground trellis, as the surrounding felts and rugs, auspicious red ornamented with multihued vegetal motifs symboliz-ing terrestrial fecundity. The ger is conceived as the vitalizing union of male and female (Shakhanova 1992:159), in which the wooden struc-ture is shaped by men and the woolen felts by women.[1] In pitching a tent, men and women work together. Trellis sections are first extended, interlocked, and fitted to the door frame. Cane screens are then attached to the exterior of the trellis walls. In very large gers putting up the roof

---

[1] Felt is manufactured by placing fluffed-up wool evenly over a mat, sprinkling it with hot water, and then rolling it up to be tied on the back of the horse during the next day's trip. The following evening, the wool is rewetted, rolled in the opposite direction, and returned to horseback for further conditioning. With this alternation, the vibration of the horse mashes and kneads the wool until it becomes densely matted and, mixed with goat hair, impermeable (Barber 1999:37).

wheel may be accomplished by a man on horseback, though usually a forked pole is deployed to raise the wheel and the thick upper felts; the same pole later can be utilized to stabilize the structure during storms, and it also fulfills important ritual functions. The family works together to secure the connection of roof wheel and roof struts, then starting left of the doorway begins raising and tying in place the great sheets of felt that cover the framework on the outside. While white felts are preferred, white wool must be selected and is therefore expensive, so mixtures of different colored fleeces are encountered. But white felt is the ideal insulator against heat gain and loss. Insulation is aided by the nearly hemispherical shape of the tent, which affords the minimum surface area to enclose a given horizontal floor space. This economy of space in turn minimizes the amount of wool covering needed to be felted and the bulk of materials to be transported. While the fire burns inside the tent, the round shape allows all parts to be heated equally.

Tents are routinely pitched with the door facing south to receive maximal sunlight, but also for protection against the strong winds that blow from the north. In summer the floor may be bare, but in winter rushes are strewn on the ground below the floor felts for extra insulation. The hearth is located slightly fore of center. Impregnation of felts by smoke in winter causes them to change to pearly brown; it also makes them more waterproof. The sun through the aperture above the roof wheel casts a segment of light on the floor or sides of the tent. As this light segment travels around the tent interior in the course of the day, it acts as a sundial. The circular floor is divided into four quarters relating to the sunrise and sunset and corresponding to the four cardinal points. The rear of the tent opposite the doorway is the sacred or ceremonial part of the dwelling. Distinguished guests are received there with dignity, and this is where in summer many trunks, the finest rugs, kilims, and applique felt hangings, often decorated apotropaically with tassels and talismans, are displayed. The space between the doorway and hearth is the profane half; animals being tended and visitors of low status, squatting on their heels, remain here. One half of the tent (the right as seen from the rear) is regarded as the male domain for the storage of horse trappings, harness, saddlery, and water. The goat or sheepskin sack containing *airak*[2] (fermented mare's milk), along with the churning stick to introduce the old culture into the new milk, is strung nearby. The

---

[2] Mongolian term for lightly fermented beer made from mare's milk. In Turkic it is known as *kumiss*.

other side is reserved for cooking utensils, women, and young children. This structural division is conceptual, not physical, but nevertheless clear (Andrews 1997:29–35, 48). A wife often weaves in the family tent, her responsibility to produce the close-fitting woolen garments that provide warmth against the icy winds of the steppe and protect legs from chafing while riding; trousers clearly were a steppe invention, an adaptation to equestrian life. A horizontal loom often is staked to the ground, a large rug occupying half the floor space. Carpet knives discovered in late Bronze Age graves of Central Asia date the origins of pile carpet weaving to at least 1400 BC. The horizontal loom is more easily transported than the vertical loom; it may be dismantled, rolled up, tied to a pack animal, then reassembled many times before the carpet is completed. This creates different tensions in the warp threads, which results in the slightly irregular shape characteristic of tribal rugs (Macdonald 1997:15, 19–20).

In the nomad wedding ceremony, the ger's pole and roof wheel assume great symbolic significance. Groom and bride both exchange ritual statements in which the man standing alongside the pole declares he is the satellite of the woman's moonlike round roof wheel. There is thus mythological comparison of the pole as the male force, the roof wheel as the woman's womb, and the ger conjoining the two essences as in the act of impregnation and conception. The spot in the ger where the wheel is hoisted aloft by the pole is called the umbilicus, and during childbirth the pole, together with a horse's bridle, provides a supporting structure for the woman in parturition. The placenta, wrapped in felt, is placed on the roof wheel, the circumference of which is decorated with triangular pendants to ensure fertility. A golden eagle inside the ger or a studhorse tethered outside affords protection against evil forces (Shakhanova 1992:161–165). As will be seen, the circularity of the domed ger, as microcosm of the universe and focus of cyclical rebirth and regeneration, is also reflected in steppe funerary symbolism and in later epochs in monumental architecture across Eurasia.

On the steppe, the status of women is high. The family hearth, the very center of the ger, is referred to as "grandmother," the protective spirit of the family and clan. On striking camp, as clan grandmother, the mistress of the tent is responsible for protective rituals in transferring the fire coals to the new encampment and their division among clan members. Among nomads, fire is metaphor for birth, and the rituals revolving around the hearth are generative in relation to the continuity of clan, family, and herds (Jacobson 1993:188–189). When it is time to move on to the next pasture, belongings are bundled in an efficient manner. The tent trellises are loaded in pairs on either flank of a camel, struts stowed on top, felts placed across the back, and the roof wheel laid horizontally on top of all. Alternatively, collapsed tents with belongings may also be transported on carts drawn by oxen, horse, or mule. For the great chieftains, large permanently constructed gers were mounted on carts drawn by as many as 20 oxen. These imposing structures are known for the first millennium BC from Scythian and Sarmatian artwork and recorded historically for the Mongols, Turks, and Tatars from the twelfth to seventeenth centuries AD (Hildinger 2001:8).

Steppe Technology and Weaponry

Prior to the Indo-European equestrian dispersal across the steppes, no human being had ever traveled such vast distances overland with such rapidity. Let us then examine the mechanical innovations that aided these lightening migrations and made possible the efficient transport of nomad impedimenta. In Eurasia, the spread of wheeled technology was so swift that it is impossible to determine whether there was a central point of diffusion or multiple independent inventions; most likely, the bentwood sled of the Mesolithic was the predecessor of the wheeled vehicle. Earliest evidence of the disc wheel comes from a fourth-millennium model found in Bikova, Bulgaria (Clutton-Brock 1992:12), but between 3500 and 2500 BC wheeled transport had become generally adopted from western Europe to India. The earliest wheeled vehicles were constructed with one pair (as in carts) or two pairs (as in wagons) of wheels with their axles, either both turning together or with fixed axle and freely rotating wheels. Harnessing a pair of draft bovines was accomplished by a central pole with the yoke bearing on the withers or attached to the horns. When equids – donkeys, onagers, horses, and their hybrids – were subsequently employed in draft, this yoke harnessing persisted with little modification, even though it was ill suited to equid anatomy and reduced the animal's traction force. Disc wheels of the carts and wagons were either single piece or composite. The composite, sometimes of two but more typically of three planks rounded at edges with tightly fitting dowels and internal tubular mortices (Piggott 1992:17–18; Fig. 3.2), was not achieved with stone or flint (Piggott 1983:25). Sophisticated new metal tools, shafthole axes, axe-adzes, adze blades with asymmetric cutting edges, chisels, and gouges had to be invented to produce the tripartite wheel (Piggott 1983:58).

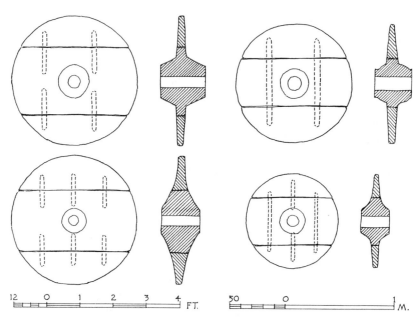

FIGURE 3.2. Tripartite disc wheels: top, from Trialeti barrows 5 and 29; bottom, from Lchashen and Ner Getashen, Armenia (Piggott 1968:fig. 7).

Later, lunate openings were deliberately fashioned to lessen the weight of the solid wheel (Piggott 1983:25); another attempt to lighten the wheel was the introduction of the crossbar type, a single diametric bar traversed at right angles by two slender "cross bars" (Littauer and Crouwel 1977:95).

As we have seen, beyond the Urals, c 2100 BC the Sintashta-Petrovka sites showed burials of spoke-wheeled chariots accompanied by two-horse teams (Anthony 1995:561). More complete evidence of chariotry is available to us from a slightly later site at Lchashen, near Lake Sevan between the Black and Caspian seas. Dating to c 1500 BC, two superbly preserved chariots displayed in fine detail a rectangular chariot box mounted over a midplaced axle. Most remarkably, revolving freely around the fixed axle were wheels with 28 spokes (Shaughnessy 1988:201; Fig. 3.3). Alongside horse and horsehide burials, bronze bits were recorded "with a linked mouthpiece and openwork disc or wheel-shaped cheekpieces" (Piggott 1974:18). This new vehicle differed from its predecessors, the cart and the wagon, in that it represented an essentially new, light, resilient conveyance, designed not for transport of heavy loads but for speed and maneuverability in war, hunt, or

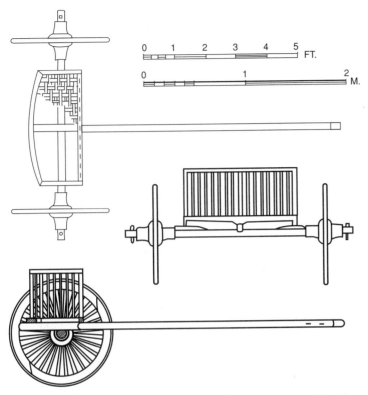

FIGURE 3.3. Measured drawings of chariot from barrow 11, Lchashen. Courtesy History Museum of Armenia (Piggott 1974:fig. 1).

ceremony. Mounted on two spoke wheels, intended for a minimum of persons, and drawn by two or more horses harnessed to a central draft pole, the chariot was a prestige vehicle, par excellence, interred only in burials of elite members of an increasingly hierarchical society. Its sophisticated technology brought both economic and political advantage. With its military muscle, the chariot came to be regarded as a sacred vehicle, indeed as a conveyance of the gods (Littauer and Crouwel 2002:48).

The three basic components of this amazing new vehicle, forerunner of the modern automobile, were the box to carry the driver and combatants, an axle and wheel assemblage, and a harnessing assemblage. The box, to accommodate a standing crew of one or two (later three), was enclosed by sides or railings, normally open in the rear. The spoked wheels were mounted onto the axle between tubular bushings fastened with linchpins. Spokes radiated from a central hub and were mortised in a bentwood felloe (Shaughnessy 1988:192–193). Bentwood technology required the wood, cut to shape, to be soaked overnight, then heated in a vertical structure over the hearth, at which point it was bent by leverage to the correct curvature on a pegged bench, then held in shape between stakes on the ground for several days until ready for construction. In the course of the second millennium BC, bronze and iron fittings would be used on vehicles. The draft pole was also mounted off the axle, running forward under the chariot box, then curving upward until it reached a little above the wither height of the horse, where it connected perpendicularly to the transverse or yoke (Piggott 1983:29, 90). This arrangement, derivative of bovine harnessing and restrictive of horse capacity, with time was partially rectified by the introduction of the yoke saddle to adapt the vehicle yoke to horse anatomy (Anthony and Vinogradov 1995:40). This was accomplished by suspending from the yoke two inverted V-shaped yoke saddles, designed to fit neatly over the neck of the horse, forward of the withers. By lying along the animal's shoulders, the legs of the yoke saddle transferred at least part of the pressure to this area. The horses were then secured to the yoke saddle by leather straps that ran separately across the neck of the horse and to its mouth to join with the organic or metallic bit. Additional horses would be fastened only by traces, their tractive power proportionately reduced. But in that these outer animals experienced less pressure, they tended to set a faster pace, thereby stimulating the yoke animals to increase their speed (Littauer and Crouwel 1979:29, 85; Shaughnessy 1988:193). The rapid success of the chariot across the steppes was evidenced by innumerable petroglyphs of multi–spoke-wheeled chariots with teams of two, three, or four horses from the Caucasus in the west across the Pamirs, the Mongolian Altai to the Gobi desert in the east, showing clear examples of yoke saddles and midplaced axles (Littauer 2002a:106–109, 112–115; Shaughnessy 1988:205).

Also a product of sophisticated wood-bending skills, the bow was the primary weapon of the steppe nomad. The recurved composite bow, adopted toward the end of the second millennium BC probably in response to the need for a short bow for use in hunting on horseback, was an important component of the nomad's success and mobility. Ironically, this instrument not only facilitated more efficient predation but eventually allowed cavalry to supersede the chariot as a method of warfare. Unlike the western straight-staved, simple bow, which employed a stave cut to utilize different parts of one piece of wood, the composite bow used a combination of materials to withstand tension and compression. It required a great deal of work. The central bowstave was first cut from wood selected for its ability to absorb glue well, typically maple or mulberry. The central grip section was joined by fishtail splices to a pair of bow arms, to which tips were affixed. A single piece of long horn was glued to the belly of the bow, tied into an arc, then left to dry for two months. Gluing was undertaken preferably in the cool and wet of winter, so that drying should be gradual. Next, sinew from the leg of a deer was beaten into fibers, soaked with glue, and applied to the back generally in two layers. Tied once again in an even more recurved arc with tips together and cord secured to the handle, the bow was left for another two months. Small shims of wood or bone might be inserted under the horn plate of the limbs should these separate slightly from the center grip.

Tillering, adjusting the bow so that limbs curved uniformly when drawn, followed. When a limb was too stiff it was filed gently. This was repeated until the bow arms bent evenly at a full draw, ensuring an accurate shot. To waterproof the sinew, thin strips of bark or leather were applied diagonally. The result was a bow mechanically superior to all others: sinew has a tensile strength four times that of wood and horn a compressive strength twice that of hardwood. This meant the bow was shorter yet drew the same weight and transferred more energy to the arrow, shooting it further and faster. Its shape held another advantage over the straight-staved, simple bow. The tips of the recurved bow were relatively inflexible, functioning somewhat as levers and making the bow smoother to shoot; minute deviations in length of the draw did not detract from arrow accuracy or velocity. While ideally suited to hunting from chariot or on horseback, this light, short, recurved composite bow was in fact a lethal artillery weapon early adapted to mounted warfare. Tales abound of the amazing accuracy at long distance of steppe equestrian archers. Often recounted was the tactic of feigning a retreat, using the nomads' amazing ability to shoot backward at their pursuers over the horse's tail in the famed "Parthian shot." Horse and bow together delivered to the steppe warrior the devastating combination of speed and maneuverability coupled with the ability to kill from afar, allowing the mounted steppe nomad to engage in wide-ranging military tactics that were to confound pedestrian and chariot armies alike (Hildinger 2001:21–23, 35).

The Scythian composite bow of the first millennium BC was carried in a bowcase always combined with a quiver (*gorytus*), containing

300 light arrows of reed or wood with bone, bronze, and later iron points, often poisoned. Other weapons comprised daggers, battle axes, curved swords, lances, darts, lassos, whips, and slings. Wicker or hide shields were strengthened by metal straps. Protective scale armor was worn by horsemen and sometimes their horses (Rolle 1989:65, 74; Sulimirski 1993:155–156).

The Horse – Sacred Symbol of Rebirth

But metal items were not always strictly utilitarian. Designed to celebrate the nomadic lifestyle, many horse and chariot trappings and belt accessories, previously fashioned from bone and stone, were now rendered in bronze, silver, and gold; as ceremonial objects they were finely worked and intricately decorated (Bunker 2002:7–8). Migrating across the steppes, Indo-European pastoralists had intermarried with the sparse hunting populations encountered along river valleys. Much of the early hunters' sacred steppe lore had been incorporated into shamanic ritual observances. Mythology reflected this complex interaction between the forces of nature, men, and the supernatural. These beliefs were given visible form in flourishing ornamentation in which zoomorphic imagery was paramount, an art form known to our modern world as "animal style" (Brentjes 2000:259).

As the first men to hunt on horseback, the nomads superbly registered in their art the speed and vitality of the prey animal – the stag in flight, its body tense, its head high, eluding the hunter. The animal's pose varied. Other times the herbivore was serenely recumbent, the predator menacingly crouched or coiled, or predator and herbivore were entwined in deadly combat: clutched in the raptor's talons, a caprid writhing in death agony; two camels wrestling, each biting the other's rump; the horse attacked by a ferocious panther; the deer's fantastic antler tines efflorescing into birds' heads (Jacobson 1993:11, 53–55). The motif of animal combat or predation has been interpreted by Rudenko (Thompson 1970:xxiv) as reflecting the dualistic struggle between good and evil as propounded in Persian Zoroastrianism. Depiction of ferocity and death was juxtaposed with birth and life. Many images clearly evoked fertility and procreation, with ithyphallic features and popular themes of animal copulation, possibly to ensure propagation of wild game and livestock (Bunker 2002:18), but also, as argued by Jacobson, to celebrate the cyclic rhythms of death and rebirth.

Jacobson, in her analysis of early steppe art, has identified an ancient cervid goddess, the female elk, as the embodiment of the forces of rebirth and regeneration. Across millennia, to accommodate the inflow of new cultural elements, this image shifted to syncretic form (Jacobson 1993:3, 92). Over time, the elk was replaced as the source of life and guardian of death by the deer, ambisexual, its rack of antlers swept back in great waves over its lithe body (Jacobson 1993:20). A focal symbol of cosmogenesis, the deer's branched antlers, often foliate in shape surmounted by birds, formed the tree of life (Jacobson 1993:85–87). As equestrian nomadism supplanted hunting, the composite image of the deer-horse emerged (Jacobson 1993:4), the deer acquiring the long equine torso, the horse the deer's towering antlers.[3] The horse became the cosmic animal, associated with gold, the sun, and the heroic warrior. Chariot and wheel, emblematic of the sun disc, furnished the vehicle of the gods (Jacobson 1993:129–131). Intertwined with antler and tree-of-life imagery, the horse served as the steed on which the dead made their journey to the next world (Jacobson 1993:86) and was an integral component of steppe funerary observances. These early steppe themes and imagery of death and rebirth, together with the concept of the horse as a cosmic symbol, would persist across Eurasia to shape the religions of Hinduism and Buddhism and would also extend westward through Zoroastrianism to influence Christianity and Islam.

Steppe Kurgans and Ritual Burial

Given the high mobility of pastoralist adaptation to the steppes, nomads left very little in the way of settlement remains. In their elaborate rituals of life and death, however, they did construct huge monumental kurgans, sometimes far from major rivers, in order to enshrine their ancestors. It is interesting to note the response of the steppe king Idanthyrsus to Darius's query as to why the Scythians avoided battle with the Persians:

> Persian, I have never run from any man in fear; and I am not doing so now from you. There is for me nothing unusual in what I have been doing: it is precisely the sort of life I always lead, even in times of peace. If you want to know why I will not fight, I will tell you: in our country

---

3 *Rgveda*, Book 1, CLXIII, explicitly connects the horse to the deer, stating the horse has horns. Verse 9: "Horns made of gold hath he," and verse 11: "Thy horns are spread in all directions" (tr. Griffith 1889; cited by Mair 2007:43n).

there are no towns and no cultivated land; fear of losing which, or seeing it ravaged, might indeed provoke us to hasty battle. If, however, you are determined upon bloodshed with the least possible delay, one thing there is for which we will fight – the tombs of our forefathers. Find those tombs, and try to wreck them, and you will soon know whether or not we are willing to stand up to you. (Herodotus 2003:4:127)

Soaring high above the undifferentiated vastness of the steppe, the kurgan tumulus was held sacred by the nomads and served as marker of tribal territory and allegiance. Often surrounding the tomb was a cromlech – a circle of erect stelae, sometimes anthropomorphized, other times merely with tapered upper ends. With its shaft thrust deep into the earth the stela stood as the tree of life, ritually connecting the subterranean, terrestrial, and aerial spheres; above loomed the sepulchral kurgan, stately symbol of the world mountain.

One of the earliest kurgans, Maikop, dating to the fourth millennium BC, was situated in the metal-rich zone of the Kuban River, north of the Caucasus. Over 10 m in height, it was the funeral mound of a pastoralist chieftain, who in exchange for cattle driven south received valuable objects from the newly formed cities of Middle Uruk, Mesopotamia. The chieftain's tunic featured 68 golden lions and 19 golden bulls, potent symbols of Near Eastern might. Also worn was a diadem of golden rosettes and elaborate necklaces of precious stones – turquoise traded from as far away as Tajikistan, carnelian from western Pakistan, and lapis lazuli from eastern Afghanistan. Maikop was in fact a filter through which southern innovations reached the steppes: arsenical bronze tools and weapons, lost-wax metal casting, early textiles of cotton – domesticated in India c 5000 BC, and possibly the wagon. In return Kuban copper, silver, lead, and gold ores flowed south. And perhaps northern sheep, bred to produce long wool, were first introduced into the Near East at this time. In a Late Maikop grave, a frieze of 19 horses was painted in red and black colors on stone (Anthony 2007:263, 289–294; Piotrovsky 1974a:12).

More than 2,000 years later Alexandropol, a colossal kurgan constructed in the Dnieper region, measured over 20 m, twice the height of Maikop. Inside were found the burials of 15 horses with innumerable gold or silver ornaments. One horse was interred apart in a posture typical of animal-style representation: legs drawn up under body, head and neck stretched forward (Piotrovsky 1974b:27). As a consequence of equestrian mobility and far-flung contacts, there were many shared features among steppe cultures. Along with their similar subsistence practices, the nomads possessed a common world view that nurtured the spread of religious beliefs and artistic forms. Over the centuries, as the pastoralists extended their exploitation of the grasslands eastward, the kurgan with its associated complex of monumental tombs accompanied them. Elaborate political theater surrounded the funerals of their chieftains. Spectacular animal sacrifice and lavish distribution of meat were central elements in recruiting and incorporating new clients. In public feasts, heroic or praise poetry validated in song the Indo-European language as a vehicle for communicating with the gods (Anthony 2007:343). Despite certain local distinctions, these tumuli with their recurrent horse rituals attest to a common steppe culture reaching from the Pontus across the Urals to the Altai-Sayan.

The most extensive steppe horse burials are known from the eighth-century-BC Arzhan tombs in the Sayan mountains, where a gigantic circular drum-shaped cairn, 110 m in diameter and 4 m high, overlay radially constructed timbers. A king and queen, richly adorned with sable and gold ornaments, were centrally interred in an enormous wooden edifice, the floor strewn with horse tails and manes. Lines of logs, like spokes of a gigantic wheel, radiated out from the center. With cross pieces forming concentric lines, the entire structure was divided into 70 trapezoidal compartments, in which there were mass human and horse burials, the 138 horses all saddled and bridled, probably gifts from tribal units subordinate to the king. At the edge of the tomb was a semicircle of 300 stone graves each containing a horsehide burial, evidence of a lavish ceremonial feast. A total of 450 horses in all had been sacrificed. The Arzhan kurgan presents clear evidence of an elaborate sun cult. The king, bedecked in gold, was located at the center of a huge wheel symbolizing the sun or solar chariot. The steeds accompanying him were placed in strictly defined groups within the structure, indicating their integral participation in the rite. Horses were on the one hand the sun's inner essence; on the other they were the means by which souls were to reach the luminary (Piggott 1992:112–114).

Arzhan was not unique:[4] solar sepulchral shrines occurred elsewhere in the eastern steppes, some dating to the second millennium

---

4 Alongside the fifth-century-BC tomb of Duke Jing of the state of Qi (in modern Shandong), there exists an even larger sacrificial pit, where more than 600 horses, lined up in pairs, extend over a distance of 200 m. That horse-poor China should conduct such an elaborate sacrifice only underscores the extraordinary prestige attached to the horse (Mair 2007:41n).

BC. At Qawrighul in the Taklimakan desert, the surfaces of six male graves were each adorned with seven concentric rings radiating out in a solar configuration measuring 50–60 m in diameter (Mallory and Mair 2000:137).[5] Horse-sun association is linked to the otherworldly nature of the horse. At a gallop the horse appears to fly and as such is believed to be intermediary between worlds, conveying the soul of the deceased from earth to heaven. In mountainous areas very often sanctuaries were dedicated to the "heavenly steed," and pictographs of horses appeared high on cliff sides. Fire, the earthly manifestation of the sun, was also important in funerary ritual. The central tomb structure was sometimes burned, often with total or partial cremation of the deceased. A ring of fire might be lit around the central platform or as many as forty mounds containing hearths would surround the kurgan, bearing evidence to the belief in a circular universe and its fiery essence, isomorphic with later Vedic creed. Burning the deceased was a sacrifice to the gods, since the tongues of flame, like horses, would transport the soul to heaven. These dramatic customs all echo the widespread Indo-European belief in the rite of cremation. Gold, the color of the celestial orb, was also repeatedly associated with burial, royalty, and divinity. In multiple chiefly burials across the steppes, the deceased was literally clad in gold. Accordingly, later Achaemenid kings were interred in gold sarcophagi; in the wider Aryan world Agni and other ancient Indian deities were golden-skinned, and the Buddha Sakyamuni's body, radiant like the sun, shone with gold (Litvinskii 1987:518–521).

Regalia of the Pazyryk Kurgans

The most phenomenal finds of ceremonial materials, which provide dramatic insight into life of the steppes, have been obtained from the Pazyryk cemetery in the eastern foothills of the Altai. There, excavation of five elite kurgans has allowed us to reconstruct the magnificent funeral rites of tribal chieftains from the fifth to third century BC. Due to the increasing demand for steppe horses from the urbanized centers of China and the satrapies of the Achaemenid empire, occasioned at this time by the switch from chariot to cavalry warfare, massive breeding of

---

[5] In one, as many as 894 upright posts were utilized. As Mair (2007:25) has posited, in treeless steppe or desert, a circular configuration of posts may well stand for the sacred groves of western Eurasia.

FIGURE 3.4. Decoration on saddle cover from Pazyrk, barrow 1 (Rudenko 1970:pl. 113).

horses was underway (Thompson 1970:xxv). Mainstay of the economy, the horse featured spectacularly in funerary ritual, in the ritual passage of the dead to the next world (Rudenko 1970:56).

The richness of the Pazyryk remains in large part is due to the region's severe climate, where long winters and short summers with night frost fostered conditions ideal for the formation of kurgan congelation, as a consequence wonderfully preserving tomb contents. Accompanying frozen mummies were rich assemblages of grave goods, in particular textiles that in the absence of written language operated as a coherent system of symbols, evoking images of myth and legend. Fantastic animals prominent in folklore were depicted, as for example a bird-griffin with jagged comb ruff gripping an elk in its talons (Fig. 3.4) or a lion griffin leaping upon a mountain goat (Rudenko 1970:235). Saddle blankets (*shabrack*) were especially elaborate; on one the entire surface was decorated with applique designs of five stylized deer antlers signifying rebirth, their roots coming together as a circle, their tines radiating outward (Barkova 1978:50–51). An elaborate felt wall hanging depicted a splendidly attired rider astride a saddled and bridled horse (Fig. 3.5). But by far the most remarkable woven item recovered from the Pazyryk

FIGURE 3.5. Felt wall hanging from barrow 5, depicting rider mounted on a saddle with bridle (Rudenko 1970:pl. 154).

kurgans was a polychrome pile carpet, almost 4 m square. Of great historic and aesthetic value, it is the most ancient complete woolen carpet in existence; from the great skill with which it was executed, it is clear that carpet weaving had been practiced long before 300 BC. While the carpet was incontestably of steppe manufacture, the design showed undoubted Achaemenid influence in that its border of 28 mounted riders paralleled the 20–30 emissary groups from tributary nations flanking the approach to the Apadana at Persepolis (Macdonald 1997:25). Also interred was a multistringed harp, probably bowed and prototype of instruments emerging a millennium later in Persia and China (Lawergren 1992:102). Anticipating the international Silk Road trade of the next millennium, Chinese articles were also present: exquisitely embroidered silk textiles. During this epoch, the Chinese principalities to the east were embroiled in great political strife, the steppe nomads varyingly allied with different Chinese warlords. One striking Chinese import at Pazyryk was a canopied carriage, conceivably part of the dowry of a Chinese bride. This four-wheeled carriage, token perhaps of military alliance between warlord and nomad, was 3.3 m in overall length; each wheel had 34 spokes and measured 1.8 m in diameter (Fig. 3.6). A draft pole was attached indirectly to the axle by means of a bow to allow flexibility in turning for a team of four horses, two harnessed by yoke and yoke saddles, and an outer pair by traces. The sophisticated construction of this prestige vehicle showed affinities with

FIGURE 3.6. Reconstruction of carriage (with yoke saddles) in barrow 5 (Rudenko 1970:pl. 131).

both western and eastern traditions of transport (Piggott 1992:130–132; Rudenko 1970:189–191).

The human remains at Pazyryk indicate that the people were predominantly Europoid but with East Asian admixture (Rudenko 1970:45–47). Warring was prevalent; one chieftain had been scalped, the skin above his forehead slashed from ear to ear. It was a proud steppe custom to adorn the horse bridle with scalps of slain enemies (Rudenko 1970:221). Another noble warrior, of Mongoloid extraction, wore a large false beard. As evidenced even today in the case of the Taliban, the full beard in Central Asia has long symbolized manly strength and dignity. One further form of decoration was tattooing in the vividly flowing animal style of the steppes (Mair 2005:74). While many human burials had been mercilessly ransacked by robbers, no concerted attempt had been made to disturb the horse burials, with the result that much of the horse regalia remained intact. The Pazyryk bridles were sophisticated but differed from modern bridles in lacking straps at the chin (Rudenko 1970:120). The saddles at Pazyryk were true saddles but rudimentary in character. In its evolution, the saddle was earlier preceded by the saddle cloth to absorb sweat, then by the contoured pad that conferred both stability to the rider and protection to the horse's barrel. The Pazyryk saddles were more advanced in that they consisted of two fully stuffed leather cushions attached to a felt underpad, with rigid bow arches to the front and rear of each cushion (Fig. 3.7). Breast and haunch attachments prevented the saddle from slipping forward or backward on the steep mountain gradients; spacers held the cushions apart to stop them from pressing on the horse's withers (Hyland 2003:52). There were no stirrups, and the horses were unshod (Thompson 1970:xxvi–xxvii). The finest saddle horses were richly caparisoned with shabracks, masks, and headdresses carrying high crests of deer antlers. Such exotic finery was clearly beyond mere conspicuous display. In effect Jacobson (1993:64–67) argues it constituted a semiotic system whereby the transition from life through death to rebirth was mediated by the articulation of symbols sacred to the deer goddess and tree of life. In elaborate antlered headdress, the horse represented the fusion of these sacred images.

Scythian Rituals of Sacrifice, Dismemberment, and Regeneration

While incredibly rich data have been retrieved from funerary kurgans, from these remains we can only tentatively reconstruct steppe ritual observances. For more detailed information, we need turn to Herodotus's fourth book of *History*, detailing the Scythians of the fifth century BC. From his accounts, we learn that steppe women held important positions as priestesses; they also courageously participated in military operations. In military graves, female Amazon warriors equipped with scale armor and weapons often occupied the central and most richly adorned position (Melyukova 1990:111–112; Sulimirski 1993:190). Tomyris, widow of the Massagetae king, swore "by the Sun our master," to whom the horse was sacrificed as an offering of "the swiftest of mortal creatures to the swiftest of gods." With her steppe cavalry this Amazon queen defeated the Persian army, killing Cyrus the Great in 530 BC (Herodotus 2003:1.214–216).

As reflected in internal coloration of the nomads' tent, Scythian cosmology comprised three levels: eternal fire, the heavens, and earth. In the creation myth, golden objects hurled down from the sky by the fire goddess Tabiti[6] defined societal groupings. The golden chalice of ritual libation designated the rulers and priests; the golden battle axe, the warriors; and the golden yoke and plow, the herders and farmers. Targitaus, offspring of the cosmogonic marriage of heaven and

[6] Known as Tarayati in Iran and Hestia in Greece.

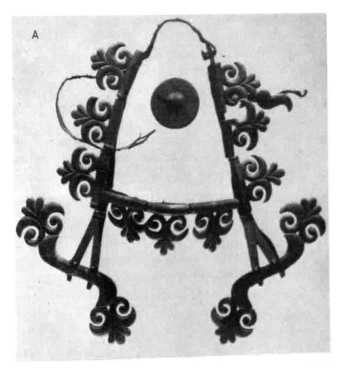

FIGURE 3.7. Bridle (a) and saddle (b) from barrow 1 (Rudenko 1970:pl. 79).

earth, had three sons. As symbols of the three zones of the cosmos, they approached the golden treasure. But when the two eldest sons reached toward the priceless items they burst into flame. Before the youngest, the fire died, permitting him to possess the sacred objects.

Thus Colaxais, signifying "Sun king," inherited the realm, and the three brothers became ancestors of the three strata of Indo-European society, social order mirroring heavenly structure (Herodotus 2003:4.5). The Scythians assiduously guarded this sacred gold, performing sacrifices in its honor. Once a year, in elaborate reenactment of the primordial creation myth, vast offerings of horses and sheep were sacrificed to the god of war, symbolically enshrined as a sword surmounting a huge brushwood pyramid. The structure was a cosmogram representing the universe, the iron sword the *axis mundi*, the god image uniting the world of god and the world of man (Raevskii 1987:146). War captives were commonly enslaved or exchanged in trade, but for every hundred war captives, one prisoner would be selected for sacrifice according to sacred ritual. The throat of the sacrificial victim was slit, his right arm cut off and tossed in the air. This act of mutilation and dismemberment was to appropriate the martial vigor of the defeated enemy and to transmute that power toward Scythian victory in future battles (Lincoln 1991:202–203; Herodotus 2003:4.62). The skull of an especially hated foe might be fashioned into a drinking vessel; lined with gold, as a symbol of transformation and regeneration, the trophy skull would be used in toast to seal an intertribal treaty (Rudenko 1970:221).

Herodotus also provided us with a firsthand account of the funerary rites surrounding the death of a Scythian king. The royal corpse was ritually cleansed, embalmed, and then, arrayed on a wagon, transported to all the locations of his domain. At each encampment, the bearers were received with great lament. Mourners would "cut a piece from their ears, shave their hair, make circular incisions on their arms, gash their foreheads and noses, and thrust arrows through their left hands" (Herodotus 2003:4.71). Each group in turn drove the funerary carriage to the next location, where the same formalities were repeated until all subjects had commemorated the royal corpse in this traditional manner. Accompanied by a strangled retinue of servants and concubine, the king was then interred in a pit prepared at the outermost limits of his territory. Finally the high tumulus was constructed by the people amidst frenzied competition to make it the most great. Further ceremonies took place after one year had elapsed. Fifty of the finest horses were killed, gutted, and placed on frames. Fifty of the late king's attendants were similarly treated, their bodies as riders supported by vertical poles on the framed horse carcasses in order to escort their chief to the next world (Herodotus (2003:4.72). In the middle of the steppe, this circle of impaled riders and horses formed a sacred grove around their deceased king

FIGURE 3.8. Buzkashi played c 1900 in the hills of Samarkand (Kalter 1997:185).

(Mair 2007:30–31). Thus, by ritual visitation of each encampment, the cortege defined the territorial extent of the tribe. The followers, by inflicting self-mutilation – limited sacrifice – identified with the sacrificed retinue and mourned the death of their king. But alive, they celebrated royal rebirth by avowing their loyalty to his successor (Lincoln 1991:194). Erected at the boundaries of their territory, the kurgan was the symbol of their pride and political continuity.

The Nomad Ritual of Buzkashi

Equally, dismemberment and transformation were practiced in yet another steppe ritual that persists until the present. In times of the Achaemenids, Iranians played the equestrian sport known to the modern world as polo; it is even recounted that in a contest against Turanian invaders the legendary prince Siyavush galloped so fast and hit so hard that the ball in an instant flew face to face with the moon (Spencer 1971:1). Still today, in many parts of the steppes, the tribal form of this game, *buzkashi*, continues to be played with the carcass of a goat, calf, or sheep (Fig. 3.8). Whitney Azoy witnessed these ritual contests among the Pushtun and Uzbek tribes during the 1970s. The buzkashi contests he observed typically were organized to mark festive events such as a wedding or puberty initiation. The sponsor of the game was necessarily an eminent personage, with a large extended family to shoulder the subsidiary activities of organizing a gathering of hundreds of tribesmen. He needed to command the respect of the local people, who would be required to provide hospitality to the numerous participants in the game. And his reputation had to be such that he would attract from afar many competitors, who would arrive bearing rich gifts to be awarded as prizes during the contest. His distinguished sponsor's role was to maintain at all times a demeanor of decorous hospitality. He was assisted by a lieutenant, often a younger brother, whose responsibilities were to umpire the game and to resolve any disputes that might arise. Buzkashi facilitated at the regional level the periodic aggregation of nomads, habitually scattered over a vast area. It was also a means by which a man's stature and influence in society might be enhanced – that is, if all went well.

At the commencement of the game, the calf was ritually slaughtered, completely decapitated with all four hooves severed. Evisceration was gauged according to weight appropriate to the contest. A light, fully eviscerated calf promoted a fast game of equestrian prowess, whereas the heavier, less eviscerated calf tested superior muscular strength of the contestants. Competitors often numbered in the hundreds, sometimes a thousand. Supposedly any player could position himself anywhere, but in practice only the tribal champions, backed by a local leader and his retainers, through sheer strength advanced sufficiently close to the center, where they were able to grab the calf. Before each bout, the local crier would announce the award. Then the horses reared forward buffeting one another, as their riders lunged toward the calf carcass. Musicians played primitive flutes and drums as accompaniment to the contest. The struggle was most turbulent when the carcass was underfoot. The longer the contest persisted, the higher the umpire raised the prize. Finally a competitor would wrest the carcass free of the ground and ride swiftly to deposit it beyond the crowd of horsemen, where he was awarded his prize, noisily acclaimed by the crier, and applauded by the crowd. The game would then resume. On occasions two riders, seizing the calf simultaneously, might rip it apart. In the ensuing furor whips and drawn knives would be brandished. Alternatively, an entire tribal group might leave contemptuously, displeased at an umpire's decision. At midday a break would be arranged for spirited horse racing. At the end of a day, fierce competition occurred over the final possession of the mangled gristle and bone of the carcass, a source of sanguinary pride.

The evening would be spent midst feasting and hilarity in anticipation of the next day's equestrian combat (Azoy 1982:31–70).

As can be seen, in the tradition of the steppes, buzkashi was integral to the formation of alliances in warfare. It brought together large numbers of nomads ordinarily dispersed across the steppe. It provided an opportunity for pan-tribal communication at many different levels. It tested the internal organization of the group hosting the event. It challenged the virility and equestrian skills of every participant. It validated the leadership of competing champions. It fostered loyalty to a group's victor. And it allowed the nomads to assess the spirit and horsemanship of other groups competing. Success in hosting the games brought the chieftain/sponsor respect at home, renown abroad, and ready partners in warring. Failure either to organize the event successfully or to participate boldly in the contest earned only scorn and hostility. From the ritual slaughter of the calf and the mangled bloody carcass sprang new links of trade and friendship, new alliances for war.

EXPANSION FROM THE STEPPES TO
SOUTHWESTERN AND SOUTHERN ASIA

INURED TO THE BLIZZARDS OF WINTER AND THE SEARING DROUGHTS of summer, with rapid wheeled transport the pastoralist tribes penetrated and adapted to every ecological niche on the steppes, developing thriving economies, experimenting with iron, engaging in far-flung trade, and communicating over vast distances. With the perfection of the war chariot, what had previously been gradual infiltration of sparsely populated or unoccupied territories now became large-scale expeditions. Compelled by great herds of horses to change pastures regularly and driven by a one-sided economy, steppe pastoralists everywhere established economic links with sedentary agriculturalists. As warrior elites emerged, hostilities intensified. Internal warfare, and also climate fluctuations, compelled tribes to migrate long distances, resulting in great ethnic movements (Harmatta 1992:367–368). Masters of interior Eurasia, the horse charioteers next invaded beyond the steppes. To the west, south, and east, horsepower traversed earlier protective barriers, the inhospitable deserts circumscribing the nuclear centers of rich alluvium, where great sedentary civilizations flourished. The advance south by Indo-Europeans followed two principal routes: one taken largely by centum speakers from the western steppe into Anatolia and the Near East; another by Aryan satem speakers from the heart of Central Asia into India and Iran. In both arenas, the evolution of the war chariot is traced from its original function as a mobile firing platform, through that of the massed-charge assault force, to the Persian scythed attack vehicle. Invaders from the steppes not only attacked mighty urban centers and disrupted ancient economies, they also went on to found their own powerful states. Later, with the adoption of military cavalry, their horsemen overwhelmed the alluvial civilizations restricted to the riverine environments of the Tigris-Euphrates, Nile, and Indus by establishing far-ranging empires that spanned many lands from India to the Mediterranean and introducing across these diverse territories their language, religion, and culture.

In contrast to the vast sweep of the steppes, ancient civilizations of the Near East were concentrated along the Tigris, Euphrates, and Nile rivers, where, due to inadequate rainfall, the extremely fertile alluvium was cultivated by means of artificial irrigation. In this area of high-density settlement, by the third millennium BC, intensive organization of labor and urbanism had developed: brick-built towns, with a centrally located cult temple and fine edifices decorated with public art. Extensive trade networks were in operation whereby manufactured items such as fine textiles were exchanged for all-important metals, imported from distant regions. In these highly differentiated, economically complex societies, a surplus was necessarily produced to support centralized authority together with its strong bureaucratic and priestly apparatus, whose prestige was validated by conspicuous displays of affluence. By Middle Uruk, cylinder seals had appeared as a symbol of chiefly authority. In the economic administration of fields and warehouses, both writing and numeracy were utilized: cuneiform on clay tablets in Sumer; hieroglyphics and hieratic on papyrus in Egypt. But these inventions were not limited to administrative bookkeeping. Numbers featured equally in mathematics, architecture, astronomy, and calendrics, as did writing in medicine, veterinary science, pharmacology, history, poetry, hymns, the great epic of Gilgamesh, and the legal code of Hammurabi. In religion, powerful godheads gained ascendancy over local pantheons, and eventually monotheisms emerged. From these cultural and economic underpinnings the first militaristic states evolved, their thick-walled fortresses as much instruments to impose unified rule by suppressing internal convulsion as staging posts for territorial expansion (Nissen 2006; Murnane 2006).

EARLY INDO-EUROPEAN INVASION ACROSS THE NEAR EAST

The Hittite State in Anatolia

From domestic horse bones reported in Khabur, northern Syria, and the first appearance of a word for horse in cuneiform texts of the Ur III period, we know that by the end of the third millennium BC steppe horse culture had penetrated the Near East (Oates 2003:117). From the Eurasian steppes, various groups had migrated south toward this nuclear area of earliest civilization, destroying Akkad in 2300 BC (Macqueen 1996:18). In Anatolia at Alaca Huyuk, chiefly kurgan burials from 2200 BC have been uncovered containing solar discs and theriomorphic standards characteristic of the Pontic steppe region. By early second millennium BC, Assyrian cuneiform tablets additionally showed that Indo-European languages[1] were spoken across Anatolia (Bryce 1998:12–13, 17). The first Indo-European language to be written was Hittite in cuneiform. The Hittites, who arrived in Anatolia with armed priestesses from the steppes (Sacks 1995:19), worshipped a rider-god, Pirva,[2] and sacrificed horses at the burial of a king or queen (Kuzmina 2007:333). A high priestess presided over the cult of the sun goddess of Arinna, associated mythologically with the stag and horse as symbols of renewal. As such, Arinna exhibited dualistic qualities: a bright side by day, when she accompanied the weather god across the heavens, and a dark side by night, when as nocturnal mistress of the Underworld she traveled from the western to the eastern horizon (Kristiansen and Larsson 2005:283–286). The Hittites monopolized the iron ores concentrated in the mountains immediately south of the Black Sea. At this time iron was rare, due to the fact that techniques of smelting and producing the high temperatures necessary for working this metal were not widely understood. The Hittites would remain preeminent in iron making, an industry over which they exercised strong political control (Gurney 1975:83). By the eighteenth century BC a proto-Hittite state united much of eastern Anatolia, effectively undermining the Assyrian economy (Bryce 1998:42) such that Assyria was absorbed by Hammurabi's expanding Babylon (Macqueen 1996:20). A century later, the capital was established at the impressive fortress of Hattusas; with high ramparts and massive gates this architecture would characterize all future Hittite fortifications wherever they were constructed (Gurney 1975:110–111). In 1595 BC the Hittite king Mursilis I sacked both Aleppo and Babylon (Macqueen 1996:44). Destined to endure five centuries, the Hittite state in its heyday extended from the Aegean to the Euphrates (Bryce 1998:16).

---

[1] The Anatolian language group, known to history as Luwian, Palaic, and Hittite (Nesite), was centum but likely derived from the western steppe before 4000 BC, constituting therefore a fringe group isolated before the fragmentation of the PIE terminal continuum.

[2] Pirva has been compared to the Lithuanian god Perkunas and the Slavic deity Perun.

The Chariot in Warfare

In the course of the second millennium BC, the horse-drawn, spoke-wheeled light chariot, implemented earlier at Sintashta-Petrovka, would now make its appearance in Europe, the Near East, Iran, and India, reaching China later in the millennium. As was seen earlier, battle wagons and carts had long been employed in the Near East, but were heavy with solid wheels and drawn by donkeys or hybrids of ass and she-onager. That they were deployed in war is graphically evidenced on the "Standard of Ur," where helmeted and armed warriors in wagons were depicted traversing a battlefield strewn with the prostrate and bleeding bodies of the defeated enemy. But, not highly maneuverable, these vehicles were limited to level and open ground. Likely they served in the hunt, but in war they functioned more as mobile arsenals or elevated command posts; they certainly were not agile enough to perform as attacking units. Tires, of rawhide or wood reinforced with hobnails, were important in protecting the tread and improving traction, but also in consolidating different parts of the wheel. Metal tires, of copper or bronze, were encountered at Susa, but were not "sweated on" as were later iron tires (Littauer and Crouwel 1979:19, 32–33). For the first time in the Near East there was mention of the "ass of foreign mountain countries" – the true horse – a more fleet, spirited animal by far than its onager or donkey predecessors (Shaughnessy 1988:211). Evidence of early conquest by horse and chariot was found among the Hittites, but also among the Hyksos, the Kassites, and the Mitanni-ruled Hurrians (Gurney 1975:104). At the beginning of the seventeenth century BC, the Hyksos, probably a Semitic people, had introduced the horse-drawn chariot along with the mounted war goddess Astarte to Egypt, a land they dominated for over a century (Cotterell 2004:96). In the sixteenth century BC, the seminomadic Kassites occupied Babylonia, securing it militarily with horse and war chariot. Probably a century or so earlier, the Indo-Aryan Mitanni,[3] led by a class of *maryannu* war charioteers, migrated into Hurrian territory in northern Syria. As a small elite group, the Mitanni ruled over a large indigenous culture, introducing there a perfected form of the chariot and a breed of horse most suited to chariotry (Harmatta 1992:372). A Mitanni seal of the fourteenth century

---

3 Distinct from the centum-speaking Indo-Europeans penetrating much of Anatolia from the west, the Mitanni, satem speakers, had invaded from the eastern steppe.

featured the figure of a winged centaur (Padgett 2003:129) – an artistic rendering perhaps of an early high-speed steppe equestrian? Wherever it penetrated, the two-horse chariot immediately created a revolution in warfare, making speed the determining factor in battle.

The Hittite army was an efficient military machine. The supreme commander was the king, who assumed a prominent role in any fighting. Military service was a feudal obligation rewarded by distribution of booty. Hittite armies transported supplies and equipment by means of baggage trains of donkeys or bullock carts. As in Vedic practices, a deceased king was borne to his funeral pyre in a wagon. But the vehicle of attack for the Hittites was the horse-drawn chariot, light in weight and highly maneuverable. Hittite military success lay not just in possession of the war chariot, for clearly by mid-second millennium BC many of their opponents had also acquired it, but in the manner in which the Hittites adapted the basic design to reconcile speed and maneuverability with firepower and security. One method adopted by the Egyptians had been to have the chariot driver clad in scale armor for protection, with reins tied around his waist, wielding a bow and arrow (Fig. 4.1), a javelin case affixed to the side. Alternatively, the chariot was manned by a team of two, driver and warrior. The chariot was thus a mobile firing platform, from which medium- and long-range missiles could be projected into enemy ranks (Gurney 1975:105–106). The Hittite perspective on chariot warfare was somewhat different. To meet the demands of chariot control, offensive warfare, and self-defense, the Hittites developed a deep enough vehicle to transport a three-man crew: a driver, a warrior, and a shield-bearing soldier to protect the crew. Crew members wore helmets and armor; horse flank, back, and neck were similarly protected by scale armor. In addition to bow and arrow, the chariot fighter was equipped with sword or spear, thereby achieving tactical advantage in hand-to-hand fighting at close quarters. The chariot was used to combat other chariots, to panic green infantry, and to run them down once they had broken rank (Beal 2006:548). In the seventeenth century BC, the Hittites successfully blocked access to the besieged city of Ursum with a cordon of 80 chariots and infantry (Moorey 1986:204).

In 1931, French cavalry commandant Lefebvre des Noettes published practical experiments he had conducted to demonstrate that the harnessing of ancient chariots was three times less efficient than a modern harness. As previously noted, chariot pole-and-yoke draft was derived from the ox wagon. Yet equid anatomy contrasts markedly to the prominent withers and low thick neck of the ox, in that horses have longer,

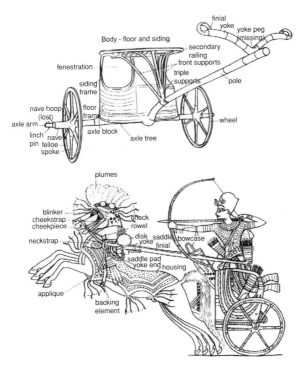

FIGURE 4.1. Sketch of an Egyptian chariot (Littauer and Crouwel 1985:fig. 2). Reproduced with permission of Griffith Institute, University of Oxford.

slenderer necks, set high at a completely different angle. Attached to the yoke, the archaic throat-and-girth harness placed a girth around the belly and posterior costal region of the horse combined with a throat strap that diagonally traversed the withers, allegedly compressing the muscles of the sternum and the trachea beneath. Lefebvre des Noettes maintained that whenever the horse extended its head forward to pull a heavy load in exertion, its breathing was impaired. However, Littauer (2002b) pointed out that Lefebvre des Noettes had omitted to consider an important device – the yoke saddle. Lashed to the yoke with thongs, this was a wishbone- or chevron-shaped wooden object designed to adapt the yoke to the narrower equid neck. Basically, it prevented the yoke from slipping back behind the withers and allowed the upper shoulders to exert forward pull on the yoke, thereby alleviating pressure on the horse's throat. Evidenced in the Middle East, in petroglyphs across the steppes, in Kurgan 5 at Pazyryk, and as far east as China, the yoke saddle was widely utilized. Spruyyte (1983:26–31, 40), working

97

with a reconstructed model of the chariot found in Tutankhamen's tomb, was able to validate the relative efficiency of yoke saddles in pulling heavy loads. But while this harnessing proved adequate in the case of the light chariot, it still failed to capture the full strength of the horse. As will be shown later in the book, more than a millennium would elapse before superior harnessing methods were developed, and many centuries more before these became universally adopted (Littauer 2002b:479–484).

Most chariot wheels of the Near East differed from those of the steppes by having far fewer spokes: four initially (sometimes of bronze), but six by the fourteenth century BC (Littauer 2002b:486). Whereas the steppe spoke wheel was made with spokes mortised into a separate cylindrical nave, late-second-millennium-BC Egyptian chariots featured another type of construction: the integral nave, in which the spokes formed a composite part of the nave (Spruytte 1983:26). Also around this time, the Near Eastern axle shifted from the center of the rider's box to the rear edge. While this placed more weight on the horses, it endowed the vehicle with greater fore-aft stability, reducing the danger of the occupants' being thrown out on sharp turns. Another modification in later Neo-Hittite and Assyrian chariots was a front-to-back partition down the center of the body, providing combatants an extra wall against which to brace. In the seventh century BC, the Assyrians would actually deploy a four-man chariot team (Littauer 2002c:80).

Training of the Chariot Horse

While considerable expertise went into the design and construction of the war chariot, extraordinary attention was also accorded the care of horses. A horse training manual was recorded in cuneiform on clay tablets c 1360 BC by Kikkuli, a Mitannian. The Mitanni prince Sativasa of the Hurrian kingdom had concluded a treaty with the Hittite king Supilluliuma in which they invoked among others the Indo-Aryan gods Indara, Mitrasil, Nasarianna, and Uruvannassil, corresponding to the Indra, Mitra, Nasatya, and Varuna of the ancient Rgvedic hymns. Not only that, many Mitanni personal names of kings, chariotry terms, and colors of chariot horses were Indo-Aryan terms, and many such loan words were employed in the horse training manual. Moreover, animal style art, so characteristic of the eastern steppes, first appeared in Anatolia at this time (Mallory and Mair 2000:257).

Kikkuli's manual, designed for the instruction of the formidable char-iotry corps maintained by the Hittite king, revealed the extensive dis-cipline exercised over a seven-month period in the preparation of the chariot horse. The first few days were a trial intended to eliminate from the outset horses unfit for Kikkuli's rigorous course. In the morning, the horses were harnessed and required to pace 18 km and gallop 120 m; on the way back they were made to run 180 m. Unharnessed, the horses were rubbed down, watered, and each given a handful of clover, two handfuls of barley, and a handful of chopped grass mixed together. In the evening they were driven at a pace 6 km and at a run 120 m. At the stable they were again rubbed down, watered, and given three hand-fuls of green chaff; later a bushel of boiled grain was added. Coming off grass to a sparse if concentrated diet, the horses craved bulk. At night therefore they were muzzled to prevent their eating the bedding or chewing the manger. This training was continued, extending dis-tances, intensifying effort, alternating gaits, and maintaining a varied diet. After sweating, rugs were put on, and the horses were each given one pail of salted water and one pail of malted water. Other days water was withheld to accustom the animals to thirst. The horses regularly swam in the river. The entire training was conducted in pairs, not only in the chariot but also in the slow pacing during which the horses were yoked but driven by a groom on foot. "The teams were inseparable, if one horse was a casualty the survivor would only accept another yokefellow after considerable re-training" (Dent 1974:56–59). Superb chariotry would enable the Hittites not only to dominate Asia Minor but also to extend their armies to the borders of Egypt.

War Chariots of Kadesh and Troy

In their exodus from Egypt, the Israelites had no horses. With hateful memories of the Pharaoh's chariots, they came to regard the horse as a beast fit only for pagan foes. Jewish law in fact prohibited horse breed-ing by the king: "he shall not multiply horses to himself, nor cause the people to return to Egypt to the end that he should multiply horses" (II Samuel 18.9; Deut. 18.6; Piggott 1992:69). Israel was situated in hilly terrain generally unsuited to chariotry; thus the armies of Israel were without chariots until late in David's reign, when the king captured 100 chariots from the Aramaean king Hadarezer (II Samuel 8:3–4; I Chronicles 18:3–4). There are also biblical references to the chariots of

David's sons Adonijah and Absalom, although it is noted that Absalom rode a mule, probably in observance of the traditional prohibition against horses for royalty (II Samuel 13:29; 18:9). In contrast, during the reign of Solomon when Jerusalem controlled much of the region west of the Euphrates with far-flung trading contacts, the royal stables boasted thousands of stalls for horses and chariots; there is some evidence also for the ridden horse in battle. But Solomon was criticized for tolerating non-Hebrew practices. Soon after his death, from internal friction the kingdom split in two halves, Israel and Judah. Weakened, these polities were vulnerable to attack from Egypt (I Kings 4:26; II Chronicles 9:25; Margolis 1969; Yadin 1963:284–287).

Hittite influence extended throughout the Near East. King Solomon obtained many horses and chariots from Anatolia (Aubet 2001:49), sent Egyptian steeds to the Hittite king, and had Hittite wives (Gurney 1975:1–2: Wood 1998:170; II Chronicles 1:7, 17). The Hittites similarly attempted interdynastic marriage with Egypt, as when the royal prince Zannanza was dispatched to marry Ankhesenpaaten, Akhenaten's third daughter, widow of Tutankhamen; the prince was assassinated, however (Gurney 1975:31). The Hittite state also fought a decisive war with Egypt. This contest was fought in 1286 at the battle of Kadesh on the banks of the Orontes River. Previously, c 1700 BC, the Hittite king Anittas had faced an army of 1400 infantry and 40 chariots; in the fifteenth century BC Thutmose III of Egypt had captured 894 enemy chariots at the battle of Megiddo. Now in the thirteenth century BC, determined to crush Egyptian military aggression against his Syrian territories, the Hittite king Muwatalli II was to deploy no fewer than 3,500 chariotry in tactical charges against enemy lines; it is believed the Egyptians had amassed a comparable number of chariots (Shaughnessy 1988:211–213). The Egyptian army was composed of four divisions, Ramses II leading the way with a single division, the Amum, and the other three dispersed over a considerable distance to the rear. The pharaoh advanced recklessly. Misled by Bedouins in league with Muwatalli, he crossed the Orontes solely with the Amum, which in surprise attack the Hittite chariotry surrounded in ever-constricting circles. Faced with the imminent rout of his forces, Ramses launched a daring counterattack. Fortunately for the pharaoh, upon the success of the Hittite initial assault, the discipline of the motley groups of mercenaries and vassal troops had broken down, succumbing to loot and plunder. Finally, with the arrival of two other divisions, Ramses was able to save his army from devastating defeat at the eleventh hour. Heavy losses were sustained on both sides. But on numerous temple reliefs at Luxor, Karnak, and Abu Simbel, Ramses claimed overwhelming victory. Reality differed, however. After fending off the Hittite onslaught, Ramses immediately retreated far south, pursued by Muwatalli, who succeeded in recapturing much territory from the Egyptians (Bryce 1998:256–264). Yet the war was not a total success for Muwatalli either. During his preoccupation with Egypt there had appeared extensive unrest in the lands of northwestern Anatolia (Macqueen 1996:49–50), a region known as the Troad, more familiar to us perhaps as Troy.

In the lands adjoining the Aegean, the influx of Indo-European speakers with horse-drawn chariots can be dated to approximately 1900 BC, as evidenced by Gray Minyan ware throughout the Troad and across the Greek peninsula. The contenders in the Trojan war most likely were descendants of these invaders from the steppes, who arrived around the Aegean at approximately the same time (Taylour 1983:14–17). From Hittite archives, it is possible to gain some insight into the approximate time of the Trojan confrontation. King Muwatalli (1306–1282 BC), in order to concentrate attention on his Syrian campaigns against Egypt, had drawn up treaties to enforce the allegiance of vassal states in western Anatolia. These states were Arzawa, Mira, Asuwa (Asia), and Wilusa (Ilion); in the last case the agreement was negotiated with none other than Prince Paris Alaksandu of Taruisa (Troy). Hittite records also indicate protracted involvement of Ahhiyawa – Achaean Greeks – in western Anatolia from the fifteenth to the thirteenth centuries BC and repeated attacks on Troy toward the end of this period. The Achaeans, it appears, long had had commercial and cultural contacts with Milawata (Miletos), a prosperous region of rich arable soils and dense population south of the Maeander River. From this base the Achaeans sought to extend their influence to adjacent regions of western Anatolia (Bryce 1998:394–396), sacking cities on the mainland and offshore islands (Wood 1998:23). That Troy should have been the major target of these hostilities can be understood from its strategic position on the Hellespont that allowed it to exact heavy tolls from passing ships or actually to prevent passage to the rich lands around the Black Sea and access to the lucrative trade of the Pontic region. The ancient Greeks, it would appear, were well familiar with the nomads of the steppes, as evidenced by the mention of "milkers of mares" in the *Iliad* (Melyukova 1990:98). Troy also commanded the chief route linking the Near East with the metal resources of central Europe (Bryce 1998:397–398). One further attraction might have been Troy's fine horses cited in Homeric poems and its citizens' fame as horse breeders; Hector was known as "tamer of horses." The prevalence of horse rearing has been confirmed in archaeology by large finds of horse bones in Troy VI (Wood 1998:166).

Conceivably, then, the siege of Troy occurred for reasons rather more prosaic than an amorous prince's abduction of a queen whose beauty "launched a thousand ships." Homer's *Iliad*, written down 500 years after the event, likely compressed the long hostilities between Greece and the Asian mainland by representing the final episode of the siege as 10 years of battle on the plains outside the city of Troy. For 3,000 years the Trojan war has provided Europe the most important source of inspiration in the arts, literature, and music. It was a decisive struggle between a European power on one side and an Asian power on the other, in which all the small Greek nations rallied around Agamemnon and the peoples of Hittite Anatolia repeatedly sent reinforcements to Troy. In this great epic, Helen was the daughter of Zeus, who as a swan had seduced Leda, wife of Tyndareus, King of Sparta. Of unsurpassed beauty, Helen wedded Menelaos, brother of mighty Agamemnon, king of Mycenae, but later eloped with Paris, son of Priam of Troy.

Confronted by this delict, Menelaos summoned the kings and princes of the Greek polities. Wealthy Agamemnon assumed the responsibility of commander in chief, and Achilles of Phthia joined as the most formidable fighter in the Achaean Greek army (Woodford 1993:13, 25). Once the armada had embarked, though, Achilles soon grew to resent Agamemnon's authority. When his concubine Briseis was abducted by the king, Achilles, enraged, vowed neither he nor his soldiers would further aid the Achaeans. On the battlefield, meanwhile, Menelaos had leapt from his chariot to challenge Paris to single combat, in which the Greek overcame the Trojan prince; however, the goddess Aphrodite plucked Paris away in a cloud to escape safely to Troy. With Briseis restored to him, Achilles later authorized his confidant Patroclos to lead Achaean troops against Troy. Wearing Achilles' armor in the fighting, Patroclos was slain by Priam's eldest son, Hector. To avenge the tragic death of Patroclos, Achilles returned to battle, mercilessly slaughtering a host of Trojans. He then advanced on Hector, pursuing him three times around the walls of Troy. Finally, Hector turned to make a stand and was killed by Achilles, his body dragged by the heels behind the chariot through the dust to the Greek ships (Thompson 2004:36, 40, 48–49, 53–54).

Achaean funerary ceremonies observed many of the sacrificial rites practiced by nomads on the steppes. The body of Patroclos was cremated on a 30-m-high funerary pyre together with the sacrifice of 12 captive Trojans and 4 horses. Funerary games were organized in which men competed for magnificent prizes. Every day at dawn, for 12 days, Achilles dragged the corpse of Hector tied to the back of his chariot three times around the funerary tumulus. In the ceremonial chariot race run to commemorate Patroclos's death, five great warriors cast lots in a helmet shaken by Achilles. Antilochus's lot was drawn first, then that of Eumelos, Menelaos, Meriones, and Diomedes; they lined up accordingly, ready to ride across the plain to the goal and back again (Buckley 1851:422–428; 23.161–360).

> Then they all at once raised their lashes over their steeds and struck them with the reins, and cheered them on with words incessantly; but they rapidly flew over the plain, far away from the ships, swiftly and beneath their breasts the excited dust stood up, raised like a cloud or a whirlwind; whilst their manes were tossed about by the breath of the wind. Sometimes, indeed, the chariots approached the fruitful earth, and at others bounded aloft; but the drivers stood erect in the chariots, and the heart of each of them, eager for victory, palpitated. (Buckley 1851:429; 23.363–375)

The course was not without incident. Apollo, enraged with the son of Tydeus, shook the goad from his hands. In defense of Diomedes, Athena restored his lash and invigorated his steeds. Then, catching up to the son of Admetus, the goddess broke the yoke such that his mares ran off the road, dashing Eumelos to the ground. Antilochus drove his chariot with such cunning that Menelaos objected that he had obstructed him by cutting in. Meanwhile Diomedes, the bravest of warriors, bounded ahead of the others to win the race (Buckley 1851:429–430; 23.376–436).

The *Iliad* ends with the return of Hector's body to Priam, but the story of Troy, drenched in the blood of endless warfare, was continued in the *Odyssey*, the Greek tragedies, and Virgil's *Aeneid*. In later hostilities Achilles was shot in the heel by the expert archery of Paris, who in turn fell to the celebrated bow of Heracles wielded by the Greek Philoktetes. In apotheosis, Achilles ascended the heavens in a chariot drawn by two winged horses. Desperate for Achaean victory, wily Odysseus of Ithaca devised a cunning scheme. He had the craftsman Epeios fashion a huge hollow wooden horse, which was to be left standing on the Trojan plain as an offering of thanks to Athena for the Greeks' safe return home. Under cover of night, led by Odysseus, a picked force of Greeks climbed into the horse's belly; meanwhile the remainder of the forces burned camp and launched their ships seemingly to return home, but in fact to set sail for the island of Tenedos. Believing the Achaeans to have departed, the Trojans decided to appropriate this powerful talisman for themselves. Midst great rejoicing the horse was hauled into Troy. As the night wore on, the warriors inside the horse escaped and gave the signal to the waiting fleet, which sailed back and advanced unchallenged; together the forces inside and outside the city were able to sack Troy. On an altar, king Priam was mercilessly murdered; Hector's son, Astyanax, was hurled to death from the rampart walls; Hector's wife, Andromache, and all the royal women were enslaved (Woodford 1993:85, 104–109). The epic enshrined the political turbulence, rivalry, and heroism of an ancient era: a European Achaean military force pitted against the powers entrenched on the Asian mainland – an intercontinental struggle oft to be repeated in the millennia ahead.

The Appearance of the Military Steed in Battle

The collapse of the Hittite state traditionally has been attributed to massive migrations of peoples across Anatolia and the Levant to Egypt in the twelfth century BC. Wide-scale movements continued in western Anatolia between 1100 and 700 BC, as Phrygians migrated in from the north, probably pushing Luwian speakers southward down the Aegean coast; Armenians penetrated eastern Anatolia somewhat later. Maritime transportation of horses by the Phoenicians was undertaken at this time (Aubet 2001:49; Bryce 1998:367, 389). It is entirely possible that the development of the Greek alphabet from the Phoenician consonantal system of writing occurred in this very environment where Semitic Phoenician and Indo-European Luwian were spoken and written side by side, then transmitted westward to the Greek trading settlements on the Aegean Coast.

Another important development, the emergence of the ridden horse in military context, occurred in the Near East around this time. During the second millennium BC, the horse as a mount had at first been viewed with distrust. In Mari, King Zimri-Lim (1779–1761 BC), when planning a trip to the Akkadian cities, was advised by his courtier to avoid the risk of mounting a horse. He was encouraged to "drive in a chariot. Or, if you must ride, ride a mule. For only thus will you preserve the dignity of your royal position" (Drews 2004:48). Horses were very expensive, a single steed worth seven bulls, 10 donkeys, or 30 slaves (Hyland 2003:15; Kuzmina 2007:135). As early as the fifteenth century BC, the Hittites on occasion deployed dispatch couriers on horseback or, when rapid movement was required, light mounted auxiliaries in the execution of scouting or surprise tactics. This was depicted on an Egyptian relief in which several Hittite horsemen are shown wearing plumed helmets and armed with bow, quiver, and shield (Beal 2006:549; Gurney 1975:106). The aftermath of conquest, however, was one area in which systematic use of the horse was made in organizing the deportation of thousands of people (and their livestock) from conquered territories across hundreds of kilometers to distant regions of the Hittite realm. This relocation of population served primarily to reduce the threat of future rebellion in subjugated lands but was also geared to repopulation of sparsely inhabited lands, labor in state work projects, and garrisoning frontier posts (Bryce 1998:236–238).

The transition from riding a horse as a means of transportation to actual mounted warfare probably was not a simple one. By 1000 BC, the Medes, Iranian-speaking immigrants from the central steppes, had arrived on the well-watered southern shores of the Caspian Sea. Pottery models show saddles and indicate that the horses ridden by the newcomers were large. From horse bones found at Hasanlu in Azerbaijan it is known they measured about 14 hands (Drower 1969:475). No doubt on the steppes extensive selective breeding had been practiced to produce a larger horse capable of carrying a warrior armed with combat weapons. It is not altogether clear though why the adoption of massed military riding in the civilized nuclear areas was so slow in development. Horses certainly are tricky to handle, and conceivably a monarch's fall in public could be construed as loss of status or even an ill omen. For the inexperienced horseman, the challenges of acquiring riding skills, mastery of the horse, competence with weapons on horseback, and then proficiency in maneuvering the horse in combat may have seemed insurmountable. In that most battles were deliberately conducted on level terrain, likely it was more practicable and a lot less perilous to remain ensconced in the chariot box, ready to launch long-range weapons.

However, attempts were made by some warriors to fight on horseback. But, as can be seen on the Assyrian bas-relief, these attempts conserved elements of military chariotry, where one fighter wielded the bow and arrow while the other, as driver, controlled the reins of both horses (Fig. 4.2). Finally, in the ninth century BC, Near Eastern cavalry received a major boost. During the Assyrian campaign led by Tukulti Ninurta II (890–884 BC) against Urartu, the mountainous trails encountered were too precipitous for chariots. In that this territory was more suited to the ridden than to the driven horse, the Urartians had already adopted cavalry, having relatively direct access north and east to the nomadic herds of the steppes. It was in these Urartian lands that Assyria first acquired its cavalry horses. Graphic representations from the succeeding reign, that of Ashurnasirpal II (883–859 BC), show nomad enemies competently riding, twisting around to shoot an arrow at a pursuing chariot. The intermittent encroachment of nomads north from the steppes no doubt provided powerful incentive for the transference from wheels to horseback (Drews 2004:65–66; Hyland 2003:7, 79–80).

As cavalry use in the Near East increased, expertise improved from the two-horseman team to the independent rider mounted in a more balanced fashion. An important development of the first millennium BC was the widespread replacement of the organic bit by metal bits, at first bronze but later iron. From Europe through the Middle East to the eastern steppes, men everywhere adopted more efficient methods of bridling. In contrast to the solid, straight bar of the earliest metal bits, now the mouthpiece or snaffle was jointed, with two bronze canons cast as an interlinked pair. A few forms were severely punishing, featuring barbed mouthpieces or tacked cheekpieces. Others were elaborately ornate, such as those produced by the Luristan metallurgists, who specialized in lost-wax bronze casting (Drews 2004:79, 85, 89–90). With more secure control, cavalry became a disciplined strike force, each rider a formidable combatant. Acquisition of horses rose dramatically as the Assyrians procured fresh horses from the nomad territories beyond the Zagros, south of Lake Urmia. At Qarqar in 853 BC, a Levantine confederation fielded 3,940 chariots against the Assyrian king Shalmaneser III; in this battle we have the earliest documentation that 1,900 cavalry troops participated. Mounted cavalry thus came to form an essential part of the Near Eastern fighting force. By the time of Sargon II (721–705 BC), the Assyrians had many more times cavalry than chariotry (Drower 1969:475; Hyland 2003:94–95; Shaughnessy 1988:213).

Toward the end of the eighth century BC, Cimmerian cavalry from the steppes erupted through the Caucasus to invade Anatolia, where they sacked Urartu. In 679 BC the Cimmerians attacked Assyria but were

FIGURE 4.2. Assyrian driver-horseman controls reins of archer's horse as well as his own (Littauer and Crouwel 1979:fig. 76).

beaten off by King Esarhaddon. Following the southern Black Sea coast westward, the Cimmerians confronted Midas of Phrygia at Gordion, forcing his suicide in 678 BC (Diakonoff 1993:93–95). Scythians too entering West Asia in the seventh to sixth century BC undertook devastating raids and exacted tribute from towns in Mesopotamia and Syria. With entreaty and bribery, the Egyptian pharaoh Psammetichus finally stalled their advance in Palestine (Herodotus 2003:1.105; Melyukova 1990:99–100). But these invasions by Aryan speakers from the steppes are really the subject of the next section, to which we now turn.

ARYAN EXPANSION FROM THE STEPPES THROUGH CENTRAL ASIA

In the earlier discussion of the Indo-European homeland, it was noted that c 3000 BC, largely as a consequence of horsepower and wheeled transportation, the Yamnaya population dispersed in all directions, resulting in the west-east split of centum and satem languages. Subsequently, c 2000 BC, the latter, the eastern subdivision of Indo-European languages, proto-Aryan, split into the ancestral branches of West Aryan and East Aryan. In this section, we will examine the cultures of these Aryan-speaking equestrians, many of whom migrated from Central Asia to southern Asia. First a brief note on the term *Aryan*, which refers not to the pernicious propaganda of a Nazi master race maniacally devised by Adolf Hitler. It properly references in a western zone the Indo-European languages spoken in or around Iran and earlier on the steppes, and secondly in an eastern zone the Indo-European languages spoken mainly on the Indian subcontinent. The latter Indo-Aryan languages today are spoken primarily in the north to middle part of the subcontinent, for example, Punjabi, Hindi, Urdu, Bengali, and Nepali.[4] As noted above, the Mitanni language very early extruded west to northern Syria. And Romany, the language of the Gypsies, was carried west from northern India during the Middle Ages; ironically Gypsies, who migrated through Persia into southeastern Europe between the eleventh and fourteenth centuries AD, are the only true Aryan speakers recently to have inhabited Europe. It is noteworthy that the Aryan name of today's modern state of Iran evolved from the Avestan tribal name *aryanam* through *eran*. The Persian king Darius I was descended from an *ariya* family, and the Medes were formerly called *Arioi*; this term is widely used in Indo-Aryan languages to designate members of the community. Cognates also occur in Indo-European languages outside the Aryan branch: in second-millennium-BC Anatolia it signified kinsmen in Hittite (Mallory 1996:36, 125–126; Parpola 1988:116). In modern days far to the west among the Irish it denotes the country Eire and the language Erse.

Aryan Migrations South

The migrations of Aryan speakers south from the steppes toward India extended over a thousand or more years, probably starting at first as the slow infiltration of stock breeders interacting peacefully with indigenous groups but later culminating in the massive intrusion of organized armies of charioteers who sought to dominate local polities (Harmatta 1992:368). Parpola (see Chapter 2) has identified the proto-Dasas as the first Aryan speakers to move south c 1900 BC from Bactria with their horses, chariots, and sharp weapons (Parpola 1988:101; 1999:191–192). In the Dashly 3 cult center of northern Afghanistan, the structure of

---

4 Dravidian languages today are spoken almost entirely in southern India. However, the continuing presence of some Dravidian Brahui speakers in Pakistan, Afghanistan, and Iran suggests the existence, prior to Indo-Aryan intrusion into the subcontinent, of a wider Elamo-Dravidian language grouping, possibly linking Elam in the Near East to the Indus Valley civilization.

the *tripura* (threefold fort) strikingly reflected the tripartite[5] partition of Indo-European socio-cosmology; in future centuries its sacred circle conjoined with the square would be manifested in the *mandala*, the Tantric cosmogram of later Buddhist and Hindu traditions (Litvinskii 1987:517). At the sacred fire altars of this ceremonial complex, animal sacrifice, especially that of horses, was practiced (Foltz 2000:25). The Dasas subsequently spread through the Bolan pass to the Sindh, Punjab, and upper Ganges, disrupting trade and the collection of taxes in these centralized polities (Parpola 1988:96, 101; 1999:200–201).

A century later Sauma-Aryans, known to have practiced cremation on the steppes, migrated south as evidenced in the archaeological record by chiefly tombs with models of battle chariots, flourishing metallurgy, proliferation of weapons, and elaboration of fire and sauma cults (Parpola 1999:188). Sauma (Indo-Aryan *soma*, Iranian *haoma*) yielded the cultic draft of immortality that inspired poets, priests, and warriors. In the *Rgveda* more than a hundred hymns were dedicated to Soma, the third most invoked deity (Mallory and Adams 1997:494–495). Another feature recounted in the Vedas is evident on the famous golden bowl of Hasanlu discovered near Lake Urmia and dated to 1500–1000 BC. In the lower register appeared a hero combating a god within a mountain that ended in a three-headed dragon. This corresponds to Indra's slaying of the three-headed Visvarupa. It also has a counterpart in the Iranian *Avesta*, where the name of the three-headed monster was *Azi*, frequently depicted on Bronze Age seals of Bactria and corresponding to the Vedic *Ahi* "snake, dragon," Indra's demonic enemy (Parpola 1999:186). Following the Sauma-Aryan migrations, repeated movements of Aryan Rgvedic and Vedic peoples moved south toward India, at Pirak on the Kachi plain; terra-cotta figurines of mounted horsemen indicate regular travel on horseback (Parpola 1988:150–151). The early Iron Age was signaled by the appearance of Yaz I culture (1500–1000 BC), as the smelting of iron daggers and arrowheads spread from the steppes across the Iranian plateau through Baluchistan to India. Along the Ganges, iron axes were used to clear vegetation and iron plows to till soil impervious to earlier copper and bronze tools. Soon after Aryan intrusion, trade in Chinese silk would first be introduced into northern India. And in the Deccan Plateau (800 BC), megalithic stone circles with burials have been found surrounding a central mound. In these graves lay sacrificed

---

[5] The tripartite division of society into priests, warriors, and herders as evidenced in the ancient Scythian creation myth discussed in Chapter 3.

horses elaborately fitted with iron bits and copper ornaments and trappings, closely paralleling ancient funerary practices of the faraway steppes (Parpola 1999:196–199; Wolpert 1993:37–38; Yu 1967:166).

Thus in the course of a thousand years, southward migrations of Indo-Aryan charioteers significantly impacted southern Asia. While the horse and chariot wrought military and political upheaval, efficient stock breeding and the introduction of iron strengthened the economies of these lands. But changes were not only political and economic in nature. The invaders also brought with them from the steppes their religion, in which the horse and war chariot featured dramatically in the cosmic symbolism of myth and ritual. These holy texts provide insight into the sacred beliefs and practices of the past.

The Rgveda

Estimated to date from 1500 to 1000 BC, the *Rgveda*[6] was transmitted orally from generation to generation by priestly memory and recitation. In written form, the *Rgveda* comprises 10 books (*mandalas*) of sacred Sanskrit hymns of praise (*suktas*) to the gods, recited or chanted during ritual sacrifices in which the horse often served as the central oblation. The hymns extol the noble role of the horse in war: "His mane is gold: his feet are of iron; and fleet as thought, Indra is his inferior (in speed)" (Macdonald 1982:4, 56–57).[7] Apart from the great cultural beauty of its hymns, the lexica of the *Rgveda*, the earliest corpus of Indic religious literature known, furnish the main sources for the reconstruction of ancient Indo-Aryan vocabulary (Mallory and Adams 1997:306). Not only that, but because of its antiquity, the *Rgveda* allows us to trace correspondences with mythical traditions of other steppe cultures, migrating at this time into Europe and Anatolia. Reminiscent of the great open skies of the steppes, the great Sky Father *Dyaus-pitr* appears in the early verses. This "oldest of gods" is derived directly from PIE *dyew pater* and has cognates in Greek *Zeus-pater*, Latin *Ju-piter*, and Germanic *Tyr*. Again common to Sanskrit, Greek, Celtic, and Germanic traditions, the *danastuti* is a short coda of verses, frequently featured in Vedic hymns, that praises the generosity of a patron of sacrifice.

---

[6] The *Rgveda* (*rg* "verse" and *veda* "sacred knowledge") is the most ancient collection (*samhita*), but the *Sama*, *Yajur*, and *Atharva* are Vedas of a slightly later date.

[7] Indra was the first Vedic deity to mount the horse.

Other elements earlier venerated on the steppes are similarly anthropomorphized. Engaged in amorous adventures, Indra plays the primary role of mythic ruler (O'Flaherty 1987a:214; Watkins 1995:73). Driving his battle chariot and horses, wielding the *vajra* thunderbolt weapon, and leading his band of *Maruts* (storm warriors), Indra is king of the gods, overlord of other kings, and conqueror of enemies. As the symbol of sovereignty on earth, he plays an important part in battle rites, leads the army, and fights against all rivals and demons (Singh 1997:31, 48–49). From his glorious exploits, we learn how the Vedic gods aided the Aryans in their battles over different river valleys and helped destroy the forts of their enemies. As such, the *Rgveda* provides some insight into the invaders' "epic" journey from the Asian steppes to the plains of India. Furthermore, in his numerous victorious combats over adversaries, Indra furnishes the mythic prototype for later warrior heroes of epic reality (Watkins 1995:55, 304). Two outstanding epics of the first millennium BC are the *Ramayana* and *Mahabharata*. In the first, Rama's quest for his abducted wife Sita, in which he is aided by his brother Laksmana, parallels that of Menelaos and Agamemnon in Homer's *Iliad*. Several centuries later, the *Mahabharata* recounts the victory of divine forces over the demonic. On the historic battlefield of Kuruksetra, conflicting ideals are expressed as the warrior Arjuna faces his own kinsmen among the enemy; grief-stricken, he prefers to be slain rather than to kill. But his charioteer, the avatar Krisna, evocatively sings the *Bhagavadgita*, finally persuading Arjuna that it is his military duty to fight this terrible war (Hiltebeitel 1987:119).

Everywhere, the horse chariot is thought to control the sun.[8] Its association with celestial bodies and spectacles offers an explanation of cosmic movement. The locomotion of the sun as chariot is in part responsible for the emergence and sustenance of life. The chariot symbolizes the dawn, bringing succor to human settlement and illumination to a world engulfed in darkness, evil, and ignorance. Juxtaposed, the gods Agni[9]

---

[8] This is also evidenced in the fourteenth-century-BC model of a three-axle chariot at Trundholm, Denmark, which is depicted drawing the sun across the sky (Fig. 6.2). Three-axle carts were also rolled in Vedic rituals (Kristian Kristiansen, personal communication, 2008).

[9] Derived from the Indo-European root *egnis*, Sanskrit *agni* "fire" has cognates in Latin *ignis*, Lithuanian *ugnis*, and Hittite *ak/gnis*. Agni in *Brahmanas* of the mid-first millennium BC becomes centrally related to Prajapati, the primordial creator. Superseding Indra, their joint figure becomes the cosmic person projected into being through dismemberment (Findly 1987:133–134).

and Soma represent the fiery and watery elements of the earth. The light and heat of Agni, the golden fire deity with flaming hair and beard and shining eyes, are manifested in the chariot's force and movement. Both fire and chariot emerge out of wood. Rekindled Agni appears as the horse. A martial symbol of world rule, the horse is carrier of the gods, the white horse drawing the chariot as the primeval force that moves as fast as light (Heesterman 1987:222–223; Singh 2001:150, 166–169). Sacred fire of course was worshipped across Indo-European societies, tended by six vestal virgins at the shrine of the fire goddess Vesta in Rome and dedicated to the goddess Hestia in the Greek *prutaneion*; indeed when ancient Greeks left to colonize new lands they always carried sacred fire from the mother city to rekindle in the new settlement. From India through Greece to Rome, cremation was considered a transition to immortality, particularly in the example of Heracles' apotheosis on the funeral pyre winning him eternal youth among the gods of Olympus. In later Hinduism and Buddhism, self-immolation by fire would be undertaken for moral or political reasons (Edsman 1987:341, 343–345).

Prominent throughout Vedic ritual, the horse also is seen as instrumental in the acquisition of secret knowledge. In the *Rgveda*, Indra revealed the sacred mysteries of honey mead (*madhu*) distillation to the fire priest Dadhyanc, engaged in devout prayer and meditation. But the god threatened to decapitate Dadhyanc should he divulge this information to any other. The divine Asvin twins, desirous of learning the secret, pleaded to be Dadhyanc's pupils and promised to protect him by cutting off his head and replacing it with a horse head, at which point Dadhyanc imparts the secret knowledge. The god then cuts off the horse head, for which the twins substitute Dadhyanc's real head (Singh 2001:152–153). The Asvins (*asvinah* horsemen) are two youths, appearing varyingly as brothers or twins, who are depicted as supernatural charioteers – the chariot being typically manned by a pair, the driver and the warrior (Heesterman 1987:222). Because the Asvin twins are *divo napatah* (sons of the Indo-European sky or sun god), their epiphanies are horses. In their equine form, they are the divine steeds that draw the solar chariot. The sun god is the solar charioteer, and the wheels of his carriage are the sun. At dawn, yoked to the golden chariot, the Asvins accompany the sun on its daily course. The Divine Twins perform wondrous feats of rescue and healing that reverberate across all major Indian epics and legends. They too are attributed supernatural powers of fertility and as such are associated with the paired male sexual organs, the testicles.

Evidence for the worship of the Divine Twins, however, ranges beyond India, far west across Eurasia to the Atlantic, where themes of their exploits have penetrated all levels of Indo-European religious and folk beliefs. As solar steeds, they share a consistent relationship with the dawn goddess, who appears as their, mother, sister, or consort. In Irish myth, the goddess *Macha*, often shown seated on a horse but also linked to the Celtic divine mare *Epona*, is forced, in an advanced stage of pregnancy, to run a race against the king's fleetest horses. Expectably, the horse goddess wins the race but prematurely gives birth to twins. Germanic legends are spiced with the adventures of the Divine Twins, as seen in the Anglo-Saxon founders of the kingdom of Kent, *Hengist* "stallion" and *Horsa* "horse." As is well known, the twins Romulus and Remus are the mythical founders of Rome. The Greek heavenly twins are the demigods Castor and Polydeuces, whose strong equine associations are manifested in the monikers "good horsemen," "white colts," and "Zeus's white ponies," underscoring their relatedness to other Indo-European traditions. Their sister Helen's name is etymologically connected to the sun god *Helios*; abducted by Paris, she was of course rescued by two brothers, Menelaos and Agamemnon (Mallory and Adams 1997:161–165).

The Vedic Asvamedha Horse Sacrifice

In our discussion of the Eurasian steppes, from the Pontus to the Altai mountains, horse sacrifice and head-and-hoof offerings were repeatedly noted in funerary contexts. In the Indo-European diaspora, horse veneration and sacrifice featured as a continuing custom over the centuries among many groups. In humid, subtropical India, where ecological conditions were generally unfavorable to horse breeding (Kuzmina 2007:339), horse sacrifice was less frequent. Nevertheless, an extraordinarily lavish horse sacrifice was celebrated at the investiture of a monarch. In the scriptures of the *White Yajurveda*, we are fortunate to have an historic account of this ritual. Of all Vedic ceremonies the supreme sacrifice was the *asvamedha* (*asva* "horse," *madho* "drunk" or "strength"), in which the horse, representative of the sun illuminating the world, was anciently offered to the warrior deity Indra, and later to Agni-Prajapati. The sacrifice was performed to gain prosperity for the kingdom. The sacrificial victim was a stallion, ideally white with a black spot on its forehead, symbolizing the eye of Prajapati. In the flower of youth, the sacrificial horse brought unbounded vitality; its speed represented virility. Dedication ceremonies took place a full year before the actual sacrifice was enacted. Just before the full moon of the spring equinox, the king, accompanied by four wives, arrived to transfer power to one of four officiating priests, each party of four representing the cardinal directions. The stallion was offered libations and then released with a herd of 100 geldings toward unconquered horizons in the north. The ceremony concluded with recitals and invocations, following which the king must sleep a full sun year in the embrace of his favorite wife, but without consummation. Sexual abstinence was observed in order to redirect cosmic energy.

The stallion was entrusted to four groups of 100 nobles whose duty was to protect its virility by preventing it from approaching a mare, entering the river, or returning before the time of the asvamedha. In all else it was left to roam at will. All kingdoms entered by the stallion must be conquered by the guardians for the king. Any chieftain opposing the horse's wanderings must be attacked and defeated. Having thus redefined in the course of the year the new frontiers of the king's realm, the stallion returned to a bloody sacrifice of five males: a man, a horse, a bull, a ram, and a goat. A sacrificial fire altar was then constructed (*agnicayana* "piling the fire"), derivative perhaps of the brushwood pyramid or portable stone altars utilized by steppe tribes (Fuchs 1996:17–23). In the lowest level of the hearth-altar were immured the heads of the five sacrificed males, suggesting a funerary tumulus possibly ancestral to the future Buddhist *stupa* (Findly 1987:134; Heesterman 1987:231). To appreciate the significance of these devotional steps one must understand that, in Vedic cosmogenesis, from godly oneness emerged terrestrial diversity. That is, in creation, divinity fragmented into progeny. The asvamedha repeated this primordial rite, but in reverse. In earthly ritual the human sacrificer mutilated his surrogate, the sacrificial victim, so that through immolation by sacred fire the scattered and dismembered offering would be transformed and reintegrated with the godhead. From mundane multiplicity, archetypal unity would be restored. Thus while the sacrifice celebrated primeval origins, at the same time it strove to promote world renewal (Snodgrass 1985:47–48).

The morning of the sacrifice, the sun was venerated as it appeared above the horizon. Amidst hymns, the stallion was yoked with other horses to a gold-studded war chariot. The king, in war attire brandishing a bow, drove the chariot into a lake. The stallion, its mane and tail decorated with pearls, was soothed by the priests and finally suffocated.

The dead horse was laid out, its legs to the north, its head to the east. The remaining domestic animals were sacrificed; wild animals were released into the forest. The monarch's four main wives and one daughter with her lady companions approached the stallion to perform ablutions. The senior wife then lay down under a blanket to have intercourse with the horse while the priests, the other three wives, and daughter exchanged obscenities. In dividing up the corpse, no bone was broken. The horse was ceremonially dismembered with gold studded knives and offered to different deities, its sacred blood poured into the fire as sacrifice. At the sacrificial dinner, all ate the flesh of the horse roasted on spits. Later, after bathing, the king promiscuously distributed among the priests his four main wives, his daughter, and her lady companions. As symbol of the sun, the horse in sacrifice celebrated cosmic death, renewal, and regeneration of prolific life, the juxtaposition of fire altar and lake water highlighting the cosmogonic drama of the event (Fuchs 1996: 23–26).

Practices analogous to the Indic asvamedha were observed among other Indo-European speakers, particularly rituals involving the killing of white stallions, which recorded over many centuries and across great distances suggest a protean mythic core. In Greece, Demeter, often depicted with a mare's head, mated with Poseidon, to whom white horses were sacrificed. Alternation of fire and water was also evidenced in the myths of the Valkyries, female warriors on winged horses charged with the transport of deceased warriors across the sky, where Brunnhilde rode her white horse through a wall of flames to her death, at which point the waters of the Rhine flooded the world. *Epomeduos* (compound of "horse" and "mead" comparable to the term *asvamedha*), an Irish sacrifice celebrated at the inauguration of the king of Ulster, was recorded in the twelfth century AD by the Norman monk Geraldus Cambrensis, utterly shocked by the obscenity of what he beheld. The horse was a mare, and it was the king that coupled with her. From the sacrificial horsemeat, in a cauldron a broth was prepared in which the sovereign apparently immersed himself; the king also drank some of the broth after which it was distributed to the populace (O'Flaherty 1987b:463–465; Mallory and Adams 1997:278). On the steppes among Altaic-speaking tribes, horse sacrifices exhibiting features reminiscent of the ancient Indo-European rituals have persisted until recent times among the Cumandins and Buryats. Many of these rites retain the same erotic elements and themes of ritual death, dismemberment, and regeneration.

Aryan Equestrian Migrations West

As we have seen, in the course of the second millennium BC, there had been a general movement of pastoralists south from the steppes. In the west, the Srubnaya culture had veered across the Urals away from the Potapovka-Sintashta complex of the mid-Volga-Tobol drainage, extending southwest as far as the Dnieper in the Ukraine (Anthony 2007:435). Ecological crisis on the western steppe during the last quarter of the millennium accelerated further southern migrations of these Iranian speakers through the Caucasus and along the Caspian shores toward Margiana and Bactria. With the transition to nomadic stock breeding, horse riding had become widespread. These mobile tribes of the steppes and Iran would elevate horse riding to a high military art – terms for rider, horsecloth, bridle, saddle girth, and tail belt all being of Iranian origin (Kuzmina 2007:139). On the desert borders, the mobile steppe nomads launched frequent raids against oasis settlements, their military superiority allowing the horsemen to dominate the sedentary populations. Following this turbulent confrontation, a certain segment of steppe folk succeeded in imposing their Iranian language on the oasis inhabitants, at the same time adopting many elements of settled life (Kuzmina 2007:431–432). With the arrival of steppe nomads, the early Iron Age in Central Asia (1300–800 BC) was under way, as evidenced by iron beads, sickles, and axes. Many Iranian-speaking tribes would continue as pastoralists across the steppes of Eurasia, to emerge in history as the nomadic Cimmerians, Scythians, and Sarmatians on the western steppes and Massagetae, Wusun/Alans, and Saka in the east. In Central Asia, others would populate the urban oases of Khorezm, Sogdia, Ferghana, and Tashkent. Still others would press on to the Iranian plateau (Kuzmina 2007:157, 425–426).

As to be expected in light of their common steppe origins, Iranian religion shared many traits in common with Vedic beliefs. Both Indo-Aryans and Iranians venerated the tree of life and the great mountain standing at the center of the world (Gnoli 1987a:279). Society revolved around *mairiia*, war bands of unmarried men engaging in sacrificial rites and ecstatic practices, ever disposed to undertake daring offensives. Cognate of Vedic *marya* and characterizing many Indo-European groups,[10] this warrior cult is most familiar to us in the west as

---

[10] Other Indo-European parallels of this war cult were the Ephebes of ancient Athens, the Krypteia of Sparta, and the Diberga of the Irish (Mallory and Adams 1997:31).

Mannerbund. The widely held concept of three ritual fires corresponded to the societal subdivisions of priests, warriors, and pastoralists (Gnoli 1987b:581). Fire and water formed the basis of daily sacrificial acts (Iranian *yasna*, Indo-Aryan *yajna*). Fire was the source of warmth in bitter steppe winters; the hearth fire, the means of cooking and sustenance for family members, was ritually carried as live embers from campsite to campsite, and on the arid steppes water made all life possible. But instead of cremation, from ancient times there existed the Iranian rite of exposing the corpse in a barren place where vultures and scavenging beasts quickly devoured it (Boyce 1987:12, 14).

The earliest attested Iranian language, Avestan, takes its name from the holy book of the prophet Zarathustra (Zoroaster), who toward the end of the second millennium BC forged a religious system of great strength. Thought to have originated in northeastern Iran, in the most ancient sections, called *Gathas*, the *Avesta* displays the same archaic characteristics as the *Vedas*, the grammar being largely identical with the oldest *Rgveda*. It is therefore assumed that only a few centuries separated the two great works (Mallory 1996:52; Skjaervo 1995:161–162). Lauding great heroes on horseback, the later parts of the *Avesta*, *Yashts*, contributed an enduring element to Iranian culture, the epic tradition. Derived in part from ancient Aryan mythology and in part from the heroic deeds of *kavis* (kings) and champions, legends described the creation of the world, the first man, and the first king in battles against an evil usurper and Turanian enemy nomads. But in his wanderings, Zarathustra had witnessed brutal acts of violence, where nomadic war bands attacked communities to pillage, slaughter, and rustle cattle. He therefore introduced many reforms into his religious thinking. He had a deep longing for justice, for moral laws to be applied to the weak and strong alike so that order should prevail. The lie (*druj*) was the foulest of social behaviors, as was debt; truth (*asha*) was virtue. To achieve virtue, man had the obligation to care for others through adherence to a threefold ethical code of good thoughts, good words, and good deeds. Through the merit of individual ethical achievement, one could attain paradise. At death, merits and transgressions were weighed. If the bad prevailed, the individual fell to hell; if the good predominated, the individual was judged worthy of heavenly paradise (Boyce 1987:4, 9, 77; Gnoli 1987c:412–413).

Central to these beliefs was *Ahura* (Sanskrit *asura*) *Mazda*, literally Lord Wisdom, surrounded by six radiant beings, *Amesha Spentas*, lesser spirits that formed a heptad with Ahura Mazda himself, the supreme unity of beneficent godhead. In the beginning, the one creator god existed from which all other beneficent beings emanated. The genesis of the world occurred in seven consecutive creations: sky, water, earth, plant, animal, man, and fire. Seven communal high feasts dedicated to Ahura Mazda and the six Amesha Spentas honoring the seven creations were observed annually. The seventh, *Nawruz* (New Day), occurring at the spring equinox, celebrated fire – the pervasive life force. As the last of seven feasts, it looked to the Last Day as the ultimate triumph of good, the New Day of eternal life (Boyce 1987:20–21, 33–34). Venerated in sanctuaries, fire ever bright and living was elevated on a pedestal as the eternal warrior flame combating darkness, vice, and ignorance (Boyce 1987:51, 65). Because they instigated greed, destruction, and bloodshed, Zarathustra demoted the *daevas*[11] to evil demons. *Angra Mainyu*, the epitome of ignorance and evil, was Ahura Mazda's primary adversary and the reason for all the sorrow and suffering endured in life (Boyce 1987:20). In later centuries these twin concepts evolved into Ohrmazd and Ahriman. By offering the hope of redemption to the virtuous persevering in the face of adversity, Zarathustra's teachings broke with aristocratic and priestly tradition. His philosophy extended the hope of salvation to the humble but threatened the mighty, if unjust, with extinction. He therefore encountered political opposition and was forced to seek asylum in the kingdom of Kavi Vistaspa, whence his new religion spread throughout Iran (Boyce 1987:30–31). But Zarathustra was apprehensive that he would not live to see the Last Day. He therefore prophesied the coming of his successor, the *saoshyant* (savior), who would lead mankind in the final battle against evil. His followers fervently believed the messianic saoshyant would be born of the prophet's own seed miraculously preserved in the waters of a lake, where a virgin would bathe and conceive (Boyce 1987:42).

Because of the all-pervasive opposition between good and evil, Zoroastrianism frequently is characterized as a dualistic religion; in its main emphasis on a supreme being, however, it clearly sowed the seeds of monotheism. Incontestably a powerful and original thinker, Zarathustra dramatically impacted the course of human spirituality. Zoroastrian beliefs formed a highly original model that upheld human worth and dignity and exercised a strong influence well beyond the Iranian world, both to the east and to the west. The worship of one

---

[11] Later diffusing across Indo-European languages as "diavolo," "devil," and "teufel."

supreme god, the seven days of genesis, the concept of angels and demons, the everlasting flame, the prophesy of the coming of a messianic savior, virgin birth, the last day of judgment, heaven and hell, adherence to a moral life that combined spiritual vision with a strict code of behavior observing purity laws: these tenets were to shape the religious practices not only of Persians, Medes, Parthians, Sogdians, and Khorezmians but also the religions of Judaism, northern Buddhism, the Gnostic faiths, Christianity, and Islam (Boyce 1987:1; Foltz 2000:32; Gnoli 1987b:581).

Ancient Iranians

A significant segment of Iranian speakers thus continued past the urbanized oases of Central Asia to infiltrate the Iranian plateau, south of the Caspian. Migrations of the next half millennium would lead to equestrian conquests over a vast area, in the west culminating in the Achaemenid empire that would extend thousands of kilometers from India to the Aegean and to North Africa. From the thirteenth century BC onward, skirting the central desert, the Iranian nomads wandered with their herds over northwest Iran. The lands they inhabited provided good horse pastures; in fact, Nisaya (the Vale of Borigerd south of Ecbatana/Hamadan) became the breeding grounds of the finest horses of antiquity, derived from earlier elite Andronovo stock (Kuzmina 2007:149). A highly nutritious legume fodder, a species of clover known as Medean grass and today named alfalfa/lucerne, grew there; its protein level reached 20 percent, more than double that of most hays. With excellent diet and selective breeding Nisaean horses achieved superior growth, reaching their full genetic potential (Hyland 2003:30). But in the ninth century BC, the Iranians were confronted by militaristic Assyria. In 834 BC, Shalmaneser III recorded on a black obelisk at Nimrud his encounter with the Parsua (Persian) nomads in the eastern foothills of the Zagros and the Medes on the plains below (Humphreys 1991:16). *Parahshe* in early Semitic referred to "land of horses" (Daniel 2001:3). From these Iranians, Shalmaneser extracted tribute in the form of horses and iron, for which he had an insatiable demand in order to feed the expansionistic Assyrian war machine. Following the lines of the Zagros mountains, the Persians later migrated south around the Elamite city-state of Anshan not far from the Gulf. Later, when the Assyrian Ashurbanipal destroyed Elam in 646 BC, the Persians would occupy Susa (Humphreys 1991:17).

As was previously mentioned, during the eighth and seventh centuries BC Cimmerian and Scythian nomads roamed unhindered across the Near East storming many cities. By 625 BC, however, the Medean king Cyaxares had succeeded in expelling marauding Scythians north of the Black Sea. Adopting the ballistically superior Scythian archery, Cyaxares proceeded to integrate into his confederation Iranian territories as far away as Sogdiana and Thatagus (Cook 1993:220; Diakonoff 1993:92, 119–121). Allied with the Babylonian Nabopolassar, Cyaxares sacked Assyrian Assur and then Nineveh in 612 BC. Cyaxares next invaded ailing Urartu, an action that brought him into conflict with the Lydian king Alyattes. Their battle in 585 BC, one of the most famous of antiquity, ended with a negotiated settlement after the contending armies, cowed by an eclipse of the sun, hastily recognized a frontier along the river Halys (Humphreys 1991:18–23). Meanwhile, in the south of Iran, Persia at one point had become a vassal state of Medea. However, inheriting the kingdom of Anshan, c 550 BC Cyrus II challenged Medean suzerainty by refusing tribute to Cyaxares' heir Astyages. A large segment of the Medean army defected to Cyrus, who occupied Ecbatana, seized its treasure, and assumed the title *Shahanshah* (Great king, king of kings; Daniel 2001:37).

The Achaemenid Equestrian Empire

Cyrus the Great accorded the Medes a form of partnership and sought to bolster the unity of the two peoples. He consolidated the two armies to meet the challenge from Lydia 2,000 km away. King Croesus, fabulously wealthy and responsible for the invention of metal coinage, had taken advantage of the Medean collapse to cross the Halys in breach of the treaty with Cyaxeres to invade Cappadocia. Cyrus pursued Croesus to Sardis, where he stormed the citadel (Humphreys 1991:24). Cavalry now dominated the battlefield, and the Persians, a nation of riders, were taught three things: "to use the bow, to ride a horse, and to speak the truth" (Herodotus 5:113). By defeating Croesus, Cyrus inherited suzerainty over the Greek city-states of Ionia, which, mindful of their links to Greece, would not readily submit to invaders from the east. But their settlements, strung out along a rugged coast, were too isolated to withstand the Persian landward attack and one by one succumbed to the Achaemenids' superior weapons and equestrian speed and surprise in intercepting, flanking, and attacking infantry. As successful in the east as in the west, Cyrus also consolidated Medean territories as far away as remote Gandhara, adjacent to the Indian world beyond (Humphreys 1991:25). By 539 BC Babylon too had fallen. This last conquest brought Cyrus control over all the former dependencies of the Babylonian empire, vast territories extending to the Mediterranean and to the borders of Egypt.

Persia was punitive to the extent that entire towns in rebellion were exiled to Central Asia, as occurred in the case of Ionian Greeks and Egyptians (Frye 2001:90). Deportation of these populations across vast distances was accomplished through equestrian control. Medea also overflowed with captive slaves, who under the Achaemenids were employed in construction, agriculture, and personal service of the aristocracy. Tribute in young boys from the satrapies was also levied for royal service as eunuchs, whereby these youths might attain positions of importance in provincial administration (Diakonoff 1993:136–137). But Cyrus II is generally known to history as a benevolent ruler. Many a vanquished king was restored to office within his empire. Earlier conquest among the Near East riverine states had always been brutal, in which opponents were tortured, temples destroyed, and holy images desecrated to symbolize subjugation. By contrast, Zoroastrian religion, recognizing the great Sky father, opposed enclosing within walls divinity whose dwelling place was the whole world. The two great plinths at Pasargadae attest to the tradition of worship under the open sky. At Zela, an artificial mound was the world mountain for people to ascend and pray. In sacred precincts fire was exalted in altars, the establishment of dynastic fire marking the enthronement of each new king. Cyrus benevolently tolerated the free exercise of religions throughout his dominions (Boyce 1987:60; Daniel 2001:38), encouraging his subjects to lead orderly and devout lives according to their own faiths.

The most famous instance of Cyrus's clemency involved the Jews. In 587 BC Jerusalem was sacked by the Babylonians, its temple destroyed by Nebuchadnezzar II, and the people led away into slavery. Freed by Cyrus in 559 BC, some Judeans returned to Jerusalem, others chose to remain in Babylon as free citizens of the new Persian empire, and still others elected to try their luck in the Persian-controlled lands to the east. The Judeans entertained warm feelings toward Cyrus for permitting the rebuilding of their temple in Jerusalem, and the prophet Isaiah hailed him as benefactor "anointed of the Lord." Beginning in this period and continuing through Parthian times, many concepts of Zoroastrianism permeated Judaean religious thought, later evolving into Judaism.

During this postexilic period, in striking parallel to the Persian concept of Ahura Mazda, Isaiah for the first time celebrated Yahweh as creator of the universe, maker of all things, creatures, and man. Eschatological ideas such as a messianic savior, resurrection, the last judgment, and angels and demons were borrowed from the Persians. The dualistic concepts of heaven and hell first appeared in Israelite texts in the post-Babylon period, and Angra Mainyu or devil was initially mentioned as *ha-satan* in the book of Job. In the book of Esther, Teresh and Zeresh reflected the demons Taurvi and Zarik of the Avesta, representing the opposition of the lie (*druj*) to the king's law (*data*). *Frashokereti*, the final catastrophe, similarly was evidenced in the post-Babylon apocalyptic writings of the books of Ezekiel and Daniel. And the perpetual flame on the altar was first described in postexilic Leviticus. These Iranian ideas no doubt entered Jewish culture through the mediation of Jews immersed in the Iranian world and were then transmitted westward to communities on the Mediterranean, where they subsequently influenced Christianity and Islam (Daniel 2001:38–39; Edsman 1987:342; Foltz 2000:30–34). Certainly the Iranian concept of fire as the radiant life force is reflected in the saintly halo of Buddhism, Christianity, and Islam. Additionally, the Avestan sacred number of three is evident in Christian thought in the holy trinity and the epiphany of the three Magi following the star at Christ's nativity. Dismemberment and sacrifice are portrayed in Christ's scourged and broken body on the cross at Mount Calvary, and regeneration and renewal, in his resurrection from the dead after three days and ascension to heaven.

As we have seen, Cyrus died on the steppes in a hard-fought battle against the Amazon warrior queen Tomyris of the Massagetae. History has tended to view him as a humane ruler and astute statesman. He rose from relative obscurity to forge an empire of unprecedented dimensions, yet to an unusual degree he respected the ancient civilizations he had conquered. In 530 BC his embalmed body was laid to rest in a gold coffin; a carving of the sun, symbol of immortality in a luminous paradise, signaled his Zoroastrian faith, as did the fire altar at his nearby palace. Each month a horse, as special creature of the sun, was sacrificed for Cyrus's soul (Boyce 1987:52–53). Cyrus's eldest son, Cambyses, his cavalry aided by Bedouin camels carrying precious water across the Sinai desert to Egypt, took the Persian conquest far up the Nile to Ethiopia, later turning to Libya and Cyprus (Humphreys 1991:31). During the young emperor's campaign abroad, a Magi priest in Medea staged a palace coup, proclaiming himself king. In his haste to return to Persia, Cambyses fatally impaled himself on his own sword while mounting his horse. At the Persian court, a cabal of seven Persian nobles resolved to overthrow the impostor and have one of their number assume the throne in his stead. In order to determine the new sovereign, it was necessary to receive a sign from the sun god via his sacred animal, the horse. The nobles agreed to meet at dawn and that the rider of the first horse to neigh after sunrise would be king. Darius, it seems, was not willing to leave this to chance. On the eve of the meeting, his clever groom Oebares led a mare in heat to the meeting place and allowed Darius's stallion to cover her. The next morning as the horses approached the place the stallion, responding to the mare's scent on the ground, whinnied in anticipation, thereby winning Darius the throne (Hyland 2003:109–111). Once again, as in the asvamedha, we see the interplay of the horse, eroticism, and the sun in the inauguration of kingship.

There followed a general slaughter of Magi throughout Medea; this strife between Persian and Mede and the potent symbolism of Darius and the six nobles, evocative of Ahura Mazda and the six Amesha Spentas, bespeak a religiopolitical confrontation of high intensity. Gaining immediate control of the Nisaean horse-breeding grounds, Darius I went on to successfully suppress nineteen rebellions and to overthrow nine kings. At the famous rock of Behistun, engravings in the cliffside depicted Darius confronting the captured enemy kings. To provide the official account of his controversial accession, inscriptions were written in three different languages: Babylonian (Akkadian), Elamite, and Old Persian. This trilingual inscription was instrumental in the subsequent decipherment by linguists of the three ancient languages. A leading figure in this decipherment was the nineteenth-century British diplomat Sir Henry Rawlinson, who, dangling from ropes, copied down the inscriptions carved high on the cliff face 150 m above the ground (Comrie, Matthews, and Polinsky 1996:170; Wood 2002:192). Darius I went on to extend Persian territories northward by capturing in pincer movement Skunkha, the king of the "Pointed Hat" Scythian nomads. He subsequently gained further victories in Libya, Thrace, and India, thereby extending his equestrian empire to encompass 50 million people (Daniel 2001: 41). Divine and universal ruler, the Achaemenid king still on many occasions adhered to ancient steppe practices. At festivals the Shahanshah held audiences in a vast cosmic tent of round awnings called the "Heavens." This tradition was to persist long on the steppes, where medieval Mongol and Chinese rulers would similarly conduct imperial audiences in ornate tents accommodating over a thousand people (Smith 1950:81).

If Cyrus II was the founder of the Achaemenid empire, Darius I certainly was its main architect, organizing his territories into 20 provinces, each paying taxes and tribute to a central government and under the jurisdiction of an official satrap. But Darius's vision of government exceeded that of the circumscribed riverine state. His nomadic ancestry stopped him from being rooted in a single capital and spurred him instead to routinely move across the cosmopolitan lands he governed. Far-ranging, in winter he resided in Susa, the former Elamite capital; in summer in Ecbatana, formerly the Median capital; in fall, Babylon; and in spring, Persepolis. He respected the diverse traditions of his dominions, freely selecting from among them whatever innovation he deemed useful. The Phoenician navy was adopted whole. Transportation was critical as much for security as for the promotion of trade and commerce. Darius repaired and extended roads begun by the Assyrians, most notably the Royal Road, well guarded and policed, stretching 2,600 km from Sardis to Susa. Fast-riding travelers could speedily cover great distances, stopping when fatigued at post houses to change horses and to receive provisions; a postal service delivered messages to far-off destinations. Such efficient travel and communication helped fuse Iranians and other peoples into a unified culture. At the core of his new army stood the exclusively Persian elite bodyguard of the king, the 10,000 Immortals. In times of war, from the different satrapies composing the empire, large contingents of warriors assembled, each with their own weapons and manner of combat.

Darius recognized the importance of codified law and economics for the well-being of his people. He introduced into his empire metal coinage used earlier in Lydia, thereby revolutionizing the economy by putting it on a monetary rather than a barter basis. Wide economic innovation included the standardization of weights and measures and the systematization of a monetary system using gold and silver coins of specific weights (Daniel 2001:41–42). In agriculture, the aridity of the Iranian plateau was tackled by the development of long underground aqueducts (*qanats*) that took advantage of the natural slope of the basins (Daniel 2001:10). To promote the opening up of barren lands, families were allowed to reap the benefits for five generations before relinquishing the land to the crown (Cook 1993:288–289). Across the empire, Semitic Aramaic was established as the official lingua franca.

Different peoples including the Indians and the Nabateans of the Sinai[12] adapted this system of writing, derived from Phoenician consonantal script, to their own languages during the Achaemenid period (Comrie, Matthews, and Polinsky 1996:178–179, 195; Frye 1953:37). Not satisfied with the extensive land empire his cavalry had won in war and his horsepower maintained in peace, Darius also sponsored exploration of the coastlines from the Indus to the Mediterranean. Under the guidance of Scylax of Caryanda, in 30 months an expedition sailed down the Indus River to the delta and then across the Indian Ocean to Egypt. This voyage of discovery was followed by the construction of a canal completed in 497 BC from Bubastis on the Nile to the Red Sea at Suez, wide enough for two ships to pass. To document the cosmopolitanism of Darius's rule, it is interesting to note that graphic representations of Saka cavalrymen stationed in Egypt showed Mongoloid features (Cook 1993:255).

To display the splendor of the world's greatest empire, between 520 and 450 BC the Achaemenid kings commanded the construction of a national spiritual sanctuary in the Persian heartland at Parsa, known today as Persepolis. Situated on a high terrace of natural rock 12 m above the plain, the royal palace stood oriented to the sunrise of the spring equinox. The ascent to this monumental platform was by means of a double reversing stairway, so wide and low horses could easily be ridden up. To the south lay the Apadana with its two ceremonial stairways, one on the north and the other on the east. The facade of each stairway depicted a carefully staged procession in which courtiers, soldiers, and peoples from all corners of the empire brought tribute to the Shahanshah (Wilber 1989:36, 40–42). Enthroned on high, on the verge of apotheosis, the Persian hero-king appeared with an entourage of cosmic divinities, receiving votive offerings from his subjects on occasion of the Nawruz festival. Sculpted at the head of this procession were high dignitaries of the empire, preceded by horses and two splendid chariots, one for Ahura Mazda, the other for the Shahanshah. The tributary groups followed, bringing animals from their lands, the most frequent being horses, camels, and cattle, though the Libyans came bearing an elephant tusk and leading a kudu, and the Ethiopians offered an okapi. All across the facade one thing, however, was apparent. While Persian cavalry had successfully vanquished the Middle East from Libya to the

---

[12] Probably the Nabatean Aramaic script evolved into the Arabic writing system.

Crimea, Central Asia to the Persian Gulf, and the Aegean to the Indus, so too, it appears, had equestrian trousers! For millennia skirts had been the proper attire for men throughout the ancient world, but Zoroastrian priests had retained from the steppes the long-sleeved fitted jacket, trousers, and boots. From the Apadana reliefs, it is clear that nomad trousers, altogether more decorous in mounting and dismounting than the short tunics of the Mediterranean, were now being worn by men of different lands (Boyce 1987:67; Wilber 1989:72, 74, 79–85, 98).

Europe's Defiance of Achaemenid Equestrian Might

The large-muscled Nisaean warhorse from the steppes thus secured for the Persians success in campaigns across all of southwest Asia and on to North Africa. Triumphant, Darius now set his sights even further west – to Europe – where, as fate would have it, the Persian invasion was destined to turn out rather differently. Seeking to establish a base north of the Danube from which to launch an assault on Mediterranean Europe, in 513 BC Darius crossed the Bosporus to undertake an invasion of Scythia. Once Darius had traversed the Danube, though, the Scythian steppe horsemen, determined not to fight an open battle with his well-organized army, lured him into the depths of their territory, always keeping one day's march ahead, destroying forage, and blocking wells. Meanwhile the nomads merely resorted to guerrilla tactics, skirmishing with the Persian foraging parties and driving them back to the protection of the infantry, with which the nomads would not close. The Scythians even contemptuously chased a hare they were hunting across the Persian vanguard and then disappeared. Darius's immense army, men and animals alike, suffered greatly. After two months and hundreds of kilometers of futile marching, Darius had no alternative but to abandon his camp, leaving the sick and wounded to their fate. Saved only by the loyalty of the Greek guards on the bridge of the Danube and lucky not to have met the same fate that befell Cyrus fighting the Massagetae, Darius finally returned to Sardis with a corps of men, one-tenth the original number (Burn 1993:301–303; Humphreys 1991:34).

Emboldened by this defeat, in 499 BC the Athenians, allied with the Ionians, burned Sardis. Furious, Darius dispatched emissaries to demand symbolic earth and water submissions from every known Greek state. The Spartans threw the Persian herald into an execution pit; the Athenians tossed theirs down a well. To punish the cities that had insulted his majesty, Darius mounted an amphibious expedition carrying cavalry in specialized horse-transport craft with doors that let down to form a landing ramp (Burn 1993:309, 315–316). In 490 BC the 600-galley armada landed 40 km from Athens at Marathon, where the plain offered ideal terrain for cavalry, in which the Persians were overwhelmingly superior. But cavalry played no part in the ensuing battle, since by the time the Athenians had reached the southern plain the Persian horses had reembarked to make a preemptive assault on unprotected Athens. At Marathon, outnumbered, Miltiades led the Greek attack. The heavy-armed hoplite infantry charged the enemy flanks at the run, driving them in disarray back to the ships. A battle that should have been won was lost, primarily through lack of cavalry. The runner Pheidippides, at the cost of his life, brought to Athens the news of the Marathon victory (Humphreys 1991:35; Hyland 2003:112–113).

This bloody repulse at Marathon hardened Persian resolve to conquer Greece. In 480 BC Darius's son Xerxes led another invasion in which contingents from all satrapies and subject nations participated, their cavalry comprising 80,000 horses. Thermopylae, a pass too narrow in which to deploy cavalry effectively, was defended for three days against nearly a million Persians by 300 valiant Spartans, but betrayed by Trachis, they were annihilated, their remains to be entombed under a monumental tumulus. Xerxes then advanced through Attica to lightly defended Athens, where he burned the Acropolis. But, relying on the Greek fleet, Themistocles lured the Persian navy into a trap in the straits of Salamis where the invader was defeated. Almost concurrently at Himera, the Greeks of Sicily destroyed the Punic Phoenician fleet allied with Xerxes. A year later Greece triumphed over the Persians at Plataea, the disciplined, heavily armed infantry of the Greek phalanx defeating the frontal attack of Persian mounted troops; the Greeks also destroyed the Persian navy at Mycale. Victory thus won for the Greeks control over the Hellespont and Bosporus, just as they had wrested it from Asian Troy 700 years previously. This would not be the last time a seafaring nation held continental horsepower in check. As will be seen in later chapters, other coastal kingdoms in the Pacific and Atlantic would successfully halt equestrian military expansion. After Salamis, Himera, and Mycale, Greek naval supremacy in the Mediterranean opened up every port to Greek trade, attaining a prosperity that freed Europe from the imperium of Asian despotism. Unburdened with alien tribute, Greek city states developed their own political institutions. Greek commercial enterprise secured the wealth that financed the great era of intellectual, artistic, and scientific achievement known to the West as the Golden

Age (Daniel 2001:47–48). Devastated by the Persian occupation, Athens was entirely rebuilt under Pericles. Great architectural works were lavishly constructed and adorned by sculptural masterpieces of Pheidias, Polycleitus, Cresilas, Phradmon, and Myron. Anaxagoras and Philolaus examined the heavens; Philolaus pursued the celebrated number theory of his teacher Pythagoras, while in philosophy Socrates laid the way for Plato and Aristotle. And in Athens's civic theater seating 15,000 spectators, the extraordinary dramas of Aeschylus, Sophocles, Euripedes, and Aristophanes were enacted.

But the Trojan War between Europe and Asia was never quite over; intermittently the struggle between Greece and Persia continued. Both sides too were plagued by conflict: the Delian league was periodically ruptured by intercity rivalry, and Persia was divided by court intrigue. In an attempt to usurp the throne of his brother Artaxerxes in 401 BC, Cyrus recruited 10,000 Greek mercenaries. Defeated at the Battle of Cunaxa, the Greeks refused to surrender and escaped instead across Anatolia. Organizing the cavalry, Xenophon led the retreat over the mountains of Kurdistan to the Black Sea. After five months of successful cavalry maneuvers against enemy armies and guerrilla bands, across foodless plains and perilous passes in which brave men perished in deep snows, the Greeks finally sighted the sea; below them lay the Greek colony Trapezus (Trebizond). To celebrate, a great horse race was organized that featured galloping down a cliff and back uphill midst great cheering. The heroic exploits of the 8,600 men who had eluded death were recorded in the *Anabasis*. News of the Greek triumph spread throughout Hellas – persuading Philip two generations later that well-trained Greek cavalry could defeat Persian forces many times its size. Unwittingly, Xenophon prepared the ground for Alexander to take the fight to the Persian heartland (Durant 1966:459–461).

Son of Philip II of Macedonia and the princess Olympias, and claiming descent from Achilles, Alexander considered the *Iliad* a viaticum of military art. During his campaigns he always carried a copy annotated by his celebrated tutor Aristotle, at night placing it next to the dagger under his pillow (Worthington 2003:17–18). As a youth Alexander excelled in sports; on horseback he was an accomplished bowman and fearless hunter. When all others failed to tame the giant Thessalian horse Bucephalus (Oxhead), the twelve-year-old prince noted that the horse shied from its own shadow. Repositioning the animal so that the shadow fell to the rear, he was able to mount it. At which point his father remarked prophetically: "My son, Macedonia is too small for you, seek out a larger empire." Alexander was to treasure this horse for the next 20 years (Lane Fox 1974:48).

During the fourth century BC, the Greek city-states came under the hegemony of Macedonia, which extended from the lower Danube to the Aegean and from the Adriatic to the Black Sea. Adjacent to the steppe, the Thracian territories had always possessed superior horses, but during the advance of the Asian forces, the Persian stud had also sired fine horses there. Philip (lover of horses) and his son were the first Greeks to make consistent and extensive use of cavalry, introducing on the battlefield far-reaching reforms that placed their army at the forefront of military technology. The Macedonian cavalry known as "the King's Companions" was trained to fight in tight formation; backed by these 800 feudal barons at the Battle of Chaeronea in 338 BC, Philip's innovative and audacious tactics won the day. Eighteen-year-old Alexander had led the cavalry charge down the valley to overrun the Thebans, thereby facilitating Philip's rout of the remaining Greek army (Sacks 1995:56). Consolidating Macedonian control of the Greeks in the League of Corinth, Philip prepared to invade the Persian empire in order to liberate the Greek cities of Asia Minor. Following Philip's assassination by his lover Pausanias, Alexander succeeded in restoring order (Worthington 2003:65) and in 334 BC led his army, some 30,000 infantry strong with 5,000 cavalry, from Thrace across the Hellespont. At Cape Sigeum, Alexander was the first to leap ashore, hurling his spear into the ground in his resolve to end the struggle between Europe and Asia. He viewed his expedition as comparable to the fabled exploits of the Achaean Greeks and believed he was retracing the steps of Achilles, completing the work his ancestor had begun at Troy. At Ilion he sacrificed at the tomb of Protesilaus, the first Achaean to have fallen. Crowning the graves with garlands, he honored the great Trojan War heroes and then with his inseparable companion Hephaestion raced around the tombs of Achilles and Patroclos (Stoneman 1997:17, 25–26).

At Granicus River in the Troad, the Macedonian army defeated a Persian advance force of the western satraps. Although outnumbered, Alexander denied the Persian cavalry the space to attack his flanks and rear, forcing it instead to fight at close quarters, for which the Greek thrusting spear was better equipped. From riderless horses running loose after the battle, Alexander replenished his cavalry with superior Lydian stock. He then traveled south to liberate the Aeolian and Ionian cities (Lane Fox 1974:122–123, 129–130; Stoneman 1997:27–29). En route, he visited Gordion in Phyrgia, where according to legend whoever untied the knot of bark attached to the ancient wagon of King Gordius would become lord of Asia; Alexander slashed the knot with his sword (Badian 1993:428). The Macedonians and Persians met at Issus on the Syrian plain in 333 BC. Darius III led a huge heterogeneous force of 600,000 on its processional way preceded by the holy chariot of Ahura Mazda and sacred embers of eternal fire (Boyce 1987:64; Humphreys 1991:60). Darius's cavalry numbered 30,000, Alexander's only 5,000. But the coastal plain at Issus was too narrow to deploy the full strength of the Persian cavalry effectively. Cunning use of their lesser cavalry force played a major part in the Macedonian victory. Once within missile range, Alexander led the Companion Cavalry across the Penarus River and hit the Persian left. The Thessalian heavy horse under Parmenio then reinforced the Greek horse that had lured Darius's cataphracts across the river. The cataphracts disintegrated and fled across the Penarus in retreat, followed by the Persian foot soldiers. The King's Companions then attacked the Greek mercenaries, 8,000 of whom forsook Darius to return to Greece. Darius panicked and fled the battlefield. The Macedonians captured the Damascus royal treasury and a large haul of Persian war horses, the heavy muscled Medean Nisaeans, which more than replaced the Macedonian horses lost (Badian 1993:430–431). Alexander continued down the Phoenician coast to Egypt, where he was welcomed as liberator and crowned pharaoh, paving the way for the Ptolemaic dynasty. On the west delta, Alexander founded a new capital, Alexandria, both port and naval base. Along the coast Sidon had surrendered peaceably, but Tyre and Gaza had resisted. Enraged by this defiance, Alexander had the feet of the Gaza commander bored and fitted with metal rings; in vainglorious memory of Achilles, Alexander dragged the Persian tied to the royal chariot at full speed around the city (Durant 1966:541, 544).

The Greeks then pursued Darius across the Tigris to Gaugamela, where in 331 BC they faced the monarch's 200 newfangled scythed chariots. The chariot charge was broken up by a volley of javelins and its drivers cut down (Littauer and Crouwel 1979:153). Outnumbered, Alexander's cavalry was hit hard by the Scythians and Bactrians, whose fully armored horses and men revealed Greek weakness in defensive equipment. Ferociously determined, the Greeks refused to cede ground, attacking squadron by squadron until the Thessalinians finally routed the elite Persian cavalry (Hyland 2003:153–154). The way to the Persian homeland now lay open. Alexander entered victoriously Baghdad, Susa, and Parsa, seizing enough bullion from treasuries to fund a lifetime of campaigns. At the ceremonial capital of Parsa, he burned the richest of all cities of the world to the ground. Was this devastation merely the finale of all-night revels or planned retribution for Xerxes' firing of the Acropolis? Perhaps it was Alexander's fury at seeing, on his approach to Parsa, 800 Greeks who had suffered branding on the forehead, mutilation of ears and nose, amputation of limbs, and gouging out of eyes at the hands of the Persians (Durant 1966:545–546; Humphreys 1991:62). Heading north Alexander attacked, unsuccessfully, the Saka and Massagetae along the Jaxartes. These steppe nomads allied with the Sogdians provided the most formidable military opposition encountered by Alexander in all his advance through Asia, killing 2,000 of his men. As a military power, the Sogdians were finally crushed by Alexander but in the millennium ahead would reemerge as major political players in the international trade across Central Asia (Lane Fox 1974:314–316; Badian 1993:454–456).

Hoping to extend the empire further south and equipped with a scientific staff of geographers, botanists, and other scholars, Alexander invaded India. His scientists did not only report on the lands they traversed; they also relayed to the subcontinent ancient knowledge from Mesopotamia and the Aegean. Following the 600 BC Babylonian initiative of regularly employing wedge-shaped triangular marks as placeholders when tallying numbers, the Greeks had substituted the lowercase omicron – a hollow circle – for this function. Stimulated by this Greco-Babylonian system of annotation transmitted during the Alexandrine invasion, Indian mathematicians by the fifth century AD would advance to develop the revolutionary construct of the zero (Seife 2000:39). Crossing the Indus in 326 BC, Alexander confronted Porus, King of the Pauravas, whose powerful army included elephants capable of disrupting cavalry forces. In Alexander's army now rode the elite Persian detachments of Bactrian and Scythian horse and mounted archers. In the ensuing melee of massed chariot and cavalry charge, the Macedonian foot soldiers wielded 5-m-long pikes tipped with sickle-shaped cleaves or loosed missiles at the elephants, which, injured, ran amok trampling Indian and Macedonian alike (Wood 2002:37–38). In victory, Alexander treated Porus with respect, reinstating him as vassal king. But in the hostilities Bucephalus, Alexander's warhorse during campaigns of more than a decade, had died from wounds received during his master's final battle. Founding a city in honor of his gallant steed, Alexander led the funeral procession to lay his horse's remains in a ceremonial grave. In battle Bucephalus had been adorned with golden horns as befits a charger named Oxhead. More than a thousand years later Marco Polo would encounter legends of horned horses belonging to rulers between the Oxus and the Pamirs (Lane Fox 1974:361–362: Worthington 2003:154).

Returning via the Makran desert, Alexander lost thousands of men in his trek across this rocky wasteland between India and Persia. Back in Susa, however, he soon became impressed by the way the Great Kings had organized their empire. He realized he could achieve greater permanence for his conquests by reconciling Persian nobles to his leadership and appointing them to administrative positions. In this manner, as Greco-Persian emperor, he would preside over a realm where Greeks and Persians would coexist on equal footing. He therefore settled thousands of Greek colonists across Mesopotamia and Persia. To further the fusion of west and east, Alexander also embarked on a policy of self-deification, requiring all to recognize him publicly as the son of Zeus-Ammon and adopting the Achaemenid tradition of the nomads' cosmic tent as the place of appearance for the divine king of kings. No doubt by following these measures, Alexander sought to overcome the heterogeneity of his empire by providing a common unifying faith. What he certainly accomplished was transmission to the classical world of the west the concept of a divine and universal ruler enthroned beneath a sky canopy. From the world tent of Alexander, the Roman and Byzantine emperors derived the golden and jeweled baldachin under which they orchestrated their state appearances as the supreme ruler. Alexander continued to plan explorations and conquests, but his beloved companion Hephaestion had died at Ecbatana. The two often had shared the same tent and in battle always fought side by side. Achilles had not long survived Patroclos, nor did Alexander long outlive Hephaestion. In 323 BC in Babylon Alexander died at age 33 (Durant 1966:547–551; Smith 1950:82).

Alexander's dream of Greco-Persian unity, however, was not to endure; Macedonian territories were immediately divided among his generals, of whom Seleucus emerged the most competent. As thousands of Greeks settled across Asia, temples, gymnasia, theaters, and hippodromes were built to accommodate the colonists. Thus, Greek philosophy, science, literature, art, law, and sports impacted Asia, but Asia also impacted Greece. Alexander had dispatched westward large numbers of clay tablets inscribed with 3,000 years of Mesopotamian scholarship, inviting Jewish scholars to settle in Alexandria. Here in the age of Hellenistic learning, Ptolemy would build the Museum, where writers, astronomers, physicians, botanists, and mathematicians conducted research and experiments, and also the Library to house their great works and translations of the masterpieces of Babylonian, Jewish, and Egyptian learning. Across the Mediterranean world, great scholarship flourished. In geometry Euclid c 300 BC wrote his famous *Elements*, in which he perfected a method of progressive exposition and demonstration. Viewing science as a key to understanding the universe rather than simply a practical tool, Archimedes of Syracuse devoted himself to every branch of mathematical science. His formulation of the relation between the surface and volume of a sphere and its circumscribing cylinder was his finest work. He was also famed for developing the hydrostatic principle and the Archimedes screw. Aristarchus of Samos hypothesized that the earth rotated and revolved around the sun in the circumference of a circle. Hipparchus of Nicaea alternatively proposed an elliptical orbit but then switched his support to geocentric cosmology, upheld throughout the later Islamic world and European Middle Ages. Much of Hipparchus's work is known to us from Claudius Ptolemy's *Almagest*; in fact, Ptolemaic astronomy should probably be called Hipparchian. Working with Babylonian models, Hipparchus improved astrolabes and quadrants, the chief astronomical instruments of his time; he discovered the precession of the equinoxes; he invented the method of determining terrestrial position by lines of latitude and longitude; he calculated the length of the year within $6^{1}/_{2}$ minutes; and he created early trigonometry. Eratosthenes of Cyrene, by comparing at noon on the summer solstice the differential position of the sun at the Tropic of Cancer and at Alexandria, some 800 km to the north, was able to calculate the earth's circumference as 39,689.64 km.[13] He also predicted that by staying on the same parallel one could pass from Iberia across the Atlantic to India (Durant 1966:627–637).

Cosmopolitan Hellenism thus made some progress toward the cultural fusion envisioned by Alexander. But storm clouds were soon to loom on the horizon. To the north, Parni equestrian nomads of the steppes were filtering through the Elburz mountains to challenge the Seleucid rule that succeeded Alexander. From the Achaemenid and Macedonian campaigns, it is clear that military cavalry had now superseded chariotry on the battlefield. In contrast to many thousands of cavalry forces, Darius III and Poros had each deployed merely a couple of hundred chariots – the Persian chariots scythed. In Phrygia, 301 BC

---

[13] Modern computation is 40,075.16 km.

at Ipsus, in a conflict involving 45,000 cavalry, 100 scythed chariots would remain undeployed. The war chariot finally disappeared from the Mediterranean arena. In the west, Rome would shortly be locked in brutal combat with formidable Carthaginian cavalry invaders before emerging triumphant to consolidate an empire in Europe, Asia Minor, and North Africa even greater than the Achaemenids'. The hostile worlds of east and west were already mobilizing for their next armed confrontation. But in his bold sweep east, Alexander's cavalry had bravely laid the ground for the emergence of the Rome-Byzantium era and the subsequent spread of Christianity (Adcock 1957:50; Humphreys 1991:68–71).

CHINA AND THE STEPPES BEYOND ITS BORDERS

EQUESTRIAN CHINA

As the horse-drawn chariot had radiated from the steppes westward across Europe and southward to the Middle East and India, so too during the second millennium BC it traveled eastward to China. Its impact there in many ways was quite comparable to that in the west; politically it accelerated the pace of militaristic expansion and consolidation of territory. Yet ever plagued by chronic shortages of warhorses for her military, China (Table 5.1) persistently maneuvered along its northwestern borders, attempting to import the much-coveted horses from the steppes. During the second and first millennia BC, the situation was complicated by constant warring in the northwestern borderlands, which, despite lower population densities on the steppe, led to repeated pastoralist invasion from the north and diffusion of new technologies south into China. Toward the end of the era, border hostilities between China and the nomads resulted in major upheavals across the steppes, propelling different tribal groups great distances south toward India and west toward Europe (Mair 2005:46–47). Through these nomad migrations, for the first time Chinese inventions and exotic items came into contact with western civilizations; in turn western ideas and products flowed east. In China, the shift to food production had occurred a little later than in the west, with the earliest rice domestication taking place in the seventh millennium BC on the lower Yangtze and millet a millennium or so later along the Yellow River (Smith 1995:123, 134). But by far the most spectacular early Chinese invention was sericulture, dating from the fifth to fourth millennium BC. Derived from the larvae of the domestic moth (*Bombyx mori*) fed on mulberry leaves, silk thread woven into exquisite fabrics would be a major element in trade enacted

TABLE 5.1. *Early Chinese Dynasties*

Shang	1570–1045
Western Zhou	1045–771
Eastern Zhou	770–221
Spring and Autumn period	770–475
Warring States period	475–221
Qin	221–210
Han	206 BC–AD 220
Western Han	206 BC–AD 9
Eastern Han	25–220
Period of Division	220–581
Sui	581–618
Tang	618–906

through equestrian contact between the western world and the Orient (Wood 2002:28–31).

Arrival of the Horse in China

As noted in Chapter 2, c 3600 BC the migration of the Afanasievo culture from the Pontic-Caspian brought agro-pastoralism east to the Altai region, whence in the course of the third millennium BC cattle, goats, and sheep diffused southward to northern China; the domestic horse arrived there later, toward the end of the second millennium BC (Mair 2003:163). Western impulse also stimulated Chinese culture in the area of metallurgy. China's earliest celts, socketed spears and arrows, and single-edged knives find their prototypes in the Andronovo and Seima-Turbino complexes of ethnically non-Chinese cultures along China's northwestern periphery. In northerly Chinese provinces, ornaments for the first time were made of gold, in place of the traditional, prestigious jade (Kuzmina 2007:251, 254–255; 2008:105). Unheralded by any previous type of wheeled conveyance, the first chariots to reach Anyang, China, appeared abruptly, fully formed at the Shang capital during the reign of Wu Ding c 1180 BC in association with bronze knives and bow-shaped objects (Bagley 1999:202, 208). From the two dozen pits excavated (Thorp 2006:171), it is apparent that Shang chariots, drawn by two-horse teams, were a product of the same sophisticated technologies of heat bending, gluing, and joining as used in western Asia, at the same time displaying remarkable similarities in details of construction and horse gear: "nave, nave hoop, axle sleeve, axle block, linch pin, pole-end block, pole saddle, curved yoke, yoke saddle, cheekpiece, bits, whip stock," and plaited leather floor (Mair 2005:69). The most distinctive features of the Anyang chariots were the numerous wheel spokes (between 18 and 26, far greater than the 4, 6, or 8 of the Near East) and the axle mounted not to the rear of the box but midway between front and back, showing closest affinity with mid-second-millennium BC chariots encountered in the west at Lchashen in Armenia (Bagley 1999:206–207).

It seems the Shang did not at first deploy the chariot in combat but utilized it rather as an elevated mobile command platform, from which a general could survey his troops during hostilities. Adorned with heraldic banners, oxtail tassels, and tinkling harness bells, the chariot later would alternatively serve as prestige conveyance in ceremonial displays and grandiose hunts (Bunker 1995a:26). A rare item imported from the northwest, the horse was restricted exclusively to chariot traction and reverentially interred in magnificent funerary context. Also buried in these tombs were sacrificial offerings of cattle, sheep, and humans (Fig. 5.1). Of the hundreds of human skeletons unearthed, some had been bound and buried alive, many had been decapitated, and others had been severed at the waist or chest with limbs butchered. From ritual oracle-bone inscriptions, it is known that Shang armies seized rich booty in horses and weapons from the northwestern steppe regions. In all probability, the sacrificial victims were prisoners captured in these northern battles (Kuzmina 2007:257; Thorp 2006:189). But some frontier tribes were semipacified; from these allies the Shang court obtained the horse trainers, veterinarians, drivers, wheelwrights, and grooms to maintain the vehicles and equestrian gear that the Chinese so imperfectly understood (Bagley 1999:207–208). The dramatic impact the horse was to have on East Asia can be assessed by the near unanimity in use of the Indo-European term for horse across diverse cultures: Chinese *ma*, Japanese *uma*, Korean *mar*, Tungusic *murin*, Mongolic *morin* (Mair 2003:179). Such broad similarity indicates a single source and rapid diffusion.

As had occurred earlier in the Near East, the light horse-drawn chariot would soon make its mark in battle. In 1045 BC, the Shang were overthrown by the Zhou. The Shang defeat has been attributed to Zhou tactical use of the chariot as an agile combat machine deployed in large numbers. At Muye, the Zhou faced a numerically superior

Shang infantry, but with 300 war chariots and the composite bow they decisively routed the enemy. Wen, founder of the Zhou dynasty, was recognized by Mencius, second sage of Confucianism, "as a man of the Western Yi" (barbarians), that is, of steppe origin. In the centuries that followed, the massed chariotry-against-chariotry style of combat spread throughout the rest of China. By the Spring and Autumn period, four-horse chariots had become widespread, and even small states were capable of fielding several hundred chariots in war (Lu 1993:831; Mair 2005:56; Shaughnessy 1988:228–231). The Zhou also introduced from the steppes the concept of the "mandate of Heaven" that bestowed divine right on the meritorious ruler. In the interests of political stability, the Western Zhou organized a defense system against the border tribes by constructing along the northwestern frontier a series of watchtowers, utilizing smoke signals by day and fire by night (Bunker 1995a:27). But nomad influences continued to permeate the borders. From western centers across the steppes, iron was first introduced into China c 800 BC. In metalwork, images featured bearded Europoids with prominent long noses, thin lips, and round eyes. And from a bronze fitting dating to the eighth century BC, we glean the first irrefutable evidence of efficient horse riding during the hunt in East Asia: two mounted hunters depicted pursuing a hare. Also retrieved from the same site at Nanshangen, Inner Mongolia, was a representation of horse-drawn chariots deployed in hunting deer (Mair 2003:169–171; So 1995:47). Exotic animal-style combat motifs were also featured in the decor of northern Chinese bronze vessels and belt plaques. Inspired by the nomad fascination with color and precious metals, Chinese weapons became dramatically ornamented with rare metals and stones (Bunker 1995a:28; 1995b:55). Finally, though, Zhou control in the west was eclipsed by an alliance of pastoralists with rebel states, displacing the seat of government eastward to Loyang, away from the marauding nomads of the borderlands.

The Eastern Zhou was historically divided into the Spring and Autumn period and the aptly termed Warring States period. During this classical period of Chinese history, as scholars traveled widely in search of a new political order, contending political schools emerged, of which Taoism, Confucianism, and Legalism were the most prominent. While the Taoism of Lao-tzu saw in nature the ultimate curative powers for social and political malaise, Confucius believed in the superiority of antiquity and emphasized the importance of *li* (ritual) and

FIGURE 5.1. Chariot burial, Guojiazhuang M52, Anyang. Yinxu 4, eleventh century BC (Zhongguo Shehui Kexueyuan 1988:pl. 4). Courtesy of Chinese Academy of Social Sciences, Institute of Archaeology.

ren (benevolence), arguing for the need of strong ethical considerations in government. Xunzi, by contrast, argued that man was innately bad and that *ren* was only achievable through the defeat of the authentic self by means of strict control and constant discipline. His dogmatic approach inspired Han Feizi's formulation of Legalist doctrine. More of a statecraft or realpolitik, the harsh realism of Legalism maintained that a populace had to be compelled or enticed by the rule of law, specifying punishment and reward for every type of behavior (Wright 2001: 22–26, 34).

From the fifth to third centuries BC, the feudal states of the Chinese heartland fought interminably among themselves for military and political supremacy. In the course of these wars, minor adjustments were made to the chariot. The wooden chariot box was mostly rectangular, but occasionally oval, especially when made of rattan. The box was reinforced by a railing 30–40 cm high for spearmen to lean or hold on to during battle; its floor sometimes was woven from leather straps in order to reduce bouncing at high speeds. Mounted on the 300 cm long axle, the large wheels, now with 25–28 spokes, measured 125–140 cm in diameter. The wheel's hub, thickened and lengthened to accommodate multispoke insertion, was additionally reinforced with bronze, as were the connection of the draft pole to the yoke and that of the yoke to the two chevron-shaped yoke saddles. Bronze was fitted throughout the chariot to strengthen areas subject to particular stress, but the metal was also deployed in rich ornamentation in order to enhance the glamour of the vehicle. It seems chariots, graded by degree of decoration, were formally recognized as symbols of status, awarded by Chinese rulers, along with horses, banners, and slaves, to meritorious warriors and supporters (Lu 1993:826–827, 830–831, 836).

But if the Chinese states fought endlessly among themselves, they fought equally as often with the steppe nomads persistently encroaching upon their borders (Capon 1983:8–10). An abundance of non-Chinese artifacts in tombs during this period indicates fairly vigorous trade relations between "the steppe and the sown" (Bartold 1927). Nomad horses and cattle typically were brought to market in the fall when the animals were fat and could profitably be exchanged for agricultural products. In the event the Chinese failed to open their markets, the nomads raided aggressively when grain was harvested (Bunker 1995a:24–26). By 484 BC, horse-mounted warriors had made their first appearance on steppes northwest of China (Shaughnessy 1988:227). These horsemen were amazingly mobile, moving rapidly from one point of attack to another and almost always directing superior forces against the slower Chinese defenders, necessarily scattered the length of the frontier (Waldron 1990:32). The three northern states of Qin, Zhao, and Yan actually built walls against nomad incursions (Frye 2001:121). It is known with certainty that by 307 BC steppe mounted warriors had been used to attack the Chinese heartland, since at that date King Wuling of Zhao, in order to address this military threat, formally instructed his people to learn the arts of horseback riding and archery, decreeing for the army the adoption of equestrian attire, namely, sleeved jackets and trousers (Yu 1990:118–119); the edict was none too popular with the Zhao elite, whose long, flowing robes were emblematic of high rank (Creel 1965:651). Just as with Achaemenid cavalry expansion where, as shown on the Apadana, men in southwest Asia came to relinquish skirts and to don pants, so now at the far eastern end of Asia the Chinese too were compelled, not only to adopt archery from the saddle, but to modify their dress accordingly.

The Qin Equestrian Conquest of China

During the turbulent Warring States period, the most dynamic of the principal states was Qin, where Legalist policies had transformed a feudal aristocracy into a centralized government. Relatively isolated in the Wei valley of northwestern China, protected by mountains and the Yellow River, its natural geography made Qin easy to defend but difficult to capture (Capon 1983:12). From this base, equipped with iron and bronze weapons and deploying chariots and cavalry, Qin Shi Huangdi (first sovereign emperor of China) undertook a long series of military campaigns that ultimately unified the warring kingdoms into one imperial state. Rapid horse communication and transport allowed national boundaries that would define China for the next 2,000 years to be established and defended. In unifying his diverse territories, like Darius of Persia 300 years earlier, Shi Huangdi embarked on an ambitious program of large-scale road construction across China, affording an efficient network of highways for pack and vehicular transport: horse-drawn for officials and merchants, donkey and ox draft for cargo. Mules standing as high as 16 hands were also utilized. Clearly, as horse culture effloresced, parallels between southwestern and far eastern Asia did not stop at the adoption of trousers. Additionally, reform of the written language was undertaken; characters were made universal throughout the empire, and a standard script ("small seal") was used in all official communications. Major efforts were made to impose standards of uniformity on coinage, weights, and measures, even the axle lengths of carts (Roberts 1999:23; Wright 2001:45–47; Yu 1967:30–31). Besides land routes, water transportation was improved. While Darius, to complement his equestrian land empire, had built a canal from Bubastis to Suez to facilitate maritime trade, similarly in China canals were constructed for transportation as well as irrigation. The Linzhu canal, connecting the Li River of Guangxi with the Xiang River of Hunan, was to play a key role in future overseas trade. It allowed foreign commodities from the port of Panyu (Canton) to be transported entirely by water route to the Yangtze River region, thereby stimulating maritime commerce (Yu 1967:29). Under equestrian control, Chinese populations were relocated to colonize underdeveloped regions, where efficient iron plows opened up new lands for Chinese agriculture. In the north, under the

direction of the general Meng Tian, a vast army of half a million convicts constructed a "great wall"[1] as defense against nomad incursion,
joining together the earthen walls built by the smaller polities during
the Warring States period (Roberts 1999:24).

In sum, Shi Huangdi was an exceptional ruler who accomplished the
unification of China, but he was also despotic, cruel, and obsessed with
the fear of death. Recruiting over 700,000 conscripts, slaves, and prisoners from all parts of his realm (Ledderose 2001:273), he initiated the
construction of a magnificent necropolis. A model of the cosmos, his
funerary tumulus measured 515 m from north to south and 485 m from
east to west. In nearby pits, encompassing a total area of 25,833 m²
(Blansdorf et al. 2001:31, 33), in strict military formation guarding his
tomb was a huge contingent of 7,000 life-size terra-cotta figures of soldiers bearing swords, spears, and crossbows, 500 cavalry and chariot
horses, and over 130 battle chariots (Capon 1983:42). Also interred was
a spectacular royal carriage complete with canopy, crafted in bronze at
one-half life-size scale. The bridles displayed on the small but sturdy
Mongolian cavalry horses demonstrated China's debt to the steppe
nomads. Developed by the Black Sea Scythians in the sixth century
BC, the bit type fitted with S-shaped cheekpieces had diffused eastward across the steppe and reached China during the late Eastern Zhou
period, the same time horse racing was introduced (Bunker 1995a:29).
Qin cavalrymen were also using saddles with retentive molding at can-
tle and pommel, a haunch breeching strap, and central girth (Hyland
2003:53) – and they were wearing the nomads' long pants and short
boots. During the Qin campaigns across China's varied terrains, cavalry
came to dominate the battlefield. Militarily triumphant, Shi Huangdi
successfully established the political model for future dynastic govern-
ments. But his rule had been harsh and his subjects pushed to the limits
of their endurance. After his death, following four years of civil war, a
commoner but brilliant war leader won a decisive victory in 202 BC to
become Gaozu, the first Han emperor (Wright 2001:50).

Earlier it was noted that Wen, founder of the Zhou dynasty, was
of known steppe origin. Chinese historians subsequently report that
emperors Shi Huangdi, Gaozu, and Guangwudi, founder of the Later
Han, all displayed the non-Sinitic traits of prominent long nose, deep-
set eyes, and bushy beard and eyebrows. Not only that – apparently so

---

[1] The Great Wall of China, familiar to us today with its stone towers, ramparts, and
crenellations, dates mainly from the Ming Period (sixteenth century AD). The unified
wall of the third century BC was a more modest earthen construction (Waldron 1990:26).

did many of their subjects! According to Qin law, as a form of corporal mutilation, shaving off the beard was the most commonly inflicted punishment, deliberately designed to debase a man's standing (Mair 2005:70–73). As the reader will see, catastrophic events of future centuries will demonstrate how deep an insult this was to male pride.

Xiongnu Nomads

Across China's northern borders, steppe nomads inhabited a vast swath of marginal lands extending from the Gansu corridor to the Ordos desert. Many of these tribes spoke Indo-European languages, as evidenced by Sinitic words derived from Indo-European stems, such as *ma* "horse" or "mare," *che* "wheel," and *$^*m^y ag$* "magician" or "soothsayer." In fact, for centuries Iranian-speaking Magi (Old Persian *magus*) had been employed by Shang and Zhou courts to foretell the future, to offer sacrifices, and to perform astrological calculations (Bunker 1995a:21; Mallory and Mair 2000:326). But by the end of the third century BC, the Xiongnu nomads had emerged as a real power to be feared, reputedly amassing for battle 300,000 mounted archers. Instrumental in this military expansion was their charismatic leader, the *chanyu* Modu, who had united the tribes of the east Asian steppes into one large confederacy. The story of his succession reflects the manner in which he ruled and the unwavering loyalty he commanded. It seems Tumen, Modu's father, favored a younger son and, seeking to dispose of Modu, sent him as hostage to the Yuezhi (a tribe believed to be Tocharian speakers), then attacked the Yuezhi. Modu thwarted his father's gambit by escaping on a fast horse. In reward, he was given the command of 10,000 bowmen, whom he trained assiduously, disciplining them to shoot without question at whatever he himself aimed at with a whistling arrow. Modu first aimed at his favorite horse, then at his favorite wife; those who failed to shoot as ordered were instantly executed. When none of the men balked as he aimed at his father's finest horse, he was confident of their discipline. In revenge, he shot his whistling arrow in his father's direction during a hunting expedition; his men expectably followed suit. Modu finally eliminated all others who had conspired against him. He then successfully attacked the Yuezhi, forcing them to emigrate westward from Gansu; c 175 BC his generals routed the Yuezhi from the Tarim, displacing them west to the Ili valley. Modu's son, Laoshang, allied with the Indo-European Wusun of the Tian Shan and c 162 BC ousted the Yuezhi from Ili, expelling them even further west toward

Sogdiana. As is customary on the steppes, Laoshang fashioned a gilded goblet from the skull of the slain Yuezhi king (Yu 1990:120, 127). It is worthy of note that at this time the Chinese recognized the unequivocal superiority of the Xiongnu horses. One Chinese official, Zhao Zu, commented, "In climbing up and down mountains, and crossing ravines and mountain torrents, the horses of China cannot compare with those of the Xiongnu" (Creel 1965:57). Chinese merchants made a practice of acquiring unusual exotic silks to be used in exchange for large numbers of Xiongnu horses (Creel 1965:658).

Lightening cavalry maneuvers by the Xiongnu in combination with repeated defections in the borderlands by Chinese officials and merchants, politically amphibious in their dealings, critically undermined Han imperial rule in the northern territories (Yu 1990:122). To counteract this situation, Gaozu decided to negotiate for peace with the nomads and sent envoys to establish the *heqin* policy as a framework for relations between the two states. Originally, there were four major provisions of this policy. It was agreed a Han princess would be married to the chanyu, simply stated "brides for bribes"; from China there would be fixed annual payments of silk, wine, grain, and other foodstuffs; the two states would be coequal; and the Great Wall would be observed as the official boundary. These were generous terms that benefited Modu enormously. In the steppe economy of extensive mobile pastoralism, to exploit all available pastures animals were necessarily highly dispersed and as a consequence unpredictably vulnerable to theft, disease, and climatic extremes of drought or blizzard. Modu's power was limited by the inherent fluidity of his nomad economy. To counteract this internal weakness the chanyu now moved to develop a more secure economic base by financing the nomadic state with resources external to the steppe. Thus in the heqin extortion of products from China, the chanyu deployed the subsidies to reinforce his power across the steppes and to consolidate a supratribal confederacy. By controlling the redistribution of Chinese goods to the various tribal leaders he gained political stability not otherwise attainable. His prestige enhanced by the Han princess consort symbolizing his political equality with the Han emperor, Modu dispensed luxury items to reward the support of his military elite. Similarly, he bestowed rich gifts on newly dominated tribes to win over their full allegiance, lavishly entertaining his followers with the 200,000 L of wine so generously provided by the Chinese. Alternatively he employed Han silk as a form of currency to trade in distant markets (Barfield 1989:45–47). In later years, the emperor Wen actually opened

Chinese borders to nomad trade by establishing markets at strategic spots along the Great Wall.

But behind even the most peaceful Xiongnu-Han relations lay the threat of violence. The Xiongnu purposely alternated war and peace, so as to constantly remind the Han government that peace treaties were cheaper and less disruptive than border wars. In effect, military campaigns were much more costly for the Han to conduct than for the nomads. Small groups of mounted steppe warriors could penetrate deep into the Chinese heartland, deliberately causing much devastation to terrorize the Han, then retreat rapidly back across the desert, making pursuit difficult and expensive. In good steppe tradition the nomads avoided any initial confrontation, drawing Chinese troops deep into the inhospitable desert and attacking only when their pursuers were exhausted and supplies depleted. It was remarkable that the Xiongnu polity numbering barely a million could confront the Han empire of 54 million so effectively. Their "trick or treat" extortionist strategy of alternate trading or raiding in order to increase subsidies and trade privileges influenced not just border authorities but decision making at the highest imperial levels (Barfield 1989:49–50; Bunker 1995a:26).

Chinese Equestrian Expansion

Under the Han, Chinese economy prospered as important social reforms were introduced and major technological inventions occurred. Perhaps the most extraordinary accomplishment was China's utilization of iron technology, relayed from the steppes by the nomads. Building on their expertise with bronze, the Chinese successfully advanced techniques for casting iron. The addition of 6 percent phosphorus to the iron mixture lowered the melting point from the normal 1130°C to 950°C. Coal generated efficient heat (Temple 1999:42). From a running stream, water-wheels transmitted power to large bellows, which helped blast furnaces attain the high temperatures necessary to melt iron. Cast iron, a process by which the metal was made fully molten and poured into molds to produce implements, utensils, and armaments, was an extremely efficient and cheap method of manufacture. Artisans further developed innovative ways to modify iron by altering its internal structure to improve strength and ductility in a complex metallurgical process called malleabilization. Thus the manufacture of cast iron and steel was initiated by China between the sixth century BC and the first century AD; steel was produced simply by reducing the carbon content of iron (Flemings

2002:115–117; Maddin 1988:xiv). Many improved agricultural implements were invented during the Han period. Animal-drawn, the latest
malleable plows were extremely sturdy, with a sharp-pointed central
ridge to cut the ground and wings sloping gently upward to throw off
the soil in order to reduce friction. An adjustable strut additionally regulated plowing depth, which could be altered to suit whatever soil condition was encountered. Confucian officials rapidly moved these new
tools and intensive hoeing and row cultivation methods to the underdeveloped frontier states, contributing directly to economic expansion.
And by 100 BC, the imperial state had established huge iron foundries
in most provinces, later erecting cast-iron buildings, one 90 m high.
But iron manufacture, by far the most significant sector of Han industry, not only stimulated construction and agricultural development;
it also strengthened the military power of the Chinese by providing
superior armor and armaments for their armies (Temple 1999:15–19, 44;
Yu 1967:21–24).

Strengthened militarily but continually plagued by Xiongnu depredation, the martial emperor Han Wudi realized that in order to counter
the threat from the steppes, China needed to establish military alliances
with nomad enemies of the Xiongnu. In 139 BC Wudi sent a delega-
tion led by Zhang Qian to contact the Yuezhi, the Tocharian-speaking
peoples to the west, who in the wake of their defeat by Laoshang
had fled toward Bactria, arriving c 160 BC on the upper Jaxartes in
the province of Ferghana. Traveling across the prosperous oasis states
of the Tarim, Zhang Qian was first captured by the Xiongnu; escaping, he succeeded in contacting the nomadic Wusun (perhaps related
to the Sarmatians), Indo-European speakers also disaffected with the
Xiongnu and reported by Chinese historians to be red bearded and blue
eyed (Grousset 1970:29). Among the Wusun, Zhang Qian encountered
the "heavenly horses," steeds far superior to the horses possessed by
the Han. Later arriving in Bactria, Zhang Qian met with the Greater
Yuezhi, whom he found prosperous but unfortunately no longer eager
for a confrontation with the Xiongnu. His trip was not in vain, however, for soon he examined in the Ferghana valley the fabled "blood-
sweating"[2] horses, which were even more outstanding than the horses
of the Wusun. Returning to China many years after his initial departure,
he submitted to the emperor a comprehensive report on the geography

---

[2] This is probably due to a parasitic infection (*Parafilaria multipapillosa*) that causes minor
bleeding of the skin and makes the foamy sweat of the galloping horse appear pink.

of the western lands. Zhang Qian's explorations stimulated much interest at the Han court, which saw great opportunities in terms of markets for prized Chinese goods and, of course, access to the nomads' superior breeds of horses from Central Asia (Mallory and Mair 2000:55–58).

Having already received from the Wusun gifts of heavenly horses (Creel 1965:661), Emperor Wudi next authorized expeditions to obtain the even more superior Ferghana horses to counter the incessant raiding of the Xiongnu mounted warriors. But as far west as Parthia, peoples deferred to the Xiongnu and provided all manner of goods on demand. By contrast, in their travels the Chinese met only with resistance and were charged exorbitant prices for needed food and horses (Yu 1990:128). Finally in 102 BC an extraordinarily provisioned expedition comprising 60,000 warriors was dispatched over 4,000 km of steppes to lay siege to Ferghana. After 40 days the Chinese were successful in acquiring some 3,000 of the Ferghana horses. Unfortunately, not all the men and horses succeeded in reaching China alive, but the venture was deemed victorious (Levine 1999:6–7) and the emperor was at long last elated at obtaining high-quality horses to improve the breeding stock of his imperial stables (Creel 1965:661, 663). From the Gansu province, a bronze statue of a Ferghana horse in flying gallop, held aloft on the wing of a swallow, attests to the Han equation of the horse with magical flight. It seems that the Han emperor had other motivation for acquiring the heavenly horses besides military conquest. Wudi was obsessed with the idea of his own immortality and associated the heavenly horses with the powerful, mythical dragon, emblem of imperial China. As emperor, son of Heaven, he expected to be transported by a pair of these miraculous steeds to the heavenly home of the Immortals in the western Kunlun mountains. A hymn was composed in his honor:

The Heavenly Horse comes down,
A present from the Grand Unity,
Bedewed with red sweat,
That foams in an ochre stream,
Impatient of all restraint
And of abounding energy.
He treads the fleeting clouds,
Dim in his upward flight;
With smooth and easy gait
Covers a thousand leagues.
    (Waley 1955:99; in Wood 2002:56)

We cannot say whether the emperor was successful or not in this his final endeavor. But where he was most successful was in his contact with Central Asia and the acquisition of superior equine stock for the Chinese army. From this point on, effective trade occurred between China and Ferghana, with 10 caravans a year traveling along what was destined to become the fabled Silk Road (Mallory and Mair 2000:60–62).

In the first century BC, the Han shrewdly exploited a struggle between two Xiongnu brothers over the right to succession. Two separate Xiongnu kingdoms resulted, corresponding roughly to Outer and Inner Mongolia. Allied with the Southern Xiongnu, the Han with their superb Ferghana horses defeated the northern nomads, driving them west from the Tarim. As noted earlier, previous Xiongnu aggression, in what has been termed the "domino effect," had expelled the Yuezhi from the Tarim into Bactria, where in turn Saka nomads were pushed southeastward into southern China (Mallory and Mair 2000:329). This time, however, these Xiongnu migrations were to impact not just east Asia and Central Asia but also the west. The Northern Xiongnu now displaced the Indo-European Wusun from the Ili valley westward across the Eurasian steppes, where some as the Ossetes found refuge in the Caucasus; other Wusun continued on to western Europe where as the Alans they occupied parts of southwestern France and Spain. Moving across Central Asia behind the Wusun toward Russia, the Xiongnu first harassed Sasanian Persia, then emerged in the fourth century AD as the Huns[3] under Attila's command to threaten the Roman empire from Hungary (Wright 2001:59–60). These Xiongnu and Wusun migrations across the Eurasian landmass probably constituted the first major movement of northeast Asian steppe nomads westward, thereby reversing the dominant west-east movement of steppe pastoralists of the previous three millennia.

With the Northern Xiongnu departure, the Han, more secure within their borders, now focused on developing the imperial cavalry force. A vigorous program of horse breeding was instituted. Veterinary medicine was practiced from an early date. In many states, government officials were recruited for the procurement and rearing of horses; in fact

---

[3] Modern Standard Mandarin "Xiongnu" in the Han period was written with two graphs and pronounced *hyong-na*, closely resembling the name Hun. This is confirmed by old Sogdian merchant letters found in Dunhuang attributing the sack of Ye and Loyang in AD 307 and 311 respectively to fighting between the Huns (*xwn*) or Southern Xiongnu and the Chinese (*cyn*), a fact corroborated by Chinese historical records (Sims-Williams 1996:47).

many nomads were employed as grooms and trainers. Official records were kept, registering government horses and grading their quality. But intensive farming left little room for pastureland in the middle of China proper, where horse rearing was criticized on the grounds that it removed vital land from agriculture and interfered with the people's livelihood. Borderlands were more suited for pasture but alas more vulnerable to nomad raids. Thus, there would always be recurring shortages of horses in China. Despite the huge bureaucratic apparatus, the horse did not flourish there, and peasants made poor cavalrymen. A spirited mount does not perform at its best unless there is fine rapport between horse and rider (Creel 1965:669–671). The Chinese could not compare to the nomad, who almost from infancy learned to ride sheep, to shoot birds and rats with bow and arrow, later on horseback to shoot foxes and hares, and then as a young man to act as armed cavalry in time of war (Sima Qian; Wright 2001:55). But the Chinese revered the horse; at the Han and Tang courts 100 prize horses, adorned with unicorn heads and phoenix wings, caparisoned in silver and gold with precious jewels woven into their manes, danced intricate steps in time with the music, with heads tossed high and tails beating (Wood 2002:80). The Chinese government, recognizing that war horses were the chief commodity needed from trade, first manipulated silk exports, then later artificially inflated the price of tea beyond its borders, appointing a Tea and Horse office in order to enhance China's buying power of horses. Of course both products were, to the wily nomad's advantage, traded further west, where because of their rarity the value increased with distance from China (Creel 1965:666, 668). But, by late Tang, the Chinese were paying the exorbitant price of one million bolts of silk for 100,000 horses per year, a drain on the imperial economy that no doubt contributed to Tang downfall (Mair 2003:163).

Even with these concerted measures to bolster horse importation from Central Asia, China really had no reliable military solution to the threat posed by the nomads. Beginning in the fourth century AD, north China was ruled by invaders of nomadic stock, who for 200 years divided the region into small states. In fact, in AD 317 it was descendants of the Southern Xiongnu under the leadership of Liu Yan who overthrew the Western Chin and founded their own alien dynasty (Creel 1965:664–665; Yu 1990:143–144). The most famous general of the Han period, Ma Yuan, acknowledged his military debt to the horse by having a bronze statue of a horse inscribed, "Horses are the foundation of military might, the greatest resource of the state" (Creel 1965:659). In the eleventh century AD, these words were again echoed by the eminent official Song Qi:

> The reason why our enemies to the north and west are able to withstand China is precisely because they have many horses and their men are adept at riding; this is their strength. China has few horses, and its men are not accustomed to riding; this is China's weakness.... The court constantly tries, with our weakness, to oppose our enemies' strength, so that we lose every battle.... Those who propose remedies for this situation merely wish to increase our armed forces in order to overwhelm the enemy. They do not realize that, without horses, we can never create an effective military force. (Creel 1965:667)

Attempts begun by the Chinese to outmaneuver the equestrian nomad – the silk-for-horses trade to supply the cavalry needs of the Chinese army – would continue into the Ming dynasty. For well nigh 2,000 years, intermittent warring between the nomadic world of the steppes and the agricultural world of China would continue in which China periodically reconstituted itself, as northern nomads "conquered and ruled over parts of China, and sometimes all of China, more than 70 percent of the time" (Mair 2005:49; Wright 2001:54–55).

EQUESTRIAN CULTURES OF COSMOPOLITAN CENTRAL ASIA

The horse then had played an integral role in the imperial unification of China, expansion of Chinese rule to the Tarim, and the extension of trading relations westward to Ferghana. Beyond China's borders, on the steppes great herds of horses continued to flourish. Far from constituting a barrier to civilization, the dynamic nomad culture furnished a bridgehead across Central Asia whereby goods and ideas flowed between east and west, linking the Far East to the Indian hinterland and to the Mediterranean world – economically and spiritually. To appreciate the high mobility of these Central Asian societies, let us recap briefly. Alexander's military conquest in Central Asia had left the Seleucids in control as far east as Bactria, where many Greek colonists settled. These outposts of Hellenism exerted a powerful influence on the surrounding regions. But as mentioned in Chapter 4, early in the third century BC, from east of the Caspian, Parni nomads began infiltrating the former satrapy of Parthia, finally killing the Seleucid governor in 250 BC. By midcentury their Parthian state, centered around Merv, had extended eastward across the Iranian plateau, expelling the

Greco-Bactrians across the Hindu-Kush. In these borderlands, Greek and Indian cultures merged as the Greco-Bactrian general Menandros (150–135 BC), benevolent ruler of Buddhist subjects, engaged in the *Milindapanha,* a philosophical dialogue in Platonic style, with the Indo-Greek monk Nagasena. But nomadic invasions continued as the Parthians also found themselves vulnerable to attack from Saka nomads who penetrated the area around Sistan (Sakaistan) (Foltz 2000:44; Frye 2001:111–112, 117). The heterogeneity of artistic styles in funerary items of Afghanistan reflected this highly diverse cultural situation. Among the many gold objects recovered by archaeologists were representations in the styles of Greek realism, steppe animal-style combat, Parthian hieratic, and sinuous Indian depiction. A profusion of deities was similarly evident in religion (Frye 2001:129–130). Even the legend of the Trojan horse was present but reinterpreted as a wooden elephant; however, unlike the gullible Trojans, the besieged were not so easily hoodwinked (Foltz 2000:46). Last to invade these territories of mixed populations were the Tocharian Yuezhi; in little more than a century they had forged the Kushan state, a rule in Central Asia that united the cultural strands of nomadic, agricultural, and urban traditions. Incorporating Samarkand, Bokhara, and Ferghana in the north, the Kushans maintained a thriving trade with Kashgar, Yarkand, and Khotan in the east. They sent envoys to Rome in the west, and by AD 100 Kushan gold coins were struck at the same weight as the Roman *denarius.* By the second century AD, Kushan control extended south across the border regions to Kashmir and central India (Frye 2001:133–137).

From Vedic Roots, Buddhism Travels North to China

Sometime during the sixth century BC, in the Great Renunciation, Siddhartha Gautama, on his snow-white steed Kanthaka and accompanied by his faithful charioteer Channa, escaped his palace in Kapilavatthu. Having undergone six years of severe austerities in order to achieve enlightenment, as Buddha he preached a doctrine that had developed against the background of Brahmanism but eschewed caste. His teaching was based on Four Noble Truths: Life is suffering. The cause of suffering is desire. There is a way to end suffering. That way is to follow the eightfold path of righteousness. In what was the first large-scale missionary effort in history, his devout followers traveled throughout India and beyond carrying the Buddha's message and constructing *stupas* (shrines, temples) (Wolpert 1993:49–51). Of ancient origin, the stupa is most likely derived from the steppes, the brushwood pyramid of the Scythians or earth tumulus piled as a funerary monument with a tree or wooden post planted in its center, representative of the tree of life upon the world mountain. Stupa in the *Rgveda* signified a collection of flames of fire and in Brahmanism early denoted a heaped-up mound of brick and earth that constituted a hemispherical dome (Joshi 1996:vii), not unlike the quadrant circle of the Sintashta tholos or the agnicayana hearth of the asvamedha horse sacrifice. Stupas often were adorned with wheels and sometimes were sustained aloft by them. Not infrequently stupas were constructed on a terraced platform with a wheel-shaped base: a solid hub with concentric circles or with 12, 18, or 32 radiating spokes, also with stone gates marking the cardinal points (Kuwayama 1997:126–135).

It is hardly surprising that the wheel featured prominently in the religious life of the Vedic peoples. It was of course the wheeled chariot that propelled them from the deep steppe far south to fertile India and facilitated their conquest of sedentary groups. The chariot spoke wheel symbolized conquering progress and expanding sovereignty. In Sanskrit *cakravartin*, "the one who turns the wheels," signified ruler. The circle or wheel was the universal symbol of unity. On the steppes beneath the roof wheel of their round tent the ancient nomads slept close to the warming fire each night. And in their cyclic migrations to exploit the seasonal riches of the vast steppes, they transported their families by wheeled wagon, the solar roof wheel perched atop their belongings. The revolving wheel as symbol of the sun was linked to the concept of rebirth. As it spun through the universe, the sun dispelled ignorance. The sun was seen as a chariot, its twin wheels turning on an axle tree. This axis mundi tree of life connected the wheel of earth to the wheel of heaven. The wheel's turning symbolized the ceaseless flux of phenomena, the sun as origin of time and source of the year, the revolution of the planets, and the movements of the constellations.

The central point on the ground of the stupa was the *omphalos* (navel or fulcrum) of the world. It marked the place of communication and passage, the gateway to the heavens, and the path along which supernatural grace flowed to the world from the omnipotent sun. The swastika, aniconic representation of the Buddha, was homologous with the wheel. In some stupas the four entrances turned at right angles to form a swastika, thereby implying cosmic rotation (Snodgrass 1985:19–20, 80–82). The ritualized motion of circumambulation in a clockwise direction around the stupa was also mimesis of the sun's movements, passing through the four directions and seasons of the year (Snodgrass 1985:33). In Vedic thought, reincarnation (*samsara*, the wheel of birth and death that turns forever) entailed a succession of existential states, the nature of which were determined by the law of *karma* from the net results of good or evil deeds in prior existences. One reaped in the next life the fruits of past action. Only through adherence to moral and cosmic law (*dharma*) did the individual achieve enlightenment (Long 1987:266). Similarly in Buddhism the wheel of the law (*dharma-cakra*) rotated around the central point of eternal truth perceived by the Buddha with his eye of omniscience (Snodgrass 1985:85). At death, the body of the Buddha was cremated, his mortal remains distributed among the clans to be immured in stupas across their lands (Joshi 1996:viii). Empowered by the relics of the Buddha sealed within, as symbol of enlightenment, the stupa defused the forces of chaos and promoted order in nature and the cosmos (Cook 1997:3).

Of course, transmigration and rebirth were philosophical constructs not only prevalent in Indo-Iranian religions, but also current on the steppes extending west to the Celtic cultures of Europe[4] and south to the Greek archipelago. From Greek mythology, we know that Orpheus received from Apollo the first lyre. When his wife Eurydice died of snakebite, Orpheus daringly defied death and ventured into the underworld, where he charmed Hades with his music. Allowed to take Eurydice back to the world of light, upon looking back Orpheus tragically lost his love forever. Torn to pieces in Bacchic frenzy by the Maenads on Mount Pangaeus, like Buddha, Orpheus was dismembered, his death giving rise to a mystical cult with beliefs that all living things underwent transmutation (Detienne 1987:112–114). Different theses of metempsychosis were later explored by the mystic-mathematician Pythagoras and Greek philosophers Empedocles and Plato (Long 1987:268).

In the turmoil of the Seleucid era, to escape Parthian equestrian invasions from the north, many Greco-Bactrians had fled south to seek refuge in Buddhist monasteries of the Indian frontier region. With this influx from the west, Hellenic art was introduced into the Buddhist domain. Refugee Greco-Bactrian artists well versed in techniques, styles, and mythology worked under the tutelage of Indian monks to

---

[4] In the first century BC, Julius Caesar encountered belief in transmigration among the Gauls.

depict realistically the events of the Buddha's life. Under the natural-ist influence of classical Greek art and sculpture, Buddha for the first time was portrayed in human form (Mustamandy 1997:17, 24–25; Stone-man 1997:96). Around the circular stupa, stone panels were intricately carved of Buddhas and Bodhisattvas[5] with flame halos (Wood 2002:41). With time this elaborated stupa evolved into the multistoried pagoda (Sanskrit *dhatugarbha* "womb of relics") in which the steppe tree of life component was most evident in its foliate spire and parasols (Cook 1997:6). The integration and adaptation of Hellenic form resulted in the flowering of an original art style, Gandhara, in which Indic deities intermingled with Olympian gods attired in Greek drapery. Perhaps the most famous of these works from Hadda, Afghanistan, is the equa-tion of Heracles with the thunderbolt-wielding Vajrapani, guardian of Buddha and slayer of lions. With a lion skin over his left shoulder and thunderbolt in his right hand, a curly-haired, bearded Heracles is seated on a stone throne, his head turned respectfully toward Buddha (Mustamandy 1997:22–24). This syncretism of Indian and Greek ele-ments furnished the basis for the subsequent development of Buddhist art in China and elsewhere. The Gandhara art style, both dynastic and religious, reached its maturity during the Kushan reign, particularly under the patronage of the sovereign Kanishka (AD 78–144), who built pagodas 13 stories high, topped with solar-like gilded copper discs (Wood 2002:41).

From India, Buddhism was transmitted north to Central Asia along routes earlier established by the nomad invaders, then eastward along the equestrian highway of the steppes to China. In that the regions traversed were peopled by Indo-European speakers, it is clear that the Buddha's message spread fairly easily across these related languages. At Bamiyan, beside the colossal statue of Buddha (so tragically dyna-mited by the Taliban in recent years) stood a smaller Buddha sur-mounted by the Iranian sun god Surya driving a chariot drawn by four horses (Geoffroy-Schneiter 2001:12). Balkh in Bactria and Merv in Margiana became prominent Buddhist centers. During the first century BC, the Mahayana (Greater Vehicle – a pan-Buddhist move-ment) emerged in Central Asia, where many texts were composed and where the intermingling of many cultures and ideas doubtless exerted

---

5 The Bodhisattva of Mahayana Buddhism embodies the concept of a compassionate savior who, pausing at the threshold of nirvana, vows to be reborn as many times as necessary to become a full Buddha for the sake of helping all mankind obtain liberation from sorrow and salvation through his grace (Foltz 2000:42; Wolpert 1993:72).

powerful stimuli. Cross-cultural influences operated in all directions. Through Greek channels, Indian concepts moved westward to impact the Mediterranean world. Iranian soteriological notions appeared particularly influential during the Kushan period, when the most popular image was of the Maitreya or the future Buddha, showing clear parallels with the Zoroastrian saoshyant savior. Legend has it that a Buddhist monk from Kashmir traveled to the Tarim during the Mauryan emperor Ashoka's reign (269–232 BC). Buddhism reached China in the first century AD, when two missionaries arrived with a white horse bearing a felt figure of the Buddha and the Sutra of Forty-two Chapters. To commemorate this event, the Eastern Han emperor erected the White Horse temple outside Loyang. The first missionary actually named in Chinese sources was a Parthian monk, An Shigao, who organized early systematic translations of Buddhist texts into Chinese. He introduced the regimen of mental exercises (Sanskrit *dhyana*, Chinese *chan*, Japanese *zen*) and, consistent with the Iranian tradition of soothsaying, was reputed to be knowledgeable in western astronomy. Accounts tell of Buddhist rites being practiced in conjunction with Taoist observances (Foltz 2000:40–50). However, due in large part to the resistance of educated officials, who scorned Buddhism's appeal to the illiterate lower classes and found its renunciation of the world incompatible with Confucian importance of family, Buddhism would blend only slowly with Taoism and Confucianism to become the philosophical triad of Chinese civilization (Roberts 1999:45). Buddhism first reached the forbidding mountains of Tibet via Nepal; later, when Tibet gained control of the Tarim oasis towns, the Tibetan people became exposed to Chinese Buddhist ideas from the east (Foltz 2000:58).

On Horseback West Meets East – the Silk Road

With the equestrian traffic of Buddhist missionaries and pilgrims, communication was regularized between west and east, and trade intensified. What originally had begun as the direct exchange of nomad horses for agriculturalist grain now swelled into a massive flow of commerce, unprecedented in its volume and variety, in that era unmatched by any continent on the planet. The consolidation of the Kushan kingdom, with its Greco ties to the Mediterranean, its Yuezhi ties to the eastern steppes, and its Buddhist links to southern Asia, bridged the gap between Occident and Orient. The term *Seidenstrasse* was coined in 1877 by the German explorer and geographer Baron Ferdinand von Richthofen for not one but several ancient routes of international trade that extended over the 8,000 km of landmass between the Chinese empire in the east, the civilizations of the Mediterranean in the west, and India in the south. These routes, imperiled by sandstorms that delivered sudden death, traversed inhospitable terrains where temperatures ranged from –40°C in winter to 38°C in summer and the annual rainfall was a mere 200 mm or less (Wood 2002:9, 16, 75).

Silk was not the first textile to be traded; it was preceded by wool, linen, and importantly cotton, domesticated in India c 5000 BC. But the extraordinary silk fiber, woven into patterned fabrics of exquisite beauty, surpassed all others. By the time of the Han dynasty, silk was produced in a variety of weaves: taffetas, satins, brocades, and gauzes (Wood 2002:28). These gossamer fabrics were not always well received in the west, however, with critics remarking that Greek ladies clad themselves in silk only to appear unclad. In Rome, Seneca the Elder, appalled by the transparency of fine silks, denounced women for flaunting their nakedness in public, "hardly less obviously than if you had taken off your clothes" (Wood 2002:30). Despite such opprobrium, wealthy Romans were voracious consumers of this tantalizing fabric, even adorning the Colosseum with silk drapes; in the first century AD they paid dearly for it in gold and silver, estimated by Pliny to be as much as 100 million sesterces a year (Grotenhuis 2002:16).

The availability of silver and gold and the abundance of copper coinage signaled flourishing economic conditions (Frye 2001:187). Rome sent ornamental blown glass to the orient, in exchange receiving musk, rubies, diamonds, and pearls from China (Wood 2002:14). Also exported eastward were amber from the Baltic; red coral from the Mediterranean; sables, ermines, and fox furs from Khorezm; silver from Persia; precious stones from Khotan; lapis lazuli from Afghanistan; ivory from India; and ostriches from Syria and Arabia. Gold was transported south from Central Asia to India. And Yuezhi merchants continually traded Central Asian horses south to India and Southeast Asia (La Vaissiere 2002:79). Everywhere nomad horses commanded a very high price, and early in the Tang dynasty, the Persian game of polo was played at the Chinese court by both men (some of them bearded) and women at a special polo field within the palace. At a polo ground alongside the Silk Road a stone tablet was inscribed. "Let other people play at other things, the king of games is still the game of kings" (Spencer 1971:1). Luxuries were not the only items of trade. All kinds of animals, birds, plants, and fruit were traded. Spices and herbs were traded westward. Spinach, pistachios, and vines were imported to China from Persia; also imported were raisins, almonds, melons, hazelnuts, and alfalfa grass as forage from Ferghana; sesame, peas, onions, coriander from Bactria; saffron from India; and fagara pepper from the Mediterranean. Utilitarian objects introduced to the Orient were chairs from Rome and Persia and the "barbarian" bed (actually a small, folding camp chair). In all societies, slaves were an important commodity of trade, mostly sold into domestic slavery although some tilled the land (Frye 2001:154, 195; Wood 2002:26, 59, 80–87, 141).

Along routes that started from the ports of the Levant, crossed the Euphrates to Bokhara and Samarkand, continued on to the Tarim oasis towns, then finally extended through the Gansu corridor to the Chinese capital Changan (Xian), trade passed through many territories, fiercely guarded for mercantile and political reasons (Frye 2001:156). Until the Mongol period, no one made the complete one-way trip; rather, one caravan gave way to the next. Prices soared as taxes were levied and the numbers of merchants involved increased. In the midst of this melee, the merchants of Sogdiana emerged as the dominant entrepreneurs of the Silk Road. Adept at dealing with the nomads, much of the Sogdian merchants' success came from their commercial representation of the political powers that ruled the steppes. In the Central Asian towns, bazaars were built complete with caravanserais, warehouses, and shops where craftsmen plied their wares. Trading colonies were established along the routes, also deep in the interior of China. There developed an institution peculiar to Central Asia, the military slave. These slaves were trained to guard the home of a wealthy merchant while the master was abroad on a trading mission. With time these defensive units developed into the private armies of dignitaries; this practice later was adopted by the Umayyads, Abbasids, Samanids, and Ghaznavids and later became highly institutionalized with the Mamluks of Egypt (Frye 2001:185–186, 195–196).

In contrast to most other peoples along the eastern Silk Road, very few Sogdians were Buddhists. Their dominant creed was a local Zoroastrianism. A cult of the Fravashis honoring the souls of the ancestors was observed as was widespread lamentation for the dead, where mourners slashed their faces with knives in a manner reminiscent of the Scythian funerary ritual and, as we shall later see, not dissimilar from the Shiite Ashura ceremony. Comparable mutilation in mourning practices is reported as far east as Khotan in the Tarim (Frye 2001:189–190; Mallory and Mair 2000:79).

Thus in Sogdiana, on the fringes of east and west, in keeping with the Zoroastrian tradition of Cyrus, there existed a climate of religious tolerance. Shortly another religion would travel along the Silk Road, this time from far western Asia – Christianity. As is well known, Christianity first emerged as a movement within the Jewish society of Roman Palestine. But many of its interpretations of history were rejected by Jewish scholars who proceeded to solemnly formulate the rabbinical tenets familiar to us today as Judaism. Doctrinal disputes also occurred within Christianity, one major disagreement erupting into the monophysite-dyophysite debate of the fifth century AD during which Cyril, patriarch of Alexandria, engaged in massive court bribery in order to persuade the Council of Ephesus to denounce a rival bishop, Nestorius, as heretic. Nestorius's following in Syria subsequently seceded to form the Nestorian church. Challenging western orthodoxy, Nestorianism thus found refuge along the Silk Road to become the dominant doctrine of Christian Asia.

Although Syriac was the liturgical language of the Nestorian church, the religion was disseminated in the Iranian Sogdian language, the lingua franca of the Silk Road. In addition, from their commercial dealings in different lands, Sogdian traders knew many foreign languages, which equipped them well in the task of translation (Foltz 2000:63–63, 67–68). Sogdian and Iranian merchants and missionaries carried Nestorianism as far east as China. One priest, Alopen (Abraham), delivered scriptures translated into Chinese so the emperor would understand. But the Nestorians did not win many Chinese converts, despite their concerted attempts at syncretism, evidenced in the famous 3-m-high Nestorian monument in Changan of a Maltese cross on high, resting on a Taoist cloud, with a Buddhist lotus flower beneath (Foltz 2000:71–72, 85; Wood 2002:118).

Jews also participated in the Silk Road. As was mentioned earlier, following the Babylon diaspora, Jews had moved north and east to explore trade prospects in the lands conquered by Persia, many settling in the towns of Khorasan. One group, the Radanites (Persian *rah-dan* "one who knows the way"), whose itineraries ranged from Spain to China, trafficked slaves from the northwest lands of the Slavs and the Saxons. This slave trade brought them into contact with the Turkish Khazars, occupying the Volga delta, the Don and Donets, whose territories served as a transit point for captured slaves. The Khazars' control of this important northern offshoot of the Silk Road made them ideal middlemen between west and east, in that they enjoyed symbiotic relations with Iranian settlements to the southeast. Perceiving the commercial benefits, the Turkish Khazar elite converted to Judaism at the end of the eighth century AD, although their khan and most of the population adhered to their original shamanic practices. This conversion facilitated trade contacts with Jewish communities strung along the eastern Silk Road (Foltz 2000:101–102). The Khazars were also allied with the Byzantines, constituting their major line of defense against incursion from the steppes by securing the Balkan and Caucasian approaches to the empire. The Khazars, visited by Jews from as far away as Egypt and Spain, were to exert an important influence on the development of Russian Jewry (Golden 1990:265–267).

Yet another important religion of the Silk Road was Manichaeism, which had its origins in Persia in the third century AD. Derived largely from the Gnostic dualistic tradition equating good with spirit and evil with matter, Manichaeism appealed to intellectual elites by purporting to achieve salvation through knowledge. Again the Sogdians played a major role in the transmission of this faith eastward, Samarkand becoming a vigorous Manichaean center with commercial contacts reaching deep into northern China. Intermediaries with the Turkish tribes, the Sogdians organized extensive horse rearing on the grasslands of the Ordos, where they staged huge fairs to provision the Tang military with mounts. As on the steppes, the funerals of these prosperous merchants were marked by elaborate ritual, in which the caparisoned, riderless horse symbolized the deceased. But during the eighth century AD, Turkic unrest in northern China provoked imperial retribution, with the result that Sogdian communities were subject to brutal massacre (La Vaissiere 2002: 212–218; Lerner 2005:17). Notwithstanding, Manichaeism once more gained state sponsorship under the Uighur Turks, north of the Tian Shan. By adopting this religion, the Uighurs may have wanted to signal their political independence from China, or as citizens of the Silk Road they may simply have wanted to promote commercial trade with the west through the Sogdians (Foltz 2000:73–80). Religious movement was not just in a west-east direction: hundreds of Chinese Buddhist pilgrims also traveled westward to the holy land of India to visit sacred sites, to study in Buddhist monasteries, and to procure scriptures for translation into Chinese. Of these the most famous was Xuanzang, who in AD 629 traveled through Kashmir to India, where he sought guidance at the most distinguished Buddhist institutions. After 16 years of study, he returned midst acclaim to the Chinese capital, where he presented to the imperial court a vast collection of sacred relics and texts

(Mallory and Mair 2000:82–83; Wood 2002:100–104). But whereas Buddhism eventually came to be widely adopted in China, the other faiths, Zoroastrianism, Nestorian Christianity, Judaism, and Manichaeism, all introduced into China via equestrian trading networks, did not make much headway with the general populace. They remained largely confined to the expatriate merchant communities they served, where religion was good for trade and vice versa. In the mid-ninth century AD, xenophobic rulers banished these other foreign religions from China, although Nestorianism would be reinstated by the Mongols a few centuries later (Foltz 2000:81).

But goods, crops, and religions were not the only elements to reach China from the west. In a lighter vein, jugglers and acrobats sold in the slave markets of the Roman Orient were in constant demand in Changan circuses (Wood 2002:53). Entertainers were also eagerly sought from the Tarim oasis towns, where Tocharian was still spoken, people were light complexioned and blue eyed,[6] and Tarim women in good nomad style wore vests, belts, and trousers and rode horseback like their men (Mallory and Mair 2000:79). One striking import from the west was the ultralong tubular sleeves worn by female dancers depicted in 700 BC Greece, where ancient myths tell of bird-maidens bringing fertility, and evidenced across the steppes as far as the Tarim basin. First introduced into China during the Han dynasty, as "water sleeves" they came to feature most dramatically in traditional Chinese opera (Barber 2002:66–70). Of all the Tarim, the Kucheans were especially renowned for their musical talent, excelling on flutes and stringed instruments, precursors of the violin. Again, wooden soundboards of early psaltery had been widely implemented across the Eurasian steppes from ancient times, the earliest depiction of a stringed instrument dating to the fourteenth century BC in Hittite Anatolia. So impressed were the Chinese by the western instruments that the Tang emperor Xuanzong completely overhauled the instrumentation of China to accommodate Kuchean music (Mallory and Mair 2000:76).

Via Nomadic Central Asia, China's Early Impact on the West

If China absorbed selectively from the west "heavenly horses," metals, cultigens, technology, musical instruments, religion, and art forms, it guarded its own inventions jealously and warily exported its products

---

[6] Although now interspersed with Mongol types.

westward. As was seen earlier, to gain horses China deployed inspectors to artificially inflate the price of tea abroad. China also controlled its traders by means of passports that specified destination, purpose of travel, and type of merchandise carried (Wood 2002:59). In terms of the Silk Trade, the earliest evidence of silk in the west dates to c 1000 BC and was uncovered by archaeologists in Egypt (Wilford 1993: C1, C8). By 400 BC significant numbers of silk textiles were being traded by the Sarmatians and other Iranian tribes west to the Greek colonies of the Black Sea (Barber 2002:58). Exquisite silks of course were encountered in the 300 BC Pazyryk burials of the Altai. Notwithstanding this brisk business, the Chinese succeeded in retaining their monopoly over sericulture for many centuries. Finally, despite imperial decrees carrying the death penalty against the exportation of live silkworms and mulberry seeds, those precious items were smuggled out to Central Asia and the process of sericulture was revealed to the west (Grotenhuis 2002:16). According to legend, a Chinese princess, bequeathed as bride to the ruler of Khotan, c AD 440 concealed silkworm eggs in her coiffure. There in the Tarim, local silks were woven in the distinctive *ikat* weave with wavelike stripes produced by tie-dyeing the warp threads so that the pattern was the warp. Later, Nestorian monks carried silkworm eggs hidden in a walking stick from Central Asia to Byzantium in the sixth century AD (Wood 2002:151). Nevertheless, even after the practice of sericulture had spread to the west, Chinese silk remained highly valued for its superior quality and delicate designs. One further material invented by the Chinese was paper. Dating to the second century BC, paper was actually the residue of finely pounded fibers of hemp, flax, or the bark of the mulberry tree, suspended in a solution. When the liquid was drained away, the resultant thin deposit at the bottom was allowed to dry. Crude, durable paper was used for curtains, toilet paper, mosquito nets, kites, clothing, wall paper, and light body armor. In the first millennium AD it came to replace silk and bamboo as a medium upon which to write (Mallory and Mair 2000:321).

Yet other inventions were in the sphere of equine harnessing. As noted previously, yoke harnessing was originally designed for paired bovid draft. Also known as throat-and-girth, this mode of harnessing was anatomically inappropriate for equids and did not efficiently exploit the full tractive force of the horse, necessarily utilizing yoke saddles to alleviate pressure on the trachea (Needham 1965:312). To capture the superior strength of the horse, not just its speed, radical improvements needed to be made in harnessing technology. As early as the fourth century BC, the Chinese achieved a significant breakthrough in this area. From paintings on a lacquer box of that period, we know that the yoke was placed across the horse's chest, from which traces connected it to shafts. Somewhat later, this hard yoke across the chest was replaced by a more satisfactory breast strap, commonly termed "trace harness." This arrangement placed the weight of the load not on the neck but on the horse's sternum and collarbones, which were far better able to withstand the strain, allowing a single horse to pull a more robust vehicle carrying several passengers (Temple 1999:21). A later important innovation, questionably evidenced on a painted molded brick sometime before the first century BC but definitively depicted in the Northern Wei cave-temple frescoes of the fifth century AD, was the collar harness. It may be that this horse collar was originally conceived as an artificial "ox hump" to which the yoke was initially attached. It has alternatively been suggested that, in the shifting sands of the Gobi where traction is problematic, the collar might have been inspired by the Bactrian camel's pack saddle, a felt-covered wooden ring upon which baggage was piled; steppe nomads of course were expert in felt manufacture. At any rate, the collar, at first stiffened but later thickly padded to prevent sores from developing on the animal's back, bore principally on the sternum and attached muscles, linking the line of traction directly to the skeletal system and as a consequence freeing the respiratory channel. With traces connecting it directly to the vehicle, the contoured collar harness afforded the most efficient system of haulage for equids. To illustrate this, one especially telling example, often quoted, is that while ancient Egyptian, Greek, and Roman chariots, of minimal size, with cutaway sides, accommodating two persons at most, were often drawn by four horses, contemporary Han chariots, with heavy upcurving roofs, frequently carrying as many as six passengers, were usually drawn by a single horse (Fig. 5.2). In the third century AD, the Chinese also invented the whippletree. This was designed particularly for multiple draft, even accommodating odd numbers. It consisted of a piece of wood placed behind the animal, attached to traces at each end and by its middle to the vehicle. These ingenious gadgets (Fig. 5.3) greatly aided advances in Chinese agriculture, eventually to make it the most productive on the planet. In the west, these inventions in harnessing would have a comparably beneficial effect – although many hundreds of years later (Needham 1965:305, 313, 321–327; Temple 1999:22–23).

The modern metal stirrup first appeared in China in the first millennium AD. The earliest known experimentation with metal stirrups,

FIGURE 5.2. Han breast-strap harness, c 147 AD (Needham 1965:fig. 541). Reprinted with the permission of Cambridge University Press.

however, was much earlier, dating to the fourth-century-BC Scythian kurgan at Kul Oba in the Crimea, where on a gold torque terminal a hook stirrup's bulbous outer end, inner shank, and chain links for suspension were clearly displayed; a similar hook stirrup image was encountered in Kushan territory in AD 50. The earliest figured evidence for nonrigid stirrups was encountered in India: a soft strap for the whole foot at Mathura in 50 BC and a soft big-toe stirrup at Sanci in the first century AD. These strap or rope stirrups may have served simply as a mounting device or a place to rest the rider's dangling feet; the

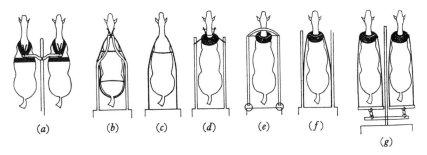

FIGURE 5.3. Modes of equine harness: (a) throat-and-girth harness; (b) Han breast strap with shafts; (c) later breast strap with traces; (d) and (e) early collar harnesses; (f) modern collar harness; (g) whippletree (Needham 1965:fig. 570). Reprinted with the permission of Cambridge University Press.

whole-foot soft stirrup is still occasionally utilized even today in Central Asia. Unfortunately, the disadvantage of the soft stirrup was the danger of dragging a thrown rider. As seen in the Achaemenid Cambyses' self-impalement while mounting, getting astride the increasingly larger horse while fully armed could be problematic! The obvious remedy was to set a rigid tread in the soft loop, which in time evolved into the complete wooden stirrup, later to be sheathed in metal as in northeast China in the fourth century AD. Finally, in the fifth century AD, China manufactured the cast-iron stirrup, permitting a more heavily armored rider to mount a bigger horse. The additional lateral support the iron stirrup provided facilitated the development and deployment of the lance and saber from horseback (Littauer 2002d:439–446). Wielding formidable weapons, the equestrian warrior could now avoid becoming unseated during the heaviest onslaught of battle. Appreciating its utility, the nomads quickly adopted the complete metal stirrup, which effectively increased the rider's stability and lethality with bow and arrow.

Both trace harness and stirrups were transmitted to the west via Central Asia by the Mongol Rouran or Avars, reaching Byzantium around the sixth century AD. The breast strap, which the Ostrogoths may early have introduced into Italy (Needham 1965:319), spread across eastern Europe during the seventh century AD, arriving in western Europe in the eighth. Finally, the horse collar diffused west at the turn of the millennium. With curved hames fitting snugly to the neck and chest, this contoured collar effectively extracted maximal motive power from the horse in plowing the wet sod soils of northern Europe (White 1962:63–65). Stirrups from seventh century AD Avar graves in Hungary, close in form to contemporary Chinese specimens, attest to the startling rapidity and directness of equestrian transmission from east to west (Littauer 2002d:450). White (1962:1) has argued it was the stirrup that allowed the military action of heavy cavalry and made possible the rise of the medieval European knight with couched lance. The West thus benefited enormously from these marvelous Chinese inventions traded over thousands of kilometers of nomad routes across the steppes. The transmission of papermaking westward from China to the Muslim Near East and on to Europe, however, would require yet another actor in Central Asia.

EQUESTRIAN EUROPE – SOLAR EDIFICES, HIPPODROMES, AND ARTHURIAN CHIVALRY

Early Indo-Europeans in Europe

While horse cultures invaded sedentary civilizations from North Africa across Asia to China, comparable pastoralist migration took place at the other end of Eurasia. As discussed in Chapter 2, starting in the mid-fourth millennium BC, Indo-Europeans with the horse had moved west from the Pontic-Caspian region into agricultural Europe. Lured no doubt by the lush environment of the Danube valley, equipped with wheeled vehicles, they had continued across the Balkans into central Europe, where stone stelae depicting their Indo-European gods were erected and funerary tumuli marked their path. Likely, this territorial encroachment did not at first entail massive invasion but rather consisted of migrations of mobile bands, heavily dependent on animal husbandry, which in many areas caused the abandonment of earlier, long-settled Neolithic tells. The intruders constructed defensive sites, the most famous of which was the hilltop settlement of Vucedol in Croatia, where two houses were surrounded by a high wooden palisade; such forts also served as centers for the manufacture of metal weaponry (Gimbutas 1997a:358–363; Mallory and Adams 1997:44).

By the third millennium BC, the ox-drawn plow and four-wheeled wagon had become widespread, and mixed farming was prosperous. Between 2600 and 1900 BC a highly distinctive assemblage of artifacts achieved broad distribution across eastern, central, and western Europe, and Britain: pottery bell-shaped beakers, probably for the consumption of mead and intricately decorated with cord-impressed and incised designs. These were found in burial mounds, frequently in association with copper knives, tanged and barbed flint arrowheads, and stone wrist guards. It seems that these objects spread so rapidly, not so much as a result of population movement, but rather because, in an increasingly ranked society, they were prized status possessions belonging to individuals substantially wealthier than their fellows, to be exchanged as bridewealth, inherited as heirlooms, or used as funerary adornment (Fagan 1986:410–413; Harrison 1980:9–10). And for the first time in central and western Europe, the domesticated horse was common, in some sites amounting to 36 percent of the animal bones encountered; paired horse skulls and later chariots appeared in ritual funerary contexts. The mobility the horse conferred was of unquestionable significance for transport, trade, and war, facilitating interaction between areas where no prior contact existed (Harrison 1980:55, 67). Tin-copper alloys of bronze produced in central Europe soon spread westward. These bronze-working centers, active in long-distance trade, also served as locales for redistribution of many other goods (Fagan 1986:413). As a mechanism of expansion, the introduction of the domesticated horse into Europe thus ushered in a period of rapid social change and technological progress; it also resulted in the new formation of cultural groupings from which the Indo-European languages – Greek, Italic, Celtic, Germanic, Albanian, Baltic, and Slavic – would evolve. In the course of the next two millennia, these Europeans would develop their own indigenous civilizations, which in turn would be subject to future nomadic incursions from the steppes.

Prehistoric Solar Edifices

One notable characteristic of the early Indo-European invasions was their circular edifices, sharing many features in common, hundreds of which extended across Europe to the British Isles (Gimbutas 1997a:364, 366). Notable among them were the round tumuli or megalithic tombs of the newcomers in which warriors were buried with their battle-axes. These kurgan burials, already familiar to us from the Eurasian steppes, replaced the long barrows of earlier inhabitants. Also timber circles, resembling somewhat the wooden structures discovered at Qawrighul in Tocharian Tarim and at Arzhan in the Sayan mountains (see Chapter 3), were widely distributed and consisted of formal predetermined arrangements of numerous wooden uprights possibly supporting an impressive superstructure. These buildings, punctuated by elaborated points of access and egress, frequently contained ritually charged materials, such as corpses ceremonially exposed to carrion birds

(Stover 2003:59), and showed cardinal or equinoctial orientation. A third phenomenon, the megalithic circle, encompassed much of the above, often having both round barrows and timber circles, and in many ways was an essential amplification of the more ancient kurgan sepulchral form. As sites of celestial worship, these imposing stone monuments in a preliterate era were the centers of epic traditions, of ceremonies, festivals, processions, and sacrifice. The most dramatic of these ancient shrines was the great hypaethral sun temple of Stonehenge, a site of astronomical observation, again an activity extensively practiced by the steppe pastoralists. By the second millennium BC, Stonehenge, situated in the middle of the great Salisbury plain of southern Britain, was the power center of a great kingdom; it controlled the rich tin mines of Devon and Cornwall. From as far away as the Mediterranean, the seafaring Mycenaeans would be avid importers of this valuable British tin. Britain's prehistoric Wessex industrialists also specialized in the manufacture of hard bronze axe heads for export (Stover 2003:81).

Initial construction at the Stonehenge shrine was marked by a circular ditch surrounding an area of round tumuli. Starting around 2500 BC, huge megaliths were procured for this colossal monument. The first to be erected were bluestones, igneous rocks, which were transported over hundreds of kilometers to the chalk upland from the Preseli mountains of southwest Wales. Since many mountains intervened, it is likely that part of the route was by water along the Welsh and Cornish coasts (Souden 1997:34, 82–83). One wonders what motivated the gargantuan effort of hauling megaliths over such great distances. Evidently, it was precisely at the latitude of Stonehenge that solar and lunar alignments intersected.[1] In a later astonishing feat of engineering and design, huge 40 ton blocks of extremely hard sandstone were assembled to form an exterior sarsen circle, the megaliths capped with a continuous ring of lintels. Inside this enclosing wall was a circle of bluestones, within which were positioned a horseshoe of five great sarsen trilithons and an inner horseshoe of bluestones. Both horseshoes opened to the northeast, aligned with the sunrise at the summer solstice. Contrastingly, the sunset at the winter solstice was framed between the uprights of the great trilithon. Stonehenge thus marked the extreme points of the solar annual trajectory. Another stone from faraway Wales, the Altar

---

[1] Four station stones formed a rectangle, the longer sides of which marked the direction of the moonrise and moonset at their farthest point, intersecting the solar alignments at right angles.

Stone, was positioned at the center of this extraordinary configuration (Fig. 6.1). The mica platelets of this exceptional piece of rock glittered like myriad mirrors in the sunlight as it stood at the focal point of the entire setting (Souden 1997:36–39, 122).

In his discussion of Stonehenge, Stover insists that the monument conserved many elements of the chiefly megalithic tomb. Stonehenge was in fact a collective cemetery of many centuries, an ancestral tomb. Stover's point, however, is that its architecture resembled that of the chambered funerary grave of the steppes – but with the mound cover removed. Towering above the plain, it was an outdoor, freestanding version of the sepulchral tomb. Atop the sarsens, lintels, unknown in other prehistoric sites, recalled the roof slabs over the burial chamber of a subterranean grave. The outer sarsen ring resembled the steppe cromlech circle of stones (Stover 2003:51–57). As on the steppes, concern for death, sacrifice, and regeneration was evident. Carved chalk phalluses emblematic of human fertility and rebirth have been uncovered (Souden 1997:113). Human sacrifice was also practiced at Stonehenge. The skeleton of a young man was discovered dating to 1800 BC. He had been shot at close range from behind, at least one arrow penetrating the heart. Five tanged and barbed arrowheads lay within his rib cage, one stuck in the back of the breastbone. From Strabo, a geographer of Augustan Rome, it is known that Druid priests performed human sacrifice by stabbing the backs of their victims and foretelling the future through interpretation of their death throes. Other forms of sacrifice were impaling and immolation, for which an immense wickerwork effigy was constructed. Cattle, wild animals, and humans were sealed inside the wicker structure and incinerated as an offering to the gods (Stover 2003:94–96). Timber circles in the vicinity of Stonehenge were similarly associated with sacrifice. One anciently comprised six concentric rings of timbers; a large building of the same diameter as the dome of the Pantheon, it probably supported a roofed rotunda with an open atrium in the middle. At the center of this prestigious monument under a low flint cairn lay the sacrificial remains of a three-year-old girl whose skull had tragically been split in two with a stone axe, perhaps as a foundation offering. Radiating out from this central shrine, rings of animal bones occurred with startlingly regular patterning: domestic animals were interred in the inner circles, wild animals in the exterior rings (Castleden 1993:84–88). Conceivably represented here at the world umbilicus center of six circles was the tiny cleft-skull sacrificial link to divinity; the widening circles of variant animal bones possibly

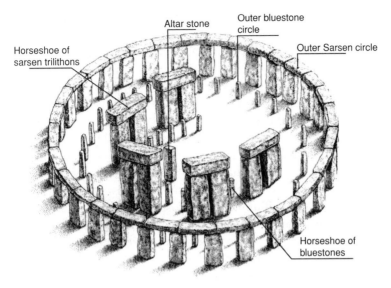

Altar stone

Outer bluestone circle

Horseshoe of sarsen trilithons

Outer Sarsen circle

Horseshoe of bluestones

FIGURE 6.1. Stonehenge circles and horseshoe with altar stone at the focal point (Souden 1997:39).

expressed a progression away from this sacred cosmic hub, outward toward the wildwood.

Researchers have commented on the circuitous course of the ceremonial avenue as it wound its way up around barrows, screens, and banks toward the Stonehenge monument. The procession, a common element in many religious observances, is a formal ritual whereby an ordered assembly of persons moves toward a focal point in a prescripted manner. The curved nature of the ceremonial approach ensured that the entrance to the megalithic circle came into sight just at the final stage of the uphill climb; then the irregular positioning of the bluestones within the sarsen ring forced the celebrants into a spiraling movement around the inner perimeter of the central shrine (Souden 1997:32–33, 42). One wonders at the purpose of this tortuous route! But let us remember the stupa of faraway Gandhara, its architecture suggestive of cosmic movement, and the accompanying religious enactment of circumambulation around the shrine. Perhaps also at Stonehenge the circuitous approach of the practicants and their spiral passage within the shrine emulated the trajectories of the celestial orbs they worshiped. As will be shown, in the centuries ahead many other solar edifices, open to the elements or emulating the firmament, dramatizing the sun's rays, would soon soar into the skies of Europe.

In considering the ritual observance of the midsummer solstice at Stonehenge, Meaden has emphasized the uterine symbolism of the horseshoe of sarsen trilithons facing the rising summer sun. Within the inner horseshoe, stag antlers – strong images of rebirth – were interred. In this sanctum sanctorum stood the gigantic 3-m-high Altar Stone, its myriad mica platelets capturing the first light of day and sparkling fiery red in the sunrise. Outside the abdomen of the shrine in front of the northeast entrance to the outer sarsen circle was located the Heel Stone, the precise height and distance from the circular earthwork to project at midsummer sunrise a long shadow deep into the heart of the monument. Meaden argues that as the sun rose at its most northerly point of the year, its light first illuminated in cosmic intercourse the entire Altar Stone. But almost immediately the Heel Stone partly eclipsed the sun's rays, its shadow[2] darkening the lower part of the Altar Stone and impregnating the fecund earth. This dramatic spectacle of rising sun and moving shade symbolized the hierogamous marriage of the sun and earth, thus ensuring worshipers the fertility of their women, animals, and crops and the safety of their world (Meaden 1997:103–108).

As the ceremonial center of an economically powerful kingdom, a solar observatory, an ancestral tomb, and the site of annual fertility rites, Stonehenge, according to Stover's (2003) analysis, also featured prominently as an important political forum. At the death of the monarch, nobles would convene in assembly to elect his successor. Stover believes Stonehenge served as the election court where the new king was formally chosen. It was also customary at these gatherings to organize funeral games to honor the deceased ruler. Just north of the monument, William Stukeley in AD 1723 discovered a *cursus*,[3] that is, a 3-km-long, 100-m-wide raised earth platform between a parallel pair of banks with rounded terminals and two funerary tumuli at the western end. Stukeley suggested this linear earthwork was a chariot racetrack (Souden 1997:46–47). Possibly, this was the site where funerary games were conducted in memory of the dead monarch following the election of his successor. Certainly, historical accounts of Celtic festivals all underscore the salience of horse racing during political assemblies. Also telling evidence comes from elsewhere in Europe, in Poland, where it

---

[2] In Brahmanism, the shadow of a tree falling upon the earth is thought to have phallic fructifying power.

[3] Many other *cursi* are known from ancient Britain; one in Dorset measures 10 km in length.

FIGURE 6.2. Trundholm cult chariot (John Lee, National Museum of Denmark).

was reported that in investiture ceremonies, at the finish line of the race-course the embalmed body of the deceased king was elaborately laid out, surrounded by his worldly goods, an envied prize for the winner of the race (Stover 2003:113–115).

The horse and chariot as solar symbol of renewal is also seen in the famous second-millennium-BC Trundholm chariot miniature from Denmark, which featured a horse pulling a sun disc, both mounted on a rod and carried by three pairs of four-spoke wheels (Fig. 6.2). Like the Hittite sun goddess of Arinna, this cult object displayed dualistic qualities. The disc consisted of two convex circular halves. Only one half, though, was covered by gold sheet to symbolize the daytime sun; the darker back signified the sun's nocturnal passage from the west through the underworld to the new day of the eastern horizon (Kristiansen and Larsson 2005:294–295).

Celtic Migrations across Europe

During the Urnfield era (c 1300–900 BC), skills in bronze metallurgy reached new heights; sometime after 1000 BC, ironworking techniques were introduced from the east. The Hallstatt culture, developed during the late Bronze Age, by the early Iron Age had become identified with the Celts. Hallstatt was characterized by horse-riding warriors with long slashing swords, a far more devastating weapon than the cutting sword. Hill forts and sumptuary burials with ceremonial wagons were common across Europe (Haywood 2001:31–32; Litton 1997:28–29). These ceremonial wagons were solidly constructed but had small wagon boxes that were suited for neither speed nor heavy transport. In funerary association with richly ornamented horse harnesses, these wagons often were elaborately decorated. As suggested by the seventh-century bronze *Kesselwagen* from Strettweg, Austria (Fig. 6.3), it is likely these wagons were prestige objects involved in cultic practices and, as such, served as cosmological symbols (Pare 1992:217–218). The Strettweg wagon model shows a central female figure uplifting a ceremonial vessel, accompanied by stags, practicants, and mounted warriors with spears (Egg 1996).

Apart from ceremony, there had been significant developments in wagon construction as a functional vehicle for agriculture. Wheels, carrying between 6 and 10 spokes, were now equipped with iron hoop tires. This was accomplished by hammer forging a hoop to the exact size of the felloe, heating the hoop over fire to expand the metal, then fitting it, red-hot, over the wheel. After cooling, the tire would shrink to a tight fit, holding together nave, spokes, and felloe. Another innovation on the four-wheeled wagon was the pivoted front axle, whereby two traction rods were riveted to the front axle, with a wooden crossbar fixed between the two central perforations of the cylinder-headed rods. As seen on the Dejbjerg wagon, the perch of the vehicle was then attached by a single iron kingpin to the middle of the crossbar. In this manner, the pole and the front axle were rigidly connected yet were able to pivot freely around the kingpin in order to facilitate turning (Pare 1992:128–130).

As commerce developed between Europe's northern rivers and the Greek colony of Massalia (Marseilles), Hallstatt cultures shifted southwest to control the trade routes along the Rhone valley. Luxury items were imported, most notably wine. With the introduction of viticulture, the donkey first entered western Europe. It is interesting to note that as the African donkey dispersed north to colder latitudes, it became a shorter-limbed, stockier, shaggier animal than its slender desert progenitor. These changes reflected variation in morphology evidenced in many mammalian species of wide distribution whereby in colder, northern climes there is a tendency to develop a heavier body and limbs (Bergmann's rule) and shorter extremities (Allen's rule) (Clutton-Brock 1992:61). Through these trade contacts, the Mediterranean world

FIGURE 6.3. *Kesselwagen* wagon model from Strettweg, Austria. Romisch-German-isches Zentralmuseum.

first became aware of the Celts, named *Keltoi* by the Greeks and later *Galatae* (Gauls) by the Romans (Haywood 2001:33). During the seventh century BC, Celtic migrations moved south toward the Mediterranean. Lepontic Celts traversed the Alps into the Po valley of northern Italy (Haywood 2001:15). Other Celts crossed the Pyrenees to Iberia, where the Celtic language became established alongside the indigenous non-Indo-European tongues of Basque, Iberian, and Tartessian. In Celtic areas, horsemen fibulae were popular, and a gold torc in filigree with figures of a winged horse was also found in burial (Haywood 2001:44–45; King 1998:26).

Originating in west central Europe during the fifth century BC, a second great equestrian culture of the Celts, La Tene, by 300 BC had spread as far west as the Atlantic and east to the Don River (Haywood 2001:34). The Celts gloried in display. La Tene weapons, armor, portable artifacts, and horse trappings were richly ornamented in a curvilinear art style, to a degree reminiscent of steppe animal-style art, in which forms metamorphosed freely into other forms: "leaves become faces, animals become plants, figurative representations melt into abstract swirls, whorls and trefoils" (King 1998:22, 28). In elaborate tumulus burial, the deceased was arrayed on his war chariot surrounded by weaponry (Litton 1997:32). As a preliterate society, the Celts placed high value on oratorical prowess. The Druids with their retinues of soothsayers, bards, and astrologers held an important position in society. They were trained to master an enormous body of orally transmitted verse comprising religious lore, law, magic, and history (Haywood 2001:64). As philosophers, they explored nature and the universe, believing in the immortality and transmigration of souls. As in Zoroastrianism, speaking the truth was integral to Druidism, also honoring a debt, and fulfilling a sacred oath. Like the Persian Magi, Druids conducted religious rituals in the open air, often in sacred groves rather than in temples. Lugh was the primary sun god–warrior deity, widely propitiated with offerings of animal and human sacrifices. Many Celtic settlements were named after him: Lyons, Laon, and Leiden (Litton 1997:33–37).

As among other Indo-European groups, there were three tiers in Celtic society: *ri* (warrior aristocracy), *drui* (priesthood), and *aire* (husbandmen). *Wid* as in *Rgveda* meant wise or seer; *druwid* meant thrice wise.[4] This tripartite division corresponded to Indo-Aryan *kshatriya*, *brahmin*, and *vaishva*; Roman Gallic *equites*, *druids*, and *plebs*; and medieval nobles, clerics, and serfs (Stover 2003:68–71). Female status was high, and Celtic women (like steppe women) often fought alongside men in battle. On horseback, the Celts wore brightly embroidered shirts and pants (Latin *bracae* "breeches") topped by a woolen tartan cloak. More militarized than Hallstatt, c 400 BC an early La Tene invasion crossed the Alps to found the settlement of Mediolanium (Milan) (King 1998:15, 28, 30) and to attack Etruscan towns, rendering them vulnerable to later Roman expansion. The Celts also sacked Rome in 390 BC and extracted a huge indemnity, subsequently settling the Po valley, which was named Cisalpine Gaul after them (Haywood 2001:36). Recovered from defeat and resolved to bring the Gauls under control, in 225 BC Rome confronted a major Gallic army as it swept down the peninsula, estimated by Livy to comprise 20,000 Celts on horseback and in chariots. In the vanguard the warriors fought, naked, adorned only with gold torques, belts, and armlets to show their contempt for death. It was also customary for one of the leaders, brandishing his spear, to

---

[4] In Indo-European texts, warriors are often termed "thrice strong."

advance and challenge the bravest of the enemy to single combat. In song the warrior would extol the manly virtues of his ancestors, proclaiming his own brave deeds, while denigrating his opponent in order to demoralize his spirit (Ritchie and Ritchie 1985:29, 35). At Telamon, the Roman legions won a decisive victory against the Celts; they further consolidated their conquest by establishing Roman colonies in the northern territories (Haywood 2001:43).

Celtic tribes also moved east across the Balkans and Carpathians. On Macedonia's northern border in 336 BC they had their famous meeting with Alexander the Great, who asked them what they feared most. They replied they feared the sky might fall in, reflecting their awe of the almighty sky god. By and large, relations with Alexander were peaceful; but in the political chaos that followed his death, the Celts raided Thrace and Macedonia and killed king Ptolemy Ceraunos in 281 BC, predictably making a trophy of his head. Emboldened, they surged southward past Thermopylae to attack the sacred city of Delphi, where many Greek states had their treasuries, but were forced into a retreat in which their leader Brennus was killed. Such was the Celts' reputation for ferocity that 20,000 of them were invited by king Nicomedes of Bithnyia to serve as mercenaries against the Seleucid king Antiochus I. Defeated, they settled in Phrygia, later expanding eastward into Cappadocia. This territory – Galatia (land of the Gauls/Celts) – became a client kingdom of Rome in 64 BC and was annexed into the empire in 25 BC. It appears that the Galatians adopted much of the indigenous Anatolian culture but remained sufficiently distinct ethnically to receive an epistle from St. Paul and, as late as the fourth century AD, were recognized by St. Jerome as speaking the same language as the Gauls (Haywood 2001:25, 37–41). To this day, the Celtic language continues to be evident across Europe in place names beginning with *Ga* or *Wa*, such as Galatia in Anatolia, Wales in western Britain, Wallachia in southern Roumania, Galicia in northern Spain, and of course Walloon, meaning Gaul and designating the modern Belgian, now French-speaking ethnic group. Goidelic Irish and Scottish and Brithonic Welsh are still spoken in the British Isles, as is Gallic Breton in the west French peninsula of Brittany (Haywood 2001:15).

The Horse in Greek War and Myth

The Greeks of course appeared earlier than the Celts in Europe, having migrated from the steppes to their southern peninsula at the beginning of the second millennium BC. In 1104 BC Achaean Greece was invaded by Dorians equipped with superior iron weapons. Despite the presence of iron, the horse-drawn chariot, unsuited to the mountainous terrain of mainland Greece, was never used there in the full-speed, massed charge that in earlier centuries had been the mainstay of Near Eastern warfare conducted on leveler battlefields. In Homeric times it seemed the chariot functioned rather more like a taxicab, transporting a prominent warrior into the thick of the fighting, then drawing back to a prudent distance, ready to provide a speedy exit should this be required. In the warfare of Greek classical times, great emphasis was placed on the hoplite close-set formations of heavy-armed, javelin-hurling citizen infantry. Only the very rich could afford to raise horses, and even these were small breeds. As a result the cavalry contingent in a polis army typically was limited in size, although the horse-breeding plains of Boeotia, Thessaly, and Greek Sicily were able to produce cavalry corps of larger substance. The Greek cavalry weapons were the 6-ft-long spear for jabbing, thrust overhand down from the shoulder, and the iron saber for slashing. Besides scouting and escorting the supply column, the Greek trooper in combat was responsible for guarding the vulnerable infantry flanks. In retreat his role was critical in pursuing a fleeing enemy or conversely protecting his own foot soldiers. The knight was equipped with cuirass and shield, but his steed was not strong enough to be armored. As a consequence, as the rider wheeled around in the midst of the melee, his horse was vulnerable to the thrusting spear of the enemy. Later, of course, the military reorganization of Philip of Macedonia and subsequent conquests of Alexander would introduce Persian tactical innovation and the larger Nisaean horse to Hellenistic cavalry (Sacks 1995:54–55). But one invention, at least, that did reach Greece from the east certainly in the eighth century BC, if not earlier, was the light racing chariot. Horse and chariot racing enjoyed immense popularity. Three- or four-horse chariots competed abreast, negotiating dangerous turns around the course and providing tense excitement to the massed spectators (Greenhalgh 1973:27).

While Greece lacked the vast grasslands and great horse herds of the Achaemenids, Greek myth and ritual nonetheless were replete with equestrian imagery. In early antiquity, peoples south of the steppes must have viewed the mounted steppe warrior astride his fleet steed with amazement, imagining a fabulous creature, half human, half animal. In the thirteenth century BC, an Assyrian cylinder seal depicted a winged centaur with the torso of a bearded man hunting gazelles with

FIGURE 6.4. Middle Assyrian cylinder seal impression of winged centaur hunting gazelles (Padgett 2003:fig. 2). Princeton University Art Museum.

a dog in front (Fig. 6.4). The winged archer-centaur with a scorpion's tail of course later became the zodiac symbol for Sagittarius (Padgett 2003:6, 129–130). In Greek myth, the centaur was a wild, woodland creature inhabiting mountain ridges, gorges, and caves in remote regions of Thessaly and Arcadia. Centaurs represented uncultured life before the establishment of Greek law and polis. They were not regarded as evil, but rather as rough, traveling in packs, prone to drunkenness and overeating, with unbridled sexual appetite and proclivity to violence. Yet there was ambivalence: in some respects the centaur was hospitable, possessed certain noble qualities of the horse, and thus stood astride the two worlds of nature and of man. The centaur's form varied. It might be represented by a fully human forebody combined with the hind legs of a horse. Alternatively, the forelegs might also be equine, in which case the centaur often was winged. The best-known myth about the centaurs, mentioned in Homer's *Iliad* and *Odyssey* and depicted on the southern metopes of the Parthenon, told of their battle with the Thessalian Lapiths. The gathering started as a friendly feast to celebrate the wedding of King Pirithous, but the centaurs, becoming drunk and unruly, attempted to rape the Lapith women. In the ensuing fray, outraged at Eurytion's insult to Hippodamia, Pirithous defeated and expelled the hairy brutes to Mount Pindus. Similarly, Heracles shot Nessus with poisoned arrows when the centaur tried to rape the hero's second wife, Deianeira, as he carried her across a river. Nessus avenged this deed by entrusting to Deianeira the blood-soaked garment that would cause Heracles' death. However, Cheiron, represented with human forelegs sometimes with hooves, always was a munificent centaur, renowned for his wisdom, friend to men, and tutor to Greek heroes Jason, Asclepius, and Achilles (Sacks 1995:56). Half horse and half god, this wise mountain dweller was immortal. Though often representing the barbarian enemy, the centaur on occasions displayed a noble character; its erect human torso and equine underbody personified perhaps the bifurcate nature of humanity, that is, man's virtue but also his darker, bestial side.

By contrast, the winged Pegasus, snow-white horse of the dawn goddess Eos, was the heavenly, mythic steed associated with the constellation of stars. Offspring of Poseidon, Pegasus was born when Perseus struck off the head of his mother, the Gorgon Medusa. With incredible speed he ascended to the seat of the Immortals and lived in the palace of Zeus, for whom he carried thunder and lightning across the skies. Apollo and the Muses of music, poetry, and the arts often rode him, but no mortal ever dared until the gods bade Bellerophon slay the Chimera. Athena herself had tamed and bridled Pegasus. Advised by a soothsayer, Bellerophon spent the night in the temple of Athena. The goddess appeared to him in a dream, instructed him to sacrifice to Poseidon, and bequeathed to him a golden bridle. Upon awaking, Bellerophon performed the sacrifice and with Athena's bridle succeeded in catching and mounting Pegasus. Once having slain the Chimera, emboldened by his triumph, Bellerophon attempted to fly on his winged horse to Olympus. Furious, Zeus caused a gadfly to sting Pegasus; as the horse bucked Bellerophon fell downward to earth. Pegasus was also associated with the well of Hippocrene. As the Muses sang during a song contest, the heavens, the seas, and the rivers all enraptured stood still to listen, and Helicon itself rose upward in ecstasy. At Poseidon's command, Pegasus stopped Mount Helicon's rise by kicking it with his hoof. From the impact of Pegasus's hoof there arose Hippocrene, the fountain of inspiration of the Muses (Smith 1925:664–665).

Another equestrian figure that fascinated the Greeks was the hard-riding female Amazon warrior of the steppes, reputed to be expert in tracking game and to rejoice in battle. According to legend, to facilitate drawing the bow, the right breast was seared off during childhood – hence the name breastless (Greek *amazoi*) (Warner 2000:204). To breed, the Amazons were reputed to mate periodically with foreign males, discarding any resulting male babies. Over the centuries Amazons featured conspicuously in Greek legends and in Greek art were usually depicted wearing Scythian-style pants, armed with bow, ax, sword, and crescent-shaped shield. Legend describes how the beautiful Amazon queen Penthesileia, daughter of the war god Ares and Otrera, after Hector's death led an army of tribeswomen from the steppes to aid Priam during the siege of Troy. Amazon courage in battle reduced the Greeks to dire straits. Finally, in combat with Achilles, the Amazon queen was pierced by the champion's sword. Even as she sank mortally wounded, Penthesilea's beauty fired the heart of her victor with passionate love. In his ninth labor, Heracles, at Eurystheus's bidding, traveled far to fight the Amazon Hippolyta in order to acquire the girdle bestowed on the queen by Ares (Devambez 1970:354; Seyffert 1995:298, 468). The Athenian hero Theseus actually succeeded in abducting the Amazon queen Antiope and defeated her outraged followers when they besieged Athens. The Amazons worshipped Artemis, virgin goddess of the hunt and one of the cruelest deities of Greece's dark pantheon of chthonic death and rebirth. When the hunter Actaeon sighted the goddess bathing naked, she transformed him into a stag, so that his own hounds pursued him, ripping him to pieces. She dispatched the Caledonian boar to ravage the Greek countryside. Associated with speed, agility, and violent death, Artemis stood for fierce autonomy, for which her impregnable virginity was the symbol. Her cult was celebrated at the great temple of Ephesus. The Amazon of the steppe thus exerted a strong influence on Greek imagination, representing a savage, irrational force that threatened the ordered Greek world. Amazonomachy, as portrayed on the west metope of the Parthenon, would come to symbolize Greece's defeat of the Asian invader (Sacks 1995:19; Warner 2000:202).

The tamer of Pegasus, virgin Athena, with her spear and round shield, was the martial goddess of Attica. Repeatedly linked with horses, Athena was often shown on Attic vases driving horses and chariots; she was also thought to have initially fashioned the bit, taught the Athenians horsemanship, and helped build the Trojan horse. An ancient deity, as noted in the *Iliad* (2.549–551), Athena had long been honored by a rich temple, and it was her foster son Erichthonios who reputedly invented the chariot race and founded the *Panathenaia* in her honor. Throughout the year, many festivals were offered to Athena Polias, protectress of Athens, but by far the most extravagant was the Panathenaia, celebrated annually with contests in music, theater, gymnastics, and equestrianism. Entering the city, the long joyous procession followed the ancient Sacred Way, 10–20 m wide to accommodate the elaborate cavalry and chariot displays (Neils 1992:13, 18, 21–22; Neils 2001:190). Earlier, our analysis of the Indo-European festival at Stonehenge emphasized the spiraling rather than direct path of worshippers into the timber circle and megalithic shrines; a similarly circuitous route was followed in the Panathenaia. Having encircled the city and crossed the Agora diagonally, the procession climbed the steep north slope, turning on the ramp to enter the Acropolis from the west through the magnificent Propylaea. As the Temple of Athena faced east, just as at Stonehenge, the procession by necessity perambulated the entire sanctuary, winding around the Parthenon to its highest point to reach the Erechtheum. There, the richly woven *peplos* textile was presented to the goddess, and at the finish of the torch race in which runners from the ten tribes of Attica participated, hundreds of animals were sacrificed, set aflame by the victorious torchbearer. The significance of this ancient rite was rebirth, the transfer of sacred fire to ignite the sacrifice at the goddess's altar. Finally the public feasted on the roasted flesh of the sacrificial offering (Neils 1992:24).

In Athens, the breeding and racing of horses, which necessarily entailed the maintenance of costly equipment, was emblematic of wealth and status. Famous generals maintained extensive stables, employing champion riders in competitions. Victory in races rewarded the owner with prestige and contacts in influential circles of society. Because of the aristocratic associations of horse and chariot, the equestrian events always preceded the less prestigious athletic competitions. It was entirely appropriate that hippic performances featured so prominently in Athena's festival, since we know from the *Iliad* (23.388–406) of the goddess's enthusiasm for chariot races and her ready disposition to intervene on behalf of her champion Diomedes during the Trojan games. The Sacred Way of Athens frequently was referred to as the *dromos*, indicative of its original use as a racecourse; in fact, excavations have uncovered five square limestone bases spaced at regular intervals at the northwest corner of Agora that appear to be the starting line of a racetrack. Prior to the ascent to the Parthenon, to honor the hero tombs of the Achaean era, equestrian contests were conducted in the Agora, adorned with murals of the Trojan War. To commemorate the funeral games Achilles long ago organized for the slain Patroclos, the *apobates* was staged; in this most dangerous of contests the runner reenacted Homeric war practices by mounting and dismounting a moving chariot (Neils 1992:18–21). On the Parthenon frieze, the splendid figures of the *apobatai*, sometimes armored or simply with helmet and shield, but most often nude, immortalized this dramatic martial display. In addition to the apobates, these competitions from ancient times included the two- and four-horse chariot races, the javelin throw from horseback, the chariot race throwing the javelin at a target, and cavalry contests. For these events Athenian horses were adorned and equipped for war.

Marble equestrian statues, although relatively rare in archaic Greece, were commonly positioned on the fifth century BC Acropolis. In fact, most of the frieze and upper porches of the Parthenon temple were decorated by prancing horses and dashing chariots. In conjunction with Athena, Poseidon was patron of Athens. The only Olympian to ride horseback, he was also god of horsemanship. After the battle of Salamis, Poseidon was recognized as superior in naval battles, while Athena was always superior in wisdom. Chariots flanked these deities on the west pediment of the Parthenon, where the contest between Athena and Poseidon for the land of Attica was represented. Poseidon had struck the Acropolis rock with his trident to produce a marvelous salt spring. But Athena was judged victor when she caused the first olive tree to grow, giving Greece food, oil, wood, and prosperity. The theme of Athena Hippia and Poseidon Hippios was reflected in the combat scenes of the metopes, which symbolized the triumph of western civilization over eastern barbarism: on the south Lapiths versus Centaurs; on the west the Amazons fighting on horseback; and on the north the Trojan war (Neils 2001:189–191). Enshrined on the east pediment, facing the sunrise, was the birth of Athena from Zeus and their Olympian conquest of the Tritons.[5] Beneath was depicted the sun god Helios, like Indra driving a four-horse chariot, emerging at daybreak from the waters of Okeanos. His horses were full of vigor, wildly tossing their heads in the spray in all eagerness to fly across the sky (Cook 1984:47–49). As in other Indo-European epics, the vital centrality of equestrian spectacle, the sacrifice of fire, and the emergence of the sun god signaled Attic renewal and revitalization. Atop the Acropolis earth mountain, the olive-wood cult statue of Athena represented the sacred tree of life.

Cavalry Wars between Rome and Carthage

Greece's neighbor Rome, of course, came to the world stage much later than Hellas. As did Greece, Rome had to deal with Gallic invasions. Similarly, Rome also had to contend with another older and richer power across the Mediterranean in North Africa, Carthage. By the end of

---

5 Greek rendering of the Indo-European epic of the devas against the asuras.

the second millennium BC, the Phoenicians, Semitic-speaking mariners from Byblus, Tyre, and Sidon, had begun trading contacts with Tartessus at the mouth of the Guadalquivir River in Spain. On the lengthy voyages between the Levant and Iberia, the Phoenicians established intermediate trading posts along the southern Mediterranean coast, founding Carthage in 813 BC. At Gades (Cadiz) a sumptuous temple was dedicated to Melqart/Heracles. In the Mediterranean many islands were captured, and Carthage preyed piratically on the trade of Greek Massalia with Gaul and that of the semi-Greek towns of Saguntum and Ampurias in northeastern Spain (Aubet 2001:191–192, 218, 260).

As Carthage grew rich from shipments of copper, iron, and silver from Spain, it also developed commerce with the Garamantes, chariot-riding oasis inhabitants of Fezzan deep in the interior of the Sahara desert (Herodotus 2003:IV.183), who controlled the trans-Saharan trade. Numerous engravings of spoke-wheeled chariots have been found deep in the Sahara desert, some as far south as the copper mines of southern Mauritania (Garlake 1990:118). Also traded across the Sahara were elephants, ivory, salt, gold on pack mules, and Negro slaves raided from the south. It is reputed that in 596 BC the Egyptian pharaoh Nechao financed Phoenician circumnavigation of Africa and in 490 BC the Carthaginian Hanno established colonies and trading posts along the Atlantic coast of northwest Africa to gain access to the valuable gold of the southern savannas. This maritime venture, however, was opposed by the ancestors of the Afro-Asiatic Berbers, the Pharusii, nomads who rode across the desert with water skins strapped under the bellies of their horses. Middlemen in the gold trade, the Pharusii relentlessly attacked these competitor Punic colonies along the Atlantic coast (Levtzion 1980:124–126). Not a great deal is known about these ancient horsemen of the Sahara, but perhaps we may glean a hint of their technology from remote nonislamized regions of North Africa, particularly the Jos plateau region. There, in the twentieth century, Ron tribesmen still rode bareback with a simple rope knotted around the horse's nose. Alternatively used was a noseband, comprising two curved iron bars joined by an iron ring. The bar placed under the horse's chin was commonly spiked to exert a severe curb pressure whenever the rein was pulled. Another Jos custom was to cut the center of the horse's back, so that the raw and bleeding surface, like cement, would afford the rider a grip that otherwise would be lacking; this incision ultimately formed a callous pad that protected the horse's spine. At the death of a chief, sacrifice of horses and human victims was also practiced, and the deceased was even buried wearing the skin of his favorite horse as a shroud (Law 1980:93–95, 167). According to Strabo (Geog. 17.3.19), during the first millennium BC, the area in Africa between the Gaetulians and the Mediterranean was extremely verdant with vast herds of horses raising 100,000 foals a year (Hyland 1990:177). Thus by the third century BC, Mediterranean Carthage was politically strong, its capital crowded with a quarter of a million inhabitants and fortified by a triple wall 14 m high, accommodating 4,000 horses, 300 elephants, and 20,000 militia (Durant 1971:40–41).

Initially Rome won Messana, Sicily, from the Carthaginians. In response, the Carthaginians advanced northward across Spain to attack the semi-Greek port of Saguntum. Thinking to take advantage of Celtic resentment of the Romans after the Battle of Telamon, in 218 BC Hannibal with an army of 50,000 infantry, 9,000 cavalry, and elephants crossed the Ebro, only to encounter there Gallic tribes loyally defending their trade contacts with the Greek ports. Due to the hostility of these Transalpine Gauls and the later difficulties of maneuvering elephants through the precipitous passes of the Alps, the Carthaginians reached Italy with only 20,000 infantry, 6,000 horses, and far fewer elephants. Fortunately for Hannibal, the rebellious Cisalpine Gauls welcomed the Carthaginian forces as allies. Along with the best of his own horsemen, Hannibal thus commanded Libyan-Phoenician, Numidian, Spanish, and Celtic cavalry, exceeding by far in ratio of horse to infantry anything the Romans had ever fielded in battle. The Romans were ignominiously defeated at Pavia and Trasimene; by 217 BC Hannibal controlled all northern Italy. Foremost in the fighting was his Numidian cavalry, whose superb rapport with their horses allowed them to ride without head restraint, leaving both hands free for combat. Riding without bridle, guiding their nimble horses with body movements, a withe around the neck, and taps of a stick, they repeatedly engaged in lethal charge, disperse, and re-form tactics (Hyland 1990:80, 173–175). Heading south in 216 BC, Hannibal gained another major victory at Cannae, Apulia, where facing Roman numerical superiority of 80,000 infantry, the Carthaginian lured the Romans to fight on a broad plain ideal for his stronger cavalry of 10,000 horsemen. When the Gallic center gave way under Roman might, Hannibal in the thick of the fray ordered his veterans to close in on the flanks and his cavalry to attack the legions from behind. Surrounded, the Romans were near annihilated, the Numidians tearing the fleeing Romans from their horses' backs. Throughout the Carthaginian invasion, the repeated defeats inflicted by Hannibal's superior cavalry had given Rome a protracted lesson in the importance of the horse in warfare. Hannibal's superb use of the cavalry definitively ended Roman reliance on infantry and reshaped military tactics for the next 2,000 years (Bagnall 1990:191–194).

Following his victory at Cannae, Hannibal concluded an alliance with Philip V of Macedonia in the hope that all Greece would unite with him in the defeat of the upstart Roman republic. But far south in the peninsula, many of Hannibal's Gallic allies deserted him for their northern homes, leaving the veteran Carthaginian troops vastly outnumbered. Hannibal requested reinforcements from home, but the Romans had invaded Spain, making fresh support overland unlikely, and a gale disrupted a fleet of 100 ships carrying critical supplies. Victorious in Spain, the young Scipio, freshly elected consul, sailed to Africa. Recalled to defend Carthage, Hannibal met the Roman general at Zama in 202 BC and repeatedly countercharged the superior cavalry of the Numidian king, Masinissa, now allied with Rome. His efforts were in vain: with inferior numbers of cavalry, for the first time in his life Hannibal lost a battle, but he succeeded in eluding capture, then encouraged Carthage to sue for peace. The outcome of the Second Punic War changed the entire western Mediterranean. It reunited the whole Italian peninsula under Roman rule; opened up maritime routes and foreign markets to Roman ships; permitted Italian dependence on extorted grain from Spain, Sicily, and Africa; and delivered Spain's precious mineral wealth to Rome. The resultant burgeoning economy provided the finances for intensive militarization. Access now to the herds of fine horses from North Africa and Iberia equipped Rome well for future equestrian expansion across the European continent (Caven 1980:250–254).

Resistance to Rome and the Boudican Revolt

After triumph at Zama, Rome moved swiftly to avenge Macedonian perfidy. In a scant 50 years, all of Greece and Macedonia were annexed as Roman provinces and Rome's imperial supremacy was ruthlessly established across the Mediterranean. But elsewhere in Europe, the Celts did not take docilely to Roman rule. In 154 BC, led by Viriathus, the tribes of Lusitania (Portugal) rebelled and for eight years vanquished every army sent against them; a decade later the Numantian Celts of central Spain similarly revolted. Finally in control of Iberian wealth, to secure the strategic land route between Italy and Spain, in 125 BC the Romans invaded and annexed southern Gaul. By the first century BC, prosperous agriculture across the region had stimulated the development of *oppida* townships, which regulated craft production and trade. Peace, however, was not destined to last. In 73 BC the Italian peninsula was racked by a rebellion of slave gladiators led by Spartacus, a Thracian whose horse inspired great fear in battle. Spartacus defeated the Roman consuls sent against him, but in 71 BC he faced the combined forces of Crassus and Pompey. Defiant, at the time of battle Spartacus sacrificed his own horse, then plunged into the midst of Crassus's army, killing two centurions before being cut down (Shaw 2001:131–136); 6,000 of his followers were cruelly crucified along the Appian Way. Further north, German tribes had invaded Gaul, and from Noricum (Austria) Celtic Boii joined over 300,000 Helvetians in their migration west from the Alps to the lands near the Bay of Biscay (Haywood 2001:60). All this threatened to destabilize Roman Gaul. At this time of extreme political turbulence, the surest way to power in Rome was through success in war. In 58 BC, Julius Caesar audaciously embarked on the conquest of northern Gaul, first pursuing the Helvetii in a brutal campaign and forcing them to return to their Swiss territory. Next he attacked the Germans just west of the Rhine, where he was victorious. Caesar immediately organized the northern lands under Roman authority, mobilizing rapidly to crush any Gallic resistance he encountered. In 55 BC Caesar invaded Britain ostensibly to discourage the islanders from providing further aid to their kin in Gaul. Back in northern Italy in the winter of 52 BC, Caesar received word that the Averni chieftain Vercingetorix had organized an uprising of some 300,000 Gallic tribesmen. Separated from his main army, in disguise Caesar rode desperately from south to north across all of Gaul to rejoin his legions and to fight a week-long bloody battle until Vercingetorix surrendered and the rebellious Gauls were enslaved. This triumph over the enemy at Alesia added five million people and a territory twice the size of Italy to the Roman empire. It also gained Caesar the reputation of a relentless warrior and elevated him to new heights of wealth and political power (Goudineau 2001:13–15; Simon 1996:169–187).

Perhaps the most heartrending Celtic rebellion against Roman dominion occurred in Britain. Caesar's expeditions there in 55 and 54 BC had been largely reconnaissance raids. A century later in AD 43, 40,000 Romans under Aulus Plautius crossed the Channel and conquered extensive territory in southeast England. Not all tribal leaders resisted the Roman advance. Some found it expedient to come to terms with the new order and received from the emperor Claudius large sums of money (Sealey 1997:5; Webster 1978:54–55). As seen repeatedly on the European mainland, the training, discipline, and superior equipment of the Roman army made it superior to any Celtic force, even one many times its size. Rebellious Britons fared poorly in pitched battle against Roman military discipline. But tribal leaders quickly found guerrilla tactics to their advantage, consequently retreating west beyond the river Severn, where thickly wooded terrain afforded protection against the Roman cavalry (Webster 1978:24–25). Following the death of Claudius, a temple was planned for the emperor's deification, and Britons were required to contribute to the financing and construction of the temple. The fact that an alien cult was being imposed on Britain brought bitter condemnation from the Druids, who traveling from tribe to tribe became an important political force in fomenting revolt. Other grievances abounded. Young men were forcefully drafted to serve as auxiliary units in the Roman army. Grants of Britons' land were apportioned to retiring Roman veterans. And the monies presented to leaders by the late emperor were perfidiously recalled as loans, with the result that many Britons found themselves subject to land expropriation and eviction (Sealey 1997:13–17; Webster 1978:89). The culminating incident was the shameful violence perpetrated against the royal family of the Iceni, a tribe early allied with Rome. Upon the death of the Iceni king, unscrupulous Roman officials, with little heed for the subtleties of treaties, confiscated the Iceni estates. The outraged queen Boudica (meaning *victory* in Celtic) was summarily stripped and flogged as a common criminal; as captive slaves her two daughters were gang-raped by legionaries (Webster 1978:87–88).

When Boudica's rebellion erupted in AD 60, the military governor, Suetonius Paulinus, was campaigning in North Wales against the Druids (Sealey 1997:30). From an elaborate 300 BC chariot burial at Wetwang in the East Riding of Yorkshire, it is known that women warriors were of long-standing tradition in Britain. Amazon queen Boudica led her allies against the capital Camulodunum (Colchester). Elsewhere the chariot in warfare had been outmoded, but the Britons continued its use much as in Trojan times. They approached from all directions throwing spears to create confusion in enemy ranks. After penetrating the cavalry, the warrior leapt from the chariot to fight on foot, and the driver withdrew from the fray, positioning the chariot advantageously should escape be required (Webster 1978:29). The Britons engulfed the town at first onslaught, forcing the Romans to retreat within the walls of the unfinished temple; within two days all defenders had perished. Led by

Boudica in her chariot, the army then moved south to attack undefended Londinium (London), wreaking universal destruction, slaughter, and horrendous atrocities in which women's breasts were hacked off and stuffed in their mouths.

Eighty thousand Romans and their allies were slain before veteran of North African and Iberian campaigns, Suetonius Paulinus, returning from Wales with his legions, met Boudica at Mancetter, Warwickshire. Paulinus chose the battleground site shrewdly. The woodland behind it prevented any large-scale outflanking movement or infiltration from the rear; the open plain in front with little cover allowed for optimal military maneuvering. Most importantly, the immediate approach was through a narrow defile that compelled the Britons to advance in a front of decreasing width and increasing compactness. As the Britons surged into the defile, the legionaries unleashed thousands of javelins into the air, designed to penetrate enemy shields so they would be discarded. Then with shield close to the body and short sword drawn, the Romans closed into a line of tight wedges against the attackers. This wedge formation drove great clefts into the Britons and inflicted brutal slaughter. Cavalry units on each wing charged with lances and swords, cutting down in flight from behind or rounding men up to be shackled for the slave market. With these lethal tactics, imperial military discipline prevailed and the British forces were routed, perhaps as many as 50,000 slaughtered by 12,000 Romans. With legionary reinforcements from Gaul, Paulinus relentlessly pursued the rebels (Webster 1978:89–101). But in the north opposition would persist for centuries to the extent that Hadrian in the second century AD was forced to build a wall 112 km long from the Solway Firth to the mouth of the Tyne to defend against Scottish attack. Today a bronze statue of Boudica, a tall, red-haired woman with her chariot symbolizing resistance, flanked by her two daughters, stands on the Thames embankment (Sealey 1997:13–14). Two thousand years ago, no Roman would have suspected there would be future queens, one a redhead and another named Victoria, who would lead island Britain to imperial power greater than Rome.

Roman Equestrian Might

As we have seen, under Achaemenid rule many satrapies adopted the equestrian pants of the steppe nomad. Not so the Greeks, who opposed the Persian enemy's attire on the grounds it impaired their sexuality. Similarly, the Roman military positively viewed askance the colorfully embroidered pants of the Celts. Notwithstanding, Gauls and Britons kept their breeches, their character, and for a while their language. But the Latin alphabet, adapted c 600 BC from the Greek, now spread literacy across western Europe. Gaul became the conduit through which classical learning and Christianity were to be transmitted to northern Europe, although certain Celtic cults became popular with the invaders, notably worship of the horse goddess Epona by the Roman cavalry to ensure the safety of their steeds. As Latin triumphed, Roman rule brought about rapid urbanization. Prosperity developed as industry advanced. Towns had paved and drained streets, amphitheaters, and public baths. Roads, bridges, aqueducts, and waterways were constructed by Roman engineers. Horse racing and other dramatic spectacles were presented. Augustus's peaceful annexation of Noricum, Pannonia, and Illyricum brought the remaining Celts south of the Danube under Roman rule. For four centuries to come, these Celts would protect the Mediterranean world from direct barbarian invasion out of the steppes (Haywood 2001:59–61).

The network of trunk roads covering the Roman equestrian empire totaled an amazing 85,000 km. Rome maintained communication with the provinces by means of chariot service based on posting stations by which officials, mail, and freight traveled. *Mutationes* were established along the route where animals could be changed and *mansiones* where travelers would stay overnight. In military expeditions, thousands of baggage mules laden with supplies or hauling ballistae and other machines plodded along under the protection of mounted escorts. Military couriers galloped along the sides of the road. Astride extremely fast horses and with repeated changeovers, these riders were able to cover 385 km in one day (Hyland 1990:250–254). Due to Carthage's prolonged presence in Iberia, superb foundation stock had been developed there that later was reared in Italy on imperial estates. Thus African and Spanish bloodstock came to feature prominently in Roman cavalry and racing (Hyland 1990:74, 173). As Rome grew, equines came to play an increasingly significant role in military operations. For a nation intent on far-flung conquests, the horse possessed many admirable qualities, namely, durability, speed, weight-carrying capacity, and the ability to forage on the move, all of which aided in the domination of other societies (Hyland 1990:64–66). Typically in military maneuvers, horses were used for nighttime reconnaissance. In daytime, front, back, and on both flanks, the cavalry formed a protective shield around the marching column of infantry, baggage animals, officer remounts, and ballistic vehicles. Crack cavalry units and the cream of the infantry were positioned in the rear to guard against surprise attack (Hyland 1990:164). As Rome expanded east and west, the great distances involved dictated rapid troop movement that only mounted horsemen could deliver. The Roman cavalry was based in Milan, and the extensive road system crisscrossing the empire allowed this mobile force traveling at sustained speed to nip a revolt in the bud before it spread to the wider populace (Hyland 1990:192–193).

During battle the horseman had constant need for sudden spurts and stops and equally quick turns and levades. To accomplish all phases of these movements the firm support of a rigid saddle was highly advantageous. Without the brace of this secure seat, the rider was unable to harness adequate power to deliver maximum thrust of his handheld weapon or projectile. The early prototype of the tree saddle was seen at Pazyryk, and it is known that the Scythians used a firmly constructed saddle. The Gundestrup cauldron of the second century BC also showed the Celts mounted on a horned saddle. It is possible, though, that the impetus for the tree saddle may have come from the Sarmatian *clibanarius* of the steppes. Whatever its provenance, by Roman times the saddle had evolved in such a manner that the two edges of the tree or framework formed a hard ridge under the rider's inner thigh, requiring that a thick pad be placed underneath. The natural fibers of the padding allowed for sweat absorption and protected against pressure and friction. The Roman saddle was attached with breast and haunch straps. The tree saddle, constructed with four horns, greatly increased mount capability and significantly enhanced cavalry effectiveness. In combat, by locking the right thigh under the right horn, the rider could maintain his position with greater security. In an overhand missile throw the front horns served as a brace. The horns also assisted rapid negotiation of both uphill and downhill slopes (Hyland 1990:131–135).

In terms of armor, the chanfron of leather or metal protected the horse's head and the peytral the chest. The Romans did not customarily fight fully armored as the Parthians and the Sarmatians did, the reason likely being that the cataphract and clibanarius horse carried a major disadvantage, namely, heat stress, suffered far more readily by the heavier Roman horse. From the steppe grasslands, the Parthians and other Iranians had access to vast reserves of remounts (Hyland 1990:145, 148, 155), an advantage not shared by the Romans. The Sarmatian nomads had developed a distinctive form of equestrian combat, that of the fully armored rider on the fully armored horse. Quite unlike the Scythians, their approach to war was one of shock combat, a mode of fighting destined to dominate the European arena for centuries to come. They fought with *contus*, a heavy lance and broadsword. As armor, they wore a long-sleeved coat and pants so that the extremities as well as the torso were protected. Their early armor was made of scales of bronze, iron, or occasionally horn or hoof, riveted in overlapping rows on cloth or leather backing. It was sword proof, arrow proof, and, critical for horse riding, flexible; even their horses were protected by scale covers and bronze-studded leather chanfrons. Later, scale armor would be replaced by chain mail, adopted probably from the Celts. The Sarmatians fought against Rome as much as they fought with them. In AD 175, the Sarmatian Iazyges sided with the German Marcomanni and Quadi to invade Pannonia but were decisively beaten by the emperor Marcus Aurelius, who in his time of triumph assumed the title Sarmaticus. In the wake of this victory 8,000 Sarmatian Iazyges cavalrymen were impressed into the Roman army, 5,500 of whom were stationed in Britain to guard Hadrian's wall against the troublesome Picts and Scots. Few of these nomads returned to the steppes; instead, following their period of enlistment, most settled at the Roman cavalry fort of Bremetennacum Veteranorum in northern England. As shown on Trajan's column in Rome, The Lizard (Sauromata) was the totem of these Sarmatians. Its effigy flown on a serpentine banner, writhing in the wind, possibly popularized the concept of the mythical dragon in Britain (Hildinger 2001:47–51; Littleton 1995:265; Nickel 1974:151). The Iazyges, like their ethnic cousins the Sarmatian Alans, who reached western Europe a couple centuries later, were also known for their *tamgas*, sacred symbols emblazoned on their helmets, shields, and other items of equipment (Littleton and Malcor 1994:8, 13). These insignia may have contributed to the early birth of heraldry.

Besides Africa and Iberia, Rome levied horses from many other tribes: Gaul, Thessaly, Thrace, Cappadocia. Horses were raised on *latifundia* in the most fertile areas of Italy. Lucerne/alfalfa, the prized fodder of the Nisaean horse, was introduced from Medea to the Italian peninsula. This highly nutritive fodder significantly increased the size and quality of the bloodstock to the extent that export of the Italian horse was prohibited by law to prevent subject peoples from upgrading their own stock for cavalry use (Hyland 1990:17–21). In summer, horses were pastured in the mountains, where the rocky ground toughened their hooves, an important factor in an extended empire of diverse terrains. To protect the hoof, the Romans commonly utilized a hipposandal, a smooth iron plate bent over to form loops at each end that were secured by leather straps. An early iron horseshoe, attached by nails, is thought to have been adopted from nomads by German tribes during the second century BC and later may have been used in a few northern Roman provinces. Veterinary medicine was widely practiced, and everything was done to ensure breeding success (Forbes 1956:515; Hyland 1990:36–37). In terms of preparation for war, from an early age the horse was conditioned for battle and subjected to the clamor of arms, war drums, and trumpet calls. In riding, it was exposed to a variety of terrains, required to leap trenches, and made to swim rivers (Hyland 1990:108–109). Alongside horse rearing, mule breeding was another massive industry to support troops on campaign.

Solar Edifices of Rome

So much of Rome's time, money, and resources were invested in breeding fine horses that this promoted another national activity: horse and chariot racing. In fact, many horse ranches were dual purpose, catering to both the army and the racetrack. Training the racehorse started in the third year, with racing beginning in the fifth year and continuing until the horse reached 20 years of age. Every major city in the empire boasted a flourishing circus housed in a monumental edifice. Wealthy landowners maintained stables for hunting and sport, the civic-minded among them contributing generous gifts to the cursus in order to advance their public careers. But racing itself was governed by a plethora of rules, civic, political, and religious, with annual race days traditionally occurring during sacred festivals. Situated in the valley between the Aventine and Palatine Hills, the largest racetrack in Rome was of course the Circus Maximus, 650 m overall in length, 220 m wide. The central *spina* around which horses turned some was 233 m long; since each race normally entailed seven laps, the distance covered was about 3 km (Hyland 1990:204, 215–217).

The Circus was dedicated to the sun, its name associated with the goddess Circe, daughter of the sun. From the union of Circe and Odysseus was born Latinus, ancestor of all the Latins. According to Tertullian, the first circus spectacle was given by Circe in honor of the sun, her father. This solar association of the circus was of great antiquity. From earliest times, hypaethral temples to the sun and the moon had been present in the valley close to the circus, like Stonehenge their roofs open to the sky and light, so the divinities would enter these sanctuaries by their rays. But in the political upheavals of Rome in AD 64, not only was the Temple of the Moon burned down, but the Temple of the Sun actually served as a center of conspiracy. Nero paid homage to the sun for revealing the plot by erecting new temples to the sun and moon within the Circus Maximus directly overlooking the finish line, thereby linking the solar deity to victory as patron of the circus, the supreme charioteer. The triumphant pose of the victorious charioteer thus paralleled the majesty of the sun god. At the semicircular end of the racetrack stood the monumental three-bay arch, commemorating the military victories of Titus. Surmounted by a chariot, the arch symbolized the vault of heaven and the sun's traversal of the sky and triumph over darkness, to be perennially celebrated by horse and chariot racing in the racetrack (Humphrey 1986:91–95, 120, 122).

The spectators applauded with passion the exploits of their hero jockeys and charioteers, who enjoyed the same fame as today's baseball or soccer champions. Horses were awarded bronze medals for their performance with which they were later buried at the racetrack. Racing associations were divided into factions, each with a color dedicated to the seasons and the gods. Whites and Reds initially symbolized winter and summer but later became White for Zephyrs, Red for Mars, Blue for the sky/sea, and Green for earth. Racing mania gripped rich and poor alike as contestants fought for supremacy in the race. The perils of the *naufragia* (shipwreck) were ever present as collision inevitably brought down horses and riders in a tangle of harness straps and splintered chariots. If unable to cut himself loose, the driver would be dragged along amidst thrashing hooves, a danger to every charioteer on the track. Many valiant horses and men perished in this endeavor (Hyland 1990:205, 224). The intense competitiveness of the racetrack, like the rigors of warfare itself, engendered an unrelenting search for superior equine strength and speed. Drawing on the finest stud of their empire and selectively intermingling genes, breeding of the Roman horse laid the foundation bloodstock on which Europeans of later ages would depend.

Other spectacles for which Rome was famous were animal hunts (*venationes*) and gladiatorial contests (*munera*). Like equestrian races, the latter had its origins in ancient funerary ceremonies in which sacrificial practices persisted similar to those of the steppes. War captives or slaves purchased expressly for the event were immolated at the funeral. A more ancient rite was to expose the sacrificial victim to wild animals to be torn to pieces. These practices evolved into the gladiatorial pair, *munus*, who would fight before the tomb of a fallen soldier. By 183 BC funerary ceremonies in the Roman forum featured over 60 gladiatorial contests. Later, these rites to commemorate valiant warriors became celebrated as public games in solar elliptical arenas (Vismara 2001:21–23). Finally amphitheaters appeared. In the center of Rome, the Colosseum, the imperial amphitheater where foreign dignitaries were entertained, was regarded not only as Rome's navel, but the world's navel (*umbilicus mundi*) as attested by apocalyptic oracle:

> *Quando stat Colysaeum stat et Roma,*
> *quando cadet Colysaeum cadet et Roma,*
> *quando cadet et Roma cadet et mundus.*[6]
> (Coarelli 2001:19)

But an earlier solar edifice had preceded Vespasian's Colosseum in the center of Rome. In AD 64 in the wake of the fire that devastated the city, Nero had constructed the extraordinary palace *Domus aurea* (Golden House), its walls covered in gold and inlaid with precious stones and mother of pearl (Lugli 1968:8). For this despot of cosmic aspirations, rectilinear architecture was too limited in its formal repertory. Instead, he drew inspiration from the hypaethral Temples of the Sun and Moon, newly introduced into the Circus Maximus. For Nero's Golden House, his architects devised a revolutionary design that daringly utilized the centralized morphology of vaulted space. At the very center of the edifice was the octagonal hall of the sun-god emperor, its central vault rising gradually from octagon to seamless dome, culminating in a broad oculus. In the airy sun-illuminated aula below, space, shape, light, and structure became one cosmic theatre for the Roman emperor (MacDonald 1976:54–55).

It is not clear quite where and how the first dome originated. As we have seen, the round kurgan sepulchral mound (the earth mountain) extended across the entire swath of the Eurasian steppes as far west as Britain, where Stonehenge, the ancestral tomb and solar temple, arose in the third millennium BC. Also, throughout Europe, from antiquity to civilization, domical – conical-tholos, hemispherical, hoop-shaped – tombs abounded. At the oracle at Delphi, the omphalos was represented as a round hut with a cupola marking the tomb of a legendary god-king (Smith 1950:6, 75–76). In its transformation from prehistoric shelter

---

6 "When the Colosseum stands firm, Rome too stands firm; when the Colosseum falls, Rome too falls; when the Colosseum falls, both Rome and the world fall."

to tomb to shrine, Smith proposes that the domical structure of the ancient ancestral dwelling is venerated as a cosmic symbol of tribal unity. He has even suggested that the stimulus for adoption of the domical shape in ritual or mortuary context may have come from the round, domelike cosmic tent of the steppes. Earlier it was noted that the Achaemenids, descendants of the steppe, brought to the classical world the concept of the divine and universal ruler and the imperial practice of conducting audiences in a great celestial domed tent. Both ideology and rite were adopted by Alexander and later incorporated by Roman and Byzantine emperors into the ceremonial baldachin canopy of their state appearances. The domical baldachin was similarly reported by Philostratus for Parthian Persia:

> the ceiling of which was constructed in the form of a dome like the heavens, covered with sapphire stone, this stone being intensely blue and of the color of the sky ... and in its heights are the images of the gods in whom they believed, and they appear golden. (Smith 1950:81)

Persian precedents may have inspired Nero to represent himself as the incarnation of the sun-god and to construct his Domus aurea as a sun palace, thereby introducing the dome with its celestial symbolism into Roman imperial architecture (Smith 1950:82).

A later important piece of imperial domical architecture symbolizing cosmic and political unity was the Roman Pantheon *templum deorum omnium*, constructed in the Campus Martius during Hadrian's reign between AD 118 and 128 (MacDonald 1965:95–96). No building of the time was more structurally ingenious – its dome was built up by pouring successive rings of concrete against a temporary hemispherical dome of wood. Once dried, the concrete interior was ornately decorated by armies of marble and bronze workers (MacDonald 1976:42). The golden marble of the rotunda, the marble and porphyry circles and squares of the glowing pavement, and the geometry of the soaring canopy inspired awe (MacDonald 1976:34–35). The central oculus 45 m above, 62.80 m square, illuminated the building in which statues of gods and emperors stood (MacDonald 1965:110–111). With its cyclopic eye, the Pantheon was designed to capture light, to manipulate the great beam of solar radiance that poured in from the heavens, giving life to the building. Drenched in light, expanding and revolving with the sun, in its cosmic rotundity this temple of the world expressed all the ambition of the Roman state (MacDonald 1965:119–121). With solar circle set at the center of the whole, the planetary symbolism of the Pantheon spoke of immanent universality and was to influence architecture more than any other building (MacDonald 1976:11).

Equestrian Invasions from the Steppes

Rome was destined not to be eternal. Its demise in the west was in no small part hastened by the migration from northeast Asia of the nomadic Huns, who reached the Volga and Oxus c AD 355. Although there has been less than consensus on this point, the Huns now are identified with the Xiongnu who left the Chinese borderlands driving the Sarmatian Wusun and Tocharian Yuezhi before them. As we know, the Yuezhi headed south toward India to found the Kushan empire. Moving west, the Wusun became known as Alans and occupied territories previously inhabited by the Scythians. Arriving in Europe, the Huns absorbed some of the Alans but forced some, the Ossetes, to take refuge in the Caucasus and others to move through Russia into the Balkans; shortly we will discuss the Sarmatian myths of the Ossetic refugees in the Caucasus. Not only were the Huns a dominant force in propelling different tribal groups in domino style across the Eurasian steppes, they were also responsible for causing major upheavals and dislocations among Germanic tribes in central Europe. Arriving on the Danube, the Huns attacked the Goths who had spread from the Baltic down the Vistula. Defeated, the Visigoths surged south, despoiling all of Thrace to confront and destroy the imperial army and its eastern Roman emperor Valens on the plains of Hadrianople in AD 378. The Visigoths later invaded Greece and Italy, forcing the western emperor Honorius to retreat to Ravenna, protected from the barbarian cavalry by its walls and marshes. For the first time in 800 years, midst mayhem and pillage, Rome fell to the enemy. By AD 414 Ataulf had established a Visigothic kingdom in Gaul with its capital at Toulouse (Durant 1950:24–28, 35–37).

Meanwhile, in response to Roman withdrawal of legions from beyond the Alps to defend Italy against the Goths, the Sarmatian Alans formed an alliance with the Germanic Vandals and Suevi and crossed the Rhine to plunder Belgium, Gaul, and Aquitaine. Many Alans settled in southwestern Gaul, as is evident from the popular male names Alan and Alain, meaning fierce warrior, and the toponyms Allainville, Alaincourt, and Alencon-Orne (Littleton and Malcor 1994:234). In AD 409 the Vandals, Alans, and Suevi, 100,000 strong, invaded Spain (Littleton 1995:264). The havoc and destruction inflicted on Europe during those years was memorialized in the vernacular by Gregory, Bishop of Blois, when he denounced the excesses of the French Revolution as "vandalism," likening its terror to the destruction and atrocities perpetrated centuries earlier by the Vandals (Onesti 2002:12). In two years the equestrian invaders swept across the Iberian peninsula from the Pyrenees to the Straits, giving their name to the province of Andalucia and extending their conquest to the African coast (Carr 2002:26–28). Unable itself to intervene militarily, Rome bribed the Visigoths of southwestern Gaul to recapture the Iberian territories for the empire. In AD 429, under attack from the Visigoths, 80,000 Vandals and Alans chose to follow their leader Gaiseric *"rex Vandalorum et Alanorum"* to Africa. Moving expeditiously along the North African littoral, the invaders, Arian Christians themselves, were joined by rebellious Moors resentful of Roman rule and Donatist heretics long persecuted by orthodox Christianity. Rome signed a treaty in AD 435 ceding much of this territory to the barbarians and in AD 442, after Gaiseric had seized Carthage, recognized the independent North African kingdom. The Alans, originally the Sarmatian Wusun of the distant Ili valley who c 162 BC allied with the Han against the Tocharian Yuezhi, now with the Vandals controlled the second largest metropolis of the civilized world. They had arrived victorious in North Africa by traversing the entire Eurasian steppe and the breadth of the European continent, then traveling from the British channel to the southernmost tip of Europe's most westerly peninsula. But expansion did not stop there. With aggressive sea power Gaiseric conquered the Baleares, Corsica, and Sardinia, invading the coasts of Sicily, Italy, and Spain; no one knew where his cavalry-laden ships would land next. This unbridled piracy culminated in the sack of Rome in AD 455 (Bright 1987:10–11).

Behind the Alans, the Huns too had migrated with their flocks and tents westward across the steppes onto the Hungarian plain. Archaeology of their graves has shown the Huns to be primarily of Mongoloid extraction although with some Europoid admixture. Coming increasingly in contact with Rome, they had fought alongside the Sarmatian Alans as mercenaries in the imperial armies. In combat the Huns used the lasso as a weapon. Hun-Alan joint tactics consisted of encircling maneuvers of far-shooting Hun equestrian archers complemented by Alans fighting at close quarters with heavy lances and long swords. This combination of light and heavy cavalry, previously used by the Parthians, would again be employed successfully in the twelfth century by the Mongols (Hildinger 2001:63–64). In AD 434 two brothers, Bleda and Attila, politically controlled Hun territories that extended from west of the Rhine to the steppes north of the Black Sea, as a consequence threatening both halves of the Roman empire. Fearful of invasion, Theodosius II sent his best envoys to negotiate with the brothers. At the confluence of the Danube and Morava rivers, Bleda and Attila pitched their richly decorated tents opposite the Roman fortress, insisting on negotiating on horseback, from which neither brother deigned once to dismount during the entire conference. The resulting treaty of Margus required Constantinople to allow Hunnic merchants equal trading rights in the frontier zone and to increase gold payments to the Huns from 160 to 320 kg a year (Howarth 1994:36–37). If the Huns were not, as some contend, the actual Xiongnu,[7] one cannot help but notice that Bleda and Attila's behavior toward Byzantium showed a remarkable resemblance to Modu's "trick or treat" bargaining with the Chinese Han empire a few hundred years earlier. The Huns later extended their rule to the Caspian, and in AD 448 Attila's armies attacked Thrace and Illyria, taking thousands into slavery and forcing Theodosius II to increase the annual tribute threefold (Hildinger 2001:68).

Having bled the eastern Roman empire, Attila turned west and found an unlikely pretext for war. The sister of Valentinian III had been seduced by a chamberlain and banished to Constantinople. Desperate to escape a regime of fasting and penitence, she sent her gold ring to Attila, who interpreted this as a proposal of marriage. He immediately claimed Honoria along with half the western Roman empire as her dowry. When Valentinian protested, Attila declared war and in AD 451 led half a million men to the Rhine, attacked the towns of Trier and Metz, laying waste to the surrounding area, and then advanced toward Orleans. The general Aetius, allied with the Visigoth Theodoric I and the Alan Sangibanus, met Attila at Troyes. The fighting was ferocious, but Aetius at the end did not press the advantage he had gained, preferring only to discipline and not to destroy the Huns, since he needed them to counterbalance the Alans and Visigoths, both of whom he distrusted. Predictably the Huns resumed war the following year, invaded Italy, destroyed Aquileia, and exacted tribute from Milan. To escape Attila's cavalry, the peoples of Padua took refuge in the swamps of the Adriatic, where they founded the city of Venice. Attila advanced toward Rome, but plague had broken out in his army. He therefore elected to withdraw his army to Hungary, where he consoled himself by taking a new young

---

7 Probably Xiongnu elements were present but intermixed with other tribes encountered on their trans-Asian migration.

wife. In the accompanying festivities, inebriated, he probably suffered a ruptured artery in his head during the night, and suffocated in his sleep (Durant 1950:40–41; Hildinger 2001:69–72).

There followed a funeral according to ancient steppe tradition. Attila's body was placed in a silken tent pitched on the plains over which he had led his cavalry to war. Champion horsemen, chosen for their prowess from among the tribes, galloped wildly around him as in a circus to gladden the heart of their dead king. In celebrating his burial with great revelry, the Huns mixed grief and joy in an extraordinary manner. The mourners cut their hair and slashed their faces with their swords, so that the great warrior be mourned not with the tears of women, but with the blood of men. The sepulchral mound was heaped up and his body laid within, covered with gold, silver, and iron, the tribute of all nations. The weapons, gems, and other precious articles he had stripped from his enemies were placed in the grave, as were his attendants who were sacrificed over his body (Thompson 1996: 164–165).

Attila's empire disintegrated after his death. Hun military techniques were to persist, however, incorporated by the Byzantines into their armies along with federate Huns. But the steppes did not remain quiet for long. In the sixth century another nomad invasion from Asia took place. The Mongol Avars advanced across Pannonia to fortify their capital near Buda, calling it the Ring; their terrorization of central and eastern Europe would only end with Charlemagne's victory in AD 796. In the east the Byzantine emperors were better equipped to deal with the new menace. Repeatedly, the Avars attacked east Rome but without success. With chain mail, lance, broadsword, and now the Hun recurved composite bow used from the saddle, the east Roman trooper was well experienced with steppe warfare. He knew the hardiness of the nomads, their long-range archery, ambushes, encircling tactics, feigned retreats, and sudden returns. One innovation the Avars brought from eastern Asia was the metal stirrup. This was immediately adopted by the Byzantines, and its use spread rapidly to the Franks and across Europe. It has been claimed that the stirrup was the most important invention of the Middle Ages, in that it conferred greater stability to the heavily armored rider, with lance and long saber. On the other hand, we know that both the Parthians and the Sarmatians rode in full armor with heavy lances without stirrups. But in lance combat, there was always the danger the rider might be toppled by his own blow. The stirrup averted this problem by allowing the rider to grip the lance in a couched position, that is, held in the right hand and braced under the arm, whereas previously the lance had been held loosely. With this firmer grip, the equestrian warrior was able to attack an adversary not solely with the strength of one arm but with the full force of the charging horse, the saddle with a raised and reinforced back preventing him from being impelled backward over the crupper. This high-speed charge with couched lance was of prime significance in the development of medieval knightly warfare.

The Arthurian Epic – Chivalry in the West

In the Avars' wake, the Russians, Bulgars, and Magyars continued to advance from the steppes, eventually to suffer defeat. To ensure the salvation of these pagan subjects, the imposition of Christianity became Byzantium's moral obligation as missionaries were dispatched north. Practically, conversion operated as a device to tame the barbarian invaders and to facilitate their absorption into civil society. Further west, however, mass migrations of Germanic peoples totally engulfed the continent, and the Dark Ages descended on western Europe, to endure there for a half millennium. With the disappearance of centralized Roman rule from faraway Britain, the Celts were invaded by Picts and Scots from over the northern mountains and Angles, Saxons, and Danes from across the North Sea.

Out of this conflict arose the legends of King Arthur and the Knights of the Round Table – part Celtic, part Christian, perhaps even infused with more ancient Indo-European lore. Several key figures of these tales are transparently Celtic. The name of Arthur's father, Uther Pendragon, in Welsh signifies "Glorious Head of the Troops." Arthur's queen, Guinevere, is named after the fertility goddess (Welsh *Gwenhwyfar*, Old Irish *Findabair* "Born on the White," cf. Greek *Aphrodite* "Born on the Foam"). Arthur has been linked to Riothamus, a shadowy king of the Britons who waged military campaigns in Gaul (Mair 1998: 297, 299). But in 1925, Malone advanced the claim that the name Arthur was not Celtic in origin, attributing it instead to Lucius Artorius Castus, commander of the Sarmatian auxiliaries posted in Britain by the Roman emperor Marcus Aurelius. Furthermore, he contends that as Sarmatian auxiliaries joined with Celtic tribes to repel the barbarian from Britain, they contributed certain Iranian elements to the legend of their leader. In fact, it is quite possible that the tales of King Arthur represent a mythic composite of different war leaders' exploits in their resistance to the foreign invader. The name Arthur may have persisted over centuries of warring to denote "military chieftain," in much the same way as Caesar elsewhere became Kaiser or Czar (Nickel 1974:151).

In this great epic, young Arthur, barely past puberty, accompanied by his loyal paladin Sir Kay,[8] rode to the site where a miraculous sword had appeared and, where others before had failed, demonstrated his readiness for knighthood and his right to Uther Pendragon's throne by pulling the weapon from the stone. As we have seen, veneration of swords as divine was deeply rooted in the nomadic steppe tradition, where a sword embedded in the ground, rock, or altar symbolized the axis mundi and claim to territory; indeed, the tribal god worshiped by Sarmatians was a sword stuck upright in a stone (Littleton 1982:58–59; Nickel 1974:152). The feudal king Arthur and his queen Guinevere reigned over the court of Camelot, thought by some to be situated at Roman Camulodunum but more likely located midst the megalithic tumuli and hilltop fortresses of the northern or western regions, where Britons retained autonomy longest (Haywood 2001:90). From legends collected by Georges Dumezil (1930) from among the Sarmatian Ossetes of the Caucasus,[9] it has been observed that later aspects of Arthur's life show certain affinity with the adventures of the Nart hero Batraz (Littleton 1979:329). When accompanying the magician Merlin to the Lady of the Lake, King Arthur received a second sword, Excalibur.[10] Arthur retained this supernatural weapon until the hour of his death, its magical powers allowing him to perform miraculous feats. Similarly, Batraz acquired an Excalibur-like sword also from a mystically endowed woman, his aunt the seeress Santana. In the Nart sagas Batraz, wielding his mighty weapon, avenged his father's death and led his band of followers on wondrous adventures (Littleton 1995:264–265). Sung over the centuries by bards in Britain, comparable legends of the Celtic West told how Arthur *dux bellorum* defended Britons. These tales recounted noble deeds of ancient heroes: undertaking perilous adventures midst

---

[8] Possibly the legendary warrior Kai Khosrau of the Avestan *Yashts* (Littleton and Malcor 1994:126, 143).

[9] As noted earlier, the Ossetes found refuge from the Huns in the Caucasus. Today the Ossetes number half a million, still speak their northern Iranian language, and retain their Sarmatian myths. Over decades, the heroic Nart legends were collected by Georges Dumezil. Most recently these narratives have been studied by John Colarusso (2002).

[10] The earliest form, "Caliburnus," derived from Latin *chalybs* (steel) and Greek *Kalybes* (Sarmatian smiths) (Nickel 1974:152).

remote castles hidden in dark forests, searching for holy treasure, rescuing damsels in distress, and destroying dragons and other monsters. Orally transmitted over the generations, these tales were constantly enriched by folklore.

One important cycle of the Arthuriad was the Quest of the Holy Grail, which combined spirituality with chivalric and romantic adventure. Underpinning the mysticism of the grail was the concept of the cosmic circle and life's cyclic journey from birth to death. The symbol of a circular vessel as a source of sacred power was very ancient in Indo-European lore. During the first millennium BC, steppe tribes from the Don River to the Altai ritually utilized circular cauldrons to prepare sacrificial food for communal meals on calendar festivals (Kuzmina 2007:404). The firmament was widely thought to be an upturned bowl covering the earth, with the sun and the moon as vessels filled with divine beverage. For the Greeks the concept of circular vessel was fundamentally the *Krater* or fiery cup, the matrix of creation "in which was mixed the light of the sun." In Buddhism, the Tibetan goddess Narokhachoma drank blood from a human skull in rituals of transformation. In the west, the word *graal*, meaning a serving platter, carried the connotation of plenitude and may refer back to Celtic sagas in which great heroes banqueted in the abodes of the gods. Already familiar to us from the cosmic stew of the Epomeduos festival (see Chapter 4), the Celtic cauldron was the symbol of inspiration and rebirth. On the Gundestrup cauldron, the theme of rebirth was evident in the procession of warriors killed in battle waiting to be brought back to life by being dipped head-first into the cauldron by the god Cerunnos. King Arthur himself early went in search of the grail-cauldron, but like so many of his knights he returned empty handed (Mahoney 2000:9; Matthews 1981:8–9, 51, 78). By contrast in the Ossetic Nart sagas, Batraz, in his quest, succeeded in gaining stewardship of the sacred Nartymonga, a cauldron-like chalice (Littleton 1979:327).

During the fifth century Christian missionaries spread north to evangelize Europe, and Alans, Sarmatian settlers in France, accompanied these monks. Around this time, Sir Lancelot (Alanus a Lot)[11] entered the Arthuriad driving the typical Sarmatian *charrette* (cart) (Littleton and Malcor 1994:98). Under the influence of Christianity, the ancient Celtic imagery became overlaid with themes of Christ's sacrificial death and

---

[11] The Lot River drainage was a region heavily settled by the Alans.

rebirth. The grail became associated with the Eucharist and the chalice from which Christ drank at the Last Supper, when in the form of bread and wine the disciples ate of Christ's body and drank of his blood (Matthews 1981:30). To represent the Table of the Last Supper, the magician-enchanter Merlin constructed the Round Table. This *tabula rotunda*[12] was ascribed supernatural powers and linked by iconography to the wheel of fortune, but it was also a chivalric institution. To obviate the contentious rivalries of bellicose barons, the king led his court to assemble in a circle of 50 knights, all bound by the rules of chivalry (Biddle 2000:17). Over time, the number of knights increased. Then one Pentecost, when all were assembled, there was an extraordinary roar of thunder and the palace became illuminated a hundredfold. The Holy Grail appeared veiled, floating on a beam of sunshine; all were transfixed by the beauty of the spectacle before it miraculously disappeared. The knights then pledged to undertake the holy quest and set out on horseback from Camelot carrying relics of the saints. But the search for the Holy Grail was surrounded by codes to be solved, by taboos, and by severe penalties for presumption or ignoble action. Only the pure were eligible, and they were required to undergo ordeals of courage and faith to accomplish their goal. Lancelot succeeded in approaching the vessel, but because of his adulterous love for Arthur's queen Guinevere, he was rejected and temporarily blinded. Only three men were able to contemplate the true grail and partake of its mystery: Galahad, the sinless virgin knight; Perceval, who had learned the use of arms and horsemanship from the warrior women Witches of Caer Loyw; and Bors, the modest ordinary man (Matthews 1981:6–7).

When Lancelot returned to Camelot to resume his sinful love with Guinevere, war ensued between the lineages of Arthur and Lancelot, extending as far as Brittany/Armorica. Many knights of the Round Table were slain, and Arthur was mortally wounded in battle (Pastoureau and Gousset 2002:10). As he lay dying, the king bade Sir Bedivere throw his sword Excalibur into the sea. Twice the knight attempted to deceive his lord by concealing the sword, but Arthur, detecting the lie, insisted. The third time, Sir Bedivere obediently hurled the sword into the water. Marvelously, a hand appeared from the depths and seized Excalibur, then sank slowly beneath the waves. When this event was reported,

---

[12] In the first Round Table there were 13 seats, of which the last, that of the traitor Judas, was left vacant. This *siege perilleux* was maintained in later tables.

the king knew it was his time to part and passed on a barge to the isle of Avalon, the Celtic otherworld. In amazing parallel to this Excalibur episode, the Ossetic Batraz, after slaughtering many of his own people, announced to his Nart followers that his own death was imminent and that his magical sword must be consigned to the sea. In similar fashion, the Narts initially tried twice to hide the sword but finally following orders flung the wondrous weapon into the waters. As in the case of Excalibur a prodigious event occurred: a violent storm raged, lightning streaked across the skies, and the waves rolled blood red. Knowing this, the dying leader willingly left this life (Littleton 1995:265). Whether transmitted by the Sarmatian Iazyges and Alans across Eurasia to Britain or derived from a common ancient Indo-European tradition of heroism, the analogous structures of the Celtic and Ossetic myths are striking: the internecine battles, the mortal wound, early deception of the leader's dying wishes, the final relinquishing of the miraculous sword, the phenomenal seizure of the mighty weapon by the waters, and the war leader's passage to the otherworld.

The dramatic upheavals expressed in the Arthurian legends reflected the continentwide *volkerwanderung* that swept aside classic Rome and propelled Europe into the Middle Ages. The disappearance of central-ized Roman rule from western Europe resulted in political fragmenta-tion that fostered the development of feudalism in military response to territorial aggression. In this near-moneyless system, the monarch retained numerous knights at his court but also distributed large tracts of land to nobles, who themselves granted territories to lesser knights. This land was sufficient to support the knight's family as he practiced mounted combat in preparation for war, while his vassals worked the soil and served as infantry. The system was characterized by loyalty expressed in oath that in time of hostilities the knight would render military service to his noble master, who in turn was obligated to the sovereign. These land grants were hereditary, with military duty passing from father to son. The same was applicable to church lands, which too furnished knights to the king during wartime. Heavy cavalry would become the battle arm of medieval warfare; cavalier, *chevalier*, and *caballero*[13] – all derived from the Latin vernacular of horseman – reflected the distinction of nobility and gave rise to the western institu-tion of chivalry (Hopkins 2004:22, 26).

---

[13] Germanic *Knecht* and Old English *cniht* signify military follower.

Arthur's fame was not restricted to Britain, nor to the Dark Ages. To escape the invasions of the Angles and Saxons from the north, many Celtic Cornish and Welsh fled across the English Channel to settle along the north and west coasts of Brittany. They took with them a wealth of legends lauding their noble king Arthur and the exploits of his knights-errant. These songs and stories were carried across northern France and in the twelfth century were immortalized in the Old French romantic poetry of Chretien de Troyes at the court of Champagne. Writers of diverse nationalities composed later works detailing the separate romances of the Arthuriad that spread widely across medieval Europe. In recent centuries, renewed interest in these medieval ballads and romances by Sir Walter Scott and Wordsworth fueled an Arthurian revival led by Alfred, Lord Tennyson, whose *Idylls of the King* attained immense popularity during the Victorian era. The grail continued into the twentieth century in T. S. Eliot's *The Waste Land* (Mahoney 2000:3, 37, 41; Barber 1979:2–3). To this day, the Arthurian epic still inspires plays, musicals, operas, even films, such as *Star Wars*, where Jedi Knights with light sabers defend the weak against oppression.

Byzantium – Equestrian Bastion of Christianity in the East

As barbarian invasions from the north and east convulsed Europe, imperial rule shifted from Rome to Byzantium. Just as Celtic kingdoms would be the outposts of Christianity in the west, so Constantinople would be its citadel in the east, albeit a beleaguered one. As we have seen, eastern Rome was repeatedly confronted by new emigres from the steppes. But there was a more ancient foe further east – Persia. As early as 54 BC, Marcus Crassus,[14] envious of Caesar's and Pompey's victories in the west, as governor of Syria was ambitious for military conquest in the east. Disdaining the king of Armenia's advice to enter Parthia through the mountains, Crassus instead marched across the plains to Carrhae, there to tackle the formidable Parthian heavy and light cavalries. In steppe fashion the Parthians, shooting nonstop from afar, encircled the Romans. Crassus thought to endure this, expecting the arrows soon to be exhausted, but camel trains brought up fresh supplies of arrows. Then Crassus's son Publius charged the Parthians with 1,300 cavalry, archers and legionaries; deceived by a feigned retreat, his force became separated from the infantry and was totally destroyed.

---

[14] Conqueror of the Spartacus slave revolt.

The following day Crassus himself was treacherously slain, his head removed to play Pentheus in Euripides' *Bacchae* at the Parthian court. It was the worst military rout for Rome since the days of Hannibal, and Persia would persist as a formidable Asian foe for centuries to come (Hildinger 2001:42–46).

The city first known to the classical world as Byzantium but later as Constantinople was founded in 658 BC by early Greek colonists. In AD 324 Constantine, reuniting the two halves of the Roman empire, sought for himself an eastern capital better situated to defend his Asian borders against the Sasanian Persians – successors to the Parthians. At this time, Constantine also concluded that the empire, in its decadence, needed new spiritual force and decided to fuse Christianity with Greco-Roman religion. Devoted to the god Apollo, whose cult prevailed among followers of Zarathustra, the emperor was a tolerant monotheist. He therefore reversed the earlier policy of persecution and granted free religious and civil rights to Christians. Combining the spiritual power of Christ with the temporal authority of Caesar, he was to rule, semidivine, over church and state. By linking Christ with war in this manner, Constantine launched a Greco-Roman Christianity that in its spread across Europe would absorb as local saints many other Indo-European deities. Aiming at a syncretism of diverse philosophies, Constantine imported from across the empire the finest ancient sculptures to grace public spaces. In the center of the Forum, to the accompaniment of chanted *Kyrie Eleison*, an immense gold statue of Constantine as the Apollo sun god was mounted on a porphyry column 30 m high; the rays from his crown shining upon the city were thought to embody nails from the true cross. The emperor's mother Helena had traveled to Jerusalem, where excavating at Cavalry she had uncovered the crown of thorns, the true cross, and other holy remains. Constantinople would be the guardian city of these sacred relics. Upon succession, Constantius II continued his father's plans in constructing in AD 360 the great basilica of *Hagia Sophia* (Holy Wisdom) (Kinross 1972:16–18, 20), thereby incorporating into the Christian church the Zoroastrian concept of Ahura Mazda (Lord Wisdom).

Thousands of workmen raised sea walls as fortifications and with artists constructed sumptuous buildings. At the secular axis of the Byzantine world in the popular heart of the city, the Hippodrome was erected to accommodate 70,000 spectators in honor of the public passion for horse racing. In its center stood the bronze serpentine column from Delphi commemorating the Greek victory over the Persians at Platea in 479 BC. At inauguration, a golden chariot drew the gilded statue of the emperor around the Hippodrome; his imperial *kathisma* box was adorned with four horses of gilded bronze, ancient sculpture of Lysippos. Great festivals were celebrated with exhibitions of exotic fauna, animal hunts and fights, and athletic contests. But the 24 horse and chariot races provided the greatest excitement, the jockeys and charioteers in different colored garb receiving the heated applause of the crowds. In Byzantium high office was restricted to an aristocracy of *comites* and *duces* appointed by the all-powerful emperor. Only at the Hippodrome could the populace express political petition or dissent. It could request favors, demand reforms, accuse abusive officials, even criticize the emperor himself in the dignity of his imperial seat. Since there was much rivalry among the competitors, the emperor easily maintained his authority by playing off one faction against another. The equestrian factions, far from being mere sporting associations, had evolved into the equivalent of political parties that reflected real social, economic, and religious cleavages within the population. From the principal four, Red, White, Green, and Blue, there had emerged into prominence the Blues and Greens, whose polarization expressed the rift between Christian orthodoxy and monophysitism, the religious controversy prevailing at that time. These factions were also called on to perform the important military duties of defending the walls of Constantinople in times of barbarian attack and on occasions even proclaimed emperors. In AD 532, burdened by heavy taxation, political corruption, and economic discontent, the Blues and the Greens joined forces in the Nika revolt in an attempt to depose the emperor Justinian. The rebels raged through the city during a week of frenzied destruction. Hagia Sophia, part of the imperial palace, and other public buildings were burned to the ground. The general Belisarius finally routed the insurgents, slaughtering 30,000 on the floor of the Hippodrome (Cameron 1976:2, 46; Kinross 1972: 18, 27).

In the sixth century, Constantinople, with a population of one million, was the richest, most beautiful city of the civilized world. Committed to restoring his capital after the riot, Justinian resolved to build an even mightier church than Constantine's. Never before had construction been undertaken on such a large scale. The creation of Hagia Sophia called, not merely for the technical skill of the engineer, but for the intellectual vision of the scientist and the imaginative perception of the artist. Four centuries earlier the Roman Pantheon had relied on concrete, rigid enough to resist the thrusts in the structure. But the Byzantines built in bricks and mortar, materials too flexible to counter the stress of the dome on the vaults and supporting arches, requiring therefore the reinforcing devices of buttresses, barrel vaults, and half domes. In Hagia Sophia the spherical dome finally attained its true form. Over 30 m in diameter, resting on four triangular curved pendentives, it appeared not to be supported by masonry but as a celestial tent to be suspended from heaven (Kinross 1972:35, 43–45). So brilliantly did the gilded surface of the roof flash that gold seemed to flow from the dome in a molten stream, like the Holy Spirit flying down from heaven. Set on a triangular headland facing east, this spiritual lighthouse commanded the confrontation west and east of two continents, Europe and Asia. Poised between the Black and Aegean seas, Hagia Sophia stood at the center of the known world (Kinross 1972:14–15).

Just as extraordinary igneous rock was transported over hundreds of kilometers in construction of the solar temple at Stonehenge, to ensure that the Church of Holy Wisdom surpassed all other, priceless building materials were procured from all parts of the empire as far west as Gaul. Marble of every hue was obtained from the most famed sources. Through the dome's corona of 40 windows played a heliophany of light, sending piercing rays of sun into the vaulted interior (MacDonald 1962:36). The brightness of Hagia Sophia was further heightened by gold mosaic – 4 acres in all – that decorated the ceiling and the surfaces of the vaults and arches, then in turn was reflected in the walls and floors of polished marble. Light was further diffused throughout the church by a thousand lamps and candelabra hovering at different levels across the chromatic void (Kinross 1972:36–37). Below the great dome, in the center of the nave was the omphalos (earth navel), a great disc of dark marble set in a square frame. A millennium after the great Colosseum lay in ruins, Justinian's solar edifice would stand to proclaim Rome's might to the world.

On the day of inauguration, Justinian ceremonially left his palace in a four-horse chariot to perform the ancient sacrifice of 10,000 birds, 600 stags, 6,000 sheep, and 1,000 oxen and to donate 30,000 bushels of meal to the needy. In a ceremony to be repeated on the same date each year for the next nine centuries, the emperor with the patriarch led the procession into Hagia Sophia as the first rosy beams of light entering the church leapt from arch to arch, chasing away deep shadows. The nobles followed chanting hymns of praise to the sacred drama. Ancient fire temple of the sun, now Christian basilica, Hagia Sophia stood at the eastern edge of Europe, its dome/earth mountain crowned by Christ's gilded cross/tree of life. In AD 553 earthquakes damaged the eastern arch. By AD 563 the church was restored and stabilized (Kinross 1972:15, 45), as well it needed be strengthened – for the turbulent millennium that lay ahead.

ARABIAN CONQUEST FROM THE SOUTH

TURN OF THE ERA TO MID-FIRST MILLENNIUM AD

Throughout its history, Byzantium had repeatedly repelled assaults by nomads from the Eurasian steppes and advances from Persia in the east, but in the seventh century AD it would face yet another nomad, this time from the south. From the sands of Arabia, Muslim equestrian armies would soon surge north to defy the civilizations of eastern Rome and Sasanian Persia. Constantinople, the beleaguered citadel of Christianity, would stand firm against Arab offensives from both land and sea. But Persia would fall to the nomad invader and convert to Islam. In time, though, Persia would resurge to reassert its Zoroastrian identity, reshaping Islam in the process. Equestrian tribes from the Asian steppes and African deserts would also convert to and invigorate Islam. But before we turn to the Arab invader from the south who shortly would dominate the arid and semiarid lands of Asia and North Africa, let us first view briefly the imprint on the Middle East left by three millennia of Indo-European invasions.

Crossroads of Continents

For thousand of years, equestrian armies had swept across this region from the north leaving their mark on territories from the Jaxartes and the Indus in the east to Anatolia in the west. As we have seen, by the time of the Seleucids these lands represented a vast commingling of cultures. Following Alexander, Greek had replaced Aramaic as the lingua franca and the Greek alphabet was adapted to the Indo-European languages of greater Iran. Yet Zoroastrianism existed alongside Hellenic polytheism as high-turbaned Magi tended great ever-burning fire altars in temples where Greek cultic statues were venerated. A longing for the Zoroastrian cosmic savior influenced Gnostic and Jewish thought, and in this epoch even Jews proselytized widely. Armenia, an independent kingdom paying tribute to the Seleucids, served as a buffer state between east and west; the Armenians worshipped Ahura Mazda but later in defiance of the Sasanians embraced Christianity. In Bactria, the Kushans, while preserving their fire sanctuaries, issued coins bearing Zoroastrian, Greek, and Buddhist deities. Becoming more Indianized, they adopted Prakrit and patronized Buddhism. As Mahayana Buddhism spread northward through Central Asia, it flourished in the Iranian borderlands as a rival to Zoroastrianism, at the same time incorporating the Zoroastrian concept of the saoshyant savior as the future Buddha Maitreya (Boyce 1987:83–90).

Nowhere was the extreme cosmopolitanism of this region more highly epitomized than at the sepulchral tumulus of Commagene (today Nemrud Dagi). While the monumental basilica of the Christian Hagia Sophia stood facing east from the very edge of Europe, across Anatolia in the southeastern mountains of the Anti-Taurus there rose yet another solar temple, the tomb of Antiochus I of Commagene (69–34 BC). Kummuha-Kummuhu, the city kingdom of second-millennium-BC Hittite-Assyrian texts, had endured for centuries on the fertile west bank of the Euphrates River, along with other Neo-Hittite kingdoms strung out across southern Anatolia into northern Syria. With the Alexandrine invasion and Seleucid reconquest, it had become hellenized to Commagene. Freed of Seleucid dominion in the second century BC, after brief independence, Commagene in AD 72 was incorporated as a province into the Roman empire by Vespasian, who deposed king Antiochus IV on account of his political intriguing with the Parthians against Rome. In the ancient tradition of the distant steppes, the hierothesion of Antiochus I was a conical tumulus 150 m wide and 45 m high, but set atop a 2,100 m mountain summit, as a landmark clearly visible at great distance from all directions. From its elevated height, it commanded a vast panorama of deep gorges and ridges, traversed by caravan routes to and from the Parthian empire (Sanders 1996:17–20). As with so many other Indo-European shrines, worshippers from afar converged on the cult center of Antiochus I, undertaking the arduous ascents along the winding, processional trails to the mountaintop sanctuary, where they performed sacrificial rites before the sepulchral tumulus (Sanders 1996:92–93). Nor was the superluminary orb absent. At dawn each day, the rays of the rising sun struck the peak in dazzling illumination, igniting the eastern side of the mountain, its limestone tumulus and statues a fiery red. Centrally enthroning a colossal Zeus-Ohrmazd[1] flanked by other tutelary Greco-Persian deities, the massive tumulus blended Anatolian traditions with Hellenistic and Iranian elements (Sanders 1996:31). Starting with Alexander, stelae to the south detailed the Macedonian and Seleucid ancestry of Antiochus, while stelae to the north showed his Persian and Commagenian ancestors beginning with Darius the Great (Sanders 1996:2–4).[2]

Long, long after Antiochus's death, this region would continue to be split between west and east. In AD 224 Parthian rule in Persia ended with their defeat in battle by Ardashir, son of Sasan, priest of Persepolis. Driven by religious fervor, Ardashir resolved to destroy western influence and to reconquer the empire of the Achaemenids. Thus under the Sasanians, Zoroastrianism was reinforced, the fire cult elaborated, and the army refurbished with its backbone of cavalry. In 260 Shapur I attacked Antioch, captured the Roman emperor Valerian – to use him as a foot stool from which to mount his horse – and deported thousands of Roman prisoners to forced labor in Iran. As the Sasanians advanced across Armenia to the Tigris, Persian power and prosperity grew. To ensure the loyalty of his allies, the sovereign Ohrmazd III distributed silvered platters on which, as the deity Ahura Mazda, he is depicted enacting on horseback the famed "Parthian shot" against the evil Ahriman, represented first as a lion ready to pounce then slain beneath the horse's hooves. By the mid-first millennium, the most enlightened Sasanian monarch Khosrau I (Chosroes) had instituted many reforms in irrigation, land reclamation, and scholarly learning. Khosrau was also an accomplished polo player, as was his beautiful consort Shirin. The poet Nezami wove a beautiful love story around the two monarchs' polo matches with their courtiers. From Persia polo spread to Byzantium, Arabia, Tibet, China, and Japan, where the polo stick featured prominently in the heraldry of those cultures. Declaring holy war against Christians, Khosrau II sacked Jerusalem in 614, massacred 90,000 Christians, and captured the most holy relic of the True Cross. On both sides, no longer were rulers indifferent to the beliefs of their masses. By means of a hierarchically organized clergy, each emperor vigorously promoted religious conformity across his realm, with warfare

---

[1] As noted earlier, Ohrmazd is the later term for Zoroastrian Ahura Mazda, literally Lord Wisdom, directly analogous to Hagia Sophia, Holy Wisdom.
[2] Obviously, genealogical legerdemain on the part of Antiochus.

assuming an increasingly religious character and religious deviation equated with political dissidence. Within 10 years, the Byzantines countered the Sasanian offensive. In retaliation for the desecration of Jerusalem, the new emperor Heraclius destroyed Clorumia, the birthplace of Zoroaster, and extinguished the sacred light; by repulsing all armies sent against him he succeeded in regaining many of his former territories. Thus after four centuries of inconclusive, unremitting conflict, thoroughly depleted, the imperial armies of both powers had fought to a complete stalemate (Durant 1950:142–147; Harper 2007:25; Spencer 1971:2–3).

Byzantine and Sasanian Imperial Policies toward Arabia

South of the two empires lay Semitic Arabia, since the third millennium BC an intermediary in the long-distance maritime trade between the Indus Valley and the Middle East. By the end of the third millennium BC, the one-humped camel or dromedary had been domesticated in Arabia; by the end of the second, camel nomads had established a highly prosperous trade in spices and incense with Mesopotamia (Schwartz 2006:256). In the course of the first millennium BC, the dromedary dispersed north to the Middle East, east toward Persia and India, and west to Africa, reaching the Sahara a few centuries before the turn of the era. As Midianite cameleers (*aribi*) advanced north through biblical lands, their herds inflicted great damage on the agricultural fields of settled populations. These migratory nomads roamed the deserts of Arabia and adjoining territories, leading their flocks of sheep, goats, and camels from one watering hole to another. Advances in saddle technology rendered the dromedary highly efficient in transport. Faster than the Bactrian camel, the dromedary was capable of carrying burdens up to 200 kg at a pace of 2–3 km per hour and in raiding could be ridden over distances of 65–80 km per day. Due to its low tolerance for extreme cold, however, it never wholly replaced the Bactrian camel in Central Asia, although hybridization of the two types occurred. But in warfare, even at a gallop, the dromedary could never deliver the momentum and impact of the cavalry charge. While fighting with lance from camelback was practiced, it was not the easiest mode of combat since the camel was notoriously unresponsive to rider command. In armed hostilities, everywhere the warhorse was the preferred steed. Thus, in the waterless desert, the dromedary came to fulfill the important function of supporting horses, which to conserve energy during travel were tied to the cinch of the camel's saddle and mounted only at time of attack. The Arab's camel transported containers of water for horse consumption. It also provided as much as 10 kg of milk per day for horse nourishment en route; additionally in time of dire emergency its stomach could be slit to access its reserve of water (Bulliet 1990:99; Hill 1975:34; Kohler-Rollefson 1996:282, 286–291).

Not all Arabia was desert, however. Horses were raised in oases and in the green valleys of the central Nejd tableland. Along the monsoon lands of the southern coast urban culture flourished. Situated at the crossroads of ancient commerce, these beautiful towered cities competed for control of the trade in silk, cotton, spices, aromatics, ivory, and gold from India, Africa, and China. This rich traffic then traveled along caravan routes to the shores of the Mediterranean. The most valued item of this commerce were the wootz steel ingots from India, for which imperial Rome had readily traded silver and gold to make their famous short swords. Iron had reached India in the later stages of the Indo-Aryan invasions. But as early as the mid-first millennium BC, the Indians at Hyderabad had devised techniques that far surpassed merely heating iron in a forge to absorb carbon from burning charcoal. They had learned to fill clay crucibles with small pieces of wrought iron combined with wood and leaves from specific plants. Sealed on top with a layer of clay, the crucibles were placed in pits 1 m deep filled with charcoal and were air-blasted to high temperatures for several hours of firing. As the iron melted, carbon of the plant material became evenly distributed throughout the molten liquid, producing the highest quality steel ingots in great demand all over the civilized world. Indian methods of steel manufacture were kept secret for centuries, but triumphant Arab cavalries would carry this superior steel technology as far west as Toledo (Raymond 1984:78–80).

Byzantine and Sasanian imperial policies toward Arabia therefore were twofold: to contain the predatory southern nomads on the one hand but also to gain control of their lucrative trade routes. To accomplish the former, alliances were forged with powerful Arab tribal confederations, such as the Ghassanids and Lakmids of Syria and Iraq. Equipped with imperial weapons and warhorses, these troops could deliver harsh reprisals to tribes 800 km distant in the Arabian interior (Donner 1981:43–49). In pursuit of their latter objective, the Byzantines established Christian churches and monasteries in the north, while the Persians appointed governors along the Gulf coast. Confrontation between the two rival empires dominated the politics of the era, yet neither could subjugate the peninsula. In 522, Byzantium encouraged Christian Abyssinian invasion of Jewish Himyar in southwest Arabia. In 575, Persia countered by sending an army into Yemen (Durant 1950:156). Clearly by the late sixth century AD tensions in the Gulf region were escalating.

The Prophet Muhammad

In the marginal lands of Arabia, outside the jurisdiction of any state, one means of establishing a power base was the *haram*, a religious site controlled by descendants of the pious founder of a cult. Since violence was forbidden in the sacred precinct of the haram, the settlement often thrived as a market town of commercial transactions, in which members of the holy family gained social prominence in adjudicating political disputes. The trading networks participating in these markets were bound by strong religious ties to the amphictyonic center and thereby developed a firm regional economy (Donner 1981:34–36). Near the west Arabian coast, Ukaz was one such market center; the holy sanctuary of the *Kaaba* was located nearby at the Mecca cult center. The Quraysh tribe appointed the priests and guardians of this shrine, managed its revenues, and controlled the government. At the beginning of the sixth century, the Quraysh were divided into two factions: one led by Hashim, a rich merchant and philanthropist, the other by Umayya, his jealous nephew (Hitti 2002:184–185; Kennedy 2007:44).

Great-grandson of Hashim, Muhammad ibn Abd Allah was born in Mecca in 570. Early orphaned, he was reared by his uncle Abu-Talib to be a caravan leader. At the age of 25 he entered into the employ of Khadijah, a rich widow whom he married. Their daughter Fatima later married Muhammad's cousin, Ali, son of Abu-Talib. Accustomed to meditate, Muhammad experienced visions of *Jibril* (Gabriel), from whom he received god's command to reject all idols. In AD 613, convinced of divine revelation, he advocated attainment of salvation in the next world through adherence to the faith of the one god, charity to the poor, and strict sexual modesty. Many of his visions dealt with social injustice, which attracted people of lower social stature. On his miraculous Night Journey, Muhammad was transported in his sleep from Mecca to Jerusalem, where the winged white horse Buraq awaited him at the Wailing Wall of the ruined Jewish Temple. Astride Buraq, the Prophet ascended through the seven levels of heaven (*miraj*) to speak with Allah, Moses, and Jesus, thus linking Islam with the two older

religions. Elevated to a supreme state of consciousness, this peak defin-
ing experience set the Prophet on the inexorable course of his life mission
to establish Islam. Muhammad's family was immediately supportive,
but the new faith drew strong criticism from Mecca's mercantile community, long accustomed to receive substantial revenues from pilgrims
worshipping the Kaaba's diverse tribal gods.

Muhammad's message, however, found sympathetic ears in the citizens of Yathrib, who invited him to arbitrate some factional disputes. In
622 his flight to that city (later Medina) was known as the hegira (*hijra*)
and marked the beginning of the Muslim calendar (Donner 1999:6–9,
23). In Medina, he received further revelation – the Koran. Several battles ensued between Mecca and Medina. Eventually a truce was reached
with the treaty of al-Hudaybiya in 628, which permitted Muslims to
make the pilgrimage to Mecca. Muhammad's intimate knowledge of
the economic circumstances of the nomads and the several political
marriages he had contracted with them enabled him to form military
alliances with tribal groups. With their backing, Muhammad in 630
marched on Mecca, which he occupied without bloodshed (Donner
1981:62–63). The Prophet declared a general amnesty, treating his enemies leniently. He then inaugurated a monotheist sanctuary by destroying all idols around the Kaaba, except the Black Stone. In control of the
ancient market and agricultural center of Hijaz on which the surrounding nomads depended, Muhammad now commanded the tribesmen's
staunch support; he also had established far-flung contacts across the
peninsula. Thus the Quraysh clan and the towns, oases, and tribes of
Arabia concluded a nonaggression pact, their profession of loyalty constituting submission (*islam*) to the will of Allah. The five pillars of Islam
(*arkan al-islam*) laid down by the Prophet were *al-shahadah*, the primary
profession of Islamic faith in god's unity "*la ilaha illa Allah; Muhammad
rasul Allah*" (there is no god but Allah; Muhammad is his messenger); *al-
salat*, the statutory prayer and praise of Allah directed toward the Great
Mosque of Mecca five times a day; *al-zakah*, compulsory payment of
yearly tithe to provide alms for the needy; *al-sawm*, the monthlong fast
during Ramadan, the ninth lunar month of the Islamic calendar; and
al-hajj, the annual pilgrimage to Mecca during the twelfth or last month
of the Islamic year, to be fulfilled at least once in the lifetime of a believer
(Ozigboh 2002:41–46). In 632 Muhammad died, having founded a new
Arab state but without leaving a male heir. During his life, he sought
to restrain idolatry and superstition. Combining elements of Judaism,
Christianity, and his native creed, he forged a monotheistic religion that,

simple, clear, and strong, afforded Arabs a means to transcend tribal affiliation and to achieve political unity with a common code of laws.

Military Expansion of the Islamic State out of Arabia

But in the wake of the Prophet's death, many tribes felt their contract too had expired and no longer wished to pay the tax they had previously contracted. In the face of this *Ridda* – apostasy or blasphemous repudiation of Islam – Muhammad's successor Abu Bakr, the first caliph, sent armed troops led in large part by the ruling elite of settled townships. Every Ridda movement challenged the hegemony of the embryonic state based at Medina and threatened Islamic domination of the Arabian peninsula. Two years of campaigning completed the process of political unification that Muhammad had begun. After the ceaseless military activities of the Ridda wars, Abu Bakr's forces had come to assume almost the character of a standing army. The political consolidation he attained by traditional and innovative means had succeeded in bringing the nomadic element firmly under state control, thereby harnessing the full military potential of the Arab population (Donner 1981:84–90).

One effect of the Ridda wars had been disruption of trade in Arabia, placing many nomads in dire economic straits and prompting extension of tribal raiding into the Fertile Crescent. The communities in the marginal desert lands north of the peninsula had blood ties with the Arabs. There were enticing economic benefits to be gained: acquisition of new lands, taxes on conquered populations, booty in wealth or slaves, and political consolidation of the Arabian tribes in the fringe territories of Syria and Iraq – all of which would bring the Muslims into direct clash with the Byzantine and Sasanian empires (Donner 1981: 6, 271). Following one confrontation with the Byzantines, the Arab general Khalid ibn al-Walid was redirected from Iraq by the caliph to relieve hard-pressed Arab forces in Suwa. Between the Arabs and their destination in Syria lay five nights and six days of totally waterless desert. The Bedouins did not possess sufficient water skins to supply water for the men and horses over that distance. To overcome this obstacle, by initially withholding water they forced the thirsty camels to drink copious amounts, then tied the camels' mouths to prevent their chewing cud and contaminating water in the stomach. During travel each day a specific number of camels were slaughtered, their stomachs slit to provide water to the men and warhorses (Donner 1981:121–122). Khalid's successful advance into Syria in 634 revealed the Arabs' astounding effectiveness on the desert steppe. It also demonstrated the high control exercised from the caliph's capital at Medina and clearly showed that the Muslim advance was a coordinated series of military operations. With the military zeal of the *jihad* (holy war) and Khalid's tactical genius, the Muslims successfully dominated the open countryside of southern Syria. Equipped with arms looted from the former Persian protectorates on their peninsula, the Arabs, agile horsemen, fought effectively with a lot less drinking water and attacked at the hottest time of the day (Nicolle 1994:20, 89). Inured to the hardships of the desert, they were ably led and disciplined. Arab victories were, no doubt, in part due to religious zeal, but in fact, both Byzantium and Sasanian Persia were corrupt and in considerable political turmoil. Byzantine persecution of Nestorian and Monophysite sects had alienated large segments of the Syrian and Egyptian populations, even the military garrisons (Durant 1950:188).

The most important battle between Islam and Byzantium occurred at Yarmuk, near the Sea of Galilee, in 636. In preparation for the hostilities, the second caliph, Umar ibn al-Khattab, had ensured the systematic collection of warhorses from the conquered Syrian territories. The Yemeni provided war camels and formidable swords of wootz imported from India (Nicolle 1994:20, 40). The Christian Armenian field commander, Vahan, first attacked both flanks while holding the center. Events initially went badly for the Arabs, who once in full retreat, according to legend, were shamed into resuming the offensive by their womenfolk wielding tent poles. Days of fierce fighting ensued. At a critical point, the Byzantine cavalry was separated from the main army when the Arabs captured the bridge over the Wadi Ruqqad. Penned in between the Ruqqad and Yarmuk gorges, the Byzantines' only avenue of escape was to scramble down the ravines in a retreat during which many perished (Nicolle 1994:69–77). Yarmuk was a complete rout of the numerically superior and better equipped Christian army, a stunning triumph for the Arabs, and a miraculous demonstration of divine favor for Islam.

Horses of the Deserts

There is no firm agreement where the Arabian horse originated, although it is more generally thought that it first appeared in North Africa and then spread to Arabia, rather than vice versa. As was seen in Chapter 1, there is abundant evidence of ancestral asses and zebras in Africa but no fossils of the wild horse *Equus ferus*. While primary domestication of the donkey occurred in Africa, the domesticated horse was introduced there from elsewhere. As detailed in Chapter 4, the Hyksos first brought the warhorse and chariot from southwestern Asia into Egypt in the seventeenth century BC. Earlier, in the discussion of the spread of the domestic donkey from Africa to northern Europe, it was remarked that in the colder climes this animal developed a heavier body and shorter limbs. Precisely the opposite seems to have occurred in the introduction of the horse to Africa. The northerly Eurasian steppe was the natural habitat of the wild horse, where the native Przewalski horse is a stocky animal with a heavy head and short ears. Similarly, the famed Nisaean horse of the Medes from the Caspian region was fully fleshed and ram headed. In the course of its diffusion from the steppes southward to the Near East, in accordance with Bergmann's and Allen's rules, the horse in its biological adaptation seems to have become a more gracile animal with long, fine limbs. Remains of horses from seventeenth-century-BC Sudan and fifteenth-century-BC Thebes exhibit the same fine limbs characteristic of horses in Egypt and Arabia today. And both skeletons share a feature in common with the modern Arabian horse, namely, five lumbar vertebrae in contrast to the customary six of other domestic breeds. At Mileiha in the United Arab Emirates, 2,000 years ago Arabian horses were elaborately interred with bejeweled trappings. Frequently in ancient paintings, Egyptian horses appear bedecked with ostrich plumes, their elegant limbs, slender bodies, and small heads showing a remarkable resemblance to the modern Arabian horse. Their slighter build most likely was an adaptation to dry, hot desert conditions (Bin-Sultan al-Nahyan 1998:7; Clutton-Brock 1992:80–83).

From Pharaonic records, we are also aware of horse presence elsewhere in North Africa, for at the battle of Perire in the thirteenth century BC the pharaoh Merenptah was attacked from the west by horses and chariots of a coalition of Libyans, Achaeans, and Dorians. Probably around this time, the domestic horse and chariot were first imported into the Sahara. Across the Saharan oases, over 200 rock paintings dating from 1500 to 1000 BC have been discovered of riders or horses pulling chariots, the chariot depiction showing distinct affinities with Mycenaean-style art, the horses spread-eagled in the distinctive "flying gallop" (Hyland 2003:31). As major routes traversed the Sahara to the copper and gold mines of the south, at Dhar Tichitt-Walata there is clear evidence of prolonged hostilities between invading horsemen and indigenous oasis farmers. By the latter part of the first millennium BC, all traces of earlier Negroid herders and sorghum and millet agricultural-ists had disappeared, to be replaced by *tifinar* inscriptions, Libyo-Berber pre-Islamic tombs, and paintings of mounted warriors, indicating equestrian nomad conquest from the north. Elsewhere in the Sahara, c 300 BC rock paintings of cavalry reflected a general transition from chariots to cavalry, followed shortly by the introduction of the domes-ticated dromedary to the Sahara (Levtzion 1980:5–6, 12–13). The bulk-transport efficiency of the dromedary, mainly as a pack animal but also in draft and plowing, would displace wheeled vehicles in North Africa and much of the Arab world (Law 1980:160). Its high efficiency across the Sahara would also inhibit transmission of the wheel to southern Africa.

As trans-Saharan trade flourished, the Negro kingdom of Wagadu arose in the Sahel to control the sources of gold and its traffic northward. A centralized polity, Wagadu employed cavalry as a striking force in its armies. Military superiority was additionally asserted through the use of iron, which by 300 BC had spread over most of the Sahara. With horses, iron swords, and iron spears, the Soninke elite of Wagadu raided and enslaved their Negro neighbors who possessed no iron and fought only with ebony staves (Levtzion 1980:13–14). With time, though, these Negro tropical root-crop agriculturalists would acquire the new iron technology that starting in the first millennium AD would allow them to clear the dense tropical rain forests with increased efficiency. This devel-opment, in conjunction with the adoption of the southeast Asian crops taro and bananas, facilitated a series of migrations of Bantoid tribes-men south and eastward, to occupy the major part of continental sub-Saharan Africa (Clark 1970:214–216; Vansina 1996:15). This widespread movement of cultivators across the Congo basin may have in part been an escape from the equestrian slavers from the north. Because of the trypanosome diseases borne by the tsetse fly, the warhorses from the savanna kingdoms could not survive deep in the equatorial rain forest and were therefore unable to pursue the fleeing agriculturalists. There has been some speculation as to why the Bantu, in their subsequent expansion over the southerly African savannas, did not domesticate the zebra. But later, such attempts by the Boers showed the zebra, like the onager, to be highly resistant to domestication (Diamond 1999:164, 171–172).[3]

Thus, the domesticated horse, present across the Sahara from the second millennium BC onward, never extended south much beyond the savanna belt. In North Africa, however, it thrived. In antiquity we learn of the desert horse from the Carthaginians, whose formidable Numidian cavalry in the third century BC inflicted such resounding defeats on the Roman armies. The African, Libyan, and Numidian horses shared similar genetic makeup with the horse we know today as the modern Arabian and were used extensively by the Carthaginians to upgrade Spanish stock during their occupation of the Iberian peninsula. In Africa, Arabs would hunt ostrich, elephant, and giraffe on horseback. With a long-arched neck, concave forehead, straight nasal profile, and large, somewhat protruding eyes, the Arabian horse had a deep body culminating in powerful quarters; the hocks, well set down, gave the horse power and ability to maneuver. Renowned for its intelligence, the Arabian was the swiftest and toughest of horses. It remained healthy on little fodder, achieved the fastest speeds, and displayed extraordinary stamina (Bin-Sultan al-Nahyan 1998:8; Hyland 1990:24–27, 209; Law 1980:163).

Following the Muslim victory at Yarmuk, the Bedouin warrior emerged from the Arabian peninsula on his tough, nimble steed, preferring to ride mares in battle, as opposed to stallions, since they were less apt to challenge other horses. Well accustomed to the precariousness of the desert, fed a daily diet of camel milk and dates, the Arab's horse showed a hardiness and grace under the most trying conditions. Its distinctness was intensified and maintained by long inbreeding in an environment demanding toughness and alertness. The desert tribes' respect for endogamy was mirrored in their close supervision of horse-breeding practices. An *asil* (purebred) mare was only ever covered by an asil stallion. When raiding into enemy territory, the Arab sewed up the mare's vagina to prevent her mating with an inferior stallion. The Bedouin believed in telegony. Should the mare be covered by a non-asil horse, it was feared that all future foals would be contaminated

---

[3] Eighteenth- to nineteenth-century Boer experiments showed zebras did not have the right build for comfortable riding and lacked the stamina of horses in pulling wagons and coaches (Child 1967:6–7). Even though eccentric Lord Walter Rothschild may have coursed flamboyantly through London in a carriage drawn by zebras, the zebra as it matures is known to be a highly irascible animal; it has a vicious bite, easily evades the lasso, and injures more modern zookeepers each year than tigers do.

by impure blood. In birthing, the cherished asil foal was not allowed to fall to the ground but caught and caressed as an infant. Mare and foal shared the men's tent, the mare's neck often a pillow for its master. The foal was weaned after a month, then fed camel milk and later barley (Amirsadeghi 1998:18–19). Backed by the water-carrying, bulk-transporting dromedary, the cavalry forces of Islam would spread in all directions across desert regions to Central Asia and India and across North Africa to the Atlantic Ocean.

EQUESTRIAN EXPANSION OF ISLAM EASTWARD

The Byzantines evacuated northward, leaving all roads open. With their victory at Yarmuk, Muslim forces spread out across the Middle East, forcing capitulation of cities often without encountering serious resistance. In fact, numerous Arab-speaking communities, chafing under imperialist tyranny, readily accepted the rule and then the faith of the invaders, in town after town throwing open the gates and welcoming their Muslim liberators with songs and dances (Foltz 2000:91). In those early wars, the Arabs soon gained advantage over their enemies through the superior mobility afforded by dromedary support of the horse. By using the desert for passage, raiding base, and refuge, they were able to cover long distances rapidly and to concentrate their forces at the point of greatest danger. Their central stratagem was to mount surprise attacks across the desert borders. In situations of adversity they could retreat back into the desert, without fear of Byzantine or Persian pursuit, to await a more favorable opportunity to rally. With these tactics, their rear and lines of communication were safe from enemy interference and their dispatch of reinforcements was free of hazard (Hill 1975: 41–42).

At the battle of Qadasiya in 637, Sasanian elephants at first caused consternation in invader ranks. Soon, however, the Arabs retaliated by lancing the animals in the eyes and slashing the girth of the howdahs to bring the enemy crashing to the ground. As reinforcements from Syria arrived, the third night was spent attacking under cover of darkness. Fighting continued into the fourth day, when a sandstorm blew in the faces of the Persians, allowing the desert nomads to overwhelm their blinded foes and kill the Sasanian general Rustam. Once across the Euphrates, the Tigris halted the Arab advance eastward for several weeks. Finally, a force of horsemen forded the river. Then the army followed to capture the royal palace at Ctesiphon. In 642, their cavalries won a triumphant victory at Nihavand in the Zagros. Routed, never again did the Sasanians field a major army in battle (Glubb 1964:197–199, 202–203, 251).

Moving thus across Asia, Islam extended southeast to the Sind in the lower Indus and northeast to Samarkand. In 750 a quarrel broke out between the *chabish* of Taskent and the *ikhshid* of Ferghana, both rulers vassals of the Tang emperor. When the Chinese governor of the Western Regions intervened to sack Tashkent, the Muslim governor of Samarkand marched against the Chinese. At Talas in 751, in mid-battle Turkish Qarlug tribal auxiliaries defected to the Arabs with the result that the Chinese were crushed and withdrew permanently from Central Asia. A far-reaching consequence of Talas was that among the Tang captives were experts in paper manufacture, a Chinese invention of the second century AD. The Arabs immediately recognized the high utility of this new material, produced from fibrous plants beaten into pulp and later dried into thin sheets. Paper rapidly replaced the less flexible and more costly parchment, assuming the name of its ancient predecessor, papyrus. Through the Arabs, this innovation spread west with revolutionary economic and cultural ramifications. Paper manufacturing was initiated in Baghdad in 794; Egypt in 800; Spain in 950; Constantinople, Sicily, and Italy in the twelfth century; and northern Europe in the thirteenth century (Soucek 2000:67–69).

Throughout Islamic expansion, *ribat* (garrisons) were established in key areas, later becoming the nuclei of new cities, such as Kufa, Basra, Merv, and Qayrawan, where scholars would emerge as *ulama*, guardians of Islamic values. Arabs were initially concentrated in these fortified settlements, separated from the vanquished peoples they ruled, and given religious instruction; in return for military service they received government stipends, graded to reflect length of adherence to Islam and superior cavalry performance in battle (Crone 1996:11–12). In dealing with subject populations, Islam made provision for *dhimmi* "peoples of the book," namely Jews, Christians, and to some extent Zoroastrians, allowing practice of religion, retention of place of worship, and release from military service on payment of a poll tax (Hitti 2002:170–171). There was no comparable fiscal discrimination against *mawali* (clients), voluntary converts to Islam, thereby creating an economic incentive for embracing Islam (Crone 1996:16–17). With time, however, the prohibition against agriculture was dropped and abandoned lands were made available for settlement in frontier zones. In the wake of this development, from the soil-poor deserts of Arabia, waves of migrations fanned out north and east, hungry for arable lands.

The Umayyad Caliphate and the Shia Schism

The Arab conquest was extraordinarily successful, with assimilation to Islam proceeding at a prodigious rate. But midst this military success, political discord arose. In 656 the third caliph, Uthman, was assassinated in Medina, triggering a civil war waged mainly by opposing factions of the Prophet's tribe, the Quraysh. The Hashimite clan recognized Ali ibn Abi Talib, cousin and son-in-law of the Prophet,[4] as the next caliph. His nomination, however, was bitterly opposed by Uthman's kinsmen of the Umayyad clan, led by the governor of Syria, Muawiya, son of Abi Sufyan, Muhammad's chief enemy. At the Battle of the Camel near Basra, Ali's party – *shiat Ali* or Shia – initially emerged victorious. But in 661 Ali was assassinated by the Kharijites, a sect renowned for its martial piety. Muawiya then poisoned Ali's elder son, Hasan, and as caliph founded the Umayyad dynasty at Damascus (Donner 1999:15–16), where the Great Mosque would be built and where the Arab metal smiths, now familiar with Indian methods, produced quality wootz steel for the fearsome swords arming Muslim warriors in their conquests.[5]

Husayn, Ali's younger son, however persisted in championing the cause of the House of Ali. Following Muawiya's death in 680, the second civil war erupted. The dead Hasan's younger brother was invited to assume the leadership of a powerful Shiite group in Kufa. Husayn had married a Persian princess, the captured daughter of the last Sasanian emperor, Yezdegird III. In *Muharram* (the first lunar month of the Islamic calendar), he with his entourage of family and followers set out from Mecca. But on the plains of Karbala the party was ambushed by the Sunni forces of Yezid, son of Muawiya. Although defeat seemed certain, the small band of 72 was determined to fight the mighty, 4,000-strong opposing army. For 10 days in the searing heat of the desert, while all attempts to procure water from the Euphrates were blocked by the enemy, the Imam's companions resisted. The siege drew to its bloody end on the tenth day (*Ashura*). Their heroism notwithstanding, as women and children looked on in terror, all the men – Husayn,

---

[4] Ali had married Fatima, Muhammad's daughter.
[5] In this process titanium was blended into the steel to render the flexible blade with the highly prized damascened, water-patterned finish (Raymond 1984:80).

his relatives, and his devoted supporters – were pitilessly slaughtered in the most barbarous manner. Their heads were severed and spiked on spears, their corpses trampled under the hoofs of the Umayyad horses; then Husayn's head with halo was presented as prize trophy to the new Umayyad caliph, Yezid (Homayouni 1976:1–2). At Karbala, the site of the massacre of Husayn's family, the Shia built a shrine to honor the bloody sacrifice. This battlefield and the tombs of both Ali and Husayn became sites of sacred pilgrimage for Shiites throughout the Islamic empire. Islamic society now found itself divided between two bitterly opposed factions: the Sunni, who upheld the Arabic tradition of succession by election as expression of Allah's will, and the Shia, who espoused succession by inheritance through blood ties to Muhammad. The great schism of the Shia dates from this conflict (Fig. 7.1).

The Twelve and Seven Imams

Whilst all Arab attempts to seize Constantinople failed, Umayyad rule brought great prosperity to the Islamic empire. Yet because of Umayyad usurpation of the caliphate, tribal enmities between Umayyads and Hashimites persisted, as Alids and their Shiite partisans fomented many uprisings, praying that Allah would send a *mahdi* (savior) to redeem them from the Umayyads' impious rule. However, it was not the Alids but the Abbasids, another branch of the Hashimite family, who provided that leadership. Abu al-Abbas, great-great-grandson of an uncle of Muhammad, launched a revolt from Khurasan. In 750, when Damascus fell to his siege, he ordered all Umayyad princes hunted down and executed. This was artfully accomplished by declaring an amnesty, inviting 80 Umayyad leaders to a banquet, then treacherously assassinating them during the meal. Carpets were spread over the bodies and the feast resumed by the Abbasids, to the music of their enemies' dying groans (Hitti 2002:285–286). In repudiation of the fallen Damascus regime, the splendid new imperial capital of Baghdad was established east on the Tigris as a symbol of Abbasid political supremacy. This shift of power eastward meant a greater role would be played by non-Arab Muslim converts. Mostly Iranians schooled in Sasanian statecraft, these men as political administrators were to introduce Persian urbanity and refinement to the court. After a century of subjection to the Arab invader, Persia would again come to dominate the Middle East, albeit through the new prism of Islam (Crone 1996:22; Donner 1999:24–25).

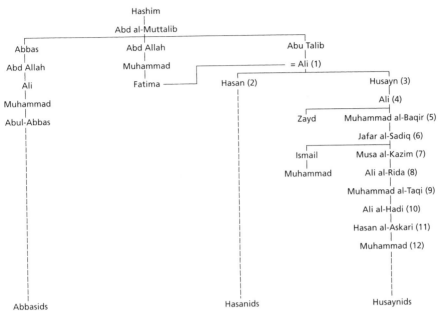

FIGURE 7.1. Genealogy of the Hashimites, the family of the Prophet Muhammad (Crone 1996:20). Reprinted with the permission of Cambridge University Press.

But while the Shiites had supported the Abbasid overthrow of the Umayyads, the Alids had not gained political power, and Baghdad remained predominantly Sunni. Still a powerful sect, the Shia declared that Muhammad had designated Ali as his imam successor, denounced the first three caliphs, rejected the Umayyads and Abbasids, and claimed that solely descendants of Ali and Fatima were rightful claimants to the prerogatives of the caliphate. Before death the imam communicated to his successor the sacred knowledge and divine authority to lead Islam. It was anticipated that the imam would bring justice and peace in place of tyranny and restore the true Islam to the world (Lewis 1967:24). There was, however, dissension among the ranks of the Shia, from which two major groupings emerged:

- The *Imami* or "Twelver" Shiites recognized 12 imams. The eighth imam was Ali al-Rida, whose tomb at Mashhad in northeastern Persia is venerated as the glory of the Shiite world. The line ended in 874 when the twelfth imam, Muhammad al-Mahdi, still an infant, went into occultation in Samarra. Again reflecting the ancient Zoroastrian tradition of Persia, it was anticipated that as the Mahdi/savior, the twelfth imam would return at the end of time to lead all Muslims in righteous preparation for the Last Day of Judgment. The belief in the imam Mahdi was central to the Shia millenarian dogma of the return of the Mahdi (Donner 1999:44; Crone 1996:20).

- The "Sevener" Shiites recognized only seven imams. Around 760, the sixth imam, Jafar al-Sadiq, named as successor his eldest son Ismail. But the nomination was rescinded, and a younger brother was appointed instead. Some Shiites maintained that the nomination was irreversible and recognized Ismail or his son Muhammad as the seventh and last imam. In the ninth century, these *Ismailis* or "Seveners," led by Abdallah ibn Qaddah, maintained that Muhammad ibn Ismail would return as the Messiah. In essence, the Ismailis proclaimed that the Imamate had not ended in 874, there never ceased to a living imam even though his identity might not be known, and the Mahdi would emerge as the savior of Muslims. At initiation into the sect, the devotees pledged secrecy and absolute obedience to the Grand Master (*Dai-d-Duat*) with the expectation that the Mahdi would establish universal equality and fraternal love on earth. An Iraqi, Hamdan ibn al-Asrath, known as Qarmat, succeeded Abdallah, plotting to overthrow the Arabs and to restore the Persian empire. These *Qaramita* (Carmathians) recruited thousands of followers, forged a mystical, communistic religion, and embraced a liberal interpretation of the Koran (Donner 1999:44).

These major sects within Islam persist to the present. While the Sunni represent the majority of Muslims, the Twelver Shiite congregation today is concentrated mainly in Iran and southern Iraq. The Sevener Ismailis, now peaceable, recognize the Aga Khan as their imam and, estimated in the millions, they extend from the Indian subcontinent across the Middle East to Africa.

The Epic Drama of Taziyeh – Opera on Horseback

To this day, more than a millennium later, every year Shiites commemorate the tragic deaths of Ali, Hasan, and Husayn in the reenactment of *Taziyeh* passion plays in veneration of the first three imams. These tragedies reflect passionate ethnic and religious rivalries that have simmered for centuries. For the Shia, Ali and his descendants were imams – exemplars, infallible incarnations of divine wisdom, successors to the prerogatives of Muhammad, and critical to salvation. Doubtless influenced by Zoroastrian concepts of rebirth and prophesy that the saoshyant savior would arise from sacred seed at the end of time (Lewis 1967:22), the Shiites regarded Ali and Husayn as holy figures, perhaps not unlike the Buddhist notion of the repeatedly incarnated Bodhisattva. The term *Taziyeh* means mourning, sympathy, and consolation, and its theatrical performance focuses on the siege of Karbala. Amazingly, this ritual drama is utterly unique to the religious world of Islam, which everywhere prohibits figural representation of animate form. Its roots necessarily are sought not in the Semitic traditions of Arabia but in Persian precedents. Sandwiched between the extraordinary dramaturgical traditions of Greece and India, the Parthian court produced Greek tragedies, as we know from earlier mention of Crassus's posthumous performance as Pentheus. Contrastingly, it is two indigenous tragedies, deeply rooted in ancient Persian tradition, that dramatically anticipate many features of the *Taziyeh*. Sung for centuries by Parthian bards before being committed to writing, the epic *Memorial of Zarer* recounts how a devoted warrior of the faith protected Vishtapa, the holy king of the Zoroastrian church. Like the passion of Imam, Zarer heroically faced a massive enemy army. and was treacherously slain on the battlefield . As in the *Taziyeh*, future calamities were foretold in the actor's early forebodings, prophesies, and laments. Couched in elegy, these revelations prepared the emotional mood of the audience for the inevitable doom of their hero. While the opposing armies are different, it is clear that the *Memorial of Zarer* served a religious and cathartic function comparable to that of the later Islamic *Taziyeh*: a valiant warrior, inspired by the fire of his faith, confronts the mighty army of an evil opponent, falls tragically in battle, and is passionately lamented.

An even earlier precursor to the *Taziyeh* was the tragedy of Siyavush. Of prehistoric tradition, it predated Zoroastrian reform but was incorporated into the *Yashts* and later recounted in the *Shahnameh*. It tells of the fate of a Persian prince cruelly murdered in distant Turania. Confiding in his pregnant wife, Siyavush too forecasts the catastrophe about to befall. In martyrdom he was to be thrown down like a sacrificial animal, mutilated, his throat slit, his face slashed to shreds. As Siyavush was buried amidst great cosmic upheavals, from Sogdiana to Khwarizmia, minstrels rendered beautiful songs. In their heartfelt lament the people wildly hit and cut their faces (Yarshater 1979:89–93). Perhaps a still more ancient antecedent to the *Taziyeh* theater of mourning can be seen in the funeral celebrations of the equestrian warriors of the Eurasian steppes, when on the death of a king, the tribes formed ceremonial processions to escort the wagon-hearse of their sacred hero-king. At the time of burial, horse and human sacrifices were performed and in wild lament the mourners would slash and tear their flesh.

As we know, mounted warriors of the steppes invaded both Anatolia and Iran, with the horse, all important on the battlefield, featuring centrally in their religion. Across these lands, centuries later, from the icy mountains of the north to the scorching deserts of the south, a funeral lament similar to that of the steppes was observed during the first 10 days of Muharram. The Islamic Shia in colorful attire and with much pageantry, in processions marching or mounted on horseback, enacted the events of the Karbala tragedy. Living tableaux of bloodied martyrs, their bodies butchered by simulated amputations, were paraded through the streets on wheeled platforms (Chelkowski 1979:3). On camels, women and children rode weeping as Yazid's prisoners, their heads and faces painted to appear bruised as if wounded by arrows (Baktash 1979:105). Standards and banners of ancient war were followed by the finest horses, equipped with costly armor, harnesses, and all manner of weapons and shields suspended from the saddles (Mahjub 1979:140). Mock battles were mimed by hundreds of armed actors, some performers showing extraordinary dexterity in swordsmanship and other combat techniques (Shahidi 1979:43). At times, club fights were fought in order to pilfer the standards of other processions; if in the turmoil a man died it was thought his soul passed immediately to heaven (Baktash 1979:104). Other devotees clad in white formed processions of flagellants, who in time with the clash of cymbals beat their backs with iron chains till the flesh was lacerated and streaming with blood; others scourged their bare backs with metal whips. Still others struck their heads with daggers and swords, making the blood spurt copiously, spattering their shirts bloody red. These crimsoned clothes were worn throughout the festival and later were buried in consecrated ground. To the accompaniment of funeral music, spectators with faces blackened and hair disheveled beat their bared chests midst the moaning, wailing, and keening of the crowd (And 1979:240–242).

Thus, the very earliest rendering of funerary lamentation for the deceased heroes of Karbala occurred at the folk level, enacted among the Shia by pious common folk. But by the tenth century, with Shia ascendancy under the Buyid dynasty in Baghdad, even more impressive Muharram ceremonies were officially promoted. Much later, when

Shiite Islam was established as the state religion of Safavid Persia, commemoration of Husayn's martyrdom became a patriotic duty. *Takiyeh* (arena theaters) were constructed as a public service by the wealthy, the design maintaining the Muharram tradition of "street theater" and dramatic interplay between actors and spectators. A raised platform occupied the center of the theater; at its heart stood the *kalak* (altar) betraying Zoroastrian origins (Peterson 1979:73). Surrounding the stage was a circular band of space along which, for example, Husayn mounted on his white horse might gallop to signal change of time, location, or journey. Corridors ran through the seating area from the outer wall to the central stage, allowing entrance of armies and processions of horses, camels, or vehicles. Subplots, duels, and skirmishes were played in unwalled peripheral arenas behind the spectators, the side actor occasionally engaging in dialogue with a main actor or, at the moment of dramatic climax, plunging precipitously through the audience to gain center stage. The takiyeh theater in the round symbolized Umayyad encirclement of Husayn on the plains of Karbala and as such represented the Shiite omphalos (Chelkowski 1979:4–5).

To lead up to the culminating martyrdom of Husayn, the *Marriage of Qasem* was usually performed between the fifth and tenth days of Muharram. Qasem is the son of Hasan, Husayn's elder brother, who was poisoned shortly after their father Ali's assassination. It was Hasan's wish that Qasem be married to Husayn's daughter Fatima. Both youngsters are still in their teens, but Husayn, recognizing that their deaths are imminent, orders the wedding. Festive preparations unroll for the wedding, as the beribboned nuptial tent is erected and sweets are ceremonially passed among the audience. Suddenly the riderless horse of Husayn's son Ali Akbar appears, portent of the youth's death on the battlefield; Fatima shrieks and the entire takiyeh is transfixed. Qasem rushes out, only to return leading the warriors bearing the body of Ali Akbar high on their shields to center stage. Weeping, the audience rises to sing dirges with the performers. Spectators near the funeral procession attempt to assist the bearers; those not close enough stretch out their arms in symbolic gesture. The body is laid down opposite the nuptial tent. Husayn laments the death of his son by kissing the stirrups and saddle of his horse. On one side of the stage mournful funeral rites are performed, while on the other the wedding is joyfully celebrated; the audience alternates between crying and laughter (Chelkowski 1979:5–6; Humayuni 1979:23). Drums of war sound as the couple leave for the bridal chamber. Alone, the groom takes leave of his bride. Mindful of

his fate, he confides that their union will be consummated on the Last
Judgment Day. This tragedy within a tragedy ends with Qasem departing for the battlefield. Husayn wraps a shroud over his son-in-law's
wedding clothes, authorizing his entry in the jihad, where the youth
fights valiantly (Humayuni 1979:14–15, 20). But, fatally wounded, he
finally falls from his horse. Pleading to see the face of his beloved one
last time, Qasem is brutally beheaded by Shemr, the enemy general. This
tragic tale of unrequited love transports the audience to great depths of
emotional anguish.

On Ashura, the tenth of Muharram, the day of martyrdom of the
imam Husayn, processions appear from all directions, the horses bearing a single green turban. People hang a flask around their necks to
give water to others, in this way to ease the thirst of Husayn oppressed
(Baktash 1979:105–106). The twelfth-century poet Badrud-din Qavami
elegizes the cruel end when Husayn is finally beheaded by the evil
Shemr, shameless offspring of adultery (Mamnoun 1979:160):

> The ignoble shut thee away from the water of the Euphrates;
> They mingled thy blood with the dust of Kerbela.
> The enemies of faith lay in ambush for thy life;
> Not a friend or acquaintance was left to thee –
> Neither a kind person to befriend thee,
> Nor a hard heart who would show thee respect.
> Thy breast torn open, throat cut, hands cast down,
> Head sundered from the body, rolling in the blood and dust.
> They rode their horses over thy beloved breast,
> O thou who in the entire world wert like the Prophet in distinction.
> How could thy body be trampled by the hooves of horses,
> When the breeze would not dare to cast pollen upon thy rosy face? . . .
>
> (Eqbal 1979:197)

As the murdered bodies of the imam's children are heaped onto the
stage, again hundreds of devotees beat and wound their heads, spot-
ting the ground with blood till it appears a field of poppies (Baktash
1979:106). So appalled is all of nature at these inhuman acts that a lion,
not the ferocious predator but an actor clothed in the actual skin of a
lion (Shahidi 1979:43) holding Husayn's flag in its mouth, treads softly
the pile of corpses, throwing straw over its head and gently pulling out
arrows from the bodies of the dead martyrs (Wirth 1979:35). Finally a riderless white horse appears, on which are perched two white doves symbolizing the souls of Hasan and Husayn (And 1979:240). The *Taziyeh*, a

tragedy of epic dimensions, thus reenacts the eternal drama of hero and villain, pure and corrupt, the Zoroastrian forces of good and evil. In the larger context of equestrian ritual ceremony, its poignant and desperate imagery supports a deep meaning, the darkness of sacrifice and the light of salvation (Hanaway 1979:187–188).

Abbasid Caliphate and Turkic Incursion

When the Abbasids deposed the Umayyads in the mid-eighth century, they controlled an empire that stretched from the lower Indus west across the Middle East and North Africa to Spain. They represented the greatest power in the Islamic world. In the 200 years of their golden age, there would be a great flowering of arts and sciences as scholars and artists flocked to the Abbasid courts, seeking patronage for their work. The caliphs established the style for all Muslim rulers, and the administrative systems they developed served as model for all successor regimes (Kennedy 2004:xix). But the Abbasid caliphate was ever alive with religious strife. Shia-Sunni enmities persisted and would flare up periodically in open war. War was also waged externally as *ghazis* (fighters for the faith), seeking to extend the boundaries of Islam, attacked Turkic nomads in the north, Christians in the west, and Hindus in the south. To recruit manpower in these hostilities, the Abbasids relied heavily on imported slaves, the majority of which were the Turkic *ghulam* or *mamluk* from the steppes. Superb cavalrymen, the Turkic ghulam became the warrior preferred above all other military elements in caliphal service (Ayalon 1994:1). Well accustomed to frontier warfare, these Turkic warriors over time would usurp the power of the Abbasid caliph and, on the fringes of the empire, overthrow indigenous Iranian and Indian rulers to build mighty empires of their own (Bosworth 1975:196).

With the transfer of power to Iraq, the second Abbasid caliph, al-Mansur, erected a splendid new capital at Baghdad, dedicating himself sedulously to reorganizing both government and army. During his rule and that of his son and successor al-Mahdi, swift military action was taken against Alid pretenders. Summer campaigns were also waged against the Byzantines, who during inter-Arab conflicts had recovered much Muslim-conquered territory in Anatolia. Having driven the Greeks back to Constantinople by 784, the fourth Abbasid caliph, Harun al-Rashid, would preside over the brilliant court of *A Thousand and One Nights* fame (Bosworth 1996:277). Following his death in 809, fratricidal warfare ensued in which his elder son al-Mamun emerged the victor. Al-Mamun's royal patronage of the arts, sciences, letters, and philosophy surpassed even that of Harun. From Constantinople and Alexandria, he obtained ancient texts of the Greek masters and paid a corps of scholars to translate these works into Arabic. He also established an observatory and academy of sciences in Baghdad (Mottahedeh 1975:72–73).

But, in the course of the ninth century, a politico-military trend became evident in which the caliphs appointed governors to outlying provinces. And by 874, Transoxania and Khurasan were ruled by a fully autonomous Samanid dynasty of local Sogdian origin, tracing its descent from the Sasanians. Devout Sunnis, the Samanids modeled their administration on that of the Abbasids; the Samanid courts of Bokhara and Samarkand in fact rivaled Baghdad as centers of learning. Yet the Samanid domain differed starkly from the heart of the caliphate. Their region formed the northeastern bastion of the Iranian world against the mass incursion of nomads from the steppes of Central Asia. Border areas bristled with some 2,000 ribat forts, these barriers against the infidel Turk manned by ghazi volunteers from Samanid territories. Since earliest Islam, the austere ribat had furnished a center of military training and religious indoctrination for the Muslim warrior. Besides this frontier defense, the Samanid emirs personally commanded punitive expeditions onto the steppes, to capture immense booty of men and horses. Slaves were the chief reward of these forays (Bosworth 1973:30–31). Turkic mounted archery – the rapid firing of arrows from a swiftly moving and maneuvering horse – was a highly skilled art, one that only those brought up to it from an early age could master. With time, mendicant Sufi missionaries wandering the steppes would convert many Turks. But upon capture or purchase, the Turkic youth was immediately indoctrinated in Islam and, in training schools maintained by the Samanids, rigorously prepared for military or administrative service. Thus, large numbers of tribal nomads were imported from the steppes into Islamic lands, most of whom found employment as military guards in the service of caliphs, emirs, or provincial governors (Kennedy 2001:123; Frye 1975:150).

Within the Abbasid caliphate, the military slave institution dated back to the time the early caliphs first reduced the pay of free Arab *muqatila* forces, using the money saved to buy Turkic slaves (Bosworth 1973:99). This process was accelerated by al-Mutasim, who upon accession in 833 built up an army of 30,000 troops, half of which were Turkic ghulams. Because these ghulams became embroiled in clashes with the citizenry and military elements of Baghdad, who resented the nomads usurping the elite role of cavalry in the army, al-Mutasim relocated his capital north to Samarra, where his armed forces would be more securely accommodated. Deracinated from their homeland, segregated from the local populace, the ghulams owed direct loyalty to their ruler. But as their numbers and political clout increased, it was the Turkic military commanders who made and unmade caliphs, placing their favorites upon the throne as docile puppets (Bosworth 1996:278–279; Kennedy 2001:122, 126). Shortly before his death in 892, caliph al-Mutamid, hoping to curb ghulam power, restored the caliphal seat to Baghdad. But here the caliphate was even further diminished in 945, when the Shiite Buyids invaded from the Caspian highlands to reduce the Abbasid caliph to a mere figurehead (Mottahedeh 1975:85).

Mounting Turkic power was also apparent in Samanid territories. In 961, the Turkic commander of the Samanid forces staged a putsch upon the death of his emir. Unsuccessful in placing his candidate on the throne, Alptigin withdrew to the eastern fringes of the empire, where with a small force of his own ghulams and Tajik ghazis he captured the citadel of Ghazna. His son later was invested governor by the emir of Bokhara. But after several years of upheaval, Alptigin's son-in-law Sebuktigin assumed control of Ghazna to reign for 20 years. A Qarlug Turk, he had been captured by an enemy tribe, sold to a slave dealer, and then purchased by Alptigin for service in his guard. Quickly distinguishing himself in combat, by age 18 he commanded 200 ghulams. Accompanying his master to Ghazna, he had played a prominent role in the hostilities. In 994 Sebuktigin invaded Khurasan, where he was victorious. To strengthen control over the province, his son Mahmud established headquarters in Nishapur in response to pressure from the Karakhanid Turks who had invaded the Jaxartes valley (Bosworth 1973:37–44). But as Samanid power weakened, the two Turkic foes found it expedient to divide up the spoils and partition the Samanid domain. In 999, the Karakhanids definitively occupied Bokhara, bringing the Iranian dynasty to an end, while Mahmud successfully extended his dominion over territories south from the Oxus to the Gulf (Frye 1975:159).

But Ghazna was also to serve as the springboard of Turkic equestrian expansion into the subcontinent. These southern infidel lands promised an infinitely richer plunder than the bare northern steppes. Legitimized by caliphal approval and ostentatiously espousing the cause of Sunni orthodoxy, Mahmud undertook decades of ceaseless campaigning over vast stretches of southern Asia to gain lasting reputation as the great ghazi warrior for the faith. He would purge religious dissidents at home and persecute Hindu idolators abroad (Bosworth 1975:168–169). Each winter, armies of regular troops swollen by thousands of booty-hungry ghazis from all parts of the eastern Islamic world would descend onto the plains of India. His victories opened up the floodgates of the north-western passes, through which for centuries streams of Turkic invaders from Central Asia would pour onto the northern plains of the sub-continent. Tactically, the cavalry was the most important force in the Ghaznavid army because of its mobility, ability to charge the enemy, and usefulness in skirmishes; the infantry was valuable in pitched battles and sieges. For the Somath expedition (1025–1026), Mahmud's troops comprised the customary nucleus of slave guards, 30,000 cavalry, plus volunteers (Bosworth 1973:114). His invasions essentially entailed plunder raids in which Hindu temples were systematically despoiled to provide bullion for the sultan's gold and silver coinage. Tens of thousands of slaves were captured to be sold to slave merchants converging on Ghazna from all parts of western Asia. Some slaves were incorporated into the army, where Rajput fighting qualities were highly valued (Bosworth 1975:179–180).

Mahmud's exploits in India were a remarkable military achievement; at the time of his death the Ghaznavid empire had attained its fullest extent. But by 1030 another warring nomad tribe had gathered on the northern steppe horizon. Oghuz Turks, the Seljuks, in their spoliation of the region quickly brought economic life to a standstill. In 1040 Mahmud's successor, Masud, confronted the nomads at the ribat of Dandanqan. There, Masud's numerically superior army was routed by 16,000 Seljuk cavalry, Khurasan was abandoned, and Masud retreated toward India. This collapse of Ghaznavid defenses inevitably attracted more Oghuz tribesmen from Central Asia. Already converted to Sunni Islam on the steppes, the Seljuks advanced west across Iran to Iraq. Ousting the Buyids from Baghdad in 1055, their sultan (secular ruler) Toghril effectively liberated the Sunni caliph al-Quaim from his Shiite overlords, to assume the role as protector of the caliphate (Bosworth 1968:16, 19, 22, 46). Thus, by the mid-eleventh century Arab power in the Abbasid caliphate had significantly diminished. Operating on the eastern fringes of the empire, Ghaznavid and Seljuk equestrian campaigns in the Middle East – the former forging an invasion route for subsequent Timurid and Mughal conquests of northern India, the latter ever advancing westward – had effectively set the pattern of Turkic political domination over much of the Islamic world for many centuries to come.

EQUESTRIAN EXPANSION OF ISLAM WESTWARD

Just as Muslim militarism convulsed much of western Asia, so too Arab western expansion across Africa followed shortly after the Prophet's death. Arab victories cannot be attributed to their masses, for they were vastly outnumbered by their enemies. The Arabs' strengths were their religious fervor and their astonishing military mobility, afforded by the Arab warhorse and dromedary support in the desert. Both men and horses were accustomed to living off the meager diet of Bedouin existence. Hardy and resourceful, without supply train they traversed barren and inhospitable lands, traveling at night with the bright light of the desert stars – even fighting at night (Kennedy 2007:371). In Egypt, Alexandria finally fell to siege in 641; meanwhile al-Fustat, Cairo of the future, was established and the 130 km canal between the Nile and the Red Sea was reopened, permitting direct navigation between the Indian Ocean and the Mediterranean. South in Nubia, a treaty was concluded at Dongola in 642 that laid the foundation for the Muslim slave trade in Africa. The treaty stipulated that a mosque be maintained in the center of town and required each year the delivery of 360 male and female adult slaves, all in good health and without blemish (Heers 2003:27). The earliest slaving of Negroes in Africa of which we have record dates to the sixteenth century BC, shortly after the acquisition of the horse, when Eighteenth Dynasty Egypt procured slaves from the Land of Punt (northern Somalia). Later historical data attest to large numbers of Negro slaves in the Persian Gulf region centuries before the rise of Islam (Patterson 1982:150). But with the Muslim advance into Africa, this ancient trade intensified as Arabs swept down the Nile valley to the Sudan and across the Red Sea down the East African coast to Zanzibar. Christian caravans to the Holy Land were savaged, their pilgrims enslaved. From Ethiopia to Fezzan to Chad, in every location the annual tribute exacted was the same, 360 adult slaves. First gathered in castration centers, this human chattel was then trafficked to destinations in the Arab states, the Mediterranean, and Egypt (Heers 2003:28–31).

To protect Egypt from Byzantine flank attack, 40,000 Muslim troops traversed Cyrenaica and Tripolitania from 643 to 647. The islands of Cyprus and Rhodes were also attacked. In 670, Uqba ibn Nafi founded the important Muslim garrison town of Qayrawan in Ifriqiya. But here the momentum of the advance faltered. Realizing the capture of Carthage would give the Muslims control of the Mediterranean, Byzantium sent a fleet and hefty troop reinforcements. In 680, Uqba led an expeditionary force of several thousand men across North Africa, engaging in numerous offensives against both Berber and Byzantine foes. Finally, the Arabs reached the Atlantic (near Agadir), where Uqba rode his horse deep into the water, declaring but for the ocean he would wage jihad even further afield! Returning from the western edge of the continent, in the Aures mountains in confrontation with a large force of Berber cavalry, he found the martyrdom to which he aspired. Led by the Zanata prophetess Kahina, native Berbers continued to put up fierce resistance to the Arab armies. It was thus not until 698 that Carthage was subdued. Enslaving tens of thousands, the Arabs pursued their conquest west along the North African littoral to capture Tangier in 708. Less than 70 years after leaving Egypt, Muslim power now extended 7,000 km from Central Asia to the Atlantic (Kennedy 2007:211–223). As North Africa was brought under Islamic rule, successive waves of Jewish migration moved from the Near East into the western provinces of the caliphate. Under the Abbasid dynasty, the Babylonian Talmud had emerged the dominant doctrine, its *midrash* (centers of learning) extending to Qayrawan, which in the ninth century would achieve considerable prosperity (Cohen 1987:149–151).

Having reached the Atlantic in their western conquests, the Arabs began to move south into the western interior of the African continent. Deep in the Sahara, Afro-Asiatic Berber pastoralists, dominated by the Sanhadja tribe, controlled the oases for their camel pastures. These equestrian nomads also filled the important role of guides and protectors of trans-Saharan caravan trade between the Mediterranean littoral and the southern desert fringe where, due to danger of disease to their camels and horses, goods were transferred to donkeys and human porters for transit to the equatorial forests. In the trans-Saharan trade, slaves and gold were the major products. Alluvial gold deposits were encountered primarily along the headwaters of the Senegal, Niger, and Volta rivers. Additional products traded north were salt, copper, and ivory to be exchanged for horses, weapons, and textiles; cowrie shells imported from the Indian Ocean often served as currency (Garlake 1990:118–120).

Another form of currency were the human slaves themselves. In later wars for control of the caravan trade, horses, sometimes numbering 10,000 or more, were an indispensable force in the armies of the savanna.

Yet, due to the extreme climate, these animals were ever subject to serious disease, needing to be replaced as frequently as every two years. The price of one horse was 15 to 20 human slaves. Therefore in order to replenish cavalry, regular raids were mounted against the southern Negro populations in order to realize many thousands of captives each year. To conserve the element of surprise, a band of some 20 men would leave their horses about a kilometer outside a settlement to be raided. Concealed, they then lay in wait close to a well, near a village route, or crouched amid the cultivated fields often guarded by children, ready at the appropriate moment to pounce upon their victims. Other times a mobile force of horsemen and cameleers would surprise an entire village at dawn, seizing fit individuals to be dispatched northward, massacring the weak and elderly (Heers 2003:64–67). In the Sahel the war horse, vital for the control of gold, also drove the slave trade.

Islamic Advance across the Iberian Peninsula and Defeat at Poitiers

Poised between the Atlantic and the Mediterranean, the tide of Islamic conquest turned north. In the east Byzantium would continue to defy Muslim advance for many centuries to come, but in the west Spain furnished an alternate route to assault Christian Europe. In 711 an army led by the Berber commander Tariq ibn Ziyad landed near Gibraltar or *Gebel al-Tariq* (the rock of Tariq).[6] A second army under the governor of North Africa, Musa ibn Nusayr, followed. Internally divided, Visigothic Spain was without strong political leadership. Their king Rodrigo faced the battle-hardened Arabs and Berbers at Guadalete, where he was slain. Following his defeat, Sevilla, Cordoba, and Merida fell, then Toledo and Zaragoza, with considerable loss of life and devastation of the surrounding countryside. Only those towns that offered armed resistance to the Muslims were subjected to the full rigor of Islamic custom: summary execution of adult males and enslavement of women and children. Towns that submitted to the conquerors were assured their safety and freedom to practice their religion. As in the Middle East, so in Spain, Islamic law permitted Christians and Jews, as "peoples of the book," to exercise their religion. In return the populace was required to pay a poll tax, partly in money and partly in agricultural products. These taxes did not exceed those levied under the Visigoths. Such terms allowed

---

6 In the same year, Muhammad ibn Qasim invaded Daybul on the lower Indus (Kennedy 2007:299).

Muslims, without garrison obligations, the mobility to advance over wide territories. By 720 all the lands of the peninsula were subjugated by the invaders except Asturias,[7] where a Christian revolt had defeated the Arabs at Covadonga. The Muslims established the government of their conquered territories in Cordoba, naming the new Islamic land al-Andalus (Fletcher 1992:17–19; Halsall 2003:84).

Obedient to the imperative of expansion in search of booty and slaves, the Muslims continued to mount forays deep into Gaul. In 732, the Arab governor, ravaging territories he passed through, led his elite Berber cavalry as far north as Poitiers. Finally, in 733 on the plains between Poitiers and Tours, he was met by the Merovingian army headed by Charles Martel. After seven days of fierce fighting, the Franks opened a passage to the camp of spoils. A large cavalry force immediately withdrew from the Arab army to defend the spoils, then disorder broke out. Thousands of Muslims were killed. The Arab army retreated during the night, never again to mount a large-scale raid on France. In fact any further offensive northward was prevented by Al-Andalus's preoccupation with the 741 great Berber rebellion in the Maghreb over the brutalities of the slave trade (Enan 1940:57–59; Kennedy 2007:321–323). Thus, Martel's victory was a decisive check to Arab conquest that rescued and protected Christian Europe. From this encounter with the Arab invader, Martel recognized the strategic importance of cavalry to repel the Muslims permanently. Previously the Franks had fought to some extent on horseback, but now the great Mayor of the Palace moved to augment the numbers of military horsemen in his army. In medieval Europe this objective could only be accomplished through the acquisition of additional lands for horse rearing. To realize his goal, therefore, Martel confiscated vast areas of ecclesiastical properties, which he then distributed to retainers on the condition that they train and equip themselves for cavalry service in his army; any failure in this responsibility resulted in land forfeiture. Quite apart from furnishing horses and costly arms, the knight's primary pride and duty was prowess in the saddle – no part-time occupation. Starting from puberty, mounted combat required strenuous physical conditioning and long technical training in riding and use of the lance and shield; the military exercises of jousting of course evolved into the spectacular tournaments of the twelfth century. Households of great lords became schools where youths, as hostages for their father's loyalty, were trained in

---

[7] Destined to become the kingdom of Leon in the ninth century and eventually Castile.

the chivalric arts, learning the *noblesse oblige* traditions of their profession, knightly rivalry in feats of arms, and the discipline of the combat squadron.

These measures greatly strengthened Frankish military force. Mounted cavalry enabled the later Carolingians to effectively combat Muslims in Provence and to establish power in German territories (White 1962:4–5, 31–32). While campaigning in Saxony in 777, Charlemagne received an embassy from the Arab governor of Barcelona, announcing his rebellion against the emir of Cordova and requesting Frankish support. Assembling a large army in Aquitaine, Charles advanced south toward Zaragoza. But the military venture misfired and the Franks had no alternative but to withdraw. Retreating through the Pyrenees, Charles's forces were ambushed in the pass of Roncevaux. This ambush of the Frankish troops was later avenged by Charlemagne's son, Louis, who conquered Barcelona in 801 and established the Frankish march of Catalonia (Fletcher 1992:29–30; Owen 1973:31).

The Song of Roland

The tragic rout of the Frankish forces at Roncevaux inspired the most somber of French epics, the *Chanson de Roland*. The *Chanson de Roland* was the earliest and finest of the medieval *chansons de geste*, songs of deeds to celebrate the Christian holy wars against the Muslim enemy, in which Charlemagne was portrayed as the champion of Christendom surrounded by his court of Twelve Noble Peers, embarking on fantastic expeditions with his majestic white beard waving in the wind. These early French epics probably evolved from popular songs that in the wake of an important battle spontaneously acclaimed the heroic feats of great warriors. At first orally transmitted, with time these short ballads were elaborated poetically into legend, in simple flowing lines of verse. Plying the great pilgrim routes to shrines such as Santiago de Compostela, gifted minstrels gleaned local heroic traditions and wove them into epic form. To hold the rapt attention of his listeners, the wandering minstrel, in the castle or marketplace, on his fiddle would strike up a recurring melody with a strong beat, perhaps at first reciting his lines, then at moments of high tension or pathos bursting into song. Gesture and mimicry played a vital part in these tales of betrayal, disaster, and revenge, as the minstrel modulated his voice to each dramatic action, ringing with triumph at infidel death, lamenting the tragic loss of the Christian hero (Owen 1973:39–40).

In August 778, Charlemagne returned to France through the Pyrenees. As his army passed through a narrow winding gorge, a horde of Basques descended on the last section of the baggage train loaded with loot, forcing his rearguard into a valley and slaying them to the last man. The twelfth-century *Roland* epic, however, diverges somewhat from the events of the original coup in that the Basques are replaced by an evil Spanish king leading an infidel army later abetted by the Cairo emir of all Islam. As feudal vassal, duke of the Breton Marches, nephew of Charles, and first of the Twelve Noble Peers, Roland is committed to the honor of his king, country, and family to the point of death. He therefore volunteers to command the dangerous rearguard defense of the column. Outnumbered, but flanked by his staunch friend Oliver and the archbishop Turpin, Roland leads his men in desperate resistance against the overwhelming enemy (Owen 1973:31, 34, 37). Inspired by their leader's great physical strength and victory over the giant Ferragut, the men fight to the death. In midst of the carnage, Roland steadfastly refuses to ask for assistance.

> Count Roland gripped his sword dripping with gore.
> He has well heard the Frenchmen's dire lament.
> And feels his own heart bursting with great grief.
> To the pagan he said: 'God give you woe!
> You have slain a man for whom I claim high price.'
> He spurs his steed on to a fiery pace;
> For gain or loss he clashes with his foe.
> . . . .
> The count strikes him so violent a blow
> That to the nasal the whole helm is split;
> He slices through the nose, the mouth and teeth.
> The trunk and hauberk of Algerian mail,
> Through the gold saddle with its silver bows,
> And deeply down into the charger's back.
> (Owen 1972:67; CXXIII 1629–1635, CXXIV 1644–1649)

One questions here the noble dedication of the Christian warrior. Is this valiant commander not tainted with pride and ambition for renown and, as such, blinded to the welfare of his soldiers whose fates depend on him? Finally Roland blows his ivory horn, Oliphant, until blood bursts from his temples. Charles hears and turns the main army to the rescue, yet the dark hazardous mountain route impedes the Franks' progress. Mourning over the corpse of Oliver, Roland is urged by the dying archbishop to escape to safety. Instead the noble warrior continues the fray until all his attackers have fled. With his last strength Roland breaks his jeweled sword, Durendal, against a rock to prevent the enemy from using the mighty weapon. On the hilt are sacred relics, which gave the sword formidable supernatural powers in the service of Christian holy war. Mortally wounded, Roland holds up his glove to God as a sign of loyal vassalage. The flower of his Frankish knighthood destroyed in this tragic rearguard action, Charles never again mentions the names of his closest military leaders slain in the Pyrenees. In France, the emperor breaks the news to Aude, Roland's betrothed and sister of Oliver, who falls dead at his feet. As a great epic, the *Chanson de Roland* continued to inspire great valor in the Christian armies of France. To embolden the Normans in their invasion of England at the Battle of Hastings in 1066, heroic words were sung by the minstrel Taillefer of Charlemagne, Roland, Oliver, and the knights that died at Roncevaux. For centuries to come medieval knights would emulate the reckless courage and chivalry of Roland (Owen 1973:37, 39).

The Heavy-Armored European Knight

Following Roncevaux, Charlemagne went on to wage many wars of expansion across Europe, in the 790s dramatically conquering the Mongol Avars, who as a major power had occupied the Danube basin for 200 years (Halsall 2003:144). The Avars of course had introduced the metal stirrup from China across the steppes to central Europe in the late seventh century. The ninth-century St. Gallen Psalter showed Carolingian cavalry with saddles almost identical to the Roman era, but equipped with stirrups (Hyland 1994:7). A superior horseshoe providing a far better grip on the hoof finally appeared around the ninth century AD in both the Yenisei region of Siberia and Europe to become widely utilized by the eleventh century (Clutton-Brock 1992:13, 73). With the stirrup, the Frankish knight developed on horseback a mode of attack that combined the strength of the rider with that of the charging stallion, augmenting human energy with animal power. Earlier techniques of combat had featured the spear wielded at the end of the arm and delivered with the power of the biceps. But with the greater stability in the saddle afforded by stirrups, the western knights developed the capability of carrying with one arm a long, heavy lance, firmly couched between the upper arm and body, to inflict on the opponent a blow of unprecedented force (White 1962:1–2). Long before, on the steppes, the

Sarmatian clibanarius without stirrups had wielded the two-handed
lance that at the most critical moment of battle necessitated laying the
reins on the horse's neck and controlling the animal with the knees. By
contrast, the Frankish utilization of the couched lance at rest allowed
the knight at all times to exert rein control over his steed and also
to carry a kite-shaped shield on his left arm, efficiently operating in
both offensive and defensive modes (White 1962:8–9). As shown on
the Bayeux Tapestry, these sophisticated techniques served William the
Conqueror well in 1066 at the Battle of Hastings, when his Norman
knights defeated the Saxons. Earlier it was noted that equids in northern, colder climes assume huskier proportions. Centuries before, Julius
Caesar had admired the larger Gallic horses, noting their effective role in
draft (Hyland 1994:3). In time, as heavier armor developed for the new
form of mounted shock combat in which the bulk of the horse served as
a battering ram, a much larger horse became necessary. With this larger
Frankish horse capable of sustaining enormous weights, often in excess
of 180 kg, the full complement of armor for knight and horse evolved
along with heraldic devices on helmets, shields, and banners to identify
each totally armored equestrian warrior. With the massed charge with
couched lance, early tank warfare had arrived (White 1962:33)! North of
the Pyrenees arose mighty Frankish power, the forces of which over the
course of the next few centuries would fight alongside Spanish Christians to reclaim the Iberian peninsula in the west and would also sail
across the Mediterranean to challenge the heart of Islam in the east.

Al-Andalus

South of the Pyrenees, Islam, however, was to be entrenched in Europe
for many centuries to come. Muslim migration into the peninsula probably consisted of as many Berbers as Arabs, who likely marrying indigenous women formed a mixed culture from the start. For the most part
Christians at first did not rapidly convert but lived side by side with
Muslims in large Mozarab communities that acquired much Arab culture but remained staunchly attached to the Christian religion. Jews,
earlier persecuted by the Visigoths, were concentrated in the cities,
finding Islam a system whereby they could prosper while practicing
their own faith. Connected through marriage with their coreligion-
ists in Provence and North Africa, they became the most successful
merchants of Spain (Grabar 1992:4, 6–7). In 755, Abd al-Rahman, the
only Umayyad to escape the Abbasid massacre, arrived in Spain; from

Cordoba he and his successors in both emirate and caliphate would rule Al-Andalus until 1030. Umayyad rule transformed the economics of southern Spain. Mineral resources of mercury, iron, and lead were actively exploited; Toledo became the center of important wootz steel manufacture in the west. Revolutionary agricultural techniques were introduced, the cultivation of rice in particular hitherto unknown in the western Mediterranean. Exotic textiles were produced, and gold and ivory, acquired on the edges of the Sahara, were crafted into luxury objects. There was a wealth of productivity and exchange as Al-Andalus became a rich exporter of consumer goods.

But by the ninth century, as social and political tensions mounted, Christian resistance against Islam grew. In response, the Umayyads took measures to suppress the rival religion's rhetorical powers by demolishing Christian bell towers. Erected instead was the tower minaret, soon to be ubiquitous in Al-Andalus, where the cry of the muezzin came to dominate the townscape. For generations bells would remain a controversial item between Christian and Muslim. After sacking Barcelona, in his reprisals against Christians during the tenth century, despotic al-Mansur razed the Christian sanctuary at Santiago de Compostela in faraway Asturias-Leon, depopulating entire towns and deporting Christians as slaves. On the shoulders of Christian captives, he had transported the shrine's enormous bells to Cordoba, to be suspended as lamps in the mosque (Dodds 1992:17–18, 24).

But European slaves were a commodity far more valued than bells and under Islam were trafficked in vast numbers. While Vikings slaved along the Atlantic coasts, from their bases on captured islands of the Mediterranean, the Muslim fleets mounted raids on Languedoc, Provence, and the Mediterranean and Adriatic coasts of Italy. Sometimes as many as 200 ships converged on a port, establishing in Christian territory fortified camps from which predatory horsemen would scour far into the interior, abducting slaves, looting, and plundering (Heers 2003:12–14). In northern Europe, pagan captives were taken from Scandinavian and Slavic lands to the centers of castration at Verdun and Prague, thence under the control of Jewish and Christian merchants southward to the ports of Al-Andalus and the entrepots of North Africa. In Al-Andalus, *saqaliba* (Slav eunuchs) became an important part of the military elite and a major political force. The Byzantine emperor Leon V formally interdicted the slave trade but was flagrantly defied by Venice, which readily preyed on Saracen lands in revenge for Muslim raids. Just as African slaves were herded in the thousands across the Sahara to markets on the Mediterranean or Red Sea, so too European slaves were transported by traders of many faiths to Arab lands in the south (Grabar 1992:4–7; Heers 2003:16–21; Kennedy 2001:159).

As immense wealth from the slave trade and gold from south of the Sahara flowed into Al-Andalus, Cordoba became a great cultural center rivaling Baghdad (Fakhry 1999:284), its library reputed to have housed more than 400,000 volumes. In spite of their opposition to Abbasid political power, the Hispano-Umayyad caliphs vigorously emulated the opulent palatial arts of Baghdad and Samarra. The original Cordoba mosque had been constructed from spolia acquired from Christian churches and Roman civic buildings. Intent upon reasserting his Umayyad heritage and displaying caliphal authority, Abd al-Rahman III ordered the Cordoba mosque refurbished in ceremonial imitation of his ancestors' Great Mosque at Damascus. His son al-Hakan II had the *qibla*[8] wall adorned with mosaics, petitioning skilled artisans from Constantinople to execute this task; anxious for potential allies against Baghdad, the Byzantines complied. As glowing mosaics visually evoked the original Umayyad mosque, Koranic inscriptions were introduced, their aniconic vocabulary weaving an intricate path through the abstract jungle of geometric and vegetal shapes. This rhetoric both disseminated the word of Allah and projected the image of Muslim victory, while buttressing links between the old and new dynasties of Syria and Al-Andalus (Dodds 1992:19–23).

Arabic Efflorescence

Across the Islamic world, from east to west, mosques soared high in the skies, the gold and azure of their domes denoting their sanctity, their interiors elaborately decorated with mosaics, marble paneling, and brilliantly gilded ceilings. One of the first major Islamic monuments, the Dome of the Rock, under the caliph's sponsorship was built in 692 by Byzantine architects and artisans on the remains of Solomon's temple in Jerusalem, its mosaic iconography of vegetation and skies relating to the garden of paradise promised to Muslims (Blair and Bloom 1999:253, 266). Over the centuries, in a thousand mosques from Samarkand to Cordoba, Arabic became the official language. But Arab horses sped not only a new language, religion, and architecture across Asia to Europe;

---

[8] The direction of the Kaaba shrine in Mecca toward which all Muslims turn in ritual prayer.

as we have seen, with the Islamic conquest went many new cultigens, industries, and inventions. The remarkable Chinese invention of paper manufacture adopted by the Arabs greatly promoted the development of calligraphy, bookmaking, rapid dissemination of information, bookstores, and public libraries. As the shrewd Arab quickly absorbed the ancient cultures of the lands he conquered, there was new emphasis on learning. Employing Arabic as the universal language of communication, philosophers and scientists from the borders of China to the Atlantic pursued knowledge in diverse disciplines and engaged in an exchange of ideas unprecedented in earlier civilizations (Dallal 1999:158). Surveying lands from Zanzibar through India to China, al-Masudi provided a biology and geography of his explorations. Al-Idrisi, geographer at the Norman court of Sicily, composed a world map, including in his treatise, *Kitab nuzhat al-mushtaq*, mention of the rich North Atlantic fisheries and men living in lands beyond the ocean in houses of whalebone (Dallal 1999:183, 185; Fagan 1991:19).

An extremely important innovation occurred in mathematics, where the Arabs' intellectual inheritance was preponderantly Babylonian and Greek. But with the Ghaznavid invasions south, the Muslim world also came under the influence of India (Dallal 1999:160–161, 184). As mentioned in Chapter 4, by the fifth century AD, the Indians had adapted their numbering to a base-ten arithmetic system using the Greek omicron in combination with nine digits to represent units, tens, hundreds, thousands, and so forth. In this Hindu system, hitherto unknown to the West, the name for the hollow circle was *sunya*, meaning empty, which the Arabs translated to *sifr* (cipher), Latin transformed into *zephirus*, and Italian abbreviated to *zero*. Standing with other digits to form a numeral, the zero enabled the mathematician to add, subtract, multiply, and divide much faster than with an abacus. A profound idea, indeed held by many to be a major human accomplishment and turning point for technology, the zero permitted negative numbers, conceptualized the void and the infinite, and, by lending great ease to complex computations, dramatically stimulated the growth of mathematics (Seife 2000:67–70, 73–74). Just as steppe equestrians had carried important Chinese silk and stirrups across Eurasia, so now the revolutionary Hindu concept of the zero would also spread throughout the Old World. Using these Hindu numerals, al-Khwarizmi[9] or Muhammad ibn Musa (780–850) issued a dissertation known in its Latin form

9 Popular name derived from his birthplace, Khwarizm, south of the Aral Sea.

as *Algoritmi de numero Indorum* (Al-Khwarizmi on the Numerals of the Indians); with time the term *algorithm*, a corruption of his name, came to signify an arithmetical system based on decimal notation. A giant in mathematics, al-Khwarizmi also formulated the earliest trigonometrical tables, provided analytical and geometrical solutions of quadratic equations, and compiled astronomical tables. In 979 the astronomical tables of al-Khwarizmi were adapted to the meridian of Cordoba and this knowledge spread north to Christian Europe. Algebra, *al-jabr*, owed its name to the Arabs. The application of diverse mathematical disciplines to one another transformed methods of reasoning and fostered advances in many branches of science (Fletcher 1992:71). While Buddhist and Hindu travelers sped the zero along the Silk Road east to China, Muslim equestrians carried the concept westward (Kaplan 2000:91), where Hindu numerals were popularized in Europe by the Pisan merchant Leonardo Fibonacci, accustomed to trade with North Africa. Impressed by the efficiency of the zero, Italian merchants seized upon the new system, which under commercial pressure quickly spread across the continent (Seife 2000:78–79).

Another accomplished scholar from Khwarizm, al-Biruni (973–1048) extended his research to many disciplines. He wrote more than 150 works on astronomy, mathematics, metallurgy, geography, history, and philosophy. Equipped with revolutionary new tools, al-Biruni exhaustively probed specialized topics: shadows, gravity, and coordinates of geographical locations. His astronomical observations were remarkable for their accuracy and range. Expensive precision instruments were devised for astronomers: astrolabe; armillary spheres; compass boxes, cartographic grids; quadrants with a radius of 9 m; and sextants with a radius of 20. In Toledo, al-Zarqali improved many of these instruments and demonstrated for the first time the motion of the solar apogee with reference to the stars. Copernicus would later acknowledge his debt to al-Zarqali's treatise on the astrolabe (Dallal 1999:168–169, 181).

Many Muslim hospitals were built complete with apothecaries, and physicians were required to abide by Hippocratic and Galenic codes of professional conduct (Dallal 1999:201). Arabic medicine was particularly strong in therapy and medicaments. Chemistry as a science was practically created by Muslims. They introduced controlled experimentation, precise observation, and recording. They invented the alembic, defined alkalis and acids, analyzed many substances, and manufactured innumerable drugs (Durant 1950:244–247). In the Samanid courts, one outstanding figure in the field of medicine was al Razi or Rhazes (844–926), who compiled an encyclopedic medical survey of diseases, treatments, and clinical observations; also important was ibn Sina or Avicenna (981–1037), who achieved a systematic synthesis of medical knowledge through the rigorous application of theoretical principles (Dallal 1999:203–204). There was comparable ferment in the field of philosophy. Avicenna was also renowned as a philosopher and much influenced by Aristotle and al-Farabi (878–950), whose great work *Al Madina al Fadila* (Ideal City) dealt with the individual's perpetual struggle against others (Hobbes's *bellum omnium contra omnes*). Avicenna sought to reconcile popular belief with logical reasoning. His style of writing was fluid and incisive, as a consequence extending the influence of his work throughout medieval learned circles to the distinguished Jewish philosopher-physician Maimonides and to Averroes in Spain. Fleeing Almohad persecution across Spain and North Africa, in Egypt Maimonides would write his major work, *Guide of the Perplexed*, in which he sought to achieve a synthesis between Judaism and Aristotle (Cohen 1987:155; Fakhry 1999:275). Everywhere there was high mobility and efficient communication among scientists. Horse-sped, scientific knowledge diffused rapidly over large segments of the educated elites, across different regions of the Islamic world, and beyond. In Spain and Sicily, Arab, Jewish, and Christian scholars quickly translated Arabic works into Latin for the benefit of Europe.

Berber Cavalry Rebellion from Africa

But while great art and science flourished under Islam both east and west, nomads were stirring on yet another southern periphery. In the decades following the Abbasid transfer of the caliphate from Damascus east to Baghdad, political fragmentation occurred in the Muslim west of North Africa. Enriched from the trade in gold and slaves, one by one, provinces along the Mediterranean came to establish their autonomy. Here renegade sects would arise to threaten both Abbasid and Umayyad caliphates. In Tunisia, Kutama-Berber followers of the Shia doctrine of seven imams overthrew Aghlabid rule. Hailed as the Mahdi, the promised messianic figure, Obeidallah ibn Muhammad c 909 arrived from Arabia to assume kingship of Qayrawan. Claiming descent from Fatima, daughter of the Prophet, he named his dynasty

Fatimid. Wresting power away from puritanic Kharijite Arabo-Berbers, from the northern gates of the Sahara, Fatimid horsemen seized control of the 3,000-km-long eastern routes to the southern gold fields. Utilizing this immense gold wealth to finance campaigns against the Abbasid caliphate in Baghdad, the Fatimids deployed vast amounts of money to build a "propaganda network" in preparation for their conquest of Egypt (Levtzion 1980:127). In 969 they transferred their capital to Qahira (Cairo), later extending their rule over Arabia and Syria. Tax revenues from Egypt's rich farmland, the nonstop flow of African gold, and maritime trade with the east fortified the Fatimid caliphate for the next 200 years. Midst this great affluence, the caliph al-Hakim, intoxicated with power, in 1005 saw fit to order the persecution of Jews and Christians and the destruction of many of their buildings, including the demolition of the Church of the Holy Sepulcher in Jerusalem. His cruel acts would have repercussions in the years ahead as contributory cause of the Crusades (Donner 1999:45–47).

All was not tranquil elsewhere in North Africa. In response to Shiite Fatimid and Buyid domination of former Sunni populations, the early eleventh century saw a zealous revival of orthodox Sunni Islam. Because in this westernmost corner of Islam there existed considerable religious heterodoxy, the missionary Abdallah ibn Yasin was dispatched to indoctrinate the equestrian Sanhadja of the western Sahara. As in the east, ribat-fortified religious centers had been established along the Islamic frontiers in Africa, where devout Muslims could honor Allah and extend the kingdom of Islam by fighting infidels. Under Ibn Yasin's stern tutelage, the nomads developed into a tough disciplined fighting force. Known as *al-murabitun* (ribat fighters of jihad), later as Almoravids, they rallied many desert tribes to their cause. As a Sunni reform movement, the Sanhadja between 1054 and 1059 succeeded in vanquishing their Zanata Berber political rivals, capturing Sidjilmasa in the north and Awdagust in the south. With these two termini of the trans-Saharan gold route under their authority, they controlled all the trade of northwest Africa (Fig. 7.2); unfortunately they suffered a setback when Ibn Yasin was killed at the battle of Kurifalat (Hrbek and Devisse 1988:347–348).

SANHADJA TO THE SOUTH. Ibn Yasin was succeeded by Abu Bakr, who led his tribal cavalries and cameleers south to suppress uprisings in *Bilad al-Sudan* (Lands of the Black People) between Lake Chad and

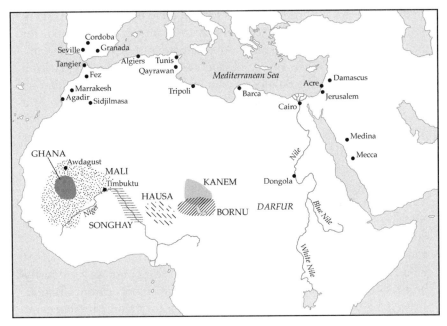

FIGURE 7.2. Almoravid extension south from Sidjilmasa across the Sahara to Ghana. Later Negro cavalry kingdoms of the savanna.

the Atlantic, converting the rulers of Wagadu, now Ghana,[10] in 1076 and enforcing Sunni orthodoxy by eliminating all remaining forms of Shiite and Kharijite Islam (Levtzion 1980:45). By strengthening the staging posts along the connecting routes between Morocco and Senegal, Almoravid equestrian militarism succeeded in integrating the different economies of the region into the political unity of the Maghreb (Hrbek and Devisse 1988:361). Thus ancient Ghana, long accustomed to its fabulous wealth in the gold trade – its king appearing at audiences bedecked in a golden headdress surrounded by 10 horses adorned with gold trappings – in the twelfth century would flourish as an independent Muslim kingdom (Bovill 1958:81). By mid-thirteenth century, however, Ghana was in decline, as Mali emerged the dominant power along the Niger River, its trading chains extending from the Sahel to the sources of gold

[10] As early as the eighth century, ancient Wagadu had been contacted by Arab traders, who were permitted by the Negro king to establish residence in a special sector of his capital Kumbi-Saleh. In the course of trading, some local people were converted to Islam, and the kingdom in the Sahel came to be known as Ghana by the Arabs.

in the south. As Muslim merchants continued to establish trading centers throughout the region, conversion to Islam became essential for peoples of the savanna wishing to participate in this prosperous commercial network. When Tuareg nomads seized Timbuktu in 1433, Mali was superseded in the Sahel by Songhay, and in the central Sudan by Kanem-Bornu and Hausa, whose fortified towns would protect the gold trade.

In these cavalry kingdoms, Muslim traders and religious leaders would regularly consult with the different rulers, who as early recipients of Islamic teachings greatly expedited the process of islamization (Levtzion 1999:476–481). These were militaristic kingdoms, constantly vying with their neighbors. Cavalry, the striking force of their armies, appears early to have been composed of free men, whose commanders were rewarded by gifts and estates from the king; in later times cavalry forces would include both slave warriors and mercenaries. Small horses could be bred locally above the latitude 12°N. Larger horses were costly and needed to be imported from the northern Berbers or from Dongola in exchange for slaves. By the mid-fifteenth century, along the Senegambian coast, the Portuguese too had begun supplying horses to the kingdoms of Jolof and Mali, the exchange rate 14 slaves per horse. The Arab historian al-Ulmari reported that the king of Mali commanded a force of no less than 10,000 cavalry (Law 1980:10, 41, 51, 148; Levtzion 1985:154). Everywhere, the warhorse was the symbol of wealth and high political status. With the buildup of military power came improvements in weaponry. Later, iron helmets and coats of mail were introduced to complement archery, spears, and swords, thereby attaining a definitive edge over pagan adversaries (Adeleye 1976:558); in the extreme heat quilted cotton armor was also used. The principal cavalry weapons were the lance for thrusting and the hurled javelin; although less important, a broad-bladed slashing sword was carried for hand-to-hand combat, as were cudgels and battle-axes. Surprisingly, little archery was used by mounted troops in West Africa (Law 1980:112, 127–129). In this territorial expansion, Muslim power from the Sahel would reach south to the fringes of the tropical forest, but not far beyond. Cavalry, a fearsome force in the deserts and savannas, could not operate effectively in the humidity of the tropics. The high cost of transporting hay there was prohibitive. And in the southern areas of West Africa, the horse could not withstand the infection *Trypanosoma brucei*, transmitted by the tsetse fly and causing fatality within three months. Periodic fluctuation of the tsetse belt northward at times even affected the savanna kingdoms, resulting in the weakening of cavalry forces and decline in military strength. Furthermore, tropical vegetation presented insurmountable obstacles to effective cavalry offensive; bamboo traps were easily set along forest paths to trip advancing horses. From very early colonial reports, it is known that the Ijesa forested country of Yorubaland on multiple occasions had proven to be a graveyard for cavalry armies invading from the north (Law 1980:76, 79–81, 139–140).

SANHADJA TO THE NORTH. As Abu Bakr campaigned and consolidated Muslim power in the south, the Sanhadja cavalry led by his cousin Yusuf ibn Tashfin aggressively attacked northward subduing semi-islamized Berber groups and establishing a military camp at Marrakesh, which would grow rapidly to become the Almoravid capital in 1070. From 1075 to 1083, Ibn Tashfin conquered all of Morocco and western Algeria, finally securing the Gibraltar strait (Hrbek and Devisse 1988:351). Almoravid authority spanned vast distances and the gold trade rose to a new peak. But in Al-Andalus, the Hispano-Umayyad caliphate had collapsed in civil war with rebel Berbers and was replaced by various Taifa kingdoms, which due to incessant internecine feuding failed to gain significant political power. In response to Taifa pleas for aid in repelling the northern Christian armies, Ibn Tashfin led his frontier fighters into Al-Andalus as Toledo was being taken in 1085 by Alfonso VI of Castile and Leon. In spectacular defeat of the Christian forces, the Almoravids halted the enemy advance at the battle of az-Zallaqa (Sagrajas) near Badajoz in 1086. Continuing Almoravid victories on the battlefield kept the Christians at bay in the north but failed to regain Toledo. During Almoravid rule, the economy boomed as increased supplies of copper, iron, and silver were exported from Morocco and vast quantities of African gold reached Al-Andalus across the straits (Hrbek and Devisse 1988:363). Almoravid dinars were of pure gold and therefore in great demand throughout Europe. The Almohads, another revivalist group who challenged the Almoravids in North Africa and invaded Al-Andalus in 1147, continued to maintain the same high standard of gold coins (Levtzion 1980:129). Thus, on the western fringes of empire, two Berber equestrian dynasties from the deserts of North Africa stemmed the onrush of Christian armies for over a hundred years. In 1212 at the battle of Las Navas de Tolosa, however, the Almohads suffered a crushing defeat at the hands of the crusading princes of Leon, Castile, Navarre, and Aragon (Curtin 1970:35–36). Once again fragmented into small principalities, Al-Andalus was ever vulnerable to Christian depredation. In 1236 Ferdinand III removed the cathedral bells suspended in the Cordoba mosque and sent them back to Santiago de Compostela, this time on the backs of Muslim prisoners. At this point, the Nasrids were the only remaining Islamic dynasty in the Iberian peninsula. High on a hill above Granada, from their splendid city-palace of the Alhambra they would rule until 1492 (Dodds 1992:18).

TURKIC-INVADER CONVERTS TO ISLAM AND CRUSADER OPPONENTS

WHILE ARAB FRONTIERS IN THE WEST WERE REPEATEDLY CHALLENGED during the Middle Ages by Spanish and Frankish Christians from the north and Saharan Berbers from the south, there was comparable turmoil in the east as vast movements of Turkic peoples swept out of Central Asia. These migrations were in many ways a continuation of the earlier Hun and Avar nomadic journeys across the Eurasian steppes, in which tribe after tribe of Altaic speakers from the east displaced Iranian speakers westward. As noted earlier, in the Persian national epic, the *Shahnameh* (Book of Kings), this ethnic confrontation was even depicted as a polo match between the invading steppe forces and the followers of the legendary Persian hero, prince Siyavush. The *Shahnameh*, three times the length of the *Iliad*, emphasized this eternal struggle between Iran, settled and civilized, and the pastoral steppe, dominated by nomads. In the wake of Arab conquest, like the *Taziyeh*, the *Shahnameh* epic reasserted Persian identity by recalling its Zoroastrian heritage. Written in Persian, employing a modified form of Arabic script, the poem echoed the tense conditions of the Samanid period and the changing nature of the Middle East at the end of the first millennium AD as Turkic tribes invaded from the steppes (Donner 1999:40).

The Shahnameh

The *Shahnameh*, comprising some 60,000 lines of rhyming verse in the poetic tradition of Persia's Zoroastrian ancestors, was composed by the tenth-century poet Abul Qasim Mansur, later known as Firdausi. From Avestan antiquity across ages of Iranian civilization to the Arab conquest of the Sasanians, it recounts the exploits of heroes and kings, describing the splendor of their armies and the devastation of their wars.

253

In Zoroastrian tradition, it opposes the purity of light to the forces of darkness, ever upholding the principles of righteousness. As in the case of the *Vedas*, these verses were transmitted orally over the centuries. It was not until the enlightened reign of the Sasanian monarch Khosrau I in the sixth century AD that a systematic attempt was made to compile these legends in the Pahlavi text of *Chodainameh* (Book of Sovereigns). Research into the epics continued under the Samanids. In the tenth century, the poet Dakiki was assigned to render the tales in verse but was murdered by a Frankish eunuch. Firdausi, from the landed gentry of Khurasan, a class regarded by many as custodians of Iran's ancient traditions, took his place. Following Samanid defeat, in 1010 he reluctantly dedicated the completed work to the Turkic sultan Mahmud of Ghazna, whose forces had overrun much of Persia. But palace intrigue resulted in the poet's receiving only meager payment for his work. After delivering a scorching satire on the Ghaznavid sultan, Firdausi fled the court to seek refuge on the Caspian coast (Gottheil 1900:iv–vi). Years later, the sultan Mahmud, waging a campaign in India, was awaiting rebel response to his demand for surrender. In the suspense of the moment he turned to his minister for comment. The man, an admirer of the *Shahnameh*, quoted a couplet:

> And should the reply with my wish not accord,
> Then Afrasiyab's field, and the mace, and the sword!
> (Browne 1977:137)

So struck was the sultan by the pungency of the verse, he insisted on knowing the poet's name. When reminded of his shabby treatment of Firdausi, he was filled with remorse and promptly dispatched indigo to the value of some 60,000 gold dinars – one for each line of the *Shahnameh* – to Tus, the poet's birthplace to which he had returned. But as the royal camels bearing the gift approached the city, Firdausi's corpse was borne out for burial. His daughter disdainfully refused the bounty (Browne 1977:137–138).

Of the many dramas contained in the colossal narrative of the *Shahnameh*, few are so vivid as the exploits of the great hero Rustam, who was known in Saka legends as far east as the Tarim. Destined from birth to become the guardian and savior of his people, he was a paragon of justice and courage. His lifetime spanned 600 years and the reigns of eight shahs, many of whom were indebted to Rustam's heroic deeds for control of their throne. A semidivine being, gigantic in stature,

Rustam nevertheless did not represent total perfection. He too was subject to human weaknesses and the inevitable forces of destiny that often posed challenges of great moral conflict (Lillys 1958:3). Paradoxically as kingmaker, the hero Rustam was a living challenge to the concept of kingship, even though all his adventures – but one – were dedicated to upholding it. This dialectic between king and hero appears to be a fundamental theme that can be traced back to the remotest Indo-European traditions; its cognates are seen in many language groups. In Greek, Heracles, in the service of Eurystheus king of Argos, was obliged to undertake 12 labors at the behest of one inferior to him as hero. Just as Achilles, king of remote Phthia, resented Agamemnon's authority over all Achaeans, so Rustam, local king of remote Sistan, in turn during the Kayanid dynasty would be critical of Kai Kaus's headstrong foolishness that inevitably led to untold troubles requiring Rustam's heroic intervention (Davidson 1994:6, 12, 100–101). Both Heracles and Rustam were supermen, albeit with sympathetic human proclivities, ever engaged in gripping adventures combating evil and championing good. But hauntingly similar rivalries between hero and king were also evidenced in the Celtic legends of Lancelot and King Arthur, in the history of El Cid and the Castilian monarch Alfonso, perhaps even in the stubborn heroism of the Frankish knight Roland, himself a Celtic outsider from Brittany, vis-a-vis his emperor Charlemagne.

At the very beginning of the epic, there was a confrontation between the idolatrous peoples of Arabia and Assyria and Feridun, the first Indo-European. As in the Scythian myth of Targitaus, Feridun too had three sons, Silim, Irij, and Tur, for whom respectively he divided the world in three: Europe in the west, Iran as world center, and Turan on the eastern steppes (Gottheil 1900:37). In Rustam's adventures, the Turanians, a barbaric horde inhabiting the fringes of the earth, appear as the most hated enemy; their king Afrasiyab was created by evil to destroy Iran. As attested in the earliest Avestan tradition, the Turanians were rival Indo-Europeans, their daring mairiia warrior cult combating Iran. Later they assumed a more composite character and came to be equated to the Altaic Turkic tribes persistently threatening the Iranian borders (Davidson 1994:103–105). The whole poem deals with the unceasing efforts of the kingdom of darkness to subdue the kingdom of light. Ohrmazd is represented by Iranians; Ahriman, by devils, fiends, or sorcerers that harass Iran. Like Heracles, Rustam displayed incredible strength, as a boy overcoming a white elephant that had broken loose. Facing the crazed beast alone, Rustam slew the elephant on the spot with a crushing blow. Rustam was also responsible himself for choosing his marvelous piebald colt *Rakhsh* (Lightning) from his father Zal's great herds (Lillys 1958:6–8). With a lion's heart and tiger's strength, astride Rakhsh, Rustam sped toward the Turanian enemy (Gottheil 1900:113):

> Excited by his master's cry,
> The war-horse bounded o'er the plain,
> So swiftly that he seemed to fly,
> Snorting with pride, and tossing high
> His streaming mane.
> (Gottheil 1900:114)

At full gallop, Rustam lassoed the evil Afrasiyab out of his saddle.

Dispatched by Zal to rescue Kai Kaus's army, Rustam embarked on a perilous journey during which he underwent seven ordeals or trials. Throughout these adventures, the fine horse Rakhsh, lauded by Rustam as his throne, defended his master with strength and courage. In a forest, having feasted on roasted onager, Rustam sank into a deep sleep. When a lion emerged from the bushes, Rakhsh fought off the beast about to devour them, grasping it in his teeth and trampling it underfoot. Another time the valiant steed tackled a dragon; unable to defeat it, he awoke Rustam in time from his slumber. As the hero engaged the raging monster, the horse bit its shoulder, distracting it so that Rustam was able to cleave the dragon's head with his sword. Rustam also grappled with a wicked sorceress and finally succeeded in killing the White Demon, thus freeing his sovereign Kai Kaus from imprisonment (Gottheil 1900:93, 93–102).

Once, on a solitary hunting expedition, Rustam awoke to find that Rakhsh had been abducted. Arriving on foot at the nearby kingdom of Samangan across the Turanian border, Rustam was entertained lavishly at the palace by the king, who immediately organized a search for the steed. In the middle of the night a beautiful girl came to Rustam's chamber. She was Tahminah, the king's daughter who had rejected many suitors, hoping Rustam one day might come. She declared her love for him and her desire to bear his child. If he would have her, Tahminah promised she would restore the horse. They were married the following day. Rustam departed, entrusting his signet as token. Should the child be a boy Tahminah would tie the signet around his arm. Their son Suhrab was born and grew to be as big and strong as his father (Gottheil 1900:115–120).

But Rustam's fine romance ended in tragedy. Tahminah had prevented news of Suhrab's birth from reaching Rustam, for fear her son would be trained for war. But her son demanded to know of his father and eventually learned he was the great hero Rustam. Suhrab impulsively decided to overthrow both Kai Kaus and Afrasiyab and then with his father jointly rule both kingdoms. But wily Afrasiyab directed Suhrab against Kai Kaus. Suhrab began his campaign by attacking a Persian stronghold defended by the fair Amazon Gurdafarid, who with her great beauty tricked Suhrab into letting her escape to warn Kai Kaus. A Persian army was sent against the Turanians. Thus, after many years, Suhrab and Rustam met on the battlefield. Without full knowledge of each other's identity, they fought with javelins, scimitars, and maces, culminating in a wrestling match. Suhrab succeeded in flinging Rustam to the ground, sat astride him, and drew his dagger for the fatal blow. Rustam quickly countered that the customs of battle dictated that a victor in wrestling might only kill his adversary on the second throw. The chivalrous youth accepted his plea. The next day Rustam returned to the fray, dashed Suhrab to the ground, and not giving him a second chance stabbed him in the chest. As Suhrab lay dying, he swore his father Rustam would avenge his death. Demanding proof, Rustam then recognized the seal on his son's arm. Crazed by his discovery, the champion sank into deep desperation (Robinson 2002:32–35). At Suhrab's last expiring groan,

> Now keener anguish rack'd the father's mind,
> Reft of his son, a murderer of his kind;
> His guilty sword distained with filial gore,
> He beat his burning breast, his hair he tore.
> > (Gottheil 1900:153)

In the Turanian camp, tragically Tahminah too received news of her son's death and blamed herself for concealing his birth from Rustam:

> The strong emotion choked her panting breath, . . .
> Then gazing up, distraught, she wept again,
> And frantic, seeing 'midst her pitying train,
> The favourite steed – now more than ever dear,
> The hoofs she kissed, and bathed with many a tear;
> Clasping the mail Sohrab in battle wore,
> With burning lips she kissed it o'er and o'er;

His martial robes she in her arms compressed
And like an infant strained them to her breast.

(Gottheil 1900:156)

Hostilities continued between Iranians and Turanians. Rustam met opposing warriors in individual challenges, captured, and killed in the furor of battle. But Afrasiyab repeatedly eluded the Iranians until finally the infamous ruler and his brother were captured and executed by the noble warrior Kai Khosrau, son of Siyavush and grandson of Kai Kaus (Gottheil 1900:246). Kai Khosrau of course has been equated with Arthur's trusted paladin Sir Kay, linking the Arthuriad with the *Shah-nameh* as well as the Ossetic legends. But Rustam also had to contend with treachery at home. Isfandiyar, son and heir apparent of shah Gush-tasp, attempted to take Rustam captive. Rustam tried unsuccessfully to mollify the prince, but in the inevitable clash between the two men Rustam shot the aspiring shah between the eyes with Simurg's deadly forked arrow (Robinson 2002:74–76). This "killing of the king by the kingmaker" constituted a fundamentally unnatural deed and as such sealed Rustam's fate (Davidson 1994:12–13).

As foretold by the wondrous bird Simurg, the slayer of Isfandiyar was to be pursued by anguish (Davidson 1994:140). Rustam finally was ensnared by his half brother Shaghad in conspiracy with the king of Kabul. Huge pits were dug and planted with long, sharp spear points, then covered with grass. Upon Rustam's arrival, knowing of the hero's fondness for the hunt, the king invited him to join the chase. The con-spirators' villainy complete, Rustam rode out to his doom. As the hero approached the hunting grounds, his noble steed Rakhsh, detecting the smell of freshly dug earth, jibbed, then began to move cautiously between the skillfully concealed pits (Robinson 2002:77). Impatient, Rustam tapped Rakhsh lightly just as the horse was attempting to avoid the traps. As Rakhsh stumbled, both rider and mount fell into the trench cunningly crafted by the assassins, to be brutally impaled below. Fatally wounded, Rustam requested a bow against marauding lions. Shaghad complied, but Rustam grasped the bow with such strength that the half brother fearfully took refuge behind a tree. Drawing the bow to his ear, Rustam summoned his last strength to shoot the arrow straight through the tree to instantly kill the treacherous Shaghad. News of Rustam's tragic fate spread rapidly, and a great outburst of anguish resounded throughout Iran. As a final farewell, men of all ranks in homage poured roses and musk at his feet. Mourners shed tears of blood. Never was a funeral more extraordinary! Rustam's death marked the end of a noble era (Lillys 1958:13, 30).

Equestrian Invaders from the East

The turbulent tensions of Firdausi's *Shahnameh* clearly reflect the regional upheavals occurring in eastern Islamic lands, in terms of hostilities among Iranian petty dynasties as well as concerted resistance to nomad encroachment from the steppes. With Seljuk domination of these territories in the eleventh century, it is necessary to recognize, however, that Seljuk military leadership and Turkic migrations were different although related phenomena. As did Toghril, the succeeding Seljuk sultans to a large degree continued to depend on Turkmen for their armies, and the Turkmen recognized the Seljuks as their royal leaders, but there was plenty of friction between the two parties. The Seljuks therefore continued the established practice of recruiting slave mercenaries to fill the core of their army, opportunistically allying with different nomad groups for specific campaigns. At the same time, they directed tribal migrations away from fertile alluvium near Seljuk-controlled towns, encouraging the nomads to raid in frontier (often Christian) zones. Thus while the Sunni sultanate controlled a loose empire from Transoxania to Iraq, the Turkmen did not stop at Baghdad but continued their migrations into Anatolia, defying the Byzantine fortresses. In this joint Turkic advance westward, the light-framed mounts of the Seljuk sultan Alp Arslan in the summer heat at Manzikert outmaneuvered the heavy-armored cataphracts of Byzantine emperor Romanus IV Diogenes, effectively ending Christian domination of eastern Anatolia in 1071. After a complex struggle for power among the Seljuk clans and the Armenian, Turkic, and Kurdish chieftains, Byzantine resistance in western Anatolia also ceased. The Seljuks then expanded into Syria at the expense of Fatimid Egypt. By the late eighties, the greatest of Seljuk sultans, Malik Shah, was gazing across the Bosporus at Constantinople. To the south, a rival clan, the Seljuks of Rum, consolidated power in Konya (Iconium), a major center of Sufism (Donner 1999:54–55; Hyland 1994:53).

Equestrian Invaders from the West

Thus, in the idiom of the *Shahnameh*, at the beginning of the second millennium AD, nomadic Turanian invaders from the steppes had prevailed over civilized Iranians. One further invader, however, was missing in the Middle East, Salm, the first son of Feridun – or more specifically, his European descendants from the Occident. Unbeknownst to Firdausi writing in the tenth century, in effect soon to arrive in the Near East would be great armies of western knights from Europe. Different factors, from earlier Shia Fatimid desecration of holy shrines in Jerusalem, which had outraged western Christendom, to repeated Byzantine losses in Anatolia and the final Turkish advance to the Bosporus, led to the phenomenon of Christian Crusader invasion of the Holy Land. In 1095, alarmed at Seljuk successes in Asia Minor, the emperor Alexius I Comnenus sent delegates to Pope Urban II urging Latin Europe to help repel Sunni Muslim encroachment (Irwin 1996:43). Politically isolated from the West since the schism over papal authority of 1054, the Byzantine emperor appealed to Rome to assist the Christian East, offering a reunion of the Greek and Latin Church against Islam and stressing the strategic importance of confronting the infidel on Asian soil, rather than allowing the Turkic invaders to swarm through the Balkans to besiege the capitals of western Europe. Troubled by internecine warring within Europe, Urban now hoped to stop the infighting among knights at home by directing their aggressive impulses toward the Muslims. Already the Spanish Christians with the help of Frankish knights had seized Toledo from the Moors in 1085, pushing back the borders of Al-Andalus. In 1091 the Normans had succeeded in conquering all of Sicily from the Arabs. The pope therefore responded to Alexius's plea in 1095 at the Council of Clermont by appealing energetically to the faithful to recover the Holy Land from the infidel and to liberate eastern Christendom from the scourge of Islam. He offered hefty inducements to Christians for the duration of the war, freeing the serf and vassal from fealty to their lord, exempting soldiers from taxes, and granting a plenary indulgence remitting all sins to those who should die in battle. Christian martyrs were promised Paradise (Durant 1950:431, 586–588). Popular reaction to the pope's declaration was extraordinary. Knights expended large sums of money on horses, armor, and weapons to equip themselves for the long campaign. In the spirit of the Cluniac vision of pilgrimage, younger knights received financial assistance from their rich elders and alms were distributed among poor pilgrims (Armstrong 1991:150).

THE FIRST CRUSADE. One immediate consequence of the pope's appeal was the Peasants' Crusade, which during its march across Europe in the spring of 1096 unleashed unspeakable violence against the Jews of the

Rhineland, the first of a series of pogroms that would characterize crusading activity. Later in the year, the forces of the First Crusade some 30,000 strong arrived in Constantinople, led by the brother of Philip of France and Godfrey of Bouillon, descendant of Charlemagne. The Byzantines were so impressed by the collective charge in formation by the Frankish knights that Anna Comnena, daughter of the emperor, exclaimed "a Frank with a lance in his hand could punch a hole in the walls of Babylon" (Hopkins 2004:38). Alexius offered transport and military aid in crises in exchange for the Crusaders' oath of allegiance that all lands taken should be held in fealty to Constantinople. It appears though that both parties had distinct reservations about honoring such a pledge; the leaders of the First Crusade had far grander territorial ambitions than merely intervening on Byzantine behalf in the Near East, and Byzantium was at times most reticent in providing promised support for Crusader endeavor. Having the sheer good fortune to arrive shortly after the death of the last great sultan Malik Shah, at a time when the sultanate was rent by dissension among rival kinsmen, the Latin Christians won easy first victories against the Seljuks. They were able to advance to Antioch, Tripoli, and Acre; to capture Jerusalem from the Fatimids in 1099, brutally massacring the Muslim and Jewish inhabitants; and to establish for western Christendom a chain of Crusader principalities along the Syrio-Palestinian coast (Irwin 1996:43).

Thus, the First Crusader forces to arrive in the Holy Land followed the land route across Europe to Constantinople whence they were shipped across the Bosporus. The Byzantines had long experience in maritime horse transport, for centuries having deployed their troops to Asia Minor and North Africa, most recently having carried their Norman mercenaries over the Straits of Messina to assault Muslim-held Sicily. Their vessels, *Dromons* or *Triremes,* were equipped with large openings in the stern with ramps for easy embarking and disembarking of horses, the transports being backed onto the beach for this purpose; ramps could also be lowered from the side of the ships. But during the First Crusade, the Christians experienced acute shortages of mounts. After the long siege of Antioch, the Crusaders could muster no more than 200 horses, and many were reduced to riding into battle on pack animals (Asbridge 2004:233). In order to increase the number of horses available to their armies in later Crusades, Byzantine techniques of marine transportation were adopted by Latin Christians, and as transports improved and capacity increased, large quantities of horses and mules were shipped directly from western Europe to the eastern Mediterranean. On-board stabling provided mangers, stall rails, esparto grass bedding, and stabilizing underbelly slings for the horses. Early transports stabled 20 horses in one row below deck at the center of the ship with room for a groom to pass between. Once the animals were on board, the entrance hatches were caulked to make them watertight. Later vessels accommodated 30 to 60 horses. On long-distance voyages, frequent landings were necessary for airings and to load fresh water on board. A horse normally consumed four gallons of water a day. Confinement in the hot, humid, restricted space below deck greatly increased this intake. Enforced inactivity aboard ship caused muscle wastage. Also, mental stress resulted from rough weather conditions experienced during sea travel. Having endured these hardships, horses arriving by sea to Outremer required well over a week to regain fitness. Notwithstanding these difficulties, over the next 200 years, large contingents of cavalry horses would be shipped to the kingdom of Jerusalem. But these shipments from Europe were never sufficient to supply all needed mounts and baggage animals. Syria was good horse-breeding country; therefore, horses could be alternatively purchased, seized in raids, captured in battle, paid as ransom, or received as rent for land or gifts from fortified cities to avoid assault. In times of heavy battle casualties, knights of necessity had recourse to mules and donkeys (Hyland 1994:143–148).

WARRIOR MONKS. An interesting development in the early life of the Christian principalities was the establishment of the religious orders of warrior monks. The elite military order, the Knights Templar, was founded in 1119 by king Baldwin II of Jerusalem and housed in a wing of his palace near the former Jewish temple from which the name derives; with time subsidiary temples were organized outside Jerusalem. In a period when the Crusaders controlled only a few strongholds, French knights led by Hugues de Payens formed this religious community in order to protect pilgrims to the Holy Land threatened by robbers and highwaymen. The Templars wore the distinctive regalia of a white surcoat marked by a red cross, each knight taking vows of poverty, chastity, and obedience to the Grand Master who headed the order. The Templars' numbers rapidly increased partly because of the Cistercian writings of St. Bernard de Clairvaux, which introduced the military edge to monasticism, establishing a corps of knights obedient to the pope in order to counterweigh the power of European nobility as well as to serve as troops in defense of the Holy Land. This synthesis of knight and monk retained certain elements of the ancient Indo-European mairiia/Mannerbund – band of unmarried warriors operating on the fringes of society – substituting Christ for the wolf-god Woden and heaven for Valhalla. In Bernard's political vision, the Christian crusade, requiring sacrifice both in the monastery and on the battle field, was a sacred quest (Seward 1972:3–4). The kings and queens of Europe also donated great properties and wealth to the order, financing temples across Europe and the Holy Land. Their extraordinary military capability enabled the Templars to act as bankers, securely transporting bullion across many lands. In 1139 Pope Innocent II established the order directly under his papal authority.

During the eleventh century, Italian merchants from Amalfi had similarly established a hospital in Jerusalem and hostels along pilgrim routes to treat invalids. But with the success of the Templars, early in the twelfth century these Hospitalers of St. John of Jerusalem were reorganized to combine military duties with ministering to the sick; the Hospitalers were distinguished by a black surcoat marked with a white cross. Perhaps more cosmopolitan than the Templars, they also incorporated Turcopoles, local men of European father and Syrian mother, as light cavalry (Howarth 1993:96–97). Later in the twelfth century they were joined by the Teutonic Knights. During the Crusader siege of Acre, German merchants formed a fraternity to tend the wounded, later establishing a hospital; the fraternity in turn was converted to a religious order of knights like the Templars, with the distinctive garb of white mantle marked with a black cross. Far from their homeland, segregated in their strongholds, imbued with the Cistercian ethic of poverty, chastity, and strict military discipline, these orders constituted a resolute standing army in the Holy Land.

Equestrian methods of the Latin cavalry and the Muslim *faris* (mounted warrior) differed. In the crusading era, the European horse stood approximately 15 hands and weighed between 545 and 590 kg. By comparison the Turkmene horse had the same height but weighed only 360–400 kg; the Arab horse was even lighter. The western knight rode straight legged in order to deliver the most powerful thrust with his heavy lance, his saddle so high off the horse's back that rider was fairly insensitive to animal body movements. Turks and Arabs rode in a more balanced manner with bent knee, the leg absorbing some of the thrust's shock. As a consequence there was closer interaction between rider and mount. The Saracens' lighter horse could stop dead in its stride, then whirl around on its hocks to dart in any direction. In contrast, the bigger, heavily armored European horse, trained for the shock charge en masse, lacked skill in quickly maneuvering in narrow confines. The couched lance used in a close-packed *conrois* of knights demanded discipline and unit cohesion that would topple the foe from the saddle, even over-throw the horse. The Crusaders' massed charge in fact was devastating but required space. Their couched lance technique was adapted with modification by the Saracens. In turn, with the capture of the lighter-built Saracen steeds, the Crusaders during their sojourn in the Holy Land also acquired certain eastern techniques (Hyland 1994:8, 113–114, 117; Nicolle 2001:31).

In contrast to the secular knights, whose comportment at times might seem reckless and, like that of Roland, given to feats of individual valor, the military orders displayed exemplary discipline. Colorful, costly clothes and richly decorated equipment, so characteristic of medieval knighthood, were prohibited to the monk. Hunting was forbidden and racing only rarely permitted. Mock jousting and half-speed lance attack without casting weapons were approved and taught the knight to posi-tion his horse accurately; the exercise also built confidence in the horse to charge. Penalties for rule infraction were harsh, underscoring that disobedience in combat was worse than defeat. Templar supremacy in battle was achieved through strict compliance with military rou-tine. To drink water required permission, for so often the well or river was the site of cleverly planned enemy ambush. An elite guard of 10 knights protected the standard in battle, with a spare furled banner at hand to which the troops would rally in the face of disaster. While the Templar standard still flew, no brother would retreat. Close combat, the Templars' specialization, was conducted astride stallions. So valorous was adherence to discipline that many men and horses fell in battle. The Saracens both admired and feared the fortitude of the fighting orders of monks (Hyland 1994:159–164).

Neither the Abbasids nor Seljuks evinced much interest in pursuing jihad against the western invaders, leaving Muslim resistance to the Crusaders' neighbors in the Levant. In 1128 Imad ad-Din Zengi was installed by the sultan of Rum as *atabeg* (governor) of northern Syria, then a patchwork of petty rival states. In the course of his remorseless military campaigns, Zengi imposed unity on these territories. The elite of the multiethnic Saracen armies were soldiers of slave origin, while the majority comprised free-born Arabs, Turks, or Kurds, subject to the *iqta* land grant system (Hyland 1994:114–115). The Arab Bedouin had the reputation of hard-riding light cavalry, inured to hardship in the deserts. Kurds were famed for their swordsmanship and fought as tribal units or individual mercenaries. Like all steppe peoples, the Turks were militarily important as horse archers. Their archery was based on shower shooting in volleys. In practice they trained by aiming at a straw animal rolled downhill in a cart. While charging at full speed 30 m from the enemy, the Turkic archers, holding arrows and bow in the left hand, were competent at shooting level, upward, or downward as fast as five arrows in two and a half seconds, before snatching another five arrows from the quiver. The archer dropped the reins as he shot, but with a strap attached to a finger of his right hand he would quickly regain them again. The faris used his spear in various ways. In the traditional two-handed form he slacked the reins as he lowered the spear, then dropped them as he struck the enemy. Later he too would employ the couched lance method of his Crusader enemy. Sword fencing was highly sophisticated, delivering on horseback blows of terrifying impact and precision (Nicolle 1997:11, 13).

THE SECOND CRUSADE AND THE RISE OF SALADIN. In 1144 Zengi, atabeg of Mosul, with a heterogeneous army captured the Christian principality of Edessa (Irwin 1996:44). In reaction to this major defeat by the Muslims, the Second Crusade led by Louis VII of France and his queen Eleanor of Aquitaine set out from Europe, arriving in Antioch in 1148. The monarchs were received by Raymond of Antioch, who promptly became Eleanor's lover. Conrad of Germany also arrived in the Holy Land, but with only a remnant of his original army. Alarmed at the buildup of Zengid forces, the Christians decided to attack Damascus, but their siege resulted in a complete fiasco, entailing extensive loss of life. After the Second Crusade departed for Europe in disgrace, Zengi's son and heir Nur ad-Din (1146–1173) mobilized a jihad of defense against the Latin invaders, slowly conquering Syria and encircling the Christian states, finally making Damascus his capital in 1164 (Armstrong 1991:219–221).

The Zengids also intervened in the ailing caliphate of Egypt, whose military leaders were contending for the vizier's position of power, the actual strength behind the Fatimid throne. Nur ad-Din dispatched a force under his trusted Kurdish general, Shirkuh, to assume the post of vizier. When Shirkuh died in 1169, he was succeeded by his nephew, Salah ad-Din, also a Kurd (Iranian speaker). Saladin (as he became known to the West) now governed Egypt on behalf of Nur ad-Din. As seen in the last chapter, Shia had earlier gained political ascendancy in Egypt as the official faith of the Fatimid caliphate of Cairo, in hostile opposition to the Sunni Abbasids of Baghdad. With the ailing Fatimid caliph too sick to resist, Saladin in 1171 replaced the Fatimid Shia faith of Egypt with orthodox Sunni Islam. Opposition to his daring move, however, came from an unexpected quarter, the Iranian sect of the Assassins, an extremist offshoot of the Ismaili Sevener Shiites, whose center of operations was based in the Elburz mountains of northern Persia. There, a 3,200-m-high fortress, Alamut (Eagle's Nest), was a center of military education from which the Shia waged a campaign of terror against opponents of their faith. Founded in 1090 by Hasan ibn al Sabbah to advance the cause of the Ismaili revolution, the holy warriors murdered prominent Sunni political and cultural leaders (Donner 1999:49). Obliged to submit faithfully to the Grand Master's will to die if necessary, the jihad was undertaken by *hashshashin* – from which is derived the English word *assassin* – referring to the alleged practice of adherents' consuming hashish to induce mystical visions of paradise before facing martyrdom. Terrorism was adopted by this sect as a sacred religious duty. These radical terrorists of medieval Islam spread to strongholds across the Middle East. From Masyaf, a mountainous redoubt in Syria, their envoys approached King Amalric of Jerusalem, proposing an alliance between Christians and Shia against the Sunnite Saladin. Amalric agreed. The Crusaders already knew the Assassins' legendary leader in Syria, *shayk al-jabal*, as the "Old Man of the Mountain." Masters of clandestine murder, in their suicidal fervor the Assassins would make formidable allies. Saladin, however, was successful in foiling their various plots to assassinate him (Howarth 1993:128).

After Nur ad-Din's death in 1174, Saladin moved out of Egypt with 700 horsemen to occupy Damascus, justifying his rule in Syria and later Mesopotamia by prosecuting jihad against the Crusader states (Irwin 1996:44). As a ruler, Saladin displayed great integrity and stern orthodoxy of faith. Returning to Egypt, in Cairo he inaugurated the Ayyubid dynasty and ruled with justice and diligence. He was always accessible to his people and never ceased to make his saddle his council chamber, in battle often moving through the ranks accompanied only by a page leading his warhorse. He introduced an educational program into the army whereby the *hadith* was read to the assembled troops; further discussion of these scriptures ensued as the mounted cavalry advanced toward the enemy (Armstrong 1991:237–240). At first Saladin contented himself with minor forays against the Christians, but an incident in 1183 provoked his pious wrath. A Frank, Reginald of Chatillon, determined to kidnap the Prophet Muhammad's body and smash the Kaaba, with a band of adventurers sailed down the Red Sea, then rode to Medina with horses purchased from the Bedouin. The force was intercepted by the Egyptians. Reginald eluded capture, but many of his companions were executed in public displays. Their deliberate attempt to violate the sanctity of Islamic holy sites was provocation in extreme (Regan 1998:57–58).

In retaliation Saladin besieged Reginald's castle at Kerak. The siege failed but was marked by a chivalrous gesture so characteristic of Saladin. At the time, a marriage was being celebrated, and its festivities continued even while the walls were being pounded by rocks from eight mangonels. The Franks courteously sent out festive foods to Saladin, who responded by ordering his soldiers not to bombard the part of the castle where the young couple would spend their wedding night (Howarth 1993:142). Saladin's gentility and noblesse were evident on many other occasions. Despite the many hardships endured, Saladin's honor would remain unsullied (Regan 1998:128). Inevitably, though, a decisive confrontation between the two armies was to be fought, and so in the summer of 1187 Saladin crossed the Jordan River. The Christians were encamped at Sephoria, a well watered and pastured site. When news came that Saladin had laid siege to the castle of Tiberias, thereby endangering Count Raymond's wife, the knights' reaction was to immediately aid this damsel in distress. Some dissented, however, recognizing the folly of abandoning their strong location. Notwithstanding, by royal decree the army struck camp at dawn. Meanwhile the Saracens had moved to the village of Hattin 180 m below. Between Sephoria and Hattin lay 19 km of glaring, waterless white limestone over which the Christian knights rode in heavy armor under the merciless midsummer sun. Detachments of fast mounted archers rode out from the Saracen camp to harass them, almost successfully separating the Templars from the main army. By nightfall the wind had risen. Having encircled their enemy, the Muslims ignited the dry brush, causing the smoke to billow over the already dehydrated Franks. The next day the infantry made a desperate dash to the Sea of Galilee gleaming below, only to be cut down in droves. The cavalry fought bravely, several times breaking the Muslim lines, finally making the last stand on the Horns in defense of the king's red tent and the True Cross. But the king's tent was overturned;

Guy, king of Jerusalem, was captured; and the True Cross was dragged in the dust. Saladin showed the Templars and Hospitalers no mercy, beheading those not slain in battle and personally executing Reginald of Chatillon (Howarth 1993:149–153). On October 2 of that year, the day Muslims commemorate Muhammad's Night Journey, Saladin conquered Jerusalem. This time the sultan displayed great clemency. There was no killing, no plunder, many thousands were released; only those not able to pay the low ransom were enslaved. Most of Jerusalem's defeated sought refuge in Tyre; this peninsular port was twice besieged without success by Saladin and thus stood as the rock of Christian resistance against Saracen domination (Armstrong 1991:258–259).

THE THIRD CRUSADE. The Third Crusade involved the kings of both England and France, Poitevin Richard the Lionheart and his Capetian rival Philip Augustus. Both deeply distrusted each other's designs on their respective European kingdoms and were only reconciled to undertake the crusade on condition of the other's participation. Richard, an excellent horseman and swordsman, was the son of the irrepressible Eleanor of Aquitaine, who upon her return from the Holy Land divorced Louis VII to marry Henry II of England. A third monarch participating in the Third Crusade was Frederick Barbarossa, Holy Roman Emperor, who during his papal coronation had initially refused as secular ruler to perform the customary rite of holding the pontiff's bridle and stirrup, in helping him to dismount. When the kiss of peace and consequent crown of empire were withheld by Pope Hadrian IV, Frederick was forced to comply with this customary reverence. In 1189 Barbarossa led 100,000 men toward the Holy Land but unfortunately was drowned fording a river in Cilicia (Armstrong 1991:262–264; Durant 1950:662–663). For their part, Philip and Richard wintered jointly in Sicily. There Richard secured from the king Tancredi 1136 kg of gold in settlement of the dowry of Richard's sister Joanna, widow of Tancredi's predecessor. Early in 1191 both monarchs set sail for Outremer. But the ships were blown off course and the English landed on Cyprus, which Richard conquered. With the riches of Messina and Cyprus in his holds, Richard continued to Saracen-held Acre. Acre had been under siege by the Christians for more than 19 months (Howarth 1993:162–165).

To speed up the offensive, Richard, affluent from the proceeds of his maritime adventures, offered bonuses for stones removed from the fortifications. In early July the garrison capitulated. As Richard inspected Acre, reveling no doubt in the glory of his conquest, he noted a foreign banner flying from a rampart. Upon learning it belonged to Duke Leopold of Austria, he ordered it torn down. Richard and Philip acted on the assumption that each would take half of the conquests. Few Germans were present at Acre, and Leopold's retinue was minimal. Too poor to attract more knights to his banner, Leopold had no alternative but to return home. This royal temper tantrum, however, would cost Richard almost his life and England a pretty penny (Gillingham 1999:224–225; Regan 1998:164). The terms of peace presented to the Saracens required that the True Cross along with named Christian prisoners be returned by the end of the month; Muslims would remain hostage until all terms were fulfilled. But it appears that Saladin prevaricated. By late August Richard's patience was exhausted. He had 2,700 Muslim prisoners massacred in full view of the Saracen troops in the hills. Whether this was enacted simply in reprisal for the Christians slain at Hattin or as a necessary measure given the risk of leaving large numbers of enemy troops behind is unclear. At any rate within 48 hours Richard was headed south toward Jerusalem with his army, in its vanguard the elite corps of Templars, their white mantles emblazoned with the red cross of martyrdom; in the rear guard rode the Hospitalers (Howarth 1993:166–171).

The Christians followed the old Roman road south along the coast, supported by the Pisan supply fleet. Stretching three miles along the Roman road, Richard's battle formation was exemplary. Halfway to Ascalon, the two armies joined battle at Arsuf. The Christians held like rocks against Saracen attack; then as the trumpets sounded the knights, division by division, swung through the infantry in a thundering charge of their great armored horses, Richard in the forefront. Even the mobility of the Saracen horsemen could not save them from the weight of the Christian charge, as Saladin's biographer recounts:

> On our side the rout was complete. I was myself in the centre: that corps having fled in confusion, I thought to take refuge with the left wing, which was the nearest to me; but when I reached it, I found it also in full retreat and making off no less quickly than the centre. Then I rode to the right wing, but this had been routed even more thoroughly than the left. (Regan 1998:173, 180–182)

At Arsuf in pitched battle, Richard decisively defeated Saracen forces vastly outnumbering the Crusaders, his triumph demonstrating to Christians that Saladin was not invincible. Saladin himself changed tactics from that point on, resorting more to a rearguard, scorched-earth policy. Enthusiastically the Latins marched on toward Jerusalem, but halted a mere 12 miles from their objective. With the Holy City well within their grasp, the Templar and Hospitaler knights in consultation with native barons unexpectedly argued against the conquest. Mindful that the Crusaders would soon return to Europe, these monkish warriors recognized the vulnerability of this great inland city to recapture by Saladin, given the Christian occupation of only a narrow coastal strip of maritime ports. They urged instead a negotiated solution (Howarth 1993:173–175).

But a truce was not immediately realizable. Saladin, committed to the preservation of Jerusalem for Islam, shrewdly assessed Richard's position. The months passed in alternating acts of aggression and overtures for peace. Following the Christians to the coast, Saladin took the town of Jaffa. Lionhearted, Richard at once sailed to Jaffa, where with only a small number of knights he led the charge against the Muslim army. The Muslim troops were so awed by the king's bravery that none dared challenge him (Gillingham 1999:18–19). Richard also engaged in diplomacy and forged a close friendship with Saladin's brother al-Adil. Unbeknownst to Joanna, he offered his sister to the Kurdish prince in marriage. Each leader shone as a model of chivalric virtue. But it was a military stalemate. Finally in 1192, a peace treaty was signed in which it was agreed that Christians could visit the holy shrines of Jerusalem and that Muslim and Christian traffic would pass freely through one another's lands. On the advice of the commercially minded Venetians, Pisans, and Genoans, Christians became reconciled to a much diminished coastal kingdom stretching from Jaffa to Beirut with its capital in Acre and its king, Conrad of Montferrat, still wistfully called King of Jerusalem. Eight days after his election, however, Conrad was knifed to death by the Assassins, followers of the Old Man of the Mountain, for having pirated one of the sect's cargo ships in the Mediterranean (Armstrong 1991:266–271). Richard the Lionheart left the Holy Land almost immediately. His co-crusader Philip Augustus had invaded the borderlands of Richard's French territories, and in England his brother John was intriguing to usurp the realm. Warned that enemies lay in wait along his route, Richard sailed first to Corfu, then switched to a smaller vessel, which was shipwrecked on the northern Adriatic coast of Italy. His party was thus forced to continue the journey overland disguised as pilgrims. But the dashing young king did not travel easily incognito. Passing through Austria, he was recognized in 1193 and captured by Duke Leopold, whose banner he had cast aside at Acre. Fifteen months later the immense ransom delivered for his release by England helped finance the construction of the Vienna battlements, fortifications that in centuries ahead would protect central Europe from invasion by other Turks from the east (Gillingham 1999:231–232).

THE FOURTH CRUSADE AND THE SACK OF CONSTANTINOPLE. While the Third Crusade failed to recapture the city of Jerusalem and left behind fragile Christian possessions, the Fourth Crusade, which began auspiciously with European nobility flocking to take the Cross, never even reached the Holy Land but instead degenerated into war with Byzantium. In the West, Christians had blamed the failure of the Crusades to secure Jerusalem on the perfidy of the Greeks. For their part the Byzantines had viewed with equanimity the mutual weakening of the West and Islam in their warring over Palestine. Envenomed by theological schism, enmity between West and East had intensified. But there was also internal friction within Byzantium. In 1201 the emperor Isaac was unseated in a coup and blinded by his brother. Hoping to benefit from these circumstances, the Germans and Franks developed a scheme to install Isaac's son Alexius on the Byzantine throne in exchange for Constantinople's reinforcing the Fourth Crusade with a force of 10,000 men. In Venice, the near-blind doge Dandolo, who to protect his lucrative eastern markets of timber, iron, and slaves had secretly promised Cairo sultan al-Adil to divert all Crusaders from Outremer, now consented to transport by sea 4,500 knights, 9,000 squires, 20,000 infantry, and 4,500 horses to Constantinople. Maritime troop and horse transport had clearly made significant advances. Thus 50 Venetian war galleys headed to Constantinople, first stopping along the Adriatic to raid the rival Hungarian port of Zara (Armstrong 1991:383–385; Kinross 1972:70). The Greeks resisted the Latins energetically, but the Crusaders, mounting a full-scale assault, took Constantinople in triumph, looting its cathedrals, palaces, and libraries. Familiar with the city as merchants, the Venetians knew where the finest treasures lay. Along with priceless works of art and jewelry, Constantine's four magnificent gilded bronze horses were plundered from the Hippodrome to adorn the parapet on the facade of St. Mark's Cathedral in Venice. Churches were also rifled of their coveted sacred relics, which were profitably peddled in western Europe. King Louis IX erected the Sainte-Chapelle to house the Crown of Thorns along with a part of the True Cross. Soissons obtained the Veil of the Virgin, the heads of St. John the Baptist and St. Stephen, and the finger St. Thomas had inserted into the side of Christ; Chartres, the head of St. Anne; and Amiens, another head of St. John the Baptist. The plunder, mostly of hard gold and silver, amounted to seven times the annual revenue of England at that time (Kinross 1972:71–77).

It was not until 1261 that the Greeks finally restored a Greek emperor to the throne of Constantinople. But the two centuries of political strife between West and East Christendom had taken their toll and undermined the vitality of the Greek world. The empire that had tamed the Hun, Sarmatian, and Avar invaders from the steppes, dominated the north African coast, countered the onslaught of Sasanians, and withstood the repeated assaults of Umayyad, Abbasid, and Seljuk Islam never recovered from the sack of Constantinople by the Fourth Crusade. The blow dealt Byzantium by its fellow Christians gravely weakened the empire in a manner that only hastened her final conquest by the Ottoman Turks. Naval supremacy in the Mediterranean now passed from Byzantium to Italy, as Italian fleets and their Barcelona and Marseilles allies transported pilgrims and warriors to the Holy Land, supplied Christians in their garrisoned forts, and imported back to Europe luxury oriental products. Facilitated by new banking techniques learned from Byzantium and Islam, western industry expanded to achieve prosperity (Durant 1950:606, 612–613). But also very significantly, for the first time protracted military invasion with cavalry was conducted over long distance by sea, not simply short stops from Europe's southerly peninsulas to nearby foreign coasts. Crusader ships crammed with tens of thousands of war horses, riders, and their equipment spanned the entire breadth of the Mediterranean, from western Europe to the Near East. This invasion of eastern Mediterranean shores by mounted warriors from the Christian west, the establishment of coastal forts against indigenous armed resistance, and the provisioning and reinforcement of colonist populations for an extended period of two centuries prepared western Europe well for later maritime expansions with equestrian might that would extend much further afield than the Mediterranean.

The Enduring Legacy of the Equestrian Warrior Orders

Thus, for over a century, the Christian offensive against Muslim Arab, Turkic, and Kurdish troops in the Near East, already torn by Sunni-Shia rivalry, only escalated the political turbulence of the region. Frankish behavior had alienated eastern Christians. Christian knights had intrigued unscrupulously against one another, their princes allying with Saracen leaders. A Christian king had conspired with the notorious Assassin sect. And the Fourth Crusade had sacked Byzantium. Nevertheless, the equestrian forces engaging in this conflict would have enduring impact on future political developments. Ethnically distinct, embracing different religions, yet in amazing parallel, these frontier horsemen would struggle for centuries to define the boundaries of their respective faiths in Europe, Asia, and Africa.

EGYPTIAN MAMLUKS. As the Fifth, Sixth, Seventh, and Eighth Crusades continued well into the thirteenth century, invading Christians now encountered opposition from a new military force, the Mamluks. Upon gaining control of Egypt, Saladin had introduced this slave corps into his army; subsequently the Ayyubid sultanate greatly augmented the contingents of Mamluks under its command. The Mamluks, responsible at Mansurah for the rout of the Seventh Crusade under saintly Louis IX, in 1250 demanded greater powers in the Egyptian government. When this was refused, they staged a coup, assassinated the Ayyubid sultan, and founded a new Mamluk dynasty. The Mamluk sultans extended their patronage to the holy cities of Mecca and Medina, and as will be seen in the next chapter, in 1260 at the battle of Ayn Jalut succeeded in halting the Mongol advance into the Near East. They were also unrelenting in waging holy war against Christians in the Levant. And in 1291, Mamluk conquest of Acre and other Frankish-held cities and fortresses marked the end of Crusader presence in Syria and Palestine (Hildinger 2001:159–161).

Mamluk, derived from the Arabic word meaning "owned," refers to the long-standing practice, first adopted by the Umayyads and critical in their military expansion, of procuring youths from nomadic Turkic tribes to serve as slave soldiers. As noted in the previous chapter, once Transoxania was islamized, peoples of the northeastern frontiers were instrumental in capturing or purchasing large numbers of slaves from steppe tribes. Puberty was judged to be the most appropriate time for purchase. At that age the youngster had already acquired many of the riding and combat skills characteristic of the steppes. Yet still tractable and amenable to being molded to suit the interests of a new master, the youth was taught Arabic, converted to Islam, and as adept horse archer incorporated into Muslim armies. Segregated from other military elements, the Mamluk naturally developed strong loyalties to his warrior corps and enjoyed exclusive status in the army (Ayalon 1975:55–56; Patterson 1982:308).

273

Egyptian Mamluk military training was grueling and, as indicated by the *furusiyya* manuals of drill and instruction, required mastery of the skills of lancer, archer, and swordsman. In order to build up arm muscles, the Mamluks practiced slicing at lumps of clay as many as 1,000 times a day (Irwin 1999:240). Well armored in chain mail, the rider employed different methods of tilting. Like the Sarmatian style of the steppes, the Khurasan method entailed two hands, in which the right hand held the butt of the lance and the left secured the head of the lance with the rider leaning slightly to gain protection from the horse body; this double hold could be reversed and the lance used in short thrusts and retraction. The Damascus hold was more rigid, the lance grasped by the right hand and couched under the armpit. In archery the horseman placed five targets to both right and left, then galloped past shooting at them, each time moving the targets closer. Polo was considered the most strenuous practice for war, in which horse and rider together would prepare their hearts for the perils of battle, turning, defending, charging, struggling with the adversary, snatching the ball, racing free – maneuvers to hone the daring and dexterity of the successful warrior in combat (Hildinger 2001:156–158). Manumission was generally performed around the age of 18. Upon receiving uniform, horse, and arms, the young warriors were attached to emirs of different ranks or assigned to the sultan himself. Only royal Mamluks could rise to the rank of emir; only Mamluks manumitted by the reigning sultan could succeed to the sultanate. The perpetuation of this equestrian oligarchy, with the horse and horsemanship as backbone of their rule, was assured by the continual arrival of new adolescent slaves from the steppes (Hrbek 1977:40–41).

The greatest of Mamluk sultans, Baybars, as just ruler of Egypt and Syria strengthened the navy and cleared roads, harbors, and canals. Monopolization of the foreign spice trade represented a primary source of the economic and financial might of Egypt. Once again, Cairo was the most affluent, bustling city west of the Indus. Nor did Baybars, a Kipchak Turk, forget his steppe origins. In Cairo he built two superb hippodromes (*maydan, mayadin*) expressly to accommodate furusiyya exercises, encouraging others to follow his example by practicing rigorously twice a week (Hildinger 2001:167). Baybars greatly enlarged his army, increasing it from 10,000 to a reputed 40,000 horsemen. The Mamluk army thus became one of the best in the world, its victories in the Near East over Crusaders and encroaching Mongols earning it a reputation for invincibility (Amitai-Preiss 1995:71, 139, 215–216).

Egypt's might under the Mamluks was further evidenced in its monumental architecture, Ayyubid style enriched by Syrian and Persian influences brought in by artisans fleeing the Mongol onslaught. Mosques, hospitals, mausoleums, mayadin, and madrasas were constructed with rich facades and stucco carvings (Clot 1996:288–301). Previously, Sunni Seljuk and Ghaznavid Turks had dominated western Asia and northern India – in 1192 Ghaznavid successors, the Ghurids, with their Mamluk warriors penetrated deep into the Hindu heartland to topple Delhi (Lawrence 1999:399–400). Similarly, religiously motivated Berber nomads of western Africa had forged the Muslim Almoravid empire from the Senegal River in the south, north as far as the Ebro River in Spain. Now, Kipchak Mamluk military power would extend from Syria southward down the Nile, and Muslim influence would advance east across the desert to Chad.

During the Fatimid and Ayyubid dynasties, nomadic Arabs had always constituted a turbulent element in Upper Egypt. Under Baybars, however, their uprisings were systematically put down by the better trained and equipped Mamluks. As a consequence, many nomadic tribes migrated southward, creating an explosive situation in the Nubian borderlands. In response to Nubian aggression, Baybars in 1276 launched a punitive expedition against Dongola to defeat the Nubian army, this event contributing directly to the decline of Nubian Christianity and the deterioration of Coptic Christian status in Egypt. The subsequent disintegration of Nubia facilitated the great Arab breakthrough to pasturelands between the Nile valley and Lake Chad, resulting in the islamization of the Nilo-Chadic Sahel. In 1324 on pilgrimage to Mecca, Mansa Musa, king of Mali of the Niger, visited Cairo, displaying his wealth and generosity by distributing as gifts enormous amounts of gold, with the result that the price of the metal significantly depreciated. The sultan presented him Arabian horses equipped with Egyptian saddles and bridles. Musa also purchased 30 Mamluks as his bodyguard to return with him to Mali. Every year, as great caravans with as many as 12,000 camels traveled between Egypt and Mali, peoples across the Sudan increasingly looked toward Cairo as the commercial center of the Muslim world (Hrbek 1977:76–79, 90; Law 1980:121).

For over 200 years, Mamluk Egypt was to reign as the most powerful state in the Near East. Toward the end of the fourteenth century, Circassian Mamluks from the Caucasus began to replace the Kipchaks, whose numbers had dwindled. But in 1516 against the Ottomans the Mamluk army suffered a severe defeat at Marj Dabiq outside Aleppo.

The decisive factor was Selim the Terrible's masterly use of artillery; the concentrated fire of his 150 cannons wrought total destruction on the bravely charging Mamluk cavalry (Clot 1996:173–174, 194–195). Later modernized under the Ottomans, the elite Mamluk regiments would continue intact, in time to infiltrate and dominate the highest levels of Ottoman society. Thus when Napoleon invaded Egypt in 1798 he was confronted by a Mamluk regime that would be ousted only in 1811 by Mehmed Ali (Clot 1996:322–326).

The Mamluks were not the only military order to survive from medieval times into the modern era. The western orders of monks, whose military discipline, we have seen, retained elements of the mairiia warrior band, fought on in Outremer almost to the end of the thirteenth century. Despite failure in the Holy Land, the monks were destined to exert a significant influence on their political environment in shaping the future of Christian Europe. While bitter adversaries on the battle-field, in this age of equestrian expansion, these warriors of different faiths nevertheless shared many organizational traits in common. Like the ribats of Islam's steppes and deserts, the warrior monks would build their own castles in Europe's northern forests and along her southern shores in order to defend and expand Christendom. Crusading fervor would continue among Europe's chivalric elite as they adapted with ingenuity to novel strategic circumstances, combining horsemanship with naval ventures against invaders from the east. Just as their ghazi counterparts – Arab, Berber, and Turkic frontier horsemen – fought with fervor and ferocity to transmit Islam to Central Asia, India, and the North African hinterland, so the Christian warrior monks would struggle long and hard to define the borders of Europe, even its colonial extension overseas.

TEUTONIC KNIGHTS. The Teutonic knights early moved their operations north to extend Christendom across eastern Europe. Initially they helped King Andrew II of Hungary to protect his Transylvanian border-lands against the Cuman/Kipchak Turkic nomads by constructing castles. But their quick success met with opposition from Hungarian nobles, who expelled the knights from the region – an error, it would seem, on the part of the Hungarians, for a strongly garrisoned lower Danubian basin might well have prevented the catastrophic defeat Hungary suffered a couple of decades later at the hands of invading Mongols (Urban 2003:34–36). In 1226, the Hohenstaufen emperor Frederick II in the Golden Bull of Rimini rewrote their constitution by which the

Teutonic knights were no longer beholden to the pope but directly dependent on the emperor's order (Armstrong 1991:422). Subsequently, with a volunteer lay army recruited from central Germany, the knights helped the Polish duke Conrad I against the pagan Prussians of the lower Vistula. With much bloodshed, the crusader armies overran the Balt Prussian tribes. Pledged to poverty and obedience, the celibate Teutonic knights endured the freezing cold of the long northern winters, in time settling secular knights and peasants on vacant lands, attracting German burghers to found new towns, and assimilating surviving Prussians through a process of germanization (Urban 2003:56–57).

The northern crusade continued into Balt Livonia and even attempted invasion of the Christian Orthodox states of Russia, where the brothers aimed to control the valuable river trade in furs, ores, amber, and timber. But in the 1242 battle on frozen lake Peipus, the Teutonic knights and their allies were soundly defeated by Prince Alexander Nevsky of Novgorod. The knights subsequently directed their campaigns south against Balt Lithuania (Nicholson 2004:46–47). In this barren wilderness, massive flooding in spring and summer restricted equestrian warring to the depths of winter, when the snow was hard and the marshes iced over. From every Catholic state in Europe, knights flocked to this northern crusade against pagans and schismatics. In this enterprise, the centrality of the cult of chivalry was epitomized by the symbolic use of the *Ehrentisch* (table of honor) in sealing the knights' brotherhood in arms (Housley 1999:272–273). Teutonic military aggression persisted even after Lithuania had embraced Christianity, provoking that country's enmity, and also that of Poland, which with its loss of Gdansk had been cut off from the sea. The order suffered a devastating defeat by these two nations at the Battle of Tannenberg in 1410, subsequently losing its capital at Marienburg in 1466.

Just as Teutonic efforts had helped reconstitute central Europe in the wake of the Mongol cataclysm, following the Ottoman victories at Kosovo in 1389 Teutonic knights aided the Hapsburgs in their operations along the Balkan front. The Turks first attacked Vienna in 1529, raiding annually along the frontier until their final siege of the Austrian capital in 1689. Logistically, the Ottoman army could march out of Istanbul only when the grass was high enough to feed its horses. Austrian troops deployed to remote border castles, under the command of the Teutonic order, were instrumental in tactically delaying the Turks' advance northward, the knights thus playing a vital role in the defense of western Europe (Urban 2003:274). Under Protestant pressure in the north, Teutonic influence markedly declined. Their estates later secularized by Napoleon, the order today exists as different chapters engaged in charitable clinics across central Europe.

HOSPITALERS. When Acre fell in 1291, the Hospitalers briefly sought refuge in Cyprus and then in 1309 established their headquarters in Rhodes, from which island they terrorized Muslim shipping in the Mediterranean for two centuries and withstood repeated attacks from Mamluks and Turks. In 1522, Suleiman the Magnificent personally led a massive naval bombardment of Rhodes; 7,000 Hospitalers endured a siege of six months against 200,000 Turks. Finally, their fortress in ruins, the knights were allowed to withdraw from the island – a bitter defeat for the West (Edbury 1999:298–299). Bequeathed Malta by the Holy Roman emperor Charles V in 1530, they founded hospitals for the care of the sick. But Suleiman again pursed them, laying siege to Malta in 1565. Vastly outnumbered, under their grand master Jean Parisot de la Valette, they heroically defended the approaches to Sicily and Naples, ultimately to repulse the Ottoman invader. In 1571, the Hospitalers joined the fleets of the Holy league of the Papacy, Spain, and Venice to score a major naval victory against the Turks at Lepanto. The knights continued into later centuries as a cosmopolitan medical organization and supranational military-naval force in the Mediterranean (Housley 1999:288, 290). Finally dislodged from Malta by Napoleon in 1798, the order became based in Rome, where today the Knights of Malta devote themselves to medical activities around the globe.

TEMPLARS AND THEIR SUCCESSORS. Both Hospitalers and Templars possessed rich estates distributed across the length and breadth of Europe. They were active in the administration of these properties, improving agricultural methods and expanding economic and commercial operations in order to finance their military commitments. Like the Teutonic knights in eastern Europe, the two orders were also active in developing marginal lands in the west – along the Anglo-Gaelic frontier in Britain and the Christian-Muslim frontier in the Iberian peninsula. The Templars, in particular, had maintained a long-term presence in the Portuguese and Spanish kingdoms. In Portugal, they received their first castle (recovered from the Moors) in 1128 and in 1147 participated in the takeover of Lisbon (Nicholson 2001:91–92). Coming to the aid of the Spanish kingdoms, early in the thirteenth century both Templars and Hospitalers played a significant role in the capture of the Balearic Islands and in the conquest of Valencia. However, due to demands in the Holy Land, the Templars were unable to supply sufficient troops for the Christian rulers' needs. As a consequence the kings approved local military religious orders. The order of Calatrava was founded in 1158 (Martinez Diez 2001: 64–65, 77). In the 1170s the orders of Alcantara and Santiago were established in Leon. Calatrava and Alcantara both lived by celibate Cistercian rule; the Order of Santiago observed the milder Augustinian canons. Receiving *encomiendas* (landed estates), the knights pursued the aggressive policy of driving the Muslims out of the peninsula. The knights' wealth and influence made it vital for the crown to control the Spanish orders (Luttrell 1999:328). Thus, kings were careful to endow different foundations in order to ensure that no one institution became too powerful. Portuguese kings took advantage of European knights sailing to the Second and Third Crusades in order to mount attacks on Muslim-held cities in Portugal (Nicholson 2004:28–29) Alternatively Spanish and Portuguese knights were deployed in naval operations to control the Straits of Gibraltar and in later raids on north Africa (Forey 1999:179; Luttrell 1999:329). Templars, Hospitalers, and the Spanish orders all participated in the critical battle of Las Navas de Tolosa to win a resounding victory against the Almohad caliph al-Nasir (Martinez Diez 2001:82–83).

In contrast to the Teutonic and Hospitaler knights, the Templars did not survive to confront Napoleon. This brotherhood of warrior monks, which had fought for Christ in the Holy Land, pursued Cathar heretics in France, and combated Moors in Iberia, was the highest disciplined army in the western world. Templar castles were the strongest buildings known, used as places of deposit for money, jewels, and documents, their equestrian networks facilitating the transfer of goods from one locale to another (Forey 1999:191–192). Yet unlike the Hospitalers, they supported no hospitals, no schools. Templar financial power, armed might, and allegiance to the papacy offended the embryonic nationalism of Philip IV of France. Chronically short of funds, he coveted their immense wealth. Accused in 1310 of immorality and heresy, the knights were tortured to secure confessions, their properties confiscated by the state. After brutal torment, many, including their grand master, Jacques de Molay, were burned at the stake (Howarth 1993:14–18), their awful fate perhaps portent of the religious persecutions soon to engulf Europe – and future European territories overseas. Nevertheless, the

Spanish orders would continue to provide combat troops to the long, bitter campaigns of the *Reconquista*.[1] In 1491, the knights of Santiago delivered 1,000 of the 10,000 horses assembled at Granada (Luttrell 1999:328). And in 1519–1521, the fleet of Ferdinand Magellan, Knight Commander of the Order of Santiago, circumnavigated the globe.

[1] The Christian reconquest of Muslim Spain.

FROM THE STEPPES, THE ALTAIC NOMAD
CONQUEST OF EURASIA

THE MONGOL EQUESTRIAN EXPANSION ACROSS EURASIA

As we have seen in western Asia, the horse nomads of the steppes –
in Firdausi's verse Turanians – repeatedly invaded the settled agricultural lands to the south. The Seljuks, foes of the Crusaders, were
but one of numerous Turkic tribes infiltrating the Middle East during
medieval times. In comparable manner, at the eastern end of the steppes
other nomads were invading China. Amidst the chaos accompanying
the fall of the Tang in the tenth century, a nomadic Altaic-Mongol-
speaking people, the Qidan, established the Liao dynasty in northern
China (Table 9.1). Pursuing the ancient policy of pitching one barbarian horde against another, the Song dynasty in the south encouraged
an Altaic-Tungusic-speaking people from Manchuria, the Jurchens, to
eradicate the Liao. The Jurchens complied but much to the Song's ire
continued their advance into northern China to found the Jin dynasty.
China thus was divided into three sovereignties: the Song in the south,
the Jin in the north, and in the northwest the Tanguts, a Tibetan herder-
agriculturalist people who in 990 had secured independence from the
Song to establish the kingdom of Xixia in Shaanxi and the Ordos
(Saunders 2001:35–37). Shortly, however, the sedentary states of both
Persia and China would be swept away by a mighty tide of equestrian
invasions out of the steppes. In preceding chapters, we saw that the
horse was originally domesticated on the steppes' borders, and we have
followed diverse nomad migrations from the steppe periphery into the
civilized heartlands. In this chapter we will examine a nomad invasion
originating on the furthermost margins of the northeastern steppe, the
military might of which would engulf the vast breadth of the Eurasian
landmass.

TABLE 9.1. *Later Chinese Dynasties*

Liao	907–1125
Jin	1126–1215
Song	960–1278
Yuan	1279–1368
Ming	1368–1644
Manchu	1644–1911

A Mongol, Genghis Khan was orphaned early in life and as an outcast scavenged for survival on the most desolate fringes of the steppe world. He grew to maturity in a climate of extreme tribal turbulence, where he experienced every type of deprivation and violence. Amazingly he survived, his descendants to become emperors of numerous territories. Although illiterate, one by one he learned to outwit and outfight the hostile tribes that threatened Mongol life, finally forming against all odds a grand confederation of steppe nomads. Aged 50, he turned his disciplined cavalry against the sedentary civilizations that for centuries had exploited steppe peoples. On multiple fronts across continents, he waged a war of swift assault and terror, devising new fighting techniques, utilizing new weaponry, and deploying siege craft as had no nomad before him. With no more than 100,000 horsemen he conquered lands from the Pacific to Muscovy. Over this vast area great roadways were protected for intercontinental commerce. Spanned by a rapid post relay system, distant countries were organized into the world's largest free-trade zone over which international law was established. Educational institutions, teachers, priests, lawyers, and doctors were all exempted from taxes; aristocratic privilege and abuse were abolished and replaced by a system of individual talent and achievement (Weatherford 2004:xvi–xix).

The Epic of the Horsehair Spirit Banner

The details of Genghis's extraordinary career come to us in a document known as the *Secret History of the Mongols*, compiled shortly after Genghis's death by persons familiar with his early life. Passages in alliterative prose indicate that these were probably first chanted at tribal gatherings before being committed to writing. The title denotes the chronicle to be sacred to the Mongols, replete with tribal lore and commemorating the epic deeds of the Great Khan. The document was likely systematized during Khubilai's reign, when under the influence of Chinese practice, during the Yuan dynasty scholars were assigned to render the historical record in both Mongol and Chinese (Saunders 2001:193–194). One copy of this work remains today. From it we learn that the Mongol people originated in the mountainous region of Burkhan Khaldun at the headwaters of the Onon, Kerulen, and Tula rivers. Through genealogies full of fantastic and mythical elements, the Mongol tribes and lineages traced their descent from this distant, legendary past. Their mythical ancestors provided a fictive kinship whereby biologically unrelated segments of the population through genealogical manipulation could establish political ties.

The most ancient Mongol lineage was the Borjigin, which in the twelfth century united steppe tribes against the Jin. In hostilities against the Jurchens and Tatars, leadership passed to the Tayichiud lineage but later reverted to the Borjigin, as such infuriating the Tayichiud (Allsen 1994:330–332). Yesugei, a Borjigin, in the 1160s with his brothers abducted his bride-to-be, Hoelun of the Onggirad lineage, from a Merkits tribesman. In battle with the Tatars Yesugei then slew an important warrior. Returning from war, he found that Hoelun had given birth, the infant ominously clutching in his right hand a large clot of blood. On Hoelun's first son the father bestowed the dead Tatar warrior's name, Temujin, later to be known to the world as Genghis Khan. Shortly thereafter, Yesugei was poisoned by a band of Tatars. Before his death, Yesugei had achieved a certain level of local leadership (Man 2004:63–68, 72–73). But life was precarious in this bleak region, each family alert for the opportunity to destroy a weaker group. The followers of Yesugei were not disposed to recognize his son as their chief. Prominent in this defection were the Tayichiud, still harboring a grudge. They decamped, depriving Hoelun, a co-wife, their six sons, and a daughter of their herds; Yesugei's close kin followed. Hoelun courageously seized the *tugh* (the stallion-tailed standard of their clan) to pursue on horseback and to harangue the deserters. This spirit banner consisted of hair from the finest stallions tied to the shaft of a spear that Yesugei had always planted outside his ger to stand as perpetual guardian of the camp. The horsehair twisting and flowing in the wind captured the power of the sun and sky, transmitting their vital power to the Mongol warrior, ever egging him onward to far-off pastures. But without the economic support of their kinsmen, the two widows had to fend for their families in the desolate region of the Upper Onon. Fatherless, Temujin would grow to maturity in conditions of extreme want and hardship (Grousset 1966:42–43; Onon 2001:62–63).

Growing up, Temujin would experience camaraderie and loyalty but also tragedy and betrayal. He first forged a close friendship with a Juriat Mongol named Jamugha, with whom as *anda* (ally) he swore an oath of eternal brotherhood. By the age of four all Mongol youngsters could ride; together the two youths engaged in wrestling while standing bareback. From horseback Temujin and Jamugha practiced throwing lassos and shooting arrows at dangling targets blowing in the wind (Grousset 1966:44; Man 2004:74). As Yesugei's sons grew older they contributed to the family sustenance by hunting birds and marmots. It was in this context that a violent confrontation occurred between Temujin and his half brother Begter. The eldest of Yesugei's sons, Begter, was intent upon asserting his status over Temujin. Already he had appropriated Temujin's catch of a lark and a fish. Unwilling to assume subordinate status, Temujin quickly took his revenge. Approaching Begter from opposite directions, he and a younger full brother with bow and arrows shot their half brother dead. Hoelun fiercely reproached her sons for the murder of her stepson, especially at a time when the family was vulnerable to outside attack. But Temujin was obdurate. As he was to show later in life, he was not a man to suffer lightly a challenge to his pride (Onon 2001:66).

Hoelun's fear of hostile attack was well founded. Shortly after Begter's death, the Tayichiud kidnapped Temujin, whom they held hostage in a wooden yoke to secure his arms. The youth suffered every humiliation and privation but, aided by his father's old ally Sorqanshira, finally succeeded in escaping. Reunited with his family, he was next set upon by bandits who made off with eight of their nine horses. On the remaining horse, Temujin pursued the raiders and recovered the stolen animals (Grousset 1966:48–57). Emboldened by this success, Temujin traveled to his mother's Onggirad clan to claim his affianced bride. His wife Borte brought with her as dowry a valuable sable coat, which Temujin deployed in order to reestablish ties with his father's former anda, Toghril, *khan* (tribal leader) of the Keraits tribe. Recognizing the young man's legitimacy, the chieftain extended his protection; his patronage encouraged Temujin's kin, previously defectors, to return with their herds to the Borjigin. But again disaster struck: in revenge for Yesugei's kidnapping of Hoelun, the Merkits captured Borte. Accompanied by his anda Jamugha, Temujin caught the Merkits off guard. Borte was rescued unharmed, but pregnant by the Merkits chief. Temujin accepted the child, Jochi, and recognized him as his son. Borte proved to be an intelligent and resourceful wife, a major force in Temujin's subsequent rise to power (Allsen 1994:335–336; Onon 2001:76–91).

But rivalry was soon to surface between the two youthful allies. The *Secret History* recounts how when traveling together with their followers Jamugha announced that they should divide the herds. He would encamp near the mountains with the horses and Temujin should herd the sheep and goats on the lower ground. Temujin interpreted this as a move on Jamugha's part to establish his ascendancy within the group. The distinction between aristocrat and servitor depended on equestrian prowess and military skills. Wealth in horses was the means by which a chieftain would lead his tribe to war and booty. Acting upon Borte's advice, Temujin split with his former comrade-in-arms to follow an independent path, taking with him many of Jamugha's followers and their herds (Dupuy 1969:6; Man 2004:89–90). Chagrined at his former ally's rise to power, Jamugha attacked the Mongols at Dalan Baljud. The battle was indecisive, but at the end Jamugha brutally boiled alive 70 captives in iron cauldrons. His pointless cruelty alienated many of his of his former adherents, who defected to Temujin (Saunders 2001:50). By contrast, Temujin in his defiance and determination to overcome the odds inspired the allegiance of other talented individuals and, as we have seen, through good leadership retained their loyal services. Out of the political chaos of feuding nomads Temujin would painfully forge a new tribal confederation.

Emergence of Mongol Power

In 1196, the Jin dynasty, weary of Tatar encroachment to their north, in typical imperial barbarian-against-barbarian maneuver organized a coalition of Keraits, Mongols, and Jurchens against the Tatars of the Onon-Kerulen region. For Toghril and Temujin, this was an opportunity to wreak revenge on their traditional enemies. The Tatars were soundly defeated, and from their ranks Temujin recruited additional warriors. The Mongols also marveled at the luxury of the goods seized from the Tatars, particularly the rich gold brocade. Temujin on this occasion adopted a Tatar orphan, whom he gave to Borte to raise as his fifth son. The Jin honored the two khans' military performance by bestowing the title *Ong* (prince) on Toghril (Allsen 1994:338). Temujin repeatedly confronted the Naimans, Merkits, and Juriats, finally eradicating the

Tayichiud in 1201. One Tayichiud warrior, a famous archer, had succeeded in wounding the warhorse of Temujin. Captured, he was brought
before Temujin. Admitting his deed and asking mercy, he swore loyalty
to the Mongols. Temujin admired the youth's mettle. Bestowing upon
him the name *Jebei* (arrow), he invited him to ride by his side. Jebei
was to become the greatest of Temujin's generals (Grousset 1966:106–
107). But a final score remained to be settled, the showdown with the
hated Tatars. For this operation, Temujin sternly ordered his army to
desist from looting during hostilities, threatening any offender with the
harshest punishment. Looting created confusion on the battlefield. It
also served as an obstacle to total victory, often allowing defeated troops
to reassemble for counterattack. Instead, Temujin intended to centrally
control the distribution of booty after the battle, in the same way as game
was distributed in the traditional Mongol communal hunt, apportion-
ing it fairly among participants but also to widows and orphans. His
offensive in 1202 against the Tatars resulted in a complete rout; his
father's tragic death was finally avenged (Weatherford 2004:50–51).

But treachery was afoot. With Temujin's repeated successes in eastern
Mongolia, relations with the Ong khan had become strained; Toghril
with his son Senggum set a trap for the young warrior at a wedding feast.
En route to the celebration, Temujin received intelligence of the planned
assassination and together his small retinue fled east. Usually steppe
warriors desert a general in retreat, but although vastly outnumbered
by pursuers Temujin's companions never faltered (Hartog 2004:24–26).
They were saved from starvation by successfully hunting a wild horse.
On the treeless steppe, they made a fire from dry dung and a bag
from the horse's hide and, placing heated rocks in a mixture of water
and meat, so cooked their meal. To the men the propitious appearance
of this horse, the most revered animal of their universe, symbolized
divine intervention. Henceforth the sacrifice of a horse would precede
all major Mongol battles. A devout shamanist, Temujin worshipped
the sky and mountains, but his companions were varyingly Christian,
Buddhist, and Muslim. By drinking together from the bitter waters of
Lake Baljuna, they celebrated a covenant by which Temujin swore an
oath never to forget his followers' loyalty. At the nadir of his military
experience, he drew strength from the heterogeneity of his followers,
a vibrant force that would nourish the rise of his empire (Weatherford
2004:57–58). Reinforced by Mongol contingents, Temujin overwhelmed
the Kerails in a three-day battle. Temujin now reorganized his army on
a decimal basis. This had previously been attempted on the steppes in

the third century BC by the Xiongnu, regarded by the Mongols as their ancestors – *Hun-nu* (people of the sun). But now Temujin rigorously enforced decimal organization, as much to achieve political control as to ensure military discipline. He divided the army into *arbans* (squads of 10 warriors), sworn never to forsake another in battle. Ten arbans constituted a *jaghun* (company), 10 jaghuns a *mingan* (battalion), and 10 mingans a *tumen* (army) of 10,000 (Hildinger 2001:118). The Mongols marched west to the Altai, where they defeated the Naiman forces allied with Jamugha. Temujin then transferred his capital westward to Karakorum, historically the core territory of Modu of the Xiongnu, the first steppe empire. A Uighur was appointed Keeper of the Seal and instructed to adapt the Uighur alphabet (derived from the Sogdian) to the Mongol language. The Uighurs, originally nomads themselves, had settled the oases of eastern Turkestan, absorbing much of the culture of the Tocharians. Employed as scribes, officials, and merchants they were to exercise a strong influence on Mongol political culture during the empire's formative stages (Allsen 1997:6).

In 1206 a *khuriltai* (tribal gathering) was convened to celebrate the formation of the new powerful confederation that extended across the Mongolian plateau from the forests in the east to the Altai mountains in the west and from the southern deserts to the northern tundras. The *khagan* (khan of khans) was honored at the foot of the sacred mountain of Burkhan Khaldun, where mythical progenitors the blue-gray wolf and the fallow doe originally begat the ancestor of all Mongols. Present were leaders of all recently affiliated tribes as well as Temujin's customary entourage of *noyan* (commanders – close kinsmen and loyal allies). The first ritual enacted was the raising of Temujin's tugh battle standard flying nine horse tails. In Mongol tradition, the number nine augured good fortune, and the unfurling of the tugh publicly acclaimed Temujin's charisma. Seated on felt blankets, Temujin was lifted on high to celebrate his sovereignty over "peoples of the felt tent." In Mongol cosmology, sovereign power was conferred on an earthly ruler by Tengri, the sky god and principal deity of the nomads. Temujin's spectacular rise to power was therefore seen as a manifestation of celestial might and his sovereignty a mandate from heaven. Mongol military expansion was believed to be divinely sanctioned, and all nations were expected to submit to Mongol suzerainty; any state opposing their dominion defied god and deserved direst retribution (Allsen 1994:342–343). In grand spectacle, amidst drumming, chanting, and sprinkling airak in the air and on the ground, the chief shaman Kokchu bestowed on the Mongol leader the formal title of Genghis Khan, meaning Universal Invincible Ruler. With gers stretching for kilometers in all directions, the ceremonial games of the *naadam* commenced, involving contests in Mongolian throat singing, horseracing, wrestling, and archery.

Genghis Khan expanded his personal bodyguard to 1,000 to serve simultaneously as protectors and stewards supervising daily activities. At his court, hostage sons of vassal leaders were also trained as administrators. From Hoelun, the Mongol leader learned that his chief shaman, angling for a position of influence in the new administration, had intimidated his younger brother Temuge. Genghis, who had seen his father's younger brother depart with the Tayichiud leaving Hoelun and her children to their fate, would not tolerate such outsider interference in his family and ruthlessly ordered the shaman's back broken (Saunders 2001:50, 53). To coordinate the functions of the newly expanded administrative system, he appointed Shigi Khutukhu, the Tatar foundling adopted into his immediate household, as Grand Judge. As the highest legal authority in the land, the judge's duties entailed the apportionment of subject peoples, life-and-death decisions over the guilty, and maintenance of the *Koko Debter* in which all judicial decisions and the khagan's own legal pronouncements were recorded as precedents (Allsen 1994:344). Genghis believed in the ultimate supreme law of the Eternal Blue Sky over all people. In promulgating these laws of the Great *Yasa* (law), Genghis had prohibited hunting during the breeding season and contamination of streams and rivers; he further made animal rustling a capital offense, banned kidnapping of women as cause of conflict among Mongols, and declared total religious freedom. He forbade treachery, theft, and adultery and advocated respect for the wise and learned and mercy for the poor and aged (Weatherford 2004:68–69).[1]

The proficiency of his fighting forces was the Mongol leader's primary concern. At 30-km intervals, stations of fresh horses were set up for his Arrow Messengers, who were swathed in bandages to absorb the vibrations of high-speed travel. To achieve high maneuverability on the battlefield, peacetime drills were regularly held in the form of hunting expeditions in which the entire army participated as disciplined units. Commanders of each unit were selected on the basis of valor in battle. Each one exercised total authority over his men and in turn was subject to strict control by his superior. To coordinate the movement of

---

[1] The Yasa would even be adopted by enemy Mamluks in Egypt in the belief that it was key to Genghis's military success (Saunders 2001:69).

large formations, commanders were required to adhere to a prearranged schedule of operations; if they failed to conform, harsh penalties ensued. Genghis's old tribal allies of demonstrated fidelity, such as the Onggi-rad, formed their own ethnically homogeneous mingans led by their own leaders. But in the case of recent adversaries, such as the Naimans and Tatars, the Mongol leader purposefully utilized his decimal system to undermine any latent tribal loyalties by assigning individuals piecemeal to heterogeneous composite units (Allsen 1994:346–347). The Mongol army consisted entirely of cavalry. The light cavalry, which outnumbered the heavy cavalry two to one, was equipped with helmet and padded leather jerkin, bow and arrows, lasso, sword or battle axe, javelins, and leather-covered wicker shield. The heavy cavalry-men rode sturdier horses, sometimes armored, and wore iron helmets with leather flaps behind and at the sides. They had complete lamellar leather body armor covered with scales or rings of iron that was significantly more flexible than that of the western knight, therefore affording greater agility; these Mongols carried bow and arrows, shield, scimitar, and lance. Each warrior was issued a shirt of heavy silk, the material of which normally preceded an arrowhead into the wound without breaking, so that the arrow could easily be extracted simply by tugging on the silk. No wounded man was abandoned in battle (Hildinger 2001:119–121). Remounts were herded behind the troops. At the commencement of battle, a screen of light cavalry preceded the army, unleashing as they came within range a volley of arrows, then moving to the rear to allow the main line of heavy cavalry to advance in a massed charge. With these forces Genghis invaded the Tanguts territory, experimenting with siege techniques in an effort to take the Xixia capital (Dupuy 1969:7–8, 28–29).

In 1210 the aging Jin emperor died. His successor Weiwang dispatched an embassy to the Mongols demanding homage. Genghis Khan responded contemptuously by spitting on the ground and leaping onto his horse (Dupuy 1969:31). The following year the Mongols moved south. Genghis Khan and his youngest son, Tolui, assaulted the eastern part of the China, the other three sons Jochi, Chagatai, and Ogedei the western. The Jin army was ambushed and annihilated in the western mountains, and agricultural lands were laid waste, causing widespread famine and pestilence. By means of swift mounted messengers, Mongol unity of command was exercised at all levels of operations extending over hundreds of kilometers. Tactical movements were controlled by black and white signal flags under the direction

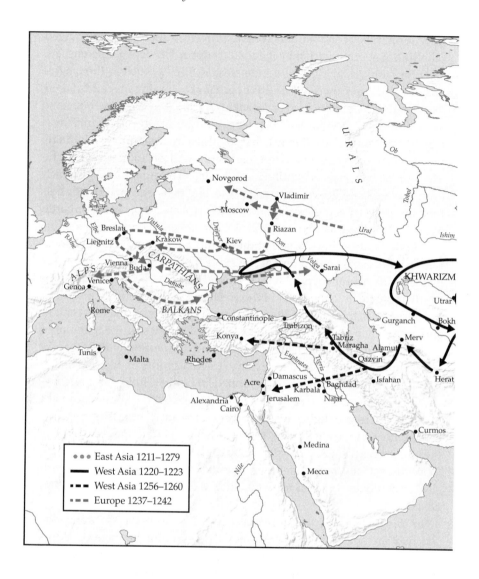

of regimental commanders; in darkness flaming arrows were used to send prearranged messages (Dupuy 1969:43–45). In 1212 the general Jebei attacked the Liao River valley, where he employed a variant of the steppe feigned-retreat tactic. Having surrounded the town of Liaoyang, he withdrew in pretended haste, leaving behind equipment and stores. The citizens hastened out to gather the booty. With the gates wide open and the walls undefended, the Mongols raced back to capture the city (Fig. 9.1).

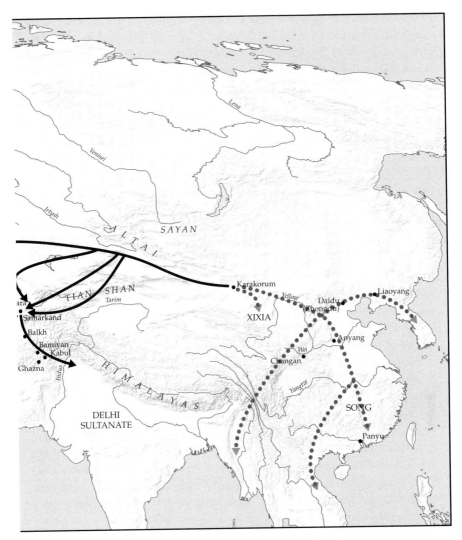

FIGURE 9.1. Thirteenth-century Mongol conquests across Eurasia.

This defeat helped ignite a rebellion among the Qidan, who promptly recognized Mongol suzerainty (Dupuy 1969:39–40). In the Jin heartland the Mongols conscripted local siege experts into their armies and adopted Jin weapons and techniques: ballista, catapult, trebuchet,[2]

---

[2] The ballista was a mechanical device that shot large arrows capable of damaging structures as well as individuals; the catapult hurled stones and flaming liquids; and the trebuchet, powered by the drop of a heavy counterweight, threw objects faster than the torsion catapult.

and battering rams. The firelance, a bamboo tube of gunpowder, was also implemented as a flame thrower to spread fire and to terrorize troops and horses (Weatherford 2004:94–95). In 1215 Zhongdu (Beijing) was sacked. Before returning to Mongolia, Genghis Khan appointed a learned scholar and scientist, the Liao prince Yelu Chucai, to advise in the administration of the newly won provinces of northern China. This sinicized Qidan scholar in time became the virtual prime minister of the Mongol empire, devising a system for levying regular taxes in lieu of the periodic raiding to which the nomads were accustomed. The Mongol general Mukhali was delegated viceroy in command of two Mongol tumens and 20,000 Qidan troops to combat the resilient Jin (Dupuy 1969:54–55).

After his lengthy absence from Mongolia, Genghis needed to settle domestic issues at home. There had been some skirmishing with the Siberian tribes in the northwest, who had failed to submit the customary tributary furs, forest products, and young maidens. Unaccustomed to fight in the thick northern forests, a Mongol punitive force sent against the tribes' queen Botohui-tarhun had been ambushed and its general killed. Genghis now employed well-planned, devious tactics to defeat the rebel queen (Weatherford 2004:102–103). Warrior Amazon queens, it seems, were still alive and well in the thirteenth century – and would continue to be. Mongol noblewomen were amazingly resourceful. Perhaps the most outstanding would be Khutulun, daughter of Kaidu, grandson of Ogedei. Prizing the traditional virtues of nomadic life, Khutulun relished life on horseback and participated in warfare. Marco Polo described her as extremely beautiful but so strong and brave no man could outdo her in feats of physical endurance and military skill. Khutulun refused to accept any suitor in marriage, unless he wagered 100 horses and defeated her in contest. One day she was challenged by a handsome young prince ready to gamble 1,000 horses in order to betroth her. In the public contest, the two combatants were fairly matched, and neither could gain the advantage until finally Khutulun flipped her contender to the ground (Rossabi 1988:104–105). Contests of this sort persist in modern Mongol festivals as wrestling on horseback and the traditional guy's pursuit of a girl (Amazon style) flailing a whip on horseback.

Militarily triumphant, in control of the immense wealth of the Silk Road that flowed through Xixia lands to northern China, Genghis Khan was content to attend to local matters and did not contemplate any fresh offensive. However, events on the western borders of his realm would soon change that. As noted in Chapter 8, on the death of Malik Shah, the Seljuk empire fragmented into a loose federation of provinces. This power vacuum had been filled by the Khwarizm-shahs, who extended their territories into Afghanistan and northern India (Saunders 2001: 40–41). In 1218 the Khwarizm-shah Muhammad sent diplomatic envoys to the Mongol court, in response to which Genghis Khan cordially expressed his desire for commercial relations (Allsen 1994:354). Shortly thereafter, there occurred what conceivably was the worst error of judgment ever – the biggest slip in world history – which led inevitably to the Mongol conquest of Persia and eastern Europe and the renewed Mongol invasion of Xixia, Jin, and Song empires. A Mongol-sponsored trade caravan consisting largely of Muslim merchants and loaded with luxury items arrived in the town of Utrar, on the upper Syr Darya, with greetings to the Khwarizm-shah. Suspecting espionage, the governor Inalchiq despoiled the caravan and massacred the merchants. Genghis Khan instantly sent his ambassador to the Khwarizm-shah to formally demand punishment of the official and restitution of the goods. Muhammad's response was to kill some envoys and to send their companions back to Mongolia with their beards shorn and faces mutilated. Genghis Khan withdrew to the sacred mountaintop of Burkhan Khaldun to consult with the eternal sky god, Tengri (Weatherford 2004:106–107). Abased thus for three days and nights, he disavowed provoking the trouble and pleaded for god's guidance. Although almost 60 years of age, finding no alternative but to avenge this deliberate insult, he declared war on Khwarizm (Allsen 1997:48–49).

Equestrian Conquests in the West

In 1219 Jochi, leading a vanguard of 25,000 men, yak skins wrapped around their horses' legs, crossed the Tian Shan at 4,000 m midst 1.5 m of snow. Genghis then divided his forces among Jebei, his elder sons, and himself so that their armies could converge on Khwarizm from four separate directions. This ingenious maneuvering of independent bodies of troops while maintaining effective communication would assure Mongol success in the campaign at hand, also in later campaigns across Europe; in fact, it would furnish a future model for modern armies as reflected in Napoleon's maxim "March dispersed, fight concentrated." Generals Chagatai and Ogedei both descended on Utrar, massacring or enslaving the entire garrison and executing its rash governor by pouring molten silver in his eyes and ears (Dupuy 1969:62–64; Hildinger

2001:129). The Khwarizm-shah had earlier wrangled with the caliph in Baghdad, who, incensed, had sent a messenger to the Mongols, followed by a regiment of captured Crusaders, petitioning Genghis to attack Muhammad. Because the soldiers were all infantry and of no use to the Mongols, Genghis released the Crusaders, who brought word of the political turmoil in Central Asia back to Europe. Because of the caliph's invitation to the Mongol leader, though, many Persian Muslims became reconciled to ally with the Mongols (Weatherford 2004:110).

While his sons were attacking border towns, Genghis Khan took a wide westward swing across the forbidding Kyzyl Kum (Red Desert). Befriending nomads en route, he was able to lead his 50,000 troops over 640 km of desolate terrain, to strike deep behind enemy lines. He traveled not with slow, hulking equipment but with a mobile engineer corps, who emerging from the desert on sighting the first trees constructed the necessary machines on the spot. Engineers built bridges to accelerate troop movement. Chinese physicians also accompanied the army, as did the Qidan Yelu Chucai in the role of astronomer and prognosticator. At Genghis's surprise appearance out of the western desert at Bokhara in 1220, the Turkish garrison was amazed and 20,000 of the men fled in panic, only to be cut to pieces by Mongol warriors stationed in wait (Allsen 2001:165; Dupuy 1969:66–67). Genghis then assaulted the citadel with sophisticated Chinese siege technology. While bombarding aerially with catapults, trebuchets, and mangonels, he had miners remove earth to undermine the walls. To heighten the psychological terror, he forced the captive comrades of defenders to fill the moat with their bodies to make a live rampart, over which other prisoners propelled the armaments of war.

In March, the four Mongol armies – Jochi from the east, Jebei from the south, Chagatai and Ogedei from the north, and Genghis from the west – advanced on Samarkand, the important commercial and cultural center of half a million inhabitants. The Mongols expected dogged resistance from Samarkand. But the city capitulated after three days, largely because the Khwarizm-shah Muhammad had fled with his family. The entire garrison of Turkish soldiers was slaughtered, the town was looted, and 60,000 craftsmen, artisans, and laborers were impressed for deportation to Mongolia. Among these were many thousands of expert weavers skilled in the production of gold cloth so admired by the khagan. Genghis Khan immediately ordered his generals Jebei, Subedei, and Toguchar, with three tumens, to pursue Muhammad to Balkh, Herat, and Merv, finally catching up with him near the Caspian, where he died in 1221 (Dupuy 1969:67–73). Jebei and Subedei then undertook an exploratory expedition westward to north Persia, Azerbaijan, and the Caucasus. Arriving in Georgia, they successfully defeated that country's cavalry and a coalition of nomads: Alans, Khazars, Bulgars, and Kumans. Near the river Kalka, they also annihilated a Russian army three times their size in one day of savage fighting. Following Jebei's death, Subedei delivered to Genghis Khan a full report of the European explorations (Dupuy 1969:85–90).

In Khwarizm, mindful of the small numbers of Mongol forces vis-a-vis the larger population, Genghis purposefully spread terror in order to frighten people into submission. At Bamiyan in the Hindu Kush, when Genghis's favorite grandson, Mutugen, son of Chagatai, was killed, everyone in the area was massacred and the valley was resettled by a Mongol regiment, their descendants to be known as the Hazara,[3] meaning 10,000 in Persian. In the fertile area south of the Aral sea, after a lengthy siege of Gurganch, the Mongols demolished the dams and flooded the entire area. By deliberately destroying the irrigation systems, they prevented farmers from returning to specific areas, thereby allowing the land to revert to pasturage in order to provide a clear route of advance and retreat for Mongol armies in future campaigns. And to reshape the flow of commerce across Asia, Genghis razed minor cities in order to funnel trade through major areas his horsemen could patrol and protect (Weatherford 2004:117–119). Midst this chaos, a clan of Turkic nomads, grazing their flocks near Merv, fled westward across Iraq to Anatolia where, granted asylum by the Konya Seljuks, they settled to become the progenitors of the Ottomans (Saunders 2001:60). Genghis Khan continued his campaign south into India, where in 1221 he allowed Muhammad's son, Jalal al-Din, who had fought like a tiger, to escape across the Indus. The Mongol leader had originally intended to invade northern India and then proceed to southern China to conquer the Song. But, as the Mongols descended into the lower latitudes and altitudes, their steppe horses sickened in the subtropical heat. Equally problematic, in the moistness of the lowlands, the Mongol bow, adapted to drier northern climes, lost its formidable accuracy (Dupuy 1969:80–81).

As camels laden with rich tribute lumbered north from Khwarizm to Mongolia, Genghis returned to the Iranian plateau in order to train his newly recruited troops in Mongol military methods. For military

---

3 During the allied invasion of Afghanistan in 2001, the Taliban likened the invaders to the Mongols and took reprisals against the Hazara.

training purposes, he cordoned off a vast area on which different armies converged from all directions for a ceremonial hunt that lasted months. Such lengthy hunts were common practice among the steppe khans. Furthermore, as far back as the time of the Achaemenids, we hear of lavish royal hunts on horseback that were every bit as much a test of horsemanship as they were of hunting skills. Basically Mongol hunting expeditions were important political events involving the khagan himself, his noble entourage, and his equestrian forces. In this collective endeavor, beaters from the army and local populace flushed the game out with pipes, drums, and fire. Meanwhile, the troops formed a vast hunting ring (Persian *nirkah*; Mongol *nerge*), which, ever constricting, drove the game before it. Strict military discipline was imposed; great care was taken that no animal escape, and the severest penalties were meted out to anyone breaking rank. These maneuvers, entailing vigorous exertion, reconnaissance scouting, and hard riding, readied men for the hardships of war. Vital to the success of the great ring hunt were an effective chain of command, accurate signaling, and rapid coordination of individuals and units. Once the ring had contracted to the diameter of a league, the army encircled the game with a pole-and-rope fence. At the bloody climax, the frantic, trapped animals were slaughtered in great numbers (Allsen 2006:23–27, 215–217).

After a region was subjugated, Genghis put every effort into rebuilding cities and reestablishing the economy. Nomads everywhere loved trade, and merchants were encouraged to resume their commercial activities under the protection of the Mongol army. Everything was done to promote vigorous international traffic as companies of traders received capital and enjoyed many rights and privileges along the routes across Eurasia. Roads were patrolled by the army, armed guards accompanied the caravans, bandits were apprehended, and oases protected against nomad raids. Yam post stations were constructed at regular intervals on main routes and stocked with food, supplies, and horses. Upon presenting passports, official travelers received refreshment and remounts to continue their journey. To further strengthen and better integrate his newly won empire, Genghis Khan introduced a land tax and customs dues. He granted freedom of worship to all religions, Buddhist, Christian, Muslim, or Jewish, thereby cultivating the goodwill of the clergy in all denominations, who in turn would preach loyalty and political support for Mongol rule. With this patronage, the Mongols harnessed the clerics' spiritual power and communication network for the benefit of the empire. Finally in the spring of 1225 the khagan, leaving his youngest brother Temuge behind, set out for home (Saunders 2001:65, 67–69).

Death of Genghis Khan

Returning to Mongolia in 1225, Genghis Khan immediately addressed the question of inheritance. He bequeathed a vast territory to his descendants, assigning to each of his four sons a portion of his conquered lands. Chagatai would inherit Turkestan; Jochi, the western regions between the Irtysh and the Volga; and Tolui, the patrimonial lands of Mongolia. Ogedei would succeed Genghis as the Great Khan. With supreme authority over his brothers, Ogedei would be responsible for administering the central government, sponsoring a court of appeal, and making decisions of war and peace. Next Genghis turned his attention to the Tangut kingdom of Xixia, which had proved to be a refractory vassal, perfidiously refusing to provide troops for his Khwarizm campaign. Such contempt for khagan sovereignty could not be left unavenged, and in 1226 the Mongol army moved south (Saunders 2001:62). Traveling across the Gobi to make war on the Xixia, the Mongols hunted wild horses, one of which charged Genghis's horse. Thrown to the ground, the Mongol leader sustained internal injuries but could not be dissuaded from pressing on with the Tangut campaign. The old warrior did not live to see its military completion, however. A brief few days before his final defeat of the Tanguts, Genghis Khan died. After his death, his body was wrapped in white felt filled with aromatic sandalwood and bound with three golden straps. Once hunting on Burkhan Khaldun midst the holy springs of the summit, the Mongol ruler had paused to rest in the shade of a great tree. Gazing up at the leafy giant above him, Genghis declared here would be his burial place, beneath the Tree of Life on the World Mountain where, at the outset of each great campaign, he had always returned to invoke the help of his great god, Tengri. On the return to Mongolia, the Great Khan's funeral procession was led by the spirit banner held aloft, the warrior's spirit ever to live on in those tufts of horsehair flying in the wind; the funerary cart was followed by the Mongol leader's horse, its bridle slack, its saddle empty (Grousset 1966:291; Weatherford 2004: xvi, 128–129). On the steppes, as microcosm of the universe, the ger was locus of the rites of passage of marriage and birth. So too in death, the khagan lay in state in his felt palace as war chiefs from every quarter of his empire arrived to pay tribute. Finally Genghis Khan was interred near the region of his birth on

Burkhan Khaldun, the mountain held sacred by all Mongols, whence flowed three rivers, Onon, Kerulen, and Tula, to water the ancestral grazing grounds below. On those slopes where in desperation as a fugitive youth he had hidden in impenetrable thickets, 40 maidens and 40 horses were sacrificed at his tomb (Rossabi 1988:7; Fig. 9.2).

Successors of Genghis Khan

In 1231, as Genghis's heir, Ogedei decided to resume the war in the east against the Jin and the Song, and in the west to suppress rebellions in Khwarizm and to effect deeper penetration of European lands. These concurrent campaigns against China, the Middle East, and Europe extended over a front more than 9,500 km long and encompassed more than 100 degrees of longitude, a feat never previously attempted in human history, nor equaled until the Allied offensive centuries later in World War II (Weatherford 2004:144). Throughout this book, in diverse geographic regions we have noted both the destructive and constructive effects of equestrian expansion. In the course of this chapter it will be shown that following this second Mongol wave of terror and devastation, these global conquerors went on to excel in many other cultural spheres beyond the military, thereby promoting extravagant intermingling of cultures across Eurasia – on a scale that effectively ushered in the modern era. Thus, while in the east Ogedei and his brother Tolui advanced across China, in the west the Mongol equestrian armies established their base on the rich grazing lands of Azerbaijan, in order to simultaneously menace the Muslim states of Anatolia and the Levant and the Christian kingdoms of the Caucasus. By 1240 both Georgia and Armenia were shattered and formally submitted to Ogedei, receiving as a consequence imperial protection for their churches. Lesser Armenia in Cilicia promptly followed the example of her northern compatriots but with the broader expectation of a military alliance between eastern Christians and Mongols against Muslims. Prospects in fact began to look encouraging for the Christians, embroiled in the Crusades, when Mongols under the noyan Baiju invaded Anatolia, at Kose-Dagh defeating the Seljuk sultan Kai-Khusrau of Rum/Iconium, who became their vassal (Saunders 2001:78–79).

But a Mongol alliance with the West was not yet to be. When Genghis had assigned the western appanage to Jochi "as far as the soil has been trodden by the hooves of Mongol horses" (Saunders 2001:80), these territories had merely been reconnoitered by Jebei and Subedei. It was now

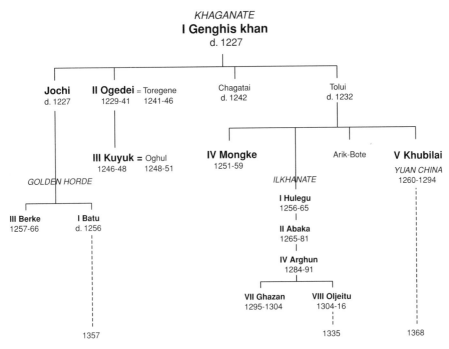

FIGURE 9.2. Genealogy of Mongol khans discussed in Chapter 9.

encumbent on Jochi's heirs, specifically Batu, flanked by his brothers[4] and also aided by the sons of Ogedei, Chagatai, and Tolui, to conquer the west – under the expert generalship of Subedei. In 1237 the Mongols moved into the Volga region and vanquished the Bulgar and Kipchak nomads, incorporating many of them into the Mongol army. Establishing their base camp along the Volga, the Mongols pastured millions of reserve animals for hundreds of kilometers across the steppe (Saunders 2001:80–82). Subedei entered Russia from the northeast, preferring to wage war in winter when icebound rivers, lakes, and marshes facilitated rapid advance. Also in winter, green grass for the horses grew beneath the snow where in summertime would lie only dry dust. The green grass also attracted game, so the armies spread out over a broad front to maximize hunting opportunities and to seek forage for their horses. Rapid messenger contact was maintained at all times. Other than the large reserve of horses, the army did not travel with a cumbersome

---

4 Batu held nominal command and would become khan of the Golden Horde, the region west of the Volga.

supply train. Each trooper had at least three remounts, when velocity was required changing horses three times a day to cover distances at speeds inconceivable to the enemy. The Mongols lived off the horse; as they traveled, they milked and slaughtered for food. They consumed a steady diet of milk and yoghurt, drank the horse's blood, and mixed dried milk paste with water, dried meat, and millet. Raw meat was placed under the saddle to make it supple and edible. As they rode, the Mongol warriors sang aloud the laws and rules of conduct. Without infantry, operating on a broad front, upon encountering the opponent the proximate unit would engage in combat while the other far-flung columns would continue to advance to the enemy's flank and rear, generally resulting, as in the great ring hunt, in encirclement and destruction (Dupuy 1969:22–25; Weatherford 2004:86–89).

The Russian princes, it seems, had learned little from the invasion 14 years earlier; still divided, they offered no concerted resistance to the second Mongol advance. From the countryside, the Mongols conscripted local laborers to fell and haul trees for the construction of a stockade[5] to encircle the besieged town. Behind their wall the attackers set up their sophisticated siege equipment to bombard the town with rocks, gunpowder, and naptha. With the firelance they launched incendiary rockets or grenades over the city walls. Once a city was captured, aristocrats were hacked to pieces, clergy burned to death, and thousands of captives forced to transport booty back to Karakorum. Prisoners dismantled the stockade for relocation to the next targeted location (Weatherford 2004:146–148). Riazan, Vladimir, Moscow, and Kiev were all destroyed; only Novgorod escaped assault because of the spring thaw and swamps that made horse approach impossible. Sweeping westward, the Mongols divided into three separate hordes. In the north the Mongols reached Breslau and Liegnitz, where at the Battle of Wahlstadt they overwhelmed the Teutonic Knights and defenders of the Hanseatic League by releasing thundering explosives to create havoc – although sustaining severe Mongol losses in combat. Having gained some respect for the heavy-lance-wielding medieval knighthood, Kaidu evaded Bohemian king Wenceslaus's army of 50,000 by heading southeast. In the south, Kadan had penetrated as far as Albania on the Adriatic. But the two branches north and south were really diversionary tactics deliberately calculated to spread terror across Europe

---

[5] The wooden version of the traditional rope-and-pole *nerge* to enclose animals in the ring hunt.

and to prevent reinforcements from arriving at what was the Mongols' real objective, the grassy plains of Hungary. Despite heavy opposition, Subedei and Batu in four days had moved over 300 km from the snow-covered passes of the Carpathians to astonish King Bela of Hungary at Buda, eastern outpost of Latin Christianity. The two armies met at the Sajo River, where the Hungarian bridgehead was awakened at dawn by "thunderous noise and flashes of fire" (Dupuy 1969). Some think this may have been the first use of the cannon in European military history. The Hungarians sallied forth to battle but were caught in a trap. Upstream, undetected, Subedei had traversed the icy river with his horsemen to lead a devastating charge against Bela's flank and rear. Cut down on all sides, perhaps as many as 50,000 Hungarians perished. The Mongols continued west almost as far as Vienna, then south, skirting Venice, protected from Mongol attack by its marshes, to raid the plains of northern Italy. But in 1242 arrived the message that 9,500 km away in Mongolia Ogedei was dead. The law of the Yasa required all princes and chiefs to return to Karakorum for the election of the new khagan (Dupuy 1969:99–108).

To the amazement of the West, over the next few months the Mongol forces withdrew from central Europe to their stronghold in Russia on the lower Volga. From his capital at Sarai, Batu established his suzerainty from Bulgaria east through Russia to Khwarizm and south to the northern Caucasus (Saunders 2001:88–89). This domain became known to the west as the Golden Horde, possibly for the elaborate golden hangings of its tents, alternatively named the Kipchak khanate since so many of its people were partly islamized Kipchak Turks. Disappointed that the loot from European cities compared so poorly to the riches of the Orient, the Mongols struck a deal with the Italian merchants of the Crimean ports to exchange their European captives for western manufactured goods. This began a rich and enduring trade with the merchants of Venice and Genoa who established trading posts along the Black Sea to harness this new source of wealth, their human cargo destined for the slave marts of the eastern Mediterranean. This seemingly lucrative arrangement backfired, however. Most of the captive Slavs and Kipchaks were sold to the sultan of Egypt to build up his Mamluk slave army. Mongols shortly would meet this army composed mostly of Kipchak Turks, skilled in steppe combat techniques and experienced in fighting Mongols. Their future meeting in Syria would have a very different outcome from the initial Mongol-Kipchak encounter on the Russian steppes (Weatherford 2004:158–159).

Ogedei's widow Toregene, a Nestorian Christian, adroitly maneuvered to place her son Kuyuk on the throne, and in 1246 an electoral khuriltai was celebrated outside Karakorum. Notables were present from all over Asia. Pope Innocent IV had also sent a diplomatic mission headed by the Franciscan John of Plano Carpini to protest the massacres committed in Europe. Arriving at Sarai almost a year after leaving Lyons, Carpini was sped by eastern horses the remaining 5,000 km to Karakorum in a scant 100 days. There Carpini reported the opulence of the *ordo ger* (tent), which accommodated 1,000 persons. The outside was white felt studded with gold nails. The tent was supported by columns covered with gold plates, and the interior roof, walls, and archways were draped with *nasij* (elaborate gold brocade). Gold as a symbol of political authority, of course, had ancient precedents on the steppes. In the Scythian myth of Targitaus, the golden objects hurled down from the heavens bestowed legitimacy on the sun king. Clearly, later nomads also venerated gold as a symbol of divine favor and imperial majesty; the Mongols swore an oath on gold (Allsen 1997:13–14, 20, 60–61, 66; Watt 2002:67–68).

The news the intrepid friar brought back to Europe of Nestorian Christianity at the Mongol court immediately prompted Louis IX of France to send a Flemish Franciscan, William of Rubruk, to Karakorum. This envoy arrived after the death of Kuyuk, a time of political friction among the princes in which Mongke, leader of the militarily strongest faction, had prevailed to become the khagan in 1251. Rubruk was privileged to participate in a theological debate in which Muslims, Buddhists, and Christians expounded their respective religions. Great lovers of contests, the Mongols had organized this symposium among rival religions along the lines of a wrestling match, in which before a large assembled audience the learned scholars in their fine robes and regalia were required to consume great drafts of airak in preparation for each new round of debate. The situation was further complicated by the fact that the Latin and Orthodox Christians regarded each other as schismatics and the Armenians and Nestorians as heretics. When nothing could be resolved through logical discourse, the Christians had recourse to singing hymns. To drown out the Christians, the Muslims resolutely recited the Koran together, while the Buddhists, aided perhaps by the airak, sank into deep meditation (Weatherford 2004: 172–173).

Rubruk, however, relayed the valuable intelligence that the Mongols were about to embark on a decisive campaign to eliminate the remaining

Muslim states. Mongke, assuming charge of the eastern war in China, in 1253 entrusted to his younger brother Hulegu the campaign to subdue Islam in the west. Hulegu first targeted the fanatical sect of the Assassins, which had terrorized the Islamic world for two centuries. Under bombardment by Chinese catapults, the Alamut stronghold in the Elburz mountains capitulated in 1256; eagles nests' elsewhere in the Middle East were all destroyed and their inmates mercilessly slaughtered. The Mongols next turned their armies against Baghdad, the seat of the Abbasid caliphate, whose thrall over millions of Muslims was an affront to the Great Khan and to Tengri. In 1258 the metropolis was taken, the caliph's treasures were seized, and the palace, mosque, and tombs of the 36 Abbasid caliphs were burned to the ground. The caliph was executed by being rolled in a carpet and kicked to death by horses. In 1259 Hulegu, flanked by Christian Georgians, Armenians, and the Crusader count Bohemund, pressed on into Syria, his armies led by the Nestorian Mongol Ked-Buka. As Aleppo and Damascus fell to the invaders, Hulegu issued the imperious command to the Mamluks of Cairo to surrender. But a distant event, the death of Hulegu's brother in China, transformed the situation. Just as Ogedei's death had saved Christian Europe, so now Mongke's death would save Muslim Asia. An armed dispute had broken out between Mongke's younger brothers Khubilai and Arik Boke for control of the khaganate, requiring Hulegu to move the bulk of his forces northward to Azerbaijan, leaving behind in Syria a small concentration of forces under the command of Ked-Buka. Cairo quickly learned of the weakened Mongol position, and the sultan Kutuz mobilized his Mamluk cavalry northward to Palestine, requesting permission from the Crusader Franks of Acre to pass through their territory. Bohemund's alliance with the Mongols had been punished by papal excommunication; the Acre Christians, therefore, mindful of the Mongols' recent devastation of Europe, conceded passage to the Mamluks (Saunders 2001:106, 109–115). In 1260 Kutuz, with his Kipchak Mamluk general Baybars in the vanguard of the 10,000-strong army, crushed the Mongols at the battle of Ayn Jalut, a turning point that stemmed the tide of Mongol advance in the west and shattered forever the dream of a Christian restoration in the Near East (Hildinger 2001:163–165). Later sultan, Baybars craftily installed a relative of the last Abbasid as puppet caliph in Cairo in order to legitimize his regime. In 1257, Batu's brother Berke succeeded to the Kipchak khanate; having embraced Islam, Berke forged an alliance with Baybars. Separated by hostile lands, Egypt and the Kipchak khanate communicated effectively by sea via Alexandria and the Black Sea ports, their union blessed by the new Abbasid caliph in Cairo. Despite the ever-watchful eye of Constantinople, this Mamluk-Kipchak alliance would remain firm as Islam regained new strength in the Middle East (Saunders 2001:115–116).

MONGOL TRADE ACROSS ASIA AND MULTICULTURAL EFFLORESCENCE

Khubilai Khan and Yuan China

Although Khubilai militarily defeated his younger brother Arik-Bote to reign as the fifth Great Khan, in all reality Mongke's death in 1259 ended the unity of the Mongol empire. The khanate of Chagatai, the Kipchak khanate, even the Ilkhanate, while originally recognizing the Great Khan's supremacy, grew to be virtually independent states in which the Mongol ruling class became slowly submerged in the local population of Turks or Iranians; solely the Ilkhans remained a political ally of the Great Khan. The long-drawn-out struggle against the Song dynasty, begun by Mongke but finalized by Khubilai, restricted the khagan's energies to China. The khagan therefore transferred the center of his empire from Karakorum to Daidu (ancient Zhongdu, present-day Beijing), his primary purpose being to restore China to the unity it had known during the Tang dynasty. By 1273 the route to the Yangtze valley lay clear; in 1275 the Mongol general Bayan defeated the Song army; and in 1279 the Song navy was beaten and the child-emperor drowned at sea. This crowning military achievement won Khubilai dominion over 50 million people. The Mongol invasion continued into Southeast Asia, where Annam, Champa, Burma, and Java would all experience Mongol suzerainty. After initial success, however, difficulties encountered there proved to be insurmountable, as the Mongols were obliged to hack their way through jungle in order to overcome native resistance. Because horses were unsuited to the torrid wet terrain, the core strength of the Mongol army – their superb cavalry – was rendered ineffective. Subject to treacherous ambush in the rainforest, these costly expeditions resulted in failure (Rossabi 1988:213–220). At home, to counter any local rebellion, Khubilai was careful to replace the winding alleys of Chinese cities with broad boulevards, wide enough to accommodate nine horsemen abreast in military maneuvers.

The Qidan Yelu Chucai, Genghis's trusted adviser, had once warned Ogedei that the empire was won on horseback, but would not be

governed on horseback. Anxious to buttress his rule of the newly conquered lands, Khubilai pursued Genghis's policy of religious tolerance.
He himself adhered to ancient steppe tradition and upheld shamanistic
beliefs, each spring celebrating the White Feast, in which herds of pure
white stallions and mares, all revered as sacred, had free run of the
summer palace grounds at Xanadu. Later in the summer, the khagan
performed the ritual horse sacrifice and the scattering of white mare's
milk to the winds as a symbol of Mongol ascendancy over the steppes
(Trippett 1974:142). In late fall or early winter, another important ritual activity was staged at Xanadu, namely, the great ceremonial hunt.
Derived from the ring hunt of the steppes, the tradition of hunting parks
in northern China enjoyed considerable antiquity. King Wu, founder of
the Zhou dynasty (c 1045 BC), inherited from his father a hunting park,
70 Chinese miles square. A millennium later, under the Han martial
emperor Wudi, the Shanglin forest park outside of Changan was more
than 200 Chinese miles in circumference. Containing within its walls a
wide variety of landforms – hills, woods, marshes, streams, ponds, and
islands – it was stocked with abundant game birds, deer, elk, antelope,
aurochs, onagers, water buffalo, camels, and elephants.

Under Khubilai, Xanadu, 400 km north of Daidu, was similarly
equipped with wild game; at its center stood an artificial hill and lake.
Here was a pristine paradise of material abundance and rich cosmological meaning: a center of origins, the beginning of mountains, the source
of waters, the homeland of plants and animals, and the original site of
kingly authority (Allsen 2006:41–47). The great ring hunt was a form of
spiritual communication in which success in the hunt was equated with
victory in war. Amidst imperial pomp, the ruler, equipped with snow-
white gyrfalcons from the subarctic, traveled in a carriage drawn by
four elephants from the subtropics. At Xanadu, as mounted horsemen
released wild animals, the emperor took aim with bow and arrow while
riding at full gallop. His was a political act, a heroic game, dramatically
advertised and celebrated. As triumphant hunter, the king assimilated
and took with him into battle the leonine strength and ferocity of the
vanquished beast. To be beloved and feared, the ruler, like the gods,
needed to be seen as merciful as well ruthless (Allsen 2006:86, 98, 162,
273). Thus in the royal hunt, the khagan demonstrated the power both
to endow and to annihilate. By establishing timber preserves and practicing game management, the emperor protected the earth and guar-
anteed fertility and plenty amidst sparseness. By organizing the hunt
with horses, hounds, tamed cheetahs, and raptors, he powerfully held

in check the wild animals that threatened the people's domestic herds and harvests. By sharing out the meat of slain animals to participants in the chase, he provided winter supplies for his poorer followers. And in times of famine, royal benevolence allowed small game to be hunted by the populace (Allsen 2006:49–50, 199). But the royal hunt was also a dress rehearsal for war.[6] When an uprising occurred in Manchuria, Khubilai used Xanadu as a military base for retaliation. Conversely, governance required periodic renewal of political ties with provincial princes and tribal chieftains, who might otherwise drift into rebellion. The pageantry of the royal hunt conducted in open countryside helped reinforce local loyalties and reaffirm imperial sovereignty over a region. Similarly along borderlands, a large-scale ring hunt, with its displays of martial prowess, military weapons, and troop cohesion, served effectively as a deterrent against troublesome enemies or alternatively as a preliminary to punitive reprisal (Allsen 2006:186, 220).

While engaging annually in ceremonial hunts and the ancient steppe tradition of the White Feast, Khubilai made no attempt to impose steppe shamanic practices on the Chinese. Instead, heedful of Yelu Chucai's advice, Khubilai prudently embraced a policy of patronage of leading religions, employing more sophisticated methods than his brother Mongke. To cultivate good relations with the Confucians, he had the Chinese classics translated into Mongolian. In 1271 from the *Yi jing* (Book of Changes) of Chinese canonical tradition, Khubilai chose *Da Yuan* ("primal force," "origin of the universe") for the name of his dynasty. Khubilai recognized the strong appeal of Taoism to the masses of the population and funded the building of many Taoist temples. He directed that his heir apparent be tutored by leading Confucian scholars and Taoist masters. Accommodation was also sought between Confucians and Buddhists in order to avoid the religious disputes that had plagued Chinese society for decades. Among Buddhists, Tibetan lamas long active in political and secular matters became Khubilai's most trusted allies. In addition to subsidies, all denominations were granted exemption from taxation and conscription.

Khubilai not only sponsored religions long entrenched in China; he also extended his patronage to creeds recently arrived from the west. In the northwest and southeast of China, he sponsored the self-governing communities of Muslim craftsmen and merchants, mostly

---

[6] The pursuit of wild onager was a foil for the exercise of equestrian swordsmanship. In a later epoch, the Mughal emperor Babur would boast of almost decapitating from horseback a fleeing onager with a single saber blow (Allsen 2006:211).

immigrants but also Chinese converts, with their own vibrant mosques, hospitals, and bazaars. Vis-a-vis Christianity, under the influence of his mother Sorkhokhtani, Khubilai employed many Nestorians at court and encouraged numerous Nestorian churches in towns across northwest China and beyond the wall. But rapid horse transport of the day brought other Christians from the west. In 1265 Khubilai lavishly welcomed the two Venetian merchants Niccolo and Maffeo Polo to his court, and on their return trip they were accompanied by the young Marco, who was dispatched across China and southeast Asia as the emperor's "eyes and ears," in time to report the marvels of these eastern lands to Europe. In further appeal to the West, in 1275–1276 Khubilai sent two Nestorian prelates, Rabban Sauma and his disciple Rabban Markos, across Asia to the Mongol Ilkhanate in Persia, whence they continued on to Europe to negotiate an alliance with the Christian monarchs against Islam. Rabban Sauma met with the Byzantine emperor Andronicus II Palaeologus, Philip IV of France, and in Bordeaux King Edward I of England. On his return he received an audience with Pope Nicholas IV before regaining Iran, where he was appointed chaplain to the Ilkhan's court (Rossabi 1994:457–465). In less than 50 years, the Mongols had ravaged Eurasia as far west as the Baltic, established control across the Asian interior, and on Asia's eastern littoral extended their reach far south to Java; now all major religions were practiced in China, and Yuan embassies reached from the Pacific to the Atlantic. The world on horseback was getting smaller fast!

To counterbalance the influence of Confucian scholar-mandarins, Khubilai declined to restore the examination system and recruited instead talented and industrious foreigners to serve as advisers, bureaucrats, and governors. Top-ranking Turkish Uighur officials provided the infrastructure between Mongol rulers and China's millions; in addition to Chinese, the decrees of the Great Khan were all published in a script adapted from the Uighur Turkic alphabet. Other Muslim immigrants from Central Asia performed a variety of specialized tasks in finance, architecture, medicine, flood control, and water conservancy (Roberts 1999:109). Khubilai also promoted Chinese culture. Under his sponsorship, printing attained wide prominence, markedly increasing literacy across the empire. Both government and private offices printed an impressive volume of books: literary works, encyclopedias, Buddhist canons, medical treatises, dynastic histories, and textbooks (Allsen 2001:181–182); the Mongol yam postal relay system only accelerated this flow of information across the nation. The Great Khan actively promoted the production of ceramics, designating entire families as hereditary households and granting potters great flexibility to experiment with new styles. The blue-and-white porcelains so characteristic of the Ming dynasty originated during the Mongol period, when the Chinese first received cobalt from the west (Rossabi 1988:169–170).

Pax mongolica and the effective protection it afforded caravans vastly increased the volume of trade along the Silk Road, intensifying and streamlining direct contact between east and west. Khubilai sponsored the construction of roads planted with willow trees to provide shade. Under good conditions an official messenger with an important dispatch could travel 400 km a day. In addition to transmitting mail, the relay posts, numbering under the Yuan more than 1,400, served as hostelries for traveling dignitaries and merchants. While these stations placed a heavy burden on the local population charged with the upkeep of the facilities, the posts were marvelously equipped with as many as "50,000 horses, 8,400 oxen, 6,700 mules, 4,000 carts, almost 6,000 boats, over 200 dogs, and 1,150 sheep" (Moule and Pelliot 1938; Rossabi 1988:124). Unlike the Chinese, who viewed traders with disdain, the Mongols energetically cultivated relations with foreigners, seeing international trade as a means to generate great wealth. Much of the overland trade was organized by *ortogh* (merchant associations), which were given preferential treatment when raising capital to finance risky ventures. Their trade was profitable to the Yuan government, for all merchants on reaching China were required to exchange precious metals for paper currency (Roberts 1999:110). Printed currency was a long-established institution in China, 10 million paper notes per annum having been issued by the Song in the twelfth century (Hobson 2004:54). Money printed on paper made from mulberry bark was quickly adopted by the Mongols. Backed by either silk or precious metals, in Khubilai's reign it became a universal currency, readily accepted throughout the Yuan realm as legal tender. Together, the issue of paper money and safe transit of goods overland furnished new impetus for trade, with the result that the ancient routes from northern China through Central Asia to the Middle East bustled with traffic (Barfield 1989:206). Extension of the imperial canal system facilitated transport of commodities from the deep interior of China. The rivers and ports of China thronged with flourishing commerce as rice, sugar, fine porcelain, silk, pearls, and precious stones were shipped westward along the south Asian coasts to the Persian port of Curmos (Hormuz), the western entrepot for Chinese mercantile activity (Saunders 2001:124–125).

The Cosmopolitan Ilkhanate – Arts and Sciences across Equestrian Asia

As Genghis's vast empire fragmented amidst the quarrels of his grandsons, the alliance between the two Toluid brothers Khubilai and Hulegu intensified against their cousins and rivals of the Golden Horde and the Chagataid khanate. As hostilities continued to erupt north of their borders, Khubilai and Hulegu were drawn into an intimate relationship, supporting each other diplomatically and militarily and exchanging envoys, commodities, and intelligence. Cultural diversity and exchange were ingredients of their success, as the two brothers created trade opportunities on a continental scale unprecedented in world history in terms of the sheer magnitude of their enterprise (Allsen 2001:13, 22–23). But trade and diplomacy under the Ilkhans extended not only eastward to China but also west to Europe.

In the Ilkhanate, Hulegu actively discriminated against Muslims, while his wife Dokhuz Khatun, a Nestorian, moved energetically to strengthen ties with European Christianity by arranging the marriage between Hulegu's son Abaka and Maria, the natural daughter of the Byzantine emperor Michael VIII (Rossabi 2002:31). Hulegu himself showered favors on Christians and Buddhists, as everywhere in Persia churches and pagodas arose symbolizing the defeat of Islam and the destruction of the caliphate. In 1285 Hulegu's grandson Arghun in communication with Pope Honorius IV offered to supply 30,000 Persian horses to a western army invading Syria to assault their common enemy the Mamluks; the papacy, however, was too preoccupied with crushing Hohenstaufen power in Italy to undertake another Crusade. Instead the Mamluks captured Acre, the sole remaining Crusader outpost on the Levantine coast, definitively ending the European presence in Syria. Despite these reverses, Latin missionaries on horseback traveled across Persia to the Far East to baptize thousands and to translate the Psalter into Mongol and Turkic (Saunders 2001:129–131, 134, 152–153). Repeated communication with the papacy, European monarchs, and their Genoese and Venetian maritime intermediaries opened Persia up to significant contact with the west. Ridding the Black Sea of piracy, the Ilkhans encouraged Italian mariners to found trading posts along its coast. Abaka's new capital of Tabriz, linked through Trabizon, emerged as a burgeoning market town on the principal route across Eurasia, a major magnate to merchants and missionaries alike. But in 1295, after a brief civil war, Ghazan inherited the throne of his father, Arghun, and embraced Islam, undertaking a royal pilgrimage to the sacred Shiite shrine of Husayn at Karbala. Buddhist pagodas and images were destroyed and Christian churches and Jewish synagogues attacked. Under Ghazan, there was a new resurgence of Islam characterized by a popular piety closely linked with Shiism, which ultimately would transform the Ilkhanate into a national Persian state. In 1303 Ghazan attempted to invade Syria but was defeated by the Mamluks. As Seljuk Rum dissolved into anarchy, from the power vacuum in Anatolia arose the Ottoman Turks. In Iran, Ghazan was duly succeeded by his brother Oljeitu and later a nephew; never again would the Iranian state be ruled by a non-Muslim (Saunders 2001:134–138).

Whether Buddhist, Christian, or Muslim, the Ilkhanate, poised between Europe and China, was the scene of incredible cross-fertilization. Clearly the ecological exigencies of nomadic life promoted borrowing and transmission. As we have seen, Genghis and his sons in their devastating sweep across Eurasia initially had scant regard for productive agricultural lands. Instead they attached enormous value to human talent and skills, which were viewed as a form of booty to be apportioned among family, much like herd animals and material spoils after a nomad raid. Genghisid brothers and cousins competed for these specialists, vital to the Mongol reconstruction effort of tapping the economic productivity of conquered sedentary lands. Once a town was sacked and its elite executed, from among the survivors the Mongols quickly selected skilled craftsmen for service to the empire (Allsen 1997:31–32). This practice of sparing artisans resulted in forced mass transfers of populations across the Mongol realm. The artisans most favored were weavers and metal workers, who, registered as hereditary servitors, were resettled in colonies or court factories (Watt 2002:63).

For the Mongol nomad, ever geared to mobility as was the Scythian before him, the most coveted items were riches that were wearable or portable on horseback. But above all, the nomad had a passion for fine textiles that publicly displayed social distinction and wealth. Woolen textiles, felts, and rugs had always played an important role in steppe cultures. During the khuriltai, textiles featured centrally in the elevation of the khagan on felt blankets to rulership over the "peoples who live in the felt-walled tents," a ceremony symbolizing Mongol ethnic nomadic roots and political core (Allsen 1997:51–52). At the apogee of Mongol power, of greatest aesthetic appeal and most treasured for their beauty were nasij (luxury textiles of gold-wrapped thread), "fabrics in which both pattern and ground were woven in gold on a silk foundation"; even the royal horses were caparisoned in silk gilt (Komaroff 2002:171). Great quantities of gold and silk were required for the weaving of these precious stuffs. Available from the Altai (golden) mountains, gold in steppe mythology held the primordial value of the sun and heavens and symbolized eternity and indestructibility. To the east Yuan China boosted its production of raw silk to unprecedented levels by an intensive program of planting mulberry trees. From the specialized workshops of Baghdad across Central Asia to the resettled colonies in the East, textile manufacture was at its peak, as traffic in human skills flowed in all directions. The Yuan established a Gold Thread Office in which westerners taught their highly specialized skills to Chinese artisans and supervised their manufacture. Craftsmen of different ethnic backgrounds working alongside one another revitalized weaving techniques and created a climate of great artistic innovation. From this cross-cultural intermingling of ideas at each center there emerged hybrid styles that became both absorbed in local tradition and diffused across the continent (Watt 2002:70–71). In ceremonial assemblies, the magnificent pavilion encapsulated the Mongols' historic rise to the world stage. The tent's felt exterior evoked the nomadic past, and its interior gold brocade dramatically expressed the Mongols' imperial success. Internationally, Mongol financial reserves were not solely in the form of bullion but also in the form of prestigious narij textiles. Gifts of these rich textiles were a spectacular element in Mongol diplomacy (Allsen 1997:55–57).

As in their ancestral Mongol homeland, the early Ilkhanid court was itinerant, moving from one seasonal camp to another during the course of the year, engaging in great tribal hunts with falcons, lynxes, and cheetahs. While enthronements and audiences of foreign envoys were conducted in splendid tents decked with pearls and jewels, permanent structures were also erected at these seasonal camps. At one major palace complex, Takht-i Sulaiman, south of Tabriz, were located several octagonal and dodecagonal buildings, believed by archaeologists to reflect the Mongol preference for polygonal structure based on the form of the nomad round tent or ger. Palace walls were lavishly decorated, often with luster-painted tiles, simulating perhaps the golden narij hangings of the ornate Mongol tent of assembly. Cultural synthesis was further evident in that some tile decorations featured mythical dragons and phoenixes, auspicious emblems showing clear affinity with the Yuan court, while others displayed figural scenes from the *Shahnameh* national epic of ancient Iran (Masuya 2002:90–99). Also boldly reminiscent of the ancestral ger were the funerary tomb towers or polygonal canopylike mausoleums marking Ilkhanid graves, such as that of Oljeitu north of Qazvin. This huge octagon 38 m across was crowned by an enormous dome more than 24 m in diameter and 53 m high. Precursor to the later Ottoman *kulliye* (funerary edifice), this monument in its sophisticated grace would be the prototype for imperial tombs built by the Mongols for centuries, down to the Taj Mahal (Blair 2002:123–124).

The Ilkhanid conquerors also set about promoting the history and cultural heritage of the lands that only two generations earlier they themselves had utterly devastated. Prominent in this effort was the compilation by the Hamadan Jew Rashid al-Din of the *Jami'al-tavarikh* (Compendium of Chronicles), which, unprecedented in scope, provided a history of the known world (Hillenbrand 2002:137, 146). But by far the most beautiful illustrated text of the fourteenth century was the *Great Mongol Shahnameh*, an illuminated rendering of Firdausi's eleventh-century magnum opus, its themes of heroism, valor in death, and dynastic succession ever grand and noble (Blair and Bloom 1994:28–30). In this monumental revival of Firdausi's national epic, the nomad conqueror not only sought reconciliation with his hostile Iranian subject but, by ambitiously reasserting Persian millennial culture, dared to assume the mantle of nobility and legitimacy of the valiant heroes and proud kings that preceded him. For propagandist reasons, many of the episodes chosen for illustration evinced a correspondence to events in recent Mongol history. As Tabriz thronged with Christian missionaries, Chinese officials, and travelers of every nationality, the universalist Mongols pioneered a new complexity of narrative techniques, interweaving gospel archetypes such as the Virgin and the Crucifixion with Buddhist images, dragons, Chinese mountains, and clouds. Even the dying Rustam was portrayed clad in Chinese imperial robes. With paintings that ranged from simple illustration, to commentary, to multidimensional works of art, the Ilkhanid masters attained a depth of expression hitherto unknown to Islamic book painting. By embracing new perspectives and pushing their medium to its limit, their achievement set the stage for the visual splendor of Timurid, Mughal, and Safavid painting of future centuries (Hillenbrand 2002:158–167).

The Mongols also aggressively promoted the sciences. In the important economic area of agronomy, new seeds and plants from Chinese agriculture, the world's most productive at that time, were acclimatized in Tabriz test facilities. Drawing on several different traditions, Iranian rice cultivation became thoroughly diversified. Conversely under the

Yuan, cultigens earlier diffused from the west now became widely popularized, resulting in a blending of cuisines (Allsen 2001:116, 120–124,
137). It is probable that *jiaozi* (dumplings) were first eaten in China in this
epoch (Rossabi 2002:26). But plants were sought for their medicinal as
well as culinary properties. Items of Muslim pharmacology were traded
east as Chinese medicines moved west. Acupuncture, pulse diagnosis,
and moxibustion were practiced at the Ilkhan court into the fourteenth
century. And in Tabriz a medical center was instituted where physicians
from different lands taught their specializations to local interns (Allsen
2001:141–156).

With this deliberate transfer of technical personnel between east and
west, the Mongols of Persia and China played a critical role in fostering
the rapid dissemination and integration of important geographic data,
particularly in the field of cartography (Allsen 2001:107–113). But as
important as terrestrial cartography might be, the nomad always held
the heavens in awe, and astronomy was of paramount importance to the
Mongols. From the political viewpoint of the khan, even a minor error in
the calculation of an eclipse would undermine his sovereign connection
to the cosmos and divine right to rule. Thus great astronomical obser-
vatories were established at Daidu and at Maragha, south of Tabriz. As
always, along with their instruments there was movement of West Asian
scientists to China and vice versa. One important result of their collaboration was the preparation of conversion tables to equate dates between
the different calendrical systems used across the empire, as important
for agriculture as for administration. Astronomers in China and Persia
continued to make observations on sunspots, occultations, and eclipses
in order to prescribe auspicious days. But in the intellectual ferment at
the Maragha school, the alternative cosmological views of the Chinese
stimulated fundamental criticism of the Ptolemaic planetary model,
challenging the reigning paradigm and prompting extensive theoretical revision that conceivably may have influenced Copernicus's work
in Poland (Allsen 2001:161–175; Saliba 1987).

The Mongol Impact across Asia to Europe

By the fourteenth century, different European monarchs had established
direct contact with the Ilkhanid court in Iran, exchanging embassies and
gifts. Renaissance women in Hungary and Italy wore the lofty silken
conical head gear characteristic of the steppes (Allsen 1997:18). Steppe
trousers and jackets became voguish in Europe, and Europeans, rather

than continuing to pluck with their fingers, began to play their musical instruments with a bow, a technique believed to have originated on the steppes of Khwarizm and Transoxania (Lawergren 1992:115). In England, 250 garters of Tatar cloth were fashioned for Edward III's Knights of the Garter, each garter embroidered with the order's motto in gold and silk. In 1331 the Cheapside Tournament was led by 16 knights wearing nasij Tatar silks and masks in the likeness of fierce Mongol warriors. Dante and Boccaccio in their writings both admired the rich gold and silk brocades from the East (Allsen 1997:1–2). And in the Knight's Tale, describing the Indian king Emetrius, Chaucer wrote:

> On a bay steed whose trappings were of steel
> Covered in cloth of gold from haunch to heel
> Fretted with a diaper. Like Mars to see.
> His surcoat in cloth of Tartary
> Studded with great white pearls; beneath its fold
> A saddle of new beaten, burnished gold.
>
> (Chaucer 1977:77)

From the verse it is clear that the intensive commerce and technical communication between the Mongol dynasties of Yuan China and the Persian Ilkhanate did not stop at the edge of Asia but extended further westward. Tabriz was the Ilkhanid gateway to Europe, and across this bridge, besides the sumptuous gold and silk nasij textiles, many products and technologies from the east flowed into Christian lands.

Chinese priority in printing is well documented, and under the Mongols printed paper currency was introduced into Iran. In terms of historical development, the sixth century AD saw the invention of xylography, by which a written sheet of paper was applied to a wood block coated with rice paste. With the paste retaining the impression of the writing in reverse, an engraver simply cut out the uninked areas. During the Tang dynasty, the first complete book, *Diamond Sutra*, was printed in 868; dramatic expansion of printing and publishing businesses followed during the Song dynasty. By the eleventh century early experimentation with movable type, earthenware and wood, took place in China, culminating in the thirteenth-century development of bronze metal type in Korea. However, due to the impracticality of working with thousands of oriental characters, little headway was made with movable type in the East. But wood-block printing was commonplace, and the Uighurs were mainly responsible for introducing their Mongol overlords to the medium of print. Under the Yuan, the Imperial Library

Directorate, established in 1273, printed as many as 1,000 copies of a book, and by the beginning of the fourteenth century several million calendrical pamphlets were produced per annum. No one knows for certain how printing technology reached the West. Rather surprisingly, Islam seems not to have been the intermediary agent. Because there were innumerable Christian embassies through Tabriz to China following Mongol expansion, the transmission of printing technology from China across Iran to Europe appears likely (Allsen 2001:176–185). As for Europe, in the wake of Mongol expansion, xylography was first evidenced in 1259 in Poland, in 1283 in Hungary, and later in Germany (Hobson 2004:185), its method identical to that of the Chinese. The early fifteenth century, however, ushered in important European advances in metallographic impression by medieval craft guilds. Metal founders experimenting with soft bronze or brass dies, engraved with letters of the alphabet, produced a lead typeface, far more durable than the woodblock and capable of rapid replication. But the final step in the development of typographic print was engineered in the Rhineland c 1450 by Johannes Gutenberg. Type pieces were arranged letter by letter on a grooved composing strip to make a complete line. The lines of type composing a page were then locked into a frame and linked for the printing press. Delivering sharp, consistently figured impressions and printing on both sides of the page, by 1475 Gutenberg's invention had achieved the major functions that were to characterize western printing for the next four centuries (Raymond 1984:106–107).

Of course, opinion still differs as to whether printing in the West represented diffusion from the East or independent invention. Similar disagreement surrounds the question of gunpowder and firearms. Again, there was a long history of gunpowder in China, whose alluvial soils were strongly impregnated with saltpeter, such that a simple fire might accidentally trigger an explosion. In the ninth century, Chinese gunpowder consisted of a mixture of saltpeter, sulfur, and charcoal in the approximate proportions of 75:14:10 and therefore differed from the petroleum-based "Greek fire" used against the Arabs in 673 during the siege of Constantinople. On contact with flame, gunpowder exploded, releasing superheated gas that propelled a projectile over distance against a target. As is well known, gunpowder in China was first used harmlessly in the manufacture of pyrotechnics for ceremonial display. But the wars in the north against the Qidan and Jurchen during the Song period prompted significant innovation in the field of explosives and incendiaries, transforming the catapult into a gun. By 1232 gunpowder was utilized in grenades, bombs, and rockets. Defending Luoyang against the Mongols, the Qidan employed the *chen tien lei* thunder bomb, "an iron vessel filled with gunpowder and discharged from a catapult by the igniting of the powder" (Saunders 2001:197), which successfully pierced the metal armor of the besiegers. In 1259 gunpowder was exploded in a fire-lance *huoquiang*, "a bamboo tube which discharged a cluster of pellets at a distance of 230 m" (Saunders 2001:198). By the time of Khubilai, gunpowder was stored in arsenals, and in the Mongol invasions of Japan in 1274 and 1281, fire-barrels, "guns with iron barrels fired by gunpowder" (Saunders 2001:198), were wielded in combat. The Mongols, always quick to learn from their enemies, under Subedei promptly adopted the thunder bomb and carried it west in their second invasion of Europe, where it is claimed a primitive cannon was deployed against the Hungarians at the battle of Sajo. Before the Mongol expansion, gunpowder was unknown in the west; during the Crusades there was no trace of its use by either Christian or Muslim. Yet, by the fourteenth century, firearms were widely employed in both Asia and Europe (Hobson 2004:59). Again the evidence suggests probable transmission of the technology by Mongols westward from China.

Yet another important innovation, the mass production of cast-iron implements, was achieved in China by the third century BC (Hobson 2004:52). Because of their superior furnace technology, reaching peak efficiency during the Han dynasty, the Chinese commanded extremely high temperatures in their blast furnaces. This, combined with the use of giant bellows and the massive burning of carbon fuel, rendered a liquid iron-carbon alloy that flowed freely from the slag at about 1150°C; steel was then produced by reducing the carbon content of the liquid iron (Raymond 1984:74–75). Prior to the mid-second millennium AD, steel and cast-iron blast furnaces were nonexistent in Europe. Manuscript evidence indicates that cast-iron blast furnace technology arrived in the Rhine Valley in 1380, followed during the next 200 years by several processes long established in steel production in China; in the west by the fifteenth century waterwheels were used to power large bellows. Again, while independent invention cannot conclusively be ruled out, there is ample evidence to suggest that as a result of the Mongol sweep of Eurasia, cluster diffusion of several technologies occurred, in which perhaps the most significant – printing, gunpowder, and cast-iron/steel technology – reached the Rhineland from eastern Asia in the fourteenth and fifteenth centuries (Flemings 2002:118). Just as earlier in the diffusion of silk, stirrups, and paper, once again the horse was the instrument of transmission. Technologically these latest advances bridged the gap between the medieval and modern eras.

SUCCESSOR STATES TO NOMADIC EQUESTRIAN MILITARISM

Viewed from the twenty-first century, it is difficult to comprehend how in the politically fragmented climate of thirteenth-century Mongolia, an illiterate leader from a small band of nomads could emerge from chaos, defeating his feuding rivals one by one, to fashion a tribal confederation that not only challenged and subdued the surrounding states but forged the largest contiguous land empire in human history. It was a feat that could only be realized by equestrian mobility. And it was of course the culmination of a process underway for millennia, namely, the invasion of sedentary civilization by the military might of the steppe nomad. But earlier it had been piecemeal! In the second millennium BC, distinct Indo-European groups had advanced separately into Anatolia, India, and Iran. In the first millennium BC, Achaemenid and Chinese empires were separately forged, with Xiongnu assaults directed mainly against Han China. In the first millennium AD from their southern deserts Arab nomads exploded across the Middle East and North Africa, but before the end of the eighth century Muslim equestrian armies were halted at Talas and the Pyrenees. Finally in the thirteenth century, Mongol invasion from the steppes struck East and West concurrently. A brilliant strategist, Genghis Khan led his superbly disciplined cavalries across the entire breadth of the Asian landmass to the borders of Europe. This vast conquest, stained by atrocious massacres, was later consolidated and extended by able generals and successor khans, save only in the southern and southeasterly peninsulas of the Asian continent, where densely forested tropical lands impeded horse warfare. With no administrative system of their own, the nomad conquerors speedily appropriated the expertise of their sedentary subjects, marshaling technologies and human talent on an unprecedented scale. Whether in the arts, sciences, religion, or warfare, without ethnic bias, the Mongols experimented freely with diversity and hybrid form. Their amalgamation of cultures and commitment to global commerce demolished barriers that earlier had isolated one civilization from another; their probing in science and industry sped ideas and inventions across continents; and their upholding of international secular law meshed cultures together in a thoroughly modern manner. Genghis's imperium was destined to endure somewhat less than 200 years, but as fallout of Mongol expansion, numerous successor states would soon emerge to define the shape of Asia in today's modern world.

Warrior Horsemen East of the Asian Mainland

First let us turn to a noteworthy exception to the general pattern of Mongol conquest in medieval Asia: a state owing its equestrian tradition to the steppes, that in its martial readiness succeeded in defying Yuan China to repulse all Mongol invasion of its territory. In Japan, the earliest record of horsemen dates to the fourth century AD, a time of tumult and upheaval in eastern Asia. While the Southern Xiongnu (Chapter 5) c 311 AD were sacking the Western Chin, other nomads, the Xianbei, attacked the Puyo stock raisers of Manchuria, driving them south domino fashion into the Korean peninsula, where they overran the kingdom of Paekche and invaded the Japanese island of Kyushu. In the *Nihon shoki*[7] it is reported that these *kiba minzoku* (horse-riding warriors) overwhelmed the local Wa population. In contrast to the preceding Yayoi era (250 BC–AD 250), in which the archaeological record showed no trace of horses, suddenly there appeared evidence of a vibrant horse culture. Common to both Korean and Japanese cultures of this epoch and betraying their common steppe origin, huge funerary tumuli (*kofun*) were constructed (Ledyard 1975:219–246; Littleton 1995:269). In these kurgan-like earthen tombs, horse trappings, weapons, iron armor, and clay figurines were interred with the deceased. The burned clay figures included representations of horses with saddles, bridles, reins, stirrups, and armored warriors wearing swords and helmets. The small metal plaques of the kofun armor showed some resemblance on the one hand to the iron plaques characteristic of first-millennium-BC steppe nomad armor and on the other to later Japanese steel plaque armor. Through the exercise of equestrian warfare, these ancient mounted warriors from the Korean peninsula moved onto the rich plain of Yamato, where they succeeded in imposing their imperial rule on the Japanese islanders (Ackroyd 1987:581; Blomberg 1994:1–3; Turnbull 2003:11–12).

As warring continued between the Korean kingdoms and Japanese islanders, measures were taken to strengthen the Japanese cavalry. To

---

[7] In the fourth century the Japanese were minimally literate. It is from the ancient books *Kojiki* and *Nihon shoki*, written in 712 and 720 respectively, that we learn of Japan's early beginnings.

meet the foreign challenge the emperor commissioned noble landowners to provide *bushi* (elite warriors) to ride horseback wielding the bow
(Turnbull 2003:13). In these formative years, a mounted warrior's proficiency focused on his skill as an archer. The earliest epic poetry refers
to "the way of the horse and the bow," and to this day *yabusame* (the
ancient martial art of the mounted archer at a gallop aiming at wooden
targets) is still practiced in Japan (Turnbull 2003:95–96). Thus, the main
weapon was the long bow composed of a wood strip between two
bamboo strips, lacquered and bound with rattan. The bow was taller
than a man, and its grip was set one-third of the way up its length, the
upper arm twice as long as the lower, thereby facilitating ease of aim
on either side of the horse's head. Arrows were correspondingly long
with different-sized steel heads. Mounted on a wooden saddle with
stirrups (Harris and Ogasawara 1990:27), the Japanese warrior came
to wear a cuirass of lacquered steel and leather scales flexibly laced
together with silk braids, sturdy enough to withstand assault but also
permitting agility on foot. Additional weapons used were the halberd
and sword. The earliest iron blades had arrived from China during the
Yayoi period (Till 1984). Initially the primitive straight sword was used
primarily for stabbing, but later it was replaced by the single-bladed
sword with curvature and a cutting edge of 1 m or more, eminently
suited for combat on horseback (Yumoto 1958:28).

Shrouded in legend, the sword occupies a central magical role in
Japanese culture. According to the ancient books, the great sun goddess
Amaterasu sent her grandson Hononinigi across the seas to rule the
land of luxuriant rice fields. Amaterasu bestowed on Hononinigi three
holy treasures, the divine regalia of the Yamato imperial house: the *Yata-
no-Kagami* mirror, the *Kusanagi-no-Tsurugi* sword, and the *Yasakani-no-
Magatama* curved jewel. Applying Dumezilian analysis to these ancient
legends, Japanese scholar Atsuhiko Yoshida argues that together these
sacred objects constituted a conception of society similar to the tripartite
structure of Scythian and Saka myth. Like the Scythian golden chalice,
the mirror represented the soul of the nation, its ruler and priesthood.
Like the Scythian spear and arrow, the sword stood for the warrior class.
Like the Scythian yoked plow, the curved jewel symbolized fertility of
the fields and multiplicity of progeny (Yoshida 1977:94–97). I suppose
it is remotely possible that the equestrian invaders who introduced this
tripartite mythology to Japan were themselves Indo-European speakers.
Far more likely, though, given that the Korean and Japanese languages
are linguistically related to Altaic Mongol, Turkish, and Tungusic, the

horsemen from the mainland were Altaic speakers who, having experienced sustained interaction with Iranian nomads on the Asian steppes, had absorbed elements of their cosmology and heroic epos (Yoshida 1977:110–111).

Another intriguing parallel possibly linking Japan to the Iranian steppes was the legend of Yamato-takeru (Brave of Yamato), the second son of the twelfth emperor Keiko, whose exploits, according to folklorist C. Scott Littleton, resemble those of the Sarmatian Ossetic hero Batraz and even the Arthurian legends of Europe. Indeed, there are uncanny similarities between the Western epics we have already discussed and the Japanese. Like Arthur, Yamato-takeru was destined for greatness from an early age. In his teens, equipped with a small sword, he stabbed two powerful Kumaso enemies to death, thereby validating his status as warrior and leader. All three great knights later received magical swords from a female figure, Arthur from the Lady of the Lake, Batraz from his aunt the seeress Satana, Yamato-takeru also from a protectress aunt, who bestowed on him his second supernatural sword, *Kusanagi*, the most sacred weapon of Japan, seized by the gods from one of the tails of the dragon Yamata no Orochi. Accompanied by a small band of loyal knights, Yamato-takeru journeyed eastward to subdue the barbarians. Successful in multiple feats of arms, he embarked on one final quest, where in confrontation with a fierce deity he was afflicted by a fatal disease. Like Arthur and Batraz, brought down to the seashore in his last hours, Yamato-takeru died tragically, departing this life as a bird to heaven (Littleton 1995:260–264). Interestingly, traces of Iranian motifs also occur in ancient Chinese myths. It would appear that just as Buddhism spread across the steppes from India to China and Japan, so much earlier Iranian influences had similarly impacted northern China, as when Magi astrologers c 800 BC played an important role at the Zhou court. Chinese legends of the first millennium BC echo themes of a grail cauldron and recount how a shining sword flung into turbulent waters was held aloft by a supernatural hand (Mair 1998:297). The traditional reverence for swords and swordsmanship may well derive from very ancient origins. Such wondrous tales of roiling waters, supernatural swords, mystical protectresses, daring adventures, conflict with powerful adversaries, and untimely death bespeak an equestrian tradition of heroism that perhaps spans the Eurasian landmass.

As we saw, the bushi initially served the Japanese emperor as elite mounted warriors. Later, equestrian warriors became attached to

FIGURE 9.3. Illustrious samurai Minamoto Hachimantaro Yoshiie (1041–1108) with bow and "Phrygian" cap (Turnbull 2003:49).

powerful landowners, and the term *samurai* came to be used. As their military power increased in the provinces, samurai lineages came to be recognized for their equestrian prowess, and there emerged a mounted warrior responsible for his own training and equipment (Friday 2003:1–2; Fig. 9.3). In the twelfth century, a fierce civil war raged for five years among samurai warlords; *sohei* warrior Buddhist monks also fought fully armored. These bloody battles were ever memorialized in the great epic *Heike Monogatari*, traditionally sung by lute-stringing, blind ambulant monks (Blomberg 1994:viii–ix, 128–129). An indelible part of samurai culture, the heroic acts of the Gempei war would serve as a benchmark, a source of inspiration to future generations as to the most noble and courageous form of warrior conduct. From the hostilities, the war leader Yoritomo emerged victorious to assume the title *shogun* (military dictator) and to uphold the martial discipline of *bushido*, which required samurai to devote themselves to horsemanship, swordplay, and archery. The new samurai military supplanted the court nobility to become political and economic masters of Japan until 1868, the emperor in Kyoto relegated to a purely religious role without political power (Turnbull 2003:14–15).

As swordplay grew in importance on the battlefield, it became customary for the samurai to challenge a worthy opponent to single combat. Seated on crested saddle, in lacquered armor with antlers or horns curving out from his helmet, the samurai in thunderous voice would recite his ancestral pedigree, followed by boasts of personal valor and threats as to how he would annihilate his adversary. The warrior challenged always responded with a litany of his own ancestors' deeds, then joined the battle. The victor in the duel finally praised the strength and courage of his slain opponent. Ancestors were revered in Japanese religion, and every warrior aspired to bring honor to his family name (Turnbull 2003:47–48). But in the face of dishonorable capture, death was preferable. Only the samurai had the privilege of carrying two swords, a long one for attack and a short one for self-destruction (Till 1984). If defeated, in *seppuku* (ritual suicide) the samurai slit his abdomen crosswise in order to release his spirit. If politically disgraced, the samurai committed seppuku at home, customarily writing a valedictory poem with blood from his belly (Blomberg 1994:72–74).

But Japanese equestrian tradition was soon to be tested by an external foe – Mongol might from across the seas. In 1274 Khubilai attempted to invade the southernmost island of Kyushu. The Japanese were not as battle-hardened as the Mongols, and, while skilled in combat, were at a disadvantage in countering the invaders' sophisticated explosive and incendiary weapons. In one day of fighting the Japanese troops were critically overwhelmed, saved only that night by a gale that cost the invaders many lives and several hundred ships (Rossabi 1988:99–103). Fired with this initial victory, the Japanese prepared to repel any future invasion by constructing formidable stone defenses. In 1281, forces of 45,000 Mongols and 120,000 Koreans invaded simultaneously from the south and the north. For two months the battles raged, but the invaders could not advance against the fierce resistance of the equestrian samurai, their legendary exploits extending the tradition of the Gempei war. Finally the war was settled by a catastrophe of nature. The island was struck by a summer typhoon, during which perhaps as many as 60,000 invaders perished, either drowned at sea or slaughtered by samurai

FIGURE 9.4. Samurai Shimazu Yoshihiro (1535–1619; shown fully armored), who led the Satsuma contingent in the Korean war (Turnbull 2003:101).

sword. For the Japanese, the typhoon (*kamikaze*) was a divine tempest sent by the gods to protect Japanese territory from enemy incursion, ever to inspire heroic self-sacrifice against invaders from across the seas (Turnbull 2003:16).

The Mongol menace greatly contributed to the intensification of martial fervor throughout Japan. The national folk epic *Shichinin no samurai* (The Seven Samurai) celebrated samurai honor and commitment to self-sacrifice. Zen Buddhism encouraged the warrior to develop a strong character. *No* drama, predominantly tragic and in keeping with the ideals of Zen, enacted themes drawn from samurai exploits and was the preferred entertainment of the military aristocracy. In their search for flawless excellence in combat, the Japanese raised military endeavor to new levels of sophistication and lethality (Fig. 9.4). Japan would emerge a formidable fighting force in the Far East, in later centuries to win wars in Korea, China, and Russia (Till 1984).

Equestrian Conquests in West Asia and West of Asia

For Yuan China, Japan's victory in 1281 was a devastating blow. Their rout at the hands of the samurai shattered the Mongols' repute of invincibility, the psychological edge of terror that underwrote their political power (Rossabi 1988:212). It is also interesting to note that the shogunate's defeat of the Yuan maritime assault took place a mere 20 years after the Ilkhanate's attempted takeover of Egypt was thwarted by another disciplined core of equestrians, the Mamluks, allied across the seas with the hardy Kipchaks of the steppes. Thus, in east and west on maritime peripheries at opposite ends of Asia, at approximately the same time, Mongol equestrian power was checked. Nor did the Yuan or the Ilkhans long endure. By the mid-fourteenth century, in the east the Yuan had succumbed to the Ming, and in the west another equestrian power arose in Central Asia.

TIMURID-MUGHAL SUCCESSORS TO THE MONGOLS. The Ilkhanate came to an abrupt end in 1335 when the khan died without heirs and his territories devolved into small antagonistic states. To the east, the Chagataid khanate was similarly split into competing segments. In 1370 a new force emerged to invigorate the greater Iranian area – Timur. As a Turk of the noble Barlas clan, early followers of Genghis, Timur would model his military campaigns on the nomadic warrior tradition of the Mongols. Lame from arrow wounds inflicted during his rise to power, he came to be known as Timur-i Lang (Turkish for "Timur the Lame") or, as transcribed in the west, "Tamerlane." Never a disciplined strategist and lacking statesmanly vision, Timur embarked on numerous campaigns of destruction without ever achieving lasting political consolidation; his exploits nevertheless dramatically impacted surrounding regions (Roemer 1993a:43, 47, 86). The Great Emir first engaged in protracted hostilities with the Golden Horde in 1391, breaking the Kipchak army at the Ural River, then pursuing it 640 km to the Volga. This offensive did much to weaken the western khanate and to prepare the ground for Russian rebellion under Muscovite leadership (Hildinger 2001:176–182). In Iran, his expeditions involved disciplinary actions against provinces in revolt, particularly Isfahan, where in reprisal for an uprising the Great Emir engaged in a program of calculated terror, slaughtering the entire population and piling pyramids of 70,000 heads outside the city walls to discourage uprisings elsewhere. Timur even ordered his cavalry to play polo with the heads of decapitated prisoners. Nothing perpetrated by the Mongols during their conquests equaled such bestial depravity (Roemer 1993a:55; Spencer 1971:4). In 1398 Timur crossed the Indus to undertake jihad against the Delhi sultanate. By releasing buffalo with flaming faggots burning on their backs, he sowed terror among the Indian war elephants, allowing his powerful cavalry to vanquish the enemy and Timur to subject his idolator Hindu captives to barbaric torture (Chaliand 2004:77). Warring against the Mamluks in 1400, the Great Emir captured much of Syria. As Timur's forces advanced across Asia Minor, the Ottoman sultan Bayezid was obliged to abandon his intended siege of Constantinople. Following devious tactics, the Great Emir inflicted a shattering defeat on the Ottomans, at the same time granting the moribund Byzantine empire a further half century of uneasy reprieve (Hildinger 2001:184–192).

Despite the scale of his conquests, Timur made the greater Iranian area the central focus of his empire, where the finest artisans from east and west were ruthlessly recruited to work on extraordinary buildings at Bokhara, Samarkand, and Herat. Great mosques were built with blue-glazed sphere-conical domes, continuing the imperial architecture of the Ilkhanate period but also proclaiming Timur's new dynastic rule. Gonzales de Clavijo, ambassador of Henry III of Castile and Leon, in 1404 visiting the Great Emir at Samarkand was amazed by the tiled multistoried kiosks and lavish tent pavilions of jeweled golden cloth midst verdant gardens. The magnificence of Timurid buildings would influence architecture far beyond Central Asia. From Turkey to India, subsequent imperial powers – Ottomans, Safavids, and Mughals – would all emulate Timur's imposing style (Blair and Bloom 1994:37–39, 53–54). Preparing next to invade China, Timur died in 1404. Fearful of continuing Timurid expansionary might, Ming China between 1405 and 1421 launched a series of six maritime explorations westward along the southerly coasts of Asia, the fifth expedition ranging as far afield as East Africa. The purpose of these voyages was to counteract Mongol political power in western Asia, by extending Chinese influence across the high seas in order to secure allies in foreign lands (Chan 1988:232–236).

Ming naval ventures notwithstanding, Timur's descendant Babur, who on his mother's side traced his ancestry through Chagatai to Genghis Khan, with his cavalries later invaded northern India from Kabul, overwhelming the Afghans of Uttar Pradesh, the Rajput confederacy, and the Delhi sultanate to establish the Mughal empire c 1526 (Roemer 1993b:127). Babur's grandson Akbar, who reigned from 1556 to 1605, was the greatest Mughal ruler, extending the empire east to the Bay of Bengal and south to the Deccan. He was also a great polo enthusiast, playing matches at night under torchlight. Even Nurjahan, the wife of Akbar's son Jahangir, was an accomplished player (Spencer 1971:3–4). Under Jahangir's son Shahjahan, there was great cultural efflorescence with the appearance of major architectural works, among them the Taj Mahal, built in memory of his favorite wife, Mumtaz Mahal, all of which showed marked influence from the Iranian northern tradition, although fused with Indian styles (Blair and Bloom 1994:279–280, 287). The Mughals reigned in India until 1857, when the British exiled their last ruler, Bahadur Shah II, to Rangoon and decapitated his two sons (Wolpert 1993:238).

SAFAVIDS – IRANIAN SUCCESSORS TO THE MONGOLS. As Timurids waged internecine campaigns in eastern Central Asia, to the west the Safavids – midst a sea of Turanians – succeeded in forging a new dynasty. Destined to last to the eighteenth century, their rule would emphasize the old political and cultural traditions of Persia, secure much of its ancient territory, and iranicize Islam to establish a militant Shiite creed as the state religion (Roemer 1993c:189–190). Shaikh Haidar claimed descent from Shaikh Safi ad-Din who had founded the Safaviyya order of dervishes to subvert fourteenth-century Turkoman influence in western Iran. Based on this folk tradition, Haidar traced his ancestry from the Prophet Muhammad through Ali's wife Fatima, professing to be the reincarnation of the Shiite imams. Haidar also claimed descent from the Sasanian royal line because of the marriage of Ali's son Husayn to princess Shahribanu, daughter of the last Sasanian emperor, Yezdegird III. In 1501 Haidar's son Ismail was crowned shah of Azerbaijan. Within a decade Ismail had established the Safavid monarchy across the Iranian region, instating the *Ithna Ashari* Twelver branch of Shia as state religion. Because the Ottoman foe was Sunni, a large majority of Persians flocked to support the Shia cause and to accept Ismail as their sovereign. As Persia reemerged as a nation, the Shia religion instilled a sense of national identity and thus served as a strong unifying force against the encroachments of the Sunni Turks. In 1514, Ismail contacted the Holy Roman Empire to form an alliance against the Turks, but communication was poor and his efforts came to naught. Facing hostilities on the eastern frontier against the Uzbeks and on the western against the Ottomans, Ismail's cavalry was critically defeated by superior Turkish artillery and firearms at the fiercely contested battle of Chaldiran outside Tabriz in 1514. That year was further complicated by the Portuguese who, following up on da Gama's circumnavigation of the Cape of Good Hope, seized the important Persian port of Curmos (Lockhart and Boyle 1978:37–39).

Continuing insecurity on the Iranian borders prompted the transfer of the Safavid court eastward to Qazvin and then to Isfahan in 1598, where shah Abbas I reigned during the most brilliant period of the Safavid era. The legitimacy of Safavid rule rested on the theological authority of Twelver Shiism and public acceptance of Abbas's anointed role as its custodian. Abbas therefore proceeded to make his new capital the political, economic, and religious hub of the nation. With an ambitious urban program, he transformed Isfahan into a wonderland of glazed tiles, soaring portals, slender minarets, and bulbous domes, flanked by boulevards, palaces, parks, and fountains in the gigantic format of a typical garden carpet. The new royal maydan, Naqsh-i-Jahan (Design of the World), covering eight hectares, was constructed for state ceremonies, archery contests, and polo. At night 50,000 lamps illuminated the maydan. On the west side at the midpoint of the Naqsh-i-Jahan was located the *Ali Qapu*, the towering royal tribune soaring 30 m high. Evolved from the traditional *talar* verandah already present in the Apadana, it provided an elevated grandstand from which royalty and guests reviewed troop parades and polo matches. When the shah scored, Ali Qapu trumpeters sounded a salute. Abbas's stone goalposts 8 yd apart continue today to be standard polo regulation. Played by Achaemenids, Sasanians, Arabs, Chinese, Byzantines, Turks, Mughals, and Safavids, polo would be encountered in future centuries by the British army in northern India, then practiced by every regiment worth its mettle. With that empire, polo would spread across the globe to become today's modern sport (Blair and Bloom 1994:183–185, 190; Spencer 1971:4–5).

OTTOMANS – TURKISH SUCCESSORS TO THE MONGOLS. As noted earlier, the ancestors of the Ottoman Turks were driven from Iran by the Mongols west into Anatolia, where they had sought refuge with the Seljuks of Konya. When these Seljuks became the vassals of the Ilkhanate, Turkish tribes continued moving westward in search of territory, where many became ghazi religious fighters on the fringes of the empire. Osman, leader of the Osmanli/Ottoman Turks, after defeating a Byzantine army in 1301, occupied Nicaea/Iznik. In the course of the fourteenth century the Ottomans traversed the European littoral, spreading across the Balkans to the Adriatic, where in 1389 they annihilated the combined Serbian and Bosnian armies at Kosovo (Field of the Blackbirds). Territories were subsequently annexed along the Danube. During these wars, the Ottomans were quick to adopt cannons and muskets from the West. Ottoman offensives in eastern Europe caused many Byzantine scholars to flee westward to Italy, taking with them important books and manuscripts in the tradition of Greek scholarship. In the consequent Renaissance, across western Europe there was a resurgence of interest in classical learning from which humanism, a new spiritual and intellectual outlook, would emerge. Finally in 1453 the Ottoman sultan Mehmed II attacked politically isolated Constantinople; its medieval walls, which had withstood over a thousand years of sieges, were no longer a match for the new monster cannons. The Greek fighting force of 7,000 was vastly outnumbered by the 80,000 Turkish troops, whose invader morale was fortified by the prospect of winning a special place in paradise upon capturing the Christian capital. After 53 days of bombardment, the seat of Caesars, the eastern bulwark of Christendom against Islam, finally fell to Asian assault, its last emperor, Constantine XI Palaeologus, plunging into the fray to perish sword in hand. As the city was given over to pillage and its population enslaved, the treasures of Hagia Sophia were desecrated; priceless gold-threaded vestments were seized to adorn Turkish horses. The great cathedral was converted into a mosque with a bronze crescent replacing the Christian cross on the summit of the dome, the city to become the new capital of the Ottoman empire (Bisaha 2004:61–63; Kinross 1972:90–102).

At age 21, Mehmed II aimed at nothing less than world conquest. Successful where numerous other commanders had failed, finally he had vindicated the first Umayyad caliph Moawiya's failure to capture Constantinople in 677. He had also avenged the Greek sack of Asian Troy millennia before and now traveled to the site of that ancient city, where he vowed to exceed Alexander and Caesar in future military campaigns. Ottoman wrath also turned against rival Islamic sects. Mehmed's grandson Selim eliminated all Shiite opposition in Anatolia by executing 40,000 followers of Shah Ismail. He next invaded Syria and Egypt, routing 4,000 Mamluk cavalry at the Battle of Reydaniyya in 1517, at which point the sheriff of Mecca presented him with the keys of the Holy Cities. Control over these ancient lands greatly enhanced Ottoman prestige. It was now incumbent upon the House of Osman as protector of the faith to extend the frontiers of Sunni Islam, which it did, relentlessly combating every form of heresy. Astride the Red Sea, the Ottoman sultan commanded vast wealth from the commerce with

India and the spice trade from the Moluccas. Turkish naval power next dominated the Black Sea, then expanded west across the Mediterranean (Inalcik 1989:33–34, 36) – while Europe trembled.

Selim's son, Suleiman the Magnificent, as leader of the most disciplined army in the world, moved swiftly to exploit his position of power. During the 1520s tens of thousands of valiant Christian knights perished as Buda fell to the Ottomans (Bridge 1983:99–100). Again in 1529 the tugh horsetail banners of war were raised as Suleiman led the Turkish army of well over 100,000 toward Vienna. No longer warring on the Asian frontier, the Turk was now threatening the heart of Europe. The elite *sipahi* (Persian "cavalryman") formed the bulk of the Turkish cavalry, complemented by *akinji* (irregular horsemen) responsible for patrolling imperial frontiers. Additionally, due to the increasing importance of firearms, the sultan had incorporated into his army *yeniceri* (janissary infantry; Turko-Persian "new army") – Christian slaves conscripted as youths from the Balkan provinces, forcibly converted to Islam, compelled to be celibate, and subject to rigorous military training. The sultan approached Vienna with the intention of wintering in that city before invading Germany in the spring (Clot 1992:15–16, 46, 64–65). Holy Roman emperor Charles V was coordinating military action in the west; here even Luther's Protestant Germans, who earlier had deemed Turkish victories punishment for papal sin, were now prepared to fight. Under Count von Salm, 20,000 troops drawn from across Charles's empire stood ready to defend the Austrian capital. But the attacker had encountered logistical problems. Suleiman's wars were no longer the lightning campaigns of the steppe nomad. The cavalry, though still at the forefront of the fighting, now was accompanied by heavy artillery and bulky wagons of explosives, most of which due to heavy summer rains had become bogged down in mud. Without heavy artillery, the Turkish bombardment of Vienna's fortifications was largely ineffective; the defenders themselves had 72 cannons and hundreds of harquebuses. By October, Turkish food supplies and ammunition were depleted; furthermore, the cold and snow had arrived. Suleiman had no alternative but to withdraw, but not before burning alive or hacking to death a thousand or more Christian captives before the walls, in full view of the defenders. As the Turkish host retreated eastward, it was persistently harassed by Austrian cavalrymen, such that many an invader, many a steed, and much equipment were lost (Bridge 1983:113–120). This was a major defeat for the Ottomans. As at Poitiers, western Europe had a narrow escape.

But Suleiman had advanced along another front. In 1523, considering the Island of Rhodes a papal vanguard for future crusades, he had attacked the Knights Hospitalers, effectively forcing their evacuation. With subsequent Ottoman control of the Balkan peninsula, the Greek pirate Barbarossa converted to Islam to become known as Khair ad-Din. As *kapudan pasha* (grand admiral), he headed the Moorish corsairs of the Barbary coast, intent on avenging their recent expulsion from Spain by raiding Christian shipping in the western Mediterranean. Thus, with little effort, the Ottomans annexed a major portion of the North African coast as far west as Algiers. One by one Khair ad-Din subdued and devastated the Venetian islands in the Aegean, enslaving thousands of Christians. Finally in 1538 the grand admiral outmaneuvered the Genoese condottiere Andrea Doria and the forces of Charles V and Venice at Preveza, thereby securing the eastern Mediterranean for the Ottomans (Bridge 1983:131–146). In the midst of these maritime offensives, Suleiman found time to confront yet another adversary, the Shiite shah of Iran. In 1534, Ottoman armies advanced down the Tigris to occupy Baghdad, later moving south to seize the sacred Shiite shrines of Karbala and Najaf. With this triumph, the capture of the ancient Abbasid capital from the heretics, Suleiman's prestige in the Sunni Islamic world soared. But for this ongoing conflict with the religious and military force of his Shiite foe to the east, Suleiman might well have successfully penetrated far deeper into Europe (Clot 1992:89–93; Inalcik 1989:38).

Steppe Nomad Legacy across Eurasia

By opening up rapid, direct communication and trade between the furthermost eastern and western extremities of Eurasia, the Mongol equestrians unquestionably left their stamp upon an emerging modern world. Their once vast, far-flung empire obviously underwent many transformations. Yet even today, the Mongol capital Ulan Bator is located just south of the mythical headwaters of the three rivers, Onon, Kerulen, and Tula, below the sacred Burkhan Khaldun mountains. Just as in the times of Khuriltais, in national festival each year, amidst kilometers of ceremonial gers, a naadam is celebrated with throat singing, archery, wrestling, and horseracing. The horse riders in the primary event are children, aged mostly under 10, all turned out in silken finery. On the opening day of the festival, in a contest designed to test their sturdy mounts, over a thousand youthful competitors race 20 km across the steppe toward Ulan Bator (Man 2004:44). The first sign of their approach is spotted as a shadow along the rim of the horizon, a shadow that rapidly spills over and down the distant hillside in the broad front of the Mongol battle charge. And not uncommonly, in the haze of dust and sweat at the finish, young Amazons ride among the lead.

To the south and east of the traditional core territory of the Mongols, the modern countries of China, Korea, and Japan and those of Southeast Asia today occupy much the same territories as at the time of the Yuan dynasty. Nation-states further west in Asia can similarly trace their history and development to thirteenth-century Mongol presence. During the Ilkhanate, Hulegu's overthrow of Abbasid Baghdad allowed Persian-speaking Iran to first emerge as a compact Shiite nation, doctrinally distinct from Arab Sunni to the west and the Altaic Turanians on its northern borders. With the Mughals, Chagataid Mongol influence extended far south into India. There, descendants of Genghis Khan reigned over an empire until 1857 when, following the Great Indian Mutiny, the British expelled the emperor Bahadur Shah II so that their new Boudica, Queen Victoria, would inherit the title "Empress of India." In eastern Europe, Russia remained more than 240 years under the Tatar yoke until 1480, when Ivan III, the Grand Duke of Muscovy, refused to kiss the stirrup of the khan, the ritual gesture of vassalage demanded by the Kipchak khanate. In the ensuing hostilities, Mongol cavalry rode on Moscow for the last time as Russia began to fight for independence, Ivan IV (Ivan the Terrible) taking Khazan and Astrakhan in the 1550s, and Peter the Great and Catherine II continuing the fight into the eighteenth century. Expanding eastward with western firearms, the czars would reverse the tide of imperialism against the Turco-Mongols, seizing for Russia nomad lands in northern Asia (Saunders 2001:168). Ironically the last ruling descendant of Genghis Khan, through Jochi and the Golden Horde, was Sayid Alim Khan, emir of Bokhara, the first city conquered by Genghis in his drive across Khwarizm. Deposed in 1920, his capital blitzed by the Bolsheviks, Turkish slaving of Russians finally abolished, Alim died in Kabul in 1944 (Weatherford 2004:xx, 263). In confrontation with European armies, as their Scythian and Mongol predecessors, the Russians would employ the time-tested ploys of the steppes, in feigned retreats luring Napoleonic and Nazi forces deep into frozen Russia, only to annihilate them in deadly counterattack.

Under the Mongol onslaught, the lands of eastern medieval Europe were leveled. Never truly recovered from these ashes, its inhabitants fell easy victims to subsequent Ottoman depredation. Successors to the Seljuks, wresting the helm of Sunni Islam from the Mamluks, the Ottomans advanced westward, intent upon completing Mongol unfinished business – the Altaic conquest of Europe. By exploiting bitter political divisions between pope and emperor, king and condottiere, the Ottomans consolidated their hold on southeastern Europe, the Levant, and the North African littoral. Finding affinity with Protestant iconoclasm, the Turkish Muslims even attempted alliances with the German princes, allowing the Protestants in exchange for their pledge of Christian solidarity to wring political concessions from the Catholic South, thereby advancing the cause of Protestantism in northern Europe (Inalcik 1989:37). Successful in holding the Arab armies at bay in Sicily and the Iberian peninsula, and spared the Mongol hurricane, western Europe had benefited initially from Islamic learning filtering north from the Mediterranean and then from the new inventions from the Far East. During the Renaissance, the development of printing dramatically cut the price of books while multiplying the number available to the public, contributing to the revival of the classics but also promoting the spread of science. To counter this latest assault on their territories by equestrian invaders from Asia, Europeans would obdurately continue to fight the Ottomans on land. But, as will be seen in the chapters ahead, nations situated at the westernmost extremity of Europe, with their backs to the Atlantic, also chose to direct their science, technology, and daring toward the oceans.

FROM EUROPE, *EQUUS* RETURNS TO ITS CONTINENT OF ORIGIN

CHAPTER 2 DOCUMENTED FOURTH-MILLENNIUM-BC HORSE DOMES-tication on the semiarid eastern periphery of agricultural Europe, sub-sequent agro-pastoralist expansion eastward, and successful nomad penetration of the furthermost reaches of the Eurasian steppes. Later chapters described how, having mastered these barren wastes, nomad armies in the millennia that followed repeatedly traversed the forbid-ding terrains that circumscribed and protected pristine centers of civi-lization, to conquer and incorporate those ancient sedentary states into far-flung equestrian empires that spanned continents. By the second millennium AD, however, another European periphery had come to exist, this time in the west. Repeatedly, nomad forces had invaded from the steppes, mercilessly ravaging eastern Europe. By contrast, western Europe survived relatively unscathed, as Christianity converted and absorbed the steppe Sarmatian, Hun, Avar, and Magyar, and Martel at Poitiers blocked the Arab surge from the south. But at the western-most extremity of Eurasia, medieval Europe was very much an intel-lectual backwater, cut off from the great cultural advances of eastern civilizations. Notwithstanding, as we have seen, important inventions reached Europe along the intercontinental highways of equestrian communication.

But, when finally Constantinople fell to the Turks in 1453, as Ottomans advanced westward across land and sea, peripheral Europe in defiance of Asian might turned to another vast expanse, the unex-plored ocean to the west. The next chapters will show how, benefit-ing from earlier probes of the Atlantic by Vikings in the north and Portuguese in the south, it fell to Spain to triumph over the ocean and to the Spanish knight on horseback to conquer the New World. In striking parallel to the ancient radiations of horsemen across the steppes, with modern navigation of the oceans encircling the globe, the maritime deployment of warhorses to strategic spots practically anywhere on the planet allowed Europeans, now equipped with steel and firearms, both to assault enemy empires of the Old World and to invade previously unexplored continents. To begin to understand these developments, let us turn to western Europe in the centuries following Islam's defeat of the Crusades in the Levant.

Europe toward the End of the Middle Ages

With the decline of Rome in the west, nomad invasions from the east, Germanic invasions from the north, and Muslim invasions from the south, politico-economic life in Europe had become decentralized, its system of communications and transportation seriously disrupted – and the final months before harvest perilously lean. Lynn White (1962:53–54, 69) has observed that the Slav introduction of the heavy plow and the ridge-and-furrow method of cultivation to Europe did much to offset the inertia of these "Dark Ages," as a consequence contributing to significant population growth from the seventh to ninth centuries. White also asserts that the arrival of the horse trace harness and contoured collar harness, originally invented in China during the first millennium BC but reaching the west from across the steppes respectively in the eighth and tenth centuries AD, further stimulated agricultural productivity. As remarked earlier, prior to these Chinese inventions in equine technology, the throat-and-girth harness, while not as throttling as Lefebvre des Noettes would have us believe, nevertheless for millennia had failed to capture the full power of the horse in traction. Because this archaic system of harnessing had proven entirely inadequate in transporting wheat even short distances from the Italian *latifundia* to the capital, imperial Rome had been compelled to rely on grain shipments from Egypt, North Africa, and Sicily in order to feed its populace (Temple 1999:21). By contrast, with the adoption of the contoured collar harness and the superior nailed iron horseshoe, the horse, so much faster than the ox, now delivered 50 percent more meter-kilograms per second in traction and moreover, having greater endurance, was capable of working two hours longer each day. The higher speed and stamina of the horse was critically important in the inclement weather of northern Europe, where often the very success of a crop depended on plowing, planting, or harvesting within a narrow time frame of favorable conditions. Deployment of the horse in agriculture also had its social repercussions. Earlier with the slow ox, farmers had been obliged to live dispersed in tiny hamlets alongside their fields. Between the eleventh and thirteenth centuries, however, peasants began to aggregate in larger villages and towns, the faster equine draft allowing them to easily haul the plow to their fields each day and also to reach outlying areas not previously cultivated (White 1962:62–66).

In a detailed study, John Langdon (1986) has disputed several of White's conclusions. While acknowledging the importance of the horse collar, he nevertheless contends that the impact of superior horse traction on agriculture was a slower, more drawn-out process than proposed by White. Langdon maintains there were multiple obstacles to the displacement of oxen by horses. In general, the horse was regarded as a princely animal, bred for riding and battle, not for the menial task of plowing. Also, in Mediterranean countries, the donkey and mule – particularly the Poitou mule, which stood more than 16 hands – were already favored for agricultural work. One certain disadvantage of the farm horse was that it consumed grain rather than grass, making it a more expensive animal to feed. This was offset, however, by the establishment of the three-field system of crop rotation, which produced larger harvests of oats, the best possible fodder for horses. Another minus was the dietary prohibition against horseflesh, preventing marketing of horsemeat for consumption. Ironically, this taboo decreased the price of horses, making them more affordable to smallholders and therefore more widely adopted. Thus, despite a variety of limiting factors, the horse gradually replaced the ox in traction, allowing both peasantry and demesne to engage in full-scale, efficient farming (Langdon 1986:96, 250–252, 259, 262).

In the twelfth century, this by no means meant total conversion to horse. The horse, long specialized in harrowing, continued in this task. It was also found that the horse excelled in plowing light soils, even stony stretches in hilly terrain; but in heavier, clayey alluvium the ox plow prevailed. Mixed teams were common; here several horses in front acted as pacesetters for the oxen behind, thereby retaining oxen strength for heavy, sticky patches but increasing plowing speed. The newly introduced whippletree greatly increased the flexibility of harnessing (Langdon 1986:1–12, 51, 100–101). Perhaps, though, the horse's main asset was its versatility: its speedy competence across the board in harrowing, plowing, and hauling – plus riding and pack work – clearly outstripped the ponderous ox.

But Langdon (1986:268) goes on to argue that even though substitution of the horse for the ox in plowing improved agricultural efficiency by cutting labor costs and setting higher levels of soil preparation, due to farmer conservatism it did not immediately lead to rising production. It did, however, permit greater regional specialization in the pastoral sector, with emphasis on cattle rearing for meat and dairy and sheep rearing for wool; as a result, the horse was a catalyst in the development of intensive mixed farming (Campbell 2007:547). Notwithstanding, Langdon insists that by far the greatest benefit achieved in the transition from ox to horse draft was in the sphere of transportation. By the end of the thirteenth century, horses would be responsible for more than 75 percent of haulage. Even more significantly, horse-hauled vehicles came to feature prominently in urban communities, producing a marked effect on the economy. Velocity of transit not only sped goods to market, it also facilitated rapid circulation of heavy gold and silver coins (Langdon 1986:270–272). Whereas earlier, transport had been primarily along inland waterways and coastal waters, beset in winter by ice and gales, now rural regions away from navigable rivers flourished as overland horse haulage delivered their valued textiles and perishable commodities promptly to burgeoning townships. In the fairs of Champagne, historic meeting grounds between northern merchants and Italian entrepreneurs from the Mediterranean, fine British wool and prized Flemish textiles were exchanged for the silk and spices of the Orient (Gies and Gies 1972:35–36). Thus, efficient horse draft and advancing farm techniques helped break down the rigid confines of the demesnial system and to lay the foundation for a more flexible economy, eventually freeing the peasantry from its feudal obligations of the past.

Thus medieval society, still composed of the three estates, church, knights, and peasantry, albeit with an emergent merchant sector, grew to be generally prosperous. By the end of the twelfth century, European rulers were extremely mobile in their journeying to visit or to war with relatives. Their castles were of outstanding importance. The lord's great wealth and prestige attracted knights to form his retinue, clerics to administer his estate, and men of letters and minstrels to entertain his court. The sumptuary demands of the court were catered to by merchants operating on an international scale, overseeing not rural cottage industries but urban professional workshops. The noble's court was the center of knightly culture where chivalric virtue and aspiration to honor and fame were defined. The knight was staunchly committed, in theory at least, to defend the church and to protect women, the sick, and the elderly. In addition to aristocrats, sons of administrators and lesser nobility now might also rise to the rank of knight by attending the court of the noble overlord, where, in addition to the military skills of battle, they acquired the social manners of knighthood (Hopkins 2004:24–34). Training a fully armored youth to wield a heavy lance while riding a horse at full gallop required years of practice. The climax of the youth's training was the dubbing ceremony at which he was incorporated into the war band of his lord (Hopkins 2004:39–42).

By the late Middle Ages the cult of chivalry, which emphasized honor, loyalty, courage, and generosity, had become richly elaborated by the warrior elite. Celebrated orders of chivalry emerged, such as in England the Order of the Garter and later in France the *Toison d'Or,* for which Philip the Good, Duke of Burgundy, selected as his emblem the Golden Fleece, regarding Jason and his Argonauts as knights-errant. Heraldry featured prominently; the simple, bold coat of arms had become infinitely complex, now a showcase for descent to be displayed on pennons, banners, and caparisons. Tournaments designed to test equestrian skills, where great lords recruited talented knights for their military campaigns, were accompanied by rich display. Since the Dark Ages, the medieval tournament had always provided the important military function of training knights for combat. But the earliest tournaments all too frequently were held in deadly earnest; the combatants, horses, and even spectators of these unregulated free-for-alls often suffered mutilation or death. Furthermore, under the guise of tournaments, the local barons of old frequently avenged personal feuds, conducting what amounted to private wars despite repeated prohibition by popes. Now with the emergent nation-state, these wasteful vendettas could no longer be tolerated by monarchs acutely concerned for the manpower and horsepower of their national armies. As a result, the tournament became a much more formalized event. With the introduction of blunted weapons, encounters between knights were bound by strict rules. Whereas in earlier times the loser forfeited his horse and armor to the winner, now fine jewels were awarded the victor. Tourneying, a knight could accumulate a significant fortune as well as a formidable reputation (Vale 1981:39, 68–71).

Chivalric meets were often celebrated in accordance with themes of the Arthurian romances, at Whitsun especially with Round Table gatherings. The English king Edward I (1272–1307) was a passionate promoter of the Arthurian ethic. In 1299 on the occasion of his marriage to Margaret of France, Edward orchestrated a Round Table extravaganza at which he played King Arthur while his knights in this courtly ritual impersonated the traditional characters of Lancelot, Galahad, Tristan, and Perceval (Dean 1987:40). This custom spread abroad, and soon the avant-garde aristocrats of Europe were receiving at baptism the names of these legendary knights. The mysteries of Christ's incarnation and death were also allegorized in the ancient myth of the unicorn, celebrated by great ceremonial hunts; part-horse, part-kid, with a single horn on its forehead, the noble beast could be tamed only by the magical power of a virgin maid (Sipress 1973:n.p.). Funerals were equally dramatized. In great pomp, a ruler's bier might be drawn by six horses caparisoned in black. To symbolize the mortality of the dead nobleman, a knight representing the deceased rode into the church to fall off his horse beside the catafalque, as weapons were broken over the coffin (Vale 2001:243–244). To commemorate the brave deeds of the warrior, an armed effigy adorned his tomb, heraldic emblems recalling his noble ancestry and military alliances; the knight's legs were crossed if he had fought in the Crusades (Vale 1981:89–90). Just as king Arthur had appeared to the embattled Britons as their messianic savior destined to liberate them from the invader, so in the warring duchies and petty principalities that one day would form the nation-states of Europe, the medieval knight emerged as the liberator of his people. In its origins, overwhelmingly of the countryside, the Arthurian legend appealed as much to the cottage as to the chateau. Chess, originally couched in the military terminology of ancient India and Persia and diffused to Europe through the Islamic world, now acquired the Arthurian characters of the king, queen, and knight. By the end of the thirteenth century even the towns had fallen under the Arthurian spell. Emulating nobility, the Hanseatic League founded societies of the Grail and of the Round Table. Great murals were painted likening knightly exploits to Alexander's marvelous explorations of the East. Palaces were embellished with great frescoes detailing the daring adventures, unrequited loves, and tragic fates of romantic heroes (Pastoureau and Gousset 2002:15–17; Vale 2001:173–174). Such medieval celebrations in turn would give way to the sumptuous festivities of the Renaissance.

The Palio of Siena

The most celebrated of these Renaissance[1] festivals was the Tuscan Palio of Siena. It appears, though, that this great feast had ancient origins. A

---

[1] Meaning rebirth – again concordant with ancient Indo-European tradition.

fragment of terra-cotta frieze from the fourth century BC shows Etruscan riders mounted bareback, brandishing the same whips that are still used in today's ritual horse race. The Palio is also linked to the founding of a Roman city. Legend tells of Senius and Archius, sons of Remus, fleeing on two horses, one white and one black, pursued by Romulus's cavalry intent upon their death. Only after a frenzied race over a great distance (a mythic *Palio alla lunga*) did the fraternal pair, in good Indo-European fashion, reach safety to found the new city (Falassi and Betti 2003:7–10). As in many Indo-European rituals, the feast projects themes of rebirth and regeneration. Every year, gold-colored earth was brought in to transform the piazza into a solar racetrack world-center. To augur good fortune in the year ahead citizens would come to this omphalos to "*pestare la terra in piazza*" (to tread the earth) (Dundes and Falassi 1975:53–54). The original "Senae" were three castles on top of three hills, and the medieval Palii were affairs of nobility, involving tournaments and horse races as training for knights in times of war (Falassi and Catoni 1983:9, 33). Fist-fighting contests also took place to prepare the people for defense of the city. With the rise of the mercantile class, tournaments and combats became somewhat less bloody and more opulent in display. In the tradition of the ceremonial ring hunt, great hunts were also organized in the central piazza, just as in the extravagant venationes of Roman times. Men pursued wild boar, deer, foxes, and hares on horseback. Within railings, the bravest young men engaged in bullfights (Allsen 2006:238; Falassi and Betti 2003:12, 15). But by far the most important event was the *la corsa del Palio* – the horse race.

Over the centuries Siena continued to observe the original tripartite division of the city, but with time smaller subdivisions arose, *contrade* (wards), to which residents owed passionate allegiance. Each contrada was the center of its neighborhood; its oratory housed the local treasures. Whereas in medieval times, knights had ridden in the Palio alla lunga, in later centuries *fantini* (jockeys; sing. *fantino*) wearing livery representative of each contrada competed in the *Palio alla tonda*, now run around the central piazza. Along with a heraldic motto, each contrada had on its coat of arms a totemic animal, derived from an allegorical bestiary. These contrada colors were paraded during the festivities of the Palio. Carried amidst the floats, they communicated precise messages known to the Siennese since ancient times. Midst the setting off of rockets and firecrackers and the sound of trumpets, hunting horns, and drums, brilliant flags were waved in dramatic aerial displays. Such "jousting" of the flags required the strength and dexterity of the fencer, as the *alfiere* (Arabic *al-faris* "mounted warrior") tossed or leapt over his multicolored ensign (Falassi and Catoni 1983:10–12, 27, 70–71).

Derived from Latin *pallium* (rectangular cloth), the term "Palio" itself designated the elaborate textile that awaited the triumphant winner at the finish of the horse race, which in time came to be known simply as the Palio. The earliest palii were costly fabrics lined with vair fur, suspended from a very tall staff and before the race displayed within the cathedral. In the thirteenth century, this gonfalon was often cloth of gold combined with velvets and silks decorated with armorial bearings and tassels. Each year a retainer, bearing large sums of money, journeyed to Venice, port of arrival of exotic stuffs from the Orient, to procure the necessary materials for the manufacture of the Palio. In later centuries, this sumptuous item was replaced by a simpler painting on silk as seen to this very day. Trials preceded the final race, and contrada supporters, singing traditional *stornelli* (chants), accompanied their horse to the central piazza (Falassi and Catoni 1983:18–19, 57). On the day of the final horse race, a solemn mass was celebrated in the cathedral. Prisoners were granted amnesty, and virtuous, unmarried women received a dowry at the expense of the community. A carnival ensued in which clowns, musicians, and poets entertained the crowds. Vassal lords were invited to an extravagant banquet, while free food and wine were distributed to the townspeople.

Before proceeding to the Piazza del Campo, each horse was blessed in the contrada chapel; should the horse defecate as the holy water was sprinkled over it, it was considered an omen of good fortune and victory (Falassi and Catoni 1983:60–61, 64). Amidst elaborate flag maneuvers, the Palio, preceded by a triumphal chariot drawn by four stately white oxen, advanced into the central piazza, to be greeted with cheers and scarf waving from the crowds (Dundes and Falassi 1975:100–101, 107–108). In the horse race, just as the Etruscans did, all jockeys rode bareback equipped with the *nerbo di bue* (whip).[2] But the Palio was not just a race; it was also a joust, a battle. Mare vaginal extract might have been smeared on the door of the stable of a rival contrada to render its horse unmanageable (Falassi and Catoni 1983:56). The whip, tool to urge on one's own horse, could also to be deployed belligerently against an enemy horse or its fantino in order to keep another contrada from

---

[2] The stripped and dried phallus of an unweaned calf, stretched to make a whip 76 cm in length (Dundes and Falassi 1975:125).

winning (Dundes and Falassi 1975:125). Or the steed might be blocked in the *parata* (block), squeezed against the outside railing in the *rinser-rata* (squeeze), or struck by a spectator. In the three circuits around the central piazza, many a jockey fell, sometimes to regain the steed and win the race. But whatever the ensuing events, the victor awarded the prestigious Palio was expected to distribute gratuities among the poor before proceeding to the celebratory dinner, where his horse was feted in honored position behind the head table (Falassi and Catoni 1983:74). Alternatively, dissension from rivals might explode into violence and the illustrious Palio be ripped to shreds (Falassi and Catoni 1983:21). The winning fantino might be beaten up by the losing contrada, or the losing fantino might be attacked by enraged members of the contrada he was representing (Dundes and Falassi 1975:131).[3] With these activities, on horseback or on foot, the Siennese practiced combat skills in readiness for the ever-recurrent warfare between rival city-states. Whatever the outcome, the festival of the Palio represented the regeneration and continuation of the Siennese community; the newly won banner in slang is still called *il cittino* (the newborn son) (Falassi and Catoni 1983:77). In today's Italian, the expression *"Fatta la festa! Corso il Palio!"* jubilantly denotes an event well organized and celebrated.

Late Medieval Warfare

While the horse always occupied a central role in display and ceremony, by the fourteenth century the time-honored dominance of the mounted knight in warfare came to be challenged by artillery and new infantry. The battles of Courtrai (1302), Bannockburn (1314), and Crecy (1346) demonstrated the devastating effects of longbowmen and pike phalanxes. The crossbow had indeed been surpassed in range, rate of fire, and accuracy by the longbow, which could drive a heavy arrow through a knight's mail and rudimentary plate armor, and kill or madden his mount. The infantry's 2-m halberd was mounted by an axe blade with a device for piercing armor and pulling a knight off his horse. The pike, twice the length of the halberd, had a 25-cm point to fend off cavalry and when used in cohesion formed an impenetrable defensive hedge. The need to offset the knight's vulnerability to these new armaments led to the development of *harnois blanc* (white armor) full plate armor during

---

3 The horse that came in second was the most disgraced and therefore recognized as loser of the race.

the latter part of the fourteenth century. As we have seen in the wake of the Mongol advance, metalworking techniques in Europe achieved a high degree of sophistication. Fine-quality iron and steel were now produced by new carburizing processes and the blast furnace. To achieve maximum protection compatible with mobility and resistance to missiles, the outer surfaces of the plate armor were submitted to hardening treatments, of which quenching while the metal was white hot was the most important. Battlefield and tournament armor were differentiated, the latter being more ornate and geared to stability, unlike field armor that necessitated mobility in battle (Vale 1981:104–107).

Techniques of fighting with the lance also changed to achieve greater penetration against the superior defensive armor. The mail hauberk and cuirass of earlier centuries failed to provide sufficient support for what now had become a much heavier weapon. The weighty lance of some 18 kg had to be lowered, aimed, and balanced while the horse sped into a gallop. To hold the mighty lance firm at the point of impact, to absorb recoil, and to stop the knight's arm from being broken by the collision, a new device was invented, the *arret de cuirasse*. With this invention, the right breast plate was equipped with a metal prong that served as a fulcrum on which to balance the lance during a charge, allowing the knight to lower his weapon from vertical to horizontal while advancing at high speed. To offset the murderous effects of the lance, the plate armor was modified to include rippling, fluting, ridges, and glancing surfaces to deflect the blow away from vulnerable areas; reinforcing pieces protected vital areas, and steel helmets covered the entire head. Horse armor was also improved with plate defenses for the chest (*peytral*), neck (*crinet*), and flanks (*crupper*), protecting against both the arrow volley and the pike hedge. Steel reinforced, heavy cavalry with the momentum and impact of the well-executed charge swept everything before it and thus won a new lease of life (Vale 1981:114–119, 128).

The Hundred Years' War (1337–1443) between England and France was the great politico-military confrontation of northwestern Europe; astonishingly its most famous knight was Joan of Arc or Jeanne la Pucelle, Maid of Orleans. Amazon of western Christendom, likened to Tomyris, Penthesilea, and Hippolyta, Joan was born in 1413 in the obscure village of Domremy, Lorraine. At age 13, while running footraces with other girls, she heard heavenly voices that called on her to take up the sword of France against England. Speed of foot and suppleness of limb of course were hallmarks of the Amazon. Also Joan's association with *arc* or bow additionally linked her to the equestrian archer heroines of the steppes and to Artemis-Diana, whose bow was the crescent moon. Like Artemis, Jeanne la Pucelle (virgin) was unassailably virgin and furthermore was reputed not to menstruate (Warner 2000:19, 200, 202). Visions of Charlemagne and Saint Louis directed Joan to the court of Lorraine, where she received her first sword. Then, like Arthur, a second sword was miraculously bequeathed her, that of Charles Martel, founder of the French monarchy and legendary defender of France against earlier Arab invaders (Warner 2000:120, 162–164).

In February 1429 the English with their Burgundian allies, in control of territories north of the Loire, had besieged Orleans with the intent of crossing the river to dominate southern France. Escorted to Chinon in the south, the Maid announced to the Dauphin, Charles of Valois, that God had bade her raise the siege of Orleans and help Charles recover his kingdom by driving out the English. Impressed by her radiance, Charles in May marched his troops to the relief of Orleans. At first the English inflicted heavy losses on the French. Undeterred, Joan rode out with her men toward the fortress of Les Tourelles, held by the English. The battle was ferocious; repeatedly the French were repulsed. Finally Joan, although wounded in the neck, rallied her men to her standard as the French surged forward to victory. Critically defeated, the English survivors immediately retreated (Warner 2000:54, 66–67).

Following her success at Orleans, la Pucelle insisted the Dauphin march north to Rheims, to be crowned king of France according to the rites of his Carolingian predecessors. Arrayed in white armor, with lance the Maid coursed her charger before the king, her weapons bright, her banner unfurled (Warner 2000:70). But in August the Dauphin agreed to a truce with Burgundy. Angered by this interruption in the war, Joan defiantly attacked Burgundian Paris but without success. Campaigning the following spring, she was caught in a pincer movement by the English and Burgundians. Imprisoned and subjected to cruel interrogation by the Inquisition, she was charged with heresy, allied with witchcraft, and burned at the stake (Warner 2000:5, 70, 75). But English hegemony over northern France had been fatally weakened. Despite her tragic end, the Maid had reversed the tide of battle. Her valiant struggle had helped restore the monarchy and forged the nation-state of France.

By the later phases of the Hundred Years' War, firearms, initially erratic and unreliable, were becoming more effective. The protracted nature of the great conflict had resulted in a kind of arms race. Large cannons of vast caliber, bombards, and mortars not only battered down fortifications; the lighter culverins and veuglaires also killed selectively from afar. Eventually artillery would sound the death knell of the armored knight (Vale 1981:131, 137). With victory in hand, French monarchs subsequently moved to organize regular mail service, repairing or constructing major paved highways to be covered by the king's messengers. But these roads were not merely for civilian traffic. Heavy mobile cannons, weighing over 2,250 kg, mounted on gun carriages, and pulled by 20 horses, now traveled these routes, requiring stronger, wider roadways and bridges (Gille 1969a:351–352; 1969b:480).

The Spanish Reconquista

South of the Pyrenees in medieval Spain, following Christian defeat of the Arabs at Covadonga in 718, Goth Pelayo had declared himself king of Asturias and so founded the Spanish monarchy. The repulse of the Muslims at Poitiers allowed Asturias later to expand its frontiers to Lusitania, Galicia, Viscaya, and in the ninth century to Leon. In the next few centuries Christian Spain would be a country divided by its mountains, provincial rivalries, and fraternal strife, where nobles conducted their affairs largely independently of kings, and bishops led their troops into war independently of popes. One unifying feature of this tumultuous era was the wondrous find by a shepherd guided by a star of a marble coffin in the mountains. The coffin contained the bones of the Apostle James, and a magnificent cathedral was built at the site. Santiago de Compostela or St. James of the Field of the Star became the sacred cult center of Christian pilgrimage. Santiago Matamoros (St. James the Moor Slayer) became the patron saint of Spain and the rallying cry of Christians struggling to regain their homeland (Durant 1950: 458–459).

But in this struggle that would last nearly 800 years, Muslim and Christian, Arab and Spaniard, became inextricably intertwined. At the beginning of the ninth century, the first Hispano-Arabic love poems were composed. This poetry explored the theme of spiritualized love, emphasizing the value of tenderness and restraint and the avoidance of gross satisfaction. With the appearance in 1022 of Ibn Hazm's *The Dove's Neck-Ring*, Andalusian love poetry reached its apogee. The emergence of this amorous poetry has been attributed to the high ratio of men to women in society in the wake of the Islamic conquest. The lure of conquest lands and riches had attracted many Arab men from the Middle

East and Berber mercenaries from North Africa. The resultant scarcity of females was exacerbated by harems maintained by wealthy Muslims and the purposeful pirating of young women along the European coasts for the slave marts of the Near East. *The Dove's Neck-Ring* is replete with instances of men's infatuation with beautiful slave girls and heartfelt desire to free them. In northern Spain there was a comparably large influx of Christian males from France and Burgundy, eager to benefit from the spoils of battle in the wars against Islam. Prominent among the Christian warriors were members of the lesser nobility and adventurers, who through exploits on the battlefield hoped to penetrate the knightly class.[4] One sure route to social advancement, though, was through marriage into nobility. But given the uneven sex ratio, young noblewomen were disproportionately rare in society. To win the affections of a rare beauty, aspiring knights perforce resorted to the romantic songs and poems of courtly love. These recitals were enacted in the public forum of social gatherings, where performance was geared to the delicate taste and approval of noble society. Increasing in popularity, this tantalizing poetry spread from Spain across Provence to northern Europe where in the late twelfth century, modeled after Ibn Hazm's masterpiece, *The Art of Courtly Love* was composed at the court of Marie of Champagne, extolling the virtue of refined, adoring, and unrequited love (Guttentag and Secord 1983:71–73).

But in this era of Christian-Muslim confrontation, the chanson de geste continued in popularity. The most famous was the Spanish national epic – *El Cantar de Mio Cid* (The Song of my Lord) – which embodied all the valor and anguish of the struggle of the Reconquista:

> They clasp their shields over their hearts,
> they lower their lances swathed in their pennons,
> they bowed their faces over their saddletrees,
> they made ready to attack them with strong hearts.
>
> You should have seen so many lances lowered and raised,
> so many shields perforated and pierced,
> so many coats of mail broken and dented,
> so many white pennants held high red with blood,
> so many good horses running riderless.
>
> (De Chasca 1976:115–116)

---

4 Castles were being built that required lower ranks of knights as guardians. These fortifications gave the name to the province of Castile.

In 1043 El Cid, from the Arabic *sayid*, meaning "lord," was born Rodrigo Diaz de Vivar of a family of middle nobility just outside Burgos. At age 15 Rodrigo went as ward to the Spanish court, where he excelled in arms and letters. Upon the death of King Ferdinand I, contrary to the Visigothic right of primogeniture, the realm was divided among the three sons, Sancho, Alfonso, and Garcia, who respectively inherited Castile, Leon, and Galicia and Portugal. Outraged, Sancho, the eldest, appointed Rodrigo commander of the royal army and proceeded to deprive his brothers of their territories. Due to El Cid's intrepid generalship and extraordinary feats in battle (for which he earned the sobriquet *El Campeador* (Champion), Sancho's forces were victorious. However, in 1072 Sancho was assassinated. Returning from exile, Alfonso VI, to win over the support of the Castilians, recognized their champion El Cid as his vassal. But just as with Rustam, Lancelot, and Roland, tensions would plague relations between king and hero. Wary of El Campeador's popularity, Alfonso denied Rodrigo any opportunity to exercise his military talents. Notwithstanding, El Cid, dispatched to collect tribute from Taifa Seville, daringly routed a Granadian attack on the emir Mutamid, only to be accused of treachery on his return to Castile. In the Castilian campaign against Muslim Toledo, in 1081 he and his knights courageously defended the most important fortress on the Duero River. Furious at his vassal's triumph, Alfonso banished Rodrigo. Yet with the Duero region strengthened, the Christians later successfully captured Toledo, most ancient venerated capital of the Visigoths.

Treated unjustly, but never wavering in his loyalty to the king, El Cid led his knights far from Castile, offering his services to Christian Barcelona. Rejected, he allied instead with the Muslim emirs of Zaragoza and won with them great conquests in eastern Spain (De Chasca 1976:19–27). Here again we see a hint of Rustam. Just as the Persian champion in his dalliance with Tahminah mingled with the Turanian enemy, so too Rodrigo fought on the fringes of his society. But south in Andalucia, Mutamid of Seville had invited Yusuf ibn Tashfin, supreme emir of the Almoravid empire that stretched from Morocco to Ghana, to invade. Yusuf inflicted a heavy defeat upon Alfonso at Sagrajas in 1086. The epic goes on to describe the diabolically tangled alliances, betrayals, battles, and defeats of the Christian king, Taifa emirs, and Almoravid invaders. Time and time again, El Cid magnificently rescued his king from disaster only to be rebuffed. But in his siege of Valencia, El Campeador successfully held the Almoravid colossus at bay. In 1094 Rodrigo again faced the Almoravids at the Battle of Cuarte,

FIGURE 10.1. El Cid lancing a bull, an etching by Goya featured as a plate in La Tauromaquia c 1815. Courtesy of the Hispanic Society of America, New York.

during which in clever ambush he defeated this hitherto invincible army. While Alfonso suffered humiliating defeats, El Cid held firm in Valencia and further fortified Christian Spain by winning more battles in the east. Dead in 1099, entombed in a monastery near Burgos, El Cid was venerated for his valor in battle, ever an inspiration to the Reconquista (De Chasca 1976:28–30, 38–49; Fig. 10.1).

By the twelfth century, four Christian kingdoms stood against Moorish hegemony in the Iberian peninsula: Leon-Castile, Navarre, Aragon, and Portugal. As noted earlier, in the borderlands between Christian north and Muslim south, different military religious orders emerged; among these, the Order of Santiago upheld the warlike motto *"Ruber ensis sanguine arabum"* (may the sword be red with Arab blood). In the ancient tradition of the *mairiia*, these warrior horsemen patrolled the lonely mesetas where no peasant dared settle for fear of Muslim raids. In time, the knights were instrumental in attracting Christian settlers to the freshly conquered territories. These monkish frontiersmen raised great herds in semiwild fashion, migrating to the high sierras in summer. Their horses were the finest in Europe – part Arabian, part North African Barb, part Iberian stock, all of which combined courage and intelligence with dramatic beauty. Their method of open-range

347

ranching, constantly involving the horse in periodic roundups, branding, and overland drives, was unique to southern Iberia and soon would be introduced to the New World. From land estates of finest pasturage bequeathed the Orders by the Spanish kings, great haciendas developed and wealth was generated. To this land of danger and economic opportunity came young men of lesser nobility to seek social advancement (Bouroncle 2000:69–70). A knight's equestrian prowess was central to his success and renown, and nowhere were horse-riding skills more proudly displayed than in the chivalric bullfight.[5] Persia had its polo; France, England, and Germany, their tournaments; Tuscany, its Palio; and Spain, its *corrida de toros*. From the caves of Altamira, we know the bull enjoyed great ritual antiquity in Spain. So famous was the Iberian bull that in Greek myth Heracles was required to steal the red cattle of Geryon from the province of Cadiz. Over the centuries the rural *capeas* (fiestas in an enclosed space) featured the bull as a symbol of extraordinary sexual power and associated its potency with human fertility. Midst the hostility of the Castilian borderlands, these fertility rites became transformed into a knightly tournament before kings and aristocrats, in which horseman and *toro bravo* were antagonists and victory was won by inflicting death on the bull (Fig. 10.2). *Romances fronterizos* (frontier epics) recounted the centuries-long contests between Christian and Moor as a chivalric Holy War, in which men achieved wealth and renown "by fighting Moors and bulls" (Bouroncle 2000:59–61, 71).

In 1147 the Almohads invaded Spain. In defense of Christendom, knights from France, Italy, and Portugal joined with Spanish Crusaders to win a glorious victory over the Moors at Las Navas de Tolosa in 1212. With the marriage in 1479 of Isabel of Castile and Ferdinand of Aragon, the two sovereigns, intent upon enforcing religious and political uniformity in their united kingdoms, requested that Rome authorize the Spanish Inquisition to combat Muslims, Jews, and heretics. One by one, the Muslim towns and fortresses fell to the Christians until finally Granada, after a nine-month siege, itself succumbed in 1492 (Hopkins 2004:92–93).

Equus *Extinct in the Western Hemisphere and* Equus *Returns*

True: "In 1492, Columbus sailed the ocean blue." Not true, however, that he discovered the New World. Columbus, it seems, missed discovering

---

5 Bullfighting on horseback, derived from the ancient capeas, continues today in Spain and Portugal as the *rejoneo*. The western rodeo is likely an offshoot of this equestrian form adapted to the ranch work scene.

FIGURE 10.2. Spanish bullfighting on horseback in the rejoneo. Drawing by Miss Torrey (Tinker 1964:39).

the New World by possibly as much as 15,000 years. Our most secure evidence of that distant epoch indicates that ancient immigrants to the New World reached North America from Asia via Beringia, the same land bridge traversed 23 million years earlier by *Anchitherium* equids and subsequently by *Hipparion* and *Equus* – although traveling in the opposite direction. In different glacial ages, water locked up in great ice sheets lowered the world's sea level, exposing sea beds as coastal plains where herbivores found fodder. From Asia, Paleolithic hunters followed the game east. But with global rise in temperatures c 14,000 BP and melting glaciers, the land bridge slowly submerged. Opportunistically, both game and hunters migrated eastward to higher land onto a continent previously uninhabited by man (Fagan 1991:67–71). Alternative routes of immigration have been proposed, such as ocean crossings in canoes along the Aleutian island chain or in skin boats along the edges of north Atlantic ice sheets – but lack sound archaeological validation. It is clear, however, that ancient immigrants to the New World, hunting large and small game, expanded rapidly to populate the entire western hemisphere, reaching Monte Verde in southern Chile c 13,000 BP, if not earlier. So successful was their technological adaptation that by 10,000 BP the megafauna on both continents of the western hemisphere were catastrophically reduced. Some scholars attribute this decline in species to warmer temperatures and increasing aridity of the environment. Whether the species were eliminated by climate change or human overkill, what is certain is that along with the megafauna, after 60 million years of equid evolution, *Equus* too became extinct in the New World (Dillehay 2000:71).

Thousands of years later, a more recent arrival to the New World came from Viking territory during the first millennium AD. In 982, Erik the Red sailed west from Iceland to discover the fertile grasslands and rich fishing banks of Greenland. Shiploads of settlers with livestock followed. The Norse sagas recount the prodigious seafaring exploits of these hardy mariners to *Ubygdir*, the "unpeopled" lands beyond the western horizon. Navigating these northern waters, Leif Eriksson explored the eastern seaboard from Labrador and Newfoundland to Vinland. Tales reached Europe of the Skraelings, who lived in houses constructed from whalebones, had no iron, and fashioned missiles from walrus tusk. The Norse, by contrast, had iron and later gunpowder. Settlements were established, sod-walled houses constructed, and farming undertaken – interrupted by skirmishes with local natives. Later attempts at more extensive colonization during the eleventh century had to be abandoned due to fatalities in warring with the local inhabitants. Intermittent contact with Inuit and Algonquian peoples extended over the next four centuries, primarily to obtain timber lacking in Greenland. But any Norse expansion inland was staunchly resisted by the far more numerous indigenous population. Interestingly, during this time period, there is no evidence whatsoever of the horse being introduced onto the North American continent. Norse settlement in Greenland endured until 1500, when piracy by hostile Basque whalers finally undermined the stability of this brave colony (Fagan 1991:15–18; Walhgren 1986:126–133).

As we have seen, in the fifteenth century in response to Timur's projected invasion of China, the Ming dynasty, in order to bolster political strength abroad, had dispatched voyages of exploration from her eastern ports. It is certainly worthy of note that at a time when equestrian nomads had extended their dominance over almost the entire breadth of Eurasia – the Mongols continuing to threaten northern China and the Turks fast advancing across Europe – nations situated at the furthermost eastern and western extremities of the continental landmass should direct their efforts toward exploration of the oceans. Just as the Ming in the Far East, Portugal and Spain, on the far southwestern periphery of Europe, were comparably engaged in oceanic exploration.

Let us turn then to these Atlantic explorations that dared to sail more southerly latitudes than the earlier Viking probe north.

It is well known that Christopher Columbus was born in Genoa in 1451, two years before the sack of Constantinople. Ottoman takeover of the eastern Mediterranean effectively abolished Venetian and Genoese trade in the Aegean and European access to spices and luxury goods of the Orient (Granzotto 1985:3). Sailing as a youth with the Genoese, Columbus survived pirate raids and shipwrecks. At age 25 he resettled in Lisbon, whence he plied the Atlantic from Iceland to Guinea. From the Norse, he heard tales of great islands to the west far across the ocean; in West Africa he experienced the seas and stars of southerly latitudes. From his Portuguese father-in-law, earlier trained under Henry the Navigator, he inherited maps and pilot books of Portugal's exploration of the Atlantic. He also gained access to the Florentine mathematician-astronomer Paolo Toscanelli's map of the world, which showed the Orient only 6,000 km west of Lisbon. Stationed two years in Madeira, the young Genoese there became familiar with midocean winds and currents. By the fifteenth century, most intellectuals in Europe had a terrestrial globe in their libraries, and as such Columbus was determined to *buscar el levante por el poniente* (to search for the east via the west); in other words he was convinced that the hostile Muslim barrier in the Middle East could be circumvented by sailing west to the Indies across the Atlantic (Collis 1989:38; Granzotto 1985:34–37, 42–46, 56–57).

Columbus first approached King John II of Portugal to finance his voyage of exploration, but failed to win his patronage (Collis 1989:45). In 1485 he moved to Huelva, Spain. There with the help of the Duke of Medina-Sidonia, wealthy financer of Spanish piratical raids along the West African Atlantic coast, Columbus submitted a petition to Queen Isabel of Castille. Isabel, who had already warred with the Portuguese over their monopoly of Guinea gold, was sympathetic, but embroiled in the final campaigns against the Moors of Granada, she was financially strapped (Granzotto 1985:67–69). Columbus desperately contacted Charles VIII of France and Henry VII of England but to no avail. Bartolomeu Dias had just returned in 1488 from his expedition around the Cape of Good Hope, and Europe's attention was focused on the eastern passage to the Orient. In 1492, however, Columbus was again summoned to the Spanish court. Granada was on the verge of surrender, and in expansionist mode, Spain was ready to take on Portugal, its rival on the high seas. Ferdinand, facing increasing pressure from hostile Turkey and Muslim North Africa in the Mediterranean, signaled his lack of interest. But Isabel felt otherwise: Castile owned the ocean! On April 17, Columbus was accorded the title Admiral of the Ocean Sea, and Spain agreed to finance three caravels in an expedition to the Indies (Collis 1989:58–63).

On August 2, Columbus's obstinate dream of more than a decade became reality. The Santa Maria,[6] the Pinta, and the Nina sailed out of Palos with their crews of experienced seamen, who were mostly Andalusian but also Basque, Portuguese, Venetian, Genoese, and Calabrian. The small fleet headed for the Canary Islands, Spanish for over a century, across a stretch of water named the Gulf of Mares for all the boats, overladen with breeding mares, that had foundered there on the way to the Atlantic colony. From the Canaries with the trade winds behind them, Columbus and his crew sailed due west across the solitary expanse of the Atlantic. Despite mutinies at sea, Columbus resolutely pressed on. After 36 days the expedition landed in the Bahamas, then navigated southwest to the Greater Antilles, always soliciting gold from the natives (Granzotto 1985:102, 110, 133, 139, 147). But disaster struck in Hispaniola (Haiti) when the Santa Maria sank on a jagged reef. Obliged to leave some of his crew behind, Columbus constructed a fort from the wreckage. Barely surviving two Atlantic hurricanes, the Nina and the Pinta returned triumphantly to Palos in 1493; flanked by "Indians" bedecked in feathers and gold, Columbus was feted in Barcelona by Ferdinand and Isabel (Collis 1989:82–83, 93–99, 105, 108–109). With the demand for gold in Europe far in excess of supply, Spain speedily financed expedition after expedition to the New World to procure this precious metal. Columbus made three further voyages. In 1493 with 1,200 men and 50 horses, he returned first to Hispaniola to find his 37 crew members slaughtered by the natives. So terrified were the natives of the newly arrived horses that they instantly fled to take refuge in the mountainous interior of the island (Collis 1989:119–121). Transported across the Atlantic, the horse would soon play a critical role in the *Conquista*[7] as the Spanish invasion continued across the Caribbean to the continental mainland. Tragically, Columbus, a far more gifted visionary than he was governor, ended his days in ill repute. Yet, only seven years after Columbus's death in 1506, Vasco Nunez de Balboa hacked his way through the jungles of Panama to gaze on the Pacific

---

[6] The Santa Maria measured 25 m in length, 3 m longer than the two other caravels.

[7] The Spanish conquest of the Americas.

Ocean. Columbus thus did not live to see the western route to the Indies he so long sought. Nor was the western continent he found in its stead named after him. That honor fell to the zealous Florentine, Amerigo Vespucci (Granzotto 1985:277–278).

Columbus did not discover the Americas, but he did discover the quickest, most direct route to America over which men and perhaps even more significantly horses, donkeys, and mules could be efficiently transported from Europe in large numbers. He discovered this route at a time when Europe, plagued by internal rivalries and invaded in the east on land and sea by belligerent Islam, had its back up against the Atlantic. Isabel, her treasury drained by decades of military effort during the Reconquista, by overthrowing Granada had disrupted trade with the Moors overland to the gold wealth south of the Sahara. Off the west coast of North Africa, maritime access to the gold of Guinea was blocked by rival Portugal. In the Near East, Ottoman Turkey exerted a stranglehold over the land and sea routes to the Orient. In desperation Spain turned to the new lands across the Atlantic. As fleet after fleet headed for the New World,[8] with the ships sailed a new kind of knight, a professional adventurer lured by the promise of booty looted from the vanquished. The conquistadors were not merely soldiers but partners earning shares in the lands they colonized. In time haciendas, courtly love poems, bullfights, and the dire Inquisition would reach the Americas. But first to arrive was the Spanish hidalgo, armed and armored in the finest steel, equipped with firearms, well trained in the military traditions of knighthood, toughened by the long bloody wars against the Moors, now flushed with final victory, and imbued with religious ardor for the new conquest ahead. With the Spaniards came hundreds of superb Spanish horses, transported thousands of kilometers across the Atlantic by devices and methods developed in the Mediterranean during the centuries of crusading and subsequently improved in choppy Atlantic waters during colonization of the Canary Islands. Even so, horses were difficult to transport. Many succumbed in Atlantic transit, particularly along the tropical, windless belt on the edge of the northeast trade winds, named the Horse Latitudes for its toll in horses. In the western hemisphere, where the horse had been extinct for 9,000 years, the European warhorse and its rider would prove to be a lethal combination in confrontation with indigenous populations,

---

[8] In 1499 alone, 30 ships brought 2,500 settlers from Spain (Hassig 1994:12).

to whom we might refer collectively, despite the distorted history and geography, as Amerindians.

Mesoamerica and the Spanish Conquest of Tenochtitlan

The Spaniards thus entered a horseless hemisphere where the inhabitants had been separated from their Old World Asian origins for some 15,000 years. Overall, cultural developments seem to have proceeded rather similarly in both hemispheres (differences will later be discussed), even though on the whole major advances such as agriculture, metallurgy, and urbanization occurred several thousand years later in the New World. In Mesoamerica by the third millennium BC beans, squash, and maize were cultivated, followed by peppers, tomatoes, amaranth, and many other crops including cacao beans used as currency (Smith 1995:157–167). Turkey, bees, and dogs were domesticated, but no other animals were raised for consumption. For 1,000 years up to the time of conquest, the wheel was utilized in small pottery toys (Fig. 10.3) from the Texas border to El Salvador; due to lack of draft animals, however, it was never deployed in transport vehicles. In North America, extensive copper working was first undertaken around the Great Lakes c 4000 BC (Moriarty 1982:n.p.). While there was an abundance of metallic ores in Mesoamerica, metallurgy was first practiced there on a small scale only c AD 650 and regionally in West Mexico by AD 800; nor did metallurgy develop autochthonously. Smelting of nonferrous metals seems to have been adopted from techniques diffused via maritime contacts from Central and South America, notably the northern Andean region (Hosler 1994:14–17). Gold and silver were used primarily for decoration. Copper was deployed as small bells, axes, or arrowheads; swords were simply wood fitted with obsidian blades.

The Olmec, the earliest Mesoamerican civilization, arose c 1500 BC in the southern Vera Cruz region and neighboring Tabasco, a major rubber-producing area. Another Formative culture, Monte Alban I of the Valley of Oaxaca, by 400 BC showed full evidence of literary texts and calendrical reckoning.[9] Two calendars were utilized. One, a secular calendar of 365 days, composed of 18 months of 20 days plus 5 additional days, tracked the earth's orbit around the sun. The other, a ritual or divinatory calendar, was the sacred count of 260 days, in which 13 numbers symbolized by bars and dots intermeshed with 20 named days. The

---

[9] The earliest forms of Zapotec writing date back to the eighth century BC.

FIGURE 10.3. Aztec wheeled toy. Courtesy of the American Museum of Natural History.

two were combined to form a 52-year cycle analogous to our century. From Zapotec territory this Calendar Round spread east to the Gulf Coast and south to the Maya lands of Central America where, certainly by 36 BC but probably earlier, the extraordinary development of the Long Count calendar took place, providing a day-to-day count from a mythical creation date of August 11, 3114 BC. Anciently adopted across Mesoamerica, this calendar reached its greatest refinement under the Maya (Coe 1993:61–62; Marcus 1992:95, 139). With vigesimal positional numeration and a glyph to indicate zero, the Maya Long Count starting from zero was superior to contemporary Old World calendars (Closs 1997:307; Seife 2000:16–18).[10] The Classic Maya (AD 250–950) were of course renowned for their rubber ball game that symbolically reenacted the struggle between celestial and infernal forces in order to assure the continuation of the sun, moon, and planets.

In Mesoamerica, as in the Old World, all centers of early civilization were situated in rich alluvial valleys. In the lacustrine Basin of Mexico, Teotihuacan rose to dominance in Mesoamerica by the early first millennium AD, its military power extending, albeit ephemerally, as far

---

[10] Because the Christian calendar was created at a time when the zero had not been conceptualized by Europeans, their calendar ran directly from 1 BC to AD 1, requiring astronomers tracking celestial phenomena to add or subtract one year manually on crossing the BC–AD barrier. This situation was of course remedied by the invention of the Julian calendar by Scaliger in the sixteenth century AD.

355

south as Guatemala. The Toltecs (950–1150) were largely a continuation of Teotihuacan traditions, although theirs was a far-flung mercantile empire, their capital Tula according to legend founded by Quetzalcoatl (Plumed Serpent) (Pohl 1999:159). In the wake of Toltec decline, many Chichimec peoples from the northern deserts migrated south, among them the ancestors of the Mexica, bearing their tribal war god, Huitzilopochtli. Ferociously warring with other Aztec Nahua-speaking groups, by 1345 the Mexica founded their own twin cities of Tenochtitlan and Tlatilulco on islands along the western lakeshore, enlarging their habitat by constructing fertile *chinampa* island gardens from mud and marsh vegetation. In the Triple Alliance of Tenochtitlan, Texcoco, and Tlacopan, the empire grew to dominate 38 tributary provinces stretching from the Pacific to the Atlantic. But it was a hegemonic empire, not a territorial one. Without animal transportation, the Mexica were unable to garrison these diverse regions. They exacted tribute, depending on their elite *pochteca* (traders) for strategic military intelligence. When a province failed to pay tribute or killed pochteca, cruel war ensued (Wolf 1966:140–141). Mass human sacrifices atop the pyramid of Huitzilopochtli followed by ceremonial consumption attended celebration of victory. It was believed that the spiritual strength of the sacrificed enemy warriors, their pulsating hearts excised, powered the sun and staved off its destruction by the forces of darkness (Brundage 1972:130–133, 217).

Across the Gulf of Mexico, by 1518 Cuban contacts with the urban Maya of the Yucatan and the Totonacs of the Vera Cruz region had furnished the Spaniards information on the availability of gold beyond the snow-capped mountains at the great imperial city of the Mexica. An immigrant to Cuba in 1509, Hernan Cortes was of tough Extremadura stock, a family that had fought its way south during the Reconquista. Successful in the importation of cattle, he was approached by Velasquez, the governor of Cuba, to lead an expedition to the Mexica (Wood 2000:24–25). In less than two weeks, Cortes readied to set sail from Cuba in 11 ships with 450 men including 13 harquebusiers and 32 crossbowmen, plus 4 falconets, 10 cannons, war dogs – and 16 horses, supported on the open decks by belly slings. Alarmed at the scale of Cortes's expedition, Velasquez attempted to intervene, but Cortes at the last minute eluded him (Hassig 1994:46–47). In Vera Cruz, on April 20, 1519, the Spaniards were welcomed by the Totonacs, who viewed the newcomers as allies in their war of liberation against the Mexica. The mood sobered, however, when Aztec emissaries arrived. In the Aztecs' honor, Cortes staged a spectacular demonstration of his horses and guns, having the cavalry charge at full tilt with swords flashing, then firing his large cannon. The Aztecs were terrified (Wood 2000:34). In the weeks ahead, Cortes's tough, sturdy, long-winded Spanish horses, with their fleetness of foot and great powers of endurance, would serve the conquistadors well. Their martial finery would impress the emperor Moctezuma upon entrance to Tenochtitlan, and their agility and courage would win decisive battles.

The invaders' path next led them through the territory of Tlaxcala, sworn enemies of the Mexica. Battle ensued, in which artillery took a terrible toll on the attacking Tlaxcalans, and horses enabled the Spaniards to make periodic forays for food. Finally, the Tlaxcalans sued for peace and after lengthy negotiation agreed to accompany the invaders to Tenochtitlan. En route they encountered opposition from Cholula, where the Spaniards massacred thousands of Chololtecs. For Cortes, this was to serve as a warning to other hostile cities; it also ensured his continued access to the coast (Hassig 1994:72–79). People wonder at the inactivity of the Mexica military during those days, but incredibly, the Spaniards had arrived in the year 1-Reed, the same year of the Aztec calendar that the god Quetzalcoatl had departed toward the east. Since it had been promised that the bearded deity would return from where the sun rises, Moctezuma had wavered, thinking perhaps the bearded Spaniards were deities of the Aztec pantheon returning with Quetzalcoatl to reclaim his kingdom. Thus Cortes's troops and Tlaxcalan allies advanced unimpeded into the Valley of Mexico, home to some 2,000,000 inhabitants. In the distance, they glimpsed Lake Texcoco bustling with canoe traffic and across it the gleaming palaces and pyramids of Tenochtitlan. This city of 200,000 residents was twice the size of contemporary Paris (Hassig 1994:84). In full battle gear the Spaniards marched along the causeway to the capital, with pomp and pageantry, the cavalry in the vanguard, the horses reeling, the ensigns agilely swirling their standards; behind followed their Amerindian allies. Cortes was received with honor and presented with gold and jewels, and his troops were housed in sumptuous quarters (Wood 2000:58).

But Cortes needed to wield control, so within a week he arrested Moctezuma, seeking to govern through him. News came that Governor Velasquez had sent a punitive expedition from Cuba. Cortes sped to the coast, where in surprise attack against the Spanish force he gained the allegiance of a large number of front-line troops, among them many

Italian and Greek veterans of Mediterranean wars. Returning to Tenochtitlan with 1,300 soldiers, 96 horses, 80 crossbowmen, and 80 harquebusiers (Diaz 1974:284), he found the situation deteriorated. In his absence, the Spaniards had massacred thousands of Aztec nobles. Cortes had Moctezuma try to pacify the Mexica crowd, but wounded in a hail of missiles the monarch died (Hassig 1994:90–94). At midnight on July 1, 1520, the Spanish contingent and their Amerindian allies attempted exodus to the mainland; their flight was detected, the alarm sounded, and hundreds of war canoes converged on the causeway. The troops hugely outnumbered, it was every man for himself. Gold, cannons, and gunpowder were all lost in the lake; Cortes barely escaped alive (Diaz 1974:301–302). While Spanish prisoners were sacrificed atop Tenochtitlan pyramids, Cortes's forces were aided by lakeside cities providing food. Fleeing north, the Spanish were pursued by thousands of Aztecs. As they climbed out of the Valley of Otumba, they were abruptly confronted by a host of warriors levied from the populous territory of Texcoco, a tossing mass of fantastic helmets and spears. Without firearms, again and again the Spanish horsemen charged the enemy in small bands, giving strength and courage to the infantry. Within sight of their native mountains the Tlaxcala fought like lions, their enemies constantly supported by fresh relays. Suddenly Cortes sighted the Mexica commander borne on a litter by noble chieftains, clothed in a rich surcoat of feathers, and crowned with a panache of splendid plumes set in gold. Calling on four of his most trusted captains, Cortes plunged headlong into battle. The five mounted lancers charged in unison, Cortes toppled the Mexica banner, Juan de Salamanca dealt the commander a death blow, and the other knights attacked the chiefs. Overpowered by the rapidity of the action, the Aztecs retreated, communicating panic to their comrades. The rest of the Spanish cavalry followed to scatter the enemy and to fight on to final victory (Diaz 1974:304–306; Prescott 2001:612–616).

As reinforcements arrived from across the Gulf, Amerindian disaffection with Mexica imperium allowed the Spaniards to further extend their power over several city-states south and west of Tlaxcala. But an unseen killer was also aiding the Spaniards. The smallpox virus had reached Mexico from Cuba. Unlike the Spaniards, who had developed a degree of immunity to Old World diseases, the Amerindians had no genetic resistance whatsoever. The resulting epidemic led to massive deaths and precipitous depopulation (Diamond 1999:210). Once introduced to the hemisphere, the dreaded virus rapidly spread overland north to the chiefdoms of the Mississippi Valley and south to the Andean area, killing thousands of Amerindians years before the Spaniards even reached these lands. Gaining control of the lake with brigantines, the Spaniards were able to enforce the surrender of numerous vassal states of Tenochtitlan, thereby depriving the Mexica of supplies and fighting power. In the final assault on the famished city, Cortes had over 900 Spaniards, some 75,000 Amerindian allies, and 86 horses (Hassig 1994:122). Amazed at the ferocity of resistance, the Spaniards fought for 80 days. Finally the cavalry broke through to the northern market of Tlatilulco; in the expanse of that great plaza within hours the hidalgos mercilessly defeated the Eagle and Jaguar warriors. The Mexica surrendered on August 13, 1521 (Wood 2000:88–91).

The Andes and the Spanish Conquest of Tawantinsuyu

The western desert littoral of South America is dissected by seasonal rivers, whose periodic floodplains from approximately the third millennium BC supported the cultivation of maize, beans, squash, and peppers. By 1800 BC irrigation projects allowed populations to move from the shoreline to prime agricultural land in midvalley habitats. In Peru, intermontane valleys were terraced with consummate skill to produce copious crops of maize and quinoa, and in the high mountains potatoes, oca, mashua, and ullucu were produced. On the high grassland (*puna*) roamed wild camelids, vicunas, and guanacos and by the third millennium BC herds of llama and alpaca, the only large mammals to be domesticated; the small guinea pig nevertheless was an important dietary item. On the eastern slopes of the Andes, coca, manioc, peanuts, and sweet potatoes were grown (Smith 1995:176–178; Morris and von Hagen 1993:17–21). As in the Old World, the earliest centers of Peruvian civilization occurred in highly circumscribed alluvial valleys. Along the central desert coastal plain, the most ancient, the Norte Chico complex, contemporaneous with the Old Kingdom pyramids of Egypt and the ziggurats of Sumer, c 3000 BC featured great monumental mounds constructed with basalt blocks, ceremonial plazas, and terraces (Morris and von Hagen 1993:37–38). Religious centers and pilgrimages facilitated the traffic of peoples and goods across areas of diverse ecological resources: in the highlands at Kotosh as early as 2000 BC, by 900 BC at Chavin de Huantar (Von Hagen and Morris 1998:33–34, 45, 212, 221), and in the first millennium AD until the time of the Inkas at Pachacamac in the Lurin valley on the central coast (Morris and von Hagen 1993:61).

Metalworking occurred much earlier than in Mesoamerica, c 1500 BC in highland Peru (Hosler 1994:16). Due to abundance of native metals and ores in the Andes, metallurgies subsequently sprung up from Argentina, Chile, and Bolivia through the Central Andes to Colombia and Central America. In Colombia 500 BC the copper-gold alloy *tumbaga* was shaped by casting, using the lost-wax technique. At Chavin by 400 BC gold repousse decoration, soldering, and welding were executed. In the first millennium AD, both arsenical and tin bronze were produced, as were copper or bronze hoes, mace heads, spear throwers, and spear points; additionally, sheet gold masks, diadems, ear spools, and filigree nose ornaments were hammered. By complex surface enrichment techniques, Andean smiths even achieved golden and silvery surfaces on copper or copper-gold-silver alloys, a feat accomplished in modern times only by complex electrochemical processes (Morris and Von Hagen 1993:215–226).

Along Peru's coast, great Andean urban societies evolved c AD 100–700, Moche in the north, Nazca in the south. Shortly after, cities developed in the southern highlands. Tiwanaku, just south of Lake Titicaca, came into power c AD 375, establishing colonies on the coast, in lowland Bolivia, and in Argentina. Around Lake Titicaca, the *waru-waru* system of raised fields was developed, the canals between its clay ridges absorbing solar radiation during the day and emitting conserved heat at night, thereby mitigating frost damage and making extensive wetlands productive. Since few trees grow on the harsh altiplano, in the monumental construction of Tiwanaku, andesite blocks weighing 130,000 kg were transported across the lake in boats made out of bundles of *totora* (reeds that grow along the lakeshore) (Von Hagen and Morris 1998:125, 213–215). Wari became dominant in the Ayacucho Basin c AD 500–750 and expanded by establishing far-flung settlements in locations where transport could be controlled and dispersed resources redistributed; precise data on these reallocations were recorded by means of the *quipu* knotted device, which under the Inka would function as an elaborate accounting system of colored pendant and subsidiary cords. With the decline of Tiwanaku and Wari in the highlands, by AD 1400 Chimu became the imperial force in the old Moche valley; from Chan Chan, its wealthy capital, it succeeded in uniting the entire north coast. Meanwhile in southern Peru various ethnic groups were jockeying for power; from this struggle the Inka emerged as the dominant regional polity (D'Altroy 2002:41).

The Inka empire Tawantinsuyu really began in 1438 with the accession of the ninth Inka Pachakuti and expanded across the southern highlands (Brundage 1963:95). During the 1460s, Pachakuti's son, Topa Inka, assuming command of the army, marched north to conquer the highlands as far as Quito, Ecuador. Turning to the coast, the Inkas then overran the Chimor empire of more than 1,000,000 inhabitants. In the south, all of Bolivia was conquered, as were large tracts in Argentina and Chile. After the death of Topa Inka in 1483, his son Huayna Capac extended the empire in northern Ecuador to the Ancasmayo River, the present-day boundary with Colombia (Lanning 1967:157–158).

The Inkas continued the highland tradition of ensuring access to far-flung resources without strict control of intervening land by allowing provinces to retain locally efficient independence. Between sowing and harvest times, tens of thousands were assigned to massive corvee work in large-scale terracing projects, construction or extension of irrigation systems, and channeling of rivers, thus opening up new state lands for agricultural production. Skilled metallurgists were concentrated around the capital, Cuzco, as were the high-grade textile workshops (Schaedel 1978:291–292, 294, 299). An elaborate structure of roads, state warehouses, and administrative cities integrated the empire. In the absence of wheeled vehicles, good road paving was not essential, and steps were used on steep slopes. In precipitous terrains, great feats of engineering were undertaken: tunnels through hills, suspension bridges across narrow ravines, and pontoon bridges across rivers in lowlands. But the pace of the llama packtrains never came close to the speed of equestrian locomotion (Mason 1957:161–167).[11] The jewel of the empire of course was Cuzco, with its great Coricancha Temple of the Sun, the whole interior covered with golden plates more than half a meter in length and adorned by the sacred golden sun image and a wondrous garden of maize fashioned in gold and silver with birds flying about and 12 life-size llamas with herders nearby, all wrought in precious metals. In Inka cosmology, "gold was the sweat of the Sun and silver the tears of the Moon" (D'Altroy 2002:298–299).

In the early 1520s, following rumors of a golden land "Biru" (Viru valley) to the south, Francisco Pizarro, also a native of Extremadura, began exploring from Panama the Pacific coast of Colombia, Ecuador,

---

[11] The llama was not suited to riding, could not carry more than 46 kg, and covered only 19 km per day (Mason 1957:140).

and Peru. In 1527, his fleet intercepted a keeled, oceangoing raft constructed of light balsa logs, covered with a platform, and powered by sail and oars. It carried objects for trade including the finest textiles; its crew of 20 or more wore jewelry of precious metals and stones. In 1531, authorized by the Spanish crown, Pizarro organized a third expedition, three ships with 62 cavalry and 102 infantry. In February 1532, the Spaniards attacked Tumbes and looted the Inka state warehouses (Patterson 1991:133–134).

The emperor Huayna Capac, in the course of his campaigns in Ecuador, had contracted smallpox, a plague that had spread overland from Mexico as far south as Cuzco. Upon the emperor's death in 1528, internecine civil war erupted between his two sons Huascar and Atahualpa. Embarking from Quito, Atahualpa, a seasoned warrior, finally prevailed at the 1532 battle of Cotopampa, but had yet to make his victorious entry into Cuzco. The arrival of the Spaniards and their possession of huge animals that ran like the wind and killed men had been reported to him. Aware of the political situation, Pizarro moved to confront the new Inka. Leading a group of 164 equipped with only a dozen harquebuses, Pizarro advanced into the cordillera to Cajamarca, where the Inka armies of 80,000 were assembled (Diamond 1999:68). Upon arrival, the famed horseman Hernando de Soto was selected with a guard of 16 mounted men to initially approach the emperor. Seated on a gold stool, Atahualpa reprimanded the Spaniards for their theft of state property. Resenting this reproach, de Soto put his mount through its most exciting paces, finally wheeling around into a head-on charge toward the royal party. The rearing forefeet of the horse so terrified the courtiers that they shrank in horror. But throughout, Atahualpa remained unblinking even though in imminent peril of being trampled; the emperor later ordered the execution of all who had panicked, as traitors to their glorious heredity (Brundage 1963:298–302).

The next day, midst a multitude of 5,000, Atahualpa returned to the city at sunset on the intelligence that horses unsaddled for the night were ineffective in war. A Spanish friar first approached to hand the emperor a Christian breviary, which Atahualpa hurled derisively in the dust. At this point a barrage of gunfire erupted, seeming like thunder and lightning to the assembled crowds. From the temple towers where they were ensconced, the Spaniards emerged on foot and on horseback, uttering their war cry, "Santiago! Santiago!" Rushing in terror from the massed charge, the Amerindians were trampled by horses or struck down by swords. Pizarro was the first to reach Atahualpa, standing guard over his prize until he was wrenched from his litter. That night perhaps as many as 3,000 were slaughtered in Pizarro's trap; those who escaped were relentlessly pursued by horsemen along the roads as Inka regiments retreated far to the north (Brundage 1963:303–305).

To provide a ransom for Atahualpa's release, the Inkas collected treasures from shrines and palaces throughout the empire. The quantities of precious jewels and metals that flowed in surpassed anything previously experienced in the New World, staggering the expectations of even the most covetous Spaniard. At Cajamarca alone, the 6,000 kg of 22.5-carat gold fed into the forges today would value $60,000,000; and the 11,800 kg of silver, another $2,000,000. Two hidalgos sped overland to secure gold in the holy city of Cuzco, encountering en route ethnic regions ecstatically celebrating release from Inka rule. Entering the most sacred huaca of the Coricancha, the Spaniards pried from the walls 700 gold plates weighing 2 kg apiece. By the time the main Spanish army arrived, every single priceless gold or silver object had been removed and ruthlessly melted down, the value of the haul in Cuzco exceeding that of Cajamarca (D'Altroy 2002:299–300). Fabulous ransom notwithstanding, Atahualpa was condemned to execution by garroting. In 1533, Manco Inka, son of Huayna Capac, was crowned emperor. His finest general, Quizo Yupanqui, in 1536 attempted to storm Lima, which was defended by two squadrons of Spanish cavalry and Amerindian allies; in disciplined charge, the Spaniards immediately annihilated Quizo and his much larger Inka army. Manco Inka himself led a rebellion to besiege Cuzco. Inka forces were again defeated by the Spaniards, who with a massed cavalry charge of 26 horsemen routed Manco's best troops. Manco Inka fled to the jungle fastness of remote Vilcabamba, out of reach of the Spanish cavalry, where Inkas ruled a rump state until 1571 (Diamond 1999:77; Patterson 1991:127–128).

Despite insurrection and factional strife, with their warhorses the Spaniards succeeded in dominating the Inka empire, the entire length of the highlands and the coast. Their incursions into the eastern tropical lowlands fared differently, however. Spanish explorers in Colombia and Venezuela brought back reports of "El Dorado," fabulous gold in the tropical rain forests. Determined to exploit this fabled wealth, Francisco Pizarro's brother Gonzalo mounted a powerful expedition, marching east from Quito in 1541. He led some 280 Spaniards, 260 horses, and thousands of native bearers with munitions and supplies (Wood 2000:192–196). In unrelenting rains the Spanish expedition spent six months wandering along the Coca River to the Napo without finding any gold, at which point most of the Amerindians were dead from starvation or maltreatment. By Christmas the men had begun to eat the horses (Wood 2000:200, 203). Francisco Orellana offered to take a brigantine they had constructed downriver to locate food for the expedition. But as Orellana headed downstream with 57 Spaniards, it became impossible for the party to return against the current. Meanwhile, Pizarro, despairing Orellana's return and fighting off fierce native attacks, marched his famished men back to the Andes. Sixteen months after setting out, only 80 of his men made it back to Quito alive. Unlike the conquest in the dry Andes, the hundreds of Spanish warhorses in the mud of the tropical rain forest were utterly useless. Gonzalo's expedition was a total failure (Wood 2000:209–216).

Orellana's accomplishment, in contrast, was a success. By February, his crew had reached the confluence of the Napo and Maranon, where they heard tales of fierce female warriors, warlike tribes they would later encounter downstream. They therefore named the river Rio Amazonas, ironically not for Isabel, Amazon among European monarchs, who had sped Spain to the New World, but after the legendary Amazon warriors of the steppes. In April a larger seagoing vessel was built and the two boats sailed on toward the sea, encountering armed resistance from the natives en route. After more than 3,200 km of perilous river travel, Orellana set sail another 1,930 km along the Atlantic seaboard to the Caribbean, reaching Trinidad in two weeks (Wood 2000:218–226). Of course the Portuguese had navigated the region earlier. The southern coast of Brazil had been sighted by Cabral in 1500; but subsequently, in establishing enclaves along the Atlantic coast for their lucrative sugar plantations, the Portuguese encountered determined Amerindian resistance that prevented their advance inland. The warhorse in fact did not colonize the Amazon; it was as unsuited to the tropical rain forest of the Americas as it was to the jungles of the Congo and Southeast Asia. Later Portuguese penetration of the vast Amazonian hinterland was undertaken mainly by watercraft, along the many tributaries of the great river. The Spaniards succeeded in advancing down the eastern flanks of the Andes to occupy the upland forested montana region. But even there, their horses could not hold their own against the indigenous peoples who early expelled the colonizers. In 1599, rebellious Shuar tribes in Ecuador massacred some 30,000 Spaniards, executing the governor by pouring molten gold down his throat until his intestines burst. The conquistadors had plenty of firearms and steel swords, but in the rain forest their cavalry failed them; for centuries they would not be able to impose their rule on the Amerindian population of the interior tropical forests (Stirling 1938:16–18).

Thus, Spanish colonization of South America was initially restricted to the Andean areas. By establishing good relations with the traditional *curaca* leaders, the colonizers maintained the excellent Inka structures of hydrology and agriculture. The Spaniards continued to loot shrines and warehouses, but as the spoils of plunder diminished they turned to the mines (Patterson 1991:132). Cerro Potosi in southern Bolivia was the richest source of silver in the world. So abundant was silver that when there was no iron replacement for worn-out horseshoes, the Spaniards simply made silver ones (Crosby 1972:81). Thousands of Amerindians were impressed into the mines. Thousands of silver bars and coins were produced by assembly-line methods and shipped north to Panama, there to be transported by mules, ancient pack animal of metals, to the Spanish galleons waiting in the Caribbean. In the 50 years following the Conquista, output of silver and gold from the Americas was 10 times that of the rest of the world. After gold and silver were depleted, baser metals – zinc, copper, tin, and bauxite – would be exploited, each contributing to the later European industrial revolution (Weatherford 1988:12–14, 51–52).

Post-Conquista Europe

For the few extraordinary gold objects that were shipped to Europe intact, a traveling exhibit was organized in order to glorify the reign of the Spanish monarch Charles I. Viewing immense sculptures of the sun and moon entirely of gold and silver, the artist Albrecht Durer, himself the son of a goldsmith, was moved to comment:

> I have never in all my days seen anything that so delighted my heart as these things. For I saw amazing objects and I marvelled at the subtle ingenuity of the men in these distant lands. (Bray 1982:n.p.)

Despite Durer's ecstatic admiration, tragically even these priceless masterpieces met the customary fate in the royal flames of Spain. Charles, of course, was also head of the Holy Roman Empire, elected Charles V in 1519. Thus, while gold and silver from the New World was bound for the port of Seville, it did not all stay in Spain. Some of the bullion was used to beautify the palaces and cathedrals of the peninsula, but fully three-fifths of it was diverted to Habsburg holdings in the Spanish Netherlands, Germany, Switzerland, Austria, and Italy (Weatherford

1988:14). Such was the magnificence of the Austrian court that Charles's brother Ferdinand I in 1562 imported from Spain the famed snow-white Andalusian Barbs for the Spanish Riding Academy in Vienna. In 1580 a stud farm was established at Lipizza where the chargers, already trained militarily to leap in the air and lash out with their hind feet at the enemy attacking from behind, now learned to perform intricate movements in time with classical Viennese music. In the grand quadrille the statuesque beauty of each of eight stallions was enhanced by a golden bridle and breastplate. In spectacular dance, the rhythmic movements of man and mount – pirouette, levade, courbette – impressed the populace with the pomp and opulence of their rulers (Tinker 1964:4, 10–11).

On a less frivolous note, the wealth garnered from the New World stimulated an extraordinary explosion of intellectual activities throughout Europe. In *Revolutions of the Celestial Spheres*, the Polish astronomer Copernicus in 1543 repudiated the old Ptolemaic system by describing the sun as occupying a central position relative to the planets, each of which was in daily motion around its axis and in yearly motion around the sun. From observations with his astronomical telescope, Galileo supported the Copernican theory. In England Francis Bacon advanced the methods of experimental science as Descartes in France extended the systematic rational method to the sciences and philosophy. In Germany, Leibniz developed integral and differential calculus. These achievements led to the Enlightenment, during which Sir Isaac Newton, in England the first scientist to be knighted for his research, laid the foundation of modern physical optics; he also formulated the three laws of motion that would become the basic principles of modern physics, culminating in his theory of gravitation. Adam Smith and Karl Marx both recognized the European conquest of the Americas as "the greatest event in history" in terms of economic reverberations around the world. Such was the influx of riches from the New World that in the first 50 years following the Conquista the amount of gold and silver circulating in Europe tripled. With this immense wealth, the old mercantile system was transformed into a true market economy. Production increased, and capital accumulated in quantities unimagined by earlier generations (Weatherford 1988:14–15).

The new money was also available to finance foreign wars. Western Europe's mastery of the oceans and riches from overseas continents would now topple the Ottoman colossus. In the Mediterranean, large investments were made to fortify the island stronghold of Malta, where the Knights Hospitalers in 1565 repulsed the attack of Suleiman the

Magnificent's 30,000 crack Turkish troops, equipped with the latest artillery. The new wealth from the Americas was further deployed to strengthen the Christian West by expanding the Spanish Mediterranean fleet. In 1571 Charles's son, Phillip II of Spain, formed an alliance with Venice and Pope Pius V against the Turks. The Christian fleet of over 200 ships carrying 30,000 men sailed for Corfu, then advanced on the Ottoman fleet at Lepanto. The Turkish galleys were ineffective against the tall western ships capable of firing broadsides; as a consequence, most of the Turkish vessels were sunk, an event celebrated throughout all Europe. Muslim naval supremacy in the Mediterranean was smashed. Swiftly, the Knights of Malta moved to disrupt enemy shipping in the eastern Mediterranean so that soon Tripoli, Tunis, and Algiers were no longer integral parts of Ottoman maritime power. The influx of American wealth into Europe also impacted neighboring economies. As gold and silver inundated the European market, the Turkish silver *akce* coin fell to half its former value, causing widespread financial distress. In 1497–1498 Vasco da Gama had rounded the Cape of Good Hope to reach India. Now in the sixteenth century, Portuguese and Spanish warships plied the Red Sea attacking Turkish territories in North Africa and diverting trade from the Near East. With their new transoceanic mobility, they outmaneuvered the Turks to deliver, through Hormuz, shipments of European firearms to Shah Abbas for his Persian campaigns against the Ottomans. Confronted with wars on multiple fronts, in a short space of time the Ottoman giant shrank from a force that had once terrorized the Mediterranean and threatened Europe to become a mere regional empire in Asia Minor (Inalcik 1973:42–49). After a near millennium of struggle between Christians and Muslims, the gold and silver looted from Peru and Mexico did more to undermine Islamic power in the world than any other factor. Not only that, following the 1519–1521 circumnavigation of the globe by the fleet of Ferdinand Magellan, silver flowed directly from Acapulco across the Pacific to Manila and China, where it was exchanged for silk, spices, and porcelain. This brought many Asian countries under the influence of the new standardized but inflated silver values, making a world economy operative for the first time (Weatherford 1988:16–17).

Competition was not limited to the Christian-Muslim confrontation. The knights of Europe scarcely left their quarrels of centuries behind on land when they headed for the high seas. Cabot, Verrazzano, Cartier, and Champlain early prowled the Atlantic in search of North American territories. In 1579 Francis Drake, sailing the South Pacific coast in the *Golden*

Hind, seized tons of gold, silver, and emeralds from Chilean and Peruvian ports and heavily laden Spanish galleons heading north to Panama. Navigating westward through the Moluccas, where he established the British right to trade in spices, then around the Cape of Good Hope, Drake arrived in Plymouth Harbor in 1580 with riches worth 1.5 million contemporary English pounds and was later knighted for his exploits by the Virgin Queen Elizabeth I. Subsequently, with the backing of the crown, the British established beachheads in the Caribbean. To replace the Amerindian work force devastated by pandemics, the Portuguese proceeded to import slaves from Africa. In the Caribbean and the Carolinas, the English operated the joint business of transporting African slaves and looting Spanish galleons. These enterprises in time led to the development of trading companies whose success spawned the banking systems and stock markets of Europe (Weatherford 1988:29–32, 37).

Europe profited, however, not just from the gold and silver treasures wrought by centuries of extraordinary Amerindian artisanship, but also from the very soil of the conquered Americas – its millennia of highly sophisticated agriculture. Tomatoes, beans, squash, chili peppers, and chocolate would enliven and enrich cuisines around the world, but of greatest impact was the Andean potato. Prior to the discovery of the New World, the Old World had depended for its staples on grains, nutritious but ever vulnerable to climatic fluctuation. In the balmy Mediterranean, the classic civilizations owed their political dominance to reliable, abundant wheat harvests every year. But in colder, northern Europe, crop failure and hunger were by no means infrequent. Potatoes, which could be grown in marginal rocky soils unsuited to grain, were soon cultivated across Ireland, England, Germany, and Poland, providing a dependable, inexpensive nutritional base[12] and a source of vitamin C. Maize fed to farm animals increased the yield of milk and eggs. These American cultigens thus fostered the population boom that would challenge the age-old supremacy of Mediterranean Europe. In the bitterly cold climate of Russia, the sturdy potato along with sunflower oil greatly improved the peasant diet, aiding the Russians in their long struggle to drive out the Mongol intruder. But American crops also thrived in the tropics and subtropics. Maize, cotton, amaranth, tobacco, sweet potatoes, pineapples, peanuts, and manioc flourished in Africa and Asia, contributing to population increases there; most importantly,

---

[12] Potatoes render more nutrition, more reliably, with less labor than grain; one hectare of potatoes provides almost double the caloric value of one hectare of wheat.

manioc grew in extremely poor soils incapable of producing another crop. And Olmec rubber would revolutionize world sports, furnish Europeans with water-resistant clothing to explore the world's jungles and mountains, and provide tires for automobiles of the future (Weatherford 1988:48, 64–75).

As agricultural yields in Europe rose, horse participation in the economy increased and larger animals were required to meet the new demands, for example, the shire horses of England and Holland. But horsepower was to play an even more critical role in transportation. In the fourteenth century, the movable forecarriage had come into prominence, making the maneuvering of four-wheeled wagons more practicable (Gille 1969:434). Possessing clear advantages over the cart, the wagon in time displaced the smaller vehicle. Less likely to overturn, the wagon could haul larger loads.

As important foreign products reached Europe's shores, even further advances in transportation were needed to distribute these valuable commodities to the nations' industries. One key invention of the fifteenth century was the modification of the wheel to a flat cone shape. This "dished" wheel provided greater strength against the sideways thrust, inevitable with the swaying of heavy wagon loads drawn over uneven surfaces (Jope 1956:552). Soon hundreds of wagons were entering and leaving European cities each week, many drawn by teams of six or eight horses, transporting loads of up to 6,000 kg.[13] These wagon carrier services were supplemented by gangs of packhorses. Horses transported greater loads by vehicle: 305 kg per wagon horse as opposed to 109 kg per packhorse. But the packhorse was faster and less seriously affected by steep gradients and poor roads in winter (Gerhold 2005:66–67).

Heavy bulk freight, necessarily conducted by water along coastlines, rivers, and inland canals, was much slower. In comparison to water, the cost of road transport was markedly higher. But the greater speed and reliability of carrier services were so appreciated by farmers, manufacturers, and merchants that an immense variety of goods were transported by road: perishable agricultural products, costly textiles, and imported luxury items (Gerhold 1993:1, 3). Even with long-distance bulk freight, the beginning and end of journeys often were

---

[13] By the 1700s, the Shire draft horse measured 18 hands and was capable of pulling 1,500 kg. Other very large draft and agricultural horses shortly to appear were Percherons, Clydesdales, and Suffolks.

overland, to and from navigable water. Thus, the two modes of transport were largely complementary; also, horses were employed towing barges along canals (Barker and Gerhold 1993:16). Horsepower further helped relocate industries to areas of cheaper labor away from major waterways. And in multistage production, it transported partial products between local centers of manufacture, thereby intensifying regional specialization and commercial integration. The wagon was the precursor of the stagecoach. Distinguished from the wagon first by its leather-strap suspension, later by laminated tensile steel springs between body and undercarriage, the stagecoach provided the first regularly scheduled passenger services over long distances. As New World wealth flooded into Europe, highways were generally improved. Drawn by four to six powerful draft horses, with frequent change of horse teams en route, the stagecoach was the speediest form of public transportation. Soon, too, the stately carriage would be *the* sumptuary gift exchanged among monarchs. With an efficient transport system and emergent national economy, London grew rapidly to become Europe's leading port. Braced for the Industrial Revolution, Britain would become the center of a worldwide empire and a developing world economy as raw materials poured in from overseas, were distributed throughout the provinces, and returned as manufactured goods to the metropolis for consumption or export abroad (Gerhold 2005:80–81,116, 158, 169, 173). And in due course, the multifunctional horse too would be exported abroad, to bolster new economies on distant continents.

As Europe's industrial and commercial demands for foreign materials soared, the conquest of the New World would serve as a model for subsequent colonial expansion around the globe. The Conquista of course had not been without a price. Many Spaniards had lost their lives in wars or at sea. But so many millions of Amerindians had perished, if not from the epidemics of smallpox, measles, and malaria that ravaged their hemisphere, then from the brutality and oppression of their colonizers. Recent hemispheric estimates indicate that the total Amerindian population of the Americas dropped from 53.9 million in 1492 to 5.6 million in 1650, a decline of 48.3 million or 90 percent (Denevan 1992:xxix). Add to this epic tragedy the forced relocation of 15 million slaves from Africa to the Americas. Such drastic truncation of thousands of years of human civilization, in terms of human suffering, exceeded even the cataclysmic slaughters inflicted by Genghis Khan and his Altaic successors.

As we have seen in the New World, Spain's conquistadors on horseback had possessed an immense military advantage over pedestrian warriors and in less than 15 years had dominated 25 million people in Mesoamerica and the Andes. The vast wealth seized blocked the tide of Islamic advance into Europe. With England's defeat of the Spanish Armada in 1588, the pendulum of power in Europe swung from the Mediterranean civilizations to the Atlantic littoral. Nations that had long exploited the Atlantic fishing banks now directed their ships to more distant oceans. From Portugal, England, France, Belgium, and the Netherlands, European gunboats, with their warhorses, trading companies, newly acquired Amerindian cultigens, and recent scientific and technological innovations financed by New World wealth, traversed the oceans to colonize Africa, southern Asia, Australia, and Oceania.

Horses of Rebellion in the Americas

Horses were not only to play an important role in conquest; they were also destined to feature prominently in rebellion. In Mexico, with the discovery of mines in Zacatecas, the frontiers of New Spain moved north. By 1550 there were 10,000 horses in the lush grazing lands around Queretaro (Crosby 1972:82). Coronado's expedition of 1540 penetrated as far east as present-day Kansas. Onate led another expedition to the American Southwest in 1598 bringing along, in the tradition of the Castilian hacienda, thousands of sheep, cattle, and donkeys and 300 horses. Finally, after 9,000 years of extinction, the horse had returned to the very canyons and mesas of North America where four million years earlier *Equus* had originally evolved. Once in its natal environment the horse prospered and multiplied. Under the Spanish yoke, the Pueblos learned how to saddle, break, bridle, and ride the new beast. Soon the more mobile Apaches of the nearby mesas utilized the horse in hunting, and thus the technology of riding was transmitted to North America. But in 1680 the Pueblos revolted and drove the Spaniards out of the Southwest until 1690. In those 10 years, thousands of Spanish horses escaped from the upper Rio Grande valley into the surrounding mountains and plains. This dispersal formed the nucleus of the great mustang herds that forever changed the history of the American West.

By 1705 the Comanche, mounted Shoshonean bands of nomadic hunter-gatherers, had emigrated onto the rich buffalo plains of Texas.

Raiding the New Mexico horse lode, they also bred horses successfully, attaining herds of thousands of animals. As on the Eurasian steppes, before the horse the prairie had few human inhabitants because the tough sod discouraged farming and the plains animals were too fleet to provide a dependable food source (Crosby 1972:102; Fehrenbach 1974:83–90, 94). As pedestrians, forest and riverine agricultural tribes on the fringes of the Great Plains had seasonally hunted buffalo by surrounding and stampeding a herd into traps or over cliffs. In contrast, the new technique of equestrian chase fully exploited the horse's ability to gallop faster than the swiftest buffalo. The horse's speed and mobility enabled the skilled hunter to single out a specific animal, ride alongside, kill at close range with bow and arrow, and move on to the next, in no time obtaining a surfeit of meat. The chase was superior to the earlier surround in that it required a fraction of the time and effort and was far more productive (Ewers 1969:159, 303–305). By 1720 many more tribes – Sioux, Arapaho, Dakota, Crow, Blackfoot – deployed the horse in hunting buffalo herds on the Great Plains well to the north of the Platte River. The adoption of the horse was advantageous in other respects. To move across the prairies, the nomadic hunters needed to transport household impedimenta. Traditionally the dog travois had been used in transportation, but now the horse travois carried heavier loads farther and faster. A horse could pack 90 kg on its back or haul 135 kg on travois in one day, four times the load of a heavily burdened dog, twice as far. Tipis of 40 buffalo skins could now be transported, replacing the earlier six-skin lodge and allowing much larger aggregations of people to operate on the plains. As powerful buffalo-hunting tribes increased in size, conflicts over hunting grounds arose. An entire Plains cultural complex emerged as intertribal wars were engendered and perpetuated by daring feats of horse raiding, counting coup, and scalping; captives were enslaved to perform domestic tasks or to be ransomed back (Ewers 1969:131, 214, 308).

While Spanish horse technology diffused onto the plains from the southwest, many inventions also spread into the continental interior from other European horsemen entrenched along the Atlantic seaboard. In 1776 there was a colonist revolt against the British throne and Paul Revere rode through the night to warn of Redcoats' approach:

A hurry of hoofs in a village street,
A shape in the moonlight, a bulk in the dark,
And beneath, from the pebbles, in passing, a spark

Struck out by a steed flying fearless and fleet:
That was all! And yet through the gloom and the light,
The fate of the nation was riding that night;
And the spark struck out by that steed, in his flight,
Kindled the land into flame with its heat.

(Longfellow 2006:49)

With these hurrying hoofbeats a new nation was born, and from the Atlantic, American settlers traversed the eastern forests to the vast expanse of the prairies. From their enclave in Quebec, the French dispatched traders and trappers across the Great Lakes down the Mississippi-Missouri drainage. Ostensibly mercantile, the French thrust exchanged muskets and ammunition for furs and skins. By operating beyond the borders of their territory in this manner, they aimed at alliance with the different tribes in order to mount armed resistance against rival Europeans in North America. As a consequence, levels of warfare on the Great Plains greatly intensified (Fehrenbach 1974:119–120). As American pioneers from the Atlantic states fanned out west onto the prairies equipped with the same covered wagons, cultigens, and domesticated animals with which Indo-Europeans six millennia earlier had expanded across the Eurasian steppes, they faced Amerindians very different from the ones encountered at the beginning of the sixteenth century by Cortes and Pizarro. The pioneers met tribes, no longer pedestrian, who strongly resented foreign invasion of their prime hunting territories and energetically resisted settler advance. The mounted Amerindian of the Plains was a formidable adversary. He had adopted the Spanish bridle and saddle, albeit a lighter rig. Both cottonwood frame saddles and leather pads stuffed with deer hair or grass, from which bentwood stirrups were suspended, were utilized. Unencumbered, the tough, wiry mustang easily outraced eastern military horses, especially over short distances. A Plains innovation was a thong slipped around the horse's neck from which the agile rider hung over the far side of the horse, shielding himself from enemy arrows and bullets (Fehrenbach 1974:95–96; Ewers 1969:81–86). The Amerindians never advanced in solid line; instead, a mass of "swirling, breaking, dissolving" riders, they thundered across the prairie unleashing a rain of arrows (Fehrenbach 1974:127). Against such a charge, massed musketry or cannon was of limited usefulness. In pursuit of retreating forces, the Plains Indian, schooled in the buffalo hunt, wielded deadly archery at full gallop (Fehrenbach 1974:128).

After the Civil War, as thousands of settlers streamed westward, treaty after treaty with the Plains tribes was abrogated by Americans covetous of acreage and precious metals. Initially, whites attempted to restrict the tribes to valueless territories, but soon this policy moved toward a war of outright extermination, in which the Amerindian food base – the herds of wild buffalo – was systematically destroyed by the now efficient breech-loading rifle. At the beginning of the nineteenth century there were an estimated 60,000,000 buffalo on the Plains; at the end barely 1,000 were left. In July 1876 tensions reached a climax when the elite Seventh Cavalry under Civil War hero George Armstrong Custer was annihilated at the battle of Little Bighorn by a combined force of Sioux and Cheyenne headed by Sitting Bull and Crazy Horse (Farb 1971:166–167). Promised a reservation in good hunting country, Crazy Horse and his starving Oglalas surrendered, only to have Crazy Horse assassinated in 1877. Sitting Bull too was forced to submit to a reservation. In 1883 when the Northern Pacific railroad celebrated driving in the last spike of its transcontinental railroad, Sitting Bull was invited to address the gathering. He berated the audience in Sioux for lying and stealing tribal territories and making the Amerindian an outcast in his own land; in 1890 he too was assassinated. Perfidy and the "iron horse" had sealed the fate of the West (Brown 1981:294, 401, 411).

In amazing parallel to events in North America, there was a comparable explosion of horses on the grassy plains of South America. In southern Chile, the conquistadors encountered fierce resistance from Araucanian tribes, who, capturing Spanish horses, had promptly adopted the new steed. The nomadic Pehuenche then transmitted the horse eastward across the low mountain passes of the southern Andes to the *pampas* (steppes), where the horse proliferated. In 1598 the 300-year Arauco war began, as the Mapuche rebelled against Governor Martin Garcia Onez de Loyola (brother of Saint Ignacio). For centuries missionizing in Chile would be conducted from a chain of Jesuit forts strung along a southern frontier. As intermediaries, the Pehuenche traded huge numbers of horses back across the cordillera, affording the Chilean Mapuche cavalries a decisive military advantage over the colonists, who had far fewer horses. In that the more northerly passes in the high Andes were precipitous and dangerous, the Spaniards did not enjoy the same ease of access to the pampas. As Spanish settlements were subjected to unrelenting raids, thousands of women and children were abducted as slaves or later exchanged for manufactured goods. In fact,

FIGURE 10.4. Gaucho with boleadora. Drawing by Alberto Guiraldez (Tinker 1964:55).

so high was the rate of miscegenation that the Chilean Coliqueo who traversed the pampas as far as the Atlantic to raid Buenos Aires were known as the "Blonde Indians" (Aldunate del Solar 1992:32–41; Jones 1999:148; Schwartz and Salomon 1999:474).

So vast were the numbers of feral horses teeming the pampas that the Tehuelche, former pedestrian hunters of the wild camelid guanaco and the rhea ostrich, now switched to mounted predation. Riding with wooden bits, saddle, and toe stirrups for their bare feet, the Amerindians adapted their *bola* weapon to equestrian hunting. The bola (or *boleadora*) comprised two or three straps of leather each bearing at one end a leather-wrapped stone ball that could be hurled at the neck or legs of a running animal to arrest its flight (Cooper 1963:14–15; Burri 1968:22). But horses were not the only introduced animals proliferating on the South American prairies: thousands of feral cattle, fierce beasts that could kill cougars with their sharp horns, also swarmed across the grasslands. During the seventeenth century on the pampa a new equestrian adventurer, the *gaucho*, emerged (Fig. 10.4) – as would later the *huaso* in Chile, the *chalan* in Peru, the *llanero* in Venezuela, and the *vaquero* in Mexico. In

375

Argentina, great expeditions set out across the pampas to hunt the feral cattle for their hides and tallow – tallow that would provide candle illumination to the European masses. Long convoys of oxcarts struggled through storms and Amerindian attacks until sighting a feral herd. Then half a dozen gauchos riding in semicircle drove off a group of a few hundred beasts. Galloping at full speed, the gaucho deftly slashed the hamstrings of a beast before him, letting it fall to the ground as he charged on to his next prey. A single man might strike down as many as 100 bulls in one day; assuredly in a few days the party would down 1,000. Work accomplished, the men gathered around to gorge on whole carcasses of beef cooking over the fires. This feast was accompanied by *mate*, a beverage made from the leaves of a Paraguayan plant served in a small gourd and sipped though a silver *bombilla* (straw). After the lavish banquet the gaucho rolled up in his poncho – ever his protection against sun, wind, and rain – to fall asleep on the open pampas beneath the stars, the saddle his pillow, the saddle blanket his mattress (Burri 1968:17, 26; Tinker 1964:53–54).

The gaucho was predominantly of Spanish blood but also Amerindian or Negro. His jacket and breeches often were adorned with silver buttons. His saddle and trappings were elaborated with exquisitely fashioned silverwork. On his richly ornamented belt he always carried a knife. Over his colt-leather boots, he wore *nazaremas* (double-goad spurs of solid silver with enormous rowels and sharp spikes). As *payador* (gaucho minstrel), he strummed his guitar to accompany impromptu singing of couplets, ballads, and *yarabi* – sad dirges of unrequited love (Burri 1968:23–24, 29). The ballad might vaunt the singer's own exploits, recounting the men he had killed in a criollo duel – a fight to the death with knives, the poncho held on the left arm as a shield. Or it might detail the life and feats of a courageous *matrero* (a gaucho sought by the police). The gaucho as outlaw was an ever-recurrent theme: the Inquisition even condemned and publicly burned the gaucho's mate leaves. In effect, the Argentinian national epic is a poem about the fugitive hero-matrero Martin Fierro by Jose Hernandez, the most famed of the gaucho rhymers. The poem recounts Martin's life of unending persecution: the compulsory military levy and attachment to a frontier fort, travails at the hands of corrupt military officials, skirmishes with local Amerindians – and his desertion. In an encounter with the police sent to apprehend him, single-handedly he defends himself with such valor that the brave sergeant Cruz sides with him against his own men in order to save such a gallant fighter. Fleeing the law, the two find they are both victims of the same injustice and seek refuge with an Amerindian tribe. Argentinians identify with this saga of their rebel hero. Over the centuries, in remote desert *pulperias* (canteens), illiterate gauchos gathered with their families to hear the epic stanzas of Martin Fierro recited by an itinerant reader or simply to listen to payador guitarists, like the medieval troubadours each trying to outsing the others (Burri 1968:48–49; Steiner 1995:225).

In the Argentine Wars the gaucho guerrillas fought with fanatical ferocity. Audaciously they lassoed Spanish sentinels at their watch, overwhelmed enemy camps by stampedes of horses, and, wielding boleadoras, captured the distinguished General Jose Maria Paz with their formidable flinging weapon. Gaucho cavalry in 1771 repulsed Portuguese invaders into Argentina from Uruguay and in 1807 joined Santiago Liniers's regular cavalry forces to recapture Buenos Aires from the British (Burri 1968:36–39; Tinker 1964:57–58). In the north, the lancers of the llanos of Colombia and Venezuela also vigorously combated Spanish Royalists. Their caudillo-chieftain Jose Antonio Paez commanded 1,000,000 cattle and 500,000 horses and mules in the Apure and in 1819 overwhelmed the Royalist cavalry at the battle of Las Queseras del Medio (Slatta and De Grummond 2003:160, 182). Without the support of Paez's intrepid llaneros, it is doubtful that Simon Bolivar would have succeeded in the national war of Liberation. Patriotic exploits transformed these rough, illiterate horsemen into romantic folk heroes whose virile virtues and adventures were extolled in song by *cantadores* across the land (Tinker 1964:58–59). The Mexican Revolution of the early twentieth century too had its vaquero heroes. The *cancioneros* of Mexico in their *corrido* songs extolled the bravery of Emiliano Zapata. During Pancho Villa's assault on the city of Celaya, at night around campfires, soldiers and *soldaderas* – incredible Amazon women who, often with a baby on their back, accompanied their men to the front and were ever ready to snatch a rifle from the wounded to carry on the fray – would listen to the verses of cancioneros. Dramatically, these songs were not of wars long past but of the day's battle, in which the conduct of generals, acts of individual heroism, and the hopes of the Revolution were eulogized (Tinker 1964:62–64).

With the annexation of Texas in 1845, the United States acquired the great plains of the Southwest with their thundering herds of feral cattle. In this epoch, the American cowboy emerged very much in the tradition of the Mexican vaquero, although centuries after his Hispano-American counterparts. "Buckaroo" was an approximation of the Spanish word *vaquero* and "cowboy" a direct translation. From the vaquero, the cowboy adopted his entire equipment: the ring bit and stock saddle the Spaniards had copied from the Moors, the latter with a horn added for roping. He wore a sombrero and chaps (*chaparreros*); he rode a bronco in the rodeo; he disciplined his horse with a quirt (*cuarta*); he roped a mustang (*mesteno*) with a lariat (*la reata*); and he called a string of horses a *remuda* and the ranch equine stock *caballada*, shortened to cavvy (Tinker 1964:50–51). Descendants of the majestic Iberian bull, longhorns were the feral cattle the cowboy rounded up as he moved west. Gauchos, vaqueros, and cowboys were the knights-errant of the Americas. Lone champion, the cowboy battled "Injuns," fought range wars, pursued cattle rustlers, and rescued heroines. Hollywood cowboy epics, whose solar themes reflect ordeals of ancient eras, have enjoyed acclaim worldwide: *Butch Cassidy and the Sundance Kid*, *Dual in the Sun*, and *High Noon*, their lyrics capturing the heroism and romance of the Wild West. In the twentieth-century chanson de geste *High Noon*, it is Will Kane's wedding day and final day as lawman. But an outlaw with his cronies is headed back to town at noon to get revenge against the sheriff. The theme of unrequited love first echoes plaintively:

> Do not forsake me, oh my darling
> On this our wedding day . . .

Bound by chivalric code of honor, however, Kane knows he must stay to face the gunslingers.

> Oh to be torn betwix' love and duty
> Supposin' I lose my fair-haired beauty
> Look at the big hand move along
> Nearin' high noon

The melancholy ballad continues; like the hero Rustam, Kane chooses likely death rather than the shame of avoiding battle:

> I do not know what fate awaits me
> I only know I must be brave
> And I must face a man who hates me
> Or lie a coward, a craven coward
> Or lie a coward in my grave.

Repeatedly betrayed by deputy and townsfolk, finally at high noon Kane moves to face the gunmen. As gunshots ring out, his bride, Amy, rushes impulsively to where one desperado has already been shot dead.

Seizing his gun, this Amazon fair-haired beauty goes in search of her husband. Ambushed, Will escapes from a stable riding low as he stampedes the horses. Amy kills one of the gunslingers attempting to shoot her wounded husband but is seized by the evil Turanian outlaw. Will walks toward his enemy ready to throw down his guns to save his bride, but as Amy struggles valiantly our champion is able to shoot his opponent dead.

HORSES ARE US

THROUGHOUT THIS BOOK, WE HAVE TRACED HORSE CULTURE FROM its steppe origins as it radiated out across Eurasia and North Africa to revolutionize Old World civilizations; in the preceding chapter we documented the impact of the warhorse on the New World, where the wild horse had long been extinct. In that the domesticated horse had influenced Old World cultures for nearly 6,000 years before it reached the Americas, it is almost as if there existed on the planet two experiments in human civilization – one horsed, the other horseless. It might therefore be instructive to compare the two hemispheres at time of contact in terms of the effects of horse presence and absence on the development of human culture. Then we might document the historical consequences of horse culture spreading to other horseless regions beyond the oceans, the horse's diverse impact worldwide, and the pluses and minuses of the enduring horse legacy we carry with us into the modern mechanized era.

Hemispheres with and without Horses

In the Old World, agriculture, metallurgy, and circumscribed alluvial civilization all preceded horse domestication. All three developments occurred indigenously in the New World, although a little later than in the Old.

AGRICULTURE. Diamond (1999) has rightly emphasized that ingenious inventions occur in every human society, but societies necessarily are constricted by the plants and animals of their environment. In Mesoamerica, agriculture developed in the third millennium BC, its trinity of maize, beans, and squash spreading almost 13,000 km across both American continents to Canada in the north and central Chile in the south. Alluvial civilizations with their intensified systems of irrigation, chinampa, and waru-waru farming arose in the circumscribed Mesoamerican and Andean areas. But without the horse the central steppes of the Americas – the prairies and pampas – remained undeveloped for agriculture and largely uninhabited, only marginally populated along forest fringes and river valleys.

METALLURGY. In New World metallurgy, native copper was first worked around the Great Lakes and pedestrian traded c 4000 BC in North America. But unlike on the Eurasian steppes, where horsepower prospected new deposits, transported metals, and disseminated new metalworking techniques, there were no horses in North America whereby copper working diffused southward. Only millennia later, c 1500 BC, was metallurgy independently invented in Peru. Interestingly, the mobility of llama herding and transport might have aided in locating minerals in the Andes and spreading metallurgy south to Chile and Argentina and north to Colombia. But in the absence of high-speed communication, it was only c AD 650, again millennia later, that metallurgy of nonferrous metals reached Mesoamerica through maritime contacts. While Amerindian metallurgists in the two nuclear areas produced great artistic masterpieces in gold and silver, there was little or no industrial communication and interstimulation between centers. Iron, although used as flux, was not indigenously manufactured in the New World. Thus the Spaniards' Toledo steel, the product of centuries-long international experimentation afforded by horse communication and transport, was met only by wooden Aztec swords set with obsidian blades and copper arrowheads and in the Andes bronze mace heads and spearpoints.

TRADE. Horsepower also affected trade on both land and sea. In the Old World Achaemenid and Qin empires of the first millennium BC, after their equestrian conquests both Persian and Chinese rulers embarked on ambitious programs of road construction over thousands of kilometers to promote trade across many regions. Darius I additionally organized the building of a canal from Suez to Bubastis on the Nile to facilitate traffic between the Indus delta and the Mediterranean. Similarly Shi Huangdi improved water transportation in his empire by building canals connecting the interior of China to the southern port of Pan-yu (Canton), thereby stimulating overseas trade. Following Han emperor Wudi's opening up of contacts with Ferghana in Central Asia and the greatly increased volume of trade overland along the Silk Road, maritime commerce also swelled between China and the West. Nor should one forget North Africa. The second-millennium-BC horse penetration of the Sahara and subsequent gold trade with the Sahel very likely spurred the first-millennium-BC Phoenician expansion along the Mediterranean littoral of North Africa and most certainly prompted the eventual exploration by Carthage of the West African Atlantic coast in an attempt to establish direct maritime access to sub-Saharan sources of gold. By contrast, in the horseless New World, Mesoamerican commodities were traded in small loads on foot by human porters who averaged per day only 23 kg over a distance of 21–28 km, carrying turquoise from Mesoamerica's furthermost northern borders in the American Southwest and cacao from Guatemala in the south. In the Andean area, llama transport made more extensive trade possible. But the llama was only able to carry 46 kg over a distance of 19 km per day, which compared poorly to the transport capability of the horse, donkey, and mule. For the swift conveyance of messages and light objects, the Inkas depended on a relay service of *chasqui* (human runners), who while amazingly fast did not come close to the 400-km-per-day capability of Genghis Khan's crack Arrow Messengers. In sum, without the existence of rapid, high-volume overland trade there was no great stimulus for bulk maritime transportation in the New World, even though watercraft on Lake Titicaca had the capability of transporting loads up to 130 tons. On the coast, the oceangoing balsa sailing rafts that plied the Pacific from Ecuador to Mesoamerica carried only low-bulk, prestige items, as did vessels in the Caribbean.

DISSEMINATION OF IDEAS AND INVENTIONS. That the horseless New World was less characterized by intensive, long-distance communication and trade meant ideas and inventions diffused less effectively than in the horse-powered Old World. Amerindian religions, whose great ceremonial temples were centers of sacred pilgrimage, were regionally delimited. As is well known, the Inka empire had no system of writing; for its imperial accounting it depended instead on the ingenious knotted quipu. But this computing device was never utilized in Mesoamerica. Conversely, neither were the writing systems of Mesoamerica ever introduced into South America. This contrasts markedly with the adoption of writing in the Old World, where following his conquests, Darius I established Aramaic with its consonantal script as the official lingua franca of his equestrian empire, thus fusing the heterogeneous population into a unified culture and spawning in nearby Arabia and India related advanced writing systems eventually used in those great civilizations. Later equestrians acted similarly. Alexander introduced the Greek alphabet to the Indo-European languages of the Silk Road. Illiterate Genghis Khan, immediately recognizing the value of writing, had Uighur script adapted to Turkish and Mongol over his far-flung empire. Another invention, every bit as important as writing, was the Mayan zero, which predated the Hindu zero by 500 years. The Mayan zero was not merely a placeholder representing an empty space but had a specific value, a fixed place on the number line. Because the Mayan calendar was created at a time when the zero had already been conceptualized, it was superior to Old World calendars. Yet whereas Old World horses swiftly sped the Hindu zero east and west across Eurasia, the Mayan zero did not extend beyond Mesoamerica and Central America. Neither did the Mesoamerican wheel! Mexico had the wheel and Peru the pack animal, but never the twain did meet.

WARFARE. The total lack of pack or draft animals also had clear political consequences for Mesoamerica, where transportation was severely restricted in terms of both load and distance. Such constraints had serious repercussions for war. It has been calculated that it was not logistically possible for Mexica armies to transport supplies for more than an eight-day round trip, obviously limiting the distance military forces could advance overland and engage in offensives. Troop movement was further hampered by the absence of formal roads,[1] compelling soldiers to travel along the narrow dirt tracks of pedestrian traders or, in order to achieve some degree of simultaneity, to strike out across country, further complicating maneuvers (Hassig 1994:15–16). Supplies could be augmented by demanding support from subordinate towns en route, but this further slowed down the pace, stripping away any element of tactical surprise (Hassig 1994:24–25). Compared to the 110-km-per-day advance of Mongol equestrian armies, Mexica progress was painfully slow. As a consequence, the Mexica never achieved the territorial empire of Persia or Rome. Mexica expanded instead as a hegemonic empire, vanquishing cities, exacting tribute, and terrorizing tributaries

---

[1] In the Yucatan, the Classic Maya had a number of formal roads.

into continued submission by its fearsome program of human sacrifice. Like Teotihuacan before them, the Mexica never ruled unchallenged over a unified region. In the west earlier in the fifteenth century the Tarascans had soundly defeated the Aztecs. In the east the Tlaxcalan confederacy was ever resistant (Hassig 1994:33–35). With their llamas and roads, the Inkas ruled a larger empire stretching 3,000 km along the length of the Andes. But without horses they too were vulnerable to rebellion. Earlier Andean states had been relatively short lived. With Huayna Capac's death, the Inka empire had split in two with Atahualpa strongly mistrusting his refractory allies on the northern coast. As the conquistador astride his tough Spanish steed moved with amazing speed over great distances, disenchanted Inka allies readily defected to the steel-armed invader.

Let us pause here to explore a brief hypothesis. What if at the end of the Pleistocene *Equus* had survived in the New World while becoming extinct in the Old World? At Los Toldos in Patagonia, Dillehay (2000:211) reports fossil remains of wild horse dating to as late as 7000 BC. This means the horse finally became extinct in the New World a mere 3,000 years before its domestication in the Old World. In the context of 60 million years of equid evolution, this time period is negligible and the proposition suggested not outside the realm of possibility. Without *Equus*, Old World civilizations likely would have remained isolated in their alluvial valleys each pursuing its unique cultural accomplishments. The Central Asian interior would have remained undeveloped, as did the windswept steppes on all other continents of the planet. Highways thousands of kilometers long would not have been constructed. No far-ranging lingua franca with accompanying script would have been introduced. No standardization of money, weights, and measures would have been established across vast areas. The great inventions of iron, paper, steel, printing, gunpowder, and the zero might never have diffused across Eurasia. And the world today would be very different. Conversely, with equids grazing the prairies and pampas of the western hemisphere, New World domestication of the horse might well have developed. With horsepower, copper working of the Great Lakes region almost surely would have diffused southward, early jump-starting metallurgy across both continents. The Mesoamerican wheel, invented originally for toys, would have facilitated the transition from pack animal to draft. As trade networks grew more extensive, metal coinage would have replaced cacao beans as currency, and a lingua franca[2] would have become established across vast trading areas, probably accompanied by adaptations of Mesoamerican writing. As literacy spread, the Mayan zero, developed half a millennium before Hindu numerals in Asia, might have reached the Andean area to enhance the computational capability of the quipu. In turn Inka engineering expertise in road, bridge, and tunnel construction would have been adopted by Mesoamericans to extend their influence across North America.

New World watercraft was highly evolved. Amerindians plied the ocean in sailed and keeled balsa rafts, transported loads of 130,000 kg across Lake Titicaca, and with fleets of swift canoes provisioned the Mexica capital, twice the size of medieval Paris. As rapid overland trade increased, maritime commerce would have swelled along the Pacific coast and across the Caribbean to the North American chiefdoms of the Mississippi Valley. Doubtless, regional conflicts would have arisen. Chariotry need not have evolved in the same manner as in the Old World, but assuredly the horse would have featured prominently in war. Hardy Amerindian mariners with horses on board might even have ventured up the Atlantic coast across Greenland to invade horseless Eurasia.

But no, the horse was domesticated in the Old World, and it was the Spaniard on horseback who conquered the New World. Guns and steel accompanied the Spanish equestrian warrior and undeniably contributed to his success. However, the harquebus of that time was erratic and very slow to reload. Of course, the Norse, with iron and gunpowder, had preceded Cortes and Pizarro to the New World, as had Columbus's castaways on Hispaniola with their guns and steel. But in 500 years of prowling the North Atlantic waters, the Vikings, scarcely novices to the art of bloody warfare, failed to establish a firm foothold on North America. Without horses, both the Norse and Columbus's handpicked crew of stalwart seamen succumbed to Amerindian counteroffensives. Gonzalo Pizarro's expedition into the Amazon was well equipped with steel and guns, but his horses, mired in the mud of the rain forest, were ineffective and his firearms of little consequence. Let us remember also that Cortes at the battle of Otumba was without gunpowder; all ammunition had been lost in the lake as he escaped Tenochtitlan. Yet dogged,

---

[2] Lingua franca, already evidenced indigenously in the widespread use of Quechua as a consequence of llama mobility, with the horse would have been even more widely manifested in trade on both American continents.

repeated charges on horseback finally repulsed the overwhelming numbers of Aztec warriors pursuing the desperate Spaniards.

The military importance of the horse can perhaps be best exemplified by the example of the Plains Indians. Spanish settlers with horses reached the American Southwest at the end of the sixteenth century, where their herds were initially raided by mounted Apache. By 1640 the Shoshonean Comanche, nomadic foragers of the arid Great Basin – people literally without farming – obtained the horse. Later, with herds of thousands, without steel or guns they dominated the southern plains of Texas, threatening the frontiers of the Spanish empire. By the end of the century the horse had reached tribes on the northern plains; another 50 years later it was in Canada and across the northern Rockies. In time, tribes acquired both guns and steel, but the bow and arrow long remained the preferred weapon of the mounted Plains warrior. In dramatic parallel the Mapuche, obtaining many more horses than the Spaniards through indigenous trans-Andean trade with the pampas, reversed the tide of European predatory expansion, terrorizing and enslaving many thousands of whites across Chile. Whereas the mighty but horseless Mexica and Inka empires crumbled in a matter of months before the Spanish equestrian invader, in both North and South America, once in possession of the horse Amerindian tribes fiercely resisted white advance for three centuries. In gaucho armies, Amerindians fought valiantly in Latin American wars of independence. Nor was the Amerindian defeated militarily in North America. At Little Big Horn in 1876, the Sioux and Cheyenne decisively routed Custer and his elite Seventh Cavalry. The Plains tribes finally lost their struggle against advancing American industrial society, largely because their subsistence environment was wantonly devastated.

Pre-Columbian Amerindians in Mesoamerica and the Andes were responsible for astonishing cultural accomplishments: wondrous artistic masterpieces that dazzled the civilized world; in metallurgy, alloys achieved later in modern times only by complex electrochemical processes; sophisticated textile manufacture; imposing architecture; major engineering feats; oceangoing ships; diverse and sophisticated farming techniques; marvelous cultigens shortly to be exported to every other continent to boost agricultural productivity worldwide; writing with pictographic, logographic, and phonetic features (Marcus 1992:19); astronomy; the world's most accurate calendar; and in mathematics, the zero. But Amerindians did not enjoy the cross-cultural interconnectivity afforded by horsepower. Without rapid communication and dissemination of ideas across continents, their superb inventions remained largely in the region of origin. Thus in the sixteenth century, the Spaniards' arrival with their warhorses, in a hemisphere where the horse had long been extinct, abruptly eclipsed two great indigenous civilizations. It need be noted, however, that the conquistador had neither domesticated the horse nor invented gunpowder or steel. The Spanish knight was simply the fortunate beneficiary of thousands of years of Eurasian and North African breeding and training of the horse for war and the diffusion over many thousands of kilometers by the horse of lethal inventions developed in numerous centers across Asia, Africa, and Europe. On the westernmost periphery of Europe, Spain fortuitously was located closest to the most direct transatlantic route to the New World.

The Impact of Equestrianism around the World

Having compared and contrasted the Old and New Worlds in terms of historical horse presence and absence, let us attempt to assess the impact of expansionistic horsepower at the global level.

RELIGION. One area in which the horse's influence is evident worldwide is in the sphere of religion. There are probably hundreds of different religions in the world, but as was seen in the indigenous Americas, most exist only at a regional level; they do not span continents. The world's most populous religions, Christianity, Islam, Hinduism, and Buddhism, however, extend over many countries and have approximately 2.1 billion, 1.5 billion, 900 million, and 376 million adherents respectively (Major Religions Ranked by Size 2005). Each of these four religions is integrally connected to equestrianism. Beginning with the most ancient, Hinduism is the end product of Vedism-Brahmanism, the religion of the equestrian Indo-Aryans, whose migrations from the steppes of Central Asia to the subcontinent began in the second millennium BC; established throughout India, Hinduism secondarily diffused by sea to Southeast Asia. Buddhism, an offshoot of Brahmanism, starting from India in the first millennium BC was carried by horse along the caravan routes of Central Asia to reach Afghanistan, Nepal, Tibet, Transoxania, Tarim, and China; it too subsequently diffused by sea to Southeast Asia. Christianity began as an offshoot of Judaism in the Near East, whence it diffused by horse in monophysite form to Egypt and Ethiopia, in Nestorian form along the Silk Road to Central Asia and

China, and in western form with the Roman cavalries to Europe; subsequently Catholic and Orthodox missionaries and Teutonic knights carried the religion to its northern European boundaries. Christianity became the rallying cause for European resistance to the Asian invader, later serving to pacify colonized people of distant continents. Rivals of Rome and Persia, the Arabs with their desert horses sped Islam east to Talas and the lower Indus, west to Toledo, and south to Ghana. Later Turkic-Mongol conversion took Islam overland to the trade termini of northern China, and as maritime commerce swelled, the religion spread overseas to the ports of Indonesia and southwest China. These four world religions emerged between 2000 BC and AD 1000 at a time when equestrian empires were being forged. Reflecting this, all four religions are replete with horse imagery: Indra had his battle chariot, horses, and thunderbolt, the white horse representing the primeval force that moves at the speed of light; Prince Siddhartha departed on his Great Renunciation astride the white horse Kanthaka, and outside Luoyang, China, the White Horse Buddhist temple was built by the Han emperor to honor missionaries arriving from the west; England's patron saint George, mounted on a white steed, battled the evil dragon; during the miraculous Night Journey, the Prophet Muhammad alighted on the winged white horse Buraq to ascend through the seven levels of Islamic heaven; and in the Shiite *Taziyeh* the riderless white horse dramatically symbolized the martyrdom of Imam Husayn. Purposefully it would seem, Christ was conspicuous in riding a donkey. All four horse-sped religions today are represented on every continent in temples, churches, and mosques, where they are spiritually embraced by 72 percent of humanity.

LANGUAGE DISTRIBUTION. The horse has also been instrumental in the spread of the world's major language groups. Today, well over one-third of the world's 6.5 billion people speak Indo-European as their first language. One might be tempted to attribute this number to recent European maritime-equestrian expansion around the globe starting in the sixteenth century. But Indo-European speakers number only 870 million, 10 million, and 24 million respectively in the Americas, South Africa, and Australasia. It appears that the vast majority of Indo-European speakers inhabits Eurasia and that this distribution is not a product of post-fifteenth-century European expansion but rather of equestrian expansion thousands of years ago. Of course with

Mongol-Turkic conquests, the explosive spread of Altaic languages,[3] extending over 100 degrees of longitude, has almost entirely displaced Indo-European from Central Asia and Anatolia. Notwithstanding, still today some seven million Iranian speakers continue to populate Tajikistan on the borders of China, and thousands more extend across Xinjiang. Within the borders of Afghanistan, Turkey, Iran, Pakistan, India, Sri Lanka, Bangladesh, and Nepal, for centuries battlegrounds of equestrian armies, there persist over one billion Indo-European speakers, coexisting with Turkish, Tibeto-Burman, Austro-Asiatic, and Arabic speakers alongside the next most populous subgroup – the 221 million Dravidian speakers mostly of southern India and Sri Lanka (Gordon 2005), survivors of the Indo-Aryan invasions from the north millennia ago.

Another large linguistic bloc in Asia resulting from early equestrianism is the category of Sino-Tibetan speakers, principally the Chinese, who number more than a billion. While Mandarin and 10 closely related Chinese languages are spoken by the majority of Chinese, there also exist several distinct non–Sino-Tibetan language families that today have fragmented distribution across southern China. Earlier these non–Sino-Tibetan speakers occupied more extensive territories in central China, as evidenced by the Austro-Asiatic loanword *jiang* "river" for the Yangtze River. This linguistic fragmentation is well documented historically in reports of the Zhou dynasty, which described ancient militaristic expansion by Chinese-speaking states into non–Chinese-speaking areas (Boltz 1999:81–82; Rawson 1999:449). Conquest was finalized c 221 BC by Qin Shi Huangdi's intensive chariot and cavalry campaigns that succeeded in unifying China into one imperial state, thus dominating and linguistically converting large segments of the non–Chinese-speaking peoples. The end result is that in contrast to the one billion plus Chinese speakers, only remnant groups of some 25 million non–Sino-Tibetan speakers remain in southern China. Just as Manco Inka's forces sought refuge from Spanish cavalry east in the Amazonian tropical forest to escape the Qin equestrian war machine, most of these Hmong-Mien (Miao-Yao), Tai-Kadai, and Austro-Asiatic speakers fled south into tropical Southeast Asia, where over 100 million of them live today, intermingled with the earlier Austronesian population (Comrie, Matthews, and Polinsky

---

3 Facilitated, of course, by the acquisition of the domesticated horse from Indo-European nomads.

1996:64–65). In contrast to other Indo-European expansions, the Chinese were able to absorb invading nomads from the steppes without relinquishing their Sinitic language. They did, however, adopt the steppe horse, chariot, and iron technology to extend their rule south and to impose their language over a vast area.

Comparable events occurred in the Afro-Asiatic equestrian expansion in North Africa. Starting in the second millennium BC, Afro-Asiatic–speaking charioteers (ancestors of modern Cushitic, Chadic, and Berber peoples) sped across the Sahara displacing Negroid agriculturalists from desert oases. Later, in the first millennium BC, iron-wielding mounted slavers attacked the Negro populations along the Sahel,[4] impelling many inhabitants of the region to move south and east through the rain forests to occupy the central and southern regions of Africa. With Muslim expansion in the eighth century AD, another Afro-Asiatic language, Arabic, diffused westward from the Middle East across North Africa. It is important to note that in all three invasions, whether Indo-European, Chinese, or Afro-Asiatic, equestrian expansion south was mainly stopped at the tropical forest. Just as soggy marshes saved Venice and Ravenna from invaders from the steppes and the spring thaw saved Novgorod, the horse, evolved in semiarid climes, was definitely unsuited to dense rain forests and jungle warfare. The Chinese repeatedly attempted expansion southward, but as we have seen, even the Mongol Yuan could not consolidate conquest in tropical Southeast Asia. In general, the linguistic map shows this demarcation: the divide on the Indian subcontinent between northern Indo-Aryan speakers and Dravidian speakers in the south; the divide in the Far East between the Chinese bloc in the north and the diverse Austro-Asiatic, Tai Kadai, Hmong-Mien, and Austronesian speakers in the tropical south; and the divide in Africa between the Afro-Asiatic speakers of the northern desert and the more southerly Niger-Congo speakers. Interestingly, the tropical-forest linguistic divide is also apparent in South America. Gonzalo Pizarro's equestrian invasion of the Amazon rain forest in 1541 was a total fiasco. Whereas Spanish equestrian expansion for the most part proceeded unimpeded across arid, highland, and temperate zones, colonization of the humid forested interior of the Amazon basin was left to the Portuguese to accomplish principally through river navigation and later firepower, a fact reflected clearly in Brazil's position on

---

[4] Horses could not penetrate deep into the African rain forest on account of the tsetse fly.

the political map of South America. Across different continents, equestrian invasions have influenced the distribution of linguistic groups to a significant degree.

Let us remember from Chapter 1 how, at the end of the Miocene, drastic global climate change adversely affected the widely successful hipparionines, specialized in tridactyl adaptation to wetlands. Increasing aridization continuing into the Pliocene selected against them and favored the *Equini*, whose monodactyly was eminently suited to drier terrains. From the above, it can be seen that in recent times the monodactyl horse, donkey, and mule have disproportionately advantaged human cultures in temperate and drier regions, allowing their inhabitants over the centuries to play a dominant political and economic role.

COLONIAL EXPANSION. By the last quarter of the sixteenth century, one lethal invention – artillery – was to sound the death knell of the armored knight. Following improvements to the harquebus, the appearance of the pistol finally drove the armored knight and his lance from the battlefield (Vale 1981:146). Poised between medieval and modern, when not astride Rocinante jousting windmills, Don Quixote saw fit to decry: "Blessed be those happy ages that were strangers to the dreadful fury of these devilish instruments of artillery, whose inventor I am satisfied is now in Hell, receiving the reward of his cursed invention" (Cervantes 1925:402; quoted by Vale 1981:129).

Having fought in 1571 with the Christian fleets at Lepanto, tasting victory at sea and recognizing the full import of the conquest of the Americas, Cervantes depicted the world in transition around him with deep satire. But if steel armor had been rendered obsolete by firearms, the warhorse had not. As New World wealth flowed back to Europe, nations of the Atlantic seaboard, previously only a side act to the classic Mediterranean, now took to the oceans. Heavy artillery, notably cannons, was mounted aboard ships. In what has been termed the "European maritime expansion," Atlanto-Europeans would navigate to the furthermost reaches of the planet, an expansion certainly with gunboats but also with that key element, the warhorse. In these explorations, the Spanish Conquista would be their model – and their primary objective to colonize new lands beyond the seas.

In the course of their grand design to outflank Islam by circumnavigating Africa, the Portuguese by 1471 had settled forts along the African coast. Unable to penetrate the tropical forest regions by horse because of the tsetse fly, the Portuguese mounted these fortifications to protect their lucrative gold trade inland against other European sea-farers (Oliver and Fage 1966:108, 113–114). But as plantation systems were developed on the offshore islands of the Canaries and Cape Verde and then introduced into the Caribbean and Brazil respectively by the Spanish and Portuguese, the need for agricultural labor increased in tropical America, and Portuguese trading for slaves ensued. With increased European demand for sugar in the seventeenth century, competition in the Caribbean between Holland, France, and England mounted, and the transatlantic slave trade correspondingly intensified. Whereas slightly less than one million Negro slaves had been landed in the Americas before 1600, close to three million were shipped in the seventeenth century, seven million in the eighteenth century, and four million in the nineteenth. For human cargo, slave traders exchanged textiles, metal goods, horses, and firearms. With guns acquired in trade, Africans from the coast ventured deep into the interior to capture slaves for export (Oliver and Fage 1966:118–121).

Earlier, it was mentioned that nineteenth-century experiments in har-nessing the zebra had been abandoned by the Boers due largely to that animal's irascibility; despite the zebra's resistance to sleeping sickness, this equid was as unsuited to traction and riding as its cousin the onager. But one is tempted to speculate what would have happened if the zebra had been amenable to domestication by Africans. Even today hundreds of thousands of zebras teem the African savannahs. Surely the his-tory of Africa would have been very different if advancing slavers had been met by zebra cavalry. As in Japan's defeat of Mongol invasions, indigenous mounted warriors wielding iron might well have repelled even invaders equipped with early firearms and thus saved millions of human victims from death or deportation in the slave trade. This could equally have been true of South Africa, where in the seventeenth century, to provision their vessels sailing on the trade winds to the East Indies, the Dutch established a small colony. The following century, Calvinist Boers with the ancient steppe assemblage of horses, sheep, goats, cattle, and covered wagons advanced northeastward across the dry veldt toward the zone of higher rainfall, displacing or destroying Khoisan indigenous people en route. On this trek the horse was critical, scouting for scarce water and protecting herd animals against ferocious predators. In 1799 the Boers reached the monsoon region, frontier of the populous Bantu agriculturalists along the Great Fish River, where-upon began the Kaffir Wars that would last a century (Oliver and Fage

1966:160–163). If the Zulu military genius Shaka had commanded zebra cavalry, there might never have been apartheid.

But instead the Boers, mounted on horseback, prevailed. At the Battle of Blood River in 1838, Andries Pretorius with a slender force of 500 defeated some 10,000 Zulu foot warriors by daringly ordering simultaneous sorties of armed horsemen from his *laager* ring of wagons (Child 1967:67). Virulent epizootic diseases prevailing across much of Africa prevented the Zulus in their hot wet coastlands from breeding horses of their own. But to assess the military importance of the horse in this setting, one need only view the unique case of the nearby Basotho, whose rugged territories in the Drakensberg mountains just outside the tropic were remarkably free from horse disease on account of altitude, thereby making horse rearing possible. By 1830 with horses and arms, Basotho mounted warriors were competently repelling the raids of their far more numerous Zulu and Boer neighbors. And in 1851 their king Moshoeshoe successfully fielded 7,000 armed cavalry against a British expeditionary force. By subsequently negotiating a British protectorate, the Basotho were able to escape apartheid – the fate of so many other southern Africans – their country to become today's independent modern nation of Lesotho (Bardill and Cobbe 1985: 9, 13–20; Child 1967:45–48). In the course of the nineteenth century, the British crossed thoroughbreds with the Arab stock early imported by the Boers to the Cape to produce the "Caper," a nimble-footed horse of extraordinary endurance, well adapted to the harsh climate of the high veldt and subsequently deployed to other British military operations overseas (Yarwood 1989:30–31). However, in their failed 1806–1807 invasions of Buenos Aires from the Cape, the British notably met their match against Liniers's spirited gaucho cavalry of the pampas. As will be seen, Britain would need horses from yet another continent in order to furnish all the warhorses required in its program of imperial expansion.

European expansion, of course, had continued across the Indian Ocean along the southern shores of Asia, where different nations competed for control of the spice trade. With the East India Company's defeat of the Portuguese in India, Britain won trading concessions from the Mughal emperor. By the end of the eighteenth century, Britain had introduced horse artillery into her armies. Early pioneered by Russian and Polish cavalries, horse artillery was first systematically developed in 1759 by Frederick the Great, whose relentless drills and discipline made artillery speed and mobility a critical element in military operations. It was soon adopted by every continental army. The French in particular made excellent use of this formidable new artillery arm, Napoleon deploying it to devastating effect in all his great victories. In this mode of combat, the guns were drawn by teams of horses, driven by men mounted on their backs postilion-wise, with some men riding on the gun limbers. This was a totally new technique of rapid maneuver that enormously enhanced the value of the cavalry. But it did more than purely support mounted action. It could be as deadly in the advance-guard work of outposts as in withdrawals, when horse artillery would delay retreat to the last second, dashing away to better terrain to resume the attack. In Buenos Aires, horse artillery under Whitelocke had not brought success. However, in Britain's overseas colonies, notably South Africa and India, horse artillery would be deployed extremely effectively (Bidwell 1973:2–3, 16–17).

It was in Assam that the British first played polo, the sport anciently diffused to India from Iran. British tea planters learned the game from the Manipuris and formed the Silchar polo club in 1859. The game with eight players to a team had almost no rules but was soon adopted by British cavalry units in India whence it spread worldwide (Singh 1971:11). Further to the east, even though engaging in oceanic exploration in response to continuing nomad threat, China had been a lot less successful than Spain in countering continental equestrian might. After their expulsion from China, the Mongols had continued to exercise considerable power from the steppe, pillaging border regions, raiding to the gates of Beijing, once even capturing a Ming emperor. Allied with these Mongol descendants of Genghis Khan, in 1644 the Tungusic Manchus invaded to conquer the whole of China (Barfield 1993:166–167). Initially, the Qing dynasty was more successful than India in opposing European penetration. Chinese resistance, however, was subverted by the opium trade, which a joint British-French military force succeeded in legalizing through imposition of the Peking Convention in 1860. Japan with its equestrian tradition staunchly resisted foreign intrusion by quickly acquiring western firearms. European colonization extended further east into the Pacific, causing epidemics that decimated the indigenous populations of Fiji, Hawaii, Tonga, Australia, and other islands (Diamond 1999:78).

In 1787 a stallion, three mares, and three colts were the first horses to arrive in Australia, sharing the rigors of the voyage from the Cape of Good Hope with British convicts. In the new penal colony the horse was at first such a scarce item that many a convict was cruelly lashed and chained into traction. With time more horses arrived, English thorough-breds but also Arab and Persian stock from India. Horses accompanied the first explorers across the Blue Mountains; stock breeders and set-tlers then pressed on into the steppe interior to traverse the continent, later deploying the camel. These vast arid lands, never before experi-enced by the wild horse in 60 million years of its evolution, now saw a rapid proliferation of feral horses – brumbies. With equable climate, abundant open grazing across rugged terrain, and cheap convict and Aboriginal labor, horse rearing thrived, nowhere more so than in New South Wales, where limestone valleys ensured good bone production in horses of surpassing beauty. "Waler" thus became the name of the Australian horse.

By contrast, in India good horses were in short supply. Historically, conquerors of northern India, whether Aryan, Kushan, Ghaznavid, Timurid, or Mughal, had derived their warhorses from semiarid regions to the northwest. On the Gangetic plain the British found the local stock inferior. Intensive agriculture allowed for no open pasture; horses were therefore hobbled for grazing, resulting in poor development of limbs and chest. Insufficient exercise in India's lengthy hot season quickly rendered mares infertile, thereby preventing breeding of indigenous stock. In attempts to procure horses suitable for war, the British fran-tically scoured nomad territories from Baluchistan to Tibet, even jour-neying to faraway Bokhara. It is known that during the sixteenth cen-tury, drawing on the ancient horse-breeding grounds of the Ferghana valley, Bokhara exported 100,000 horses annually to the Mughal empire (Anthony 2007:341; Levi 2002:58–59). British attempts at prospecting for warhorses in Central Asia, however, were thwarted by Russian encroachment and nomad turbulence in the region. To compound the problem, horse imports from South Africa had been interrupted by epi-demics of epizootic disease. In desperation, Great Britain turned to that remote arid continent on the southern periphery of the world.

Very soon into the nineteenth century, Australia was shipping tens of thousands of military horses overseas each year for campaigns in British colonies of Africa and Asia. Battling in Afghanistan against mounted warriors who were veterans of millennia of equestrian combat, Britain suffered an even more disastrous defeat than that inflicted by Argen-tine gaucho cavalries earlier in the century; in 1841 the Afghan nomads totally annihilated the British invasion force of 16,000. In India, facing opponents such as the Sikhs, whose cavalries numbered in the tens of thousands, and later confronting the Great Mutiny, the British urgently needed constant supplies of remounts for their regiments. Potent symbols of military might, cavalry and artillery horses were vital elements in Britain's rule over India's 200 million by a force of 40,000 British soldiers aided by 232,000 Indian troops (Wolpert 1993:221, 233–234). Australia supplied horses not only to the British Raj but also to the British in their intervention in the Boxer Rebellion in China; to Hong Kong, Mauritius, Singapore, and Sudan; to the Americans in the Philippines; and to the Japanese in their 1904 war against Russia. The Aussies contributed 16,357 horses to the Anglo-Boer war of 1899–1902 and 39,348 to Egypt during World War I. Between 1861 and 1931 Australia exported close to half a million horses – 355,000 to India alone (Barrie 1956:29; Colwell 1976:19–26; Yarwood 1989:25–28, 202). While Britain may have exercised gun-boat diplomacy at sea, in empire building on land it waged equestrian warfare! During the nineteenth and twentieth centuries, Britain transported across the oceans more horses to more countries than any other nation (Steele 1971:8), clearly outstripping its European rivals in colonial expansion.

Colonial Australia rivaled the American West in its coaches, horse racing, and rodeos, and later ancestral England in its fox (or dingo) hunting. From the British Indian cavalry, Australia acquired tent pegging and polo, then went on to invent its own sport, polocrosse. But just as polo was the sport of the Asian steppes, so too the game of polo came to be practiced with passion on the Australian steppe; in distant desert locales it was even played on donkeys. At the end of the nineteenth century, the Australian bard "Banjo" Paterson captured in verse the drama of the outback. His heroic epic *The Geebung Polo Club* was solemnly recited a century later by Prince Charles on an official visit to Australia:

It was somewhere up the country, in a land of rock and scrub,
That they formed an institution called the Geebung Polo Club.
They were long and wiry natives from the rugged mountain side,
And the horse was never saddled that the Geebungs couldn't ride;
But their style of playing polo was irregular and rash –
They had mighty little science, but a mighty lot of dash:
And they played on mountain ponies that were muscular and strong,
Though their coats were quite unpolished and their manes and tails
     were long.
And they used to train those ponies wheeling cattle in the scrub,
They were demons were the members of the Geebung Polo Club.

It was somewhere down the country, in a city's smoke and steam,
That the Polo club existed, called "The Cuff and Collar Team."
As a social institution 'twas a marvellous success,
For the members were distinguished by exclusiveness and dress.
They had natty little ponies that were nice, and smooth, and sleek,
For their cultivated owners only rode 'em once a week.
So they started up the country in pursuit of sport and fame,
For they meant to show the Geebungs how they ought to play the
    game;
And they took their valets with them – just to give their boots a rub
Ere they started operations on the Geebung Polo Club.

Now my readers can imagine how the contest ebbed and flowed,
When the Geebung boys got going it was time to clear the road;
And the game was so terrific that ere half the time was gone
A spectator's leg was broken – just from merely looking on.
For they waddied one another till the plain was strewn with dead,
While the score was kept so even that neither got ahead.
And the Cuff and Collar Captain, when he tumbled off to die,
Was the last surviving player – so the game was called a tie.

Then the captain of the Geebungs raised him slowly from the ground,
Though his wounds were mostly mortal, yet he fiercely gazed around;
There was no one to oppose him – all the rest were in a trance,
So he scrambled on his pony for his last expiring chance,
For he meant to make an effort to get victory to his side;
So he struck at goal – and missed it – then he tumbled off and died.

By the old Campaspe river, where the breezes shake the grass,
There's a row of little gravestones that the stockmen never pass,
For they bear a crude inscription saying, "Stranger, drop a tear,
For the Cuff and Collar Players and the Geebung Boys lie here."
And on misty moonlight evenings, while the dingoes howl around,
You can see their shadows flitting down that phantom polo ground;
You can hear the loud collisions as the flying players meet,
And the rattle of the mallets, and the rush of ponies' feet,
Till the terrified spectator rides like blazes to the pub –
He's been haunted by the spectres of the Geebung Polo Club.

(Paterson 1894:4–7)

In Australia today, as elsewhere, polo – on the Silk Road "the sport of
kings" – has become the pleasure of the megarich: princes, playboys,

and business tycoons. Polo, now regulated by many rules, is played by two opposing teams of four mounted players on a grass field 300 yd long by 160 yd wide with goals at each end. Riding at full gallop, a player scores by hitting the ball with a mallet between goalposts that still stand 8 yd apart, as in the time of Shah Abbas the Great of Persia. A game consists of six periods or *chakkars* (Sanksrit *cakra* "wheel") of 7 min duration, with intervals of 3 min between chakkars to change ponies. The game does not stop if a rider tumbles from his mount, only if his pony falls. Polo is a sport dominated internationally by the Argentines, who, proud of their gaucho heritage, hold a virtual monopoly of top ranked active 10-goal players. One wonders if modern polo grounds might not all be haunted by, in addition to the Geebung Boys, the gauchos of the pampas – perhaps even the shades of buzkashi players from the steppes.

Homo equestriens

In the early part of this book it was mentioned that while equids had evolved over a period of 60 million years, bipedal hominids first appeared a little over 6 million years ago to gradually develop the cerebral capabilities that today characterize modern *Homo sapiens*. For most of those six million years, hominids remained bipedal. Only about 6,000 years ago did the world's brainiest biped team up with the world's fastest quadruped. Most historical treatises emphasize the nuclear, sedentary nature of human civilization. This work, by contrast, has attempted to track the mobile equestrian in the course of cultural development, paying attention to periphery rather than center.

To recapitulate briefly, in the fourth millennium BC the donkey and horse were domesticated, not in the ancient nuclear centers of agriculture, but rather in marginal, suboptimal regions, the deserts of Nubia and the steppes of the Pontic-Caspian. They and their hybrids played important roles in agriculture, metallurgy, and commerce, but the horse rose to particular prominence on the Eurasian steppes, first in traversing hazardous terrains and later in equestrian warfare. As over the millennia nomads invaded from the marginal steppes to overwhelm and transform early centers of civilization, so newly equestrianized civilizations in turn vied with one another for imperial supremacy. But in the first millennium AD, Mediterranean empires were challenged from another periphery, the southern deserts, as Arab horses surged across the Middle East and North Africa. In the second millennium AD, much of Eurasia was devastated by the Mongol cyclone from the furthermost reaches of the northern steppes. In later centuries, the Ottoman successor to the Mongols advanced over land and sea to threaten Europe. To escape the Muslim stranglehold, from the westernmost fringe of the continent Spain sailed west across the Atlantic. Just as historically Asian equestrian military expansion had earlier been halted by the Greek naval victory at Salamis, island Japan's defeat of the Yuan giant, and the Mamluk-Kipchak alliance across the Black Sea, so now Spain's affront on the unknown ocean would serve as countermeasure to Old World equestrian might.

Columbus's initiative in traversing the Atlantic was in many ways analogous to the nomads' intrepid migrations millennia before across the wastes of Central Asia. From the semiarid eastern borders of agricultural Europe, agro-pastoralism had opened up the vast steppes, eventually allowing equestrian nomads to range over thousands of kilometers in their attacks on distant sedentary foes. Comparably, from Europe's far western littoral, Columbus's daring exploratory voyages and the horses he transported across the Atlantic also opened up a vast new arena for human exploitation – the high seas and the continents beyond. In subsequent maritime expansion, by transporting hundreds of thousands of horses to horseless regions around the world, Europeans successfully unlocked the resources of distant continents. Through naval mastery of the oceans encircling the continents, colonizers could now ruthlessly deploy military horsepower to trouble spots across the globe wherever needed to overcome political adversaries – whether local inhabitants of the coveted lands or rival Europeans. With this dramatic shift in geopolitics from the interior of the Eurasian land mass to the breadth of the world's oceans, conflicts between nations came to be fought on sea as well as on land. Thus the naval confrontations at the Nile and Trafalgar were every bit as decisive as the great massed cavalry battles of Austerlitz and Waterloo, the latter involving 16,000 French horsemen against 13,000 English. One final funerary equine ritual was perhaps the burial with full regimental honors accorded the warhorse of Arthur, Duke of Wellington – the military salute fired over the noble stallion's grave and a giant oak tree planted above (Brereton 1976:84). And while Paul Revere galloped through the night to earn Longfellow's immortal accolade, the American War of Independence essentially began with the defiant "tea party" in Boston Harbor; the American Civil War too commenced at sea, at Fort Sumter. Probably, the North's economic blockade of Southern ports contributed as much to the outcome of this internecine war as the cavalry charges of Union and Confederate armies did. With the increasing efficiency of artillery, equestrian warfare grew to be more perilous. The overwhelming effect of cannon fire was evidenced during the Crimean War, where Britain moved to thwart the Russian naval buildup on the Black Sea, and the charge of the Light Brigade – "the Six Hundred" – at Balaclava in 1854 was tragically memorialized by Alfred, Lord Tennyson:

> Theirs not to reason why,
> Theirs but to do and die:
> Into the valley of Death
> Rode the six hundred.
> Cannon to the right of them,
> Cannon to the left of them,
> Cannon in front of them
> Volleyed and thundered;
> Stormed at with shot and shell,
> Boldly they rode and well,
> Into the jaws of Death,
> Into the mouth of Hell
> Rode the six hundred.
>
> . . . .
>
> Cannon to the right of them,
> Cannon to the left of them,
> Cannon behind them
> Volleyed and thundered;
> Stormed at with shot and shell,
> While horse and hero fell,
> They that had fought so well
> Came through the jaws of Death,
> Back from the mouth of Hell,
> All that was left of them,
> Left of six hundred.
> (Tennyson 1987:511–513)

The very last successful deployment of mass cavalry in offensive tactics took place in the Palestinian desert in 1917, when during World War I the Australian Light Horse, shipped across the Indian ocean, charged and overran the Turks to capture Beersheba and its all-important wells. This dramatic action to defend the Suez against a capable foe was one of the most astonishing feats of the war (Yarwood 1989:180). But with the advent of tank warfare in World War II, cavalry maneuvers in battle were all but discontinued. Noble attempts by Polish cavalry forces to counter the German advance on the Eastern Front met only with disaster; horses were no match for Hitler's panzer divisions and dive bombers. In November 1941, northwest of Moscow, the 44th Mongolian Cavalry Division charged the German lines at a gallop, "stirrup touching stirrup, riders low on their horses' necks, drawn sabers over their shoulders." In 10 minutes of withering machine-gun fire, without a single German casualty, 2,000 Mongol horsemen and their horses lay dead or dying in the blood-stained snow (Brereton 1976:146, 148). Following the Battle of Stalingrad, however, the Russians successfully deployed cavalry in mopping-up operations. Remarkably, despite the twentieth century's decreasing emphasis on the horse in battle, during the twenty-first-century Allied invasion of Afghanistan, the horse once again saw combat duty with U.S. Special Forces units in the northern mountains, as did the donkey in its ancient role of beast of burden, in terrains inaccessible to motorized transport.

However, by the start of the twentieth century there had emerged yet another vast arena of human endeavor, also inspired by the horse and ever geared to greater and greater speeds – flight. On another periphery, in a North American country not yet a world power, the Wright brothers, technicians of that mechanical steed, the bicycle, launched the first successful powered flying machine at Kitty Hawk in 1904. For eons men had viewed the galloping horse as in full flight. As early as the second millennium BC men had fashioned figures of winged centaurs. Tamed and bridled by Athena, Pegasus carried thunder and lightning across the skies for Zeus. By 1914 modern winged horses – military aircraft – were carrying bombs and gunfire across the skies of Europe, as flying aces with all the daring and aplomb of medieval knights whirled in mortal combat above the trenches of World War I. By the beginning of World War II, aerial lethality had "advanced" to the level of the blitzkrieg in the obliteration of European cities. America's World War II began at the naval outpost of Honolulu, stealthily bombed by Japanese planes intent upon crippling the Pacific fleet. In the subsequent Pacific war, America was subject to suicidal kamikaze attacks by pilots, emboldened by the divine wind of their historical equestrian resistance to the invader. Half a century after the Wrights' invention, World War II ended as the United States established world dominance by aerially inflicting on Japan the thermonuclear holocausts of Hiroshima and Nagasaki. Yet another half century later, U.S. political dominance would be challenged, however, as the Pentagon and World Trade Center on 9/11 were struck in aerial raids by suicidal attackers, not ancient samurai but modern third-millennium assassins of fanatical zeal.

In considering the 6,000 years of equestrian adaptation, it was noted earlier in this book that horsepower was dual faceted: progressive yet destructive. Unquestionably, horsepower has conferred on mankind extraordinary mobility and has helped deliver phenomenal cultural achievements. Adoption of the horse has greatly increased the pace, scale, and intensity of human conflict, however. It is estimated that the Mongol invasions of China left 11 million dead. We have no figures for earlier equestrian conquests, but incontestably these too took extreme toll of human life: bloodshed, massacres, deportations, enslavement, amputation, beheadings, torture, incineration, rape, castration, famine, pestilence, and destruction. This book has documented a multitude of atrocities, and even today these horrendous crimes against humanity persist. Astride the horse, man truly has become the creature of his own imagination – centaur, part god, part beast – capable of great intellectual feats but also capable of ruthless destruction. Man's unrelenting obsession with speed continues into the modern era. After conquering the Old World from the steppes, the New World from the oceans, today with amazing celerity modern nations airlift entire armies to war zones anywhere on the planet. Man's winged technology first invaded the atmosphere; now our fiery Pegasuses hurtle through space, assuredly the arena next destined for human combat and carnage.

THIRD MILLENNIUM AD. The U.S. presidential palace, not Nero's Golden House but the White House – with its Oval Office – is situated in Washington, DC, on the Atlantic seaboard of North America, far from the steppe origins of Indo-European traditions. Nevertheless, much of the ritual that surrounds the U.S. capital is ancient. From Capitol Hill, the World Mountain, America's Temple of Jupiter, the Capitol, rises above the Potomac, its great dome emblematic of celestial blessing. Above the three-tiered dome stands the ancestral sepulchral tholos topped by the Tree of Life, not the gilded cross of Hagia Sophia but the colossal bronze Statue of Freedom. Below, in the heart of the Capitol, lies the Rotunda, crowned by the canopy of Brumidi's Apotheosis of Washington and other American heroes mingling with horses and Greco-Roman divinities in the frescoed heavens of the great dome. At the funeral of Ronald Reagan, the former president, eulogized as sun king and cowboy president, first lay in state in this solar rotunda of cyclic rebirth and political continuity. Then in funerary procession, the black artillery caisson bearing his flag-draped casket was drawn by six matched horses and followed by one lone riderless horse, since Roman times an epic symbol of the fallen warrior or deceased king. In honor of the deceased president, his riding boots were reverse positioned in the stirrups,[5] reminiscent of the European ritual of affixing a dead monarch's sword to his saddle. Then in the Scythian tradition of transporting the dead chieftain the entire breadth of the country and as the Han emperor Wudi envisaged for himself, President Reagan's casket was flown across the nation to the western mountains, where he received a sunset burial in his home state of California. At Arlington National Cemetery, a caparisoned riderless horse similarly attends the burial of every U.S. officer[6] slain in battle.

Clearly, most of us do not look forward to such spectacular ceremony in death; ritual equestrian pageantry is fittingly reserved for chieftains and great warriors. But for the rest of us, numerous equestrian elements still pervade our everyday lives. Although no longer on horseback, in keeping with our frenzied lifestyle – from fast food to high-speed Internet access to supersonic travel – men and women alike wear steppe pants, jackets, and boots. In fact, cowboy attire has long been the uniform of youth worldwide – blue jeans, nowadays as gaily embroidered as the Celtic horsemen's colorful breeches, so haughtily disdained by the Roman military. Today, the horse chariot is limited to the trotting track, and the stately carriage is pretty much reserved for British royalty or the occasional nostalgic ride around Central Park. But modern society has found itself another "sacred vehicle of heroes and the gods" – the horseless carriage. Sex symbol in youth and status emblem in adulthood, automobiles serve us daily in recreation, travel, and transportation. Economies revolve around their manufacture, and nations compete in the production of the latest streamlined models. Every year increasing numbers of cars – their engine potency measured in horsepower – teem the world's highways, their emissions along with those of industry depleting the earth's ozone layer, the massive tankers that fuel them polluting the oceans. We were only narrowly successful in saving *Equus ferus przewalskii* from extinction; as other wild species

---

[5] In funerals on the steppe the saddle often is reversed.
[6] Rank of colonel or above.

disappear daily from the earth, let us hope we can summon sufficient ingenuity to rein in our runaway technology and save our planet from global warming.

Horses are not altogether history. In undeveloped areas of the world they still perform their traditional roles in agriculture and transport and even in developed areas often are reverted to in the face of fuel crises or machinery failure. In our highly industrialized world, though, the horses with which we are most familiar are the fine animals of show jumping, horse races, polo, and hunts. The intricate dressage of the Viennese gold-bridled Lipizzan stallions, akin perhaps to the ostrich-plumed steeds of ancient Egypt or the jewel-bedecked dancing horses of Tang emperor Xuanzong, continues as spectacle to this very day. But not all horses enjoy the statuesque existence of the snow-white Andalusian Barbs of the Spanish Riding Academy of Vienna. Most horses have labored long in agriculture, industry, and war. Well into the twentieth century many thousands of pit ponies spent their entire lives working underground in mines. Of the more than one million horses and mules deployed in combat or pulling guns, field kitchens, and ambulances during World War I, less than one-tenth returned from the front. In the third millennium AD, man's world is as starkly divided as the horse's. Twenty-first-century automation may indeed have spread to economies in Asia, but half the world's population, some three billion people, currently live below the internationally defined poverty line of less than $2.00 per day, and of those, one billion live on less than $1.00 per day. Over the last 50 years, vast resources have been allocated to the exploration of outer space and the search for extraterrestrial life, while regularly each year on earth one million complex human organisms die from starvation or malnutrition. The world's richest fifth consumes 86 percent of all goods and services – more than six times that of the rest of the world (*New York Times* 1998). Despite this gargantuan inequality, the World Bank spends only 50 to 60 billion U.S. dollars a year on development worldwide, a minute fraction of the one trillion U.S. dollars expended annually on armaments by the world's nations.

As we stand on the threshold of the third millennium, looking back across history, it is as if the Trojan War never really ended: Agamemnon's triumph countered by Achaemenid imperium – then Alexander, Rome, Arab, Crusader, Mongol, Turk. The modern Middle East is ever rent by ancient rivalries: Palestinian-Israeli hostilities, Sunni-Shia conflicts, and backed by Sudanese airpower, *Janjaweed* (devils on horseback) massacres of Darfurian agriculturalists. Wars continue over vital

resources: today's Ferghana horses – the sacred petroleum that powers our divine automobile! After 6,000 years of military escalation, as
nuclear thunderbolts proliferate, perhaps we need to rein in our spirited but lethal steed? During the European colonization of the Americas,
over 50 million people died from war or disease in the space of a century and a half. In World War II 50 million died in a scant six years.
In the twenty-first century, our latest nuclear device – perhaps deto-
nated domestically – likely annihilates 50 million people in a matter of
nanoseconds. Should we not pause to rethink? In our unending quest for
acceleration, perhaps we need to seek a different form of speed – cerebral
rather than quadrupedal. A recent claim has been made (Friedman 2005)
that hostilities between nations may be reduced through the economic
interdependence afforded by modern Internet technology. Furthermore,
near-instantaneous electronic communication will allow world experts
to cooperate on issues of global warming, natural disasters, environmental degradation, endangered species, famine, epidemics, and other
crises. These electronic capabilities will bring education at all levels to
the most remote village and impoverished ghetto; similarly, medical
knowledge and surgical expertise will be shared worldwide. Maybe it
is these cerebral airways of rapid satellite communication and collaboration we need to explore next, not the "Star Wars" of galactic polo and
nuclear cavalry in outer space. As our wars continue unabated, perhaps
it is time to get off our high horse of nonstop conquest and back on two
feet on an earth racked by genocidal conflicts, depleting ozone, melting
ice caps, and disappearing coral reefs – in desperate need of a more
sapient approach to the world's challenges.

REFERENCES

Ackroyd, Joyce
 1987 Bushido. *In* The Encyclopedia of Religion. Mircea Eliade, ed. Vol. 2. Pp. 581–584. New York: Macmillan.

Adcock, F. E.
 1957 The Greek and Macedonian Art of War. Berkeley: University of California Press.

Adeleye, R. A.
 1976 Hausaland and Borno 1600–1800. *In* History of West Africa. Vol. 1. J. F. A. Ajayi and Michael Crowder, eds. Pp. 556–601. New York: Columbia University Press.

Aldunate del Solar, Carlos
 1992 Mapuche: Seeds of the Chilean Soul. Philadelphia: Port of History Museum; Museo Chileno de Arte Precolombino.

Allsen, Thomas T.
 1994 The Rise of the Mongolian Empire and Mongolian Rule in North China. *In* The Cambridge History of China. Denis Twitchett and John K. Fairbank, general eds. Vol. 6, Alien Regimes and Border States, 907–1368. Herbert Franke and Denis Twitchett, eds. Pp. 321–413. Cambridge: Cambridge University Press.
 1997 Commodity and Exchange in the Mongol Empire: A Cultural History of Islamic Textiles. Cambridge: Cambridge University Press.
 2001 Culture and Conquest in Mongol Eurasia. Cambridge: Cambridge University Press.
 2006 The Royal Hunt in Eurasian History. Philadelphia: University of Pennsylvania Press.

Amirsadeghi, Hossein, ed.
 1998 The Arabian Horse: History, Mystery, and Magic. New York: Thames and Hudson.

Amitai-Preiss, Reuven

1995 Mongols and Mamluks: The Mamluk-Ilkhanid War. Cambridge: Cambridge University Press.

And, Metin

1979 The Muharram Observances in Anatolian Turkey. *In Taziyeh*: Ritual and Drama in Iran. Peter J. Chelkowski, ed. Pp. 238–254. New York: New York University Press; Soroush Press.

Andrews, Peter Alford

1997 Nomad Tent Types in the Middle East. Part 1, Framed Tents. Vol. 1, Text. Vol. 2, Illustrations. Wiesbaden: Dr. Ludwig Reichert Verlag.

1999 Felt Tents and Pavilions: The Nomadic Tradition and Its Interaction with Princely Tentage. Vol. 1. London: Melisende.

Anthony, David W.

1990 Migration in Archaeology: The Baby and the Bathwater. American Anthropologist 92(4):895–914.

1991a The Domestication of the Horse. *In* Equids in the Ancient World. R. Meadow and H. P. Uerpmann, eds. Vol. 2. Pp. 250–277. Wiesbaden: Dr. Ludwig Reichert Verlag.

1991b The Archaeology of Indo-European Origins. Journal of Indo-European Studies 19(3–4):193–222.

1994 The Earliest Horseback Riders and Indo-European Origins: New Evidence from the Steppes. *In* Die Indogermanen und das Pferd. Bernard Hansel and Stefan Zimmer, eds. Pp. 185–195. Budapest: Archeolingua.

1995 Horse, Wagon and Chariot: Indo-European Languages and Archaeology. Antiquity 69:554–565.

1996 Bridling Horsepower: The Domestication of the Horse. *In* Horses Through Time. Sandra L. Olsen, ed. Pp. 57–82. Boulder, CO: Roberts Rinehart.

1998 The Opening of the Eurasian Steppe at 2000 BCE. *In* The Bronze Age and Early Iron Age Peoples of Eastern Central Asia. Victor H. Mair, ed. Vol. 1, Archeology, Migration and Nomadism, Linguistics. Pp. 94–113. Journal of Indo-European Studies Monograph, 26, in 2 vols. Washington, DC: Institute for the Study of Man; Philadelphia: University of Pennsylvania Museum Publications.

2007 The Horse, the Wheel, and Language: How Bronze-Age Riders from the Steppes Shaped the Modern World. Princeton, NJ: Princeton University Press.

Anthony, David W., and Dorcas R. Brown

2000 Eneolithic Horse Exploitation in the Eurasian Steppes: Diet, Ritual, and Riding. Antiquity 74:75–86.

2003 Eneolithic Horse Rituals and Riding in the Steppes: New Evidence. *In* Prehistoric Steppe Adaptation and the Horse. Marsha Levine, Colin Renfrew, and Katie Boyle, eds. Pp. 55–68. Cambridge: Macdonald Institute for Archaeological Research, University of Cambridge.

Anthony, David W., Dorcas R. Brown, and Christian George
2006 Early Horseback Riding and Warfare: The Importance of the Magpie Around the Neck. *In* Horses and Humans: The Evolution of Human-Equine Relationships. Sandra L. Olsen, Susan Grant, Alice M. Choyke, and Laszlo Bartosiewicz, eds. Pp. 137–156. British Archaeological Reports International Series, 1560. Oxford: Archaeopress.

Anthony, David W., and N. B. Vinogradov
1995 The Birth of the Chariot. Archaeology 48(2):36–41.

Armstrong, Karen
1991 Holy War: The Crusades and Their Impact on Today's World. New York: Doubleday, Anchor Books.

Asbridge, Thomas
2004 The First Crusade: A New History. Oxford: Oxford University Press.

Aubet, Maria Eugenia
2001 The Phoenicians and the West: Politics, Colonies, and Trade. Cambridge: Cambridge University Press.

Ayalon, David
1975 Preliminary Remarks on the *Mamluk* Military Institution in Islam. *In* War, Technology and Society in the Middle East. V. J. Parry and M. E. Yapp, eds. Pp. 44–58. London: Oxford University Press.
1994 The Military Reforms of Caliph al-Mutasim; Their Background and Consequences. *In* Islam and the Abode of War: Military Slaves and Islamic Adversaries. Chapter 1. Pp. 1–39. Aldershot, Hampshire: Variorum.

Azoy, G. Whitney
1982 Buzkashi: Game and Power in Afghanistan. Philadelphia: University of Pennsylvania Press.

Azzaroli, Augusto
1998 Outlines of Early Equitation. *In* Man and the Animal World: Studies in Archaeozoology, Archaeology, Anthropology, and Paleolinguistics in Memoriam Sandor Bokonyi. Peter Anreiter, Laszlo Bartosiewicz, Erzsebet Jerem, and Wolfgang Meid, eds. Pp. 41–53. Budapest: Archaeolingua.

Badian, E.

1993 Alexander in Iran. *In* The Cambridge History of Iran. Vol. 2, The Median and Achaemenian Periods. Ilya Gershevitch, ed. Pp. 420–501. Cambridge: Cambridge University Press.

Bagley, Robert

1999 Shang Archaeology. *In* The Cambridge History of Ancient China: From the Origins of Civilization to 221 BC. Michael Loewe and Edward L. Shaughnessy, eds. Pp. 124–231. Cambridge: Cambridge University Press.

Bagnall, Nigel

1990 The Punic Wars. London: Hutchinson.

Baktash, Mayel

1979 *Taziyeh* and its Philosophy. *In Taziyeh*: Ritual and Drama in Iran. Peter J. Chelkowski, ed. Pp. 95–120. New York: New York University Press; Soroush Press.

Ballou, Jonathan D.

1994 Population Biology. *In* Przewalski's Horse: The History and Biology of an Endangered Species. Lee Boyd and Katherine A. Houpt, eds. Pp. 93–113. Albany: State University of New York Press.

Barber, Elizabeth Wayland

1999 The Mummies of Urumchi. New York: Norton.

2002 Fashioned from Fiber. *In* Along the Silk Road. Elizabeth Ten Grotenhuis, ed. Pp. 57–70. Washington, DC: Arthur M. Sackler Gallery, Smithsonian Institution; Seattle: University of Washington Press.

Barber, Richard

1979 The Arthurian Legends: An Illustrated Anthology. Woodbridge, Suffolk: Boydell Press.

Bardill, John E., and James H. Cobbe

1985 Lesotho: Dilemmas of Dependence in Southern Africa. Boulder, CO: Westview Press.

Barfield, Thomas J.

1989 The Perilous Frontier: Nomadic Empires and China. Cambridge, MA: Basil Blackwell.

1993 The Nomadic Alternative. Englewood Cliffs, NJ: Prentice Hall.

Barker, Theo, and Dorian Gerhold

1993 The Rise and Rise of Road Transport 1700–1990. London: Macmillan.

Barkova, L. L.

1978 The Frozen Tombs of the Altai. *In* Frozen Tombs: The Culture and Art of the Ancient Tribes of Siberia. Pp. 21–78. Collaboration in exhibit by D. M. Wilson, Director of the British Museum; Boris Piotrovsky, Director of the Hermitage. London: British Museum Publications.

Barrie, Douglas M.
    1956 The Australian Bloodhorse. Sydney: Angus and Robertson.

Bartold, V. V.
    1927 Mesta do Musulmanskogo kulta v Bukhare. Vostochnye Zapiski 1:11–25.

Beal, Richard H.
    2006 Hittite Military Organization. *In* Civilizations of the Ancient Near East. Jack M. Sasson, ed. John Baines, Gary Beckman, and Karen S. Rubinson, assoc. eds. Vol. 1, Part 4, Social Institutions. Pp. 545–554. Peabody, MA: Hendrickson.

Benecke, Norbert
    1998 Die Wildepferde aus der spatmesolithischen Station *Mirnoe* in der Südwest-Ukraine. *In* Man and the Animal World: Studies in Archaeozoology, Archaeology, Anthropology, and Paleolinguistics in Memoriam Sandor Bokonyi. Peter Anreiter, Laszlo Bartosiewicz, Erzsebet Jerem, and Wolfgang Meid, eds. Pp. 87–107. Budapest: Archaeolingua.

Bibikova, V. I.
    1986 Appendix 3, On the History of Horse Domestication in Southeast Europe. *In* Dereivka: A Settlement and Cemetery of Copper Age Horse Keepers on the Middle Dnieper. D. Telegin, ed. Vol. 287. Pp. 163–182. British Archaeological Reports, International Series 287. Oxford: Archaeopress.

Biddle, Martin
    2000 King Arthur's Round Table: An Archaeological Investigation. Woodbridge, Suffolk: Boydell Press.

Bidwell, Shelford
    1973 The Royal Horse Artillery. London: Leo Cooper.

Binford, Lewis R.
    1972 Post-Pleistocene Adaptations. *In* An Archaeological Perspective. Pp. 421–449. New York: Seminar Press.

Bin-Sultan al-Nahyan, H. H. Sheikh Zayed
    1998 Introduction. *In* The Arabian Horse: History, Mystery, and Magic. Hossein Amirsadeghi, ed. Pp. 7–9. New York: Thames and Hudson.

Bisaha, Nancy
    2004 Creating East and West: Renaissance Humanists and the Ottoman Turks. Philadelphia: University of Pennsylvania Press.

Blair, Sheila S.
    2002 The Religious Art of the Ilkhanids. *In* Legacy of Genghis Khan: Courtly Art and Culture in Western Asia. Linda Komaroff and Stefano Carboni, eds. Pp. 104–133. New York: The Metropolitan Museum of Art; New Haven, CT: Yale University Press.

Blair, Sheila S., and Jonathan M. Bloom

1994 The Art and Architecture of Islam 1250–1800. New Haven, CT: Yale University Press.

1999 Art and Architecture: Themes and Variations. *In* The Oxford History of Islam. John L. Esposito, ed. Pp. 215–267. Oxford: Oxford University Press.

Blansdorf, Catharina, Erwin Emmerling, and Michael Petzet, eds.

2001 Qin Shihuang: The Terracotta Army of the First Chinese Emperor. Munich: Bayerisches Landesamt fur Denkmalpflege.

Blomberg, Catharina

1994 The Heart of the Japanese Warrior: Origins and Religious Background of the Samurai System in Feudal Japan. Sandgate, Folkestone, Kent: Japan Library.

Bokonyi, Sandor

1978 The Earliest Waves of Domestic Horses in East Europe. Journal of Indo-European Studies 6(1):17–76.

1994 The Role of the Horse in the Exploitation of the Steppes. *In* The Archaeology of the Steppes: Methods and Strategies. Bruno Genito, ed. Pp. 17–30. Naples: Instituto Universitario Orientale.

Bokovenko, Nikolai

2000 The Origins of Horse Riding and the Development of Ancient Central Asian Nomadic Riding Harnesses. *In* Kurgans, Ritual Sites, and Settlements: Eurasian Bronze and Iron Age. Jeannine Davis-Kimball, Eileen M. Murphy, Ludmilla Koryakova, and Leonid T. Yablonsky, eds. Pp. 304–310. British Archaeological Reports International Series, 890. Oxford: Archaeopress.

Boltz, William G.

1999 Language and Writing. *In* The Cambridge History of Ancient China: From the Origins of Civilization to 221 BC. Michael Loewe and Edward L. Shaughnessy, eds. Pp. 74–123. Cambridge: Cambridge University Press.

Bosworth, Clifford Edmund

1968 The Political and Dynastic History of the Iranian World (AD 1000–1217). *In* The Cambridge History of Iran. Vol. 5, The Saljuq and Mongol Periods. J. A. Boyle, ed. Pp. 1–202. Cambridge: Cambridge University Press.

1973 The Ghaznavids: Their Empire in Afghanistan and Eastern Iran. Beirut: Librairie de Liban.

1975 The Early Ghaznavids. *In* The Cambridge History of Iran. Vol. 4, From the Arab Invasion to the Saljuqs. R. N. Frye, ed. Pp. 162–197. Cambridge: Cambridge University Press.

1996 Notes on the Lives of Some Abbasid Princes and Descendants. *In* The Arabs, Byzantium, and Iran: Studies in Early Islamic History and Culture. Chapter 5. Pp. 277–284. Aldershot, Hampshire: Variorum.

Bouman, Inge, and Jan Bouman
  1994 The History of the Przewalski's Horse. *In* Przewalski's Horse: The History and Biology of an Endangered Species. Lee Boyd and Katherine A. Houpt, eds. Pp. 5–38. Albany: State University of New York Press.

Bouman, Inge, Jan Bouman, and Lee Boyd
  1994 Reintroduction. *In* Przewalski's Horse: The History and Biology of an Endangered Species. Lee Boyd and Katherine A. Houpt, eds. Pp. 255–263. Albany: State University of New York Press.

Bouroncle, Alberto
  2000 Ritual, Violence and Social Order: An Approach to Spanish Bullfighting. *In* Meanings of Violence: A Cross-Cultural Perspective. Goran Aijmer and Jon Abbink, eds. Pp. 55–75. Oxford: Berg.

Bovill, E. W.
  1958 The Golden Trade of the Moors. London: Oxford University Press.

Boyce, Mary
  1987 Zoroastrians: Their Religious Beliefs and Practices. London: Routledge and Kegan Paul.

Bray, Warwick
  1982 Gold-Working in Ancient America. *In* Metallurgy in Ancient Mexico. Warwick Bray, John L. Sorenson, and James R. Moriarty III, eds. N.p. Miscellaneous Series, 45. Greeley, CO: University of North Colorado, Museum of Anthropology.

Brentjes, Burchard
  2000 "Animal Style" and Shamanism: Problems of Pictoral Tradition in Northern and Central Asia. *In* Kurgans, Ritual Sites, and Settlements: Eurasian Bronze and Iron Age. Jeannine Davis-Kimball, Eileen M. Murphy, Ludmila Koryakova, and Leonid T. Yablonsky, eds. Pp. 259–268. British Archaeological Reports International Series, 890. Oxford: Archaeopress.

Brereton, J. M.
  1976 The Horse in War. New York: Arco.

Bridge, Antony
  1983 Suleiman the Magnificent: Scourge of Heaven. London: Granada.

Bright, David F.
  1987 The Miniature Epic in Vandal Africa. Norman: University of Oklahoma Press.

Brown, Dee
  1981 Bury My Heart at Wounded Knee. New York: Washington Square Books.

Brown, Dorcas R., and David W. Anthony
  1998 Bit Wear, Horseback Riding and the Botai Site in Kazakstan. Journal of Archaeological Science 25:331–347.

Browne, Edward G.
1977 A Literary History of Persia. 4 vols. Vol. 2, From Firdawsi to Sadi. Cambridge: Cambridge University Press.

Brundage, Burr Cartwright
1963 Empire of the Inca. Norman: University of Oklahoma Press.
1972 A Rain of Darts: The Mexica Aztecs. Austin: University of Texas Press.

Bryce, Trevor
1998 The Kingdom of the Hittites. Oxford: Clarendon Press.

Buckley, Theodore Alois
1851 Homer's Iliad. London: Cox Bros. and Wyman.

Bulliet, Richard W.
1990 The Camel and the Wheel. New York: Columbia University Press.

Bunker, Emma C.
1995a The People, the Land, the Economy. *In* Traders and Raiders on China's Northern Frontier. Jenny F. So and Emma C. Bunker. Pp. 17–31. Seattle: Arthur M. Sackler Gallery, Smithsonian Institution, in association with the University of Washington Press.
1995b Luxury Exports from China to the North: Sixth–First Century BC. *In* Traders and Raiders on China's Northern Frontier. Jenny F. So and Emma C. Bunker. Pp. 53–67. Seattle: Arthur M. Sackler Gallery, Smithsonian Institution, in association with the University of Washington Press.

Bunker, Emma C., with James C. Y. Watt and Zhixin Sun
2002 The Nomadic Art of the Eastern Eurasian Steppes. New York: Metropolitan Museum of Art; New Haven, CT: Yale University Press.

Burn, A. R.
1993 Persia and the Greeks. *In* The Cambridge History of Iran. Vol. 2, The Median and Achaemenian Periods. Ilya Gershevitch, ed. Pp. 292–391. Cambridge: Cambridge University Press.

Burri, Rene, with text by Jose Luis Lanuza
1968 The Gaucho. New York: Crown.

Cameron, Alan
1976 Circus Factions: Blues and Greens at Rome and Byzantium. Oxford: Clarendon Press.

Campbell, Bruce M. S.
2007 Progressiveness and Backwardness in Thirteenth- and Early Fourteenth-Century Agriculture: The Verdict of Recent Research. *In* The Medieval Antecedents of English Agricultural Progress. Pp. 541–559. Aldershot, Hampshire: Ashgate.

Capon, Edmund
1983 Qin Shihuang: Terracotta Warriors and Horses. Victoria, Australia: International Cultural Corp. of Australia.

Carneiro, Robert L.
1970 A Theory of the Origin of the State. Science 169:733–738.

Carr, Karen Eva
2002 Vandals to Visigoths: Rural Settlement Patterns in Early Medieval Spain. Ann Arbor: University of Michigan Press.

Castleden, Rodney
1993 The Making of Stonehenge. London: Routledge.

Caven, Brian
1980 The Punic Wars. London: Weidenfeld and Nicolson.

Cervantes Saavedra, Miguel de
1925 Don Quixote dela Mancha. Translated from Spanish. London: Henry. G. Bohn.

Chaliand, Gerard
2004 Nomadic Empires: From Mongolia to the Danube. Translated from French by A. M. Berrett. New Brunswick: Transaction.

Chan, Hok-lam
1988 The Chien-wen, Yung-lo, Hung-hsi, and Hsuan-te Reigns, 1399–1435. *In* The Cambridge History of China. Denis Twitchett and John K. Fairbank, general eds. Vol. 7, The Ming Dynasty, 1368–1644, Part 1. Frederick W. Mote and Denis Twitchett, eds. Pp. 182–304. Cambridge: Cambridge University Press.

Chaucer, Geoffrey
1977 The Canterbury Tales. Translated by Nevill Coghill. London: Penguin Books.

Chelkowski, Peter J.
1979 *Taziyeh*: Indigenous Avant-Garde Theatre of Iran. *In Taziyeh*: Ritual and Drama in Iran. Peter J. Chelkowski, ed. Pp. 1–11. New York: New York University Press; Soroush Press.

Chen, Kwang-tzuu, and Frederik. T. Hiebert
1995 The Late Prehistory of Xinjiang in Relation to Its Neighbors. Journal of World Prehistory 9(2):243–300.

Chernykh, E. N.
1992 Ancient Metallurgy in the USSR: The Early Metal Age. Translated by Sarah Wright. Cambridge: Cambridge University Press.

Child, Daphne
1967 Saga of the South African Horse. Cape Town: Howard Timmins.

Childe, V. Gordon
  1926 The Aryans: A Study of Indo-European Origins. London: K. Paul, Trench, Trubner; New York: Knopf.

Clark, Bill, and Patrick Duncan
  1992 Asian Wild Asses – Hemiones and Kiangs (*E. hemionus* Pallas and *E. kiang* Moorcroft). *In* Zebras, Asses, and Horses: An Action Plan for the Conservation of Wild Equids. Patrick Duncan, ed. Pp. 17–21. Gland, Switzerland: International Union for Conservation of Nature and Natural Resources.

Clark, Grahame
  1941 Horses and Battle-axes. Antiquity 15(57):50–70.

Clark, J. Desmond
  1970 The Prehistory of Africa. New York: Praeger.

Closs, Michael P.
  1997 The Mathematical Notation of the Ancient Maya. *In* Native American Mathematics. Michael P. Closs, ed. Pp. 291–369. Austin: University of Texas Press.

Clot, Andre
  1992 Suleiman the Magnificent: The Man, His Life, His Epoch. Jana Gough, ed. Translated from French by Matthew J. Reisz. London: Saqi Books.
  1996 L'Egypte des Mamelouks: l'Empire des Esclaves (1250–1517). Paris: Librairie Academique Perrin.

Clutton-Brock, Juliet
  1981 Domesticated Animals from Early Times. London: British Museum (Natural History); Austin: University of Texas Press.
  1992 Horse Power: A History of the Horse and the Donkey in Human Societies. Cambridge, MA: Harvard University Press.

Coarelli, Filippo
  2001 The Colosseum in the Urban and Demographic Context of Imperial Rome. *In* The Colosseum. Ada Gabucci, ed. Translated by Mary Becker. Pp. 9–19. Los Angeles: J. Paul Getty Museum.

Coe, Michael D.
  1993 Breaking the Maya Code. New York: Thames and Hudson.

Cohen, Mark R.
  1987 Judaism in the Middle East and North Africa to 1492. *In* The Encyclopedia of Religion. Mircea Eliade, ed. Vol. 8. Pp. 149–157. New York: Macmillan.

Colarusso, John
  2002 Nart Sagas from the Caucasus: Myths and Legends from the Circassians, Abazas, Abkhaz, and Ubykhs. Assembled, translated, and annotated by

John Colarusso with the assistance of B. George Hewitt et al. Princeton, NJ: Princeton University Press.

Collis, John Stewart
    1989 Christopher Columbus. London: Sphere Books.

Colwell, Max
    1976 Australian Pioneer Horses. *In* The Great Book of Australian Horses. Pp. 19–26. Sydney: Rigby.

Comrie, Bernard, Stephen Matthews, and Maria Polinsky
    1996 The Atlas of Languages: The Origin and Development of Languages Throughout the World. London: Quarto.

Cook, B. F.
    1984 The Elgin Marbles. London: British Museum Publications.

Cook, Elizabeth
    1997 The Stupa: Sacred Symbol of Enlightenment. Berkeley, CA: Dharma.

Cook, J. M.
    1993 The Rise of the Achaemenids and the Establishment of Their Empire. *In* The Cambridge History of Iran. Vol. 2, The Median and Achaemenian Periods. Ilya Gershevitch, ed. Pp. 200–291. Cambridge: Cambridge University Press.

Cooper, John M.
    1963 The Southern Hunters: An Introduction. *In* The Handbook of South American Indians. Julian H. Steward, ed. Vol. 1, The Marginal Tribes. Pp. 13–15. New York: Cooper Square.

Cotterell, Arthur
    2004 Chariot: The Astounding Rise and Fall of the World's First War Machine. London: Random House, Pimlico.

Creel, Herrlee Glessna
    1965 The Role of the Horse in Chinese History. American Historical Review 70(3): 647–672.

Crone, Patricia
    1996 The Rise of Islam in the World. *In* The Cambridge Illustrated History of the Islamic World. Francis Robinson, ed. Pp. 2–31. Cambridge: Cambridge University Press.

Crosby, Alfred W., Jr.
    1972 The Columbian Exchange: Biological and Cultural Consequences of 1492. Westport, CT: Greenwood.

Curtin, Philip D.
    1970 The Islamic World. Morristown, NJ: Silver Burdett.

Dallal, Ahmad

1999 Science, Medicine, and Technology: The Making of a Scientific Culture. *In* The Oxford History of Islam. John L. Esposito, ed. Pp. 155–213. Oxford: Oxford University Press.

D'Altroy, Terence N.

2002 The Inkas. Malden, MA: Blackwell.

Daniel, Elton L.

2001 The History of Iran. Westport, CT: Greenwood Press.

Davidson, Olga M.

1994 Poet and Hero in the Persian Book of Kings. Ithaca, NY: Cornell University Press.

Dean, Christopher

1987 Arthur of England: English Attitudes to King Arthur and the Knights of the Round Table in the Middle Ages and the Renaissance. Toronto: University of Toronto Press.

De Chasca, Edmund

1976 The Poem of the Cid. Boston: Twayne.

Denevan, William M., ed.

1992 The Native Population of the Americas in 1492. 2nd edition. Madison: University of Wisconsin Press.

Dent, A.

1974 The Horse Through Fifty Centuries of Civilization. London: Phaidon Press.

Detienne, Marcel

1987 Orpheus. *In* The Encyclopedia of Religion. Mircea Eliade, ed. Vol. 11. Pp. 111–114. New York: Macmillan.

Devambez, Pierre

1970 Dictionary of Ancient Greek Civilization. London: Methuen.

Diakonoff, I. M.

1993 Media. *In* The Cambridge History of Iran. Vol. 2, The Median and Achaemenian Periods. Ilya Gershevitch, ed. Pp. 36–148. Cambridge: Cambridge University Press.

Diamond, Jared

1999 Guns, Germs, and Steel. New York: Norton.

Diaz, Bernal

1974 The Conquest of New Spain. Translated by J. M. Cohen. Harmondsworth, Middlesex: Penguin Books.

Dietz, Ute Luise

2003 Horseback Riding: Man's Access to Speed. *In* Prehistoric Steppe Adaptation and the Horse. Marsha Levine, Colin Renfrew, and Katie Boyle, eds.

Pp. 189–199. Cambridge: Macdonald Institute for Archaeological Research, University of Cambridge.

Dillehay, Tom D.
2000 The Settlement of the Americas: A New Prehistory. New York: Basic Books.

Dodds, Jerrilynn D.
1992 The Great Mosque of Cordoba. *In* Al Andalus: The Art of Islamic Spain. Jerrilynn D. Dodds, ed. Pp. 11–25. New York: Metropolitan Museum of Art.

Donner, Fred McGraw
1981 The Early Islamic Conquests. Princeton: Princeton University Press.
1999 Muhammad and the Caliphate: Political History of the Islamic Empire up to the Mongol Conquest. *In* The Oxford History of Islam. John L. Esposito, ed. Pp. 1–61. Oxford: Oxford University Press.

Drews, Robert
2004 Early Riders: The Beginnings of Mounted Warfare in Asia and Europe. New York: Routledge, Taylor and Francis Group.

Drower, M. S.
1969 The Domestication of the Horse. *In* The Domestication and Exploitation of Plants and Animals. Proceedings of a meeting of the Research Seminar in Archaeology and Related Subjects held at the Institute of Archaeology, London University. Peter J. Ucko and G. W. Dimbleby, eds. Pp. 471–476. Chicago: Aldine.

Dumezil, Georges
1930 Legendes sur les Nartes. Paris: Institut d'Etudes Slaves.

Duncan, Patrick, and Chris Gakahu
1992 Plains Zebras (*Equus burchelli* Gray). *In* Zebras, Asses, and Horses: An Action Plan for the Conservation of Wild Equids. Patrick Duncan, ed. Pp. 12–15. Gland, Switzerland: International Union for Conservation of Nature and Natural Resources.

Duncan, Patrick, Oliver Ryder, Cheryl Asa, and Claudia Feh
1992 The Nature and Value of Zebras, Asses, and Horses. *In* Zebras, Asses, and Horses: An Action Plan for the Conservation of Wild Equids. Patrick Duncan, ed. Pp. 1–5. Gland, Switzerland: International Union for Conservation of Nature and Natural Resources.

Dundes, Alan, and Alessandro Falassi
1975 La Terra in Piazza: An Interpretation of the Palio of Siena. Berkeley: University of California Press.

Dupuy, Trevor Nevitt
1969 The Military Life of Genghis, Khan of Khans. New York: Franklin Watts.

Durant, Will

1950 The Age of Faith. New York: MJF Books.
1966 The Life of Greece. New York: MJF Books.
1971 Caesar and Christ. New York: MJF Books.

Edbury, Peter

1999 The Latin East. *In* The Oxford History of the Crusades. Jonathan Riley-Smith, ed. Pp. 291–322. Oxford: Oxford University Press.

Edsman, Carl Martin

1987 Fire. *In* The Encyclopedia of Religion. Mircea Eliade, ed. Vol. 5. Pp. 340–346. New York: Macmillan.

Egg, Markus

1996 Das Hallstattzeitliche Furstengrab von Strettweg bei Judenburg in der Obersteiermark. Mainz: Romisch-Germanisches Zentralmuseum Forschunginsitut fur Vor- und Fruhgeschichte in Verbindung mit dem Steiermarkischen Landesmuseum Joanneum, Graz.

Enan, Muhammad Abdullah

1940 Decisive Moments in the History of Islam. Lahore: Shaikh Muhammad Ashraf, Kashmiri Bazar.

Eqbal, Zahra

1979 Elegy in the Qajar Period. *In Taziyeh*: Ritual and Drama in Iran. Peter J. Chelkowski, ed. Pp. 193–209. New York: New York University Press; Soroush Press.

Ewers, John C.

1969 The Horse in the Blackfoot Indian Culture with Comparative Material from Other Western Tribes. Washington, DC: Smithsonian Institution Press.

Fagan, Brian M.

1986 People of the Earth: An Introduction to World Prehistory. Boston: Little, Brown.
1991 Ancient North America: The Archaeology of a Continent. New York: Thames and Hudson.

Fakhry, Majid

1999 Philosophy and Theology from the Eighth Century CE to the Present. *In* The Oxford History of Islam. John L. Esposito, ed. Pp. 269–303. Oxford: Oxford University Press.

Falassi, Alessandro, and Luca Betti, eds.

2003 Il Palio: La Festa della Citta. Siena: Betti Editrice.

Falassi, Alessandro, and Giuliano Catoni

1983 Palio. Milano: Electa Editrice.

Farb, Peter
    1971 Man's Rise to Civilization: As Shown by the Indians of North America from Primeval Times to the Coming of the Industrial State. New York: Avon Books.

Fehrenbach, T. R.
    1974 Comanches: The Destruction of a People. New York: Knopf.

Findly, Ellison Banks
    1987 Agni. *In* The Encyclopedia of Religion. Mircea Eliade, ed. Vol. 1. Pp. 133–135. New York: Macmillan.

Flemings, Merton C.
    2002 Traveling Technologies. *In* Along the Silk Road. Elizabeth Ten Grotenhuis, ed. Pp. 107–121. Washington, DC: Arthur M. Sackler Gallery, Smithsonian Institution; Seattle: University of Washington Press.

Fletcher, Richard
    1992 Moorish Spain. London: Weidenfeld and Nicolson.

Foltz, Richard C.
    2000 Religions of the Silk Road: Overland Trade and Cultural Exchange from Antiquity to the Fifteenth Century. New York: St. Martin's Griffin.

Forbes, Robert James
    1956 Roman Control of Roads and Traffic. *In* A History of Technology. Charles Singer, E. J. Holmyard, A. R. Hall, and Trevor L. Williams, eds. Vol. 2, The Mediterranean Civilizations and the Middle Ages, c. 700 BC to c. AD 1500. Part 4, Roads and Land Travel. Pp. 512–516. Oxford: Oxford at the Clarendon Press.

Forey, Alan
    1999 The Military Orders, 1120–1312. *In* The Oxford History of the Crusades. Jonathan Riley-Smith, ed. Pp. 176–210. Oxford: Oxford University Press.

Friday, Karl F.
    2003 Beyond Valor and Bloodshed: The Arts of War as a Path to Serenity. *In* Knight and Samurai: Actions and Images of Elite Warriors in Europe and East Asia. Rosemarie Deist, ed. Pp. 1–13. Goppingen: Kummerle Verlag.

Friedman, Thomas L.
    2005 The World Is Flat: A Brief History of the Twenty-First Century. New York: Farrar, Straus and Giroux.

Frye, Richard Nelson
    1953 Iran. New York: Henry Holt and Co.
    1975 The Samanids. *In* The Cambridge History of Iran. Vol. 4. R. N. Frye, ed. Pp. 136–161. Cambridge: Cambridge University Press.
    2001 The Heritage of Central Asia: From Antiquity to the Turkish Expansion. Princeton, NJ: Markus Wiener.

Fuchs, Stephen
  1996 The Vedic Horse Sacrifice in Its Culture-Historical Relations. New Delhi: Inter-India.

Gamkrelizde, T. V., and V. V. Ivanov
  1983 The Migration of Tribes Speaking the Indo-European Dialects from Their Original Homeland in the Near East to Their Historical Habitations in Eurasia. Soviet Studies in History 22(1–2): 53–95.

Garlake, Peter
  1990 The Kingdoms of Africa. New York: Peter Bedricks Books.

Geoffroy-Schneiter, Berenice
  2001 Gandhara: The Memory of Afghanistan. New York: Assouline.

Gerhold, Dorian
  1993 Road Transport Before the Railways: Russell's London Flying Waggons. Cambridge: Cambridge University Press.
  2005 Carriers and Coachmasters: Trade and Travel before the Turnpikes. Shopwyke Manor Barn, Chichester: Phillimore.

Gies, Joseph, and Frances Gies
  1972 Merchants and Moneymen: The Commercial Revolution, 1000–1500. New York: Crowell.

Gille, Bertrand
  1969 The Problem of Transportation. *In* A History of Technology and Invention: Progress Through the Ages. Maurice Daumas, ed. Vol. 1, The Origins of Technological Civilization. Part 6, Medieval Age of the West (Fifth Century to 1350). Chapter 16, Land Transportation. Pp. 431–436. Translated by Eileen B. Hennessy. New York: Crown.

Gille, Paul
  1969a Land Transportation. *In* A History of Technology and Invention: Progress Through the Ages. Maurice Daumas, ed. Vol. 2, The First Stages of Mechanization. Section 3, Land and Water Transportation. Pp. 344–360. Translated by Eileen B. Hennessy. New York: Crown.
  1969b Weaponry 1500–1700. *In* A History of Technology and Invention: Progress Through the Ages. Maurice Daumas, ed. Vol. 2, The First Stages of Mechanization. Section 5, Military Techniques. Pp. 473–492. Translated by Eileen B. Hennessy. New York: Crown.

Gillingham, John
  1999 Richard I. New Haven, CT: Yale University Press.

Gimbutas, Marija
  1997a The Fall and Transformation of Old Europe. *In* The Kurgan Culture and the Indo-Europeanization of Europe: Selected Articles from 1952 to 1993. Miriam Robbins Dexter and Karlene Jones-Bley, eds. Pp. 351–372. Journal

of Indo-European Studies Monograph, 18. Washington, DC: Institute for the Study of Man.

1997b Proto-Indo-European Culture: The Kurgan Culture During the Fifth, Fourth, and Third Millennia BC. *In* The Kurgan Culture and the Indo-Europeanization of Europe: Selected Articles from 1952 to 1993. Miriam Robbins Dexter and Karlene Jones-Bley, eds. Pp. 75–117. Journal of Indo-European Studies Monograph, 18. Washington, DC: Institute for the Study of Man.

Glubb, John Bagot
1964 The Great Arab Conquests. Englewood Cliffs, NJ: Prentice-Hall.

Gnoli, Gherardo
1987a Iranian Religions. *In* The Encyclopedia of Religion. Mircea Eliade, ed. Vol. 7. Pp. 277–280. New York: Macmillan.

1987b Zoroastrianism. *In* The Encyclopedia of Religion. Mircea Eliade, ed. Vol. 15. Pp. 579–591. New York: Macmillan.

1987c Frashokereti. *In* The Encyclopedia of Religion. Mircea Eliade, ed. Vol. 5. Pp. 412–413. New York: Macmillan.

Golden, Peter B.
1990 The Peoples of the South Russian Steppes. *In* The Cambridge History of Early Inner Asia. Denis Sinor, ed. Pp. 256–284. Cambridge: Cambridge University Press.

Goodenough, Ward H.
1970 The Evolution of Pastoralism and Indo-European Origins. *In* Indo-European and Indo-Europeans: Papers presented at the Third Indo-European Conference at the University of Pennsylvania. George Cardona, Henry Hoenigswald, and Alfred Senn, eds. Pp. 253–265. Philadelphia: University of Pennsylvania Press.

Gordon, Raymond, Jr.
2005 Ethnologue: Languages of the World. 15th edition. Dallas, TX: SIL International.

Gottheil, Richard J. H.
1900 Persian Literature; Comprising the Shah Nameh, the Rubaiyat, the Divan and the Gulistan. With special introduction by Richard J. H. Gottheil, Ph.D. Vol. 1. London: Colonial Press.

Goudineau, Christian
2001 Le Dossier Vercingetorix. Paris: Actes Sud/Errance.

Grabar, Oleg
1992 Islamic Spain, the First Four Centuries: An Introduction. *In* Al Andalus: The Art of Islamic Spain. Jerrilynn D. Dodds, ed. Pp. 3–9. New York: Metropolitan Museum of Art.

Granzotto, Gianni

1985 Christopher Columbus. Translated by Stephen Sartarelli. Garden City, NY: Doubleday.

Greenhalgh, P. A. L.

1973 Early Greek Warfare: Horsemen and Chariots in the Homeric and Archaic Ages. Cambridge: Cambridge University Press.

Griffith, Ralph T. H.

1889 Hymns of the Rgveda. 2 vols. Delhi: Munshiram Manoharlal.

Grotenhuis, Elizabeth Ten

2002 Introduction: The Silk Road, Ancient and Contemporary. *In* Along the Silk Road. Elizabeth Ten Grotenhuis, ed. Pp. 15–23. Washington, DC: Arthur M. Sackler Gallery, Smithsonian Institution; Seattle: University of Washington Press.

Grousset, Rene

1966 Conqueror of the World. Translated from French by Marian McKellar and Denis Sinor, with preface, notes, and bibliography by Denis Sinor. New York: Orion Press.

1970 The Empire of the Steppes: A History of Central Asia. Translated from French by Naomi Walford. New Brunswick, NJ: Rutgers University Press.

Gurney, O. R.

1975 The Hittites. London: Penguin Books, Allen Lane.

Guttentag, Marcia, and Paul F. Secord

1983 Too Many Women? The Sex Ratio Question. Beverly Hills, CA: Sage.

Halsall, Guy

2003 Warfare and Society in the Barbarian West 450–900. London: Routledge, Taylor and Francis Group.

Hanaway, William L., Jr.

1979 Stereotyped Imagery in the *Taziyeh*. *In Taziyeh*: Ritual and Drama in Iran. Peter J. Chelkowski, ed. Pp. 182–192. New York: New York University Press; Soroush Press.

Harmatta, J.

1992 The Emergence of the Indo-Iranians: The Indo Iranian Languages. *In* History of Civilizations of Central Asia. A. H. Dani and V. M. Masson, eds. Vol. 1, The Dawn of Civilization: Earliest Times to 700 BC. Pp. 357–378. Paris: UNESCO.

Harper, Prudence O.

2007 Silver Vessels. *In* Glass, Gilding, and Grand Design: Art of Sassanian Iran (224–642). Francoise Demange, ed. Pp. 24–28. New York: Asia Society.

Harris, David R.
1996 The Origins and Spread of Agriculture and Pastoralism in Eurasia: an Overview. *In* The Origins and Spread of Agriculture and Pastoralism in Eurasia. David R. Harris, ed. Pp. 552–573. London: University College London Press.

Harris, Victor, and Nobuo Ogasawara
1990 Swords of the Samurai. London: British Museum Publications.

Harrison, Richard J.
1980 The Beaker Folk: Copper-Age Archaeology in Western Europe. London: Thames and Hudson.

Hartog, Leo de
2004 Genghis Khan: Conqueror of the World. London: Tauris Parke Paperbacks.

Hassig, Ross
1994 Mexico and the Spanish Conquest. London: Longman.

Hausler, Alexander
2000 Review of Anreiter 1998. Indogermanische Forschungen 105:310–313.

Haywood, John
2001 The Historical Atlas of the Celtic World. London: Thames and Hudson.

Heers, Jacques
2003 Les negriers en terres d'islam: La premiere traite des Noirs VIIe–XVIe siecle. Paris: Perrin.

Heesterman, Jan C.
1987 Vedism and Brahmanism. *In* The Encyclopedia of Religion. Mircea Eliade, ed. Vol. 15. Pp. 217–242. New York: Macmillan.

Herodotus
2003 The Histories. Translated by Aubrey de Selincourt. Revised by John Marincola. London: Penguin Books.

Hiebert, Frederik T.
1998 Central Asians on the Iranian Plateau: A Model for Indo-Iranian Expansion. *In* The Bronze Age and Early Iron Age Peoples of Eastern Central Asia. Victor H. Mair, ed. Vol. 1, Archeology, Migration and Nomadism, Linguistics. Pp. 148–161. Journal of Indo-European Studies Monograph, 26, in 2 vols. Washington, DC: Institute for the Study of Man; Philadelphia: University of Pennsylvania Museum Publications.

Hildinger, Erik
2001 Warriors of the Steppe: A Military History of Central Asia, 500 BC to 1799 AD. Cambridge, MA: Da Capo Press.

Hill, D. R.

1975 The Role of the Camel and the Horse in Early Arab Conquests. *In* War, Technology and Society in the Middle East. V. J. Parry and M. E. Yapp, eds. Pp. 32–43. London: Oxford University Press.

Hillenbrand, Robert

2002 The Arts of the Book in Ilkhanid Iran. *In* Legacy of Genghis Khan: Courtly Art and Culture in Western Asia. Linda Komaroff and Stefano Carboni, eds. Pp. 134–167. New York: Metropolitan Museum of Art; New Haven, CT: Yale University Press.

Hiltebeitel, Alf

1987 Mahabharata. *In* Encyclopedia of Religion. Mircea Eliade, ed. Vol. 9. Pp. 118–119. New York: Macmillan.

Hitti, Philip K.

2002 History of the Arabs. New York: Palgrave Macmillan.

Hobson, John H.

2004 The Eastern Origins of Western Civilization. Cambridge: Cambridge University Press.

Homayouni, Sadegh

1976 *Taziyeh* in Iran. Shiraz, Iran: Navid.

Hopkins, Andrea

2004 A Chronicle History of Knights. New York: Barnes and Noble Books.

Hosler, Dorothy

1994 The Sounds and Colors of Power: The Sacred Metallurgical Technology of Ancient West Mexico. Cambridge, MA: MIT Press.

Houpt, Katherine A., and Lee Boyd

1994 Social Behavior. *In* Przewalski's Horse: The History and Biology of an Endangered Species. Lee Boyd and Katherine A. Houpt, eds. Pp. 229–254. Albany: State University of New York Press.

Housley, Norman

1999 The Crusading Movement, 1274–1700. *In* The Oxford History of the Crusades. Jonathan Riley-Smith, ed. Pp. 258–290. Oxford: Oxford University Press.

Howarth, Patrick

1994 Attila, King of the Huns: Man and Myth. London: Constable.

Howarth, Stephen

1993 The Knights Templar. New York: Barnes and Noble.

Hrbek, I.

1977 Egypt, Nubia and the Eastern Deserts. *In* The Cambridge History of Africa. J. D. Fage and Roland Oliver, general eds. Vol. 3, From c. 1050 to

c. 1600. Roland Oliver, ed. Pp. 10–97. Cambridge: Cambridge University Press.

Hrbek, I., and J. Devisse
1988 The Almoravids. *In* General History of Africa. Vol. 3, Africa from the Seventh to the Eleventh Century. M. Elfasi, ed. Pp. 336–366. Paris: United Nations Educational, Scientific, and Cultural Organization.

Hulbert, Richard C., Jr.
1996 The Ancestry of the Horse. *In* Horses Through Time. Sandra L. Olsen, ed. Pp. 11–34. Boulder, CO: Roberts Rinehart.

Humayuni, Sadeq
1979 An Analysis of the *Taziyeh* of Qasem. *In Taziyeh*: Ritual and Drama in Iran. Peter J. Chelkowski, ed. Pp. 12–23. New York: New York University Press; Soroush Press.

Humphrey, John H.
1986 Roman Circuses: Arenas for Chariot Racing. Berkeley: University of California Press.

Humphreys, Eileen
1991 The Royal Road: A Popular History of Iran. London: Scorpion.

Huettel, Hans-Georg
1981 Bronzezeitlichen Trensen in Mittel- und Osteuropa. Munich: Beck (Prahistorische Bronzefunde 16, 2).
1994 Zur archaologischen Evidenz der Pferdenutzung in der Kupfer- und Bronzezeit. *In* Die Indogermanen und das Pferd. Bernhard Hansel and Stefan Zimmer, eds. Pp. 197–215. Budapest: Archaeolingua.

Hyland, Ann
1990 Equus: The Horse in the Roman World. London: Batsford.
1994 The Medieval Warhorse from Byzantium to the Crusades. Stroud, Gloucestershire: Sutton.
2003 The Horse in the Ancient World. Stroud, Gloucestershire: Sutton.

Inalcik, Halil
1989 The Ottoman Empire: The Classical Age 1300–1600. Translated by Norman Itzkowitz and Colin Imber. New Rochelle, NY: Aristide D. Caratzas; Orpheus.

Irwin, Robert
1996 The Emergence of the Islamic World System 1000–1500. *In* The Cambridge Illustrated History of the Islamic World. Francis Robinson, ed. Pp. 32–61. Cambridge: Cambridge University Press.
1999 Islam and the Crusades. *In* The Oxford History of the Crusades. Jonathan Riley-Smith, ed. Pp. 211–257. Oxford: Oxford University Press.

Jacobson, Esther

1993 The Deer Goddess of Ancient Siberia: A Study in the Ecology of Belief. Leiden, The Netherlands: Brill.

Jansen, T., P. Forster, M. A. Levine, H. Oelke, M. Hurles, C. Renfrew, J. Weber, and K. Olek

2002 Mitochondrial DNA and the Origins of the Domestic Horse. Proceedings of the National Academy of Sciences, USA 99:10905–10910.

Jones, Kristine L.

1999 Warfare, Reorganization, and Readaption at the Margins of Spanish Rule: The Southern Margins (1573–1882). *In* The Cambridge History of the Native Peoples of the Americas. Frank Salomon and Stuart B. Schwartz, eds. Vol. 3, South America – Part 2. Pp. 138–187. Cambridge: Cambridge University Press.

Jope, E. M.

1956 Vehicles and Harness. *In* A History of Technology. Charles Singer, E. J. Holmyard, A. R. Hall, and Trevor L. Williams, eds. Vol. 2, The Mediterranean Civilizations and the Middle Ages, c. 700 BC to c. AD 1500. Pp. 537–562. Oxford: Oxford at the Clarendon Press.

Joshi, M. C.

1996 Foreword. *In* Stupa and Its Technology: A Tibeto-Buddhist Perspective. Pema Dorjee, author. Pp. vii–xiv. New Delhi: Indira Gandhi National Centre for the Arts and Motilal Banarsidass.

Kalter, Johannes

1997 Aspects of Equestrian Culture. *In* Heirs to the Silk Road: Uzbekistan. Johannes Kalter and Margareta Pavaloi, eds. Pp. 168–187. London: Thames and Hudson.

Kaplan, Robert

2000 The Nothing That Is: A Natural History of Zero. Oxford: Oxford University Press.

Keeley, Lawrence H.

1996 War Before Civilization. New York: Oxford University Press.

Kennedy, Hugh

2001 The Armies of the Caliphs: Military and Society in the Early Islamic State. London: Routledge.

2004 The Court of the Caliphs: The Rise and Fall of Islam's Greatest Dynasty. London: Weidenfeld and Nicolson.

2007 Great Arab Conquests: How the Spread of Islam Changed the World We Live In. Philadelphia: Da Capo Press.

Khazanov, Anatoly M.

1984 Nomads and the Outside World. Translated by Julia Crookenden. Cambridge: Cambridge University Press.

King, John
1998 Kingdoms of the Celts: A History and a Guide. London: Blandford.

Kinross, Patrick Balfour, with the editors of Newsweek Book Division.
1972 Hagia Sophia. New York: Newsweek.

Knowles, John, and Simon Wakefield
1992 Przewalski's Horse. *In* Zebras, Asses, and Horses: An Action Plan for the Conservation of Wild Equids. Patrick Duncan, ed. Pp. 21–23. Gland, Switzerland: International Union for Conservation of Nature and Natural Resources.

Kohler-Rollefson, Ilse
1996 The One-Humped Camel in Asia: Origin, Utilization and Mechanisms of Dispersal. *In* The Origins and Spread of Agriculture and Pastoralism in Eurasia. David R. Harris, ed. Pp. 282–294. London: University College London Press.

Komaroff, Linda
2002 The Transmission and Dissemination of a New Visual Language. *In* Legacy of Genghis Khan: Courtly Art and Culture in Western Asia. Linda Komaroff and Stefano Carboni, eds. Pp. 168–195. New York: Metropolitan Museum of Art; New Haven, CT: Yale University Press.

Kozlowski, Janusz K., and Stefan K. Kozlowski
1986 Foragers of Central Europe and Their Acculturation. *In* Hunters in Transition: Mesolithic Societies of Temperate Eurasia and Their Transition to Farming. Marek Zvelebil, ed. Pp. 95–108. Cambridge: Cambridge University Press.

Kristiansen, Kristian, and Thomas B. Larsson
2005 The Rise of Bronze Age Society: Travels, Transmissions, and Transformations. Cambridge: Cambridge University Press.

Kuwayama, Shoshin
1997 A Hidden Import from Imperial Rome Manifest in Stupas. *In* Gandharan Art in Context: East-West Exchanges at the Crossroads of Asia. Raymond Allchin, Bridget Allchin, Neil Kreitman, and Elizabeth Errington, eds. Pp. 119–171. Published for the Ancient India and Iran Trust, Cambridge. New Delhi: Regency.

Kuzmina, Elena E.
2000 The Eurasian Steppes: The Transition from Early Urbanism to Nomadism. *In* Kurgans, Ritual Sites, and Settlements: Eurasian Bronze and Iron Age. Jeannine Davis-Kimball, Eileen M. Murphy, Ludmilla Koryakova, and Leonid T. Yablonsky, eds. Pp. 118–123. British Archaeological Reports International Series, 890. Oxford: Archaeopress.
2007 The Origin of the Indo-Iranians. J. P. Mallory, ed. Leiden: Brill.

2008 The Prehistory of the Silk Road. Victor H. Mair, ed. Philadelphia: University of Pennsylvania Press.

Lane Fox, Robin
1974 Alexander the Great. New York: Dial Press.

Langdon, John
1986 Horses, Oxen, and Technological Innovation: The Use of Draught Animals in English Farming from 1066 to 1500. Cambridge: Cambridge University Press.

Lanning, Edward P.
1967 Peru Before the Incas. Englewood Cliffs, NJ: Prentice Hall.

La Vaissiere, Etienne de
2002 Histoire des Marchands Sogdiens. Vol. 32. Paris: College de France, Institut des Hautes Etudes Chinoises.

Law, Robin
1980 The Horse in West African History: The Role of the Horse in the Societies of Pre-Colonial West Africa. Oxford: Oxford University Press.

Lawergren, Bo
1992 The Ancient Harp of Pazyryk: A Bowed Instrument? *In* Foundations of Empire: Archeology and Art of the Eurasian Steppes. Proceedings of the Soviet-American Academic Symposia in Conjunction with the Museum Exhibitions. Gary Seaman, ed. Vol. 3, Nomads: Masters of the Eurasian Steppes. Pp. 101–116. Los Angeles: Ethnographics Press, University of Southern California.

Lawrence, Bruce B.
1999 The Eastward Journey of Muslim Kingship: Islam in South and Southeast Asia. *In* The Oxford History of Islam. John L. Esposito, ed. Pp. 395–431. Oxford: Oxford University Press.

Ledderose, Lothar
2001 The Magic Army of the First Emperor. *In* Qin Shihuang: The Terracotta Army of the First Chinese Emperor. Catharina Blansdorf, Erwin Emmerling, and Michael Petzet, eds. Pp. 273–307. Munich: Bayerisches Landesamt fur Denkmalpflege.

Ledyard, Gari
1975 Galloping Along with the Horseriders: Looking for the Founders of Japan. Journal of Japanese Studies 1:217–254.

Lefebvre des Noettes, Richard
1931 L'Attelage, le Cheval de Selle a Travers les Ages. Paris: Picard.

Lerner, Judith A.
2005 Aspects of Assimilation: The Funerary Practices and Furnishings of Central Asians in China. Sino-Platonic Papers 168:1–51.

Levi, Scott C.
  2002 The Indian Diaspora in Central Asia and Its Trade, 1550–1900. Leiden: Brill.

Levine, Marsha.
  1990 Dereivka and the Problem of Horse Domestication. Antiquity 64:727–740.
  1999 The Origins of Horse Husbandry on the Eurasian Steppe. *In* Late Prehistoric Exploitation of the Eurasian Steppe. Marsha Levine, Yuri Rassamakin, Aleksandr Kislenko, and Nataliya Tatarintseva, eds. With an introduction by Colin Renfrew. Pp. 5–58. Cambridge: Macdonald Institute for Archaeological Research.

Levtzion, Nehemia
  1980 Ancient Ghana and Mali. New York: Holmes and Meier; Africana.
  1985 The Early States of the Western Sudan to 1500. *In* History of West Africa. J. F. A. Ajayi and Michael Crowder, eds. Vol. 1. Pp. 129–166. Harlow, Essex: Longman Groups.
  1999 Islam in Africa to 1800: Merchants, Chiefs, and Saints. *In* The Oxford History of Islam. John L. Esposito, ed. Pp. 475–507. Oxford: Oxford University Press.

Lewis, Bernard
  1967 The Assassins: A Radical Sect in Iran. London: Weidenfeld and Nicolson.

Lillys, William, ed.
  1958 Persian Miniatures: The Story of Rustam. Rutland, VT: Tuttle.

Lincoln, Bruce
  1991 Death, War, and Sacrifice: Studies in Ideology and Practice. Chicago: University of Chicago Press.

Littauer, Mary Aiken
  2002a Rock Carvings of Chariots in Transcaucasia, Central Asia, and Outer Mongolia. *In* Selected Writings on Chariots, Other Early Vehicles, Riding and Harness. Peter Raulwing, ed. Pp. 106–135. Leiden: Brill.
  2002b The Function of the Yoke Saddle in Ancient Harnessing. *In* Selected Writings on Chariots, Other Early Vehicles, Riding and Harness. Peter Raulwing, ed. Pp. 479–486. Leiden: Brill.
  2002c The Military Use of the Chariot in the Aegean in the Late Bronze Age. *In* Selected Writings on Chariots, Other Early Vehicles, Riding and Harness. Peter Raulwing, ed. Pp. 75–99. Leiden: Brill.
  2002d Early Stirrups. *In* Selected Writings on Chariots, Other Early Vehicles, Riding and Harness. Peter Raulwing, ed. Pp. 439–451. Leiden: Brill.

Littauer, Mary Aiken, and Joost H. Crouwel
  1977 The Origin and Diffusion of the Cross-Bar Wheel? Antiquity 51:95–105.

1979 Wheeled Vehicles and Ridden Animals in the Ancient Near East. Drawings by Jaap Morel. Leiden: Brill.

1985 Chariots and Related Equipment from the Tomb of Tut'ankhamūn. Tut'ankhamūn's Tomb Series, 8. J. R. Harris, general ed. Oxford: Griffith Institute.

2002 The Origin of the True Chariot. *In* Selected Writings on Chariots, Other Early Vehicles, Riding and Harness. Peter Raulwing, ed. Pp. 45–52. Leiden: Brill.

Littleton, C. Scott

1979 The Holy Grail, the Cauldron of Annwn and the Nartyamonga: A Further Note on the Sarmatian Connection. Journal of American Folklore 92:326–333.

1982 From Swords in the Earth to the Sword in the Stone: A Possible Reflection of an Alano-Sarmatian Rite of Passage in the Arthurian Tradition. *In* Homage to Georges Dumezil. Edgar C. Polome, ed. Journal of Indo-European Studies Monograph, 3. Pp. 53–67. Washington, DC: Institute for the Study of Man.

1995 Yamato-Takeru: "Arthurian" Hero in Japanese Tradition. Asian Folklore Studies 54(2):259–274.

Littleton, C. Scott, and Linda A. Malcor

1994 From Scythia to Camelot: A Radical Reassessment of the Legends of King Arthur, the Knights of the Round Table, and the Holy Grail. New York: Garland.

Litton, Helen

1997 The Celts: An Illustrated History. Dublin: Wolfhound Press.

Litvinskii, B. A.

1987 Prehistoric Religions: The Eurasian Steppes and Inner Asia. *In* The Encyclopedia of Religion. Mircea Eliade, ed. Vol. 11. Pp. 516–522. New York: Macmillan.

Lockhart, Laurence, and John A. Boyle

1978 From the Islamic Conquest to the Qajars. *In* Persia: History and Heritage. John. A, Boyle, ed. Pp. 31–48. London: Henry Melland; British Institute of Persian Studies.

Long, J. Bruce

1987 Reincarnation. *In* The Encyclopedia of Religion. Mircea Eliade, ed. Vol. 12. Pp. 265–269. New York: Macmillan.

Longfellow, Henry Wadsworth

2006 Paul Revere's Ride. In The Oxford Book of American Poetry. Chosen and edited by David Lehman. John Brehm, assoc. ed. Pp. 47–50. Oxford: Oxford University Press.

Lu, Liancheng
    1993 Chariot and Horse Burials in Ancient China. Antiquity 67:824–838.

Lubinski, Kurt
    1928 Bei den Schamanen der Ursibirier der Kampf der Sowjetunion gegen den Medizinman. Berliner Illustrirte Zeitung, November 25.

Lugli, Giuseppe
    1968 Nero's Golden House and the Trajan Baths. Translated by John Tickner. Rome: Bardi Editore.

Luttrell, Anthony
    1999 The Military Orders, 1312–1798. *In* The Oxford History of the Crusades. Jonathan Riley-Smith, ed. Pp. 323–362. Oxford: Oxford University Press.

MacDonald, Brian W.
    1997 Tribal Rugs: Treasures of the Black Tent. Woodbridge, Suffolk: Antique Collectors' Club.

Macdonald, K. S.
    1982 The Vedic Religion: Or the Creed and Practice of the Indo-Aryans 3,000 Years Ago. Calcutta: Sanskrit Pustak Bhandar.

MacDonald, William Lloyd
    1962 Early Christian and Byzantine Architecture. New York: George Braziller.
    1965 The Architecture of the Roman Empire. Vol. 1, An Introductory Study. New Haven: Yale University Press.
    1976 The Pantheon: Design, Meaning, and Progeny. Cambridge, MA: Harvard University Press.

MacFadden, Bruce J.
    1992 Fossil Horses: Systematics, Paleobiology, and Evolution of the Family Equidae. New York: Cambridge University Press.

Macqueen, J. G.
    1996 The Hittites and Their Contemporaries in Asia Minor. London: Thames and Hudson.

Maddin, Robert, ed.
    1988 Preface. *In* The Beginning of the Use of Metals and Alloys: Papers from the Second International Conference on the Beginning of the Use of Metals and Alloys, Zhengzhou, China, 21–26 October 1986. Pp. xiii–xiv. Cambridge, MA: MIT Press.

Maekawa, Kazuya
    2006 The Donkey and the Persian Onager in Late Third Millennium BC Mesopotamia and Syria: A Rethinking. Journal of West Asian Archaeology 7(March):1–19.

Mahjub, Muhammad Jafar

1979 The Effect of the European Theatre and the Influence of its Theatrical Methods upon *Taziyeh*. *In Taziyeh*: Ritual and Drama in Iran. Peter J. Chelkowski, ed. Pp. 137–153. New York: New York University Press; Soroush Press.

Mahoney, Dhira B.

2000 Introduction and Comparative Table of Medieval Texts. *In* The Grail: A Casebook. Dhira B. Mahoney, ed. Pp. 1–115. New York: Garland.

Mair, Victor H.

1998 *Review of* From Scythia to Camelot. Religion 28(3):294–300.

2003 The Horse in Late Prehistoric China: Wrestling Culture and Control from the "Babarians." *In* Prehistoric Steppe Adaptation and the Horse. Marsha Levine, Colin Renfrew, and Katie Boyle, eds. Pp. 163–187. Cambridge: Macdonald Institute for Archaeological Research, University of Cambridge.

2005 The North(west)ern Peoples and the Recurrent Origins of the "Chinese" State. *In* The Teleology of the Modern Nation-State: Japan and China. Joshua A. Fogel, ed. Pp. 46–84. Philadelphia: University of Pennsylvania Press.

2007 Horse Sacrifices and Sacred Groves Among the North(west)ern Peoples of East Asia. Ouya Xuekan (Eurasian Studies) 6(June):22–53.

Major Religions Ranked by Size

2005 Electronic document, http://www.adherents.com, accessed December 15, 2008.

Mallory, J. P.

1996 In Search of the Indo-Europeans: Language, Archaeology and Myth. London: Thames and Hudson.

Mallory, J. P., and D. Q. Adams

1997 Encyclopedia of Indo-European Culture. London: Fitzroy Dearborn.

Mallory, J. P., and Victor H. Mair

2000 The Tarim Mummies: Ancient China and the Mystery of the Earliest Peoples from the West. London: Thames and Hudson.

Malone, Kemp

1925 Artorius. Modern Philology 22:28–35.

Mamnoun, Parviz

1979 *Taziyeh* from the Viewpoint of the Western Theatre. *In Taziyeh*: Ritual and Drama in Iran. Peter J. Chelkowski, ed. Pp. 154–166. New York: New York University Press; Soroush Press.

Man, John

2004 Genghis Khan: Life, Death and Resurrection. London: Bantam Press.

Marcus, Joyce
1992 Mesoamerican Writing Systems: Propaganda, Myth, and History in Four Ancient Civilizations. Princeton: Princeton University Press.

Margolis, Max L., ed.
1969 The Holy Scriptures. 2 vols. Philadelphia: Jewish Publication Society of America.

Martinez Diez, Gonzalo
2001 Los Templarios en los Reinos de Espana. Barcelona: Editorial Planeta.

Mason, J. Alden
1957 The Ancient Civilizations of Peru. Harmondsworth, Middlesex: Penguin Books.

Masuya, Tomoko
2002 Ilkhanid Courtly Life. *In* Legacy of Genghis Khan: Courtly Art and Culture in Western Asia. Linda Komaroff and Stefano Carboni, eds. Pp. 74–103. New York: Metropolitan Museum of Art; New Haven: Yale University Press.

Matthews, John
1981 The Grail: Quest for the Eternal. London: Thames and Hudson.

Meaden, Terence
1997 Stonehenge: The Secret of the Solstice. London: Souvenir Press.

Melyukova, A. I.
1990 The Scythians and Sarmatians. *In* The Cambridge History of Early Inner Asia. Denis Sinor, ed. Pp. 97–117. Cambridge: Cambridge University Press.

Moehlman, Patricia
1992 African Wild Asses (*Equus africanus* Fitzinger). *In* Zebras, Asses, and Horses: An Action Plan for the Conservation of Wild Equids. Patrick Duncan, ed. Pp. 15–17. Gland, Switzerland: International Union for Conservation of Nature and Natural Resources.

Mohr, Erna
1971 The Asiatic Wild Horse: *Equus przewalskii* Poliakoff 1881. London: Allen.

Moorey, P. R. S.
1986 The Emergence of the Light Horse-Drawn Chariot in the Near East. World Archaeology 18:196–215.
1988 Early Metallurgy in Mesopotamia. *In* The Beginnings of the Use of Metals and Alloys: Papers from the Second International Conference on the Beginning of the Use of Metals and Alloys, Zhengzhou, China, 21–26 October 1986. Robert Maddin, ed. Pp. 28–33. Cambridge, MA: MIT Press.

Moriarty, James R.
1982 Early Metallurgical Techniques in Southern Meso-America. *In* Metallurgy in Ancient Mexico. Warwick Bray, John L. Sorenson, and James R.

Moriarty III, eds. N.p. Miscellaneous Series, 45. Greeley, CO: University of North Colorado, Museum of Anthropology.

Morris, Craig, and Adriana von Hagen
1993 The Inka Empire and Its Andean Origins. New York: Abbeville Press; American Museum of Natural History.

Mottahedeh, Roy
1975 The Abbasid Caliphate in Iran. *In* The Cambridge History of Iran. Vol. 4, The Period from the Arab Invasion to the Saljuqs. R. N. Frye, ed. Pp. 57–89. Cambridge: Cambridge University Press.

Moule, A. C., and Paul Pelliot, trans.
1938 Travels of Marco Polo: The Description of the World (English and Latin). Translated and annotated by A. C. Moule and Paul Pelliot. London: Routledge.

Muhly, James D.
1988 The Beginnings of Metallurgy in the Old World. *In* The Beginning of the Use of Metals and Alloys: Papers from the Second International Conference on the Beginning of the Use of Metals and Alloys, Zhengzhou, China, 21–26 October 1986. Robert Maddin, ed. Pp. 2–20. Cambridge, MA: MIT Press.

Murnane, William J.
2006 The History of Ancient Egypt: An Overview. *In* Civilizations of the Ancient Near East. Jack M. Sasson, ed. John Baines, Gary Beckman, and Karen S. Rubinson, assoc. eds. Vol. 2, Part 5, History and Culture. Pp. 691–718. Peabody, MA: Hendrickson.

Mustamandy, Chaibai
1997 The Impact of Hellenised Bactria on Gandharan Art. *In* Gandharan Art in Context: East-West Exchanges at the Crossroads of Asia. Raymond Allchin, Bridget Allchin, Neil Kreitman, and Elizabeth Errington, eds. Pp. 17–27. New Delhi: Regency. Published for the Ancient India and Iran Trust, Cambridge.

Needham, Joseph, with Wang Ling
1965 Science and Civilization in China. Vol. 4, Physics and Physical Technology. Part 2, Mechanical Engineering. Cambridge: Cambridge University Press.

Neils, Jenifer
1992 Goddess and Polis: The Panathenaic Festival in Ancient Athens. Hanover, NH: Hood Museum of Art, Dartmouth College; Princeton, NJ: Princeton University Press.
2001 The Parthenon Frieze. Cambridge: Cambridge University Press.

New York Times
1998 Week in Review, September 26.

Nicholson, Helen
  2001 The Knights Templar: A New History. Stroud, Gloucestershire: Sutton.
  2004 The Crusades. Westport, CT: Greenwood Press.

Nickel, Helmut
  1974 The Dawn of Chivalry. The Metropolitan Museum of Art Bulletin 32(5):150–152.

Nicolle, David
  1994 Yarmuk 636 AD: The Muslim Conquest of Syria. London: Osprey.
  1997 Saracen Faris 1050–1250 AD. London: Osprey.
  2001 Knight Hospitaller (I), 1100–1306. London: Osprey.

Nissen, Hans J.
  2006 Ancient Western Asia Before the Age of Empires. *In* Civilizations of the Ancient Near East. Jack M. Sasson, ed. John Baines, Gary Beckman, and Karen S. Rubinson, assoc. eds. Vol. 2, Part 5, History and Culture. Pp. 791–806. Peabody, MA: Hendrickson.

Novellie, Peter, Peter Lloyd, and Eugene Joubert
  1992 Mountain Zebras (*Equus zebra L.*). *In* Zebras, Asses, and Horses: An Action Plan for the Conservation of Wild Equids. Patrick Duncan, ed. Pp. 6–9. Gland, Switzerland: International Union for Conservation of Nature and Natural Resources.

Oates, Joan
  2003 A Note on the Early Evidence for Horse and the Riding of Equids in Western Asia. *In* Prehistoric Steppe Adaptation and the Horse. Marsha Levine, Colin Renfrew, and Katie Boyle, eds. Pp. 115–125. Cambridge: Macdonald Institute for Archaeological Research, University of Cambridge.

O'Flaherty, Wendy Doniger
  1987a Indra. *In* The Encyclopedia of Religion. Mircea Eliade, ed. Vol. 7. Pp. 214–215. New York: Macmillan.
  1987b Horses. *In* The Encyclopedia of Religion. Mircea Eliade, ed. Vol. 6. Pp. 463–468. New York: Macmillan.

Okladnikov, A. P.
  1990 Inner Asia at the Dawn of History. *In* The Cambridge History of Early Inner Asia. Denis Sinor, ed. Pp. 41–96. Cambridge: Cambridge University Press.

Oliver, Roland, and J. D. Fage
  1966 A Short History of Africa. Harmondsworth, Middlesex: Penguin Books.

Olsen, Sandra L.
  1996a Horse Hunters of the Ice Age. *In* Horses Through Time. Sandra L. Olsen, ed. Pp. 35–56. Boulder, CO: Roberts Rinehart.
  1996b Prehistoric Adaptation to the Kazak Steppes. *In* The Colloquia of the XIII International Congress of Prehistoric and Protohistoric Sciences.

G. Afanasev, S. Cleuziou, J. Lukacs, and M. Tosi, eds. Vol. 16, The Prehistory of Asia and Oceania. Pp. 49–60. Forli: A.B.A.C.O. Edizioni.

2003 The Exploitation of Horses at Botai, Kazakhstan. *In* Prehistoric Steppe Adaptation and the Horse. Marsha Levine, Colin Renfrew, and Katie Boyle, eds. Pp. 83–103. Cambridge: Macdonald Institute for Archaeological Research, University of Cambridge.

2006 Early Horse Domestication: Weighing the Evidence. *In* Horses and Humans: The Evolution of Human-Equine Relationships. Sandra L. Olsen, Susan Grant, Alice M. Choyke, and Laszlo Bartosiewicz, eds. Pp. 81–113. British Archaeological Reports International Series, 1560. Oxford: Archaeopress.

Onesti, Nicoletta Francovich
2002 I Vandali: Lingua e Storia. Rome: Carocci.

Onon, Urgunge
2001 The Secret History of the Mongols: The Life and Times of Chinggis Khan. Translated, edited, and with an introduction by Urgunge Onon. Richmond, Surrey: Curzon Press.

Owen, D. D. R.
1972 The Song of Roland: The Oxford Text. Translated from French. London: George Allen and Unwin.

1973 The Legend of Roland: A Pageant of the Middle Ages. London: Phaidon Press.

Owen, David I.
1991 The "First Equestrian": An Ur III Glyptic Scene. Acta Sumerologica 13:259–273.

Ozigboh, Ikenga R. A.
2002 An Introduction to the Religion and History of Islam. Enugu, Nigeria: Fourth Dimension.

Padgett, J. Michael
2003 The Centaur's Smile: The Human Animal in Early Greek Art. Princeton: Princeton University Art Museum. Distributed by New Haven, CT: Yale University Press.

Pare, C. F. E.
1992 Wagons and Wagon Graves of the Early Iron Age in Central Europe. Oxford University Committee for Archaeology Monograph 35. Oxford: Oxford University Committee for Archaeology.

Parpola, Asko
1988 The Coming of the Aryans to Iran and India and the Cultural and Ethnic Identity of the Dasas. International Journal of Dravidian Linguistics 17(2):85–229.

1995 The Problem of the Aryans and the Soma: Textual-linguistic and Archaeological Evidence. *In* The Indo-Aryans of Ancient South Asia: Language, Material Culture, and Ethnicity. George Erdosy, ed. Pp. 353–381. New York: Walter de Gruyter.

1999 The Formation of the Aryan Branch of Indo-European. *In* Archaeology and Language. Vol. 3, Artefacts, Languages, and Texts. Roger Blench and Matthew Spriggs, eds. Pp. 180–207. One World Archaeology. London: Routledge.

Pastoureau, Michel, and Marie-Therese Gousset
2002 Lancelot du Lac et la Quete du Graal. Bibliotheque Nationale de France. Arcueil: Editions Anthese.

Paterson, "Banjo"
1894 The Geebung Polo Club. *In* The Antipodean: An Illustrated Annual. George Essex Evans and John Tighe Ryan, eds. Illustrations by Frank P. Mahony. Pp. 4–7. London: George Robertson.

Patterson, Orlando
1982 Slavery and Social Death: A Comparative Study. Cambridge, MA: Harvard University Press.

Patterson, Thomas C.
1991 The Inca Empire: The Formation and Disintegration of a Pre-Capitalist State. New York: Berg.

Peterson, Samuel R.
1979 The *Taziyeh* and Related Arts. *In Taziyeh*: Ritual and Drama in Iran. Peter J. Chelkowski, ed. Pp. 64–87. New York: New York University Press; Soroush Press.

Piggott, Stuart
1962 Head and Hoofs. Antiquity 36:110–118.
1968 The Earliest Wheeled Vehicles and the Caucasian Evidence. Proceedings of the Prehistoric Society 34(8): 266–318.
1974 Chariots in the Caucasus and China. Antiquity 48:16–24.
1983 The Earliest Wheeled Transport: From the Atlantic Coast to the Caspian Sea. New York: Thames and Hudson.
1992 Wagon, Chariot and Carriage: Symbol and Status in the History of Transport. New York: Thames and Hudson.

Piotrovsky, Boris
1974a Early Cultures of the Lands of the Scythians. The Metropolitan Museum of Art Bulletin 32(5):12–25. (Adapted from Russian text by Boris Piotrovsky, The State Hermitage Museum, Leningrad.)
1974b Excavations and Discoveries in Scythian Lands. The Metropolitan Museum of Art Bulletin 32(5):26–31. (Adapted from Russian text by Boris Piotrovsky, The State Hermitage Museum, Leningrad.)

Pohl, John M. D.

1999 Exploring Mesoamerica. Oxford: Oxford University Press.

Prescott, William H.

2001 History of Conquest of Mexico. New York: Modern Library.

Raevskii, D. S.

1987 Scythian Religion. *In* The Encyclopedia of Religion. Mircea Eliade, ed. Vol. 13. Pp. 145–148. NewYork: Macmillan.

Rawson, Jessica

1999 Western Zhou Archaeology. *In* The Cambridge History of Ancient China: From the Origins of Civilization to 221 BC. Michael Loewe and Edward L. Shaughnessy, eds. Pp. 352–449. Cambridge: Cambridge University Press.

Raymond, Robert

1984 Out of the Fiery Furnace: The Impact of Metals on the History of Mankind. South Melbourne, Australia: Macmillan.

Regan, Geoffrey

1998 Lionhearts: Saladin and Richard I. London: Constable.

Renfrew, Colin

1990 Archaeology and Language: The Puzzle of Indo-European Origins. Cambridge: Cambridge University Press.

Ritchie, W. F., and J. N. G. Ritchie

1985 Celtic Warriors. Aylesbury, Buckshire: Shire.

Roberts, J. A. G.

1999 A History of China. London: Macmillan.

Robinson, B. W.

2002 The Persian Book of Kings: An Epitome of the Shahnama of Firdawsi. London: Routledge-Curzon.

Roemer, H. R.

1993a Timur in Iran. *In* The Cambridge History of Iran. Vol. 6, The Timurid and Safavid Periods. Peter Jackson and Laurence Lockhart, eds. Pp. 42–97. Cambridge: Cambridge University Press.

1993b The Successors of Timur. *In* The Cambridge History of Iran. Vol. 6, The Timurid and Safavid Periods. Peter Jackson and Laurence Lockhart, eds. Pp. 98–146. Cambridge: Cambridge University Press.

1993c The Safavid Period. *In* The Cambridge History of Iran. Vol. 6, The Timurid and Safavid Periods. Peter Jackson and Laurence Lockhart, eds. Pp. 189–350. Cambridge: Cambridge University Press.

Rolle, Renate
1980 Die Welt der Skythen. Luzern: Verlag C. J. Bucher. (Published in English in 1989 as The World of the Scythians. Berkeley: University of California Press.)
1989 The World of the Scythians. Berkeley: University of California Press.

Rossabi, Morris
1988 Khubilai Khan: His Life and Times. Berkeley: University of California Press.
1994 The Reign of Khubilai Khan. *In* The Cambridge History of China. Denis Twitchett and John K. Fairbank, eds. Vol. 6, Alien Regimes and Border States, 907–1368. Herbert Franke and Denis Twitchett, eds. Pp. 414–489. Cambridge: Cambridge University Press.
2002 The Mongols and Their Legacy. *In* Legacy of Genghis Khan: Courtly Art and Culture in Western Asia. Linda Komaroff and Stefano Carboni, eds. Pp. 12–35. New York: Metropolitan Museum of Art; New Haven: Yale University Press.

Rowen, Mary, and Joshua Ginsberg
1992 Grevy's Zebras (*Equus grevyi* Oustalet). *In* Zebras, Asses, and Horses: An Action Plan for the Conservation of Wild Equids. Patrick Duncan, ed. Pp. 10–12. Gland, Switzerland: International Union for Conservation of Nature and Natural Resources.

Rudenko, Sergei I.
1970 Frozen Tombs of Siberia: The Pazyryk Burials of Iron-age Horsemen. Translated by M. W. Thompson. Berkeley: University of California Press.

Sacks, David
1995 Encyclopedia of the Ancient Greek World. New York: Facts on File.

Saliba, George
1987 The Role of Maragha in the Development of Islamic Astronomy: A Scientific Revolution before the Renaissance. Revue de Synthese 1:361–373.

Sanders, Donald H.
1996 Nemrud Dagi: The Hierothesion of Antiochus I of Commagene. Vol. 1. Winona Lake, IN: Eisenbrauns.

Sarianidi, V. I.
1986 Mesopotamiia i Baktriia. Sovetskaya Arkheologiya 2:34–46.

Saunders, J. J.
2001 The History of the Mongol Conquests. Philadelphia: University of Pennsylvania Press.

Schaedel, Richard P.
1978 Early State of the Incas. *In* The Early State. Henri J. M. Claessen and Peter Skalnik, eds. Pp. 289–320. The Hague: Mouton.

Schrader, O.

1890 Prehistoric Antiquities of the Aryan Peoples: A Manual of Comparative Philology and the Earliest Culture. Translated by F. B. Jevons. London: Charles Griffin.

Schwartz, Glenn M.

2006 Pastoral Nomadism in Western Central Asia. *In* Civilizations of the Ancient Near East. Jack M. Sasson, ed. John Baines, Gary Beckman, and Karen S. Rubinson, assoc. eds. Vol. 1, Part 3, Population. Pp. 249–258. Peabody, MA: Hendrickson.

Schwartz, Stuart B., and Frank Salomon

1999 New Peoples and New Kinds of People: Adaptation, Readjustment, and Ethnogenesis in South American Indigenous Societies (Colonial Era). *In* The Cambridge History of the Native Peoples of the Americas. Frank Salomon and Stuart B. Schwartz, eds. Vol. 3, South America – Part 2. Pp. 443–501. Cambridge: Cambridge University Press.

Sealey, Paul R.

1997 The Boudican Revolt Against Rome. Princes Risborough, Buckinghamshire: Shire.

Seife, Charles

2000 Zero: The Biography of a Dangerous Idea. New York: Viking Penguin.

Seward, Desmond

1972 The Monks of War: The Military Religious Orders. Hamden, CT: Archon Books. (Initially published London: Eyre Methuen.)

Seyffert, Oskar

1995 The Dictionary of Classical Mythology, Religion, Literature, and Art. New York: Random House, Grammercy Books.

Shahidi, Anayatullah

1979 Literary and Musical Developments in *Taziyeh*. *In Taziyeh*: Ritual and Drama in Iran. Peter J. Chelkowski, ed. Pp. 40–63. New York: New York University Press; Soroush Press.

Shakhanova, Nurila Z.

1992 The Yurt in the Traditional Worldview of Central Asian Nomads. *In* Foundations of Empire: Archeology and Art of the Eurasian Steppes. Proceedings of the Soviet-American Academic Symposia in Conjunction with the Museum Exhibitions. Gary Seaman, ed. Vol. 3, Nomads: Masters of the Eurasian Steppes. Pp. 157–183. Los Angeles: Ethnographics Press, University of Southern California.

Shaughnessy, Edward

1988 Historical Perspectives on the Introduction of the Chariot into China. Harvard Journal of Asiatic Studies 48:189–237.

Shaw, Brent D., ed.
    2001 Spartacus and the Slave Wars: A Brief History with Documents. Translated, edited, and with an introduction by Brent D. Shaw. Boston: Bedford/St. Martin's.

Shilov, Valentin Pavlovich
    1989 The Origins of Migration and Animal Husbandry in the Steppes of Eastern Europe. *In* The Walking Larder: Patterns of Domestication, Pastoralism, and Predation. Juliet Clutton-Brock, ed. Pp. 119–126. London: Unwin Hyman.

Simon, Andre
    1996 Vercingetorix, Heros Republicain. Paris: Editions Ramsay.

Simpson, George Gaylord
    1951 Horses: The Story of the Horse Family in the Modern World and through Sixty Million Years of History. New York: Oxford University Press.

Sims-Williams, Nicholas
    1996 The Sogdian Merchants in India and China. *In* Cina e Iran: da Alessandro Magno alla Dinastia Tang. Alfredo Cadonna and Lionello Lanciotti, eds. Pp. 45–67. Florence: Leo S. Olschki Editore, Orientalia Venetiana.

Singh, Nagendra K.
    1997 Vedic Mythology. New Delhi: APH.

Singh, Rao Rajah Hanut
    1971 A Century of Polo. *In* Chakkar: Polo Around the World. Herbert Spencer, ed. Pp. 11–15. London: Herbert Spencer.

Singh, Satya Prakash
    2001 Vedic Symbolism. New Delhi: Maharshi Sandipani Rashtriya Veda Vidya Pratishthan.

Sipress, Linda
    1973 The Unicorn Tapestries. The Metropolitan Museum of Art Bulletin 32(1):n.p.

Skjaervo, P. Oktor
    1995 The Avesta as Source for the Early History of the Iranians. *In* The Indo-Aryans of Ancient South Asia: Language, Material Culture and Ethnicity. George Erdosy, ed. Pp. 155–176. Berlin: Walter de Gruyter.

Slatta, Richard W., and Jane Lucas De Grummond
    2003 Simon Bolivar's Quest for Glory. College Station: Texas A&M University Press.

Smith, Bruce D.
    1995 The Emergence of Agriculture. New York: Scientific American Library.

Smith, E. Baldwin
    1950 The Dome: A Study in the History of Ideas. Princeton, NJ: Princeton University Press.

Smith, William

1925 A Classical Dictionary of Greek and Roman Biography. Revised throughout and in part rewritten by G. E. Marindin. London: John Murray.

Snodgrass, Adrian

1985 The Symbolism of the Stupa. Ithaca, NY: Cornell Southeast Asia Program.

So, Jenny F.

1995 Expanded Cultural Exchange: Ca. 1000-500 BC. *In* Traders and Raiders on China's Northern Frontier. Jenny F. So and Emma C. Bunker. Pp. 41–51. Seattle: Arthur M. Sackler Gallery, Smithsonian Institution, in association with the University of Washington Press.

Soucek, Svat

2000 A History of Inner Asia. Cambridge: Cambridge University Press.

Souden, David

1997 Stonehenge: Mysteries of the Stones and Landscape. London: Collins and Brown, in association with English Heritage.

Spencer, Herbert, ed.

1971 Chakkar: Polo Around the World. London: Herbert Spencer.

Spruytte, J.

1983 Early Harness Systems: Experimental Studies. Translated by Mary Littauer. London: Allen.

Steele, Nick

1971 Take a Horse to the Wilderness. Cape Town: T. V. Bulpin and Books of Africa.

Steiner, Patricia Owen

1995 The Gaucho's World. *In* Don Segundo Sombra. Ricardo Guiraldes. Translated by Patricia Owen Steiner. Critical edition. Gwen Kirkpatrick, coordinator. Pp. 215–230. Pittsburgh: University of Pittsburgh Press.

Stirling, M. W.

1938 Historical and Ethnographical Material on the Jivaro Indians. Bureau of American Ethnology Bulletin, 117. Washington, DC: Smithsonian Institution.

Stoneman, Richard

1997 Alexander the Great. London: Routledge.

Stover, Leon

2003 Stonehenge City: A Reconstruction. Jefferson, NC: McFarland.

Strabo

1961 Geography. Translated by Horace Leonard Jones. G. P. Goold, ed. Loeb Classical Library. Cambridge, MA: Harvard University Press.

Sulimirski, T.
  1993 The Scyths. *In* The Cambridge History of Iran. Vol. 2, The Median and Achaemenian Periods. Ilya Gershevitch, ed. Pp. 149–199. Cambridge: Cambridge University Press.

Taylour, William
  1983 The Mycenaeans. London: Thames and Hudson.

Telegin, D. Y.
  1986 Dereivka: A Settlement and Cemetery of Copper Age Horse Keepers on the Middle Dnieper. Oxford: British Archaeological Reports, International Series 287. Oxford: Archaeopress.

Temple, Robert
  1998 The Genius of China; 3,000 Years of Science, Discovery, and Invention. Introduced by Joseph Needham. London: Prion.

Tennyson, Alfred
  1987 The Charge of the Light Brigade. *In* The Poems of Tennyson. 3 vols. Christopher Ricks, ed. Vol. 2. Pp. 510–513. Harlow, Essex: Longman.

Thompson, Diane P.
  2004 The Trojan War: Literature and Legends from the Bronze Age to the Present. Jefferson, NC: McFarland.

Thompson, E. A.
  1996 The Huns. Oxford: Blackwell.

Thompson, M. W.
  1970 Translator's Preface. *In* Frozen Tombs of Siberia: The Pazyryk Burials of Iron-age Horsemen. Sergei I. Rudenko. Translated by M. W. Thompson. Berkeley: University of California Press.

Thorp, Robert L.
  2006 China in the Early Bronze Age: Shang Civilization. Philadelphia: University of Pennsylvania Press.

Till, Barry
  1984 Samurai: The Cultured Warrior. Victoria, BC: Sono Nis Press.

Tinker, Edward Larocque
  1964 Centaurs of Many Lands. Austin: University of Texas Press.

Travis, John
  2008 Third International Symposium on Biomolecular Archaeology: Trail of Mare's Milk Leads to First Tamed Horses. Science 322(October 17):368a.

Trippett, Frank
  1974 The First Horsemen. New York: Time-Life Books.

Turnbull, Stephen R.
  2003 Samurai: The World of the Warrior. Oxford: Osprey.

Uerpmann, Hans-Peter
  1996 Animal Domestication – Accident or Intention. *In* The Origins and Spread of Agriculture and Pastoralism in Eurasia. David R. Harris, ed. Pp. 227–237. London: University College London Press.

Urban, William
  2003 The Teutonic Knights: A Military History. London: Greenhill Books; Mechanicsburg, PA: Stackpole Books.

Vale, Malcolm
  1981 War and Chivalry: Warfare and Aristocratic Culture in England, France and Burgundy at the End of the Middle Ages. London: Duckworth.
  2001 The Princely Court: Medieval Courts and Culture in North-West Europe 1270–1380. Oxford: Oxford University Press.

Vansina, Jan
  1996 A Slow Revolution: Farming in Subequatorial Africa. *In* The Growth of Farming Communities in Africa from the Equator Southwards. J. E. G. Sutton, ed. Pp. 15–26. Nairobi, Kenya: British Institute in Eastern Africa.

Vismara, Cinzia
  2001 The World of the Gladiators. *In* The Colosseum. Ada Gabucci, ed. Translated by Mary Becker. Pp. 21–53. Los Angeles: J. Paul Getty Museum.

Von Hagen, Adriana, and Craig Morris
  1998 The Cities of the Andes. New York: Thames and Hudson.

Wahlgren, Erik
  1986 The Vikings and America. London: Thames and Hudson.

Waldron, Arthur
  1990 The Great Wall of China from History to Myth. Cambridge: Cambridge University Press.

Waley, Arthur
  1955 The Heavenly Horses of Ferghana: A New View. History Today, February: 96–99.

Warner, Marina
  2000 Joan of Arc: The Image of Female Heroism. Berkeley: University of California Press.

Watkins, Calvert
  1995 How to Kill a Dragon: Aspects of Indo-European Poetics. New York: Oxford University Press.

Watt, James, C. Y.
  2002 A Note on Artistic Exchanges in the Mongol Empire. *In* Legacy of Genghis Khan: Courtly Art and Culture in Western Asia. Linda Komaroff and Stefano Carboni, eds. Pp. 62–73. New York: Metropolitan Museum of Art; New Haven: Yale University Press.

Weatherford, Jack
  1988 Indian Givers: How the Indians of the Americas Transformed the World. New York: Crown.
  2004 Genghis Khan and the Making of the Modern World. New York: Crown.

Webster, Graham
  1978 Boudica: The British Revolt Against Rome AD 60. London: Batsford.

Weed, William Speed
  2002 First to Ride. Discover 23(3):54–61.

Wertime, T. A.
  1973 The Beginnings of Metallurgy: A New Look. Science 182:875–887.

White, Lynn, Jr.
  1962 Medieval Technology and Social Change. Oxford: Oxford at the Clarendon Press.

Wilber, Donald N.
  1989 Persepolis: The Archaeology of Parsa, Seat of the Persian Kings. Princeton, NJ: Darwin Press.

Wilford, John Noble
  1993 New Finds Suggest Even Earlier Trade on Fabled Silk Road. New York Times, March 16.

Wirth, Andrzej
  1979 Semiological Aspects of the *Taziyeh*. In *Taziyeh*: Ritual and Drama in Iran. Peter J. Chelkowski, ed. Pp. 32–39. New York: New York University Press; Soroush Press.

Wolf, Eric
  1966 Sons of the Shaking Earth. Chicago: University of Chicago Press, Phoenix Books.

Wolpert, Stanley
  1993 A New History of India. New York: Oxford University Press.

Wood, Frances
  2002 The Silk Road: Two Thousand Years in the Heart of Asia. Berkeley: University of California Press.

Wood, Michael
  1998 In Search of the Trojan War. Berkeley: University of California Press.
  2000 Conquistadors. Berkeley: University of California Press.

Woodford, Susan
  1993 The Trojan War in Ancient Art. London: Duckworth.

Woodward, Susan
  1996 The Living Relatives of the Horse. In Horses Through Time. Sandra L. Olsen, ed. Pp. 191–208. Boulder, CO: Roberts Rinehart.

Worthington, Ian, ed.
 2003 Alexander the Great: A Reader. London: Routledge, Taylor and Francis Group.

Wright, David Curtis
 2001 The History of China. Westport, CT: Greenwood Press.

Yadin, Yigael
 1963 The Art of Warfare in Biblical Lands: In Light of Archeological Discovery. Vol. 2. New York: McGraw-Hill.

Yarshater, Ehsan
 1979 *Taziyeh* and Pre-Islamic Mourning Rites in Iran. *In Taziyeh*: Ritual and Drama in Iran. Peter J. Chelkowski, ed. Pp. 88–94. New York: New York University Press; Soroush Press.

Yarwood, Alexander T.
 1989 Walers: Australian Horses Abroad. Carlton, Victoria: Melbourne University Press at the Miegunyah Press.

Yoshida, Atsuhiko
 1977 Japanese Mythology and the Indo-European System. Diogenes 98:93–116.

Yu, Ying-shih
 1967 Trade and Expansion in Han China: A Study in the Structure of Sino-Barbarian Economic Relations. Berkeley: University of California Press.
 1990 The Hsiung-Nu. *In* The Cambridge History of Early Inner Asia. Denis Sinor, ed. Pp. 118–149. Cambridge: Cambridge University Press.

Yumoto, John M.
 1958 The Samurai Sword: A Handbook. Rutland, VT: Tuttle.

Zhongguo Shehui Kexueyuan (Chinese Academy of Social Sciences) Kaogu Yanjiusuo (Institute of Archaeology) Anyang Gongzuodui (Anyang Archaeological Team)
 1988 Anyang Guojiazhuang xinan de Yindai chemakeng. Kaogu 10:882–893.

Zohary, Daniel, and Maria Hopf
 2000 The Domestication of Plants in the Old World: The Origin and Spread of Cultivated Plants in West Asia, Europe, and the Nile Valley. New York: Oxford University Press.

Zvelebil, Marek
 2000 The Social Context of the Agricultural Transition in Europe. *In* Archaeogenetics: DNA and the Population Prehistory of Europe. Colin Renfrew and Katie Boyle, eds. Pp. 57–79. Cambridge, UK: McDonald Institute for Archaeological Research.

INDEX

Abashevo, 49
Abbas I, 327, 367, 398
Abbasids, 224, 231–232, 303, 331
Acre, 268
Afanasievo, 38, 49, 55, 57, 60, 136
African wild ass, 13–14. *See also Equidae, Equus*
Afro-Asiatic, 390
Agni, 111
agro-pastoralism, 136
Ahriman, 255. *See also* Zoroastrianism, Angra Mainyu
akinji, 329
Alaca Huyuk, 94
Alans, 148, 195–196
Alcantara, 279
Alexander the Great, 128–132
Alexandria, 130
alfalfa/lucerne, 119, 190
Allen's rule, 172, 218
Almohads, 247, 251
Almoravids, 248
　　Marrakesh, 251
　　Tashfin, Yusuf ibn, 251
Altaic speakers, 115, 320
Amazons, 86, 178–179, 186, 292, 331, 342, 364, 377
Amerindian population loss, 370
Anabasis, 128
ancient riders
　　Assyrian riding duo, 106
　　BMAC (2200-1800 BC), 43
　　Kish (2400-2300 BC), 43
　　Koban (1000 BC), 63
　　Komarovka (1700-1300 BC), 53
　　Mesopotamia (2000-1750 BC), 43
　　mounted herding, 41, 47
　　mounted raiding, 44
　　Nanshangen mounted hunters (700 BC), 138
　　Pirak, 62, 109
　　relocation of populations, 105, 121
　　scouting on horseback, 105
　　Siyalk (800 BC), 63
　　Ur III (2037-2029 BC), 43
Andronovo (2000-900 BC), 49–50, 136
Arabian horse, 218, 220–221
Araucanians (Mapuche), 374
Archimedes, 133
Arinna, 94
Armenians, 104, 210
armor for the equestrian combatant, 63
　　arret de cuirasse, 342
　　chain mail, 190, 250
　　harnois blanc, 341
　　heavy armor, 242
　　iron helmet, 289
　　Japanese steel plaque armor, 318
　　Kofun metal plaque armor, 318
　　lamellar leather with iron, 289
　　padded leather jerkin, 289
　　quilted cotton, 250
　　scale armor, 78, 86, 190
　　steel helmet, 342
arms for the equestrian combatant
　　battle axe, 78, 86, 250, 289
　　bolas, boleadora, 375
　　breech-loading rifle, 374
　　broadsword, 190
　　contus heavy lance, 190
　　couched lance, 164, 198–199, 241, 264

arms for the equestrian (*cont.*)
  curved sword, 78
  dagger, 78
  firearms, 316, 326
  firelance, 292, 300
  harquebus, 329, 385, 391
  iron arrowheads, 78
  Japanese long bow, 319
  Japanese single-bladed sword,
    319
  javelin, 250, 289
  lance, 78, 164
  lasso, 78, 196, 289
  long spear for jabbing, 176
  pistol, 391
  poisoned arrows, 78
  recurved composite bow, 63, 76–77,
    138
  saber, 164
  Scythian gorytus, 77
  slashing sword, 172
  sling, 78
  whip, 78, 339, 340
arrow messengers, 288
Arsuf, 269
Arthur, 200–201, 255
  Arthuriad, 204, 320
  Batraz, Nart hero, 200, 320
  Excalibur, 200, 202
  Lancelot, 201, 255, 338
  Ossetic Nart sagas, 203
  Quest of the Holy Grail, 201–202,
    320
  Round Table, 202, 337
artisans, 310, 325
Aryan migrations, 54, 61, 108, 116
  Dasas, 62, 62n, 109
Asian wild ass, 13. *See also* Equidae,
    Equus
Assassins, 266, 270, 303
Astarte, 95
astragalus bone, 7
astronomy, 313
Asvins, 112–113, 339
Atahualpa, 362–363
Atharvana, 54
Attila. *See* Huns, Attila
Australia, 394–395, 396
Austro-Asiatic, 389
Austronesian, 389
Avars, 164, 198, 241

Avesta. See Zoroastrianism
Avicenna, 247
Ayyubids, 266
Aztecs, 356

Bactria-Margiana Archaeological
    Complex (BMAC), 43, 54
Bactrian camel, 54n
Baden, 48
Baghdad, 224
Barbary corsairs, 330
Bartolomeu Dias, 351
Basotho, 393
Battle of Hastings, 241
Baybars, 274–275, 303
Beakers, 165
beard, 85, 138, 143, 293
Beersheba, 400
Behistun, 123
Berbers, 236, 238
Bergmann's rule, 172, 218
bevel, 37–38
  Alakul-Petrovka, 38
  Botai, 37
  Sergeivka, 38
  Utyevka, 38
Bhagavadgita, 111
Biruni, 246
Bishkent, 54
Blood River, 393
blood-sweating horses, 146
Boers, 219, 392
Bokhara, 325, 331
Borjigin, 283
Botai, 35–37
Boudica, 186–187
breast strap. *See* horse power, trace
    harness
bridling, 85
  bit, 11, 33n, 37, 37f, 38, 41, 42, 64, 65, 74,
    76, 106, 142, 179, 375, 378
  cheekpieces, 37, 52, 53, 63, 74
  jointed snaffle, 106
  nose ring, 43, 52
Bubastis canal, 125, 381
Bucephalus, 128, 131
Buddhism, 306
  cakravartin, 152
  Channa, 151
  Gandara art, 154
  Gautama, Siddhartha, 151

Kanishka, 154
Kanthaka, 151
Mahayana, 154
Maitreya, 155, 210
mandala, 109
pagoda, 154
stupa, 151, 169
swastika, 152
White Horse temple, 155
Xuanzang, 159
Buenos Aires, 375, 377, 393, 394
buffalo, 372, 374
Burkhan Khaldun. *See* world mountain,
    Burkhan Khaldun
bushi, 319
Buyids, 228, 233
Byzantium, 205. *See also* Constantinople

Cabral, 364
Caesar, Julius, 185
Cajamarca, 362
Calatrava, 279
Cannae, 183
cannon, 276, 301, 344, 391, 400
cannon bone, 7
Caper, 393
carpet manufacture, 72, 84
Carrhae, 204
Carthage, 182, 183–184
castle, 276
catacomb (2500-1900 BC), 50
Cathar heresy, 279
cattle, 8, 23, 29, 34, 40, 48, 58, 80, 117, 136,
    140, 336, 348, 371, 375, 377, 392,
    396
cauldron, 115, 201, 320
Celts, 173–175, 403
centaur, 96, 176–178
centum languages, 58
Chagataids, 324, 331
chalan. *See* gaucho
chansons de geste, 239, 345, 378
    Charlemagne, 239
    Roland, 241, 255
    romances fronterizos, 348
Charge of the Light Brigade, 400
Charlemagne, 198, 241, 261, 343
chess, 338
chestnuts, 10
Chimu, 360
Chinese dancing horses, 149

chivalric bullfight, 348
chivalry, 203, 277, 336–338
    dubbing, 337
Christianity
    Arians, 196
    Donatists, 196
    Greco-Roman, 205
    Greek Orthodox, 199
    Monophysites, 217
    Nestorianism, 158, 302, 307, 309
    Papacy, 260, 263, 268, 307, 309, 367
    Protestantism, 329
Cimmerians, 116
circuitous procession, 169, 180
circumscribed alluvial states, 27, 93, 355,
    359, 380
cold-weather adaptability, 39
Colosseum, 193
Columbus, Christopher, 351–353
Comanche, 371, 386
Commagene, 210–211
Confucians, 306, 307
    Confucius, 138
conical hats, 50, 313
Constantinople, 209, 236, 244, 271, 325, 328
    Constantine, 205
    fortresses, 259
    Hagia Sophia, 206–208
    Heraclius, 212
    Hippodrome, 271
    Lysippos' golden horses, 206, 271
    Nika revolt, 206
Copernicus, 246, 366
Copts, 275. *See also* Christianity,
    Monophysites
Corded Ware, 48
Cordoba, 238, 244
Coricancha Temple of the Sun, 361
Coronado, 371
Cortes's conquest of the Mexica, 357–359
cosmic tent, 123, 132, 194
cosmology
    Celtic, 174
    Indo-Aryan, 174
    Japanese, 319–320
    medieval European, 336
    Persian, 255
    Scythian, 86–88
Council of Clermont 1095, 260
courtly love, 345
Covadonga, 238, 344

Crassus, 185, 204
Crazy Horse, 374
Cris (5600 BC), 29
Croesus, 120
Crusades, 248, 260–272
Cucuteni-Tripolye (4900-3400 BC), 29
Curmos, 308, 327
Cuzco, 361
Cyaxares, 120
Cyrus II, 86, 120, 122
   religious tolerance, 121

danastuti (coda of verses), 110
Darius I, 123–125, 126, 382
Darius III, 130
Dark Ages, 334
Delphi, 193
Dhar Tichitt-Walata, 219
dhimmi, 222, 237
diastema, 11, 37
diet, 12, 13
dismemberment, 78, 89, 122, 137, 153
   Orpheus, 153
Divine Twins. *See* Asvins
Dnieper-Donets (5100-4100 BC), 32
dog, 22, 36, 372
Dome of the Rock, 244
Domus aurea, 193
Dongola, 275
donkey, 14, 23, 24, 40, 43, 45f, 47, 95, 141, 172, 335, 388, 398, 401
   donkey seat, 44
   unsuited to riding, 24
Dorians, 176
Drake, Francis, 367
drift mine, 49
dromedary, 212–213, 216, 219, 235
Druids, 174, 186

early Islam
   Alids, 224
   Buraq, white horse, 214
   Caliph Abu Bakr, 216
   Caliph Uthman, 223
   five pillars of, 215
   Hashimites, 223
   Husayn, 224
   jihad, 217
   Muhammad, 214–215
   Nihavand, 222

Qadasiya, 221
   ridda, 216
   Yarmuk, 217
early wheeled technology, 45–46
   cart, 45, 46, 55, 73, 95, 96, 111n, 141, 308, 376
   crossbar type wheel, 74
   disc wheel, 73–74
   dispersed habitation, 45
   draught pole, 76
   early draught unsuited to horse anatomy, 46, 73, 96–97, 161
   farm efficiency, 45
   funerary models, 46
   iron hoop tire, 172
   lunate-opening type wheel, 74
   Mesoamerican wheel, 354, 383
   metal tire, 95
   pivoted front axle, 172
   rawhide tire, 95
   traces, 84
   transportation, 45
   wagon, 45, 46, 51, 52, 52f, 60, 68, 73, 95, 96, 172, 220n, 329, 373, 392, 393
el Cid, 255, 345
elephants, 131, 183, 221
encomiendas, 279
environmental devastation, 295, 386
ephedra, 56
Epona, 113, 188
equid hybrids
   hinny (jennet), 24
   mule, 24, 73, 100, 104, 191, 308, 335
   onager bred with donkey, 24, 52
   zebra bred with horse or donkey, 24
equid miniaturization, 23
equid social systems, 14–15
Equidae, 6–12
   Anchitherium, 349
   cursoriality, 8–9
   digestion, 8
   Dinohippus, 10
   Equus, 6, 10–12, 20
   Equus hydruntinus, 13, 32
   Hipparion, 9, 349
   Hippidion, 10
   hypsodonty, 8
   Hyracotherium, 7
   Leisey equids, 41
   Merychippus, 8–9
   Mesohippus, 7

Miohippus, 7, 8
monodactyly, 10
Onohippidium, 10
Parahippus, 8
Pliohippus, 10
tridactyly, 7, 10
Equus ferus przewalskii, 14, 17, 19, 40, 218, 297, 403
breeding in zoos, 18–19
capturing expeditions in the wild, 18
restoration in the wild, 19–20
Eratosthenes, 133
ergots, 10
Euclid, 133
eunuch, 121, 243, 254
exposure of dead, 51, 117

Falz-Fein, Friedrich von, 18
faris, 263
Fatimids, 248, 259, 265
Fatyanovo-Balanovo, 48
Fedorovo, 50
feigned retreat, 331
Ferghana, 147
Fierro, Martín, 376–377
fossil equids. *See Equidae*
Frederick Barbarossa, 268
French fur trappers, 373
funerary ritual involving the horse, 33–34
Alexander's funeral for Bucephalus, 131
Alexandropol, 80
Arzhan, 81
Botai horse skull circle, 36
Cyrus horse sacrifice, 122
Dashly 3, 109
Deccan horse sacrifice, 109
Europe, paired horse skulls and chariot, 166
Gross-Hoflein, 42
head-and-hoof offering, 34, 35f, 51, 53
Hittite horse sacrifice, 94
Jos horse sacrifice, 182
Khvalynsk, 34
Late Maikop, 80
Lchashen horse burials, 74
Mongol horse sacrifice, 298
Patroclos's funeral pyre, 103
Pazyryk, 86
Qin Shi Huangdi's necropolis, 142

Reagan, Ronald, 402–403
Scythian king, 88–89
Shang horse and human sacrifice, 139f
Syezzhe, 34
Varfolomievka, 35
Wellington's military salute to warhorse, 399
funerary tomb tower, 311

Galileo, 366
gang rape, 186
Gansu horse, 147
Garamantes, 182
gaucho, 375–377
Gaugamela, 130
Geebung Polo Club, 397
Genghis khan, 281–282. *See also* Temujin
exploratory probe into Europe, 295
funeral, 297
invasion of China, 292
invasion of Khwarizmia, 295
Ghana, 249
Ghazan, 309
ghazi, 233, 276
ghulam, 232
Gibraltar, 237
goat, 18, 22, 23, 34, 41, 58, 70n, 71, 89, 136, 212, 285, 392
Golden Bull of Rimini, 276
Golden Horde, 301. *See also* Kipchak khanate
Gordion knot, 129
Granicus, 129
Great Mongol Shahnameh, 312
Great Wall of China, 142, 142n
Guadalete, 237
gunpowder, 315
Gypsies, 108

haciendas, 348
Hadrian's wall, 190
Hallstatt, 171–172
Han, 142, 162
hands (measurement), 7n
haoma. *See* sauma cult
Hausa, 250
heavenly horses, 146
Heike Monogatari, 321
Hephaestion, 132
Heracles, 112, 255, 348
heroic poetry, 81

high gait, 39
High Noon, 379
hillfort, 172
Hipparchus, 133
Hittites, 94
h₁oitos oath, 60
Hmong-Mien, 389
Holocene, 10n, 13, 17, 21
honey mead (*madhu*), 112
hoof, 8
horse artillery, 393–394
horse contests
    buzkashi, 89–91, 398
    chariot racing, 103, 170, 191–192, 206
    Circus Maximus, 191
    Hippodrome, 206
    horse racing, 142, 205
    naadam, 330
    Palio of Siena, 338–341
    polo, 156, 253, 274, 324, 327, 394
    racing factions, 192, 206
    tournament, 339
horse domestication
    Botai, 35–37
    Dereivka, 32–33
    eastern Europe, 41
horse extinction in New World, 10, 350,
    353, 384
horse maritime transport, 5, 127, 261–262,
    352, 353
horse power
    carriage, 84, 142, 162, 370, 403
    cavalry, 66, 92, 106–107, 120, 125, 133,
        140, 142, 144, 183, 189, 219, 221, 236,
        241, 263, 276, 282, 289, 309, 318, 329,
        373, 377, 389, 394, 400, 401
    chariot, 51–52, 53, 66, 74–76, 96, 98, 111,
        125, 130, 133, 135, 136, 137, 139–140,
        152, 176, 182, 186, 389, 403
    contoured collar harness, 162, 334–336
    contoured pad, 85
    dished wheel, 369
    dual character of, 1–2, 245, 298, 310, 318,
        402
    furusiyya, exercise for war, 274
    hipposandal, 190
    horse shoe, iron, 191, 241
    horse shoe, silver, 365
    hunt, exercise for war, 289, 296, 306
    industrial horse transport, 369–370
    integral nave, 98

intensive mixed farming, 336
Kesselwagen cultic model, 172
movable forecarriage, 369
pack animal, 40, 44, 46, 64, 369
practice for war, 284
rapid horse transport, 336
saddle, 63, 85–86, 105, 142, 189, 241,
    373
saddle cloth, 85
scythed chariot, 130, 133, 134
speed of travel, 63, 65, 188, 308, 383
spoked wheel, 74, 75, 84, 137
stage coach, 370
stirrup
    cast iron, 164
    hook, 163
    nonrigid, 163, 375
    wooden, 164, 373
trace harness, 162, 164, 334–336
traces, 76
Trundholm sun chariot, 171
whippletree, 162
yoke saddle, 76, 84, 85f, 97–98
horse unsuited to humid tropics, 236,
    250–251, 295, 363–364, 390–391, 393
tsetse fly, 250
horseless carriage, 403
Hospitalers, 263, 278, 330, 366, 367
huaso. *See* gaucho
Hulegu, 303, 309
human sacrifice, 88, 137, 168–169, 182, 279,
    285, 298, 343
Hundred Years' War, 342
Hungary, 276
Huns, 148, 195, 196–198
    Attila, 197
Hyksos, 95

Idrisi, 245
Iliad, 128
Ilkhanate, 324, 331
imam, 225, 326
imperial road construction, 124, 141, 188
incidental riding, 44, 47, 65
India, 395
Indo-European origins, 57
Indra, 111
Inquisition, 348, 376
instruments
    flute, 90, 160
    harp, 84

lute, 321
    violin, precursor of, 160
    wooden soundboard, 160
investiture ritual involving the horse
    Asvamedha, 115
    Darius I, 123
    Epomeduos, 115
    Stonehenge, 171
Iron Horse, 374
Isabel of Castille, 351
Isfahan, 327
Ismail, 326
Issus, 130
Ivan the Terrible, 331
ivory, 182

jade, 136
Japan, 318–323
Jebei, 286, 295
jihad, 265, 325
Joan of Arc, 342–343
Jones, William, 57
Judaism, 261
    Babylonian Talmud, 236
    Khazars, 158
    Maimonides, 247
    midrash, 236
    Radanites, 158
    Rashid al-Din, 312
    Sephards, 242
    Solomon, 100

Kadesh, 100–101
Kanem-Bornu, 250
Karakorum, 302
Karbala, 224, 310, 330
Karum Kanesh II (Kultepe), 52
Kassites, 95
khagan, 287, 297
Kharijites, 223, 248
Khubilai khan, 304–308, 309
    invasion of Japan, 322
khuriltai, 287, 330
Khwarizmi, 246
Kikkuli's manual, 98–99
Kipchak khanate, 276, 301, 303,
    331
knight, 164, 260, 261, 271, 277, 333,
    337, 344, 353, 378
Kosovo, 277, 328
kurgan. *See* tumulus

Kusanagi, sacred sword of Japan, 320
Kushan state, 151, 155, 210

La Tene, 173
Lake Baljuna, 286
Las Navas de Tolosa, 348
Lchashen, 74, 137
lead mare, 40, 64
Lefebvre des Noettes, 96
Legalism
    Han Feizi, 139
Leibniz, 366
Leopold of Austria, 269, 270
Lepanto, 278, 367
Linzhu canal, 141
Little Bighorn, 374
llama, 64n, 382
llanero. *See* gaucho
long bowmen, 341
Los Toldos, 384

Macha, 113
Magellan, Ferdinand, 280, 367
Magi, 122, 123, 143
Mahabharata, 111
mahdi, 224, 226
Mahmud of Ghazna, 233–234
Makran desert, 132
Mali, 249
Malta, 278, 366
Mamluks, 273–274, 276, 301, 303, 309, 324,
    399
Manco Inka, 363
Manichaeism, 159
    Uighurs, 159
Manzikert, 259
Mapuche. *See* Araucanians
Marathon, 127
Marcus Aurelius, 190
maritime exploration, 351
maritime horse transport, 271, 272
Martel, Charles, 238–239, 343
Massagetae, 116, 122, 131
Massalia, 182
Masudi, 245
mate-defense polygyny, 39
mawali, 222
Maya calendar, 355
Mehmed II, 328
Menandros, 151
merchant associations, 308

Mesoamerican wheel, 384
metallurgy, 25–27
  Ai Bunar, copper and gold, 29
  animal style art, 78–79, 138, 151
  arsenic bronze, 360
  bauxite, 365
  bronze, 48
  bronze and iron chariot fixtures, 76
  bronze, silver, and gold horse trappings,
    78
  cast iron and steel, 316–317
  copper, 354
  copper ornaments, 33
  gold, 48, 49, 50, 80, 81, 136, 182, 213, 236,
    243, 248, 272, 302, 354, 360, 365, 367
  iron, 48, 49, 94, 116, 145, 171, 182, 219,
    319
  lost-wax casting, 50, 80, 106, 360
  metal tools, 73
  Potosi, 365
  silver, 48, 272, 354, 360, 365, 367
  socketed spears, 50
  steel, 145, 342
  tin, 44, 167
  tin bronze, 50, 166, 360
  tumbaga, copper-gold alloy, 360
  wootz steel, 213, 223, 243
  Zacatecas, 371
  zinc, 365
Ming, 350, 394
Ming maritime explorations, 325
Mitanni, 95
Mithra, 55
mitochondrial DNA studies, 40
Moche, 360
Moctezuma, 357
Mongke, 303
Mongol decimal organization, 287
Mongol prohibition on looting, 286
Mongol winter invasion, 299
Monte Alban, 354
Mughals, 325–326, 393
Muhammad ibn Abd Allah. *See* early
  Islam, Muhammad
Musa of Mali, 275

Nafi, Uqba ibn, 235
Najaf, 330
Napoleon, 276, 278
nasij, 285, 302, 310–311, 314
Natufian culture, 22

Nazca, 360
Nechao, circumnavigation of Africa, 182
Neolithic, 135
Neolithic revolution, 22–25
New World agriculture, 354, 359
  Amerindian crops revolutionize world
    agriculture, 368–369
  chinampas, 356
  waru-waru system, 360
Newton, Isaac, 366
Nilo-Chadic Sahel, 275
Nisaean horse, 119, 126, 176
No drama, 323
Norse settlement in New World, 350
Norte Chico, 359

Ogedei expansion, 298–301
Ohrmazd, 211, 255. *See also*
  Zoroastrianism, Ahura Mazda
Old World diseases, 358
  Huayna Capac, 362
Olmec, 354, 369
omphalos, 339
onager, 32. *See also Equidae, Equus*
Onate, 371
one-toed adaptation. *See Equidae,*
  monodactyly
opposition to early-riding hypothesis, 33
  antler-tine tools, 42
  no definitive pictorial representation,
    42
  pathological malocclusion, 41
Orellana, 364
Ossetes, 148, 195, 200
Ottomans, 277, 278, 295, 325, 326, 327,
  332, 353
Otumba, 358

padded digits, 7
Panathenaia, 179–181
paper, 161, 222
paper currency, 308, 314
parietal art. *See* rupestrian art
Parthian shot, 63, 77, 106
Parthians, 150, 211
passports, 161, 296
pastoral nomadism, 63
Pax mongolica, 308
Peipus, lake, 277
penning, 36
Pepkino, 44

periphery adaptation, 28
perissodactyl, 7
Persepolis, 126
petroglyphs. *See* rupestrian art
Pharusii, 182
Pheidippides, 127
Philip Augustus, 268
Phoenicians, 182
Phrygian cap, 50, 63, 321f
pig, 23, 58, 60
pike phalanx, 341
Pit-grave. *See* Yamnaya
Pizarro's conquest of the Inka, 360–363
Plano Carpini, John of, 302
Pleistocene, 10, 10n, 41, 384
Poitiers, 238
poleaxing, 36
polo. *See* horse contests, polo
Polo, Marco, 307
Pontic-Caspian steppe, 29
populous religions, 387
Porus, king of the Pauravas, 131
practice for war, 149, 339
Preveza, 330
printing, 307, 314–315
    Gutenberg, 315
proto-Finno-Ugric, 59
proto-Indo-European (PIE), 58
Prussians, 277
Przewalski horse. *See* Equus ferus
    przewalskii
Przewalski, Nikolai Michailovich, 17
Ptolemy, 132
Pueblos, 371

qanats, 124
Qayrawan, 247
Qin, 141–142
Qin Shi Huangdi, 389
Queseras del Medio, 377
quipu, 360, 382

Rabban Markos, 307
Rabban Sauma, 307
Ramayana, 111
Rawlinson, Henry, 123
Reconquista, 280
religious tolerance, 288, 305, 306–307
Renaissance, 328, 332, 338
Repin, 38
Revere, Paul, 372

Rgveda, 54, 109, 111, 117, 152
Rhazes, 247
Rhodes, 278, 330
ribat, 222, 232, 248, 276
Richard the Lionheart, 268, 270
Richthofen, Ferdinand von, 155
Roman Pantheon, 194
Ron tribesmen, 182
Rouran. *See* Avars
rubber ball game, 355
Rubruk, William of, 302
rupestrian art, 16, 50, 76, 82, 97, 218
sacred fire, 72, 82, 109, 112, 122, 209
    agnicayana hearth, 152
    cremation, 82, 109, 112, 153
    fire-goddess Vesta (Gr. Hestia), 112
    fire-priest Dadhyanc, 112
    prutaneion, 112
    torch race, 180

Safavids, 229, 326, 327
Sainte Chapelle, 271
Sajo river, 301
Saka, 116, 125, 131, 148, 151, 254
Saladin, 267
Salamis, 127, 399
Samanids, 232, 246
Samarkand, 325
samurai, 320–322
Sanhadjas, 236, 248
Santiago, 279, 347
Santiago de Compostela, 239, 243, 252,
    344
Saracens, 264
Sarai, 301
Sarmatians, 116, 161, 190, 199, 242
Sasanians, 211, 254
satem languages, 58
sauma cult, 109
Sayid Alim khan, 331
scalping, 85, 372
Scythians, 116, 120
Secret History of the Mongols, 282–288
Seima-Turbino, 50, 136
self-sacrifice
    auto-flagellation, 228
    Constantine XI Palaeologus, 328
    self-immolation, 112
    self-mutilation, 88
    seppuku (ritual suicide), 322
Selim, 328

Seljuks, 234–235, 259, 327
  Malik Shah, 259
  Toghril, 234
seminomadic pastoralism, 45
Semirechye, 50
Shahnameh, 253–259
  Afrasiyab, 255, 258
  Firdausi, 254
  Kai Khosrau, 258
  Rakhsh, 256, 258
  Rustam, 255–258, 312
  Suhrab, 257
  Tahminah, 256
  Turanians, 255
Shang, 136
sheep, 18, 22, 23, 34, 39, 41, 46, 47n, 56, 58,
  80, 88, 89, 136, 149, 207, 212, 285, 308,
  336, 371, 392
Shigi Khutukhu, 288
Shiite, Shia (shiat Ali), 223, 224, 310
  hashshashin, 266. *See also* Assassins
  Muharram, 223, 228, 229
  Old Man of the Mountain, 266
  Sevener Shiites, 226, 266
  Taziyeh, 226–231
  Twelver Shiites, 225, 326
Shire horse, 369
shogun, 321
Sicily, 260
siege warfare, 289, 292, 294
Silk Road, 148, 155, 156
  amber, 156
  diamonds, 156
  ivory, 156
  lapis lazuli, 156
  ornamental blown glass, 156
  ostriches, 156
  pearls, 156
  silkworm eggs, 161
  water sleeves, 160
Sintashta-Petrovka, 51–52
sipahi, 329
Sitting Bull, 374
Siyavush, 89, 227, 253, 258
skull trophy, 88, 144
slavery, 88, 157, 158, 160, 185, 187, 232, 234,
  235, 236–237, 238, 244, 259, 301, 330,
  345, 368, 370, 392
Socotra, 23
Sogdians, 131, 157
sohei (warrior Buddhist monks), 321

Solutre, 16–17
soma. *See* sauma cult
Song, 281
Songhay, 250
Spanish Riding Academy in Vienna, 366,
  404
Spartacus, 185
Spruyyte, J., 97
Sredni Stog (4200-3500 BC), 32, 60
Srubnaya (1800-1200 BC), 50
Standard of Ur, 95
standardization of measures, 124, 141,
  151
Stonehenge, 169
  summer solstice, 170
Strettweg wagon model. *See* horse power,
  Kesselwagen cultic model
Subedei, 295, 299, 301
Suleiman the Magnificent, 329–330
Sunni, 224, 266, 326, 330
suttee, 56
Swat, 54

Tabriz, 309, 311, 312, 314
Tai-Kadai, 389
Taj Mahal, 312
takhi (Mongolian). *See Equus ferus*
  przewalskii
Talas, 222
Tamerlane, 324–325
  architecture, 325
Tang, 156, 160, 281
Tanguts, 281, 297
Tannenberg, 277
Taoism, 306
  Lao-tzu, 138
Tarim Basin
  Europoid mummies, 55–56
  Tocharian, 56, 60
tarpan, 17
Tawantinsuyu, 361
Tazabagyab, 54
tea, 149
Tehuelche, 375
Telamon, 175
Templars, 262–263, 264, 278
Temujin, 283, 284. *See also* Genghis khan
Tengri, 287, 297
Tenochtitlan, 356
Teotihuacan, 355
Teutonic knights, 263, 276, 300

textiles
  cotton, 80, 156, 213
  linen, 93
  silk, 84, 109, 144, 149, 156, 161, 213,
    289
  woolen, 72, 83
The Seven Samurai, 323
theological debate, 302
Thermopylae, 127
tholos, 51, 152, 193
thong smoothers, 36
three-toed adaptation. *See Equidae,*
  tridactyly
timber circle, 166
  Qawrighul, 82
  Stonehenge, 168
Timber-grave. *See* Srubnaya
Tiwanaku, 360
Tlaxcala, 357
Toledo, 260
Tomyris, 86, 122
transmigration
  Celtic, 153
  Greek, 153
  Vedic, 153
travois, 372
tree of life, 79, 80, 86, 154, 297, 402
trellis tent, 67–73
  ceremony, 72, 297
  microcosm of the universe, 70
  roof wheel, 69–71
  tent wall, 68
"trick or treat" extortion, 145
Trojan war
  Achilles, 103, 129, 130, 255
  Agamemnon, 102, 255
  Hector, 103
  Menelaos, 102
  Odysseus, 103
  Patroclos, 102
  Trojan horse, 104, 151
trousers, 50, 56, 64, 72, 126, 140, 142, 160,
  174, 313, 403
Troy, 101–102
tugh, 283, 287, 297, 329
tumulus, 46, 48, 51, 67, 79–80, 88, 103, 114,
  127, 142, 152, 165, 166, 174, 210, 318
  Alexandropol, 80–81
  Arzhan, 81, 166
  cromlech, 80, 168
  Deccan, 109

Maikop, 80
Nemrud Dagi, 210
Pazyryk, 82–86

Uighurs, 287
Umayyads, 223, 242–243
unicorn, 338
Urnfield, 171
Utrar, 293

Vakhsh, 54
Valerian, 211
Vandals, 195–196
vaquero. *See* gaucho
Vercingetorix, 185
Vienna, siege of, 329
Villa, Pancho, 377
Visigoths, 195
viticulture, 172
Vucedol, 165

Waler, 395
Wari, 360
warrior band
  Diberga, 116n
  Ephebes, 116n
  Krypteia, 116n
  mairiia, 116, 255, 276
  Mannerbund, 117
  marya, 116
  maryannu, 95
Wellington, 399
White Feast, 305
winged horse, 173
  Pegasus, 178
wolf tooth. *See* diastema
wooly fleece, 23
world mountain, 80, 121, 293, 297
  Burkhan Khaldun, 283, 287, 298,
    330
  Capitol Hill, 402
  Nemrud Dagi, 210
writing systems
  Arabic, 244
  cuneiform, 93, 94
  Greek alphabet, 209
  hieroglyphics, 93
  Latin alphabet, 188
  Phoenician consonantal system, 104
  small seal, 141
  Uighur alphabet, 287, 307

Wudi, 146
Wuling of Zhao, 140
Wusun/Alans, 116, 146, 148

Xenophon, 128
Xerxes, 127
Xinjiang, 19, 55n, 389, 415
Xiongnu, 143–145, 149, 287
    heqin, brides for bribes, 144
    Modu, chanyu, 143–144

yabusame martial art, 319
yam post stations, 296, 307
Yamato-takeru, 320. *See also* Arthur
Yamnaya (3500-2400 BC), 44–49, 60
Yasa, 288, 301
Yelu Chucai, 292, 294, 304
yeniceri, 329
Yuezhi, 143, 151, 156, 195

Zama, 184
Zapata, Emiliano, 377
Zarqali, 246
zebra, 12, 14, 17, 24, 219, 220n, 392.
    See also Equidae, Equus, 11n
zero, 131, 245–246, 383
Zhang Qian, 146
Zhou, 138–139
Zoroastrianism, 254
    Ahura Mazda, 117, 205
    Amesha Spentas, 117
    Angra Mainyu, 118
    Avesta, 109, 117
    Fravashis, 157
    Gathas, 117
    Magi, 209
    saoshyant, 118
    Yashts, 117
    Zarathustra, 117, 118